Organizational Communication

Organizational Communication
Perspectives and Trends

Michael J. Papa | Tom D. Daniels | Barry K. Spiker

Central Michigan University | *Ohio University* | *Arizona State University*

SAGE Publications

Los Angeles • London • New Delhi • Singapore

For information:

Sage Publications, Inc.
2455 Teller Road
Thousand Oaks, California 91320
E-mail: order@sagepub.com

Sage Publications Ltd.
1 Oliver's Yard
55 City Road
London EC1Y 1SP
United Kingdom

Sage Publications India Pvt. Ltd.
B 1/I 1 Mohan Cooperative Industrial Area
Mathura Road, New Delhi 110 044
India

Sage Publications Asia-Pacific Pte. Ltd.
33 Pekin Street #02-01
Far East Square
Singapore 048763

Printed in the United States of America

Library of Congress Cataloging-in-Publication Data

Papa, Michael J.
Organizational communication : perspectives and trends /
Michael J. Papa, Tom D. Daniels, Barry K. Spiker.
    p. cm.
Rev. ed. of: Perspectives on organizational communication /
Tom D. Daniels, Barry K. Spiker, Michael J. Papa. 4th ed. 1997.
Includes bibliographical references and index.
ISBN 978-1-4129-1684-4 (cloth)
    1. Communication in organizations. I. Daniels, Tom D.
II. Spiker, Barry K. III. Daniels, Tom D. Organizational communication. IV. Title.

HD30.3.D33 2008
658.4'5—dc22   2007023904

This book is printed on acid-free paper.

07 08 09 10 11 10 9 8 7 6 5 4 3 2 1

Acquisitions Editor:	Todd R. Armstrong
Editorial Assistant:	Katie Grim
Production Editor:	Astrid Virding
Copy Editor:	Barbara Ray
Typesetter:	C&M Digitals (P) Ltd.
Proofreader:	Dennis Webb
Indexer:	Juniee Oneida
Cover Designer:	Janet Foulger
Marketing Manager:	Carmel Withers

Brief Contents

Contents

Preface

Our first textbook in the area of organizational communication was published in 1987 under the title *Perspectives on Organizational Communication*. Three editions with the same title followed between 1991 and 1997. This latest work is the most different in structure and content, hence the change in title to *Organizational Communication: Perspectives and Trends*. We take the unique path of describing and evaluating communication in organizations by focusing on three major perspectives for understanding organizations: traditional, interpretive, and critical. Traditionalists are concerned with the relationship between communication and organizational effectiveness. Interpretivists believe that communication allows organization members to create and recreate the system that becomes their social context. This context influences how organization members interpret their experiences and how they carry out actions. Critical scholars regard organizations as instruments of privilege or even outright oppression. They focus their attention on the relationship between the privileged classes (or privileged conditions) and disadvantaged or oppressed organizational groups. These three perspectives are used to provide insight into communication functions and structure, organizational culture, information technology; cultural control, diversity, and change; new forms of organizing such as lattices and heterarchies, group relations, leader-member relations, power, conflict, and strategic communication; and new millennium thinking about organizations.

The current book includes classic and state-of-the-art research in organizational communication complemented by commentary from corporate leaders and dozens of descriptions of communication in organizations around the world such as General Motors, Triyo Industries of Japan, Wal-Mart, McDonalds, Ben & Jerry's, Enron, IBM, ExxonMobil, Grameen Bank in Bangladesh, The Carter Center's Peace Programs, Electronic Disturbance Theatre in Mexico, Canada's public health programs, social change programs in rural India, the women's support organization Casa de Esperanza (House of Hope), and Good Works, a homeless shelter and social services organization for poor people in Appalachia.

Before proceeding with our specific description of the current book, we feel it is important to note a significant structural change that we have made. In order to more effectively structure the book according to traditional, interpretive, and critical perspectives we now have organized most of the chapters according to these perspectives. The reader will note, however, that these three perspectives do not structure Chapter 4 (*Organization Theory: Prescriptions for Control*) and Chapter 5 (*Organization Theory: Metaphors of Biology*). This was a simple decision because the material in these chapters cannot be viewed according to the interpretive and critical perspectives. Over the course of many years, these theories have been defined by traditional approaches focusing on concepts, processes, and outcomes. Traditional, interpretive, and critical perspectives structure all the remaining chapters, substantively, although in somewhat different ways. In some instances it was necessary to discuss some preliminary concepts and ideas prior to setting up the traditional, interpretive, and critical sections (see Chapters 2, 7, 8, 10, and 13). Importantly, even in these chapters, the three perspectives frame the reader's thinking about the topical subject matter. This represents a substantive shift in how the chapters were presented in previous editions. In the remaining Chapters (3, 6, 9, 11, 12, and 14), the topical discussions are structured from the beginning by the traditional, interpretive, and critical perspectives.

We open this book with a prologue in which we present an extended illustration of selected episodes from the Hurricane Katrina disaster, i.e., episodes with implications and lessons for organizational communication. The prologue provides recent and memorable case materials that we connect to particular concepts and themes in Chapter 1.

In Chapter 1, *An Orientation to Organizational Communication*, we provide our readers with the basic background and conceptual framework for the book. Specifically, we describe the historical development and current status of organizational communication as reflected in traditional, interpretive, and critical perspectives of the field. We have done more in this edition to reinforce and explain the constitutive conception of organizational communication. We have also applied each of the three perspectives to examples drawn from the Katrina prologue.

At the beginning of Chapter 2, *Communication and Its Functions,* we explain for our readers why we focus on communication function and structure (Chapter 3) so early in the book. Our rationale is that these two chapters are concerned with ideas that truly provide the foundation of organizational communication; hence their early placement in the text. In our new chapter on communication function, we describe what we mean by communication, information, and meaning, giving attention to both verbal and nonverbal behavior. We also provide a more elaborate discussion of what we mean by communication function by adding descriptions of Dance and Larson's work on communication functions, and George Herbert Mead's perspective on symbolic interactionism. Also new to this chapter are Berger and Luckmann's perspective on communication as construction and Bakhtin's viewpoint of communication as dialogic. We added a section on relational development between workers in organizations. Finally, we integrate recent work on the concept of social capital, which explains how features of social organization such as networks, norms, and social trust facilitate coordination and cooperation for mutual benefit.

Chapter 3, *Organizational Communication Structure*, focuses on formal and informal systems of communication and network characteristics. New to this edition is a discussion of diagonal communication across structural units and levels, drawing particular attention to quality circles. We also look at how information may become distorted in organizations, and we add a section on Charles Perrow's observations concerning loosely and tightly coupled systems. Next, we expand our coverage of nontraditional organizational structures such as lattice design and heterarchies. Finally, we added a brief new section at the end of the chapter, "New Communication Structures, Cultural Diversity, and Empowerment," in which we explain that workers from diverse cultural backgrounds may see organizational structures differently.

Chapter 4, *Organization Theory: Prescriptions for Control*, highlights scientific and classical management, transitional theories (Follett's administrative theory and Barnard's executive functions), the human relations movement, and human resource development (HRD).

We gave special attention to updating our descriptions of HRD and Theory Z, especially clarifying the line between human relations and HRD that we have maintained for many years. That line between human relations and HRD is sometimes misplaced in organizational communication literature, so we explain in more detail where this transition actually occurs in the history and development of management theory.

Chapter 5, *Organization Theory: Metaphors of Biology*, examines system theory, Weick's theory of organizing, Luhmann's social systems theory (new to this edition), and evolutionary psychology. Included in this chapter are updated examples and research for the section on systems theory along with new material on complexity and chaos within a system theory context. We have updated examples in the section on Weick's theory of organizing, and we also have revised and expanded the treatment of evolutionary psychology, including two new examples of organizational communication studies that use the premises and basic method of evolutionary psychology.

Chapter 6, *Organization Theory: Communication and Culture*, elevates our discussion of culture to a perspective for understanding organizations on par with the previous two theory chapters. To accomplish this we extend our discussion of what we mean by communication and culture, language, ritual, worldview, consensual and contested meanings, knowledge structures, and narratives. We address Trujillo's concept of multiple culture perspectives in this new edition and include more recent cultural studies of organizations. To clarify our cultural perspectives we added organizational examples such as Ben & Jerry's and we included a brief description of the Saturn Corporation's motto under the "Fantasy Themes" section. Finally, we added a discussion question that asks students to reflect on the type of culture that Donald Trump creates on the NBC show *The Apprentice*. This popular show provides many examples that organizational communication instructors might integrate into discussions of culture.

Nearly all of the content in Chapter 7, *Information Technology*, is revised or new material. The vast and sweeping changes that have occurred in information technology during the past decade demanded that we do this. We begin the chapter with a discussion of technology and change, and then proceed with a review of the major technology issues from the traditional, interpretive, and critical perspectives. Under the traditional perspective, we cover the use of information technology for productivity, knowledge management, and control. We describe the digital divide and review the consequences of information technology for organizational structure, for organizational processes, and for work and workers. We describe interpretive treatments of technology's influence on organizational sense making and the social construction of technology, as well as critical scholarship on the role of technology in legitimizing management authority and supporting neoliberal hegemony and global control.

Chapter 8, *Cultural Control, Diversity, and Change*, has been significantly revised. Specifically, we added organizational socialization and assimilation to our discussion of cultural control, and we included practical advice for dealing with problems associated with diversity focusing specifically on sexual harassment, racism, and making accommodations for people with a range of physical ability levels. We added sexual orientation and class to our discussion of diverse groups and we discuss contrasts among the Traditional, Boomer, Generation X, and Millennial generations. We cover the status of affirmative action programs and a discussion of recent Supreme Court cases. Importantly, we emphasize very strongly that corporations cannot ignore cultural and ethnic diversity and that they need to exhibit more of a global perspective. Finally, we end with a section on the ethics of diversity by explaining how to provide support for people who belong to diverse groups.

Chapter 9, *Group Relationships*, now includes a section on communication skills with a description of communication competence in groups. We also describe the circumstances under which group decision making is more useful than individual decision making. We identify various types of groups in this edition, including focus groups and task forces. We cover the bona fide approach in groups, and we include examples of organizational cultures that influence decision making (e.g., "the customer is always right" culture and the "protect the bottom line" culture). Finally, we discuss Giddens's structuration theory to provide insight into how groups create social structure.

Chapter 10, *Leader-Member Relations*, has a new and substantial section on transformational leadership, revised and updated material on leader-member exchange theory and research, and new material on leadership as development (i.e., mentor-protégé relationships) under the traditional perspective. We have also added material from the interpretive perspective on sense-making functions of leadership and critical treatments of leadership discourse as well as resistance discourse.

Chapter 11, *Power*, examines Weber's work on power relations and Bachrach and Baratz's two faces of power, and analyzes the community power debates by focusing on the perspectives of Dahl and Lukes. We give additional coverage to the work of Pfeffer and Clegg. Finally, we include discussions of feminist and poststructural perspectives on power. By expanding our coverage of these theorists, we provide our readers with a more complete understanding of multiple perspectives on power.

Chapter 12, *Conflict*, focuses on traditional perspectives such as interpersonal conflict and managing conflict in organizations, including a new section on principled negotiation in discussion of bargaining and negotiation. From the interpretive perspective we examine how the cultural context for conflict is influenced by gender, race, and national culture, and we also describe the emergence of dialogic culture in organizations. Finally, from the critical perspective, we present new insights into how conflict in organizations may be influenced by the contradictions between capitalism and democracy, coalitions and intergroup conflict, and the emergence of feminist bureaucracy as organized dissonance.

Chapter 13, *Strategic Communication*, is revised with a much tighter focus on the concept of strategy, different models of strategy, and their connection with organizational communication. Under the traditional perspective, we have updated the examples and illustrations in the internal communication and issues management sections, and we have linked all of this material more directly with strategy. We have added a new section on risk communication along with revised discussion and examples in crisis communication. The chapter also includes new interpretive work on strategic communication as transaction and constraints on sense making in crisis communication. Finally, we review critical treatments of strategy and hegemony, transformation and strategy, and member coping with strategic use of power.

Chapter 14, *New Millennium Thought: Perspectives and Trends*, begins with provocative insights into the end of the cheap energy era, continued population growth, depletion of the Earth's natural resources, feminist organizing, and steady-state economics replacing economic policies based on constant growth. We consider trends facing organizations in the 21st century, including the globalization of the marketplace and global competitive pressures, gender and diversity at work, quality and customer satisfaction, political and legal pressures on organizations, stress at work, an inadequately educated workforce, critical questioning of corporate values, and various stakeholder perspectives. We believe this final chapter will provide significant stimulus for discussion about the current status of organizational communication and what issues demand our attention as the 21st century unfolds.

Special Features

The book includes topical outlines and summaries for each chapter. Key terms are displayed in boldface type at or near the place where they are first defined or used in a meaningful way. Activities, discussion questions, and complete references are included at the end of each chapter.

Instructor's Resource CD-ROM

The instructor's resource CD-ROM, prepared by Wendy Papa of Central Michigan University, is a very useful tool for both experienced and new instructors. It includes lecture outlines along with PowerPoint slides for each chapter, keyword definitions, discussion questions, exam questions, activities, case studies, sample syllabi, and paper assignments and projects. Also included are hyperlinks to video clips on the Internet that complement topics covered in the book.

ACKNOWLEDGMENTS

We thank the several reviewers of the revised edition's draft; their detailed comments were very helpful to us during the revision stage of this edition.

Wendy L. Bjorklund
St. Cloud State University

Kevin James Brown
Oregon Institute of Technology

Sam Crostic
University of Nevada—Reno

Liane Gray-Starner
Marietta College

Jessica Katz Jameson
North Carolina State University

Michael W. Kramer
University of Missouri—Columbia

Virginia McDermott
University of New Mexico

John M. McGrath
Trinity University

Kami J. Silk
Michigan State University

Federico Varona
San José State University

In addition, we also thank the reviewers of the previous editions as their comments and suggestions contribute to strengthen the text:

Brenda J. Allen, University of Colorado at Denver
Stephen Banks, University of Idaho
Mary Helen Brown, Auburn University
Deborah Brunson, University of North Carolina at Wilmington
Lawrence Hugenberg, Kent State University
Fred Jablin, University of Richmond (deceased)
Michael W. Kramer, University of Missouri—Columbia
Karl Krayer, Creative Communication Network
Kevin Lamude, California State University, San Bernardino
Michael Lewis, Abilene Christian University
Don MacDonald, University of Tulsa
Renee Meyers, University of Wisconsin—Milwaukee
Vernon D. Miller, Michigan State University
R. Glenn Ray, Marietta College
Patricia Riley, University of Southern California
J. Andrew Roob, Communication Decisions
Philip Salem, Texas State University—San Marcos
Ron Sandwina, Indiana University-Purdue University Indianapolis
Jo Young Switzer, Manchester College
Charles Veenstra, Dordt College

Prologue

Well before anyone ever heard of Hurricane Katrina, Brian Wolshon, an assistant professor of transportation engineering at Louisiana State University, was working with Louisiana safety and transportation officials on the state's emergency evacuation plans, including plans for the city of New Orleans. Wolshon, an expert in hurricane evacuation, recognized that many of the city's most immobile residents (potentially 100,000 elderly and poor people) lived in the areas at greatest risk for catastrophic flooding. How could the plan ensure their safe evacuation in the event of a major hurricane? Wolshon said that this question was raised (apparently by him as well as others) during planning meetings, but "the answer was often silence" (Shane & Lipton, 2005). On August 29, 2005, Katrina shattered that silence. The city's protective levees failed, the flood waters poured in, and tens of thousands of residents were trapped with no means of escape.

Six weeks before Hurricane Katrina destroyed the southern gulf coast, Jason Jackson, director of emergency operations for Wal-Mart, was chatting casually with reporters on a tour of the company's Bentonville, Arkansas, emergency operations center. From this location, Jackson and his team track the status of Wal-Mart stores and facilities along with any major events that might disrupt their operations. On this particular July day, they were monitoring Hurricane Emily and 17 stores in the storm's path. Jackson, a former Arkansas state trooper, told the reporters, "We are prepared to deal with this type of situation" (French, 2005). His confidence appears to have been well justified. After Katrina hit, Jackson and his colleagues not only managed a speedy effort to put dozens of damaged Wal-Mart stores back into operation, but also coordinated what turned out to be the first help to arrive in many devastated communities—Wal-Mart truck drivers delivering dozens of trailers loaded with relief supplies (Barbaro & Gillis, 2005).

On Friday, August 26, 2005, the National Hurricane Center had not yet issued a hurricane warning for Louisiana and Mississippi. The official advisory of a hurricane watch for Louisiana did not occur until 10 a.m. on Saturday, and the official hurricane warning for the north central gulf coast was issued 12 hours later on Saturday night (Katrina Forecast Timeline, 2005). But center director Max Mayfield already was uneasy on Friday morning. Katrina was wallowing off the west coast of Florida and not making an expected turn toward the Florida panhandle. Among several computer models for this storm, a couple suggested that Katrina might intensify, turn northwest rather than north, and strike the coasts of Louisiana and Mississippi. This would be catastrophic because much of the land in that region, including New Orleans, lies at or below sea level. Mayfield began to make phone calls to various local, state, and federal officials (Zwerdling & Sullivan, 2005). One of these calls went to Walter Maestri at the emergency management center in Jefferson Parish, Louisiana. Mayfield told Maestri to get ready for a major hurricane. Maestri was skeptical, but Mayfield insisted, "This is real" (Zwerdling & Sullivan, 2005).

Maestri convened his own team and stressed the seriousness of the situation by saying that Mayfield "is not one of these people who runs around shouting 'wolf,' 'wolf,' 'wolf'" (Zwerdling & Sullivan, 2005). Maestri then called the deputy director of Louisiana's Department of Homeland Security. The deputy director also had received a call from Max Mayfield, but the deputy was not inclined to act hastily on Mayfield's warning because the storm was moving up the Florida coast. Maestri quickly surmised that the deputy did not really know Mayfield, so Maestri pressed the issue. "When Max Mayfield tells you to get ready, get ready" (Zwerdling & Sullivan, 2005). Governor Kathleen Blanco put the state's emergency plan into action (Tumulty, 2005). Before the end of the day, Mayfield himself called a press conference and announced his expectation that Katrina would strike somewhere along the north central gulf coast as a category 4 storm.

On Saturday, 4,000 members of the Louisiana National Guard deployed to preassigned disaster staging areas. Officials from 40 state and federal agencies, including the Federal Emergency Management Agency (FEMA), met at a Baton Rogue operations center to organize and coordinate their plans. Governor Blanco asked for and received a federal emergency declaration from President George Bush. Blanco also requested supplementary federal assistance under provisions of the Stafford Act for disaster relief on the grounds that "effective response is beyond the capabilities of the State and affected local governments" (Louisiana Governor's Office, 2005). New Orleans mayor Ray Nagin called for voluntary evacuations on Saturday, then issued a mandatory evacuation order on Sunday. Everything seemed to be coming together as intended under the general umbrella of the National Response Plan, a 426-page disaster management document approved in 2004 by 32 federal agencies and commissions as well as major nonprofit disaster response organizations such as Red Cross (Department of Homeland Security, 2004).

Despite all of these efforts, the disaster response strategy unraveled when Katrina made landfall on Monday morning. Most communications systems, including phones, wireless, and even 911 went down immediately. Police departments, fire departments, and other intended first responders themselves became victims. Agencies staged to deliver aid were isolated and uncoordinated. National Guard units waited idly for orders. Officials argued over who had authority to do what and who bore responsibility for the problems. FEMA itself seemed to be operating in a fog of confusion and misinformation (Zwerdling & Sullivan, 2005). Two weeks after the catastrophe, the director of FEMA resigned in the face of withering criticism. The president of the United States ultimately assumed personal responsibility for the failures (VandeHei & Weisman, 2005).

Why are we beginning a book about organizational communication with stories about a natural disaster? Because Hurricane Katrina was not simply a natural disaster. It also was an institutional and organizational disaster. Each of these stories and hundreds of others that can be recounted from the Katrina catastrophe or disasters such as the September 11 attacks and the Enron corporate financial and ethical meltdown offer compelling lessons about human organizations in general and organizational communication in particular.

How does a group of planning experts simply avoid answering a question as basic as the one Brian Wolshon posed about the fate of New Orleans's disadvantaged immobile citizens? How can a behemoth like Wal-Mart also be so nimble that it can deliver relief to destroyed towns before federal agencies, the military, and even the Red Cross arrive on the scene?

Why was Walter Maestri willing to act and prod others to act on Max Mayfield's uneasy hunch? What if Mayfield had just sent an e-mail instead of making personal phone calls and holding a press conference on Friday? Why did elaborate federal, state, and local response plans wilt in the heat of actual crisis? How much worse might the outcome have been if everyone had simply waited for the official hurricane warning on Saturday night?

Almost anyone might speculate about the answer to the last of these questions. The other questions and the answers to them all touch in some fundamental way on the subject of organizational communication. They point out our dependence on organizations and institutions, the centrality of communication in organizational functions, and the chaos that can occur when systems of communication and organization serve inappropriate ends or simply fail altogether.

REFERENCES

Barbaro, M., & Gillis, J. (2005, September 6). Wal-Mart at the forefront of hurricane relief. *The Washington Post,* p. D1.

Department of Homeland Security. (2004, December). National Response Plan [Electronic version]. Retrieved September 1, 2005, from http://www.dhs.gov/interweb/assetlibrary/NRP_FullText.pdf

French, A. (2005, July 20). Wal-Mart keeps eye on Emily. *The Morning News* [Electronic version]. Retrieved on September 15, 2005, from http://www.nwaonline.net/articles/2005/07/20/business/01wmdisaster.txt

Katrina Forecast Timeline. (2005). NOAA National Hurricane Center [Electronic version]. Retrieved September 15, 2005, from http://commerce.senate.gov/pdf/Katrina_NOAA_Timeline.pdf

Louisiana Governor's Office. (2005, August 27). Press release: Governor Blanco asks president to declare an emergency for the state of Louisiana due to Hurricane Katrina [Electronic version]. Retrieved September 25, 2005, from http://www.gov.state.la.us/Press_Release_detail.asp?id=976

Shane, S., & Lipton, E. (2005, September 2). Government saw flood risk but not levee failure. *The New York Times* [Electronic version]. Retrieved September 15, 2006, from http://www.nytimes.com/2005/09/02/national/nationalspecial/02response.html?ei=5088&en=86f37e1b85f29e7e&ex=1283313600&partner=rssnyt&emc=rss&pagewanted=all

Tumulty, K. (2005, September 19). The governor: Did Kathleen Babineaux Blanco make every effort to get federal help? *Time, 166*(12), 38–39.

VandeHei, J., & Weisman, J. (2005, September 14). Bush takes responsibility for failures of response. *Washington Post,* p. A1.

Zwerdling, D., & Sullivan, L. (2005, September 9). Katrina timeline: Unexecuted plans. Broadcast on *All Things Considered,* National Public Radio. Audio file retrieved September 15, 2005, from http://www.npr.org/templates/story/story.php?storyId=4839666

CHAPTER 1

An Orientation to Organizational Communication

ORGANIZATION AND COMMUNICATION

The Concept of Organization

Human beings organize in the simplest sense to get things done. We define and arrange positions or roles, then we engage in concerted action with one another by coordinating these roles to accomplish some purpose. But this idea is just the proverbial tip of the organizational iceberg. Organizations often are very elaborate and complicated forms of human endeavor. They are not only vehicles for clear, cooperative action, but also sites of conflict and confusion. An organization may have a singular mission but many different reasons for its actual existence, and these varying reasons and the forces arising from them may not enjoy a peaceful coexistence.

Unless you are literally a hermit, organizations affect many aspects of your life, and you affect the lives of others through your own involvement with organizations. Even if you work alone or in a so-called independent business, you are enabled and constrained by human organizations around you. The clock radio that jolted you into action this morning most likely was produced by an organization, i.e., in the factory of some electronics company. This morning's shower? Courtesy of your local government and the municipal employees who run the water treatment plant and maintain the distribution system as well as the utility company that provided the energy to heat that water. Breakfast? Unless you got it from your own farm or garden, it came to you through a complex system of organizations including producers, processors, distributors, and retailers. The morning news? Brought to you by a media organization of reporters, editors, technicians, and salespeople who themselves depend on other organizations to provide advertising revenue.

Before you are even on your way out the door to work or school, your life is touched in some way by various organizations. We could continue this exercise in the ubiquity of organizations for the rest of your day, but you probably already get the point. Human beings in contemporary society live in, live with, depend on, and contribute to a complex and interacting system of organizations. And we are the organizations in which we live.

Although it is common practice in the American idiom to speak of organizations as if they exist apart from the people who constitute them, this is just not the case. Yes, individuals, perhaps even entire generations of them, come and go while the organization or institution remains, but the organization is constituted, is enacted, and exists through interaction among the people who constitute it at any point in time. In other words, an organization happens through the concerted actions of its members. Inasmuch as the basis for concerted action is communication, the process of human communication is the central feature of organization. As Daniel Katz and Robert Kahn, two prominent social psychologists, observed decades ago, "Communication . . . is the very essence of a social system or organization" (1978, p. 428).

The distinction between the idea that an organization is something like a container in which human action and interaction occur and the idea that the organization *is* human interaction may seem like hair-splitting, but this distinction is very important in understanding organizations from a communication scholar's point of view. In the early years of organizational communication studies, the "container" concept was the generally accepted point of view (Conrad & Poole, 2005). Communication was something that occurred inside the organization, so communication was all about the content and flow of messages and information through formal and informal channels. We will say more about this traditional perspective later in this chapter and throughout the book. The point for now is that scholarly and even societal perspectives on organizations changed over time. Conrad and Poole describe the change concisely: "Organizational communication theorists started viewing communication as more than the transfer of information; they saw it as a complex, multidimensional process through which organizing took place" (p. 9).

Recently, the "container" concept of the organization has enjoyed a second awakening, but now in a form that is very different from its original notion. As stated by Joann Keyton

(2004), "An organization can change its physical location and replace its members without breaking down because it is essentially a patterned set of discourses that at some point in time were created by the members and codified into norms and practices that are later inherited, accepted, and adapted to by newcomers" (p. 10).

From this point of view, one would say that the "container" is this set of discursive practices, i.e., the patterned set of discourses to which Keyton refers. The idea that an organization is a set of discursive practices is difficult to grasp if you are not used to thinking this way. Fairhurst and Putnam (2004) contend that discourse and communication are not exactly the same thing, although they might be defined in about the same terms in most ordinary dictionaries. But communication involves a lot of processes and structures, including many transient and fleeting interactions. Discourse more particularly concerns the language that we use to talk about something. Discourse analysts and theorists are concerned with the uses of language, i.e., discursive practices, as well as the connection between these practices and enduring ways of thinking and acting. The organizational container of discursive practice shapes and constrains its members, although successive generations of members may change the shape of the container as well. The idea is a little complicated, but it helps to explain, for example, why Wal-Mart worked and FEMA failed during the aftermath of Hurricane Katrina. We will tell you more about discourse and discursive practices later in the book.

The Concept of Communication

So what is communication? In the past, we ourselves have defined communication essentially as a process of creating shared meaning through the use of signs and symbols. The process occurs in and among dyads, groups, and larger social structures through many means and for many purposes. This definition is okay insofar as it goes, but certainly some scholars would say that it does not go far enough. Communication is not merely a process of creating shared meaning, but also of constructing social realities in ways that are coordinated and actively managed (Pearce & Cronen, 1980). As explained by Donal Carbaugh, "Communication is socially situated meaning-making, generating pockets of coherence and community through cultural meanings and forms" (1988, p. 38).

This book is about the communication processes that characterize human organizations, processes referred to collectively as organizational communication. Our aim is to present a broad survey that will provide you with a sound foundation of concepts for understanding and discussing this subject. No one book or course is going to cover everything that you could or should learn about organizational communication. This book is no exception. It is intended only as an introduction to the field of study.

We think that this book will be more useful to you if you understand something about the background for the book and for the course in which it is being used. In order to provide that background, we need to answer three basic questions:

1. Why is the study of organizational communication useful to you?

2. How did this field of study develop?

3. What is the status of the field today?

The answers to these three questions provide background for this book and for the course in which it is being used. A really good understanding of the field depends on some familiarity with this background.

Studying Organizational Communication

You may have wondered from time to time just why you should enroll in a particular course or of what relevance and importance the course is going to be to you. In the case of organizational communication, we see at least three reasons for studying this topic:

1. You can improve your understanding of organizations and of your own experiences as an organization member.
2. You can develop awareness of the kinds of communication skills that are important in organizations.
3. The course may start you down the path to a career as a communication professional in an organization or as an academic scholar in the field.

Understanding Organizations

"I've seen all of this before, but I never had a way to make sense of it until I took this course." This is a common remark that we hear from students who have just completed their first course in organizational communication. Because organizations are constituted through communication, the study of organizational communication provides a basis for understanding virtually every *human* process that occurs in organizations. Conflict, cooperation, decision making, the use of power and authority, compliance gaining, resistance, innovation and change, morale and cohesion, relationship development, and the creation and maintenance of organizational cultures all are reflected in organizational communication.

The study of organizational communication is not intended to provide insights about *every* aspect of human organizations. It is not a study of the technology for creating a product or service or of the methods for producing and marketing these things. It is not a study of cost control and financing or of laws and regulations governing business and employment practices. Such topics can be relevant to organizational communication, and some people in the field spend a lot of time discussing them, but organizational communication primarily is concerned with the content, structure, and process of human interaction through language and other symbols in day-to-day organizational activities.

Awareness of Skills

There is broad, general agreement that well-developed communication skills are essential to personal effectiveness in organizations or, at least, in managerial, professional, and leadership positions (Munter, 2002). Review any survey of skills that organizations expect of new college graduates on entry into the job market, and you probably will find communication skills featured prominently in the list (Stevens, 2005).

The kinds of communication skills that new college graduates should possess in order to meet organizational expectations can be developed through courses in public speaking, interviewing, group discussion, and writing. Sometimes, a number of these skills are taught in one course with a title such as "Business and Professional Communication." The introductory course in organizational communication usually is not concerned with training in specific individual communication skills. It does focus attention on many of the practical demands in organization life that require good personal communication skills. These demands and the situations in which they arise are reflected in examples throughout this text.

Career Opportunities

The study of organizational communication also is important because many organizations have developed an intense interest in this subject. Leaders and decision makers in such organizations not only want themselves and others to possess good communication skills, but also want an understanding of the dynamics of organizational communication. Many apparently are convinced that there is a strong connection between communication effectiveness and organizational effectiveness (Morley, Shockley-Zalabak, & Cesaria, 2002).

Although organization leaders often understand "organizational effectiveness" only in terms of increased productivity, profits, improved work performance, customer service, or higher morale, the belief that effective communication is essential to these conditions has led to a variety of career opportunities in organizational communication.

Today, many organizations employ writers, editors, and media specialists to produce and distribute company magazines, newsletters, films, videos, and even closed-circuit television programs for an audience composed of the organization membership. People in these occupations usually are trained in journalism or media production. A flourishing training and development industry also has emerged as organizations have hired staff professionals and outside consultants to help them evaluate and change organizational communication practices. This industry includes people who teach communication concepts and skills to organization members (usually to managers and supervisors), evaluate the effectiveness of organizational communication, and help to improve interpersonal, group, and public communication processes in organizational settings (Dewine, 2001).

The demand for communication professionals in organizations does not mean that a course or even a major related to organizational communication will lead to a job in the field. Although several occupations are concerned in some way with organizational communication, students who think that they are going to get a job in something called "organizational communication" really need to understand that this label refers to a field of academic study and not to any identifiable profession. "Organizational communication" does not appear as a job category anywhere in the U.S. Department of Labor's *Dictionary of Occupational Titles*, and many employers may not even know that the field exists. In 2004, the Bureau of Labor Statistics (BLS) predicted faster-than-average growth in the early 21st century for occupations related to organizational communication, but they also noted that competition for entry-level positions will be intense. It is not easy to break into this field. Many positions in training and development began to require a Master's degree years ago, and some require a doctoral degree (Redding, 1979). If you are thinking of a career related to organizational communication, you must obtain a thorough education and be able to apply what you know. Whether or not you pursue such a career, an organizational communication course should be helpful to you in any organizational role that you may assume.

Development of the Field

Although scholars in various disciplines have studied communication in organizations for many years, the development of organizational communication as an identifiable field with courses and academic programs in university departments of communication did not begin until the 1950s. W. Charles Redding, himself a major force in the development of the field, traced its origins to a convergence of interest in "business speech" and "industrial communication" that emerged in the wake of World War II (Redding, 1985; Tompkins & Redding, 1988). By the early 1950s, doctoral students in speech departments at Northwestern University, Ohio State University, Purdue University, and the University of Southern California were producing dissertations on industrial communication. In 1952, Purdue's speech department established its Industrial Communication Research Center. Annual conferences that brought together professors of speech and communication with social scientists from other disciplines provided forums for discussion and definition of the emerging field.

Skills-oriented "how to" books on communication for managers began to appear in the late 1950s, but the concerns of the field already were expanding beyond these narrow prescriptive interests to embrace description and explanation of organizational communication processes in general. According to Redding, general academic acceptance of the field of organizational communication was signaled by several events in 1967 and 1968, which included a NASA-sponsored conference on organizational communication and the creation of the Organizational Communication Division of the International Communication Association.

The rapid emergence of organizational communication as an academic field has been accompanied by some healthy, but occasionally troublesome, growing pains. Scholars have found it difficult to create an identity for the field. At first, this difficulty arose from similarities between organizational communication and other fields of study. Later, it involved the development of several different and sometimes competing approaches to the study of organizational communication. Although both of these identity problems have been troubling, each in its own way has helped to develop and refine the field. In order to explain the point of view of this book, we must first review some of the history involved in these two identity problems.

Relationship to Other Fields

Communication scholars began to study organizations at a time when other social and behavioral sciences already had a long history of organizational research. The new field of organizational communication borrowed heavily from ideas developed in these more established disciplines. Consequently, it was difficult at times to tell the difference between organizational communication, organizational psychology, organizational sociology, and organizational behavior as fields of study. Sharing ideas between different academic disciplines is both useful and necessary in order to develop a good understanding of our world. However, ideas from one field often have to be adapted to fit the needs of another field, and organizational communication scholars frequently borrowed ideas without making such adaptations.

When psychologists, sociologists, and social psychologists began to study organizations in the 20th century, they certainly were concerned with many processes related to human communication. They often encouraged organizations to pay attention to communication and interpersonal relationships, but their explanations of organizational behavior did not focus on human communication.

For example, management theorists of that era such as Paul Hersey and Ken Blanchard (1982) often were interested in the problem of motivating employees to be productive. They relied on theories of motivation in which the behavior of individual human beings is explained as a means of meeting physical, social, and psychological needs. If asked about the role of communication in organizational behavior, these theorists might say that communication is one of several types of motivated behavior in organizations or that it is a means of motivating organization members. From this point of view, communication is only one ingredient among many in a recipe for organizational behavior. The central problem is to understand human motivation in organizations and the role of motivation in organizational effectiveness (i.e., in getting people to work more productively). Communication is merely a peripheral concern.

When the field of organizational communication imported concepts from other disciplines, it also imported their peripheral views of human communication in organizations along with a preoccupation with organizational effectiveness. Communication scholars identified dozens of elements in organizational communication, then studied the relationships of these elements to a veritable grab bag of factors in organizational effectiveness. For example, we asked questions about the relationship between organizational communication and productivity, job satisfaction, turnover, and absenteeism. Most researchers studied "economic" organizations engaged in the creation and delivery of products or services. Communication became "one more variable" that figured into organizational effectiveness.

The field's early emphasis on organizational effectiveness is understandable insofar as effectiveness has been (and generally still is) the principal concern of people in charge of economic organizations. However, attempts to relate many elements in organizational communication to various indicators of organizational effectiveness quickly produced a large body of disjointed and fragmented research (Dennis, Goldhaber, & Yates, 1978). The field consisted of hundreds of individual facts and bits of knowledge like so many pieces of an unassembled jigsaw puzzle. We needed theories of organizational communication, per se, in order to integrate and organize our work.

The need to define the field of organizational communication more clearly led to several new developments in the late 1970s and early 1980s. While many scholars worked to refine the traditional social science themes that already had developed in the field, others began to study organizational communication in ways that differed substantially from the traditional approach. Consequently, several different points of view or perspectives on the study of organizational communication were introduced in the 1980s. The description of these perspectives in the next section completes our discussion of the development of organizational communication as a field of study. This will put us in a position to answer to the final question for this chapter regarding the status of the field.

PERSPECTIVES ON ORGANIZATIONAL COMMUNICATION

There are various ways of organizing and describing organizational communication perspectives. Some scholars identify several. Others identify only two. We come down somewhere in the middle by describing three that we call traditional, interpretive, and critical. Our discussion here is essentially a synthesis of previous descriptions presented by Linda Putnam (1982) and Philip Tompkins and Charles Redding (1988).

The Traditional Perspective

The traditional perspective is so called simply because it is the oldest of the three. For many years, scholars accepted almost without question the notion that organizational communication would be studied mainly from this point of view.

Traditionalists regard organizations as objects that can be studied with the concepts and methods of traditional social science. Traditionalists believe that organizational communication is an objectively observable activity. It can be measured, labeled, classified, and related to other organizational processes. For example, suppose we want to know whether managers' styles of communicating with employees have any effect on employee job satisfaction. We think that employees will be more satisfied when managers adopt an "open" style of communication, but we are not sure. A traditionalist might answer this question through the following actions:

1. Observe and measure managers' communicative behaviors in order to classify each manager as high or low in "communication openness."

2. Measure the levels of job satisfaction among each manager's employees.

3. Statistically analyze the measurements to see whether employee job satisfaction is greater under "high-openness" managers than it is under "low-openness" managers.

Traditionalists in organizational communication often are concerned with the relationship between communication processes and organizational effectiveness. They study factors in organizational communication such as information flow within organizational networks, distortion of messages, breakdowns in channels of communication, strategies of managers and supervisors in communicating with their subordinates, and the dynamics of group problem solving and decision making. If some of these ideas are unfamiliar to you at this point, there is no need to worry. Some of the chapters that follow this one are concerned with defining and elaborating on these concepts.

The traditional perspective itself has changed somewhat over the years, so we find it useful to distinguish between early and contemporary forms of this perspective. Early traditionalists treated the organization as a machine. This machine is an engineered set of interconnected parts that operates by managerial control and depends on well-maintained communication in order to function efficiently and effectively. Managers control the machine through principles and techniques of gaining compliance and cooperation from employees. The various parts of the machine (departments, individuals) are supposed to act in a coordinated manner. Both control and coordination depend on effective communication. Communication is understood primarily as a process of sending and receiving messages. Communication effectiveness involves two conditions: (1) the processes of message sending and receiving are accurate and reliable, and (2) the message receiver understands and responds to the message in the way that the message sender intends.

This emphasis on communication effectiveness for managerial control also suggests a distinct political position in early traditionalism. There is no getting around the fact that organizations are political entities. Organizations are political because they have systems for allocating and using power and resources and because they have ways of protecting and maintaining these systems. Who has power? Who gets resources, privileges, and rewards? Which groups or individuals control the fates of others, and how do they accomplish this control? Whose interests are privileged by the ways in which organizational goals are defined and achieved? By working to produce communication effectiveness, early traditionalists implicitly privileged the political interests of owners, managers, and leaders over those of other organizational groups.

Although some traditionalists continue to embrace the early view of organizations, most have refined their perspective with more contemporary ideas that differ from the early version. The early concept of the organization as a machine gave way to the idea that the organization is like an organism, i.e., a living system (Monge, Farace, Eisenberg, Miller, & White, 1984). Organizations are more like living systems than machines in two ways. First, the idea of management control over the organizational machine sounds something like a person's running a lawn mower or driving a car. Organizations, like living systems, are a lot more complicated. They have many systems of self-regulation and control. Managerial designs and intentions are important factors, but they are not the only factors that regulate an organizational system. Internally, unions, trade and professional groups, workgroups, and even informal coalitions may exert substantial control over the organization. Externally, local, state, and federal government agencies, as well as consumer or community groups, also regulate or, at least, influence the system.

Moreover, different organizational subsystems (for example, departments, work groups, and individuals) do not generally work together in machinelike harmony. Although they cooperate to accomplish a common purpose, they also may be in conflict. They often compete for resources, assert different values, and desire different ways of ordering work and organizational life. Even "management" usually is not an undifferentiated monolith that acts with a single-minded purpose. Vice-presidents of different divisions squabble over territory. Middle managers compete with one another for rank and privilege. Leaders of different functional areas may regard each other with contempt and actively struggle over the best way to accomplish an organization's mission.

Second, organizations, unlike machines, change and adapt to change. The people who make up organizations process information and make choices based on interpretations of situations and circumstances. They plan in order to accomplish goals. They make decisions to expand or to cut back, to begin new activities, to redefine or stop old activities, and to restructure the order of the organization or to maintain it.

Traditionalists also have changed their ideas about organizational effectiveness. They are still concerned with the relationship between communication and organizational effectiveness, but they have expanded the idea of organizational effectiveness to include more than managerial objectives such as productivity and morale. Organizational effectiveness also includes the welfare of organization members in general and the overall quality of organizational life (Dessler, 1980; French, Bell, & Zawacki, 1983; Pace, 1983). This shift in emphasis changes the political position of traditionalism as well inasmuch as attention to the welfare of organization members in general means that managerial and leadership interests cannot automatically be privileged over everyone else's.

What would traditional concepts and methods in organizational communication contribute to understanding or preventing the response failures during the Hurricane Katrina catastrophe that we described in the prologue for this book? In addition to the immediate failure of electronic communications systems, many of the problems involved failures in human communication, and some of these failures may have occurred before Katrina even struck. For example, Egelhoff and Sen (1992) wrote in an organizational communication journal years ago that a crisis such as a major natural disaster will produce confusion about lines of authority and responsibility and create conditions that cannot be managed with existing operating structure and information processing capabilities. This kind of crisis "will be most effectively dealt with by decentralizing crisis management activity" (p. 465), assuming, of course, that the right resources and skill sets are available in that decentralized arrangement.

Although Egelhoff and Sen were writing about crisis management by corporations, their predictions might apply just as easily to Katrina. The 426-page National Response Plan that we mentioned earlier assumes, "Incidents are typically managed at the lowest possible geographic, organizational, and jurisdictional level" (p. 6). If an incident rises to the level of "National Significance," the Secretary of Homeland Security is supposed to step in to coordinate operations and resources, i.e., to centralize at least to some extent the management of the event. Under the plan, Governor Blanco's declaration on Saturday that Katrina would overwhelm state and local capabilities should have triggered this level of centralization before the storm hit on Monday, but that kind of coordination came much later. Moreover, much of the language in relevant law and planning documents treated the federal role as one of providing "supplementary assistance," and the governor herself used this language in her request for help (Louisiana Governor's Office, 2005).

The problem in this instance may not have been centralization versus decentralization as much as it was confusion over locus of control. Although 40 different agencies convened in Baton Rogue to get organized two days before the storm, the subsequent confusion over locus of control undermined coordination at all levels. The traditional organizational communication scholar might be disappointed, but not at all surprised that communication failed and confusion prevailed.

One also must take into account the point of view from which a structure is seen as centralized or decentralized. At one level, Wal-Mart, unhampered by entanglements and accountability within a centralized government bureaucracy, mounted a nimble response. But within Wal-Mart itself, the locus of control for emergency response most assuredly is centralized with Jason Jackson and his emergency operations team.

The Interpretive Perspective

The second important perspective is the interpretive perspective, which regards organizations as *cultures* (Pacanowsky & O'Donnell-Trujillo, 1984). When we think about the idea of a people's culture, most of us probably think about their way of life, including everything from their homes and clothing to their language and customs. Now a culture certainly includes all of these things, but it also involves a lot more. According to anthropologist W. A. Haviland (1993), "Culture consists of the abstract values, beliefs, and perceptions that lie behind people's behavior" (p. 29). This idea captures the essential difference between the interpretivist and the traditionalist. The traditionalist understands the world of social action by studying and relating observable and tangible actions and conditions. The interpretivist tries to uncover the culture that, as Haviland says, lies behind these actions and conditions.

To the interpretivist, the organization is a subjective rather than objective phenomenon. Social action is possible only to the extent that people can share subjective meanings. The culture of an organization is a network of such meanings. Thus, an organization exists in the shared experiences of the people who constitute it. This does not mean that the organization is an unreal figment of someone's imagination. It means, instead, that organizational reality is socially constructed through communication (Putnam, 1982).

Now what exactly is a socially constructed reality? It is a reality that is created and sustained through our interaction with one another. Consider, for example, the "reality" of a five-dollar bill. Objectively, it is a piece of paper with ink markings on it and worth no more than the miniscule costs of that paper and ink and the process needed to produce it. Yet you can trade this objectively worthless piece of paper for lunch at your favorite fast-food restaurant with no questions asked. Why? Because we have a socially constructed agreement about the "worth" of a five-dollar bill. Now there are many objective factors that will influence this social construction (e.g., the availability of goods and services for exchange), but the five-dollar bill is what it is only because we make it so and maintain its value in our transactions.

There is, of course, a lot more to the social construction of reality than the value of a five-dollar bill. A socially constructed reality such as a culture involves a complex web of shared meanings, filters for and shapers of our beliefs and experiences, and ways of acting toward one another as well as "outsiders." Interpretive scholars are interested in revealing the socially constructed realities of organizations. They study communication as the process through which this social construction occurs. Consequently, they are interested in the symbols and meanings involved in various forms of organizational action. Interpretivists attempt to describe the ways in which organization members understand their experiences through communication and how they enact "the organization" on the basis of shared meanings. In this sense, an organization is a negotiated order, i.e., a product of our collective discourse and transactions.

In our description of traditionalism, we illustrated how a traditionalist might try to find out about the relationship between management communication style and employee job satisfaction by measuring these two conditions and statistically analyzing the measurements. How would an interpretivist approach the problem of understanding employee experiences of managers' communication styles?

To begin with, the interpretivist probably would not ask specific questions about concepts such as "openness" and "satisfaction" and certainly would not attempt to measure these conditions. Instead, the interpretivist is more likely to ask organization members to provide illustrations or stories about their experiences. Then, the interpretivist analyzes and describes the themes that appear in these reports. These themes reveal the ways in which organization members share their experiences and socially construct an understanding of these experiences. If an idea such as the importance of openness in managers' communication happens to appear as a theme in the reports, the interpretivist might discuss it as an indication of how organization members use "openness" to understand their relationships with managers. The interpretivist's goal is to reveal those communicative activities that occur in a variety of settings to produce the unique character of an organization (Smilowitz, 1982).

How would interpretivists view organizational actions before, during, and after a crisis such as Katrina? In fact, interpretive scholars in organizational communication have studied these kinds of events and applied their concepts to explain failures and improve future response. For example, Sellnow, Seeger, and Ulmer (2002) noted that the "tendency of crisis managers . . . to see novel events according to previous experience is well documented in the crisis literature" (p. 287). They applied an interpretive use of chaos theory in a case study of the 1997 Red River Valley floods to show how this tendency inhibits effective crisis management.

How does this happen? A quest for predictability leads crisis managers to assume that their traditional methods and tools are adequate, that the current crisis can be managed like previous crises. In the 1997 Red River floods, "officials continued this strategy, despite the extreme conditions" (p. 279). They simply failed to recognize that they were confronting a novel situation. This led to a so-called cosmology episode, i.e., a collapse of organizational sense-making capability. As the flood broke a 100-year-old record, prior planning and tried-and-true methods failed. One operations manager said, "No one has ever seen this much water in the Fargo [North Dakota] area, ever. All we can do is react" (p. 279). Another admitted, "We're dealing with an unknown" (p. 279). From an interpretive point of view, was FEMA's fog of confusion during Katrina another perfect illustration of a cosmology episode?

Sellnow, Seeger, and Ulmer went on to describe how the crisis management system during the Red River floods gradually self-organized, i.e., how order reemerged from a chaotic state. A lot of self-organizing also happened at various levels of government in the wake of Katrina.

The Critical Perspective

Critical scholars differ from traditional and interpretive scholars in various ways, but one difference is especially significant: Critical scholars regard organizations as instruments of privilege or even outright oppression. They focus their attention on the relationship between privileged classes (or privileged conditions) and disadvantaged or oppressed organizational groups. They are concerned with the way in which that relationship is created and sustained through symbols and discourse. The privileged usually include owners, executives, the political elite, and even dominant ways of thinking and acting (e.g., masculine rationality). The disadvantaged or oppressed usually include workers, women, minorities, and others who are denied privilege or otherwise discounted in organizational life.

Sometimes the sources of organizational oppression seem to be located in systems of language and meaning. For example, some writers say that sexual discrimination and harassment of women in organizations arise from a language that demeans and debases women (Bosmajian, 1983). In other words, common ways of *talking* about women influence ways of *thinking* about and *acting* toward women.

In other cases, oppression seems to reside in power differences and inequalities that exist in the design of organizational structure. Discrimination against women, for example, is not merely a problem of language, but it is also a problem of physical segregation and isolation from sources of power and information (Crawford, 1977). If a woman is assigned to a "do-nothing" job, or is denied promotion and advancement, or cannot get past the boss's secretary in order to get an appointment, she faces *structural* barriers to her goals.

Not surprisingly, remedies for sex discrimination appeal to changes in both language and structure, e.g., eliminating sexist language in order to reconstruct symbolic expressions of male dominance and requiring the male-dominated power structure to integrate women into its ranks. But treating oppression as a language problem or a structure problem with palliatives directed at one or the other may miss the true nature of organizational oppression, and this is the point at which the critical perspective has something important to contribute to our understanding of organizations.

At the risk of oversimplification, we might say that critical scholars are concerned at the same time with social structure *and* with symbolic processes. Organizational oppression does not reside in structure alone or in symbols alone. It resides in the *relationship* between structure and symbols.

A good example of the linkage between structure and symbols can be found in Dennis Mumby's (1987) comments about interpretivism. Mumby, a critical theorist, agrees that interpretive research "demonstrates that organizational reality is fundamentally symbolic in nature" (p. 120), but he also believes that interpretive research is naïve because "it does little to explicate the deep structure process through which certain organizational realities come to hold sway over competing world-views" (p. 113). In other words, it does little to explain the role of symbols in dominance, oppression, and the privileging of some interests over others.

Why does Mumby make this argument, and what does he mean by *deep structure*? As he explains it, "Domination involves getting people to organize their behavior around a particular rule system" (p. 115). This rule system is the deep structure of the organization. It defines power relationships. Some of the symbolic forms that we find in organizational communication function to "produce, maintain, and reproduce these power structures" (Mumby, p. 113). Consequently, critical scholars often are concerned with discursive practices and the concept of discourse as we described it earlier.

One way in which symbols define power relations is through the systematic distortion of communication (Deetz, 1982). Tompkins and Redding point out that distortion of communication does not mean the same thing to a critical scholar that it might mean to a traditionalist. When traditionalists talk about distortion, they usually are concerned with inaccuracies or errors in information that lead to inefficiency and ineffectiveness in communication. But critical scholars regard distortion as a systematic and deliberate symbolic process through which "the owner/manager's interests are falsely joined with those of the worker in ideological communication" (Tompkins & Redding, 1988, p. 27).

As you may be expecting by now, we are going to suggest how critical scholars would contribute something to our understanding of Katrina. For example, consider the story of Jason Jackson and the Wal-Mart response to Katrina. It is not our aim here to detract from Wal-Mart's important contributions during this catastrophe, but Wal-Mart also created media awareness of these contributions. Some media organizations suggested what the corporation itself did not say explicitly, i.e., that Wal-Mart's superior systems, practices, and people enabled the company to go where others could not (Barbaro & Gillis, 2005).

Featherstone (2005) offered an initial critical commentary directed not at Wal-Mart per se but at media suggestions that Wal-Mart's Katrina response demonstrated the superiority of the private sector over government. In her own colorful use of language, Featherstone suggests that the language of this lesson on private-sector triumph versus government bungling obscures or simply ignores the consequences of systematically draining essential resources from the government agencies that are supposed to respond in such situations.

Within the company itself, stories of Jason Jackson and the emergency operations center might well become legendary as illustrations of the Wal-Mart way of doing things and the values that are important to the company's success. But critical scholars want to know whose interests these values really serve. Those of all organization members or primarily those of an elite group or class?

And how about one of the most troubling aspects of the entire Katrina episode, namely, the silences that repeatedly greeted Brian Wolshon's question a long time before Katrina about hurricane evacuation plans for the tens of thousands of immobile residents of New Orleans? Thomas Huckin may have offered some critical theory clues when he described textual silences in discourse on homelessness in 2002. Huckin discussed five forms of textual elision or silences. As a critical scholar, he was interested primarily in so-called manipulative silences, i.e., silences "that intentionally conceal relevant information from the listener or reader, to the advantage of the speaker or writer" (p. 351). Since manipulative silence manipulates only when it goes unnoticed, we doubt that it applies here, but another of Huckin's silences, namely, speech-act silence, may apply. Unlike manipulative silence, speech-act silence intends something communicative.

Maybe you have heard or even had occasion to use the phrase, "Your silence speaks volumes." In the case of speech-act silence, the listener is supposed to perceive something informative, and the speaker intends for something informative to be perceived. Now maybe this is in one sense still a form of manipulation because the speaker possesses deniability: "I never said that." Were Wolshon's expert planning colleagues saying something through their silence that they also, if necessary, could deny ever having said?

We will have a lot more to say about critical scholarship in various chapters of the book. For now, however, it is only important to know that critical scholarship, as its label implies, criticizes organizational discourse with the goal of consciousness raising and emancipation for oppressed organizational classes.

Feminism

We include feminism here as a special case of the critical perspective because feminist theory and scholarship in organizational communication also is concerned with criticism and emancipation, but feminism is focused first and foremost on the oppression of women and on patriarchy (institutionalized male domination) as the instrument of that oppression. Actually, there are several different versions of feminist theory that differ from each other primarily in their strategies for addressing the problem of patriarchy. For example, Tong (1989) and Iannello (1992) distinguish between liberal and radical feminism. Iannello says that liberal feminism aims at advancing women's rights and achieving equality by "eliminating patriarchy from the larger institutions that govern society" (p. 39). In liberal feminism, "socially constructed differences between the sexes are the chief source of female oppression" (p. 39).

Radical feminism also asserts that gender roles are socially constructed, but specifically blames "male power" (Iannello, 1992, p. 40) for that construction. Thus, according to Tong, "It is not just patriarchy's legal and political structures that must be overturned; its social and cultural institutions (especially the family, the church, and the academy) must also go" (p. 3). Under the radical feminist agenda, there is no room for any naïve interpretivist ideas about negotiated order!

Status of the Field

Having considered the major perspectives that have developed in the study of organizational communication, we can now offer an assessment of the field's present status. We think the status is best reflected in the current influence of each perspective. There are new developments that are shaping the direction of this field in this early part of the 21st century. Rather than address those in summary form here, we have saved them for the book's last chapter on future directions.

Although there are other ways of categorizing and describing the major perspectives that guide our study of organizational communication, the ones that we have labeled as traditional, interpretive, and critical seem to be the most influential (cf. Tompkins & Redding, 1988, or Miller, 2006). The traditional perspective was for many years the dominant orientation to organizational communication, but interpretive and critical approaches gained adherents very rapidly in the latter part of the 20th century. The acceptance and influence of these perspectives arose from at least two major sources of dissatisfaction with traditionalism.

First, traditionalism was responsible for the disorganized state of the field in the 1960s and 1970s. Although several major textbooks and articles attempted to assemble the jigsaw puzzle of organizational communication in the 1970s, questions remained about our ability to make sense of our own work. H. Lloyd Goodall, Jr. (1984) concluded from a review of organizational communication research in that era that different studies "read like newspapers from different planets" (p. 135).

Second, some scholars objected that traditionalism is "managerially biased" because it is concerned primarily with work organizations and with the relationships between communication and organizational effectiveness. This bias is compounded because the organizational communication scholar's audience consists mainly of managers, administrators, professionals, and, of course, college students who plan to enter similar roles. Michael Pacanowsky and Nick O'Donnell-Trujillo summed up this criticism when they argued that traditionalists try "to understand organizations better so that organizations can be made to run better. . . . What has come to count as 'better organizational function' are notions with a distinctly managerial flavor" (1982, p. 119).

Although attention to managerial perspectives and problems certainly is not wrong, many interpretivists point out that an exclusive preoccupation with these concerns results in a very narrow definition of our field of study. Much of the day-to-day communication in organizations has relatively little to do with managerial definitions of organizational effectiveness. Managerial processes involve only one slice of the organizational communication pie.

Critics of traditionalism began to turn to interpretive and critical concepts as a way of at least escaping if not correcting the problems that they saw in the traditionalist perspective. Instead of identifying dozens of communication and organizational variables, then explaining their relationships in piecemeal statistical studies, interpretivists concentrate on the communication process of constructing the meanings and frames of reference from which members experience organizational life. Critical theorists concentrate on revealing how symbols and discourse figure into systems of inequality and privileged interests.

Today, it does not appear that any one perspective dominates the study of organizational communication. While critical and feminist scholars are working on problems ranging from gendered organizing (Buzzanell & Liu, 2005) to dysfunctional organizational change efforts (Harrison & Young, 2005), interpretive research is addressing topics such as work-family conflict (Medved, 2004) and successful community building (Barge, 2003). Meanwhile, traditional scholars continue to work on issues such as factors affecting upward influence tactics (Olufowote, Miller, & Wilson, 2005), information adequacy (Rosenfeld, Richman, & May, 2004), and disengagement in workplace relationships (Sias & Perry, 2004). In any case, debates about dominance and validity of perspectives may be pointless. Important contributions to organizational communication scholarship are being made from all three perspectives, and we have tried to reflect these contributions throughout this book.

SUMMARY

Organizations are pervasive in contemporary human experience. Humans organize to get things done, but organization involves more than just accomplishing tasks. They are sites of conflict and confusion as well as cooperation and clarity. They exist for many different reasons, and the reasons are not necessarily harmonious. We tend to speak of organizations as if they are containers in which humans act and interact, but an organization is constituted and enacted through the concerted actions of its members. Hence, communication is the essence of organization. Some discourse analysts go even further by treating the organization literally as a set of discursive practices.

The study of organizational communication can be important to you for at least three reasons. It can improve your understanding of organizational life, provide you with an awareness of important communication skills in organizations, and perhaps start you on a path to a career in the field. In order to really appreciate the field, though, you should also know something about its background and the factors that shaped our approach to this book.

Organizational communication is a relatively new field of study. When it began, it borrowed ideas from other social and behavioral sciences in such a way that its focus on communication was unclear. Many critics felt that the new field was fragmented and disorganized. These problems led to at least three different perspectives of organizational communication: traditional, interpretive, and critical. Feminist theory also is included here as a special case of the critical perspective. These perspectives differ in the ways that they study organizational communication and in the assumptions that they make about the nature of organizations. Traditionalism has evolved from an early form into a different contemporary form. Early traditionalism understands organizations as machines and regards communication as a machinelike process. Recent traditionalism sees organizations as living systems and communication as a dynamic, organismic process. Despite these changes in traditionalism, interpretivism and critical theory have developed as serious alternatives to the traditionalist study of organizations. Interpretivists are concerned with the symbolic processes through which organizational reality is socially constructed. Critical theorists are concerned with the relationship between structure and symbolic processes in the efforts to criticize oppression and the systematic distortion of organizational communication.

DISCUSSION QUESTIONS/ACTIVITIES

1. What are some examples of common communication episodes in organizations? What do these examples indicate about the importance of communication in organizational life? Try to generate some examples from your own experiences in organizations, then compare them with those of another person.

2. How would you describe the similarities and differences among traditionalist, interpretivist, and critical perspectives of organizational communication?

3. What are some of the reasons that might explain the early dominance of traditionalism in the study of organizational communication?

4. According to the text, there are some questions that traditionalism is not equipped to answer. What do you think some of the questions might be? How could they be answered from other perspectives?

5. As a group exercise in class, find your own recent events such as Hurricane Katrina that offer lessons about organizational communication. Try to describe the event from traditional, interpretive, and critical points of view.

REFERENCES

Barbaro, M., & Gillis, J. (2005, September 6). Wal-Mart at forefront of hurricane relief. *The Washington Post.* [Electronic version.] Retrieved September 21, 2005, from http://www.washingtonpost.com/wp-dyn/content/article/2005/09/05/AR2005090501598.html

Barge, J. K. (2003). Hope, communication, and community building. *Southern Communication Journal, 69*(1), 63–81.

Bosmajian, H. A. (1983). *The language of oppression* (2nd ed.). Lanham, MD: University Press of America.

Bureau of Labor Statistics. (2004). *Occupational outlook handbook* (2004–2005 ed.). Washington, DC: U.S. Department of Labor.

Buzzanell, P. M., & Liu, M. (2005). Struggling with maternity leave policies and practices: A poststructuralist feminist analysis of gendered organizing. *Journal of Applied Communication Research, 33*(1),1–25 .

Carbaugh, D. (1988). Comments on "culture" in communication inquiry. *Communication Reports, 1,* 38–41.

Conrad, C., & Poole, M. S. (2005). Strategic organizational communication in a global economy. Belmont, CA: Thompson/Wadsworth.

Crawford, J. S. (1977). *Women in middle management: Selection, training, advancement, performance.* Ridgewood, NJ: Forkner.

Deetz, S. A. (1982). Critical interpretive research in organizational communication. *Western Journal of Speech Communication, 46,* 131–149.

Dennis, H. S., III, Goldhaber, G. M., & Yates, M. P. (1978). Organizational communication theory and research: An overview of research methods. In B. D. Ruben (Ed.), *Communication yearbook 2* (pp. 243–269). New Brunswick, NJ: Transaction Books.

Dessler, G. (1980). *Organization theory: Integrating structure and behavior.* Englewood Cliffs, NJ: Prentice Hall.

Dewine, S. (2001). *The consultant's craft: Improving organizational communication* (2nd ed.). Boston: Bedford/St. Martin's.

Egelhoff, W. G., & Sen, F. (1992). An information-processing model of crisis management. *Management Communication Quarterly, 5*(4), 443–484.

Fairhurst, G. T., & Putnam, L. (2004). Organizations as discursive constructions. *Communication Theory, 14*(1), 5–26.

Featherstone, L. (2005, September 16). Wal-Mart's image rescue. The National [Electronic version]. Retrieved September 21, 2005, from http://www.thenation.com/doc/20050926/featherstone

French, W. L., Bell, C. H., Jr., & Zawacki, R. A. (Eds.). (1983). *Organization development: Theory, practice, and research* (2nd ed.). Plano, TX: Business Publications.

Goodall, H. L., Jr. (1984). The status of communication studies in organizational contexts: One rhetorician's lament after a year-long odyssey. *Communication Quarterly, 32,* 133–147.

Harrison, C., & Young, L. (2005). Leadership discourse in action: A textual study of organizational change in a government of Canada department. *Journal of Business and Technical Communication, 19*(1), 42–77.

Haviland, W. A. (1993). *Cultural anthropology* (7th ed.). Fort Worth, TX: Harcourt Brace Jovanovich.

Hersey, P., & Blanchard, K. (1982). *Management of organizational behavior: Utilizing human resources* (4th ed.). Englewood Cliffs, NJ: Prentice Hall.

Huckin, T. (2002). Textual silence and the discourse of homelessness. *Discourse and Society, 13*(3), 347–372.

Iannello, K. P. (1992). *Decisions without hierarchy: Feminist interventions in organization theory and practice.* New York: Routledge.

Katz, D., & Kahn, R. L. (1978). *The social psychology of organizations* (2nd ed.). New York: John Wiley & Sons.

Keyton, J. (2004). *Communication and organizational culture: A key to understanding work experiences.* Thousand Oaks, CA: Sage.

Louisiana Governor's Office. (2005, August 27). Governor Blanco's letter to President Bush, August 27, 2005. [Electronic version.] Retrieved September 21, 2005, from http://gov.louisiana.gov/index.cfm?md=newsroom&tmp=detail&articleID=862

Medved, C. (2004). The everyday accomplishment of work and family: Exploring practical actions in daily routines. *Communication Studies, 55*(1), 128–145.

Miller, K. (2006). *Organizational communication: Approaches and processes* (4th ed.). Belmont, CA: Wadsworth Publishing.

Monge, P. R., Farace, R. V., Eisenberg, E. M., Miller, K. I., & White, L. L. (1984). The process of studying process in organizational communication. *Journal of Communication, 34,* 22–43.

Morley, D. D., Shockley-Zalabak, P., & Cesaria, R. (2002). Organizational influence processes: Perceptions of values, communication and effectiveness. *Studies in Communication Sciences, 2*(1), 69–104.

Mumby, D. K. (1987). The political function of narrative in organizations. *Communication Monographs, 54,* 113–127.

Munter, M. (2002). *Guide to managerial communication* (6th ed.). Englewood Cliffs, NJ: Prentice Hall.

Olufowote, J. O., Miller, V. D., & Wilson, S. R. (2005). The interactive effects of role change goals and relational exchanges on employee upward influence tactics. *Management Communication Quarterly, 18*(3), 385–403.

Pacanowsky, M. E., & O'Donnell-Trujillo, N. (1982). Communication and organizational cultures. *Western Journal of Speech Communication, 46,* 115–130.

Pacanowsky, M. E., & O'Donnell-Trujillo, N. (1984). Organizational communication as cultural performance. *Communication Monographs, 50,* 126–147.

Pace, R. W. (1983). *Organizational communication: Foundations for human resource development.* Englewood Cliffs, NJ: Prentice Hall.

Pearce, W. B., & Cronen, V. (1980). *Communication, action, and meaning: The creation of social realities.* New York: Praeger.

Putnam, L. L. (1982). Paradigms for organizational communication research: An overview and synthesis. *Western Journal of Speech Communication, 46,* 192–206.

Redding, W. C. (1979). Graduate education and the communication consultant: Playing God for a fee. *Communication Education, 28,* 346–352.

Redding, W. C. (1985). Stumbling toward identity: The emergence of organizational communication as a field of study. In R. D. McPhee & P. Tompkins (Eds.), *Organizational communication: Traditional themes and new directions* (pp. 15–54). Newbury Park, CA: Sage.

Rosenfeld, L. B., Richman, J. M., & May, S. K. (2004). Information adequacy, job satisfaction and organizational culture in a dispersed-network organization. *Journal of Applied Communication Research, 32*(1), 28–54.

Sellnow, T. J., Seeger, M. W., Ulmer, R. R. (2002). Chaos theory, informational needs, and natural disasters. *Journal of Applied Communication Research, 30*(4), 269–292.

Sias, P. M., & Perry, T. (2004). Disengaging from workplace relationships: A research note. *Human Communication Research, 30*(4), 589–602.

Smilowitz, M. (1982). *Ought as was in organizational reality.* Paper presented at the Second Conference on Interpretive Research in Organizational Communication, Alta, UT, August 1982.

Stevens, B. (2005, March). What communication *skills* do employers want? Silicon valley recruiters respond. *Journal of Employment Counseling, 42*(1), 2–9.

Tompkins, P. K., & Redding, W. C. (1988). Organizational communication—past and present tenses. In G. M. Goldhaber & G. A. Barnett (Eds.), *Handbook of organizational communication* (pp. 5–33). Norwood, NJ: Ablex.

Tong, R. (1989). *Feminist thought.* Boulder, CO: Westview.

Communication and Its Functions

The next two chapters in this book are concerned with ideas that truly provide the foundation of organizational communication; hence their early placement in the text. Traditionalists generally have understood the organization either as a machine or as an organism. One of the most useful and convenient ways of describing either machines or organisms is to characterize them according to their functions and structure. **Functions** are activities of a system that serve some purpose or objective. **Structure** is reflected in the linkages or relationships between elements in a system—linkages used to carry out functional activity. When these ideas are applied to organizational communication, *function* refers generally to the content, goals, and effects of communication. *Structure* refers to channels of communication or, literally, the patterns of interaction among organization members (Farace, Monge, & Russell, 1977). Although traditionalists provide us with an important perspective on communication functions, it is just one perspective. We also need to consider interpretive and critical perspectives on communication functions. Interpretivists focus on how communication leads to the construction of shared meanings. Critical theorists focus on the struggles over meaning that exist in organizations. So, we discuss the concept of communication function in this chapter, then follow with a discussion of structure in Chapter 3.

In order to discuss the concept of communication function, this chapter unfolds in the following manner. First, we alert our readers to a precaution that must be considered in any discussion of communication function: the structure-function relationship. Second, we develop our views on communication information and meaning by focusing on aspects of verbal and nonverbal communication. Third, we discuss traditionalist, interpretive, and critical perspectives on communication functions. In discussing the traditionalist perspective, we describe the production, maintenance, and innovation functions of communication. We follow this discussion with a description of Dance and Larson's communicative functions. Next, we look at uncertainty reduction and information adequacy followed by an examination of the concept of social capital. In discussing the interpretive functions of communication, we describe George Herbert Mead's perspective on symbolic interactionism, followed by Berger and Luckmann's perspective on communication as construction. Our discussion of critical perspectives on communicative functions looks at Bakhtin's views on communication as dialogic and considers how communication serves to control and manipulate organization members. Finally, we examine relationship development among workers from the traditionalist, interpretive, and critical perspectives.

A PRECAUTION: FUNCTION AND STRUCTURE RELATIONSHIP

Before we begin our description of organizational communication functions and structure, we need to discuss a precaution that you should keep in mind: *communication functions and structure are highly interrelated.* So, although we will talk about function and structure as *separate* ideas in two different chapters of this book for the sake of simplicity, these two concepts are, in fact, highly related. In particular, the communication structure of an organization is developed and elaborated in ways that serve particular purposes. For example, a traditional distinction between formal and informal communication that we will develop later in this chapter implies that the two structures often involve different communication functions. As Farace and colleagues (1977) pointed out, "Both function and structure are intimately linked together, and major breakdowns in either can render the communication system of an organization inoperative" (p. 59).

COMMUNICATION, INFORMATION, AND MEANING

The accomplishment of communication functions depends on the use of information and the meanings that are invested in that information. From the traditional point of view, information may be regarded as the basic "raw material" of communication. This raw material takes form when meaning is invested in it. Before we try to describe the basic functions of organizational communication, we need to sort out what is involved in communication, information, and meaning.

Each of us has an intuitive understanding of what is involved in human communication. After all, we communicate with others virtually every day of our lives. Yet, it is not easy to develop a precise definition and description of the communication process. The term *communication* has become such a buzzword in modern society that one can use it to mean just about anything. From the traditionalist perspective communication is *shared meaning created among two or more people through verbal and nonverbal transaction.* The basic raw material of communication is verbal and nonverbal information. When two or more human beings engage in verbal and nonverbal transaction, they are involved in generating, perceiving, and interpreting such information. To the extent that shared meaning or a common interpretation among them results from this process, communication has occurred.

This definition of communication is not unusual. Others have offered similar definitions (Goyer, 1970; Tubbs & Moss, 1980), but not everyone agrees with this approach (Eisenberg & Goodall, 1993). The idea of "shared meaning" is only one way to define communication, but we will elaborate on this definition because the key terms, at least, are common in many traditionalist definitions of communication. Then, later in the chapter, we will examine critical perspectives that define communication as involving struggles over meaning.

Information and Meaning

In a simple sense, information includes any kind of pattern that a person can observe or sense in the environment. The significance or meaning attached to the pattern may range from negligible to very substantial. **Meaning** occurs when information is placed within a context. The context may be as simple as pattern recognition or as complex as reflective interpretation, in which one piece of information is related to and understood with reference to many others. For example, consider the following markings (Figure 2.1).

Although a very small child may perceive little more than the contrast between the color of the page and the color of the markings, a normal adult will see patterns or definite characteristics such as linear and curvilinear features. Beyond these features, the English-speaking reader may assign very little meaning to these markings. If you know something about the structure of languages, you may realize that the markings represent

FIGURE 2.1   An Optical Illusion

<h1 style="text-align:center">ЭЮЯ</h1>

letters or even a word in some language. If you understand Russian, you will recognize the markings as the last three letters of the Russian alphabet. In addition to this denotative meaning, the connection between the markings and "Russian" may also evoke other feelings for you. The level of significance or meaning in each case is different, depending on the frame of reference that your experience has given you. Information provides the basis for communication. Although any perceivable aspect of one's environment is potentially informative, we are concerned with information in the forms of human verbal and nonverbal behavior.

Verbal Behavior

Verbal behavior includes speaking and writing in the code of a language system. The words in a vocabulary and the grammatical rules for arranging them in expressions are the basic features of a language system. Grammar does not necessarily mean an eighth-grade English teacher's *prescriptive* rules for how one is supposed to use language. It also includes all of the regularities that occur in the verbal behavior of a group of language users. Any mode of expression that occurs as a common usage within a particular language community represents a rule for that community. A lawyer representing a client who intends to sue you as well as some other people may say, "To protect my client's interests, I have concluded that it will be necessary to join you as a party defendant in the above styled action, to wit steps to effect this joinder have been undertaken." You may find the rules of this language to be odd and even ungrammatical from a prescriptive standpoint, but the phrase will make perfect sense to another lawyer who uses this same language. All of the words in a language are **symbols**. All symbols have three basic characteristics. They are representational, freely created, and culturally transmitted (Pollio, 1974).

A symbol is **representational** because it stands for something other than itself. Word symbols provide labels for objects, actions, and experiences. They also permit us to talk about and share conceptions of the things that they label. A word symbol is a substitute that represents an object by providing a link to the idea or concept of this object (Langer, 1942).

Symbols also are **freely created**. The relationship between a symbol and its referent (the thing the symbol represents) is arbitrary because the users of a particular language make up and choose the symbols. The founders of International Business Machines could just as easily have named the company Acme Typewriters. The referent would have been the same (although "IBM" admittedly has more flair). Human beings are continually inventing new symbols to refer to new conditions. Today, we talk about storing files on "zip disks," "microwaving" our food, and "keyboarding" on "personal computers," with meanings for these terms that were virtually nonexistent two decades ago.

Finally, symbols are **culturally transmitted**. This means that symbols are taught and learned, carried on from one generation to another within a language system. Although symbols are freely created and languages do change over time, much of the basic form and content of a language remains stable through cultural transmission. Others created most of our symbols and the rules for using them a long time before we arrived in the world. We are born into a system of symbols and language rules that imposes a particular order on our world. As we acquire the language, we acquire the order that comes along with it.

Language scholars have no problem with the idea that symbols are culturally transmitted, but the fact that language does bring with it a way of ordering the world leads many scholars to regard representation and free creation as inadequate characterizations of symbols. Symbols are more than just representative and arbitrary because language exerts a very powerful influence on the way we experience the world (Blumer, 1969; Deetz, 1973). For example, Benjamin Whorf (1957) found that Hopi Indian and English languages handle time in very different ways. The Hopi has no means for marking time that corresponds to the English use of past, present, and future tense. Whorf reasoned that the Hopi experience of time must be quite different from the experience of someone whose language affords convenient ways of carving up time according to verb tense. If Whorf is right, language is much more than a mere tool for expressing thought. Thought itself depends on language, and our notions about "reality" are products of that language. It is even possible that something that is "thinkable" in one language may be "unthinkable" in another. Avis Rent-A-Car encountered this problem some years ago when the company attempted to translate its famous "We Try Harder" slogan into the languages of other countries where Avis did business. The closest approximation in German translates roughly as "We give of ourselves more effort." Somehow, the essence of "We Try Harder" seems to be lost in the German equivalent (Pollio, 1974).

Is language an important factor in structuring our experience of organizational life? Interpretivists and critical theorists certainly seem to think so. In part, this is the point that they are making when they argue that organizational reality is socially constructed. Studies by Koch and Deetz and by Wood and Conrad provide some evidence for this point of view. Koch and Deetz (1981) reported that language systems in organizations revealed "root metaphors" that members use to order and to make sense of their experiences. For example, members might talk about and understand their organization as an efficient, well-oiled machine (mechanical metaphor), a winning team (sports metaphor), a combat group (military metaphor), or even "a big, happy family."

Wood and Conrad (1983) found that organizational languages often contain paradoxes that create double binds for members. A double bind arises from inconsistent messages that result in a "hanged if you do, hanged if you do not" outcome. Consider the manner in which members of a male-dominated management group sometimes solicit ideas from female colleagues:

> The invitation often takes the form of soliciting "a woman's perspective" or the "female viewpoint," a form which both subordinates professional expertise and peer status to gender and emphasizes the woman's difference from other

members of the group. The woman confronted with such a request is caught in a paradox. If she protests the focus on gender, she runs the risk of being labeled overly sensitive. . . . If she accepts the focus on gender, she collaborates in diminishing her image as a professional. Of course, her colleagues are caught within the same paradox of recognizing her uniqueness, yet being enjoined not to recognize it and to regard her as no different from anyone . . . of equivalent rank in the institution. (pp. 309–310)

Language and other symbol systems have two other characteristics that also are important in the study of organizational communication. First, language is ambiguous in the sense that most words and expressions can have more than one meaning. Several scholars state that much of the communication in organizations occurs in an effort to reduce the uncertainty associated with ambiguity (Goldhaber, 1993; Weick, 1979). Second, organizational communication often involves the use of group-restricted codes (Baird & Weinberg, 1981). A group-restricted code involves a specialized usage of a language. The vocabulary and rules are unique to a particular group.

Ambiguity

Ambiguity occurs as a consequence of abstract terminology, lack of sufficient detail in messages, and inappropriate or confusing use of modifiers and qualifying phrases (Johnson, 1977). Sometimes, ambiguity is accidental and unintentional, as reflected in the case of a publishing company executive who became angry when someone failed to notify the printing department about a major change in an order. The executive complained to a group of middle managers, "We've got to have better communications around here," then promptly left for a two-week vacation, thinking that the middle managers would lay down the law with employees on the importance of relaying information about any change in a project. When he returned, the middle managers could hardly wait to show him the marketing brochure describing the state-of-the-art office communications system that they had ordered (at a cost of several thousand dollars) during his absence. It was obvious that the middle managers' concept of "better communications" was quite a bit different from the idea that the executive had in mind.

Ambiguity is a common, day-to-day problem in organizational communication, and many organizations expend a great deal of energy in attempting to cope with it. Experts on oral and written expression are quick to advise people that simple, concrete language is the key to reducing ambiguity. But ambiguity in organizational communication involves more than accidental misuse of language or failure to be clear. Ambiguity occurs simply because a symbol or expression has different meanings for different people. There is no guarantee that two people will share the same meaning for a term or expression, even when it is simple and concrete. As Eric Eisenberg (1984) pointed out, ambiguity and clarity are not really embedded in messages but in the *relationship* between source, message, and receiver. Clarity exists only to the extent that "a source has narrowed the possible interpretations of a message and succeeded in achieving a correspondence between his or her intentions and the interpretation of the receiver" (p. 23).

Eisenberg also makes a convincing case that much of the ambiguity in organizational communication is quite deliberate rather than accidental. **Strategic ambiguity**, according to

Eisenberg, is not necessarily bad. In fact, it is often very useful and even essential to the organization. Strategic ambiguity helps to promote cohesion by highlighting organization members' agreement on abstract, general ideas and by obscuring their disagreements over specific details. For example, the faculty at University X is "strongly committed to excellence in teaching, research, and service." The university president likes to mention this in public speeches but never attempts to define "excellence" in these areas because different groups of faculty disagree over the specific standards.

Strategic ambiguity in organizational policies and procedures also allows organizations to adapt more readily to change. In 1979–1980, Chrysler Corporation used this form of ambiguity to cope with the public perception that the company produced low-quality automobiles. Foss (1984) noted that Chrysler quickly associated itself with Japanese products (generally regarded as high quality) by marketing the Japanese-made Dodge Colt. The little Colt was advertised as "The Most Technologically Advanced Japanese Import You Can Buy." At the *same* time, according to Foss, Chrysler *denied* its linkage to Japan in an advertising campaign for its U.S.-built K cars: "K cars are proof . . . you don't have to be Japanese to build quality cars." The strategy allowed Chrysler to capitalize on its Japanese connection as a short-term response to its quality problem until a time came when the corporation "no longer had to rely on its Japanese imports for an image of quality and desirability" (p. 82). In effect, Chrysler used strategic ambiguity to play both ends against the middle.

Finally, Eisenberg argues that strategic ambiguity is an important means for supporting status distinctions and maintaining interpersonal relationships in organizations. Consider, for example, the relationship between physicians and nurses in hospital settings. Suppose that a physician gives a nurse an erroneous or inappropriate order for a patient's treatment. If the nurse knows that the order is inappropriate, he or she is legally obligated to confront the situation. But such a confrontation challenges the physician's supreme authority over patient care and nursing actions. The nurse's only way out of this bind "is to use the doctor-nurse game and communicate . . . without appearing to" (Stein, 1967, p. 703). In other words, the nurse uses an *indirect* rather than a direct means of communicating with the physician about the problem. Instead of making an unambiguous statement that the order is inappropriate or that it should be changed (statements that would challenge or threaten the physician's authority), the nurse might say, "Doctor, I'm concerned about this order. Could you explain it to me?" This is a face-saving strategy that allows the physician to discover the problem and correct it. However, Cunningham and Wilcox (1984) noted that nurses will take stronger, less ambiguous actions if the risk to the patient is serious and if indirect strategies are ineffective in getting the physician to change the order.

The idea of anyone's being obliged to engage in these kinds of interpersonal gymnastics merely to avoid embarrassment to an authority figure is unpalatable and typical of the kind of paradox that Wood and Conrad describe. But the politics of organizational life are filled with such paradoxes. Ambiguity, as Eisenberg suggests, can be a very effective tool for managing one's way through a paradox.

Group-Restricted Codes

Whether ambiguity in organizational communication is accidental or strategically deliberate, it can be reduced only to the extent that people share the same meaning for a code. Groups and organizations often try to ensure that shared meaning will occur by adopting a **group-restricted code** that is highly specialized (Baird & Weinberg, 1981). Many professions and technical occupations use such codes in the form of "jargon"—terms and modes of expression that are known primarily to members of these groups. One's success as a member of such a group depends in part on the ability to master the group's restricted code. We know of one high-technology corporation (Intel) in which the restricted code has become so elaborate that the company issues a comprehensive dictionary of terms and expressions to new employees.

Group-restricted codes are paradoxical. They help to minimize ambiguity and promote a common identity among group members, yet they can be quite confusing to nonmembers. For example, the lawyer's jargon that we used earlier in this chapter may seem like a maze of abstractions to an outsider, but group members (other attorneys) share relatively precise meanings for the code. Even restricted codes that seem to be simple and precise to a nonmember may have "hidden" meanings that are known only within the group itself.

The influence of a restricted code in professional situations is illustrated well by the compelling case of William Borham, who in the late 1980s became chief administrator of a large mental hospital in Wisconsin. Borham had no formal education in mental health. In fact, William Borham was not even William Borham. He was really Raymond Metzgar, a former inmate in a psychiatric institution. Metzgar's familiarity with mental hospitals and his ability to speak the language of the mental health profession enabled him to deceive his employer into believing that he was William Borham, a trained clinical psychologist. The fact that Metzgar, alias Borham, became a prominent advocate for mental health programs in Wisconsin brought great embarrassment to state officials when his deception was uncovered by Chicago police after they arrested him for child molestation.

The influence of language on our interpretations of experience, on the nature of ambiguity in organizational communication, and on the characteristics of group-restricted codes should make it clear that verbal behavior and symbolic processes in organizational communication are quite complicated. This complexity increases when we consider nonverbal behavior as the second source of information in human communication.

Nonverbal Behavior

Much of the information involved in human communication is **nonverbal behavior** that occurs in forms other than the word symbols of a language. Harrison (1970) estimated that 65% of the information in day-to-day interaction is nonverbal, but the role of nonverbal behavior in communication is not as clear as the role of verbal behavior. Ekman and Friesen (1972) regarded nonverbal behavior as "communicative" only when the person who exhibits the behavior intends it as a message for someone else. In contrast, Watzlawick, Beavin, and Jackson (1967) argued that any behavior, whether intentional or unintentional, is communicative if another person perceives and interprets it.

We do not want to get into a distracting debate over when nonverbal behavior is communicative and when it is not, but defining communication as the creation of shared meaning does at least require *both* parties in the act to be aware of the behavior, attach some meaning to it, and achieve some commonality in this meaning. The perplexing and intriguing problem with a lot of nonverbal behavior is that even when we are unaware of our own behaviors in the presence of others, they may be interpreting these behaviors and acting toward us on the basis of the interpretation. The behavior itself may not always be "communicative," but it can certainly influence the communication process. With this realization in mind, we will describe three forms of nonverbal behavior that are important in organizational communication: paralanguage, body movement, and the use of space.

Paralanguage

Paralanguage consists of nonverbal speech sounds. Tone, pitch, volume, inflection, rhythm, and rate are elements of paralanguage. Paralanguage is important because the meaning of spoken expression often depends on the paralanguage cues that accompany verbal sounds. We know, for example, that feelings and emotions in spoken expression are indicated primarily by paralanguage cues (Davitz, 1964). Although there is little research on the association between specific paralanguage cues and emotions, it is intuitively obvious that we infer others' attitudes and feelings from paralanguage cues in their speech. The phrase, "What a day," spoken quickly, in a bright tone, and with emphasis, may lead us to infer that the speaker is in a jovial mood. The same phrase in a grumbling, colorless drawl suggests that the speaker is miserable.

Paralanguage also provides cues to meaning in less obvious ways. For example, distinctions between statement types often are provided in paralanguage cues. The difference between a declarative statement and a question often is indicated by the sentence structure, but sometimes can be detected only through paralanguage. Suppose that you take a work-related problem to your boss. The boss listens, then replies, "You know what to do. . . ." A downward inflection from beginning to end may suggest a declarative statement. The boss has heard the problem and is *telling* you that you know how to handle it. An upward inflection at the end could be a question. The boss is *asking* whether or not you know how to proceed. Some authorities believe that women often use paralanguage cues in ways that undermine their authority as managers and professionals, e.g., by making declarative statements sound like questions that suggest that the speaker is tentative or uncertain (Lakoff, 1975).

Paralanguage also regulates spoken expression. A pause can indicate the end of a thought or provide a cue that another party can take a turn at speaking. In this sense, paralanguage cues are like punctuation marks in written expression. Written expression also has other characteristics that correspond to paralanguage in speech. Italics and boldface type may be used for emphasis. Readers use clarity, crispness, and overall appearance of writing in making inferences about writers in much the same way that listeners use paralanguage to make inferences about speakers. The potential cues in writing may be much more limited than those available in speech because many of the devices that one might use are regarded as inappropriate in formal writing (Perrin, 1965), although anyone who has used electronic mail, computer bulletin board services, or electronic newsgroups in either a local area or on the global internet can tell you that people have adapted many typographical characters such as the almost universally recognized smiley face, :), to add style to their messages.

One of the most important functions of paralanguage in both written and spoken expression in organizational communication may be its role in influencing person perception. Several studies show that employment interviewers' hiring decisions and judgments of an applicant's suitability for a particular type of job are influenced by accent and dialect. De La Zerda and Hopper (1979) found that Hispanic Americans who speak "standard," unaccented English are more likely to be regarded as appropriate candidates for supervisory or managerial jobs than those who speak accented English. Schenck-Hamlin (1978) also found that perceptions of a person's competence, coherence, and character appeal are influenced by dialect, but the effect depends on the content of the message. Midwesterners judged "midwestern" and "southern" dialect speakers about equally on neutral topics, but a topic that evoked midwestern stereotypes of southerners led to much lower ratings for the southern dialect speaker. A "midwesterner" opposing racial desegregation was perceived as more competent, coherent, and appealing than a "southerner" presenting the same message.

Body Movement

Much of the information available in face-to-face communication is provided through **body movement**. Ray Birdwhistell (1952), a leading theorist in this area, claimed that all body movement is meaningful within the context in which it occurs. Birdwhistell believed that body movement can be subjected to systematic analysis and that the characteristics of body movement correspond to the characteristics of language. He based his concepts for the study of body movement, which he called **kinesics**, on the same ideas used in linguistics, the study of language. The idea that body movement is a kind of language has been popularized through work in kinesics, but some scholars have questioned this notion (Littlejohn, 1992).

Is body movement like a language in the sense that it has a vocabulary, grammar, and syntax? Not really, but there is no doubt that body movement has some important functions in human communication. One very useful description of these functions is a system of categories devised by Paul Ekman and Wallace Friesen (1972). Their categories include emblems, illustrators, regulators, affect displays, and adaptors.

Emblems are kinesic substitutes for verbal behavior. An emblem usually is intended to transmit a particular message, but the meaning may depend on the group that uses it and the context in which it occurs. The two-fingered "V" traditionally is an emblem for victory. During the 1960s, college students and other young people also adopted it as an emblem for peace.

Illustrators are kinesic cues that directly support speech behavior. These cues are not substitutes for the spoken word, but they help to emphasize what is being said. Illustrators include behaviors to point out, outline a form, or depict motion. In one sense, an illustrator is a kind of kinesic "visual aid." People who use many illustrators when speaking are likely to be perceived as more animated and energetic than those who use few or no illustrators (Norton, 1978).

Regulators help to control and coordinate face-to-face interaction. These behaviors include eye movements, head positions, and postures that signal taking turns in conversations. Eye contact in particular is important as a signal for seeking feedback, initiating interaction, or terminating conversations (McCroskey, Larson, & Knapp, 1971).

Affect displays are cues to feelings and emotional states. These behaviors may include facial movements such as smiles, frowns, and sneers, as well as certain postures. Facial expression seems to be a good indicator of at least six emotions: happiness, anger, sadness, surprise, disgust, and fear (Knapp, 1978).

Adaptors involve release of physical tension. These behaviors may be either the means for or the results of tension release. For instance, scratching your head may be an instrumental behavior to relieve an itch. In contrast, moment-to-moment wiggles and jiggles of various body parts may result merely from random nervous system activity.

Space

The use of **space** is a subtle but powerful factor in human social and organizational behavior that appears to vary greatly across different cultures. In general, humans seem to be territorial creatures who define and defend the boundaries of our space. We also arrange objects in space either to suit ourselves or to accomplish various purposes. Finally, we use space to define appropriate distance between people in interpersonal settings.

The formal study of the use of space is called **proxemics**. Edward Hall (1959), who developed the field of proxemics along the lines of Birdwhistell's kinesics, identified three basic types of space: fixed-feature, semifixed-feature, and informal.

Fixed-feature space involves either concrete or imaginary but stable boundaries that define territory. Goldhaber (1993) points out that there often is a close relationship between status and territory in organizations. He has identified three principles in this relationship that have the potential to influence organizational communication:

1. The higher up you are in the organization, the more and better space you have.

2. The higher up you are in the organization, the better protected your territory is.

3. The higher up you are in the organization, the easier it is to invade the territory of lower status personnel.

Whether or not the amount of space in one's territory, the ability to protect it, or the ability to invade someone else's territory are directly communicative, these conditions certainly can influence organizational communication. The allocation of space itself signifies status, and status gives one more control over initiating, structuring, and terminating interaction with others.

Offices and work areas in organizations contain many objects and fixtures that must somehow be positioned in space—desks, chairs, files, equipment, decorations. The arrangement of these objects involves the use of **semifixed-feature space**. Such arrangements may or may not be intended to transmit a particular message, but the idea of communication through placement of objects has become so popular that any arrangement is almost certain to provoke an interpretation.

If you can penetrate the well-protected territory of a high-level executive, you may find that this person's space is furnished more like a living room than an office. Presumably, such an arrangement "communicates" an atmosphere of openness and accessibility. The lower level manager with a cast-off military surplus desk, stacked with volumes of reports and positioned as a barrier behind a door to a cramped office, may be telling visitors, "Go away. I really don't have time for you." Such interpretations may be perfectly valid, but one should exercise them with caution because they presume that the person who occupies the space has a specific intent and purpose for the arrangement of objects within it. In fact, the use of semifixed-feature space may be more dependent on organizational customs and allocation of resources than on any conscious personal choice that the office occupant makes.

The final category, **informal space**, refers to the physical proximity of one person to another in interpersonal settings. Hall identified four distinct informal zones in American culture: intimate (1 to 18 inches), personal (18 inches to 4 feet), social (4 to 12 feet), and public (more than 12 feet). Most interpersonal conversations occur in the personal zone of informal space, but cultures vary in the use of this space. The Chinese seem to require more personal distance for interaction than Americans require. In turn, Americans require more than Arabs require. Most interaction in American business organizations occurs in the social zone of informal space. A Chinese visitor might find this practice to be appropriate and tasteful. An Arabic visitor might be most uncomfortable under similar conditions.

Although paralanguage, body movement, and use of space are three important forms of nonverbal behavior in human communication, researchers have identified other behaviors and characteristics of human demeanor that may also be relevant to our discussion. These include use of time, touch, clothing, and overall physical appearance (body type). Whether these behaviors and personal characteristics are communicative in the sense that we have defined communication will depend on many factors in any given situation. In any case, such behaviors certainly will influence the day-to-day process of communication.

FUNCTIONS OF COMMUNICATION

Verbal and nonverbal behaviors provide the means for accomplishing specific communication functions. There are different approaches, however, to describing the functions communication serves in organizations. Most traditional descriptions are tied to three basic processes that occur in an open system: transformation of energy and materials via input, throughput, and output; regulation of system processes; and system growth or adaptation. Farace et al. (1977) describe three communication functions that are frequently associated with these processes: production, maintenance, and innovation. We will also look at Dance and Larson's (1976) traditionalist approach to functions by focusing on the linking, mentation, and regulatory functions of communication. Next, we examine the traditionalist approach that is tied to uncertainty reduction and information adequacy. Finally, we discuss the concept of social capital.

The interpretive perspective on communication functions focuses on the subjective nature of reality and on how communicators search for and construct meanings through interaction with others. In order to understand communicative functions from an interpretive perspective, we look at the work of George Herbert Mead, and Peter Berger and Thomas Luckmann.

The critical perspective on communication functions focuses on the struggles for meaning that occur through dialogue between and among organization members and the struggles for power that are displayed through communicative action. In this section, we view the work of Bakhtin and we concentrate on how communication functions to control and manipulate workers.

Traditional Function Categories

Production, Maintenance, and Innovation

The **production function** includes any communication that controls and coordinates the activities required to produce system outputs. This means communication involved in activities that yield an organization's products or services. Such communication is "work-connected." It includes instructions for the amount and type of output to be produced, job procedures, information about workgroup organization, and reports on workgroup activity or problems in the work itself.

The **maintenance function** includes communication that regulates system processes. Regulation implies that system conditions are maintained within certain desirable or acceptable limits. Maintenance communication is concerned with keeping the organization intact and in a steady state of operation. Organizational policies or rules and various forms of deviation-correcting negative feedback serve the maintenance function, but Farace and colleagues suggested that there is more to maintenance communication than policies, rules, and negative feedback:

> Maintenance communication is that which (a) affects the member's feelings of personal worth and significance, (b) changes the "value" placed on interaction with coworkers, supervisors, and subordinates, and (c) alters the perceived importance of continuing to meet the organization's production and innovation needs. (p. 59)

Given such a broad definition, maintenance communication could include events ranging from the employee-of-the-month column in a company newsletter to many of the informal, day-to-day conversations that affect human relationships in the organization. In fact, some writers, such as Goldhaber (1993), prefer to include any communication affecting members' feelings of self-worth and quality of organizational relationships in a fourth functional category called **human**. This approach restricts the maintenance function only to regulatory processes.

The **innovation function** includes communication concerned with change in the organization. Communication in this category may involve the development of new ideas and practices as well as the means for implementing and securing acceptance of change. The changes may involve organizational mission, philosophy, structure, and functions. Generally, change implies some alteration in organizational values as well as in organizational behavior. Suggestions from organization members for changes in products, services, or work procedures; recommendations from studies of organizational needs; and long-range planning activities all involve the innovation function.

Dance and Larson's Work on Communication Functions

According to Dance and Larson (1976), human communication displays three functions: the *linking function*, the *mentation function*, and the *regulatory function*. The linking function focuses on communication used to establish relationships between the individual and the environment. More specifically, communicators use symbols to create a desired image to facilitate their linking to the environment. Through establishing a linkage to the environment, the individual is consubstantial with society. According to Dance and Larson, the linking function of communication is important across the entire life span of an individual. It is "necessary not only for the development of self but also for the maintenance of self" (Dance & Larson, 1976, p. 70).

Although Dance and Larson use the general term "environment" when describing the linking function of communication, they are more centrally concerned with the individual's social environment. Specifically, at the core of this function is people linking with other people through communication. In fact, Dance and Larson (1976) define communication as "that which ties, links, or connects any orderly relationships by providing the bond through which they may exist and may be perceived" (p. 60).

The mentation function focuses on how communication stimulates the development of higher order mental processes and leads to mental growth. The key element in speech communication is language. Importantly, at a general level, culture is both shaped and reflected by the language its members speak. In addition, at a more specific level, language allows us to express our thoughts and it serves as a tool for thought. As Piaget (1970) observed, "Language, in short, is independent of the decisions of individuals; it is the bearer of multi-millennia traditions; and it is every man's indispensable instrument of thought" (p. 75).

From Dance and Larson's (1976) perspective, language, culture, and thought are interrelated. They explain the nature of this interrelationship in the following example:

> As the maturation process continues, the child's external speech communication is gradually internalized. The presumption is that as the child says "mama" aloud, it is also saying "mama" to itself, and then progresses to saying "mama" internally without needing the accompanying vocalization. This interior representation of "mama" elevates the child's capacity for displacement, for abstraction, and for flexibility in adaptation and control of self and environment. (p. 104)

In the preceding explanation, Dance and Larson (1976) show us how using signals or symbols to interact with others in the environment sparks the development of higher mental processes. The regulatory function is the third communicative function Dance and Larson discuss. This function is "the basis for the refinement and extension to humans of the host of methods of behavior regulation that operate upon all living organisms" (p. 129). The regulatory function comprises three developmental stages: the regulation of self by others, the regulation of self by self, and the regulation of others by self. According to Dance and Larson, communication serves as a tool for regulating our personal behavior and for influencing the behavior of others. They argue:

> Speech communication always functions to regulate behavior, whether or not there is any intent by users of speech communication to control the behavior of themselves or of others. The initial acquisition of speech communication automatically limits (and thus regulates) our range of linguistic and thus behavioral options. Each language, manifested in speech communication, organizes experience differently. (p. 129)

Applied to organizations, Dance and Larson's three communicative functions are central to organizational operations. When employees use communication to link with one another, cooperative action becomes possible, people may coordinate their efforts to reach common goals, and ideas may be shared and argued over to produce creative solutions to problems. The mentation function may be observed when people communicate to solve complex problems. In fact, employees may sometimes find that the more they talk with one another to problem solve, the more effective they become at producing viable solutions. Finally, the regulatory function is an important part of people acting and communicating in predictable and agreed-on ways so the organization may reach its goals and operate smoothly. Of course we must recognize that problems such as conflict, power struggles, and deadlocks over decisions will still occur when employees display these three functions of communication. Problems may be minimized, however, when employees use communication to link together, stimulate higher order thinking processes, and regulate one another's actions.

Uncertainty and Information Adequacy

Several authorities representing the traditionalist perspective argue that the various functions of organizational communication are all related to a single, more general purpose— the reduction of **uncertainty** (e.g., Weick, 1979). Rosabeth Moss Kanter (1977) claimed that organizations (especially large, bureaucratically structured ones) thrive on predictability. Uncertainty, or the absence of predictability, is an unnerving experience to be avoided whenever possible. Hence, communication is used to reduce or at least cope with uncertainty.

Despite frequent claims that communication serves an uncertainty reduction function, we should not simply assume that this always is true. As we pointed out earlier in this chapter, Eric Eisenberg (1984) makes a convincing case that many of the messages in day-to-day organizational communication are deliberately and strategically ambiguous because *creating* uncertainty serves the purposes of particular individuals, groups, or even the entire organization. We need only recall some of the earlier examples to realize that organizational communication sometimes is more concerned with creating uncertainty than with reducing it. For example, consider the university president's speeches about commitments to excellence, Chrysler's advertising strategy to promote an image of quality, and the doctor-nurse game.

Even though different individuals and groups within an organization may try to create uncertainty for one another or even to use strategic ambiguity in ways that benefit the organization as a whole, it is probably safe to say that any given individual or group desires certainty for itself. Since information is the key to reduction of uncertainty, organization members usually are concerned with the **adequacy** of this information. Is there enough, too much, or too little information to serve organizational purposes? As Farace and colleagues (1977) contended, "*What* is known in an organization and *who* knows it are obviously very important in determining the overall functioning of the organization" (p. 27).

Although the importance of information adequacy in organizational communication has been recognized for many years, and the subject received rather intensive study in the 1970s and 1980s, problems with information adequacy continue to plague organizations today. As Spiker and Lesser (1995) note, many executives "fall into the trap of providing information on a need-to-know basis" (p. 18), i.e., they tell subordinates only what they think their subordinates need to know.

Farace and colleagues explained problems associated with information adequacy by employing Brillouin's (1962) distinction between **absolute** and **distributed information**. Absolute information refers to the total body of information that exists within an organization at any time. This information is distributed to the extent that it is **diffused** (spread) throughout the organization. Information adequacy problems may arise because a piece of information simply does not exist in the organization's pool of absolute information or because existing information is not properly distributed.

Although researchers in organizational communication have been interested in the problem of information adequacy for many years, they have made little effort to study adequacy by systematically matching an organization's information needs against *both* absolute and distributed information in order to identify the sources of adequacy problems. Many like Farace and colleagues simply assume that inadequate information usually results from distribution problems. Hence, most studies of information adequacy focus on *individual* organization members as *receivers* of distributed information.

Some researchers have evaluated information adequacy by measuring individual members' knowledge about the organization and its functions (Level, 1959; Tompkins, 1962). More commonly, researchers examine the difference between the amount of information that individual members think they need and the amount that they think they *actually receive* (Daly, Falcione, & Damhorst, 1979; Daniels & Spiker, 1983; Goldhaber, Yates, Porter, & Lesniak, 1978; Spiker & Daniels, 1981). In these studies, "adequacy" is defined by organization members' *perceptions* of the difference between what is received and what is desired.

Despite the limitations of the focus on individual rather than organizational information needs, studies of information adequacy do indicate that surprisingly large percentages of organization members consider themselves to be inadequately informed on many important topics that directly concern them. The International Communication Association (ICA) sponsored studies of 18 large organizations that found that nearly half of the members generally received less information than they wanted (Spiker & Daniels, 1981). Penley (1982), who classified all of the information topics in his study as task- or performance-related, found that 48% of the participants in his study were inadequately informed on performance topics and 8% were inadequately informed in both task and performance areas.

Spiker and Daniels's (1981) analysis of data from the 18 ICA studies revealed that information adequacy is related to members' feelings of personal influence in the organization, satisfaction with their immediate superiors, satisfaction with top management, and, to a lesser extent, satisfaction with coworkers. Furthermore, Penley (1982) and Smith and DeWine (1987) also found that information adequacy is closely related to the members' sense of identification with and commitment to the organization.

Even though organization members who consider themselves to be adequately informed generally are more committed and more satisfied and identify more closely with the organization than those who see themselves as inadequately informed, information adequacy does not always produce such positive outcomes. In a later study, Daniels and Spiker (1983) found that information adequacy on sensitive topics such as management problems, organizational failures, and organizational decision-making processes is *negatively* related to satisfaction with superiors for some organization members. That is, the more some people know about sensitive organizational issues, the less they like their bosses. Daniels and Spiker argued that this may occur because people who develop their own sources of such information become less dependent on their superiors and eventually see themselves as more knowledgeable and competent than those superiors.

Although studies of information adequacy generally have been concerned with the potential impact of adequacy on variables such as satisfaction, the most recent work has attempted to identify the conditions under which organization members perceive themselves to be adequately informed. Alexander, Helms, and Curran (1987) found that levels of communication with supervisors, administrative sources, and peers are greater for members who perceive themselves to be adequately informed than for those who perceive themselves to be inadequately informed. Inadequately informed members also were younger than more adequately informed members, and they had been employed with the organization for less time. These results may not be especially surprising, but they do suggest that information adequacy does not occur in a haphazard and unpredictable manner.

Social Capital

One important function that may be served by communication is the development of *social capital*. Social capital is a multidimensional construct (Scheufele & Shah, 2000) with a variety of interrelated definitions. One of the first published definitions came from Pierre Bordieu (1985), who stated that social capital is "the aggregate of the actual or potential resources which are linked to possession of a durable network of more or less institutionalized relationships of mutual acquaintance or recognition" (p. 248). Alternatively, Coleman (1988) defined social capital by its function as "a variety of entities with two elements in common: They all consist of some aspect of social structures, and they facilitate certain actions of others—whether persons or corporate actors within the structure" (p. 98).

There are two major differences in the definitions of social capital by Bordieu and Coleman. Bordieu explicitly points out the distinction of resources from the ability to obtain them in the social structure, whereas Coleman obscures this notion. The second difference is that Bordieu sees social capital as a tool of reproduction for the dominant class, whereas Coleman sees social capital as more positive social control, in which trust, information channels, and norms are characteristic of the community as a whole, not simply the dominant class (Dika & Singh, 2002).

Aside from some of the early notions of social capital, perhaps the most commonly referenced definition is derived from Putnam's (1993, 1995, 2000, 2001) work, in which he defines social capital as "features of social organization, such as trust, norms, and networks, that can improve the efficiency of society by facilitating coordinated actions" (Putnam, 1993, p. 167). Other scholars have come up with varying definitions that seem to encompass or include Putnam's broad classification. For example, Kawachi, Kennedy, and Glass (1999) stated that social capital is "those features of social organization—such as the extent of interpersonal trust between citizens, norms of reciprocity, and density of civic associations—that facilitate cooperation for mutual benefit" (p. 187). Social capital has also been described as a contextual characteristic describing patterns of civic engagement, trust, and mutual obligation among persons (Bellah, Madsen, Sullivan, Swidler, & Tipton, 1985; Coleman, 1988, 1990; Kawachi, Kennedy, Bruce, & Lochner, 1997; Kawachi, Kennedy, & Lochner, 1997; Portes, 1998; Taylor, 1989; Weitzman & Kawachi, 2000).

Within organizations, social capital may produce a number of benefits for employees. Social capital has been linked to occupational attainment, the provision of emotional aid (Scheufele & Shah, 2000), the functioning of democracy (Kawachi et al., 1999), and the generation and distribution of organizational resources (Sanders, 2002). In addition, Scheufele and Shah (2000) point out three functions of social capital: (1) as a source of social control, (2) as a source of group support, and (3) as a source of benefits through interlinked group networks.

In one specific study of social capital in Indian communities, Singhal et al. (2006) found both positive and negative benefits. By increasing levels of trust among villagers, establishing norms for reciprocity, and strengthening communication networks, many new cooperative actions emerged. Specifically, the community organizing activities facilitated by social capital contributed to educational programs for lower caste children, the improvement of community health, the stopping of a number of child marriages, and the promotion of gender equality. On the other hand, negative social capital occurred when people used their relational influence to limit one another's choices. In such instances, negative social capital contributed to excluding certain people from participation in prosocial action, restricting individual freedom, placing excessive demands on group members, and downward leveling norms. Clearly further investigation of social capital's effects is needed to determine the extent to which this concept contributes to cooperation for mutual benefit versus social control.

Interpretive Functions of Communication

George Herbert Mead: Symbolic Interactionism

George Herbert Mead is considered the founder of *symbolic interactionism*.[1] Symbolic interactionism has its roots in the philosophies of pragmatism and psychological behaviorism. The following ideas are central to Mead's thinking about pragmatism. First, he did not take an objectivist view of reality. This means reality is not something "out there" that can be described by an objective observer. Rather people actively create the world in which they participate. Second, there is a utilitarian element to Mead's views. Specifically, he believed that we base our knowledge of the world on what has been shown to be useful to us. Also, we define the physical and social objects we come across according to our use for them. Third, our understanding of actors we encounter is based on what they do in the world. Finally, pragmatists believe that the social world is an ongoing creation that changes and evolves as people act toward one another (Mead, 1932).

Mead used the concept of *social behaviorism* to refer to the fact that there is more to behavior than simply what we observe in a social setting. Specifically, he argued that the unit we should study is "the act." The act comprises both overt and covert aspects of human action. On the basis of this belief, Mead studied the relationship and interaction of a stimulus and the response to that stimulus (Ritzer, 1996). The relationship and interaction between stimulus and response was important to study because it is what distinguishes humans from animals. Mead argued that only humans possess mental capabilities for language, allowing them to use communication skills to decide how to respond to a stimulus.

In developing his perspective on symbolic interactionism, Mead contributed a number of important microanalytic concepts to our understanding of human action. Two of these concepts are particularly important for us to understand communication functions: *self* and *generalized other*.

When Mead refers to the self he explains that humans have the ability to see themselves as both the actor and the subject in social situations. This means that the self is *reflexive*, meaning that we can see ourselves as others see us. We develop this ability during childhood in a two-stage process. The first stage is the play stage, during which we learn to take the attitude of a particular person (e.g., a parent). The second stage is the game stage, during which we learn to take the attitude of everyone else who is part of our social world. Developing this ability allows us to function in social groups.

From the game stage, Mead developed one of his most recognized concepts, the *generalized other.* The generalized other refers to the collective attitudes of an entire group, community, or society. When we develop our understanding of the generalized other we not only see ourselves as participants in society, we have the ability to engage in shared meanings with others. In order to explain how shared meanings become possible, Mead refers to the "*I* and *Me*." The "I" is the immediate response that an individual has to others. The "Me" is the adoption of the generalized other. These concepts were central in developing Mead's theory of social control. Simply stated, when we internalize the generalized other we internalize the attitudes of the groups to which we belong, participating in shared meaning while, at the same time, contesting or not creating meanings that are antagonistic to those groups. If we apply this perspective to organizations, it means that employees participate in the creation and maintenance of a generalized other that helps sustain shared meanings, guide employee actions, and restrict choices that fall outside the collective attitudes that have been created. Thus, according to Mead, communication functions to create shared meaning, a concept we will return to in Chapter 6 when we discuss communication and culture.

Berger and Luckmann: Communication as Construction

Berger and Luckmann's (1966) perspective on communication functions extends Mead's ideas on the generalized other and offers insights into how different meaning systems are generated within society. The starting point for Berger and Luckmann is recognizing that people tend to develop repetitive patterns of behavior over the course of their lives. These repetitive behaviors or habits are useful to us because they allow us to automatically handle similar or comparable situations. The habits we develop may also be useful to other people. For example, in our relationships with others we observe and respond to each other's habits. In fact, we learn what to expect from our relationships by anticipating and depending on the habits of others. This perspective is not related only to the interpersonal relationship level, however. Berger and Luckmann argue that some habits become shared among large segments of society.

If we look within any organization, we will find a collection of shared expectations about member habits. Organizations encourage the development of roles that specify the habitual actions expected of individuals acting as organizational representatives. For an employee to legitimately assume a role, he or she must adopt these habitual actions. When others interact with that employee, they respond to him or her as a part of the organization rather than as a unique human being.

By establishing rules that govern actions, organizations contribute to the existence of societal control. In order for this control to exist over time, successive generations must be trained or indoctrinated to participate in organizations in ways that meet established expectations. In essence, an organization is both legitimized and maintained through passing on traditions and educating new generations of employees.

Once habits and behavioral expectations are passed on to successive generations, some organizations may become *reified,* meaning that members cease to recognize that the organization is essentially a human construction that may be changed. As a result of reification, members relate to the organization as if it is a natural object. Such organizations are perceived as real in the same way as we perceive reality in the "natural" world. Berger and Luckmann (1966) refer to this as "the reality of everyday life" (p. 22).

Although a given group or organization may impose a single meaning on a message, it is possible for differences in meaning to exist among different groups. To account for this, Berger and Luckmann (1966) explain that the meanings people create for messages depend on the realities of their everyday lives. For example, consider an organization that announces the appointment of an African American woman to the position of chief financial officer. To the person receiving the position, this announcement means recognition for hard work and accomplishment. For the hiring committee, this decision means the organization will move forward in making sound financial commitments. To a white man competing for this position, the announcement may mean the unfair application of affirmative action. To African American women in this company, the announcement means long-awaited recognition that members of their group may compete effectively at the highest levels of corporate governance.

Importantly, the realities of our everyday lives are intersubjective, meaning they do not develop in a vacuum. Thus, the meanings I attach to messages both relate to and are dependent on the meanings others establish around me. Every person exists within a constellation of relationships in which meanings are shared and cocreated. So, our communication environment influences the meanings we internalize.

Critical Functions of Communication

Mikhail Bakhtin: Communication as Dialogic

Social theorist Mikhail Bakhtin (1981) extended and reshaped Marx's conception of dialectics to coin the term *dialogism*. Bakhtin begins with the idea that human existence is dialogic. Explaining this perspective, he wrote, "Just as the body is formed initially in the mother's womb (body), a person's consciousness awakens wrapped in another's consciousness" (Bakhtin, 1986, p. 138). Bakhtin's language theory developed this claim further. Specifically, concerning knowledge, he claimed that "all real and integral understanding is actively *responsive*" (Bakhtin, 1986, p. 69) and that "the responsive understanding of a speech whole is always dialogic by nature" (p. 125). The reason for this is that no human may claim to produce the first or isolated utterance. Instead all human discourse "presupposes utterances that precede and follow it. No one utterance can be either the first or the last. Each is only a link in the chain" (Bakhtin, 1986, p. 136).

When attempting to understand dialogue, Bakhtin (1981, 1984) claims that we must recognize that dialectic tensions are inevitable and present in all personal relationships. Further, he believed that communication prompted by dialectic tensions allows partners to grow individually and together. Consequently, each relational impulse needs a contradictory one. By focusing on the idea of process in dialectics, Bakhtin (1981) argued that change is the only paradoxical constant in human relationships.

Bakhtin (1981) noted that everyday human action occurred at the confluence of a "contradiction-ridden, tension-filled unity of two embattled tendencies" (p. 272). These are forces of unity (the *centripetal tendency*) and forces of difference (the *centrifugal tendency*). Bakhtin (1981) explained: "Every utterance participates in the 'unitary language' (in its centripetal forces and tendencies) and at the same time partakes of social and historical heteroglossia (the centrifugal, stratifying forces)" (p. 272).

Rather than creating shared meanings, Bakhtin's critical perspective on dialogue focuses on struggles over meanings where there are multiple voices and interpretations present in a social system. This multivocality may separate people from one another rather than unify them into a consensus (Martin, 1992; Meyerson, 1991; Miller & O'Leary, 1987; Ruud, 1995). Furthermore, as Putnam and Fairhurt (2001) explain, "multiple discourses contribute to fragmentation through the way different dynamics surface in the process of organizing" (p. 114).

From the perspective of organizational culture, fragmentation through dialogue creates ambiguous cultures in which individuals and organizations have fluctuating boundaries and identities (Eisenberg & Riley, 2001). For example, Kreiner and Schultz (1993) argue that in many organizational cultures consensus is short-lived and issue specific. In such fragmented cultures there are both practical and personal struggles involved in coping with wide-scale confusion and ambiguity (Eisenberg & Riley, 2001). Consistent with a postmodern perspective, fragmentation produces "decentered" people who constantly restructure their identities (Eisenberg & Riley, 2001). Different identities are drawn on as different situations emerge. In fact, survival often seems to require a decentered person who constantly restructures his or her identity to meet different exigencies.

As an example of a dialogic struggle over meaning, consider author Michael Papa's experiences with community suppers in the rural Appalachian region of the United States. One organization that sponsored community suppers was Good Works of Athens, Ohio. Good Works (GW) is a nonprofit social services organization that offers shelter to the homeless along with a variety of services to help local people struggling with poverty. The community suppers at GW have been ongoing since 1992. The idea for this weekly event emerged when GW's Director Keith Wasserman realized that they sometimes lost track of the people who had participated in the organization's programs (as workers, volunteers, rural homeless, etc.). This supper became a reunion of sorts allowing some people to reconnect and others to meet for the first time. These suppers also provide an opportunity to rekindle and sustain friendships and to share in one another's lives. Starting from a basic idea with a simple beginning, the community suppers have become a central part of the Good Works organization with weekly suppers that often attract 125 to 140 people.

These community suppers revealed a specific dialogic struggle between unity and fragmentation. This struggle was even reflected in a single person's experience. Consider the views expressed by Shirley, a community supper participant. Her story shows both the sense of unity or connectedness she feels at the weekly supper and the isolation that is part of her life once she leaves the event.

> Shirley is 57 years old and diabetic. She opens herself up to me in the way isolated people often do, pouring out her heart because someone is willing to listen and not judge. The good Lord has been kind to her, she says, keeping her alive despite continuing health problems. She begins to cough and apologizes saying that she has a "nervous reflux" when she gets excited. This supper makes her both nervous

and excited because it is one of the few opportunities she has to meet and talk with people. Shirley lives about five miles from town. The houses are not tightly packed together like they are in town, she says, but they are not so far apart that people can't be friendly to one another. But, her neighbors rarely talk to her because, she believes, they look down on her for being poorer than they are. This upsets her because she likes to talk to people. She can't figure these neighbors out because many of them are Christian people and they should know better, but that doesn't matter. So, the community supper is her main opportunity to meet new people and talk to them. That's why she loves to come so much. (Papa, Papa, Kandath, Worrell, & Muthuswamy, 2005, pp. 261–262)

When Shirley shared her personal story, she showed how she felt connected to those around her at the supper. However, the very connectedness and unity that Shirley feels at the supper is contrasted sharply by the isolation she feels at home. So her participation in the community supper serves as a reminder of both her connection to others and her fragmented existence once she returns home. For Shirley, fragmentation and unity are experienced at the same moment, reflecting, for her, a powerful dialogic struggle over meaning.

Control and Manipulation

Different rule systems provide us with different ways of organizing our behavior. For Dennis Mumby (1987), domination and control involves "getting people to organize their behavior around a particular rule system" (p. 115). Borrowing from Gramsci (1971), Mumby says, "The process of hegemony works most effectively when the world view articulated by the ruling elite is actively taken up and pursued by subordinate groups" (p. 123). **Hegemony** refers to a relational system where one group is dominant over others. In organizational settings, such dominance occurs when a group in power (e.g., managers) convinces the oppressed group (e.g., subordinates) to identify the dominant group's interests as its own (Williams, 1977).

How does this occur? How is it that people are induced to adopt and, perhaps more importantly, *maintain* a rule system or mode of rationality that actually disadvantages them? This is where symbols and discourse come into play, particularly in a condition of manipulation that critical theorists refer to as **systemically distorted communication**.

Systemically distorted communication is a bit like magic. It is illusory. It distorts the reality of a situation. In effect, systemically distorted communication legitimizes hegemony through manipulation *by making it appear to be something other than it really is*. In developing the concept of systematic distortion, Habermas (1979) distinguished between communicative action and strategic action. Communicative action is intended to achieve mutual understanding and agreement as a basis for consensual action. Communicative action is joint action. Strategic action is a unilateral attempt at achieving one's own goals and aims. Strategic action may be open. Let's suppose that you are presenting a new policy to a management group. You expect some opposition and you want one of your friends in the group to be very vocal in supporting your proposal. If you say this to your friend in an "upfront," nondeceptive manner, you have been openly strategic. But let's suppose, in an effort to get your friend's support, you say something like this instead: "I really dread this meeting today. I think Bill and Sarah are going to give me some trouble about this proposal. You remember how those two really tried to stab you in the back last year. You know, they actually went around outside of meetings trying to line up support to try to torpedo that new marketing plan you introduced. I remember how most of the group supported it and you got it approved, but those two sure tried to kill it."

In this case, your strategic action is *latent*. Although all of the information in your statements may be factual, your real intentions are obscured. There is a "hidden agenda" in the action. If you have deliberately tried to deceive your friend about your intentions, you have engaged in manipulation. Systematically distorted communication also arises from latent strategic action, but it is more complicated than manipulation. In manipulation, one person deceives the other. In systematically distorted communication, "at least one of the participants deceives *himself* or *herself* about the fact that the basis of consensual action is only apparently being maintained" (Habermas, 1979, p. 208).

When control is established through manipulation and systematically distorted communication, the impact on employees can be significant. Annette Markham (1996) investigated a small environmental design company that she identified as Far End Design, Inc. (FED). Management at FED officially states that they value self-designed and self-managed task design (autonomy and individual creativity) and self-directed and self-managed work teams (team creativity). To accomplish this practically, management is deliberately ambiguous in their descriptions, definitions, and explanations of the job task and the work process. Management believes that this approach encourages people to work on their own. Although this sounds like a productive work environment that encourages creativity, the owner of the company yells and screams at the designers if they don't produce the designs that he thinks they should produce. Then, if the designers ask for direction from the owner, he berates them for not being autonomous and violating the organizational culture. Unfortunately, the designers reproduce this hegemonic system through their own actions. Jerry, one of the designers at FED, observed that the yelling and screaming was painful, but, "like an addiction, was constantly reproduced and sustained by the designers" (Markham, 1996, p. 414). Jerry explained: "It's just a process, it's a thing they do. They have this blow up and then everyone walks around like zombies and bitches. And then the next day, they just, it's like they take their next shot in the arm and hop right in again" (p. 414).

Control and manipulation exist in all organizations. Interestingly, workers are often trapped in control systems that they sustain through their own actions. Emancipation from these oppressive systems is possible, however. We will address potential paths to emancipation in Chapters 11 and 14.

Interpersonal Communication: Relationship Development Among Workers

Organizations, like any social system, provide opportunities for members to form interpersonal relationships through communication. These relationships may focus on the accomplishments of tasks, be social in nature, or both. Sias and Cahill (1998) conducted a study focusing on the development of friendships in the workplace. They discovered that peer friendships experienced three primary transitions: from coworker/acquaintance-to-friend, friend-to-close friend, and close friend-to-almost best friend.

At the coworker/acquaintance level, communication focuses more on work issues, with some communication of nonwork and personal topics. Caution is exhibited during this phase because of the fear of how self-disclosure will be treated. As coworkers transition to friends, there is increased discussion of nonwork and personal topics, and decreased caution. The transition to close friend is marked by further decreased caution and increased intimacy in communication. One of the workers interviewed by Sias and Cahill (1998) responded, "We became more open. I told her how I felt . . . she'd share other personal things . . . she would comfort me" (p. 288). The transition to almost best friend results in further decreases in caution, increased discussion of work-related problems, and increased intimacy. Increased levels of trust mark this stage of friendship. The friends feel free to share opinions, feelings, and personal experiences. From a functional perspective, interpersonal relationships in organizations develop much the same way they do in other social systems. Members can focus their workplace discussions on task completion and organizational issues, or they can form deeper relationships in which all topics are open for discussion.

Another way to understand interpersonal communication in organizations is to consider how such communication may be viewed from the traditional, interpretive, and critical perspectives. Starting with the traditional perspective, interpersonal communication may focus on production, maintenance, or innovation messages. Essentially, such communication would center on getting the job done, regulating system processes, or changing the organization or organizing activities in some way.

Consistent with Dance and Larson's (1976) model, interpersonal relationships in organizations may serve linking, mentation, and regulatory functions. Regarding the linking function, interpersonal relationships exist in organizations because we have a desire to connect with others. Interpersonal relationships may also exist for the purpose of stimulating our thinking about work, social, and personal issues (mentation function). Finally, interpersonal relationships can display communication that regulates the actions of organization members.

Uncertainty reduction and information adequacy may be pursued within the context of interpersonal relationships. In fact, it is within interpersonal relationships that organization members often seek information of relevance to the job and about other members. Finally, social capital is built within interpersonal relationships as organization members build trust with one other, establish norms of reciprocity, and strengthen their communication networks.

From an interpretive perspective, interpersonal relationships function to develop shared meanings that facilitate further communication and coordinated action. Interpersonal relationships also exist so organization members may actively create the world in which they participate. Finally, interpersonal relationships provide the context within which everyday lived experience contributes to meaning systems that may vary depending on the groupings of these relationships.

From a critical perspective, interpersonal relationships function to contest meanings through dialogic communication. In the process of contesting meanings, people in an interpersonal relationship shift between forces that unify and those that accentuate differences. Finally, critical theorists draw our attention to how interpersonal relationships may function to establish control and manipulate power.

SUMMARY

The concepts of communication structure and function are central ideas in the functionalist perspective of organizational communication. Functions are activities of a system that serve some purpose or objective. Structure is reflected in the linkages or relationships between elements in a system. Function and structure are closely related concepts in organizational communication. Although functionalists usually assume a direct connection between effective organizational performance and effective communication functions and structure, functions and structures of different groups and political coalitions within the same organization may clash when they pursue multiple and conflicting goals.

The term *communication* is something of a buzzword in modern society. People use the word to refer to many different human activities and conditions. Even academic scholars who specialize in the study of human communication define this concept in various ways.

Communication may be defined as shared and contested meaning formation created among two or more people through verbal and nonverbal transaction. The basic raw material of communication is information, which includes any aspect of the environment in which one can discern a pattern. Meaning occurs when information is placed within a context. Human communication is concerned with the meaning of verbal and nonverbal information.

Verbal information occurs in the spoken and written forms of a language code. This code involves a system of symbols as well as rules for how symbols are used. Symbols are representative, freely created, and culturally transmitted. Some experts regard symbols as tools for expressing thought. Others argue that thought as we understand it depends on symbols, that our knowledge and sense of reality are products of our language system. The influence of language in organizational communication is suggested by the use of root metaphors to make sense of organizational experiences, certain types of language paradoxes in organizational behavior, strategic use of ambiguity, and the prevalence of group-restricted codes.

Nonverbal information also is important in organizational communication, but the concept of nonverbal communication is troublesome because many nonverbal behaviors may be ambiguous and unreliable signs of emotional states or even random activities that occur without awareness or intent on the part of a source. Although an observer is likely to interpret such behaviors, they lead to no shared meaning. Popular notions that nonverbal behaviors are consistent indicators of specific messages and conditions that can be interpreted reliably if one knows the rules are misleading. One should exercise caution when attaching interpretations to nonverbal behavior.

Three important forms of nonverbal information are paralanguage, body movement (kinesics), and space (proxemics). Paralanguage cues such as volume, rate, rhythm, inflection, tone, and pitch help us to interpret verbal behavior. These cues also influence our perceptions of a speaker. Kinesic behaviors can be organized in five functional categories: emblems, illustrators, regulators, affect displays, and adaptors. Proxemics involves fixed-feature space, semifixed-feature space, and informal space. Fixed-feature space is essentially a territory. Territory and status are highly connected in many organizations. Arrangement of objects in semifixed-feature space can be used to convey a variety of messages. Informal space, the area in which interaction occurs, has four basic zones—intimate, personal, social, and public—that appear to vary widely across cultures.

Communication functions may be viewed from the traditional, interpretive, or critical perspectives. From the traditional perspective, communication functions to accomplish some objective such as completing tasks, stimulating higher order thinking, reducing uncertainty, or building social capital. From the interpretive perspective, communication functions to create shared meanings. Finally, critical theorists focus on how communication functions to contest meanings, establish control, and manipulate power.

DISCUSSION QUESTIONS/ACTIVITIES

1. Try over a period of a few days to construct some good notes on the dialogue that occurs among members of a student organization. Analyze the dialogue to identify the communication functions that are accomplished.

2. Is language merely representational or does it shape the way in which we experience the world? What kinds of examples can you think of in your own experience that would support either position?

3. Try to identify some instances of ambiguous communication. How do people in these situations try to cope with ambiguity? What is the final result of these coping efforts? Is ambiguity used strategically in any of these situations?

4. Observe the nonverbal behaviors of others in public settings. What information can you reliably infer from these behaviors? Under what circumstances would you consider the behaviors to be communicative?

5. Try to observe a group that uses a restricted code, then describe this code in as much detail as you can. What functions does the code seem to serve for this group?

6. Have you ever been a part of a group that could not agree on the meaning of a task, process, or event (formal event, party, etc.)? What was the discussion like? How were the disagreements resolved?

NOTE

1. Mead did not actually coin the term "symbolic interaction." Rather, his student Herbert Blumer is given that credit. Although Mead was a pioneering individual in social psychology, he did not write prolifically. In fact, his most recognized work is from verbatim notes taken by his students at the University of Chicago. These notes were published in a number of volumes with perhaps the most recognized being *Mind, Self, & Society.*

REFERENCES

Alexander, E. R., III, Helms, M. M., & Curran, K. E. (1987). An information processing analysis of organization information adequacy/abundance. *Management Communication Quarterly, 1,* 150–172.

Baird, J. E., Jr., & Weinberg, S. B. (1981). *Group communication: The essence of synergy* (2nd ed.). Dubuque, IA: Wm. C. Brown Company.

Bakhtin, M. M. (1981). *The dialogic imagination: Four essays by M. M. Bakhtin* (M. Holquist, Ed.; C. Emerson & M. Holquist, Trans.). Austin: University of Texas Press.

Bakhtin, M. M. (1984). *Problems of Dostoevsky's poetics* (C. Emerson, Ed. and Trans.). Minneapolis, MN: University of Minnesota Press. (Original work published in 1929).

Bakhtin, M. M. (1986). *Speech genres and other late essays* (Vern McGee, Trans.). Austin: University of Texas Press.

Bellah, R. N., Madsen, R., Sullivan, W. M., Swidler, A., & Tipton, S. M. (1985). *Habits of the heart.* Berkeley: University of California Press.

Berger, P., & Luckmann, T. (1966). *The social construction of reality.* New York: Doubleday.

Birdwhistell, R. (1952). *Introduction to kinesics.* Louisville, KY: University of Louisville Press.

Blumer, H. (1969). *Symbolic interactionism: Perspective and method.* Englewood Cliffs, NJ: Prentice Hall.

Bourdieu, P. (Ed.). (1985). *The forms of capital.* New York: Greenwood.

Brillouin, L. (1962). *Science and information theory.* New York: Academic Press.

Coleman, J. (1988). Social capital in the creation of human capital. *American Journal of Sociology, 94*(Suppl.), S95–S120.

Coleman, J. (1990). *Foundations of social theory.* Cambridge, MA: Harvard University Press.

Cunningham, M. A., & Wilcox, J. R. (1984). *Modifying a bind: The effects of patient harm and physician interpersonal risk on nurse communication in the inappropriate-order situation.* Paper presented at the annual meeting of the International Communication Association, San Francisco, May 1984.

Daly, J. A., Falcione, R. L., & Damhorst, M. L. (1979). *Communication correlates of relational and organizational satisfaction.* Paper presented at the annual meeting of the International Communication Association, Philadelphia, May 1979.

Dance, F. E. X., & Larson, C. E. (1976). *The functions of human communication: A theoretical approach.* New York: Holt, Rinehart & Winston.

Daniels, T. D., & Spiker, B. K. (1983). Social exchange and the relationship between information adequacy and relational satisfaction. *Western Journal of Speech Communication, 47,* 118–137.

Davitz, J. R. (1964). *The communication of emotional meaning.* New York: McGraw-Hill.

Deetz, S. A. (1973). Words without things: Toward a social phenomenology of language. *Quarterly Journal of Speech, 59,* 40–51.

De La Zerda, N., & Hopper, R. (1979). Employment interviewers' reactions to Mexican American speech. *Communication Monographs, 46,* 126–134.

Dika, S. L., & Singh, K. (2002). Applications of social capital in educational literature: A critical synthesis. *Review of Educational Research, 72*(1), 31–60.

Eisenberg, E. M. (1984). Ambiguity as a strategy in organizational communication. *Communication Monographs, 51,* 227–242.

Eisenberg, E. M., & Goodall, H. L., Jr. (1993). *Organizational communication: Balancing creativity and constraint.* New York: St. Martin's Press.

Eisenberg, E. M., & Riley, P. (2001). Organizational culture. In F. M. Jablin & L. L. Putnam (Eds.), *The new handbook of organizational communication: Advances in theory, research, and methods* (pp. 291–322). Thousand Oaks, CA: Sage.

Ekman, P., & Friesen, W. V. (1972). Hand movements. *Journal of Communication, 22,* 353–374.

Farace, R. V., Monge, P. R., & Russell, H. M. (1977). *Communicating and organizing.* Reading, MA: Addison-Wesley.

Foss, S. K. (1984). Retooling and image: Chrysler Corporation's rhetoric of redemption. *Western Journal of Speech Communication, 48,* 75–91.

Goldhaber, G. M. (1993). *Organizational communication* (6th ed.). Dubuque, IA: Brown & Benchmark.

Goldhaber, G. M., Yates, M. P., Porter, D. T., & Lesniak, R. (1978). Organizational communication: 1978. *Human Communication Research, 5,* 76–96.

Goyer, R. S. (1970). Communication, communication process, meaning: Toward a unified theory. *Journal of Communication, 20,* 6–7.

Gramsci, A. (1971). *Selections from the prison notebooks* (Q. Hoare & G. Nowell Smith, Trans.). New York: International.

Habermas, J. (1979). *Communication and the evolution of society* (T. McCarthy, Trans.). Boston: Beacon Press.

Hall, E. (1959). *Silent language.* Greenwich, CT: Fawcett.

Harrison, R. (1970). Nonverbal communication: Explorations into time, space, action, and object. In J. Campbell & H. Helper (Eds.), *Dimensions in communication* (pp. 110–146). Belmont, CA: Wadsworth.

Johnson, B. M. (1977). *Communication: The process of organizing.* Boston: Allyn and Bacon.

Kanter, R. M. (1977). *Men and women of the corporation.* New York: Basic Books.

Kawachi, I., Kennedy, B. P., Bruce, P., & Lochner, K. (1997). Social capital, income inequality, and mortality. *American Journal of Public Health, 87,* 1491–1498.

Kawachi, I., Kennedy, B. P., & Glass, R. (1999). Social capital and self-rated health: a contextual analysis. *American Journal of Public Health, 89*(8), 1189–1193.

Kawachi, I., Kennedy, B. P., & Lochner, K. (1997). Long live community: Social capital as public health. *The American Prospect, 29,* 56–59.

Knapp, M. (1978). *Nonverbal communication in human interaction* (2nd ed.). New York: Holt, Rinehart & Winston.

Koch, S., & Deetz, S. A. (1981). Metaphor analysis of social reality in organizations. *Journal of Applied Communication Research, 9,* 1–15.

Kreiner, K., & Schultz, M. (1993). Informal collaboration in R&D—The formation of networks across organizations. *Organization Studies, 14,* 189–209.

Lakoff, R. (1975). *Language and woman's place.* New York: Harper & Row.

Langer, S. (1942). *Philosophy in a new key.* Cambridge, MA: Harvard University Press.

Level, D. A. (1959). *A case study of human communication in an urban bank.* Unpublished doctoral dissertation, Purdue University, West Lafayette, IN.

Littlejohn, S. W. (1992). *Theories of human communication* (4th ed.). Belmont, CA: Wadsworth.

Markham, A. (1996). Designing discourse: A critical analysis of strategic ambiguity and workplace control. *Management Communication Quarterly, 9,* 389–421.

Martin, J. (1992). *Culture in organizations: Three perspectives.* New York: Oxford University Press.

McCroskey, J. C., Larson, C., & Knapp M. (1971). *An introduction to interpersonal communication.* Englewood Cliffs, NJ: Prentice Hall.

Mead, G. H. (1932). *Mind, self and society from the standpoint of a social behaviorist* (C. W. Morris, Ed.). Chicago: University of Chicago Press.

Meyerson, D. E. (1991). Acknowledging and uncovering ambiguities in cultures. In P. J. Frost, L. F. Moore, M. R. Louis, C. C. Lundberg, & J. Martin (Eds.), *Reframing organizational culture* (pp. 254–270). Newbury Park, CA: Sage.

Miller, P., & O'Leary, T. (1987). Accounting and the construction of the government person. *Accounting, Organizations, and Society, 12,* 235–265.

Mumby, D. (1987). The political function of narrative in organizations. *Communication Monographs, 54,* 113–127.

Norton, R. (1978). Foundation of a communicator style construct. *Human Communication Research, 4,* 99–112.

Papa, W. H., Papa, M. J., Kandath, K., Worrell, T., & Muthuswamy, N. (2005). Dialectic of unity and fragmentation in feeding the homeless: Promoting social justice through communication. *Atlantic Journal of Communication, 13,* 43–64.

Penley, L. E. (1982). An investigation of the information processing framework of organizational communication. *Human Communication Research, 8,* 348–365.

Perrin, P. G. (1965). *Writer's guide and index to English* (4th ed.). Glenview, IL: Scott, Foresman.

Piaget, J. (1970). *Structuralism* (C. Maschler, Ed. and Trans.). New York: Harper & Row.

Pollio, H. R. (1974). *The psychology of symbolic activity.* Reading, MA: Addison-Wesley.

Portes, A. (1998). Social capital: Its origins and applications in modern sociology. *Annual Review of Sociology, 24,* 1–24.

Putnam, L. L., & Fairhurst, G. T. (2001). Discourse analysis in organizations: Issues and concerns. In F. M. Jablin, & L. L. Putnam (Eds.), *The new handbook of organizational communication: Advances in theory, research, and methods* (pp. 78–136). Thousand Oaks, CA: Sage.

Putnam, R. D. (1993). *Making democracy work: Civic traditions in modern Italy.* Princeton, NJ: Princeton University Press.

Putnam, R. D. (1995). Bowling alone: America's declining social capital. *Democracy, 6,* 65–78.

Putnam, R. D. (2000). *Bowling alone: The collapse and revival of American community.* New York: Simon & Schuster.

Putnam, R. D. (2001). Social capital: Measurement and consequences. *Canadian Journal of Policy Research, 34,* 41–51.

Ritzer, G. (1996). *Modern sociological theory* (4th ed.). New York: McGraw-Hill.

Ruud, G. (1995). The symbolic construction of organizational identities and community in a regional symphony. *Communication Studies, 46,* 201–221.

Sanders, J. M. (2002). Ethnic boundaries and identity in plural societies. *Annual Review of Psychology, 28,* 327–357.

Schenck-Hamlin, W. J. (1978). The effects of dialectical similarity, stereotyping, and message agreement on interpersonal perception. *Human Communication Research, 5,* 15–26.

Scheufele, D. A., & Shah, D. V. (2000). Personality strength and social capital. *Communication Research, 27*(2), 107–131.

Sias, P. M., & Cahill, D. J. (1998). From coworkers to friends: The development of peer relationships in the workplace. *Western Journal of Communication, 62,* 273–299.

Singhal, A., Papa, M. J., Sharma, D., Pant, S., Worrell, T., Muthuswamy, N., & Witte, K. (2006). Entertainment-education and social change: The communicative dynamics of social capital. *Creative Communications, 1,* 23–35.

Smith, G. L., & DeWine, S. (1987). *An investigation of the relationship between organizational commitment and information overload/underload.* Paper presented at the annual meeting of the Central States Speech Association, St. Louis, April 1987.

Spiker, B. K., & Daniels, T. D. (1981). Information adequacy and communication relationships: An empirical examination of 18 organizations. *Western Journal of Speech Communication, 45,* 342–354.

Spiker, B. K., & Lesser, E. (1995). We have met the enemy. *Journal of Business Strategy, 16,* 17–21.

Stein, L. I. (1967). The doctor-nurse game. *Archives of General Psychiatry, 16,* 699–703.

Taylor, C. (1989). *Sources of the self: The making of modern identity.* Cambridge, MA: Harvard University Press.

Tompkins, P. H. (1962). *An analysis of communication between headquarters and selected units of a national union.* Unpublished doctoral dissertation, Purdue University, West Lafayette, IN.

Tubbs, S. L., & Moss, S. (1980). *Human communication* (3rd ed.). New York: Random House.

Wagner, E. J. (1992). *Sexual harassment in the workplace.* New York: AMACOM-American Management Association.

Watzlawick, P., Beavin, J., & Jackson, D. (1967). *Pragmatics of human communication: A study of interactional patterns, pathologies, and paradoxes.* New York: Norton.

Weick, K. (1979). *The social psychology of organizing* (2nd ed.). Reading, MA: Addison-Wesley.

Weitzman, E., & Kawachi, I. (2000). Giving means receiving: The protective effect of social capital on binge drinking on college campuses. *American Journal of Public Health, 90*(12), 1936–1939.

Williams, R. (1977). *Marxism and literature.* New York: Oxford University Press.

Whorf, B. L. (1957). *Language, thought, and reality.* New York: John Wiley & Sons.

Wood, J. T., & Conrad, C. (1983). Paradox in the experiences of professional women. *Western Journal of Speech Communication, 47,* 305–322.

Organizational Communication Structure

TRADITIONAL APPROACH TO STRUCTURE

The concept of communication structure is one of the most important ideas in the study of organizational communication. It is also one of the most complicated because the way we understand structure depends very much on the perspective from which we study it. The traditional approach to understanding communication structure dominates the organizational communication discipline, so we will spend the majority of our time focusing on this perspective. There are several different ways to think about the structure of organizational communication from the traditional perspective, but three of them in particular will give you a fairly representative review of the concept and a good idea of just how complex the concept of structure can be.

One way of thinking about structure is to define it as a system of pathways through which messages flow—the so-called lines of communication in an organization (Goldhaber, 1993; Koehler, Anatol, & Applbaum, 1981). This is the *channels perspective*, and it is the traditional definition of communication structure. If you think about this definition for a moment, it is easy to see just what it implies. Messages are regarded as concrete objects that are passed back and forth through literal channels of communication. Many scholars, even traditionalists, are uneasy about this idea because it misrepresents the dynamics of interpersonal communication. Although messages do exist in a tangible way through the written and spoken word (i.e., what Cynthia Stohl (1995) refers to as ostensive messages), in another sense, "the message" exists only in the transaction between two or more persons.

The second approach defines communication structure as the patterns of interaction among people who make up the organization. In this sense, structure depends on who communicates with whom. We will call this the *observable network perspective* in which a network "consists of interconnected individuals who are linked by patterned flows of information, influence, and affect" (Stohl, 1995, p. 18). Because these patterned flows can be observed, the second definition also is consistent with the traditional focus on objective features of organizational communication. Of course, interpretivists are quick to argue that structure is not really an objective property of communication but an idea that is shared by organization members (Trujillo, 1985).

This leads us to a third idea about structure, which really is a second version of the network idea, the *perceived network perspective*. When researchers study networks, they sometimes figure out the network structure from organization members' own reports of their linkages with others, i.e., with whom they communicate and how often. But many researchers have noted that these reports by organization members often are inconsistent with observations of the same organization made by trained researchers. So what is it that organization members are reporting if it is not the actual network? Stephen Corman and Craig Scott (1994), two network theorists, describe it this way:

> The network is a structure of perceived communication relationships. It is a kind of latent knowledge that guides members' manifest communication behavior. We believe that members' reports of communication reflect this knowledge, not their recollections of specific communication episodes. (p. 174)

Is structure an objective property or a subjective idea? Curiously, it seems to be both. On the one hand, when organization members interact, they are engaging in behavior with objective features. These features include discernible patterns that someone else can observe. On the other hand, it is also true that you generally cannot go into an organization and point to the network of communication in the same way that you can point to the network of telephones because the networks defined by interaction can be highly changeable, and any given organization member may be in many different networks within the same organization. When outside observers look at the communication network, it is a bit like taking a photograph of one particular set of interactions as it exists at a fixed point in time. When organization members talk about the communication network, they are talking about "an abstract structure of perceived communication relationships that functions as a set of rules and resources actors draw upon in accomplishing communication behavior" (Corman & Scott, 1994, p. 181). We will have more to say later in the chapter about this problem and how the ideas of observable and perceived networks can be reconciled.

The channels perspective, the idea that communication structure is a system of pathways or channels of message flow, goes hand in hand with a common distinction between formal and informal systems of organizational communication. This distinction is very useful, but it has some limitations. Some of these limitations can be overcome by viewing communication structure as a network that arises from the patterns of interaction among organization members. Because each of these ideas provides a particular way of understanding communication structure, we will review both in some detail.

FORMAL COMMUNICATION

Formal communication refers to communication through officially designated channels of message flow between organizational positions. In many organizations, the formal system of communication is specified in policy manuals and organization charts. In other organizations, the formal system is implicit, yet organization members understand it well. The United States Postal Service (USPS) and Supervalue Market illustrate this point (see Chapter 4). The USPS has explicit, written policies that define the channels of formal communication, whereas Supervalue has a system of conventions and rules learned through day-to-day experience. USPS and Supervalue also sustain hierarchical structures based on functional divisions of labor and scalar authority chains. The concept of hierarchy is so ingrained in organizational life that formal communication usually is described in terms of the three directions of message flow within a hierarchical system: downward, upward, and horizontal.

Downward Communication

Downward communication involves the transmission of messages from upper levels to lower levels of the organization hierarchy (i.e., from manager to employee, superior to subordinate). Smith, Richetto, and Zima (1972) claimed that downward communication has been the most frequently studied aspect of formal communication. Twenty years ago, there also was a great deal of evidence that most of the message flow in formal systems was downward (Tompkins, 1967).

Classical and scientific approaches to organizations considered communication primarily as a tool for managerial control and coordination. Consequently, these approaches focused on downward communication of orders and regulations from superiors to subordinates—messages concerned with production and maintenance functions.

Classical theorists assumed that subordinates would accept and comply with downward communication on the basis of superiors' legitimate authority. As the Hawthorne Studies illustrated, compliance with managerial authority is not such a simple matter. The human relations movement stressed the use of downward-communication strategies that would promote morale in the belief that satisfaction would lead to compliance with authority (Miles, 1965). Much of the research that followed human relations assumptions has attempted to determine the conditions under which subordinates comply with messages received from superiors (Smith et al., 1972).

More recently, contemporary theorists have argued that organization members have a "need to know" for their own purposes. Satisfaction of this need is important to the successful assimilation of members into an organization. As Koehler et al. (1981) argued, "The best integrated employees are those who are told what goals and objectives are, how their jobs fit into the total picture, and the progress they are making on the job" (p. 10). This idea is the basis for some of the more recent studies on information adequacy that we described earlier. For example, Penley's (1982) work focused on the role of information adequacy in bringing about members' involvement in and identification with organization goals rather than on downward-communication strategies for producing compliance with authority.

Katz and Kahn (1978) identified five types of messages that usually are reflected in downward communication:

1. *Job instructions* involving the work to be done and directions for doing that work.

2. *Job rationales* explaining the purpose of a job or task and its relationship to other organizational activities or objectives.

3. *Procedures and practices information* pertaining to organizational policies, rules, and benefits.

4. *Feedback* providing subordinates with appraisals of their performance.

5. *Indoctrination* of organizational ideology that attempts to foster member commitment to the organization's values, goals, and objectives.

Effective Downward Communication

Despite the attention that downward communication has received in management and communication research, this dimension of formal communication is ineffective in many organizations (Chase, 1970). Problems with downward communication include inadequacy of information, inappropriate means of diffusing information, filtering of information, and a general climate of dominance and submission that pervades downward communication.

Adequacy of information obtained from downward messages presents a puzzling paradox. On the one hand, downward-directed messages frequently create overload in organizations (Davis, 1972). Advances in information technology (the mechanical and electronic ability not only to manipulate information more efficiently but also to send more messages to more people) and, ironically, the importance attached to the idea of effective organizational communication have led to floods of memorandums, bulletins, newsletters, technical reports, and data in reams of computer printouts. FedEx, a company specializing in overnight delivery of letters and packages, has gleefully referred to this condition as "The Paper Blob" in its advertising. On the other hand, organization members consistently report in studies of information adequacy that they do not receive sufficient information on topics that are important to them (Goldhaber, 1993; Penley, 1982; Spiker & Daniels, 1981).

The apparent paradox is difficult to explain. One possible conclusion is that organization members receive too much of the wrong information. This does not mean that the information itself is in error. It means that much of the information that members receive may not be relevant to their personal job and organizational concerns. Farace, Monge, & Russell (1977) argued that problems in information-diffusion policies most commonly "are due to failures by managers to identify which groups of personnel need to know certain things, or to establish where these groups are supposed to be able to obtain the information they need" (p. 28). Of course, this claim, along with the Koehler et al. argument that the best integrated employees are those who are "told" about goals, the big picture, and their progress, presumes that managers are the ones who should define everybody's information needs. This assumption poses another problem: How much input should employees or subordinates have in deciding what they need and how they will obtain it? Reserving for management the exclusive right to decide who gets what information is an idea that may be unacceptable to many members of modern organizations.

The methods of information diffusion that are used for downward communication also can create problems. According to Goldhaber (1993), organizations often rely too heavily on mediated (written, mechanical, and electronic) methods of transmitting messages rather than on personal, face-to-face contact. Goldhaber, Yates, Porter, and Lesniak (1978) concluded from a review of 16 ICA-sponsored studies that organization members generally desire more face-to-face interaction. This finding also poses another paradox. How do we cope with the human need for direct, interpersonal contact when today's pressure to get more information to more people more rapidly requires us to rely on the most efficient means of communication available (i.e., paper and electronic media)?

Upward Communication

Upward communication involves transmission of messages from lower to higher levels of the organization; namely, communication initiated by subordinates with their superiors. The role of upward communication in classical theories of organization was limited primarily to basic reporting functions concerning task-related matters. The human relations movement expanded the role of upward communication by emphasizing "two-way" communication between superiors and subordinates as a means of promoting morale. Later, human resource development theories emphasized the necessity of upward communication for integration of organization members and improved decision-making processes. Upward communication is a prerequisite for employee involvement in decision making, problem solving, and development of policies and procedures (Smith et al., 1972).

Katz and Kahn (1978) point out that upward communication can provide superiors with information in the following areas:

1. Performance on the job and job-related problems.

2. Fellow employees and their problems.

3. Subordinates' perceptions of organizational policies and practices.

4. Tasks and procedures for accomplishing them.

In addition to those uses noted by Katz and Kahn, Planty and Machaver (1952) stated that upward communication can (1) provide valuable ideas from subordinates, (2) facilitate acceptance of downward messages, and (3) generally facilitate decision making by fostering subordinates' participation and by providing a better picture of performance, perceptions, and possible problems at all levels of the organization.

Effective Upward Communication

Although contemporary managers and executives praise the virtues of upward communication, actual use of upward communication appears to be limited in many organizations (Goldhaber, 1993; Tompkins, 1967). Management often does not establish effective means for upward communication. Moreover, when upward communication does occur, it may be subject to the same filtering problems that affect downward communication.

Although upward communication can be encouraged through means such as suggestion systems, systematic reporting methods, grievance procedures, attitude surveys, and employee meetings, the presence of such systems may be only a token gesture in many organizations. A story that a student told us about her first encounter with a suggestion box during a summer job at a factory is not unusual. The little wooden box hung from a supervisor's office door. When the student asked a coworker (a veteran of several years in the factory) about the box, she was told, "Don't pay any attention to that, kid. They never open it, and we never put anything in it."

Suggestion systems can be very effective when managers actively encourage their use and employees take them seriously, but our example of the "suggestion box syndrome" typifies two common research findings about upward communication. First, most organization members would rather receive information than provide information to others (Goldhaber, 1993). Second, even when subordinates make attempts at upward communication, their superiors may not be receptive to these attempts. Koehler and Huber (1974) found that managers tend to be more receptive to upward communication when the information is positive (good news rather than bad news), is in line with current policy (criticism and boat rocking are unwelcome), and has intuitive appeal (fits the managers' own biases).

Subordinates are likely to become quite dissatisfied in organizations in which superiors endorse the idea of upward communication but, in practice, actually ignore it. When subordinates develop the impression that superiors only want to hear good news and support for their own ideas, it should not be surprising that upward communication with those superiors is filtered extensively. Krivonos (1976) reported that subordinates tend to tell their superiors what they think the superiors want to hear or only what they want their superiors to hear. Information is distorted so that it will please superiors and reflect positively on subordinates.

Although several factors seem to affect accuracy of upward communication, the most important ingredient may be trust. Studies by Read (1962), Maier, Hoffman, and Read (1963), and Roberts and O'Reilly (1974) indicated that accuracy of upward communication is greater when subordinates trust their superiors. The studies by Read and by Maier, Hoffman, and Read also found that subordinates' upward mobility aspirations are negatively related to accuracy. As subordinates' mobility aspirations increase, accuracy in upward communication decreases. This finding is somewhat suspect because the method that Read used to index accuracy was rather crude. Even so, Read's research reminds us that some people who want to move up may distort information to make themselves look good or to protect their chances of promotion.

Horizontal Communication

Horizontal communication refers to the flow of messages across functional areas at a given level of an organization. Although classical approaches to organizing made little provision for horizontal communication, Fayol recognized that emergencies and unforeseen day-to-day contingencies require flexibility in formal channels. Strict adherence to the chain of command would be too time consuming in emergencies, so some provision has to be made for horizontal bridges that permit people at the same level to communicate directly without going through several levels of organization. Fayol's concept (1949) is illustrated in Figure 3.1.

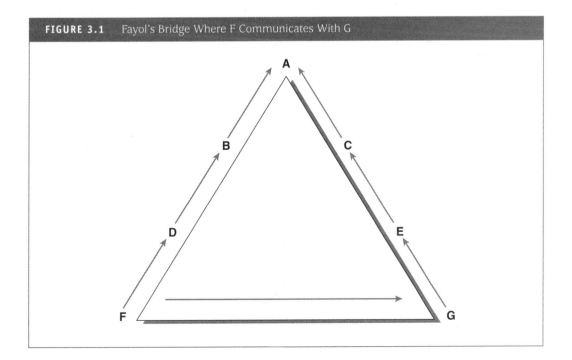

FIGURE 3.1   Fayol's Bridge Where F Communicates With G

Horizontal communication introduces flexibility in organizational structure. It facilitates problem solving, information sharing across different work groups, and task coordination between departments or project teams. It may also enhance morale and afford a means for resolving conflicts (Koehler et al., 1981). Human resource development theorists regard horizontal communication as an essential feature of participative decision making and organizational adaptiveness (French, Bell, & Zawacki, 1983).

Reliance on horizontal communication for decision making and problem solving does not mean that the process is more efficient than simple downward communication of decisions made at top levels of the organization, but horizontal communication may be more effective. As we will note in Chapter 4, this idea is emphasized in human resource development theory and applied broadly in Japanese organizations in which decision making and problem solving usually occur through horizontal communication at lower levels. The results of this process are transmitted to top management for review and approval. Ryutard Nomura (1981), chairman of the board of Japan's Triyo Industries, observed that decision making under this system can be a lengthy and difficult process, but once a decision has been made, its implementation is swift and certain. Organization members are committed to the decision because difficulties have been resolved and opposing points of view reconciled through horizontal communication before plans are presented to top management.

In the conventional Western organization, decisions are made at the top, and then orders for compliance and implementation flow downward. According to Nomura, Western-style decision making is fast because it is centralized near the top of the organization. However, acceptance and implementation of top management decisions at lower levels is slow to develop. Lack of commitment to decisions and conflicts over implementation arise at lower levels where members have been excluded from the decision-making process.

Effective Horizontal Communication

American organizations generally are unaccustomed to high levels of horizontal communication. Albaum (1964) found that any given department in an organization typically will not relay information directly to another, even when it is understood that the information is vitally important to the other department. Although Albaum's research occurred many years ago, there is little reason to suspect that conditions today are much different.

Horizontal communication problems occur because of territoriality, rivalry, specialization, and simple lack of motivation. Organizations that traditionally have functioned under rigid authority structures with fixed lines of communication may find that the values and expectations that members have acquired under such systems inhibit attempts at horizontal communication.

One inhibiting value is territoriality. Organization members who control task-related activity within a defined and fixed jurisdictional area often regard others' involvement in that area as territorial encroachment. Departments value their turf and strive to protect it. This problem may be compounded through interdepartmental rivalries that arise from win/lose competition for rewards and resources.

Some years ago, corporate executives in a national department store chain encountered territorial rivalry when they discovered that local stores within each of the company's major sales districts refused to cooperate with one another on sales promotions. For example, if Store X ran out of a sale item, it might call Store Y in the same district to obtain more. Even though Store Y would have an ample supply of the item, it would claim to be out. The explanation was simple. Local managers were rewarded only for the sales performance of their individual stores. Consequently, stores within the same sales region literally were in competition with one another as well as with other department store chains. When the company decided to provide managers with bonuses based on district-wide sales, stores within any given district suddenly began to cooperate with one another on all sorts of projects and promotions.

Specialization also may hamper horizontal communication. During the 1960s, for example, a team of experts from various fields was assembled to work on a NASA-sponsored project. The team hardly had begun its work before its members realized that they were having great difficulty in communicating. The main reason seemed to be that different specialties used the same terms in different ways. The problem was so persistent that the group finally appointed a "vocabulary committee" to develop standard definitions for all of the troublesome terms.

Horizontal communication often fails simply because organization members are unwilling to expend the additional effort that it requires. When we engage in upward or downward communication, those with whom we communicate are easy to reach because of proximity or clearly designated channels. Immediate superiors and immediate subordinates may be just across the office. We know them by name and we have well-established rules for initiating and conducting interaction with them. In contrast, horizontal communication may require contact with people in units that are well removed from our own. The channels and rules of interaction may be unclear. We do not really know these people. The need to communicate with them makes us uneasy or takes too much time, so we avoid or ignore it.

Diagonal Communication

Diagonal communication involves communication that crosses both levels and functions or departments within the organization. Although it seems only logical that this structure of communication would exist in organizations, attempts to understand, promote, and assess the effectiveness of such structures have occurred only recently. Three types of diagonal communication occur, in quality circles, lattice designs, and heterarchies. Let's take a look at each of these structures to see how it functions within organizations. We'll also assess the degree to which they promote effective communication within organizations.

Effective Diagonal Communication and Quality Circles

The quality circle (QC) concept involves creating employee problem-solving groups to improve product or service quality in organizations. The QC structure began in Japan in the late 1950s and spread to the United States in the 1970s. QCs involve small groups of employees (5 to 15 is the norm) who "meet regularly to identify, discuss, and offer solutions to problems concerning product [or service] quality and productivity" (Seibold & Shea, 2001, p. 669). Quality circles may comprise employees from the same work area, although the members usually include employees from different departments and hierarchical levels in the organization (thus creating a diagonal communication structure). In order to promote effective decision making, QC members often receive training in group process and problem-solving techniques. The QCs are then charged with preparing recommendations to improve product or service quality and productivity. Management then makes the decision about whether or not to implement the suggestions that are offered.

In general, studies of QCs indicate that most fail eventually and that when positive effects are observed they tend to be minimal (Cotton, 1993; Drago, 1988; Lawler, 1986; Lawler & Mohrman, 1987; Ledford, Lawler, & Mohrman, 1988; Steel & Lloyd, 1988; Van Fleet & Griffin, 1989). The most frequently cited reason for failure is that QC members "often lack the information needed to make viable suggestions" (Seibold & Shea, 2001, p. 671). For example, a circle may produce a good idea but circle members may not recognize the complexity of their proposal. Alternatively, QC members may offer a recommendation that works according to their understanding of organizational functioning, but it counters a new strategic mission adopted by top management.

Despite the negative findings uncovered by many researchers, there is evidence that quality circles can affect organizations in positive ways. The positive effects concern communication processes and patterns in organizations. For example, Buch (1992) discovered that QCs may open new communication relationships between employees and managers. This opening of new communication relationships may speak to the emergence of new links or to a shift from one-way to two-way communication between employees and management. More specifically, Buch reported that QC members and managers perceived that communication and teamwork improved after the initiation of a QC program.

When quality circles are effective in improving product or service quality and productivity, there appear to be certain communication conditions that must be present. Generally, Stohl (1987) discovered that the effectiveness of QCs is a product of the circle's level of connectedness with the rest of the organization. At a more specific level, QC solution effectiveness was related strongly to the number of different groups or departments in the organization to which the QC was linked (network range). In addition, managers perceived that QC effectiveness was correlated with the number of relationships that QC members had with other employees in the organization (extended network).

Effective Diagonal Communication and Lattice Design

Quality circles refer to individual groupings of employees committed to improvements in product or service quality and productivity. There may be one quality circle or many in an organization. However, even when there are many quality circles in a large organization, these circles do not reflect the entire structure of the organization. One new organizational design that does include the entire organizational structure is the lattice design.

Lattice design refers to an organization that is nonhierarchical. There are no bosses. New organization members are not assigned to a department; rather, they find a team that they would like to join. The employee then makes a voluntary commitment to achieve certain outcomes as a part of that team. In the lattice organization, direct communication is encouraged. There are no intermediaries or approval seeking. Rather than fixed or assigned authority, natural leadership emerges through fellowship among team members. Team members establish and commit to objectives and act to make them happen. Finally, lattice organizations recognize sponsors rather than bosses (Natural Leadership, 2004).

WL Gore & Associates embodies the lattice design. Founded by Bill Gore and his wife Genevieve (Vieve) in 1958 to develop commercial applications for Teflon, WL Gore & Associates now has annual revenues in excess of $1.5 billion (Natural Leadership, 2004). The organization has diversified from its beginnings as an electronic products producer (e.g., wire, cable and signal insulation) to become a manufacturer of industrial and medical products and the product for which it is most famous, GORE-TEX.

In order to sustain a team-based nonhierarchical structure, an organization may need to limit its size. Bill Gore argued that individual corporate buildings should house no more than 150–200 people. Once organizations become larger than 200, the workgroups within them begin to lose their cohesion. Because WL Gore & Associates is a large corporation that sells products internationally, they had to figure out how to grow without violating their founder's views regarding organizational size. The solution was to spawn "clusters" of plants in which each individual building houses no more than 150–200 employees. These plants are located near each other, however, "so expensive resources can be shared and functional groups of people can come together easily to share knowledge, expertise, and experience between plants" (Natural Leadership, 2004).

All Gore employees (except those at the very top) are given the title "associate." After an associate has been with the company for one year, the company contributes 15% of the associate's salary into the company's ownership plan. This significant contribution ranks Gore as one of the most generous providers of benefits in the United States. "Associates are thus significant owners of the business and are not only encouraged to behave like owners of the business but are empowered to do so" (Natural Leader, 2004).

Effective Diagonal Communication and Heterarchies

Heterarchical structures are similar to lattice designs; however, the concept of heterarchy has undergone more complex conceptual refinement. The recent emergence of heterarchical structures has been prompted by an important shift in internal and external organizational environments. Specifically, Stark (2002) argues that we are shifting away from hierarchical dependence within organizations and the relations of market independence between organizations. And, we are shifting increasingly toward relations of interdependence among networks of organizations and among groups within the organization. Stark (2002) provides us with a definition of heterarchy:

> Heterarchies are self-organizing non-hierarchical systems that are characterized by lateral accountability and by organizational heterogeneity. Heterarchy involves distributed intelligence and the organization of diversity. Restated, heterarchies encompass multiple communities of knowledge and practice that subscribe to diverse evaluative and performance criteria and answer to different constituencies and principles of accountability. (p. 2)

Why is it important for contemporary organizations to consider a shift away from hierarchy and toward heterarchy? The main reason is to respond to increasing uncertainty in organizational environments. In an era of uncertainty prompted by global competition, organizations must view innovation as central to survival. For example, how can organizations flexibly deploy resources to encourage a culture of innovation? Advocates of heterarchy believe that radical decentralization encourages innovation because every unit in the organization is engaged in innovation. Creativity is not the responsibility of a select few or of senior management. Creativity and change is everyone's job.

By increasing interdependence among organizational units, heterarchical structures increase the autonomy of work units from management. In addition, more complex interdependence heightens the need for highly tuned coordination across increasingly autonomous units (Stark, 2002). By flattening the organization's hierarchy and coordinating the distribution of intelligence across interdependent organizational units, the delegation of authority changes radically. Authority is no longer delegated vertically. Rather, authority emerges laterally (e.g., the Wikimedia Foundation).

The challenge to creating an effective heterarchy is building an organization that is capable of learning. As Stark (2002) argues, organizations "must foster a sufficiently common culture to facilitate communication among the designers, business strategists, engineers, marketers, technologists, and scientists that make up interdisciplinary teams without suppressing the distinctive identities of each. Flatten the hierarchy without flattening diversity" (p. 3).

Heterarchies draw on principles that are used frequently in quality circles. The mission of groups within heterarchies is much larger than the mission of quality circles, however. Heterarchies also exhibit similarities to lattice designs. The major difference between these two designs is the more stringent requirement in heterarchies for coordination among organizational units.

At the group level, groups within heterarchies are organized horizontally with all individuals sharing equal authority and equal responsibility. Groups within heterarchies do not act like committees in hierarchical organizations where a majority may outvote a minority (and where the minority either supports the action or leaves). Rather, within heterarchies decisions are negotiated in ways that satisfy all group members. This becomes possible because all members are equals and no one has any more authority than anyone else. In terms of decision-making process, this requires continuing discussion until a plan of action is found that will work for everyone. The plan may be implemented only when all are in agreement. The plan of action is then divided into subtasks to be executed (Future Positive, 2002).

Information Distortion From the Traditional Perspective

Communication that takes place between and among organization members may be subjected to filtering. As messages are relayed across levels of the organizational hierarchy or between departments, they may be changed in various ways. Information may be left out, added, combined, or otherwise modified as it passes through a chain of serial reproduction (Pace & Boren, 1973). Serial reproduction is the same effect that occurs in the children's game Telephone when messages are passed from one person to the next. Distortions occur as each person in the transmission series attempts to reproduce the message received for relay to the next person. Although oral messages are most easily subjected to such distortions, written messages are not immune if they are in any way relayed from level to level of the organization.

In part, distortions occur because different people have different interpretations of the same information (i.e., as a result of ambiguity) or because human beings simply have a limited capacity to process information. When attempting to reproduce a message in serial transmission, people may simply forget some of the information or "chunk" certain details together in order to handle the information more efficiently.

Organizational messages also may be filtered deliberately. Information power is a valuable commodity in many organizations. Culbert and Eden (1970) pointed out that managers often "base their power on withholding, rather than sharing, information" (p. 140), because ability to control situations and outcomes may depend on having knowledge that others do not possess. When managers do choose to share information, their subordinates may prevent it from being relayed to lower levels of the organization. Mellinger (1956) found that subordinates who do not trust a superior often choose to block that superior's messages from others.

In general, the greater the number of steps or linkages in a serial reproduction chain and the greater the perceptual differences among participants in that chain, the more likely it is that some form of message distortion or filtering will occur. The type of information also has a bearing on the extent to which it will even be distributed. In a case study of one large organization, Davis (1968) found that important information was more likely than insignificant information to be relayed by superiors to subordinates, but even the important information often was not relayed by superiors to subordinates despite the fact that the superiors had explicit instructions to pass on this information.

INFORMAL COMMUNICATION

The informal system involves episodes of interaction that do not reflect officially designated channels of communication. As defined by Tompkins (1967), the informal system is "not rationally specified." Classical and scientific theorists made no attempt to account for the role of informal communication in organizational functions and its influence on organizational life. Many classical and scientific principles of management were turned upside down when Barnard's work and the Hawthorne Studies suggested that a great deal of organizational communication is informal communication. In fact, one of the most important findings in the Hawthorne Studies concerned the influence of informal communication in developing and reinforcing performance standards, member expectations, and values at the workgroup level.

Some scholars have argued that informal communication is a substitute for an inadequate formal system. Walton (1961) concluded that informal communication systems arise when information transmitted through the formal system is either insufficient or ambiguous. Other scholars claim that the informal system is much more than a simple substitute for an ineffective formal system. Barnard (1938) and Davis (1953) argued that informal communication is an inherent and even necessary aspect of organizational life. Generally, organizational communication theorists agree that at least some informal communication is inevitable in any organization. Management efforts to stamp it out are misguided at best, although some experts urge managers to control the informal system (Hellweg, 1987).

Much of the research on informal communication is concerned with the study of grapevine communication. The terms informal system and grapevine often are used interchangeably as if they refer to the same thing (Davis, 1953; Hellweg, 1987). The use of the word grapevine as a metaphor for a communication system began during the American

Civil War in the 1860s as a description for telegraph lines that were strung through trees in such a way that they looked like grapevines. The system was not very reliable, so the term was soon applied to any form of unofficial communication (Davis, 1953).

Nearly a century later, organizational communication research indicated that patterns of grapevine communication even look something like a cluster of grapes. Consider the pattern of message flow in Figure 3.2. Person A initiates and transmits a message to B and C. B relays the message to D, while C relays it to E and F. The clustering continues as the message is diffused throughout the organization. Some participants in the grapevine act only as receivers. They do not relay information to anyone else. Others relay it to several different people.

Grapevine communication has many other important features. Susan Hellweg (1987) summarized these features in a list of 33 general conclusions that she based on a review of 19 research studies. The conclusions are somewhat cumbersome because the studies themselves are very difficult to relate to one another. Even so, Hellweg presented a comprehensive analysis of what we know about the grapevine. For simplicity, we have reorganized her conclusions under five topic areas.

1. Function and Extent of Grapevine Communication

The grapevine emerges from the social and personal interests of employees rather than formal requirements of the organization. It is the system in which most organizational communication actually occurs, emphasizing "people-oriented" information and "news" events.

2. Participants in Grapevine Communication

Secretaries and liaisons play key roles in grapevine communication, although relatively few people are grapevine liaisons, and many people who receive grapevine information do not transmit it to others. Use of the grapevine is just as prevalent among managers as it is among other groups of employees.

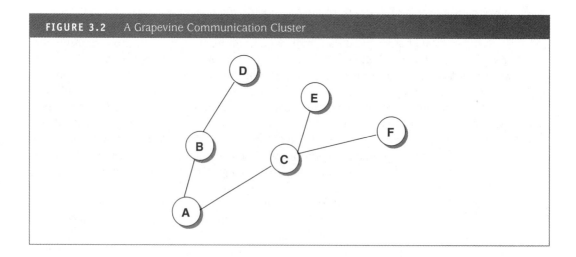

FIGURE 3.2 A Grapevine Communication Cluster

3. Patterns and Media of Grapevine Communication

Grapevine communication usually is oral and generally occurs in cluster transmission patterns. It may begin, flow, and end anywhere in an organization.

4. Volume, Speed, and Reliability of Information

Although grapevine communication usually is incomplete, information in the grapevine tends to be more accurate than inaccurate, and diffusion of information through the grapevine is fast.

5. Role in Rumor Transmission

Three types of rumors are diffused (spread) through the grapevine: anxiety rumors, wish-fulfillment rumors, and wedge-driving rumors. Rumors are distorted through sharpening, leveling, and assimilation. Once a rumor is assigned credibility, other events in the organization are altered to fit in with and support the rumor.

In general, Hellweg's review of research on grapevine communication suggests that a great deal of organizational communication occurs through the grapevine. Communication in this system is fast and more often accurate than inaccurate, although much of the information is incomplete. Grapevine communication usually is concerned with people-oriented, social information, although other forms of information are diffused through the grapevine. The grapevine serves as a rumor mill, but rumors make up only a small proportion of grapevine communication. Participants in grapevine communication include managers as well as employees and men as well as women.

COMMUNICATION STRUCTURE AS A NETWORK

Although the problems in the traditional concepts of formal and informal communication have not been resolved, they can be avoided or at least reframed to some extent by focusing on the patterns of interaction that occur among organization members, or the **communication network**. Figure 3.3 shows a diagram of a communication network. According to Noel Tichy (1981), such networks can be understood by examining four properties: member roles, characteristics of links, structural characteristics, and content.

Beginning with roles, consider the circles in Figure 3.3 as people. The lines connecting the circles are links that show who communicates with whom. The link is the fundamental unit of any network (Stohl, 1995). This particular diagram shows several distinct network roles that members of this organization assume. Assuming that the diagram represents a small organization, the communication network comprises three groups. Basically, a group is defined by members who interact more frequently with one another than with members of other groups. Most of the people in this network are *group members*. Person A is a *liaison*. A liaison links different groups but is not a member of any of the groups in that link. Individuals B and C form a *bridge* link between two groups. Unlike liaisons, people in a bridge link are group members. Person D is an *isolate* who is not linked to anyone else in the network. This does not mean that D never communicates with anyone else in the organization. It does mean that D has relatively little contact with others (i.e., the amount of interaction that D has with others is negligible in comparison to the amount that occurs among other organization members).

The links that occur between network members may be examined for reciprocity, intensity, and multiplexity. Reciprocity refers to two-way as opposed to one-way flow of messages in the link. Intensity involves commitment of linked members. For example, to what degree will a participant disregard personal costs in order to fulfill obligations (Tichy, 1981)? Multiplexity refers to the number of ways that participants in a link are related.

The structural characteristics of networks include factors such as size of the network, network density (i.e., the proportion of organization members in the network), clustering or the occurrence of dense regions in the network, stability of the network, conditions of membership in the network, and connectedness or the proportion of all possible organizational relationships that actually occur in the network.

Transactional content, according to Tichy, includes four media of exchange: expressions of affect, influence, information, and goods and services. Different types of networks have different transactional content, linkages, and structure. For example, Tichy points out that

FIGURE 3.3   A Communication Network

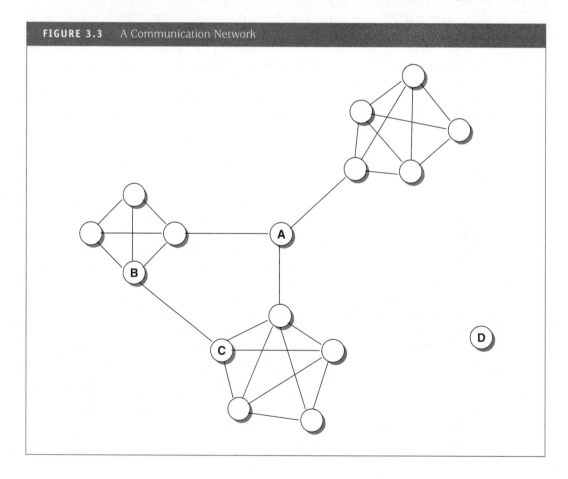

coalitions tend to deal with information and influence as content and have high reciprocity, moderate density, and clustering, but low intensity, little multiplexity, and low stability. In contrast, cliques deal with affect and have moderate intensity, greater multiplexity, low density and clustering, and high stability.

Advantages of a Network Perspective

Given the importance of structure as a concept in organizational communication, the idea that organizations can be understood as networks of communication has a powerful intuitive appeal. Cynthia Stohl (1995) has expanded this idea into a complete textbook on organizational communication. But how does a network perspective of organizational communication solve or at least help us to get around some of the problems with the traditional channels conceptions?

To begin with, it is immediately obvious that analysis of networks will allow us to tap into coupling characteristics that are difficult to see from a channels frame of reference. Being able to specify some set of formal channels and to compare that set with some sort of alternative informal system will not necessarily tell us anything about issues such as autonomy and discretion, but characteristics of networks such as density, clustering, intensity, multiplexity, and reciprocity within and between systems certainly can.

Second, a network perspective can help us to resolve the ambiguity in distinguishing between formal and informal communication. For example, Tichy (1981) and Stohl (1995) note that the problem is not so much a question of understanding the difference between formal and informal communication as it is a matter of recognizing that a formal system provides a very rough template through which enacted networks emerge. A formal system can guide and constrain emergent networks, but the emergent networks are more complex, elaborate, and varied.

Finally, a network perspective can help us to understand a little better the social construction aspect of organizational communication structure, especially when we try to reconcile the difference between the observable network and the perceived network points of view. We already have suggested that networks are paradoxically objective and subjective phenomena. A network is objective in the sense that an observer almost certainly could come into an organization and describe a set of linkages that can be called a network. Describing the communication network of the organization is another matter altogether because the network of communication just does not exist in the same static sense that the network of telephones exists. Networks enacted by organization members are dynamic and take on many different forms. When we try to talk about the communication network, we are left with Corman and Scott's (1994) observation that this is an abstract idea providing rules and reference points for members' interactions, and it may not correspond completely with any observable structure that emerges from these interactions. This is something like Tichy's idea of the relationship between prescribed and emergent networks, but the so-called prescribed or formal network is probably only one part of an organization member's abstract idea of the network. Corman talks about the network in terms of individual member's perceived communication relationships, but he also says, "It is a kind of latent knowledge that guides members' manifest communication behaviors" (p. 174). To the extent that this "latent knowledge" is shared among members, the network also exists as a social construction.

Uses of Network Analysis

The basic purpose of network analysis is to provide a picture of the patterns of interaction that define organizational communication structure. Terrance Albrecht and Vickie Ropp (1982) described several ways in which this picture can be developed:

1. Ask organization members to report the interactions that they have with one another (self-report surveys).

2. Make direct, firsthand observations of interaction patterns (naturalistic observation).

3. Unobtrusively "capture" interaction episodes on audiotape or videotape or from other records in the organization (constitutive ethnography).

4. Conduct nondirective interviews with members to obtain information that may help to explain and interpret interaction patterns.

Albrecht and Ropp argued for the use of various methods in any given network analysis because each method has specific advantages and disadvantages. Self-report surveys and interviews allow the researcher to obtain data from the organization members' perspective and to examine network structure of dyadic, group, and organization-wide levels, but analyses of member reports, as we already have noted, may yield a perceived network that corresponds only loosely with an observable network. Naturalistic observation and constitutive ethnography rely on records of current actual interaction rather than members' potentially faulty reconstructions of past events, but the scope of the analysis is restricted to dyadic and small-group levels. Unless you have an army of observers and recording devices, you just cannot be everywhere at once. The various methods also differ in the degree of structure that they impose on the situation and the kind of data that they provide for analysis.

Why go through complex procedures just to obtain a diagram of network structure? What is the utility of this information? At least three different uses of network analysis have been demonstrated in organizational communication research.

First, a network analysis makes it possible to determine the degree to which emergent networks correspond with prescribed or expected channels of communication, group structures, and member roles. Second, network analysis can identify individuals in specific network roles (e.g., liaisons and bridge links that seldom appear on formal organization charts). The presence of these linkages reveals patterns of horizontal communication between different groups and organizational units. Network analysis may also identify isolates. This may help to determine how well members are integrated into the organization.

Identification of network roles can have other important theoretical and practical implications. For example, Albrecht (1984) has reported several important differences between persons in bridge or liaison roles (linkers) and ordinary group members or isolates (nonlinkers). Her research indicates that linkers identify more closely with the organization, have a stronger connection between their jobs and self-concepts, think of their jobs in terms of teamwork and effectiveness, see a closer connection between their jobs and their salaries, and are less frustrated than nonlinkers. However, Albrecht also reported, "They [linkers] also saw their jobs more in terms of problems and pressures than did nonlinkers" (p. 545).

In addition to Albrecht's findings, other studies suggest that isolates do not contribute to organizational functions, tend to withhold information from others, and are relatively dissatisfied (Goldhaber, 1993). An organization committed to a philosophy of participation very likely would want to integrate isolates into the communication network, although there may be situations in which the presence of isolates is welcome news to an organization. For example, some universities and research institutes actively encourage a certain amount of isolation for professors and scientists in order for them to pursue research and scholarly writing.

Network analysis may also be used to reveal correlations between network characteristics and other organizational variables such as performance and satisfaction. For example, Marshall & Stohl (1993) studied the relationship of network and individual indicators of employee participation to employee performance and satisfaction. The network indicators included factors such as the size of a member's personal network (i.e., number of linkages with others) and empowerment (the number of a member's links with managers). Individual indicators of participation included the members' own perceptions of their involvement and empowerment. Interestingly, the best predictor of employee performance was the network indicator of empowerment, i.e., the number of linkages with managers, but the best predictor of satisfaction was the individual indicators, i.e., the employees' own perceptions of their participation.

A final use of network analysis lies in the study of new or "hidden" network structures in organizations. As Tichy (1981) noted, "All organizations consist of multiple networks. . . . These networks may overlap considerably or be quite separate" (p. 227). Some of these multiple networks may involve interest groups or political coalitions that are in no way identified in the rationally ordered world of the organization chart. An information network might differ greatly from an influence network, and any given member's network role may change from one type of network to another.

A study by McPhee and Corman (1995) provides a good example of this last use of network analysis. They found that networks develop around a hierarchy of member activities. Although the traditional idea of a network analysis yields a two-dimensional diagram of groups, bridge links, liaison, and isolates, McPhee and Corman's study of one organization revealed four different strata or levels in the network that clearly were tied to the demands of organizational activities. The highest level was a very dense network defined by members who were engaged in the most intensive activities. The lowest was a weakly linked network of members engaged in the least intensive activities.

Although traditionalists have not been completely oblivious to such shadowy networks as coalitions, Stevenson, Pearce, and Porter (1985) pointed out that early organizational theorists ignored these structures by assuming that all organizations have simple and well-defined goals. March and Simon (1958) were the first to call attention to conflict over organizational goals. Cyert and March (1963) extended this idea by discussing competition between conflicting coalitions that might arise in an organization, but functionalist scholars never really explored the political implications of such coalitions. Given their traditional objectives of explaining organizational effectiveness and goal setting, functionalists found it more convenient to simply treat management as a "normally dominant" coalition in order to focus on managerial control and coordination of organizational processes (Stevenson et al., 1985).

In addition to coalitions, other interest groups may provide the basis for special types of organizational networks. For example, John Van Maanen and Stephen Barley (1984) have shown that "occupational communities" can exert substantial influence over organizational dynamics. An occupational community is a group of people defined by membership in a particular profession or craft (e.g., lawyers, physicians, engineers, police, nurses). These groups develop their own networks—networks that cut across workgroup, hierarchical, and even organizational lines. Occupational communities develop and reinforce powerful values, vocabularies, and identities among their members. Because individuals' loyalties may be tied much more strongly to their membership in an occupational community than to membership in the work organization, such communities "possess a potentially useful resource to both support and oppose specific organizational policies" (Van Maanen & Barley, 1984, p. 334).

Loose Versus Tight Coupling

A focus on communication networks draws our attention to the connections that exist between and among people and units within organizations (or between organizations). However, the strength or intensity of these connections may vary significantly. One way of distinguishing between network linkages is to examine tightly coupled and loosely coupled systems. As Glassman (1973) explained, in two loosely coupled systems, either the systems have few common ties or the ties that join them are very weak. In system theory terms, highly interdependent organizational subsystems are tightly coupled. Subsystems that are related but less interdependent are loosely coupled. When an organization is based on tightly coupled subsystems, changes in one subsystem quickly ripple through others. In loosely coupled subsystems, the ripple effect of change is limited, dampened, or gradual. Any given organization might be described generally as either loosely or tightly coupled, but loose and tight coupling are two sides of the same coin. According to Karl Weick (1976), if tight coupling occurs in some areas of an organization, loose coupling must occur in others.

The distinction between tight and loose coupling is important because an organization that appears to be rigidly structured and formal may contain many loosely coupled subsystems, whereas one that appears to be informal may be tightly coupled. Weick (1976) demonstrated that educational institutions, usually regarded as bureaucracies, are very durable, loosely coupled systems. *Coupling does not depend so much on the degree of formalization in organizational structure as it does on the level of interdependence that actually exists among subsystems.*

Weick believes that the durability of successful organizations is attributable to loose coupling. Loose coupling allows for localized adaptation. When a new situation or problem arises, one area of the organization can respond without requiring organization-wide adaptation every time a change occurs in the environment. The effects of errors and failures are restricted primarily to the subsystems in which they occur.

Loosely coupled systems and the individuals within them have more autonomy and discretion than those in tightly coupled organizations. From an organizational communication standpoint, however, some of the characteristics of loosely coupled systems may surprise you. According to Weick, such organizations are relatively uncoordinated. No single member of the organization knows exactly what is happening throughout the organization as a whole, yet things get done and the organization more or less accomplishes its mission.

Loose coupling does have some potential disadvantages. It reduces benefits of standardization. It promotes diversity rather than selectivity in organizational values and practices. In other words, different groups may be doing things in very different ways. This condition may help to promote adaptation and innovation, but it also allows isolated subsystems to preserve archaic, outmoded traditions. At the same time, "loosely coupled systems should be conspicuous for their cultural lags," yet they also are "vulnerable to producing faddish responses" because so many independent subsystems have the ability to make ad hoc, isolated changes (Weick, 1976, p. 8).

The importance of reflecting on the advantages and disadvantages of loose and tight coupling varies widely depending on organizational type. Charles Perrow (1984) has given us insight into loose and tight coupling in organizations with the potential of causing catastrophic impact. He defines catastrophic impact as an organizational event that can take the lives of hundreds or thousands in one blow. Although he describes different types of organizations that may experience accidents that produce catastrophes, he spends considerable time reflecting on the nuclear power industry.

Nuclear power plants require complex systems because there are so many parts that interact to generate power and dispose of nuclear waste. In fact, Perrow (1984) states that there are often so many parts in these complex systems that, at any given time, there is likely to be something wrong with one or more parts. In a well-designed organizational system redundancy mechanisms are included so that each fault by itself does not prevent proper operation. However, in the tightly coupled systems that are common to nuclear power plants, unexpected interactions among organizational systems may lead to system failure.

Although loosely coupled systems can often accommodate failures through the use of spur-of-the-moment responses, such spontaneous reactions to problems cannot be justified when a catastrophe can result in the deaths of thousands of people. So nuclear power plants must rely on tight coupling, but how can the potential problems of this coupling system be mitigated? The designers of "tightly coupled systems must invest a great deal of effort and ingenuity in anticipating failure modes and providing safety features to permit survival and prompt recovery with minimal impact" (Perrow, 1984, p. 116).

If the concept of coupling is as important as Perrow suggests, the study of organizational communication *should be less concerned with traditional distinctions between formal and informal communication and more concerned about identifying and understanding the coupling characteristics of organizational communication networks*. These characteristics may be richer and more complex than the traditional distinction between formal and informal communication leads us to believe. We begin to get a better sense of this richness when we change our definition of communication structure from a "system of channels" to "patterns of interaction" in a network of relationships.

INTERPRETIVE APPROACHES TO COMMUNICATION STRUCTURE

The traditional distinction between formal and informal communication is useful in describing and understanding many aspects of organizational communication, but it is subject to at least two major limitations. First, there is no universal agreement on the distinction between formal and informal communication. Second, the concept of organizational structure itself may be regarded as a socially constructed reality.

Muddled Distinctions

The distinction between formal and informal communication is somewhat muddled. Most scholars make formal communication synonymous with the organization chart and informal communication synonymous with the grapevine. As Hellweg pointed out, grapevine communication usually occurs in cluster transmission patterns. Because many daily episodes of organizational communication ranging from ritual greetings to coffee break socializing do not fit this pattern, some scholars prefer a broader definition of informal communication that includes such episodes (Koontz & O'Donnel, 1955). Still others define the formal system as expected communication patterns and the informal system as actual patterns (Jacoby, 1968). Some even argue that formal communication is written, centralized (vertical), and planned, whereas informal communication is oral, decentralized (horizontal), and unplanned (Stech, 1983). None of these approaches has proven to be especially workable, so there is no one means of distinguishing between formal and informal communication that scholars uniformly accept. From the interpretive perspective, however, all communication that takes place in organizations is important to consider because it is through communication that we develop shared meanings.

Structure as a Social Construction

The concepts of formal "hierarchy" and informal "grapevine" are good examples of interpretivist notions about the social construction of reality. We often speak of formal messages "flowing upward and downward" and of rumors being "transmitted by the grapevine" as if hierarchy and grapevines are tangible things with a physical, concrete existence. Interpretivists point out that these concepts are metaphors that we use to make sense of organizational communication. After all, messages do not literally flow "up" or "down" and organizations and grapevines do not spring to life in order to "transmit" rumors.

We do not mean to suggest here that concepts such as hierarchy are just a figment of organization members' imaginations. For example, interpretivists may note that employees within a particular organization use the term "hierarchy" when they talk about their workplace. From a social constructivist standpoint, it is in conversations that take place at work that these employees construct a particular meaning of the term. Part of this meaning may involve acknowledgment of rules about who may talk to whom or who has control over resources and who does not. From another point of view, however, the predisposition to create hierarchy may very well be a "natural state of affairs" if it is an adaptation reflected in the evolved psychological mechanisms of human beings (cf. Studd & Gattiker, 1991). This possibility gains some additional credence from primatologists' observations of fundamental hierarchical arrangements in other primate species (e.g., chimpanzees) and our presumed evolutionary linkages with these species (Boehm, 1994). Such biological predispositions do not render behavior immutable, but they may influence our actions. Whether hierarchy exists as a reified social construction or as a "natural" order nudged into being through evolutionary adaptation, it is so pervasive that "it may be impossible to move beyond it in formally organized contexts" (Stohl, 1995, p. 115).

Concepts such as hierarchy and grapevine are rich in implications about power, authority, motives, intentions, and patterns of organizational communication. These terms also are embedded in the language that members of most organizations use to understand their own experiences. Our point here is that these concepts are not the only ones available for describing and explaining organizational communication.

The observations made to this point refer to general ways of taking an interpretive perspective on communication structure. A more specific interpretive way of understanding communication structure in organizations is to examine **semantic networks**. Semantic networks focus "on the shared meanings that people have for message content, particularly those messages that comprise important aspects of an organization's culture, such as corporate goals, slogans, myths, and stories" (Monge & Contractor, 2001, p. 470). In order to identify semantic networks, one would need to ask employees to "provide their interpretations of one or more significant communication messages, events, or artifacts" (Monge & Contractor, 2001, p. 470; see also Monge & Eisenberg, 1987). People who share similar interpretations are linked semantically to one another. The network identified through these "meaning connections" provides a picture of those groups of people who share common understandings. This form of analysis also makes it possible to identify isolates if there are employees who have unique, idiosyncratic meanings for messages, events, or artifacts. Liaisons and boundary spanners would be those who communicate in ways to link the meaning systems of different organizational groups.

The Relationship Between Structure and Culture

The structure of an organization may have a significant impact on organizational culture (a concept we will develop in much more detail in Chapter 6). Think for a moment about an organization that is structured as a hierarchy with strict rules about who can communicate with whom, clear areas of jurisdiction with minimal overlap, and established lines of authority and control. In this organization, violation of rules concerning organizational structure warrants punishment. For a rule-oriented person, this culture of inviolable rules may be comfortable. However, a person who values loose connections and freedom to collaborate with people working in diverse areas may feel stifled by all of the restrictions he or she faces to interact and work with others. Conversely, think of the culture that is created within a lattice-designed organization. In this culture, people are free to link with others who are committed to the same objectives. Creativity is expected and rewarded. A rule-oriented person may feel lost about how to interact in this organizational structure. A creative person who enjoys freedom and spontaneous decision making will probably feel right at home. Although these examples represent extremes in organizational structure, they do make the point that communication and organizational structure can influence the culture that develops and is experienced by organization members.

Information Distortion From the Interpretive Perspective

One of the central concerns over information distortion from the interpretive perspective is the creation of shared meaning. Given the many possible meanings that exist for complex organizational processes, there are many opportunities for misunderstandings or misplaced assumptions regarding agreement over shared meanings when such agreement does not exist. For example, Contractor, Eisenberg, and Monge (1996) conducted an examination of semantic networks in a high-technology firm. They were interested in the extent to which employees shared interpretations of their organizations' mission. What they discovered points to the difficulties of building shared meanings and building consensus over those meanings. First, they found that employees with more tenure in the organization were more likely to have actual agreement over the organization's mission. However, these employees did not perceive that others shared their interpretation of the mission. Second, employees connected cohesively in the communication network were not more likely to agree with their coworkers' interpretations of the organizational mission. However, they perceived that agreement did exist. So, the creation of shared meanings may be possible, but one must also recognize that information distortion may interfere with building consensus over those shared meanings.

CRITICAL APPROACHES TO COMMUNICATION STRUCTURE

As we observed in Chapter 2, many critical theorists are concerned with the struggles over meaning that are present in organizations. These struggles over meaning may be related specifically to communication structure. For example, consider the term "hierarchy." Taking Bakhtin's (1981, 1984, 1986) perspective, within the term hierarchy is a struggle between centripetal (unity) and centrifugal (difference) forces. When are unity more important in a hierarchy than difference and separation? When are difference and separation more important than unity? Hierarchies cannot exist without unity, nor can they exist without separation and difference. Imagine a complex conflict between organizational departments in which the struggle is over issues of how they need to be both unified and separate. This conflict is not simple to resolve. Only through dialogue will it be possible to determine how these opposing forces can coexist without tearing the units apart.

Structure and Control

According to Dennis Mumby (1987), control involves "getting people to organize their behavior around a particular rule system" (p. 115). Different organizational structures support particular rule systems that control employee behavior. In hierarchies, there are rules that govern communication relationships, patterns, and topics for decision making. When people accept the controls associated with hierarchy, they limit choices they would otherwise make freely, but they do so to receive rewards or avoid punishment. Alternatively, heterarchies govern discussions that occur within groups because there is a demand for consensus. Within heterarchies, majority decision making is not acceptable. So group members embedded within such a structure must accept the controls that are part of the system. This control may be difficult to accept as groups confront complex conflicts. However, the rule system requires the control to be internalized by members for the heterarchy to achieve its objectives.

Structure and Oppression

Scholars working from the critical perspective obviously do not deny the existence of hierarchy, but they do claim that we have reified the idea of hierarchy, i.e., we have made it to appear to be a natural state of affairs only because hierarchy serves the interests of elite groups (Deetz, 1992). When an employee's position or job classification places him or her at the bottom of the organization, how are his or her interests served by preserving hierarchy? People located at the bottom of the hierarchy are most likely to be subject to strict control and discipline. Very rarely do such workers rise through the ranks to a position of power. However, these employees reify the idea of hierarchy because they believe that no other possibilities may exist in a complex organization. They act to preserve hierarchy, guaranteeing their continued oppression, because they do not believe there is any alternative. Hierarchies are not the only structures that can create oppressive environments for workers. Remember the example we cited in Chapter 2: Far End Design (FED). FED created self-managed work teams to encourage worker creativity. However, whenever the teams produced designs that the owner disliked he yelled, screamed, and berated them. As with workers within a hierarchy, the workers at FED reified their organization's idea of self-managed work teams (a specific type of organizational structure). Their actions then supported the continuation of a system that ultimately oppressed them.

Information Distortion From the Critical Perspective

When critical theorists focus on information distortion, they concentrate on how power relationships within organizations are sustained by the distortion. In hierarchies, managers may distort information to sustain hegemony so disempowered workers act to support a system that they believe is in their best interests when, in fact, the system benefits only the managers. For example, workers may be asked to follow tedious security procedures to protect organizational property, and they passively accept punishment when there is the slightest deviation from those procedures. Management, of course, says that these procedures exist to protect everyone and that no one is above the rules. However, managers rarely have to worry about these procedures because their jobs do not require them to secure organizational property. Furthermore, managers receive economic rewards from employees internalizing this rule system that vastly exceed what the average worker is paid. Even within group structures such as quality circles, information can be distorted to preserve power relationships. One organization member may distort information about a coworker to manipulate a decision in his or her favor. The greater the motivation to preserve intact power structures, the greater the incentive will be to distort information.

New Communication Structures, Cultural Diversity, and Empowerment

The U.S. and global workforces are only going to become more culturally diverse. Increases in cultural diversity (described in detail in Chapter 8) will be prompted by previously disenfranchised workers becoming employed in a variety of organizations and by workers crossing national borders responding to employment needs. Assumptions that traditional (e.g., hierarchical) communication and organizational structures will match the worldviews and the strengths of a culturally diverse workforce may prove false. In fact, as the workforce continues to grow more diverse, we may find that certain cultural groups actually see structure differently than the traditional multilevel hierarchy. More importantly, to tap the creative potential of a diverse workforce requires drawing out their unique worldviews, skills, and abilities. The lattice and heterarchy designs described earlier in the chapter may provide just the sort of communicative structure that taps the creative potential of a diverse workforce. In both lattice and heterarchy designs, workers are encouraged to group together according to skills, interests, and workgroup culture. The flattening of organizational hierarchy inherent in both designs provides more opportunities for decision-making input into work processes and for leadership. Two important outcomes may be linked to the use of these communicative structures. First, structurally flatter, more participative structures will more effectively tap the creative potential of a diverse workforce. Second, these new structures will expand opportunities for empowerment for all workers.

SUMMARY

The concept of communication structure can be defined in at least two different ways. The traditional way treats structure as a system of pathways or channels through which messages flow. This point of view is associated with a basic distinction between formal and informal systems of communication. Formal communication usually is associated with the use of officially designated channels. Because these channels generally are specified by a hierarchical system of authority, formal communication is described according to the directions of message flow in a hierarchy (i.e., downward, upward, horizontal, and diagonal).

Informal communication usually is associated with the grapevine. Grapevine communication involves a great deal of information (only a portion of which consists of rumors), usually occurs in cluster transmission patterns, is fast, and is more often accurate than inaccurate.

Although the concepts of formal and informal communication are very useful, there is no uniformly accepted distinction between the two systems. Communication structure can be understood in other ways. In particular, structure can be defined as the actual patterns of interaction that occur among members within a network of relationships. These patterns can be studied with a technique known as network analysis, which reveals the linkages between organization members, including group structures, bridge links, liaisons, isolates, and other network roles. Network analysis can indicate the correspondence between expected and actual networks, identify patterns of horizontal communication, provide clues about the extent to which members are integrated in the organization, reveal multiple or hidden network structures, and identify the degree to which members share meanings. The technique may also be useful for inferring tight and loose coupling characteristics in an organization.

There are also insights to be gained by considering interpretive and critical perspectives on organizational structure. From an interpretive perspective, it is important to recognize that structure is a social construction. So, although employees may treat a given structure as a material reality, that structure is actually constructed and maintained through language and social interaction. Also, interpretivists draw our attention to how different organizational and communication structures affect the cultures of organizations. Critical theorists focus on the struggles over what structure means in a given organization. For example, how does employee dialogue over the meaning of hierarchy deepen our understanding of this structure and the opposing tensions that exist within it? Critical theorists also draw our attention to how organizational and communication structure controls, oppresses, and sustains existing power relations within organizations.

DISCUSSION QUESTIONS/ACTIVITIES

1. Observe some episodes of communication in an organization and attempt to classify them according to production, maintenance, innovation, and human functions. How well does the classification system work?

2. Does it really make any difference whether we define communication structure as a system of channels for messages or as patterns of interaction? Why or why not?

3. Suppose that we have asked each member of a five-person "organization" to estimate the number of times that he or she interacts with each of the other members during a specified time frame. We have entered each person's report in the matrix below by finding the row with that person's name, then recording the estimates of interaction frequency under the columns associated with the other four. For simplicity, the reports of each pair in our example are identical or very similar. For example, Ching reports 18 contacts with Monte, and Marley reports 20 with Doaks.

		Doaks	Monte	Smith	Ching	Marley
1	Doaks		5	10	5	18
2	Monte	5		10	20	5
3	Smith	10	10		10	10
4	Ching	5	18	10		5
5	Marley	20	5	10	3	

Draw a diagram that places those who interact more frequently close together and those who interact less frequently further apart from each other. Connect the individuals with lines to represent linkages. Compare your diagram to those of others in the class.

4. What are the advantages and disadvantages of structuring an organization with a lattice design or as a heterarchy? What types of people would work well within such structures? What types of people would experience difficulties in these new organizational forms?

REFERENCES

Albaum, G. (1964). Horizontal information flow: An exploratory study. *Academy of Management Journal, 7,* 21–33.

Albrecht, T. L. (1984). Managerial communication and work perception. In R. N. Bostrom (Ed.), *Communication yearbook 8* (pp. 538–557). Beverly Hills, CA: Sage.

Albrecht, T. L., & Ropp, V. A. (1982). The study of network structuring in organizations through use of method triangulation. *Western Journal of Speech Communication, 46,* 162–178.

Bakhtin, M. M. (1981). *The dialogic imagination: Four essays by M. M. Bakhtin* (M. E. Holquist, Ed.; C. Emerson & M. E. Holquist, Trans.). Austin: University of Texas Press.

Bakhtin, M. M. (1984). *Problems of Dostoevsky's poetics* (C. Emerson, Ed. and Trans.). Minneapolis: University of Minnesota Press. (Original work published in 1929)

Bakhtin, M. M. (1986). *Speech genres and other late essays* (Vern McGee, Trans.). Austin: University of Texas Press.

Barnard, C. (1938). *The functions of the executive.* Cambridge, MA: Harvard University Press.

Boehm, C. (1994). Pacifying interventions at Arnhem Zoo and Gombe. In R. W. Wrangham, W. C. McGrew, F. B. M. de Waal, & P. G. Heltne (Eds.), *Chimpanzee cultures* (pp. 211–226). Cambridge, MA: Harvard University Press.

Buch, K. (1992). Quality circles and employee withdrawal behaviors: A cross-organizational study. *Journal of Applied Behavioral Science, 28,* 62–73.

Chase, A. B. (1970). How to make downward communication work. *Personnel Journal, 49,* 478–483.

Contractor, N. S., Eisenberg, E. M., & Monge, P. R. (1996). *Antecedents and outcomes of interpretive diversity.* Unpublished manuscript.

Corman, S. R., & Scott, C. R. (1994). Perceived networks, activity foci, and observable communication in social collectives. *Communication Theory, 4,* 171–190.

Cotton, J. L. (1993). *Employee involvement: Methods for improving performance and work attitudes.* Newbury Park, CA: Sage.

Culbert, S. A., & Eden, J. M. (1970). An anatomy of activism for executives. *Harvard Business Review, 48,* 140.

Cyert, R. M., & March, J. G. (1963). *A behavioral theory of the firm.* Englewood Cliffs, NJ: Prentice Hall.

Davis, K. (1953). Management communication and the grapevine. *Harvard Business Review, 31,* 43–49.

Davis, K. (1968). Success of chain-of-command oral communication in a manufacturing management group. *Academy of Management Journal, 11,* 379–387.

Davis, K. (1972). *Human behavior at work.* New York: McGraw-Hill.

Deetz, S. (1992). *Democracy in the age of corporate colonization: Developments in communication and the politics of everyday life.* Albany: State University of New York Press.

Drago, R. (1988). Quality circle survival: An exploratory analysis. *Industrial Relations, 27,* 336–351.

Farace, R. V., Monge, P. R., & Russell, H. M. (1977). *Communicating and organizing.* Reading, MA: Addison-Wesley.

Fayol, H. (1949). *General and industrial management* (Constance Storrs, Trans.). London: Sir Isaac Pitman.

French, W. L., Bell, C. H., Jr., & Zawacki, R. A. (1983). *Organization development: Theory, practice, and research* (2nd ed.). Plano, TX: Business Publications.

Future Positive. (2002). Retrieved September 23, 2005, from http://futurepositive.synearth.net/2002/02/04?print-friendly=true

Glassman, R. B. (1973). Persistence and loose coupling in living systems. *Behavioral Science, 18,* 83–98.

Goldhaber, G. M. (1993). *Organizational communication* (6th ed.). Dubuque, IA: Brown & Benchmark.

Goldhaber, G. M., Yates, M. P., Porter, D. T., & Lesniak, R. (1978). Organizational communication: 1978. *Human Communication Research, 5,* 76–96.

Hellweg, S. (1987). Organizational grapevines: A state of the art review. In B. Dervin & M. Voight (Eds.), *Progress in the communication sciences, vol. 8* (pp. 213–230). Norwood, NJ: Ablex.

Jacoby, J. (1968). Examining the other organization. *Personnel Administration, 31,* 36–42.

Katz, D., & Kahn, R. L. (1978). *The social psychology of organizations* (2nd ed.). New York: John Wiley & Sons.

Koehler, J. W., Anatol, K. W. E., & Applbaum, R. L. (1981). *Organizational communication: Behavioral perspectives* (2nd ed.). New York: Holt, Rinehart & Winston.

Koehler, J. W., & Huber, G. (1974). *Effects of upward communication on managerial decision making.* Paper presented at the annual meeting of the International Communication Association, New Orleans, May 1974.

Koontz, H., & O'Donnel, C. (1955). *Principles of management.* New York: McGraw-Hill.

Krivonos, P. (1976). *Distortion of subordinate to superior communication.* Paper presented at the annual meeting of the International Communication Association, Portland, Oregon, May 1976.

Lawler, E. E. (1986). *High-involvement management.* San Francisco: Jossey-Bass.

Lawler, E. E., & Mohrman, S. A. (1987). Quality circles: After the honeymoon. *Organizational Dynamics, 15*(4), 42–54.

Ledford, G. E., Lawler, E. E., & Mohrman, S. A. (1988). The quality circle and its variations. In J. P. Campbell, R. J. Campbell, & Associates (Eds.), *Productivity in organizations: New perspectives from industrial and organizational psychology* (pp. 255–294). San Francisco: Jossey-Bass.

Maier, N., Hoffman, L., & Read, W. (1963). Superior-subordinate communication: The relative effectiveness of managers who held their subordinates' positions. *Personnel Psychology, 26,* 1–11.

March, J. G., & Simon, H. A. (1958). *Organizations.* New York: Wiley.

Marshall, A. A., & Stohl, C. (1993). Participating as participation: A network approach. *Communication Monographs, 60,* 137–157.

McPhee, R. D., & Corman, S. R. (1995). An activity-based theory of communication networks in organizations, applied to the case of a local church. *Communication Monographs, 62,* 132–151.

Mellinger, G. D. (1956). Interpersonal trust as a factor in communication. *Journal of Abnormal and Social Psychology, 52,* 304–309.

Miles, R. (1965). Keeping informed: Human relations or human resources? *Harvard Business Review, 43,* 148–163.

Monge, P. R., & Contractor, N. S. (2001). Emergence of communication networks. In F. M. Jablin & L. L. Putnam (Eds.), *The new handbook of organizational communication* (pp. 440–502). Thousand Oaks, CA: Sage.

Monge, P. R., & Eisenberg, E. M. (1987). Emergent communication networks. In F. M. Jablin, L. L. Putnam, K. H. Roberts, & L. W. Porter (Eds.), *Handbook of organizational communication: An interdisciplinary perspective* (pp. 304–342). Newbury Park, CA: Sage.

Mumby, D. (1987). The political function of narrative in organizations. *Communication Monographs, 54,* 113–127.

Natural Leadership. (2004). *Hewitt Quarterly Asia Pacific, 3*(2), 1–5.

Nomura, R. (1981). *West learns Japanese ways: Executives wear work clothes.* Neihon Keizai Shimbun. Tokyo: Translation Service Center, The Asia Foundation.

Pace, R. W., & Boren, R. (1973). *The human transaction.* Glenview, IL: Scott, Foresman.

Penley, L. E. (1982). An investigation of the information processing framework of organizational communication. *Human Communication Research, 8,* 348–365.

Perrow, C. (1984). *Normal accidents: Living with high-risk technologies.* New York: Basic Books.

Planty, E., & Machaver, W. (1952). Upward communication: A project in executive development. *Personnel, 28,* 304–318.

Read, W. H. (1962). Upward communication in industrial hierarchies. *Human Relations, 15,* 3–15.

Roberts, K. H., & O'Reilly, C. A., III. (1974). Failure in upward communication: Three possible culprits. *Academy of Management Journal, 17,* 205–215.

Seibold, D. R., & Shea, B. C. (2001). Participation and decision making. In F. M. Jablin & L. L. Putnam (Eds.), *The new handbook of organizational communication* (pp. 664–703). Thousand Oaks, CA: Sage.

Smith, R. L., Richetto, G. M., & Zima, J. P. (1972). Organizational behavior: An approach to human communication. In R. Budd & B. Ruben (Eds.), *Approaches to human communication* (pp. 269–289). Rochelle Park, NJ: Hayden Books.

Spiker, B. K., & Daniels, T. D. (1981). Information adequacy and communication relationships: An empirical examination of 18 organizations. *Western Journal of Speech Communication, 45,* 342–354.

Stark, D. (2002). *Collaborative organization and interactive technologies.* Retrieved September 23, 2005 from www.webuse.umd.edu/abstracts2002/stark-collaborative_organization.pdf

Stech, E. L. (1983). An empirically derived model of formal and informal communication in work units. Paper presented at the annual meeting of the International Communication Association, Dallas, May 1983.

Steel, R. P., & Lloyd, R. F. (1988). Cognitive, affective, and behavioral outcomes of participation in quality circles: Conceptual and empirical findings. *Journal of Applied Behavioral Science, 24,* 1–17.

Stevenson, W. B., Pearce, J. L., & Porter, L. W. (1985). The concept of "coalition" in organization theory and research. *Academy of Management Review, 10,* 256–268.

Stohl, C. (1987). Bridging the parallel organization: A study of quality circle effectiveness. In M. L. McLaughlin (Ed.), *Communication yearbook 10* (pp. 416–430). Newbury Park, CA: Sage.

Stohl, C. (1995). *Organizational communication: Connectedness in action.* Thousand Oaks, CA: Sage.

Studd, M. V., & Gattiker, U. E. (1991). The evolutionary psychology of sexual harassment in organizations. *Ethology and Sociobiology, 12,* 249–290.

Tichy, N. M. (1981). Networks in organizations. In P. C. Nystrom & W. H. Starbuck (Eds.), *Handbook of organizational design* (Vol. 2, pp. 225–248). London: Oxford University Press.

Tompkins, P. H. (1967). Organizational communication: A state of the art review. In G. Richetto (Ed.), *Conference on organizational communication* (pp. 4–26). Huntsville, AL: NASA, George C. Marshall Space Flight Center.

Trujillo, N. (1985). Organizational communication as cultural performance: Some managerial considerations. *Southern Journal of Speech Communication, 50,* 201–224.

Van Fleet, D. D., & Griffin, R. W. (1989). Quality circles: A review and suggested further directions. In C. L. Cooper & I. Robertson (Eds.), *International review of industrial and organizational psychology* (pp. 213–233). New York: John Wiley.

Van Maanen, J. W., & Barley, S. R. (1984). Occupational communities: Culture and control in organizations. In B. M. Staw & L. L. Cummings (Eds.), *Research in organizational behavior* (Vol. 6, pp. 287–365). Greenwich, CT: JAI Press.

Walton, E. (1961). How efficient is the grapevine? *Personnel, 28,* 45–49.

Weick, K. E. (1976). Educational organizations as loosely coupled systems. *Administrative Science Quarterly, 21,* 1–16.

Organization Theory

Prescriptions for Control

Chapter Outline

SCIENTIFIC AND CLASSICAL MANAGEMENT
> Taylor's Scientific Management
> Fayol's General Management
> Weber's Bureaucratic Theory

TRANSITIONAL THEORIES
> Follett's Administrative Theory
> Barnard's Executive Functions

THE HUMAN RELATIONS MOVEMENT
> The Hawthorne Studies and Elton Mayo
>> *The Illumination Studies*
>> *Relay Assembly-Room Studies*
>> *The Interview Program*
>> *Bank-Wiring Studies*
>> *Implications of the Studies*

HUMAN RESOURCE DEVELOPMENT
> Maslow's Need Hierarchy
> McGregor's Theory X and Theory Y
> Likert's Four Systems
> The Transition to Theory Z

Organizational behavior is as old as the human social experience. We know from history and anthropology that early African, Asian, Middle Eastern, and Native American civilizations had elaborate organizational systems for governmental, military, religious, and economic purposes. The ancient peoples who created these organizations had "theories" of organizational behavior—concepts, principles, and prescriptions for organizational structure and function. These theories generally were fitted to the needs of agrarian societies only a few generations removed from their tribal origins and adapted over time as these civilizations developed.

During the Middle Ages of Western civilization, the dominance of institutionalized religion and ordering of society into localized feudal economies produced principles of divine right and social class systems of authority and labor as guidelines for organizing. Feudal serfs (average citizens), as well as their lords, had tradition to tell them what to do in an era when the patterns of life and society were virtually unchanged for centuries (Dessler, 1980), at least until the arrival of *Yersinia pestis*, better known as the plague. During the 1300s, the plague took tens of millions of lives throughout Europe. The disease also cracked the foundations of feudal life, leaving them to be swept over by the Renaissance and, later, the Industrial Revolution.

Today, organizations in the developed and developing nations of our world function within a complex and often rapidly changing economic, legal, political, social, and technological environment. Words such as "globalization" may capture the essence of it for many of us, but humankind itself has developed this environment from four centuries of increasing commercialization and industrialization, international trade, secularization of social and governmental institutions, and compression of time and distance through technological advances in transportation and communications. In this chapter and the next two, we review theories of organization and organizational effectiveness that developed during the 20th century and are continuing to develop in today's world. This chapter addresses major developments, including scientific and classical management theory, human relations theory, human resource development theory, and some transitional theories that were ahead of their time in the sense that they provided a foundation earlier in the century for some very contemporary ideas.

When the industrialized world entered the 20th century, it was apparent that new and clearer concepts of organizational behavior would be required to deal with the complexities of modern society (Dessler, 1980). The first modern perspectives on organizational behavior were developed in the early 1900s when several prominent theorists advanced the basic principles of scientific and classical management. Scientific and classical theories envisioned organizations as machinelike objects driven by management plan and control. Individual organization members often were regarded as simple parts in the machine.

Scientific and classical theories were followed quickly by eclectic theories of organization and by the emergence of the human relations movement. The eclectic theories, which cut across several different schools of thought about organizations, were much broader than scientific and classical theories. The human relations movement actually challenged scientific and classical notions by arguing that organizational effectiveness depends more on the social processes of organization than on management design. These principles never really replaced classical and scientific views. Instead, many assumptions about organizational behavior drawn from human relations theory simply were grafted onto classical and scientific management ideas about organizational structure.

Later, new concepts in human motivation, along with influences from earlier eclectic theories and the emergence of system theory, led to human resource development theory.

Human resource development theory, based on motivational principles of the human need for self-fulfillment, began to compete with earlier human relations and classical and scientific perspectives of organizational behavior.

These theories are concerned not only with the characteristics of organizations, but also with the problems of organizational effectiveness and managerial control. They are *prescriptive* theories that indicate how organizational processes (including communication) should function and what managers are to do in order to achieve organizational effectiveness. Consequently, we have characterized the theories in this chapter as prescriptions for control. Whether or not prescriptions for organizational structure, managerial strategy, and communication always work, the pursuit of reliable methods for attaining organizational effectiveness has been a traditional concern in organizational theory. This concern carries over into the field of organizational communication.

SCIENTIFIC AND CLASSICAL MANAGEMENT

Scientific and classical theories of management represented the earliest attempts to cope with the complexities of 20th-century organizations. Three of the most influential theorists during the early 1900s were Frederick Taylor, an American engineer; Henri Fayol, a French industrialist; and Max Weber, a German university professor. Taylor published his system of "scientific management" as early as 1911. Fayol and Weber wrote classical treatises on the principles of organization and management at about the same time, although their works were not available in English translations for an American market until the 1940s. The earliest compilation of Taylor's work also was not published until 1947. These three theorists differed from one another in many of the principles that they advocated, but they shared a common idea that effective organizational performance is determined by efficient design of work and organizational structure.

Taylor's Scientific Management

Frederick Taylor was concerned primarily with the scientific study and design of work processes. Most of his principles addressed problems of work efficiency, but he also offered recommendations regarding organizational structure and processes. Essentially, Taylor (1947) advanced four ideas:

1. There is "one best way" to perform any job. The best way can be determined through scientific analysis. For example, a time and motion study can reveal the fewest number of steps and shortest amount of time required to perform a task efficiently. Experiments can determine the physical working conditions under which productivity will be highest.

2. Personnel should be selected scientifically. One should choose and assign people to tasks according to their skills or potential for developing skills.

3. Workers should be compensated on an incentive plan that pays them in direct proportion to the work that they produce. An hourly wage is inappropriate, not so much because of differences in individual productivity but because economic need is the principal factor

that motivates people to work. Workers will produce more if they realize that they will be paid accordingly.

4. Labor should be divided so that managers plan the work and workers follow the plan. In Taylor's scheme, each aspect of any task is supervised by a different "functional foreman." A given worker takes orders from any one or all of these foremen, depending on the characteristics of the task.

Taylor believed that the central problem in organizational effectiveness involved management's inability to obtain compliance from workers. He argued that if organizations followed his principles, then managers and workers would realize that they can cooperate to increase the organization's wealth and resources "until the surplus becomes so large that it is unnecessary to quarrel over how it shall be divided" (Taylor, 1947, p. 64). In other words, everybody would benefit under scientific management.

Taylor applied his principles at Bethlehem Steel Company in order to improve the work efficiency of coal and iron ore shovelers. According to Taylor's own analysis, in the third year of working under his plan at Bethlehem, the volume of material moved each day jumped by more than 350%, the cost of moving the material was cut in half, and the average pay for shovelers increased from $1.15 to $1.88. This was, by the way, $1.88 *per day*, not per hour! The results were fantastic from the standpoint of efficiency, but this particular silver lining surrounded an ominous cloud. The workforce of more than 400 shovelers was reduced to 140. Taylor himself pointed with pride to this outcome, claiming that the most important result of his plan "was the effect on the workmen themselves . . . out of the 140 workmen only two were said to be drinking men" (Taylor, 1947, p. 71). Although Taylor claimed that he did not want workers to be "brutally" discharged, he did not say what became of the hundreds of shovelers who were laid off at Bethlehem Steel.

Fayol's General Management

Whereas Taylor focused on the technical details of production work, Henri Fayol was concerned primarily with the basic principles of organizational structure and management practice. Fayol (1917/1949) offered 14 fundamental principles. Most are prescriptions for organizational structure and design.

1. *Division of work.* Each member has one and only one job to do.

2. *Authority and responsibility.* Authority includes the right to give orders and the power to exact compliance. Official authority depends on one's position. Personal authority depends on ability and experience.

3. *Discipline.* Good discipline depends on good superiors, clear and fair policies, and judiciously applied sanctions.

4. *Unity of command.* An employee receives orders from one and only one superior for any action.

5. *Unity of direction.* A group of activities with the same objective should have "one head with one plan."

6. *Subordination of individual interests.* The interests of the organization must prevail over those of any given group or person.

7. *Remuneration.* Employees should be paid fairly, in a manner that satisfies them and the firm.

8. *Centralization.* Whether decision making is centralized (restricted to higher level management) or decentralized (allocated to subordinates) depends on the organization's circumstances.

9. *Scalar chain.* The system of authority is structured as a hierarchy with clear lines of command from one level to the next, but the system must allow for departure from the chain of command when necessary.

10. *Order.* There is a place for each employee, and each employee is to be in his or her place.

11. *Equity.* Personnel should be treated with kindness and justice, but this does not exclude forcefulness and sternness.

12. *Stability in tenure.* Assuming that an employee has the ability to do a job, he or she must still have time to learn and to succeed in performing it.

13. *Initiative.* The ability to think out and execute a plan is a valuable organizational resource.

14. *Esprit de corps.* Management should strive to promote a sense of unity, harmony, and cohesion.

Fayol's ideas were based on his experience during a 58-year career with a large mining company. He spent 12 of those years as a mining engineer, 16 years as a middle-level manager, and 30 years as the company's managing director. The company was nearly bankrupt when Fayol assumed the directorship in 1888, but it gradually became a profitable model of effective management and organizational practices. The company's success helped Fayol to popularize his management theory after his retirement in 1918.

Weber's Bureaucratic Theory

Max Weber borrowed the French term *bureaucracy* as a label for his concept of the ideal modern organization. Weber believed that complex organizations in an industrial age required speed, precision, certainty, and continuity. These conditions could be realized most effectively if organizational designs were as machinelike as possible. According to Weber (1920/1947), the bureaucratic machine should have six basic features:

1. A clear hierarchical system of authority.

2. Division of labor according to specialization.

3. A complete system of rules regarding the rights, responsibilities, and duties of personnel.

4. Exhaustive procedures for work performance.

5. Impersonality in human organizational relationships.

6. Selection and promotion of personnel solely on the basis of technical competence.

Weber intended for bureaucracy to eliminate ambiguity and capriciousness in organizational life. Formalized rules, clear descriptions of authority and responsibility at all organizational levels, and predictability in human relationships should lead to several desirable outcomes. In particular, decision making should be faster, efficiency in task performance should improve, and treatment of personnel should be more equitable (fair and impartial). According to Weber, all actions in a bureaucracy are derived mechanically from rules in a rational system based on military discipline. The individual organization member "is only a single cog in an ever-moving mechanism which prescribes to him an essentially fixed route of march" (1969, p. 34).

The theories that Taylor, Fayol, and Weber developed certainly were not identical. Taylor's concept of functional foremanship in which any worker might receive orders at various points from several different superiors ran counter to the idea of unity of command that Fayol and Weber both advocated. Moreover, Fayol's attitudes toward flexibility in organizational structure, centralizing or decentralizing decision making to fit the organization's circumstances, and encouragement of esprit de corps were quite inconsistent with Weber's prescriptions for fixed, constant rules and impersonal relationships. Yet, several clear themes are common to scientific and classical management theory.

First, the organization is driven by management authority. Employees are simply the instruments for carrying out the management plan. This implies that organizational communication is merely a tool for managerial **control** and **coordination** of organizational processes. Communication involving planning and decision making is **centralized** (concentrated) near the top of the organizational hierarchy (although Fayol allowed for some flexibility on this point). Organizational policies and task-oriented messages regarding the execution of orders flow from the top down. Upward communication from subordinates to superiors serves only a reporting function to verify compliance with orders or to indicate any work-related problems.

Second, scientific and classical theorists believed that people behave according to rational, economic models. The primary motivation for work is money. If people are compensated in a fair manner, they will be more productive and more compliant with authority. Social and political motivations in organizational behavior were regarded as irrelevant or detrimental to organizational effectiveness. A rationally specified system of organization structure and functions would reduce the ill effects of group conflicts, personal rivalries, vindictiveness, power struggles, and petty egoism.

Finally, each theorist advanced a machinelike prescription for organizational design. The analogy between the human organization and the well-maintained machine performing at peak efficiency is most obvious in Weber's work, but Taylor's concept of scientific management envisioned exactly the same ideal for work processes. Even Fayol, who argued that his principles of organizational structure and management should be applied flexibly, still insisted that order, discipline, hierarchical authority, and fixed division of labor were the

TABLE 4.1	Principles in Scientific and Classical Management

Summary of Principles in Scientific and Classical Management	
Scientific Management	Classical Management
Theme: Effectiveness Is a Function of Work Design	Theme: Effectiveness Is a Function of Organizational Design

Taylor	*Fayol*	*Weber*
Effectiveness through work design	Effectiveness through flexible hierarchy	Effectiveness through bureaucracy
1. Find the "one best way" to perform each job. 2. Scientifically select and train workers. 3. Reward workers in direct proportion to productivity. 4. Managers plan, workers produce, multiple expert supervisors (functional foremen) direct various aspects of a worker's job.	1. Order is based on division of labor, unity of command and direction, but centralization will "vary according to different cases." 2. Managerial authority is derived from both official and personal bases. 3. Achieve equity through kindness and justice, but this does not exclude "forcefulness and sternness." 4. Create esprit de corps.	1. Order is based on division of labor, a clear authority structure, and a complete system of technical rules for conduct and procedure. 2. Authority is derived from a rational-legal system where each person is "only a single cog in an ever-moving mechanism." 3. Justice is derived mechanically from a code. 4. Relationships are impersonal.

basic elements in a tried and true formula for organizational effectiveness. Table 4.1 presents a summary for easier comparison of the central principles in each theory.

Scientific and classical management theories have been very influential in the design of modern organizations. Time and motion studies of the type that Taylor's followers introduced are used as basic tools to determine the most efficient procedures for task performance in large organizations. Organization charts, detailed job descriptions, and elaborate policy manuals spelling out lines of authority, work procedures, and individual rights and responsibilities are quite common in American organizations. Such documents often define channels of message flow and appropriate communicative behavior for organization members as well. For example, the U.S. Postal Service makes it clear that all official communication in the organization must conform to Fayol's principles of unity of command, unity of direction, and scalar authority:

Any communication on matters requiring discretion or policy determination shall proceed through each successive level of authority upward and downward without

> bypassing any. . . . An administrative reporting relationship establishes a
> clear line of authority between positions or units in the organizational
> hierarchy. . . . Subordinate positions never report administratively to more than
> one higher-level supervisor. (1979, sec. 153)

In other organizations, the influence of classical organizational theory is more subtle. The principles are intuitively understood rules for defining relationships among organization members—rules that generally are taken for granted. Consider the case of a large grocery store that we will call Supervalue Market. The owner, who is also the general manager, insists that Supervalue does not have organization charts and policy manuals: "We're all just one big happy family here." But the people who work at Supervalue understand that their organization has a specific structure. The store is arranged in departments. Each department has a supervisor. Every employee has a job title (checker, sacker, stocker, etc.) and a specific assignment in a designated department.

The employees at Supervalue communicate with their department supervisors on all work-related matters. In turn, the supervisors report to designated assistant managers, and the assistant managers report to the general manager. Although managers occasionally carry on casual conversations and light banter with most of the employees, they rarely speak officially with anyone except department supervisors. Supervisors relay any official information from managers to the employees. In general, different supervisors (and employees) stay out of one another's departments unless they are assigned to help out or cover for someone else. Unlike the U.S. Postal Service, Supervalue has no written policies that specify these rules. But when you go to work at Supervalue, you find out quickly from observing and listening to others that "This is the way we do it here." Even though nobody has ever published an organization chart for Supervalue, all of the members understand and use the rules to enact this organizational structure.

If we translate the implicit operating rules of Supervalue Market into an explicit organization chart, it might look something like the diagram in Figure 4.1.

Figure 4.1 illustrates a functional division of labor with different departments and job classifications for different types of work. The organization chart also specifies a scalar chain of command with lines of authority and reporting relationships from the general manager to the assistant managers, from these assistants to department supervisors, and from supervisors to employees. This type of hierarchical structure provides the basic framework for many different types of organizations, both private and public, profit and nonprofit.

Despite the influence of scientific and classical principles in contemporary organizations, these theories have been criticized extensively. Most of the critics point out that classical and scientific assumptions about human motivation are naïve. Human organizational behavior depends on many complex factors besides the desire for economic reward or blind obedience to authority. The theories also are criticized for producing rigid, unadaptive organizational structures. Hierarchies with centralized decision making, many levels of authority, and highly specialized divisions of labor can function reasonably well in a stable environment, but they lack the flexibility to adapt to change. The very fact that "bureaucracy" conjures up images of red tape, inefficiency, and indifference (features quite the opposite of those that Weber extolled) suggests that classical and scientific theorists failed to understand the social and psychological dynamics of organizational behavior and human communication.

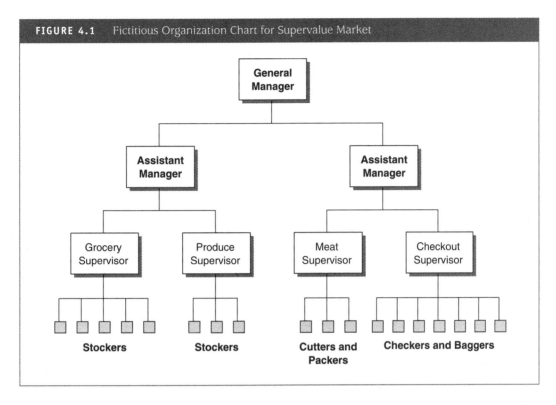

FIGURE 4.1   Fictitious Organization Chart for Supervalue Market

During the 1920s and 1930s, two developments in theories of organization and human relationships began to point to shortcomings in scientific and classical theory. One of these developments involved the appearance of two transitional theories of organization. The second development was the emergence of the human relations movement.

TRANSITIONAL THEORIES

Although scientific and classical theories focused rather narrowly on questions of organizational structure and work design, at least two **transitional theories** addressed broader concerns, including the use of power, the psychology of compliance, variability in the behavior of individual organization members, and the importance of communication in organizational processes. Mary Parker Follett introduced the first in the 1920s. Chester Barnard developed the second in the 1930s. We identify these theories as transitional because they include ideas that returned decades later in areas such as human resource development theory and system theory (to be discussed in Chapter 5).

Follett's Administrative Theory

If Mary Parker Follett's theory of administration is not easily classified, neither is Follett herself. After completing an undergraduate degree at Radcliffe and graduate work in Paris, Follett pursued an array of interests ranging from the establishment of a job placement bureau for young people that covered the entire city of Boston to lecturing at the Bureau of Personnel Administration in New York (Fox & Urwick, 1982). But we believe it was her extensive work as a community organizer and activist that most obviously influenced the development of her theory. In effect, she mastered the principles of cooperative effort in community action, then advocated the application of these principles to business organizations.

Fox and Urwick contend that Follett's theory hinges on two basic concepts. The first is the principle of reciprocal response, i.e., that human interaction always involves mutual and simultaneous influence, "and the total result is one that neither participant could have produced even half of alone" (1982, p. xxiv). The second principle is Follett's universal goal of integration, i.e., "a harmonious marriage of differences . . . that produces a new form, a new entity, a new result made out of the old differences and yet different from any of them" (p. xxv). Thus, Follett was concerned primarily with ways of building and sustaining democracy through integration of different, competing interests. In order to achieve integration of interests as Follett understood it, traditional ideas about power and authority had to be redefined. Integration of interests depends on shared power. As Follett (1982a) explained the issue,

> Whereas power usually means power-over, the power of some person or group over some other person or group, it is possible to develop the conception of power-with, a jointly developed power, a co-active, not a coercive power. . . . That should be one of the tests of any plan of employee representation—is it developing joint power? (p. 72)

Follett did not believe that power was abused only by capitalists. She also chastised organized labor and political activists, saying that management had a right "to resist any effort of the unions to get power-over" (p. 72) and that "reformers, propagandists, many of our 'best' people are willing to coerce others in order to attain an end which *they* think is good" (p. 73). Nor did Follett advocate empowerment of workers just to make employees feel better about themselves. She had learned the value of joint power in integrating different interests to produce successful community actions such as her Boston placement bureau, and she understood that successful business required the knowledge and experiences of both management and labor; that pluralistic responsibility based on function, not hierarchy or rank, is essential to organizational effectiveness.

Although "power-with" is a necessary condition for integration of interests in Follett's theory, the vehicle for integration is employee representation. She acknowledged that employee representation was in fact used in that era as a way to get employees to consent, comply, and cooperate with management plans and decisions, but Follett herself envisioned employee representation as participation in order to achieve pluralistic responsibility. Follett gave her theory an explicit communication basis not only through her concept of reciprocal response, but also by arguing that participation "requires *conference* [emphasis added] as its method" (1982b, p. 139) in joint committees of workers and managers who meet "to get from each other the special knowledge and experience each has" (p. 139). Follett died in 1933, but her idea of participation was destined to become a bedrock concept for management scholars who published human resource development theories in the 1960s.

Barnard's Executive Functions

Mary Parker Follett probably would not have accepted some features of Chester Barnard's theory, but Barnard, who said that Follett "had great insight into the dynamic elements of organization" (1938, p. 122 footnote), was one of the first important American business leaders to be influenced by her work. Barnard, who was president of New Jersey Bell Telephone and at one time chaired the National Science Foundation, apparently felt that classical theories of organization failed to provide adequate explanations of organizational behavior as he had experienced it. In his 1938 book, *The Functions of the Executive*, Barnard attempted to correct these shortcomings in three areas: *individual behavior*, *compliance*, and *communication*.

In Barnard's view, classical theorists had underestimated both the variability of individual behavior in organizations and the impact of this behavior on organizational effectiveness. Organization members are not simply so many cogs in a machine who behave predictably out of rational, economic interests. Members are individuals who differ from one another in many respects. Barnard believed that the individual is the "basic strategic factor" in all organizations and that organizational effectiveness depends on the individual's willingness to cooperate. This assumption led directly to Barnard's ideas about compliance.

Barnard regarded compliance as willingness to cooperate. Compliance in this sense requires individuals to surrender their personal preferences. An order has authority to the extent that a person is willing to surrender personal preference to carry out the order. Orders must fall within a person's *zone of indifference*, meaning that orders must be perceived in neutral terms so that they are carried out without conscious questioning of their authority. Incentives, inducements, and rewards can be used to expand a person's zone of indifference, but material incentives alone are limited in their power to effect compliance. Inducements such as status, prestige, and personal power also are necessary.

Finally, whereas Follett explicitly had linked management-employee communication with participation and representation, Barnard made communication an indispensable concept in the analysis of organizational structure. He pointed out that decision-making processes hinge on communication and described the characteristics and importance of communication in the informal organization (i.e., the interaction in a social, political, and unofficial world that is not specified on the formal organization chart). Barnard's strong belief in the centrality of communication for organizational processes is indicated in his argument that "the first function of an executive" is to establish and maintain a system of communication. According to Dessler (1980), Barnard "presented a new theory of organization structure, one that focused on the organization as a communication system" (p. 38).

THE HUMAN RELATIONS MOVEMENT

The human relations movement emerged from various currents of thought during the 1930s. The most important of these was the Harvard-affiliated human relations school of management that emerged in the wake of a complex series of industrial investigations known as the Hawthorne Studies.

The Hawthorne Studies and Elton Mayo

The first seeds of the human relations movement were sown in 1924 with a series of studies at Western Electric Company's Hawthorne Plant in Illinois. The Hawthorne Studies were conducted over a period of several years in four phases: the illumination studies, the relay assembly-room studies, the interview program, and the bank-wiring studies (Roethlisberger & Dickson, 1939). The results challenged scientific management principles by suggesting that interpersonal communication, group dynamics, and organization members' attitudes and values are more important than work structure and organizational design in determining organizational effectiveness. These studies provided the foundation for the Harvard-affiliated human relations school of management.

The Illumination Studies

The Hawthorne Studies began because an industrial engineering research group wanted to determine the relationship between lighting (illumination) conditions in a work area and worker productivity. In line with scientific management theory, the researchers believed that productivity would be greatest under some optimum or ideal level of lighting (i.e., neither too little nor too much light). They set out to find this optimum condition by experimenting with the lighting levels, but the results of the study defied explanation. Productivity increased regardless of what the researchers did to the lighting. When the light was increased, productivity went up. When the light was held constant, productivity still went up. Even when the level of light was decreased, productivity continued to increase until workers literally could no longer see what they were doing.

Relay Assembly-Room Studies

The results of the illumination studies were disturbing to engineers schooled in the principles of scientific management. In order to understand why these principles apparently failed in the illumination studies, researchers decided to isolate a small group of telephone relay assembly workers in order to study systematically the relationships between various working conditions and productivity. The studies included changes in compensation, rest periods, work schedules, and work methods. In general, productivity increased during the studies regardless of changes in the work conditions. The researchers finally concluded that the *relationship* between the researchers and the workers accounted for the results. The test-room observer had shown a personal interest in the workers, consulted with and kept them informed about changes that were being made during the experiments, and listened sympathetically to their concerns and opinions. This relationship was quite different from the task-oriented, rule-bound, impersonal manner of supervision that characterized the rest of the plant (Roethlisberger & Dickson, 1939).

The Interview Program

The results of the relay assembly-room studies led researchers to conduct interviews with thousands of employees in order to discover their attitudes toward working conditions, supervisors, and work in general. The interviews soon indicated *that people who worked under similar conditions experienced these conditions in different ways and assigned different meanings to their experiences.* For example, a given style of supervision could be satisfying to some people and dissatisfying to others.

When researchers tried to account for different reactions to similar conditions, they found that personal background and expectations contributed to satisfaction. In particular, "the meaning a person assigns to his position depends on whether or not that position is allowing him to fulfill the social demands he is making of his work" (Roethlisberger & Dickson, 1939). They concluded that *employees' attitudes* depend on the social organization of the groups in which they work and their positions in these groups.

Bank-Wiring Studies

The interview program was followed by another intensive study with a small group of employees who wired circuit banks. The purpose was to observe the effects of the work-group's social processes on productivity. The results of the study indicated that workgroup norms exert substantial influence over performance standards.

Employees in the bank-wiring study shared a clear idea of the "right" amount of output for a day's work. Production from day to day should be constant—neither too much nor too little. Even though they were paid on an incentive plan, group members pressured faster workers to slow down. Production reports were falsified to reflect either more or less output in order to maintain the appearance of a constant rate of production. The group developed an informal system that controlled and regulated the members' behavior and, at the same time, protected them from outside interference (for example, from higher level managers). The findings puzzled industrial engineers, but the workers who lost their jobs in the wake of Taylor's studies at Bethlehem Steel easily would have understood the norms in the bank-wiring group against producing "too much."

Implications of the Studies

The Hawthorne Studies occupy such a prominent place in the history of organizational research that questions about the appropriateness of the methods used in these studies and the validity of the conclusions drawn from the results have been debated for many years. For example, Carey (1967) argued that several serious flaws in the research methods prevent any reliable interpretation of results from these studies. More recently, Franke and Kaul (1978) developed a statistically based reinterpretation of the results that led them to conclusions that differed dramatically from those drawn by Roethlisberger and Dickson. According to Franke and Kaul, "It is not release from oppressive supervision but its reassertion that explains higher rates of productivity [in the Hawthorne Studies]" (p. 636).

Whatever the weaknesses that may have afflicted the Hawthorne Studies, these studies were significant because they led to the emergence of the human relations school of management under the leadership of Elton Mayo and his colleagues at the Harvard Business School. Mayo, who intensely disliked conflict and competition, tried to promote a concept of worker-management harmony (Landsberger, 1958). He was involved in the Hawthorne Studies almost from their beginning and interpreted the results as support for a "people-oriented" approach to management.

According to Mayo (1947), managers should be friendly in their relationships with workers, listen to worker concerns, and give workers a sense of participation in decisions in order to meet their *social* needs. In many respects, Mayo's advice was much like Dale Carnegie's (1936) prescription for "winning friends and influencing people." In fact, both Mayo and Carnegie have been criticized for promoting highly manipulative managerial communication strategies intended only to gain compliance from workers and to promote acceptance of managerial authority (Redding, 1979). Human relations principles *did not change* the classical features of organizations. Instead, human relations ideas simply provided a tool for management relationships with employees under traditional systems of authority and hierarchy.

Although classical and scientific management theories offer prescriptions for organizational structure and communication, they are theories of worker motivation and compliance, not theories of organizational communication. Miles (1965) pointed out that this also is true of human relations. Classical and scientific theorists believed that workers are motivated by economic need. If this need is satisfied and the organization is properly designed, compliance with managerial authority will follow. Human relations advocates stressed the importance of social rather than economic needs and urged managers to adopt communication strategies that give workers a sense of participation. According to Miles, the heart of the human relations model is the idea that participation improves morale and morale leads to greater compliance with managerial authority. Consequently, all of these theories see communication only as a managerial tool for motivating workers and controlling organizational processes.

HUMAN RESOURCE DEVELOPMENT

Just as human relations challenged some of the key assumptions in classical and scientific management, the forward-looking work of scholars such as Follett and the development of new theories of human motivation and learning led to the concepts of **human resource development** that challenged human relations. As described by Swanson and Holton (2001), human resource development (HRD) is based on humanistic values emphasizing human rationality, human perfectibility, and self-awareness. They noted that Abraham Maslow, Douglas McGregor, Rensis Likert, and others within this humanistic tradition articulated four basic assumptions that still guide HRD thinking today:

Work is meaningful.

Workers are motivated by meaningful, mutually set goals and participation.

Workers should be increasingly self-directed, and this self-control will improve efficiency and work satisfaction.

Managers are most effective when coaching, working to develop untapped potential, and creating an environment where potential can be fully utilized. (Swanson & Holton, 2001, p. 48)

We should note that scholars are not in complete agreement about where to draw the line between human relations and HRD. For example, Miller (2006) identifies both Maslow and McGregor with human relations. The line may be a little fuzzy, but our own reading of this field agrees with Swanson and Holton's. Accordingly, we begin our account of HRD with Maslow, one of the theorists who introduced the idea that motivation is not merely economic or social (the assumption in classical and human relations theories), but also tied to one's sense of self-worth and self-actualization.

Maslow's Need Hierarchy

Maslow (1954) argued that motivational needs can be hierarchically organized. His hierarchy includes five needs:

1. *Physiological needs* for food, oxygen, and other basic requirements to sustain life. These are fundamental needs at the lowest level of the hierarchy.

2. *Safety needs* for security, protection from danger, and freedom from threat.

3. *Social needs* for love, affection, affiliation, and acceptance.

4. *Esteem needs* for a sense of status, recognition, and self-respect.

5. *Self-actualization needs* to realize one's full potential as a human being. Self-actualization is the most abstract and highest level need in the hierarchy.

Maslow believed that lower level needs are stronger than higher level needs. In general, any need at a given level of the hierarchy must be relatively satisfied before the need at the next higher level is activated. Thus, a person who has reliable and stable means of meeting physiological and safety needs will become motivated to fulfill social needs, whereas a starving, homeless individual is preoccupied only with finding food and shelter.

More importantly, Maslow believed that self-actualization differs fundamentally from the other needs. Physiological, safety, social, and esteem needs are deficiency needs. They involve physical or psychological conditions that a person strives to maintain within an acceptable range—a kind of balance in which there is neither "too much" nor "too little." If you are deprived of a need such as food, the need becomes a drive (hunger) that causes behavior to satisfy the need (foraging for food). Once the need is fulfilled, the drive (motivation) is reduced and the behavior stops. In contrast, self-actualization is a growth need. The process of satisfying this need actually increases rather than decreases motivation.

McGregor's Theory X and Theory Y

As management theorists became familiar with Maslow's work, they soon realized the possibility of connecting higher level needs to worker motivation. If organizational goals and individual needs could be *integrated* so that people would acquire self-esteem and, ultimately, self-actualization through work, then motivation would be self-sustaining. According to Douglas McGregor (1960), the key to linking self-actualization with work lies in managerial trust of subordinates. McGregor identified two sets of underlying assumptions about human nature that affects managers' trust of subordinates. He called these sets of assumptions Theory X and Theory Y.

Many managers subscribe to Theory X. They believe that employees dislike work and will attempt to avoid it if possible. Employees value security above everything else, dislike responsibility, and want someone else to control and direct them. If organizational goals are to be accomplished, managers must rely on threat and coercion to gain employee compliance. Theory X beliefs lead to mistrust, highly restrictive supervision, and a punitive atmosphere.

Theory Y managers believe that work is as natural as play. Employees want to work. They have the ability for creative problem solving, but their talents are underused in most organizations. Given proper conditions, employees will learn to seek out and accept responsibility and to exercise self-control and self-direction in accomplishing objectives to which they are committed. According to McGregor, Theory Y managers are more likely than Theory X managers to develop the climate of trust with employees that is required for human resource development.

In order for human resource development to occur, managers must communicate openly with subordinates, minimize status distinctions in superior-subordinate relationships, solicit subordinates' ideas and opinions, and create a climate in which subordinates can develop and use their abilities. This climate would include decentralization of decision making, delegation of authority to subordinates, variety in work tasks to make jobs more interesting, and participative management in which subordinates have influence in decisions that affect them.

As described by Miles (1965), the human resource development concept is based on a model that differs greatly from human relations. Here, participation leads to better performance, better performance improves morale, and morale feeds even more improvement in performance. The end result of human resource development is not so much compliance with managerial authority as it is a form of self-development through fulfillment of organizational goals. Participation in the process presumably provides even greater motivation to accomplish these goals.

As human resource development concepts emerged, it became clear that these concepts not only involved managerial communication with employees, but also included many aspects of organizational communication in general. If an organization is to implement the principles of participative management and decentralized decision making, those who participate must have effective interpersonal and group communication skills, open and flexible channels of communication, and adequate information for a variety of organizational functions. The importance of these conditions for human resource development was stressed in the results of studies by Rensis Likert.

Likert's Four Systems

Likert (1961) argued that there are four basic types of management orientations or systems: exploitative-authoritative (system 1), benevolent-authoritative (system 2), consultative (system 3), and **participative** (system 4). Although Likert and McGregor worked independently, their ideas are quite similar. Likert's system 1 corresponds to McGregor's Theory X, whereas system 4 is similar to Theory Y. Systems 2 and 3 are located in between the other two positions. Likert's research indicated that organizations with system 4 participative characteristics were more effective than organizations based on other systems. The characteristics of system 4 include the following:

1.   Communication between superiors and subordinates is open and extensive. Superiors solicit ideas and opinions, and subordinates feel free to discuss problems with superiors.

2. Decision making is decentralized. Decisions are made at all levels of the organization through group processes. Both superiors and subordinates are able to influence performance goals, work methods, and organizational activities.

3. Information flows freely through flexible channels of communication and in all directions—upward, downward, and laterally. Information is relatively accurate and undistorted.

4. Performance goals are developed through participative management. The goals are high but realistic. Goals are supported by favorable attitudes and motivation of organization members and by organizational commitment to development of human resources.

5. Control processes also are decentralized. Organization members seek and use feedback in order to exercise self-control.

In contrast, the characteristics of system 1 are as follows:

1. Superior-subordinate communication is minimal and characterized by mutual mistrust.

2. Decision making is centralized. Input from lower levels is neither solicited nor desired.

3. Flow of information is restricted to specified channels. Information usually moves downward in the form of orders, policies, procedures, and directions.

4. Employees do not support managerial goals. The organizational climate is characterized by fear, intimidation, and dissatisfaction.

5. Control processes are exercised by management, but an active informal organization usually develops among lower level personnel in order to resist or oppose managerial control.

We are not overstating the case when we say that much of the scholarship and practice in organizational communication from the 1960s through the 1980s rested on the belief that Likert's participative system 4 represents the ideal climate for which organizations should strive. Characteristics such as those in system 4 have been advocated extensively as prescriptions for effective organizational communication. The **structure of communication** (channels and networks), **communication functions** (purposes, content, and adequacy), and the **quality of communication at interpersonal and group levels** (e.g., superior-subordinate communication, the dynamics of group decision making, and social processes) are regarded as indicators of **organizational communication climate**. Scholars and practitioners (e.g., Goldhaber, 1993; Pace & Faules, 1989) generally have equated the following characteristics of organizational communication climate with organizational effectiveness:

1. Flexible networks with open channels of communication and multidirectional message flow (upward, downward, and lateral).

2. Availability of accurate, adequate information on matters such as work procedures, evaluation of job performance, organizational policies, decisions, and problems.

3. Mutual trust, openness, and supportiveness in superior-subordinate communication.

4. Participation and cohesiveness in group decision making, problem solving, and other task-related processes under "team-oriented" or democratic leadership.

Despite the influence of human resource development concepts in the field of organizational communication, the theory is essentially a managerial approach to employee motivation. It happens to have clear implications for organizational communication, but its primary concern does not differ from earlier scientific, classical, and human relations theories: *the promotion of organizational effectiveness through prescriptions for organizational structure and/or managerial practice.* Table 4.2 presents a complete comparison of traditional, human relations, and human resource development assumptions.

Like the theories that preceded it, human resource development has been criticized for placing too much faith in the power of its prescriptions for virtually any organizational setting. One of the earliest critics was Abraham Maslow himself, who expressed concerns that his need hierarchy could not be applied to organizational behavior in the way that McGregor wanted to use it. Maslow confessed, "I'm a little worried about this stuff which I consider tentative being swallowed whole by all sorts of enthusiastic people" (1965, p. 55).

Other critics such as Lawrence and Lorsch (1969) pointed out that no one formula for organizational effectiveness will work in all situations. The conditions of effective organizational performance vary from one situation to another. This position is known as the contingency theory. Those who embrace it argue that we should be less concerned with "searching for the panacea of the one best way to organize" and focus more attention on "situational factors that influence organizational performance" (p. 1).

Are such criticisms fair? On the one hand, research and case studies in management and in organizational communication support McGregor and Likert's positions. Many studies of organizational communication have shown that conditions such as participation, openness, supportiveness, and information adequacy are related not only to members' satisfaction (Gibb, 1961; Spiker & Daniels, 1981), but also to member commitment to the organization (Guzley, 1992; Trombetta & Rogers, 1988). One good case example is American Steel and Wire Company as described by Oswald, Scott, and Woerner (1991). AS&W began operating in 1986 in an industry in which foreign competition has all but eliminated American firms, yet the company competes effectively and is highly profitable. Oswald et al. attribute AS&W's success directly to "the philosophy that people are their number-one resource and that quality and customer advantage come from the efforts of hard-working, dedicated 'entrepreneurial' employees" (p. 77). Thus, at AS&W, employees own 18% of the company, hire their own coworkers, participate in and chair "customer value teams" to solve work problems or improve performance, and receive the same benefits as managers. Employees as well as managers are salaried, and families are included in many AS&W activities.

There are many other contemporary HRD success stories among U.S. organizations, ranging from large and well-known corporations such as famed spice maker McCormick & Company, Inc., to less prominent private companies such as the relatively small but diversified Bell Group of New Mexico. Both of these organizations have evolved their own adaptations of HRD practices and participative systems, and they prominently feature these systems on company Web pages and other materials.

McCormick has several characteristics of an HRD-oriented firm, but the company especially touts its system of so-called multiple management boards, first developed at McCormick in 1932 (nearly three decades before HRD gained much visibility). The

TABLE 4.2   Comparison of Traditional, Human Relations, and Human Resource Development Assumptions About People

Traditional Model	Human Relations Model	Human Resources Model
Assumptions	*Assumptions*	*Assumptions*
1. Work is inherently distasteful to most people. 2. What they do is less important than what they earn for doing it. 3. Few want or can handle work which requires creativity, self-direction, or self-control.	1. People want to feel useful and important. 2. People desire to belong and to be recognized as individuals. 3. These needs are more important than money in motivating people to work.	1. Work is not inherently distasteful. People want to contribute to meaningful goals which they have helped establish. 2. Most people can exercise far more creative, responsible self-direction and self-control than their present jobs demand.
Policies	*Policies*	*Policies*
1. The manager's basic task is to closely supervise and control his subordinates. 2. He must break tasks down into simple, repetitive, easily learned operations. 3. He must establish detailed work routines and procedures, and enforce these firmly but fairly.	1. The manager's basic task is to make each worker feel useful and important. 2. He should keep his subordinates informed and listen to their objections to his plans. 3. The manager should allow his subordinates to exercise some self-direction and self-control on routine matters.	1. The manager's basic task is to make use of his "untapped"' human resources. 2. He must create an environment in which all members may contribute to the limits of their ability. 3. He must encourage full participation on important matters, continually broadening subordinate self-direction and control.
Expectations	*Expectations*	*Expectations*
1. People can tolerate work if the pay is decent and the boss is fair. 2. If tasks are simple enough and people are closely controlled, they will produce up to standard.	1. Sharing information with subordinates and involving them in routine decisions will satisfy their basic needs to belong and to feel important. 2. Satisfying these needs will improve morale and reduce resistance to formal authority: subordinates will "willingly cooperate."	1. Expanding subordinate influence, self-direction, and self-control will lead to direct improvement in operating efficiency. 2. Work satisfaction may improve as a "by-product" of subordinates making full use of their resources.

SOURCE: From Miles, Porter, & Craft (1966).

boards have rotating membership drawn from administrative, professional, and other employees in the company. They operate in some ways like quality circles and in other ways like conventional committees, but they are free to select and pursue any project of potential benefit to McCormick except in the area of compensation and benefits.

The Bell Group began in the 1940s as a provider of supplies to Native American jewelry artisans, but expanded that business over the years into lines serving both the jewelry industry and the high-tech ceramics industry with more than 21,000 products. The Bell Group employs 500 people, but has only three levels in its organizational hierarchy. Bell members are organized in dozens of five- to eight-person work teams. The teams often are not only collaborative by design, but also multifunctional. Each team is regarded as a business management unit, and Bell provides annual training for all members to support its culture of participative management.

Despite such successes, highly respected scholars remain skeptical of any prescriptive model that promises an effective organization, and many American companies have resisted the adoption of HRD. With pressures that range from globalization and the dynamics of international market competition to the allure of short-term gains for success-driven executives, "the performance scorecards available to organization decision makers generally ignore the human resource side" (Swanson, 2001, p. 305). Although HRD is by no means on its "death bed," Swanson contends that the movement is floundering mainly from the failure of scholars to present a coherent and integrated theoretical basis for its principles and practices. Put another way, HRD has a credibility problem among scholars that makes it easier for executives to ignore it. In Swanson's view, a coherent account for HRD can be developed from relevant psychological, economic, and systems theories, but the task of integration remains incomplete.

The Transition to Theory Z

Although many American organizations have resisted adoption of human resource development principles, these principles caught on very quickly in a country that rose from the ruins of World War II to become an economic giant in the second half of this century. That country is, of course, Japan.

The Japanese industrial establishment became an avid and committed consumer of human resource development ideas that fit very neatly with key values in Japanese culture. These ideas actually were returned to the United States during the 1980s under the label "Japanese management." According to Matejka and Dunsing (1991), Japanese management actually is based on a conglomeration of ideas that includes many American principles, beginning with Douglas MacArthur's post-World War II reconstruction plans for Japanese industry and statistical quality control techniques developed by W. E. Deming—techniques initially rejected by American industry, but widely adopted in Japan. Moreover, say Matejka and Dunsing:

> A stream of Japanese students have [sic] come to America's best graduate schools over the last few decades to learn about American Management. These students took their best ideas from our best writers and actually put them to use . . . something we still have not done. (p. 55)

It is important to note that the collectivistic Japanese culture with its emphasis on group loyalty provided a more compatible and fertile ground than the individualistic culture of American organizations for the application of human resource development theory, but the fact remains that Japanese industry actually has been more effective than American industry in putting these principles into practice. Matejka and Dunsing point out two key reasons for their success. First, the Japanese have a willingness and capacity "to think long-term and devise strategies and contingency plans to minimize . . . losses" (pp. 55–56). Second, because the Japanese manage by groups, "the rising star in Japanese Management is the one who can consistently, day after day, make decisions that do the most to benefit the entire operation. Whereas selfishness fuels the American star, selflessness drives the Japanese star" (p. 57).

The Japanese also derive some advantage from the fact that theirs is a highly homogeneous culture, but this should not be taken to mean that cultural diversity is a handicap to American industry. Matejka and Dunsing contend that our great diversity actually ensures a continuous flow of new ideas and creates great potential for small- to medium-sized companies to respond to the challenge of reinventing our economy. Lest anyone decide, however, that unquestioning acceptance of human resource development will ensure a future burdened by a multi-trillion-dollar national debt, overseas insurgencies, threats of terrorism, and natural disasters, we are obliged to note that the Japanese have had their own economic misfortunes as well. Robert Rehder (1981) noted years ago that pressures common to both Japanese and American organizations were beginning to force both groups to adopt each other's best features, resulting in a new form of organization that Ouchi has called the "Type Z" organization (Ouchi & Jaeger, 1978).

As described by Rehder, traditional American organizations depend on a highly structured hierarchical bureaucracy of the sort envisioned by classical management theorists, i.e., a system characterized by fixed positions, rigid lines of authority, centralized decision making, formalized manager-employee relationships, written orders and job descriptions, and individualized performance standards. Although traditional Japanese organizations assuredly are hierarchical, too, the hierarchy is fuzzy. Job descriptions are informal, and decision making is highly decentralized, with heavy reliance on group motivation and performance. Companies take a paternalistic interest in employees and their families. The hybrid or mixed American-Japanese system—Ouchi's Theory Z organization that Rehder regards as the future for both countries—falls somewhere between the two traditional types. Job specialization in the hybrid organization is moderate, but many functions are accomplished through project teams and task forces that may be transient and temporary. Decision making is less centralized and depends on informal consensus seeking. There is a concerted effort to integrate employee and organizational goals, but "written communications and individual responsibility continue to predominate" (Rehder, 1981, p. 67).

Since the early 1990s, events have pressed the Japanese to move even more quickly in the direction of Americanization. Powell noted in 1992 that the Japanese economy was projected to show little or no growth, an alarming condition that "could trigger profound changes in the way Japan does business" and take Japan "down the slippery slope toward the kind of short-term, run-and-gun capitalism that defined American business" (p. 53) at a time when Japanese workers and managers were openly questioning whether work and organizational commitment should be allowed to dominate their lives. Five years after Powell's warning,

Japan as well as other Asian nations slid right down that "slippery slope" into a major financial crisis from which they only recently recovered, mainly through greater regional cooperation, but also in part by modeling practices in American financial markets (Kuroda, 2005).

Exactly how far Asian regional cooperation and modeling of American financial systems will go in allowing Japan to maintain its traditional organizational values is unclear. Like America and the European Union, Japan also faces China and India as rising economic powerhouses. We all are international trading partners. We also are global competitors. And our organizational systems can be vulnerable to everything from volatility in energy prices and stock markets to terrorist acts and bird flu.

SUMMARY

When the industrialized world entered the 20th century, it was apparent that new and clearer concepts of organizational behavior would be required to deal with the complexities of modern society. The first modern perspectives on organizational behavior were developed in the early 1900s when theorists such as Taylor, Fayol, and Weber advanced the basic principles of scientific and classical management. Although the theories of Taylor, Fayol, and Weber differed from one another in some important ways, they generally envisioned organizations as machinelike objects driven by management plan and control. They assumed that individual organization members behave on the basis of rational, economic motivation.

Scientific and classical theories were followed quickly by eclectic theories, such as those developed by Follett and Barnard and by the human relations movement. Follett redefined traditional ideas about the exercise of power in order to achieve integration of different interests. She also emphasized a transactional concept of communication and active "conferencing" between management and employees to achieve pluralistic responsibility. Barnard pointed out oversights in scientific and classical theory regarding the variability of individual behavior in organizations. He argued that compliance depends on individual willingness to cooperate—cooperation that must be induced through incentives such as status and prestige as well as economic motives. His theory of organization structure treated the organization as a communication system.

The human relations movement evolved from various sources of influence, but the basic ideas are typified in the work of Dale Carnegie and Elton Mayo. Both encouraged managers to adopt a "people-oriented" approach to influence and gaining compliance. Mayo's theory was based primarily on results of the controversial Hawthorne Studies, which challenged scientific and classical notions by concluding that organizational effectiveness depends more on the social processes of organizations than on management design.

Later, the development of system theory and new concepts in human motivation led to further refinements in organizational theory. Human resource development theory, based on motivational principles of the human need for self-fulfillment, began to compete with earlier human relations and classical and scientific perspectives of organizational behavior. McGregor distinguished between Theory X and Theory Y managerial assumptions, arguing that the Theory Y orientation would lead to effectiveness through development of human resources. Similarly, Likert argued that organizational effectiveness is linked to system 4 participative management. System 4 emphasizes flexible, open communication, relatively accurate, undistorted information, and use of group decision making. Much of the scholarship and practice in the field of organizational communication assumes that system 4 represents the ideal climate for which organizations should strive. The prescriptions of human resource development theory have been criticized in the United States, but the Japanese industrial establishment has actively used HRD principles. Today, economic and competitive pressures are forcing Japanese and American organizations to adopt the best of each others' features.

DISCUSSION QUESTIONS/ACTIVITIES

1. Observe some samples of organizational communication. On the basis of these observations, would you say that the characteristics of the organization are closer to Likert's system 4 or system 1? Do these characteristics seem to have any relationship to organizational effectiveness?

2. Barnard argued that organization structure should be understood as a communication system. How does this argument differ from earlier classical management ideas about organizational structure?

3. A bureaucratic theorist assumes that an organization is like a machine. A system theorist assumes that an organization is like a living organism. If these two theorists observe the same organization and then report on what they saw, in what ways would the two reports most likely differ?

4. Compare and contrast human relations theory with human resource development theory. Which of these theories do you think is most consistent with the actual behavior of contemporary managers?

REFERENCES

Barnard, C. (1938). *The functions of the executive.* Cambridge, MA: Harvard University Press.

Carey, A. (1967). The Hawthorne Studies: A radical criticism. *American Sociological Review, 30,* 403–416.

Carnegie, D. (1936). *How to win friends and influence people.* New York: Simon & Schuster.

Dessler, G. (1980). *Organization theory: Integrating structure and behavior.* Englewood Cliffs, NJ: Prentice Hall.

Fayol, H. (1949). *General and industrial management* (Constance Storrs, Trans.). London: Sir Isaac Putnam. (Original work published 1917)

Follett, M. P. (1982a). Power. In E. M. Fox & L. Urwick (Eds.), *Dynamic administration: The collected papers of Mary Parker Follett* (pp. 66–87). New York: Hippocrene Books.

Follett, M. P. (1982b). The influence of employee representation in a remoulding of the accepted type of business manager. In E. M. Fox & L. Urwick (Eds.), *Dynamic administration: The collected papers of Mary Parker Follett* (pp. 167–182). New York: Hippocrene Books.

Fox, E. M., & Urwick, L., Eds. (1982). *Dynamic administration: The collected papers of Mary Parker Follett.* New York: Hippocrene Books.

Franke, R. H., & Kaul, J. D. (1978). The Hawthorne experiments: First statistical reinterpretation. *American Sociological Review, 43,* 623–643.

Gibb, J. (1961). Defensive communication. *Journal of Communication, 11,* 141–148.

Goldhaber, G. M. (1993). *Organizational communication* (6th ed.). Dubuque, IA: Brown & Benchmark.

Guzley, R. M. (1992). Organizational climate and communication climate: Predictors of commitment to the organization. *Management Communication Quarterly, 5,* 379–402.

Kuroda, H. (2005). *Dynamic East Asia: Progress and prospects for economic growth and regional integration.* Presentation at the Center on Japanese Economy and Business, Columbia Business School, New York, September 12.

Landsberger, H. (1958). *Hawthorne revisited.* Ithaca, NY: Cornell University Press.

Lawrence, P., & Lorsch, J. (1969). *Organization and environment: Managing differentiation and integration.* Homewood, IL: Irwin.

Likert, R. (1961). *New patterns of management.* New York: McGraw-Hill.

Maslow, A. H. (1954). *Motivation and personality.* New York: Harper & Row.

Maslow, A. H. (1965). *Eupsychian management.* Homewood, IL: Irwin.

Matejka, K., & Dunsing, D. (1991). Japanese/American management myths. *Business Horizons, 34,* 54–57.

Mayo, E. (1947). *The human problems of an industrial civilization.* Boston: Harvard Business School Press.

McGregor, D. (1960). *The human side of enterprise.* New York: McGraw-Hill.

Miles, R. (1965). Keeping informed: Human relations or human resources. *Harvard Business Review, 43,* 148–163.

Miles, R. E., Porter, L. W., & Craft, J. A. (1966). Leadership attitudes among public health officers. *American Journal of Public Health, 56,* 1990–2005.

Miller, K. (2006). *Organizational communication: Approaches and processes* (4th ed.). Belmont, CA: Thompson Wadsworth.

Oswald, S., Scott, C., & Woerner, W. (1991). Strategic management of human resources: The American Steel and Wire Company. *Business Horizons, 34,* 77–92.

Ouchi, W., & Jaeger, A. (1978, April). Type Z: Organizational stability in the midst of mobility. *Academy of Management Review, 3,* 305–314.

Pace, R. W., & Faules, D. F. (1989). *Organizational communication* (2nd ed.). Englewood Cliffs, NJ: Prentice Hall.

Powell, B. (1992, April 20). And after the fall? *Newsweek,* pp. 53–55.

Redding, W. C. (1979). Organizational communication theory and ideology: An overview. In D. Nimmo (Ed.), *Communication yearbook 3* (pp. 309–342). New Brunswick, NJ: Transaction Books.

Rehder, R. R. (1981). What American and Japanese managers are learning from each other. *Business Horizons, 24,* 63–70.

Roethlisberger, F. L., & Dickson, W. (1939). *Management and the worker.* New York: John Wiley & Sons.

Spiker, B. K., & Daniels, T. D. (1981). Information adequacy and communication relationships: An empirical examination of 18 organizations. *Western Journal of Speech Communication, 45,* 342–354.

Swanson, R. A. (2001). Human resource development and its underlying theory. *Human Resource Development International, 4,* 299–313.

Swanson, R. A., & Holton, E. F. (2001). *Foundations of human resource development.* San Francisco: Berrett-Koehler.

Taylor, F. W. (1947). *Principles of scientific management.* New York: Harper & Brothers.

Trombetta, J. J., & Rogers, D. P. (1988). Communication climate, job satisfaction, and organizational commitment. *Management Communication Quarterly, 1,* 494–514.

United States Postal Service (1979). *Organization structures manual.* Chapter 1, part 130, sec. 153.21.

Weber, M. (1947). *The theory of social and economic organizations* (A. M. Henderson & T. Parsons, Trans.; T. Parsons, Ed.). New York: Oxford University Press. (Original work published 1920)

Weber, M. (1969). Bureaucracy. In J. A. Litterer (Ed.), *Organizations: Structure and behavior.* New York: John Wiley & Sons.

Organization Theory

Metaphors of Biology

In Chapter 4, we saw how answers to the managerial problem of motivating organization members to perform developed from the mechanistic accounts of economic exchange in scientific and classical theories to satisfaction of social needs in human relations theory, and then to self-actualization and participation in human resource development. All of these theories are at some level theories of motivation, i.e., the causes of human action, and they offer prescriptions for organizational effectiveness and the conduct of management. At the same time that these theories were maturing, other theories were in development that embraced a different set of concerns by looking to the field of biology for organizational metaphors. These theories are concerned not with the managerial problem of member motivation in and of itself, but with the broader problem of understanding the structure, function, and development of human systems and the people who constitute these systems. The basic metaphor in these theories is the organization as an **adaptive organism** rather than a machine operated solely by management control. We will consider four such theories in this chapter.

The first of these theories, **system theory,** attempts to understand organizations with the same principles that are used to understand living organisms. The second and third are adaptations and extensions of system theory to human communication. Karl Weick's theory of organizing focuses on **equivocality reduction** and relies on an evolution model to explain organizing and organizational communication. Niklas Luhmann's social systems theory also incorporates evolution. Luhmann argues that social systems literally are systems of communications. The final theory is the psychosocial application of evolutionary theory in the emerging field of **evolutionary psychology**, in which evolution is not just a model to describe organizing, but a general foundation for explaining modern human behavior.

SYSTEM THEORY

System theory is the product of work begun in the field of philosophy during the 19th century and expanded by many scholars in various fields during the 20th century. Much of the formal elaboration of system theory was presented in Ludwig von Bertalanffy's *General System Theory* (1968), first published in 1956. Bertalanffy, a Canadian biologist, wanted to develop a set of concepts and principles that would apply generally to any type of system (hence, the label general system theory).

The perspective that Bertalanffy and other early system theorists developed soon was adapted to the study of organizations in works by March and Simon (1958), Katz and Kahn (1966), and Huse and Bowditch (1973). The influence of system theory in the study of organizational communication also has been substantial. For example, Farace, Monge, and Russell (1977) developed a structural-functional model of organizational communication that is drawn directly from systems principles. Even before publication of Bertalanffy's major works, Chester Barnard had presented some systems principles in his theory of organizational structure (Dessler, 1980; Littlejohn, 1992). As Monge (1982) pointed out, "Organizational communication has predominantly been studied from the viewpoint of system theory" (p. 245).

System theory provided a new analogy for the study of organizations and organizational communication—the living organism. Whereas scientific and classical scholars regarded the organization as a machinelike object operated by management control, system theorists stressed the point that organizations are more like living creatures than machines. Organizations experience birth, development, and death. They are dynamic entities that act in purposeful ways. System theory relies on several important concepts in order to explain the organismic characteristics of organizations. These concepts include wholeness, hierarchy, openness, and feedback.

System Concepts

Wholeness

A system is a set of elements bound together in interdependent relationships. Elements in a system are interdependent in the sense that they affect one another. If the relationships are highly interdependent, a change in one part of the system can lead to changes throughout the entire system. This interdependence among parts or elements results in an integrated whole.

Wholeness means that the effect of elements working in relationship to one another differs from the effect of their isolated, individual actions taken collectively. This effect is sometimes referred to as synergy—a condition in which the whole is greater than the sum of its parts. Perhaps you have experienced synergy as a participant in group problem solving. For example, a group of advertising professionals might "brainstorm" in order to generate a novel, creative idea for promoting a product. As they interact, they build on and modify one another's ideas until they arrive at a workable concept. Suppose that we ask these same professionals to generate ideas by working in isolation from one another, then we collect and list the ideas that they produce. We might see many of the same ideas that would appear in a group brainstorming session, but the list would not include ideas that emerged as a result of interaction within the group, and it probably would provide barely a hint of the final solution that the group developed. The individuals working as an integrated group (system) produced something greater than they would have produced in a simple collection of isolated, individual efforts. We cannot simply "add up" their individual actions in order to understand how they function as a system.

Hierarchy

The relationships among elements in a system are specified by rules. One of the more important rules is the principle of hierarchy. Elements are organized into subsystems. Subsystems are related to one another to form the system. The system itself operates within a larger environment. In an organization, we might think of the elements as individual human beings, subsystems as work groups, departments, or divisions, and the system as the entire organization.

As we already have seen in Chapter 3, the principle of hierarchy applies readily to most Western organizations. Even organizations that depart from traditional ideas about division of labor, unity of command, and unity of direction can still be characterized by a basic system hierarchy—elements, subsystems, system, and environment. This type of hierarchy occurs in new contemporary structures such as matrixed organizations. Matrix structures are intended to give organizations great flexibility in responding to specialized, temporary needs. Consider the case of Universal Products Company (UPC) as described by Mee (1964). UPC has four product divisions: automotive, electrical, chemical, and aerospace. Each division consists of five basic departments: production, engineering, materials, personnel, and accounting. In this form, UPC is a traditionally structured organization, but a major departure from this concept occurs in the aerospace division, as illustrated in Figure 5.1.

Aerospace has three major but temporary projects underway (Venus, Mars, and Saturn). Each of the three projects is directed by a manager who has full authority and responsibility for its completion. Each project manager has been assigned personnel from the five departments in the aerospace division. Until completion of the project, the manager decides on tasks, work schedules, promotions, and salary increases for those personnel who are assigned to the project. A purchasing agent who normally would report to the manager of the materials department now reports to a project manager as well. Sometimes, the project manager has total control over personnel assigned to a project, but a project manager's control in many matrixed organizations is shared with functional department heads in the regular line organization. In this case, any individual organization member literally participates in two subsystems at once, fulfilling functions as a regular department member and as a project team member, while reporting to two different superiors. The use of such matrix structures handily illustrates the power of organizational systems to adapt to changing circumstances.

Openness

Systems may be regarded as relatively open or closed. Open systems are characterized by active exchange with their outside environment. Organizations are open systems. They take in energy and materials (input), transform this input in some way (throughput), then return products and byproducts of throughput to the environment (output).

When the environment is stable, it is tempting to ignore the fact that organizations are open systems. Given a stable environment, an organization is able to operate in a steady, machinelike state. Its performance is regular and routine because nothing in the environment demands anything else. Under such conditions, the organization seems to be a closed, static system that is unaffected by its environment. This view is deceptively simple and can be hazardous when the environment changes in some dramatic way.

During the 1960s, executives in the automobile industry seemed to see their corporations in much the same way as their cars—well-engineered machines continually getting bigger and better through managerial design. The rise of foreign competition and the energy crisis of the 1970s quickly taught auto companies that they are, indeed, open systems faced with a demand to adapt to a changing and sometimes turbulent environment. General Motors and Ford made fundamental changes to respond to unanticipated consumer demand for smaller, more efficient cars. Chrysler was saved from bankruptcy only by government-backed loans. American Motors barely clung to life by creating linkages with Jeep and Renault. When the corporations recovered, they were smaller and leaner. Thousands of workers were laid off with no hope of ever recovering their old jobs, and many auto dealers went out of business. Today American Motors no longer exists. Chrysler merged with

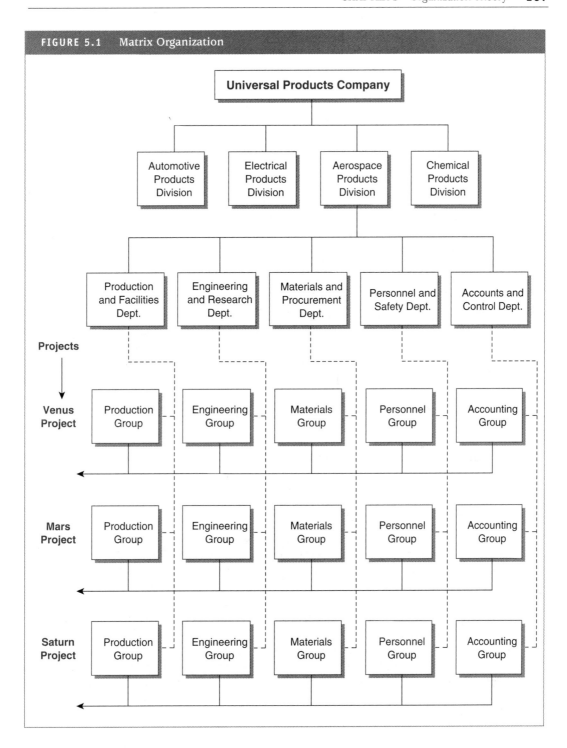

FIGURE 5.1   Matrix Organization

Daimler. By 2005, Ford and General Motors, having drifted into the complacency of their old ways during the booming 1990s, both were in trouble again.

Feedback

Open systems are characterized by two basic processes: maintenance and adaptation. Maintenance processes are regulatory. They are intended to keep certain system conditions within acceptable ranges. Adaptive processes bring about change and growth. Both of these processes depend on feedback responses to system actions that provide information for use in adjusting system conditions.

Feedback may be negative or positive. Negative feedback indicates deviations from desired conditions. The system adjusts by correcting the deviation. Maintenance processes depend on negative feedback. These processes involve the same principle of dynamic balance associated with deficiency needs in motivation. Suppose that a small manufacturing company wants to maintain a product inventory of 475–525 finished units at all times, with an ideal inventory of 500 units. If the inventory rises above 525 because sales slow down, someone sends negative feedback to the production department to ease back on production until the inventory is reduced. If the inventory falls below 475, production receives negative feedback to speed up until the shortage is corrected.

In contrast to negative feedback, positive feedback reinforces deviations rather than signaling for a correction. Positive feedback is used to create new system conditions rather than to maintain old ones. This form of feedback is the basis for change and adaptation. For example, government willingness to guarantee loans for Chrysler only if the corporation would adapt to its environment provided an incentive that led to many fundamental changes in the corporate structure, leadership, and products. If Chrysler people wanted to survive as a corporation, they were going to have to act in entirely new ways. As the changes were initiated, public acceptance and favorable market responses provided positive reinforcement for Chrysler to continue the adaptation process. Years later in 2006, Ford Motor Company, fighting for survival in globally competitive markets, announced a plan called The Way Forward (a combination of massive layoffs, plant closings, new product innovations, and changes in business practices) in hopes of the sort of feedback that helped to save Chrysler.

Of course, feedback in living, open systems is not simply a mechanical process of automatic response to deviation-correcting or reinforcing messages. Roger D'Aprix (1982) tells a story about an employee communications department in a large corporation that decided to publish an article in the corporate magazine about the company's employee compensation system. When the article was submitted to the personnel department for review, the employee-compensation manager, who feared that the story revealed too much, rejected it. The personnel department proposed a "revision" in the article that would have made it unintelligible to most readers. The employee communications department appeared to have two options: run the revised version or drop the story. The department manager chose a third path—convincing the compensation manager that most of the personnel department's fears were unfounded. The article that finally appeared in print was based on a compromise between the two managers.

D'Aprix's story is an excellent illustration of informal negotiations in management ranks, the politics of organizational decision making, and even Eisenberg's (1984) principles of strategic ambiguity. It also demonstrates several important points about feedback in episodes of communication that are acted out every day in thousands of organizations. First, deviations from desired conditions often are defined by human values instead of physical circumstances. The compensation manager's desire to conceal information about compensation decisions provided the standard for judging the acceptability of the article. Second, the recipient of feedback may choose to act on it in various ways or even ignore it. The communications manager did not simply make the changes that the compensation manager wanted but chose another action instead. Finally, organizational subsystems and individuals influence each other through *reciprocal* feedback and may employ different standards for evaluating and responding to feedback. The personnel and employee communications departments differed in their assessments of the article's acceptability. The personnel department's rejection was negative feedback. The communications department's response to rejection also was, in effect, a form of feedback. The solution to the conflict emerged from an interaction between the two departments, not from one unit's mechanical acquiescence to feedback from another.

Influence on Organizational Communication

Taken collectively, the basic concepts of system theory—wholeness, hierarchy, openness, and feedback—provide a dynamic view of organizations in action. System theory has been influential in the study of organizational communication because it places the organizing role of communication in a new light (Littlejohn, 1992). Communication is not merely an activity that occurs "within" an organization, nor is communication merely a tool for managerial control. Rather, all of the human processes that define an organization arise from communication. Relationships among individual organization members are defined through communication. The linkages and interactions among subsystems depend on communication and information flow. All feedback processes involve communication.

A good example of the influence of system theory on management and organizational theory is in the development of the contingency theory that we mentioned earlier in criticisms of human resource development theory. Lawrence and Lorsch (1969) and Joan Woodward (1958) used a system perspective in large studies of industrial companies that led them to doubt the universal effectiveness of any one approach to management and organization. Instead, Lawrence and Lorsch concluded that effectiveness depends upon the "fit" between organizational attributes and the environment, whereas Woodward found that the most successful organizations were those in which management practices were consistent with the technical processes of production, which varied across industries.

Despite the influence of system theory on management theory and the popularity of system theory in the field of organizational communication, its impact on organizational communication *research* actually has been rather limited. What does one do after declaring the newfound revelation that organizations are open systems? The field has provided only partial and incomplete answers to this question for more than 20 years (Monge, Farace,

Eisenberg, Miller, & White, 1984). We have been much more successful in talking about organizational communication with the vocabulary of system theory than we have been in using system theory as a basis for our research. At the very least, however, system theory has provided us with a different and potentially powerful set of ideas and assumptions to frame our thinking about organizational communication.

More studies these days do depend clearly on a system theory foundation. Some involve narrowly focused research problems. Lee and Jablin (1995) used basic system theory concepts to examine maintenance communication in superior-subordinate relationships, and Konopaske, Robie, and Ivancevich (2005) studied the influence of family system dynamics on managers' willingness to relocate, particularly for international or global assignments. Other studies apply systems concepts in very broad ways. Capps and Hazen (2002) showed how general systems theory can frame long-range strategic planning. Cabezas, Pawlowski, Mayer, and Hoagland (2005) used system theory as a frame of reference in literally mathematizing sustainability to link "measures of ecosystem functioning to the structure and operation of the associated social system" (p. 455).

System Theory, Complexity, and Chaos

System theory also has been dusted off and shined up again in the early 21st century because of its kinship with chaos and complexity theories in the physical sciences (Richardson, 2004). In particular, social and behavioral scientists have become interested in the tools and methods of complexity theorists and chaoticians, and system theory once again provides a working frame of reference in which to use these tools (Daneke, 2005).

We are not even going to pretend to provide a coherent account of chaos theory in this book. We are still figuring out some features of it, so we may be risking misrepresentation by way of oversimplification, but here is the basic idea. Living systems (including organizations) are quite complex, occasionally orderly, but generally turbulent and very difficult to predict. In the physical sciences, chaoticians have devised mathematical and statistical tools for nonlinear analysis that successfully locate the predictable amidst the unpredictable with at least some degree of likelihood or probability. How often have you heard a saying such as, "The only certainty is uncertainty"? As paradoxical as it seems, unpredictability is, well, predictable. The trick is not to impose a false order on organizational turbulence, but to understand turbulence as turbulence.

This trend is almost certain to generate complaints that the social sciences are yet again borrowing tools from the natural sciences that cannot be applied to social phenomena. We are taking methods developed from theories about the physical world and just using them as new toys with no grounding in theories about the social world. Daneke (2005) specifically advocates vigorous resurrection of system theory as a solution to this issue. From a slightly different standpoint, however, one might suggest that the problem with system theory all along was the absence of truly relevant research methods. The ideas looked great for application to social systems and organizations, but the right tools were not available to take advantage of the ideas. Now we have the tools. This trend is still new, and how well it works is something that remains to be seen.

WEICK'S THEORY OF ORGANIZING

One of the more important products of system theory in the study of organizational communication is Karl Weick's (1979) theory that organizing and communicating activities are directed toward the reduction of equivocality in information. Most writers refer to this theory as Weick's theory of organizing because equivocality reduction really is only one part of it, but it happens to be the most important part. Here is how it works.

Equivocality Reduction

First, we begin with the systems principle that organizations function in an environment and are influenced by the environment along with Weick's observation that late 20th-century organizational environments generally are complicated and often turbulent. As we just suggested in the previous section, change and uncertainty abound. The information that an organization must process about its environment in order to function effectively also can be very complicated and equivocal. Information is equivocal when it can be given different interpretations because it is ambiguous, conflicted, or obscure or it introduces an element of uncertainty into a situation.

In order to understand the connection between equivocality reduction and organizational communication, compare the way that we handle routine, run-of-the-mill situations to the way in which we respond to unexpected events or a crisis. Situations that we understand to be "routine" are routine precisely because they have predictable regularities. In a routine situation, a stable set of rules defines the situation and tells us how to act in that situation. Consider, for example, the rules that define placing and getting a food order at a McDonald's. It makes no difference whether the McDonald's is in Athens, Ohio, or half way around the world in Singapore; you know what to expect when you walk into one. In spite of the cultural differences between the United States and Singapore, the rules that define the McDonald's experience are essentially the same in both places. You know where to place your order, where to look for the menu, how your order will be transacted with the counter person, about how long it will take to get it, and even how your Big Mac, fries, and a Coke will taste. There is little if any equivocality in the situation. And because there is little equivocality, there is little need for communication to reduce it. The execution of your transaction at McDonald's is communicatively simple and neatly sterile, whether it occurs in Michigan or Singapore.

Now suppose that you went to a table-service restaurant instead of a fast-food place. You and your date have just finished a meal, and the server has delivered your check on a small tray. You have had two different kinds of past experiences with this procedure. Sometimes the check-on-a-tray means that the server is coming back in a few minutes to retrieve the check along with your credit card in order to handle the payment transaction for you. And sometimes it means that you are supposed to take the check to the cashier yourself. Which is it this time? Resolving this kind of uncertainty requires a bit more communicative effort. For example, you say to your date, "I wonder if the server is coming back for this." Your date replies, "Oh yes. They always do that here." You thank your date for this information, although it may have introduced another element of uncertainty, i.e., with whom did your date last dine at this restaurant?

The check-on-the-tray is an example of simple uncertainty. What happens in highly novel or equivocal situations? Crisis situations certainly are not the only circumstances in which organizations confront high levels of uncertainty and equivocality, but they lend themselves readily to our purposes here because the very idea of a crisis implies that something out of the ordinary has happened. Consider what may happen in a community that has been hit by some natural disaster such as a flood or tornado. You may have heard stories in such situations that the disaster actually "brought the community closer together" in some way. Why? Because the rules for managing routine situations are useless in the crisis. People are compelled to interact and communicate in order to figure out what do in order to manage and reduce the equivocality in the situation. Someone who is trained to respond to the specific kind of crisis (e.g., a Red Cross worker or an emergency medical technician) might not experience the same equivocality in the situation, but training is, in a sense, communicating in advance to manage the equivocality of an emergency before it actually happens. Communication still has to occur in order to figure out what will be done, even if this occurs before the crisis.

Fundamental Propositions

Of course, if you test the examples just described against the extended illustrations of the Katrina catastrophe that we used to open this book in the prologue, you may be asking whether the idea of equivocality reduction makes any sense at all. In the aftermath of Katrina, a lot of the communication required for equivocality reduction either did not occur as a result of human error, indifference, and incompetence, or it simply could not occur because the level of devastation was so great. Many months after the storm, New Orleans and other Gulf Coast communities were not just trying to recover; they were still trying to decide how to recover, recreate old order, and create new order where much of what they had was gone. And that observation leads us to three fundamental propositions in Weick's theory.

First, where environmental inputs (information) have little equivocality, organizations can rely heavily on rules to guide their responses, just as most of us probably have done at one time or another in managing our way through a transaction at McDonald's. As equivocality increases, organizations are less able to rely on rules. Second, as equivocality increases, more communicative effort is required to respond to it. This is what we often see in crisis situations, and even in an episode as simple as the check-on-the-tray. Weick has a special term for communication in this case. It is called an **interlocked behavior cycle**, which consists of a **double-interact**. Person A says something to B, B replies to A, and A provides an adjustment message (e.g., a confirmation, request for clarification, etc.) to B. For example, "I wonder if the server is coming back for this." "Oh yes. They always do that here." "Thanks. Now I know what to expect." Strictly speaking, Weick does not talk about the relationship between equivocality and communication, but the relationship between equivocality and interlocked behavior cycles. As equivocality increases, the use of interlocked behavior cycles (i.e., communication) increases in an effort to reduce the equivocality. This get us to the third point. All of this happens because equivocality makes rules less useful. As equivocality increases, we are less able to rely on rules and their routines to handle the situation.

Weick is simply describing the process in these propositions, not predicting how well interlocked behavior cycles will work, as illustrated by the case of former FEMA director Michael Brown, who was roundly ridiculed for this adjustment message in an exchange with a subordinate who was updating him on the dire situation in New Orleans. Marty Bahamonde reported to Brown, "you know the situation is past critical. . . . Estimates are many will die within hours." Brown replied, "Thanks for the update. Anything specific I need to do or tweak?" (CBS News, November 3, 2005).

The Evolutionary Metaphor

We mentioned earlier that Weick not only relies on system theory, but also uses the analogy of evolutionary processes in his theory. In the Darwinian version of evolutionary theory, known as natural selection, the members of a species exhibit **variations** in their makeup. These variations are, of course, genetic, although Darwin certainly did not know this in 1859. The connection to genetics did not occur until well into the 20th century. Some genetic variations will turn out to be more adaptive than others, i.e., they will help the organism to survive in a given environment. The fittest organisms, i.e., those whose variations are the most adaptive, get to pass on their traits through reproduction. Thus, the adaptive traits are **selected** for continuation and eventually **retained** as characteristics of the species. Natural selection explains how whales evolved from a land mammal, how humans and apes sprang from a common ancestor millions of years ago, and why bacteria develop resistance to antibiotic drugs.

The idea of using Darwin's theory of the evolution of biological organisms as an analogy to explain sociocultural adaptation has been around for more than 30 years (e.g., Campbell, 1965). This approach uses the same concepts of variation, selection, and adaptation. Here the variations are behavioral, and they occur in the face of environmental stresses. Gary Kreps (1990) explained most succinctly the premise of this theory and the way that Weick uses it:

> The most advantageous variations are selected by the cultural group for use and retained as functional attributes of the cultural group. Weick borrows this three-stage model of adaptation [variation, selection, and retention of behaviors], modifying it to the three phases of organizing: enactment, selection, and retention. (p. 113)

The idea of **enactment** in Weick's theory means that human beings do not just passively respond to conditions in an environment. We attend actively to the environment and selectively interpret it, recognizing the level of equivocality in the information that we have. The selection phase begins when we make decisions about the rules and interlocked (communication) cycles that we will use to manage the equivocality. Remember that routine rules are of little use in the highly equivocal situation, so we depend on creating communication cycles. To the extent that the cycles created in this process are successful in reducing equivocality, they are retained for future use. In effect, they become new rules that may guide the organization's actions in future situations.

Retrospective Sense Making

Our reading of Weick's theory is fairly similar to the reading provided by Gary Kreps, but, to emphasize the point that we just made about selective interpretation, all communication scholars do not read Weick in the same way, and one important variation is found in Eisenberg and Goodall's (1993) emphasis on selection and retention of *interpretations* rather than selection and retention of interlocked behavior cycles. In their reading

> Once an environment is enacted, organizing requires that participants select from a number of possible alternative explanations of what the environment means. Selection is collective sense-making and is accomplished through communication. Finally, those interpretations that are believed to work, or make sense, are retained for future use. (p. 109)

Now there clearly is some merit in looking at Weick's theory in the way that Eisenberg and Goodall do because another important idea that Weick has about organizational communication is the concept of **retrospective sense making**. Many modern management and organization theories, beginning with scientific management and classical organization theory, assume that organizational behavior is (or at least should be) rational in character, i.e., planned, calculated, and directed toward goals. Weick contends that organizational behavior is not so much rational as it is *rationalized*. What if intentions and motives do not really exist prior to action? What if they are only accounts that we construct to explain our behavior *after* we have already done it? In a simple sense, retrospective sense making means that we construct interpretations of organizational experiences and actions by reflecting on them.

The concept of retrospective sense making has something in common with the concept of socially constructed reality in the interpretive perspective on organizational communication. Both depend on the idea that human beings figure out what things mean through constitutive interpretation. We puzzle, mull over, fret, stew, and generally select, manipulate, and transform meanings to come up with an interpretation of a situation. In this sense, we construct reality. Interpretive theory adds to this the idea that much of this interpretive process is carried out through interaction with our fellow members of the organization. Hence, the result is a *socially* constructed reality.

Weick may have carried this idea a little too far by implying that human beings do not plan when most of us clearly think that we do, but consider as an example a situation that unfolded in December of 1995. President Clinton had decided to send American soldiers to Bosnia in order to support a peace agreement. Russia had signaled a willingness to join in this effort, combining its forces with the Americans under American command. At the same time, highly sophisticated, intelligence-gathering Russian submarines were detected near the coasts of California and Georgia, obviously spying on U.S. military operations at both locations. The rationalist would say that we have to get all of the facts, then work through them systematically for an explanation that fits the facts. The interpretivist would say that facts as well as explanations are constituted in the interpretation. Interpretations do not correspond to objective truths; they are instead intersubjective agreements, and Weick's theory might provide a good account of the scramble by officials in the Clinton-era White House to make sense of what the Russians were doing.

A more recent and perhaps more compelling example is the Bush administration's case for WMDs (weapons of mass destruction) as a rationale for the war in Iraq. The conspicuous absence of WMDs led partisans on the left to represent the case as a "lie" and partisans on the right to represent it as an "honest mistake." The two partisan representations and the case itself are instances of constitutive interpretation. How one determines the absolutely verifiable and unequivocal truth of the matter is not the point here. There may be elements of truth in both. The point is how constitutive interpretation and sense making occur. Many experts here and abroad had concluded from the sketchy intelligence and inconsistent details that Iraq most likely had WMDs, and former CIA director George Tenant gained infamous notoriety for calling it a "slam dunk." Interpretation might not depend as much on the cold rationality of logic as it depends on the warm comfort of affect. Put another way, will the interpretation feel right because it fits the facts, or will facts fit the interpretation because the interpretation feels right?

The concepts of equivocality reduction through interlocked behavior cycles, the evolutionary analogy of the process, and retrospective sense making are some of Weick's more important contributions to the study of organizational communication, but there are some more Weickean notions that we will discuss in later chapters. The relevance of Weick's ideas to organizational communication is so broad that Gary Kreps (1990) constructed an entire text on organizational communication around this theory and other systems principles.

LUHMANN'S SOCIAL SYSTEMS THEORY

Niklas Luhmann's social systems theory (1986, 1989, 1995) is not new, but much of his work is in German and only recently translated or still undergoing translation (Schoeneborn, 2005). As yet another variant of system theory, it has much in common with theories such as Weick's. Like Weick, Luhmann has a theory that is grounded explicitly in communication, and he also relies on an evolution model to explain social change, but he generates some new thinking about systems that is attracting considerable interest among scholars in management studies and organizational communication.

Systems as Communications

We said in Chapter 1 of this book that an organization is constituted by the joint actions of its members; that communication, as the means of joint action, is the central feature of organizations. *Actions* as such are assumed to arise out of the thoughts and intentions of *individual actors*. Individual actors together constitute an organization through their *joint* actions, and joint action occurs through communication. In Luhmann's theory, this linkage between organization and communication gets a provocative new twist. In his view, "Social systems are not comprised of persons and actions but of communications" (1989, p. 145). Now what does Luhmann mean by this?

Luhmann suggests that evolution has produced "organic" systems, "psychic" systems, and "social" systems. All of these systems are able to reproduce themselves through their own operations. The reproductive operations of organic systems are obvious, but how does reproduction occur in psychic systems and social systems? According to Luhmann (1986), psychic systems operate on consciousness and social systems operate on communications.

As Hendry and Seidl (2003) explain, "Communication is a social (for Luhmann, the only genuinely social) operation, which cannot be causally reduced to individual actions" (p. 179). What is important about the social system is not the individual utterance or intention, but the understanding produced from interactions between two or more parties, i.e., communications. In this sense, "communications" are not produced by individual actors; they are produced by the communication process. A social system can be understood only in terms of its communication system because "communications themselves determine what further communications occur" (p. 179). In other words, the communication system is self-reproducing. Schoeneborn (2005) succinctly states the implication of Luhmann's idea for organizational communication: "If we transfer this notion of social systems to *organizations,* it becomes obvious that Luhmann also understands organizations as being constituted not by their members but instead by their ability to stabilize the reproduction of a specific type of communication" (p. 7).

Episodes, Stability, and Change

You can begin to grasp Luhmann's idea a little more easily by thinking about communication in terms of episodes. The episode concept figures prominently in some theories of communication, e.g., Pearce and Cronen's (1980) theory of the coordinated management of meaning. For Luhmann, an episode is not just an "event," but a sequence of communications with a beginning and an end. An episode is recognized by the *structure* of its communications. You can think of structure as conditions that define what is possible in the episode at its beginning, at its end, and between those two markers. Structure in this sense both constrains and enables communication.

Consider the use of parliamentary procedure in deliberations in legislative bodies and some types of business and corporate meetings. Parliamentary procedure in its simplest sense is a set of rules for the orderly conduct of business in a meeting under a democratic arrangement. In parliamentary procedure, issues are settled by majority vote under conditions that facilitate open discussion and afford some protection for minority rights. Business proceeds according to some kind of prescribed order (e.g., a call to order, minutes of past meeting, reports, old business, new business, announcements, and adjournment). Members initiate actions by making motions, but only after getting recognition (permission) to speak from the chairperson. Most types of motions need a "second" from another member in order to be considered by the entire group, so a motion can "die for lack of a second." Some types of motions can be debated. Others require an immediate vote. Some can be amended. Others cannot.

Now this set of rules tells individual members and the group as a whole how to proceed, what they can do, and what they cannot do, but it does even more. It structures communications, which, in turn, structure other communications. Suppose the chair recognizes member W. Member W makes a motion. Member X seconds the motion. The chair recognizes member Y to begin the debate. Y launches into a list of three reasons why the motion is a bad idea, followed by member Z, who argues that two of Y's three concerns are completely irrelevant. And so the deliberations continue until there is a vote to dispose of the matter, and the group moves on to something else.

If you see each step here as nothing more than a sequence of individual actions, Luhmann might say that you have missed the point. Member W's motion is just an individual utterance unless it is understood as a motion by others. Absent that understanding, there is nothing to "second." Until there is the communication of a second, there is nothing for member Y to debate, and without member Y's three objections, there is nothing for Z to rebut as irrelevant.

If we stick with the rather obvious example of episodes in which communications are structured through parliamentary procedure, it is also easy to grasp Luhmann's ideas about reproduction, stability, and change in social systems. The sequences of communications in parliamentary deliberation can be replicated over and over or reproduced across a wide range of situations within a system. This is stability. At the same time, however, the basic scheme of parliamentary procedure itself has been reproduced over time with variations. In addition to the well-known *Robert's Rules of Order,* there are other notable systems of parliamentary procedure, each with its own particular features, and perhaps many less formal, modified forms used in organizations. Reproduction is not just about stability. It is also about change. In Luhmann's theory, the evolution model is invoked again. Communication systems generate mutations, then select and retain those mutations that are adaptive.

Communications and Decision Contingencies

There is much more to Luhmann's theory than we have described so far. Schoeneborn (2005) devotes an extensive discussion to Luhmann's treatment of communications as decisions and the place of contingency in decisions. He applies this idea to respond to a claim by McPhee and Zaug (2000) that three types of communication, namely, membership negotiation, organizational self-structure, and activity coordination, are essential for the constitution of organizations. Schoeneborn calls them subtypes of decisions:

> Be it the negotiation about memberships, the emergence of structures, or the coordination of organizational activities, all of these processes can be reduced to decisions in the end which are processed in the course of communication. The communication of decisions, then, is the fundamental underpinning of organizations. (p. 9)

Decisions (real ones, at least) involve choices among alternatives. After all, if there is no alternative to a course of action, where is the "decision" in taking that course of action? In a complex environment, any course of action or the likelihood of an event may depend on many factors, some known, some unknown, so in Luhmann's view, decisions involve contingencies, i.e., things that could happen, but are not necessarily certain to happen. Decisions are always contingent in the sense that we picked one alternative, but we could have picked another. Luhmann is interested in decisions made and communicated in a social context, not in the decisions of the lone individual. In this social context, we cannot really communicate decisions as such without also communicating the rejected alternatives. And decisions, rather than eliminating contingencies, generate new ones, always "opening up new possibilities to decide upon" (Schoeneborn, 2005, p. 11).

It is still a little early to know what Luhmann's theory really will contribute to the study of organizational communication, in particular, whether it will provide any insights that cannot be gained just as readily from other theories in the field. Hendry and Seidl (2003), two management studies scholars, applied Luhmann's conception of episodes to strategic planning meetings. They concluded that Luhmann's theory is no better than other theories in solving certain kinds of problems in strategic change, but it does offer a better way to study these problems because it shifts the focus from the individual phenomena of cognitive processes to the social phenomena of communication processes. This conclusion may not be big news for scholars in the field of communication studies.

EVOLUTIONARY PSYCHOLOGY

As we noted in Chapter 1, traditional, interpretive, and critical perspectives on organizational communication do not agree on very much, but they do seem to embrace one common idea: human beings become what they are through learning, socialization, and acculturation. Generally, whether we are talking about human cooperation or human conflict, learning is the mechanism that is invoked to explain why human beings think, feel, and act as they do. We can call this the presumption of **environmental determinism**, i.e., the idea that who we are and what we do is a product of environmental influences, including the physical, social, and cultural environment. The most extreme version of environmental determinism is found in theories in which humans are described as little more than passive reactors to environmental stimuli (e.g., the behaviorist school of psychology represented by B. F. Skinner). Even those theories that regard human beings as active, choice-making agents situate that choice making within cultural constraints and implicitly privilege culture as the enabler of human action (Anderson, 1987).

Because environmental determinism is so thoroughly ingrained as a bedrock premise of modern social science, any suggestion that biology, genetics, and evolution might have something to do not just with the physical characteristics of human beings, but also with our psychological and, therefore, behavioral and social characteristics is met with scalding attacks, even by some prominent evolutionists such as Stephen Jay Gould (1978). But this is precisely the suggestion with which the field of **evolutionary psychology** confronts us.

We are well aware that the material in this section continues to be controversial. Graham Sewell (2004) blamed evolutionary psychology for "the rise of Flintstone psychological thinking in organization and management studies" (p. 923). Livia Markoczy and Jeffrey Goldberg (2004) in turn accused Sewell of misrepresenting the field. David Buller (2005) argued that the empirical evidence for discoveries claimed by evolutionary psychologists is, at best, inconclusive. Frank Miele (2005) complained in response that Buller argued "like a defense attorney" trying to cast doubt on particular pieces of evidence and offering "alternative interpretations as to what might have happened" (p. 61).

Controversy notwithstanding, there are two reasons to cover evolutionary psychology in a text on organizational communication. First, although the evidence favoring some claims in evolutionary psychology may be inconclusive, the basic premises of environmental determinism itself may be wrong (Pinker, 2002). Second, it is evident that evolutionary psychology is now being applied in organizational studies and organizational communication scholarship.

Nature Versus Nurture: A False Dichotomy?

The debate over the issues in this section often is presented as the "nature versus nurture" controversy, i.e., is behavior biologically determined (nature) or socially acquired (nurture)? Early in the 20th century, the nature point of view received a great deal of attention, especially in Europe, but misuses of the work, most notably in Nazi Germany, and plain factual errors in social Darwinism, led to widespread rejection of biological or genetic explanations of human action. American scholars, who favored nurture theories anyway, essentially dismissed any role for biology at all in understanding human society. But looking at the problem only in terms of these two alternatives (nature versus nurture) misrepresents the issue (Barlow, 1991; Pinker, 2002). Although some theorists absolutely insist that human behavior is entirely a sociocultural product that has no genetic, biological basis (e.g., Lewontin, 1977), others suggest that both biology and culture shape what we are (e.g., Bouchard & McGue, 1990; Nielsen, 1994; Udry, 1995). From this point of view, insightful and productive understanding of human behavior is found neither in environmental determinism nor in biological determinism, but in the interaction between environment and biology within an evolutionary framework. If the advocates of environmental-biological interaction are correct, the nature versus nurture dichotomy is simply false, and this is essentially the position that is taken by evolutionary psychologists.

The Theory of Evolutionary Psychology

One of the major premises in evolutionary psychology is that human behavior and, by extension, culture are influenced by **innate psychological mechanisms** in human beings that did not develop under modern conditions, but evolved into their present form during the Pleistocene Epoch, which ended more than 10,000 years ago (Tooby & Cosmides, 1989). Although cultural change began to move faster than biological evolution in the Neolithic (Stone Age) period, modern behavior is nonetheless evolutionarily patterned.

Initially, what we are talking about here is the human brain, i.e., what it is, how it functions, and how it got that way. Environmental determinism embraces a *tabula rasa* (blank slate) conception of the brain as "a general-purpose mechanism, ready for social programming at birth" (Teboul & Cole, 2005). In contrast, evolutionary psychology sees the brain as a collection of domain-general and domain-specific mechanisms adapted through evolution to handle the problems confronted by early human beings (Miele, 2005).

The idea of domain-general mechanisms is easy to grasp because these include obvious functions such as memory, reasoning, and concept formation. The idea of domain-specific mechanisms adapted through evolution in our Pleistocene ancestors is where the fundamental work of evolutionary psychology begins. Identifying Pleistocene mechanisms that might continue to reverberate in modern behavior is one of the primary tasks that evolutionary psychologists have set for their field, and that effort is ongoing. Here are a few examples of the adaptive mechanisms proposed in evolutionary psychology that also have been applied specifically in organizational studies:

- Primitive emotional contagion, where the emotional state of one individual is evoked among nearby individuals through a process of automatic, subconscious mimicry.
- Reciprocal altruism, the performance of unselfish acts for the benefit of others with some expectation that the recipients will return the favor in the future.
- Preference for similarity, the tendency to prefer association with others who are similar to us.
- Sensitivity to prestige hierarchies, showing deference to more valuable group members and accepting preferential access for those members to desirable resources.

Any of these four phenomena might be explained in terms of accounts grounded in cultural rather than evolutionary terms, so the first problem in evolutionary psychology is to show how and why they could have developed through evolution as adaptive mechanisms. Assuming the case can be made, the next problem is to show how these adaptations can account for modern behavior. We will describe two studies later to illustrate how these problems are addressed, specifically for the four mechanisms in the list.

Attributing predisposing influences on modern behavior to Pleistocene psychological mechanisms does not mean that our behavior is biologically determined, nor does it deny the significance of cultural dynamics in human experience. Even our primate cousins, the *Pan troglodytes* (chimpanzees), seem to exhibit primitive forms of social learning that are at least analogous to cultural transmission in human society, for example, tool use and food-gathering techniques (McGrew, 1994). On the other hand, biological accounts of human behavior take on intuitive appeal when we see that our primate cousins share some characteristics with us ranging from empathy and conflict mediation to dominance seeking and even murder of their own kind (Liska, 1990; Miller, 1995), especially when there is no evidence that the *Pan troglodytes* "learned" how to do these things.

The point of evolutionary psychology is that human behavior arises from an interaction of the present environment with the evolutionary heritage of a past epoch, i.e., the evolved and innate psychological mechanisms of the Pleistocene with which modern human beings come into the world fully equipped. As John Tooby and Leda Cosmides (1989) explain, "By directly regulating individual behavior and learning, these mechanisms directly govern cultural dynamics" (p. 30). This statement should not be misunderstood as an argument for biological determination. It is instead a claim that human beings construct the conditions of their cultures, and the constructing behavior is influenced by an essentially Pleistocene psyche.

Tooby and Cosmides have developed one of the foundation discussions of the theory of evolutionary psychology and the generation of human culture. To begin with, there appears to be no modern connection between evolutionary adaptation and cultural dynamics. Such an admission would make environmental determinists happy, but it is coupled with the observation that much so-called culturally constructed human behavior clearly is *not* adaptive or fitness promoting under modern conditions. On the other hand, such behaviors might be predicted quite well from a knowledge of underlying psychological mechanisms evolved at a time when they would have been adaptive. How does evolutionary psychology go about doing this? Here is a simplified version of the method Tooby and Cosmides describe.

1. Identify the adaptive problems that Pleistocene humans had to solve.

2. Determine as nearly as possible how these adaptive problems might have presented themselves under Pleistocene conditions.

3. Specify the information processing conditions that must be met to solve the adaptive problem.

4. Devise models of the cognitive structures that could have evolved to solve the problem.

5. Determine which is the best model.

6. Compare the model to behavior produced under modern conditions. If the model works, it should predict behaviors that are produced by information inputs in the modern environment.

The quality of studies employing the discipline of evolutionary psychology is, to put it charitably, highly variable. Tooby and Cosmides themselves caution that one cannot simply skip steps 2 through 5 by moving directly from step 1 to step 6, and some studies appear to short-cut the method in exactly this way. Well-constructed studies, however, have produced robust predictions and explanations of behavior in modern environments with hypotheses drawn from evolutionary assumptions (Buss & Reeve, 2003).

Examples in Organizational Communication

Studies in evolutionary psychology have involved many sociopsychological phenomena, but the only ones of relevance to us are those conducted in organizational environments or addressing processes that occur in organizational environments. We will consider two recent examples here.

The first example is a study of the significance of affect (emotion) in group bonding and communication (Spoor & Kelly, 2004). As attention to human emotion in fields of social and organizational studies has gained more traction, scholars have become interested in the effects of moods and emotions in small groups. Spoor and Kelly suggest that an examination of shared affective states (emotional contagion) and means of regulating affective states in groups can inform this line of work. More specifically, they suggest "that the experience of shared affective states . . . [and] mechanisms to regulate and maintain certain affective states in groups, developed because of their adaptive value" (p. 398).

From here, Spoor and Kelly work their way through a study procedure along the lines described by Tooby and Cosmides, but with a couple of exceptions. First, only one or two alternative mechanisms beyond those of primary interest get any mention, so there is not much choosing among alternatives. Second, there is no reference to affect anywhere in Tooby and Cosmides's protocol, but affect is what this study is all about. In essence, Spoor and Kelley reason through the ways in which emotional contagion, interaction synchrony (coordination of affect and attitudes), and affect regulation would have developed as evolutionary adaptations. For example, among other adaptive benefits, the essentially automatic process of primitive emotional contagion would enable rapid communication of negative affect in the presence of danger. Regulation of affective states could serve the adaptive function of communicating status differences.

Both of these examples involve communication. The authors also go through the same exercise for group bonding. Along the way, they tie their hypothesized functional adaptations of affect to contemporary findings in small-group studies to show how the findings can be explained in terms of the adaptive mechanisms. Their illustrations include studies of emotional contagion ranging from evidence of how primitive contagion occurs in modern groups to findings such as the tendency of positive emotional contagion to improve cooperation and reduce conflict in teams. Other research examples include studies of emotional convergence in status-defined interpersonal relationships in which lower status partners did more of the converging and studies demonstrating the contribution of homogeneous affect to group stability and bonding.

The second example is a project to construct a model of organizational relationship development with predictions derived from modern manifestations of three specific adaptations attributed to early hominids: reciprocal altruism, preference for similarity, and sensitivity to prestige hierarchies (Teboul & Cole, 2005).

There is nothing novel about the ideas of reciprocal exchange, association based on similarity, and status hierarchies in modern society, but Teboul and Cole (2005) suggest that their origins are anything but modern. Hunter-gatherer societies with mutual interdependencies must have confronted problems of resource variability and scarcity. Survival depended on cognitive adaptations that responded to these problems, including among others "this for that" social exchange where "this" is offered in the present and the expected reciprocation of "that" is somewhere off in the future. Some kinds of transactions defy this model, i.e., helping persons in dire need with no little or no expectation of a return, but a different kind of adaptive mechanism presumably explains this behavior.

Early humans also faced the problem of coordinating their efforts in hunting, defending, gathering, and other cooperative tasks. If survival depended on successful coordination of collective endeavors, what adaptations occurred to effect such coordination? Teboul and Cole (2005) offer preference for similarity as one likely candidate because similarity would facilitate "development of mutual knowledge, which is essential to joint coordination" (p. 394). Evidence of this preference among humans in a range of modern research certainly does not mean that it is Pleistocene in origin, but if it was an evolutionary adaptation, it certainly is still around.

The same may be said for prestige hierarchy, and this may be the easiest of the three mechanisms to grasp inasmuch as hierarchy is evident in many domains of the animal world and pervasive in the world of primates and humans. Deference to superiors and acceptance of preferential access to desirable resources for members who are most valuable to group survival would have been functional adaptations among early hominids. Teboul and Cole cite reviews of anthropological and ethnographic records suggesting "that social groups completely devoid of prestige hierarchies of some sort have likely never existed" (p. 395). Of course, we do not always defer to the boss. But, then, neither do chimps.

Teboul and Cole weave together a rationale from these three adaptive mechanisms to make some specific predictions about relationship formation in modern organizations. Specifically, we will seek out relationships with the highest complements and highest similars available to us. Complementary relationships help us with resources. Similar relationships help us with coordination. And links to higher status individuals have more value in general. In this process, we also will differentiate between high-preference partners and low-preference partners. Seeking is, of course, not the same thing as gaining, and this model as well as its application depend on the word "available."

The authors continue the article at some length, using the predictions to explain what occurs at various stages of relationship development, suggesting evidence for the model in modern behavior, showing how the model accounts for findings in contemporary studies, and describing how it might be used in the future to generate additional knowledge about the development of organizational relationships.

SUMMARY

Several theories of organization or with the potential for application to organizational communication embrace metaphors drawn from biology or use biological principles literally in their explanations of behavior. These theories are not concerned with the managerial problem of member motivation in and of itself, but with the broader problem of understanding the structure, function, and development of human systems and the people who constitute these systems.

System theories, which view organizations as adaptive organisms rather than machines, gained wide acceptance during the 1960s in the wake of Bertalanffy's general system theory. System theories attempt to describe and explain how organizations function from the standpoint of some very general principles that are presumed to apply to all systems. These general principles include wholeness, hierarchy, openness, and feedback.

Following system theory, Weick theorizes that organizing and communicating activities are directed toward the reduction of equivocality in information. Where information has little equivocality, organizations can rely heavily on rules to guide their responses. As equivocality increases, organizations are less able to rely on rules. As equivocality increases, more communicative effort is required to respond to it. Weick discussed communication as an interlocked behavior cycle, which consists of a double-interact. As equivocality increases, we are less able to rely on rules to handle the situation and must rely on more cycles.

Weick uses an evolutionary metaphor with the concepts of enactment, selection, and retention. We attend actively to the environment, recognizing the level of equivocality in the information. The selection phase begins when we make decisions about the rules and interlocked (communication) cycles that we will use to manage the equivocality. Cycles that reduce equivocality are retained for future use.

Luhmann argues in his social systems theory that social systems literally are composed of communications, not of members and actions. Communications themselves determine what further communications occur, i.e., the communication system is self-reproducing.

The idea of episodes is important in Luhmann's theory. For Luhmann, an episode is nothing but a sequence of communications with a beginning and an end. An episode is recognized by the *structure* of its communications. Structure includes conditions that define what is possible in the episode at its beginning, at its end, and between those two markers. Structure in this sense both constrains and enables communication.

Luhmann also treats communications as decisions. Decisions involve contingencies, i.e., things that could happen, but are not necessarily certain to happen. Decisions are always contingent in the sense that we picked one alternative, but we could have picked another. Communicating a decision requires communicating rejected alternatives and creates possibilities for additional decisions.

Evolutionary psychology starts with the premise that human behavior and, by extension, culture are influenced by innate psychological mechanisms in human beings that did not develop under modern conditions, but evolved into their present form during the Pleistocene Epoch. Studies in evolutionary psychology attempt to identify Pleistocene mechanisms that might continue to reverberate in modern behavior, for example, primitive emotional contagion, reciprocal altruism, preference for similarity, and sensitivity to prestige hierarchies. These concepts have been applied to organizational communication in areas such as effects of emotions in small group and relationship development in organizational settings.

DISCUSSION QUESTIONS/ACTIVITIES

1. Observe the work of a task group at work on some sort of project, e.g., for a student organization. Is the group more like a machine or more like an organism? How well do the principles of system theory characterize the group and its processes?

2. In the same group observation above, how much of the communicative effort is directed toward managing or reducing equivocality? What kinds of conditions create equivocality for the group, and how well does Weick's theory explain the group's effort to manage equivocality?

3. The subjects of sociobiology and evolutionary psychology are rather controversial. Have a class or group discussion on this topic. From what you have read in this chapter, what are the arguments for and against biological accounts of human behavior, including organizational behavior. The Studd and Gattiker (1991) study of sexual harassment may provide a good object for discussion.

REFERENCES

Anderson, J. A. (1987). *Communication research: Issues and methods.* New York: McGraw-Hill.
Bertalanffy, L. von. (1956). General system theory. *General Systems, 1,* 1.
Bertalanffy, L. von. (1968). *General system theory.* New York: George Braziller.
Barlow, G. W. (1991). Nature-nurture and the debates surrounding ethology and sociobiology. *American Zoologist, 31,* 286–296.

Bouchard, T. J., Jr., & McGue, M. (1990). Genetic and rearing environmental influences on adult personality: An analysis of adopted twins reared apart. *Journal of Personality, 58*, 263–292.

Buller, D. J. (2005). Evolutionary psychology: The emperor's new paradigm. *Trends in Cognitive Sciences, 9*(6), 277–283.

Buss, D. M., & Reeve, H. K. (2003). Evolutionary psychology and developmental dynamics: Comment on Lickliter and Honeycutt (2003). *Psychological Bulletin, 129*(6), 848–853.

Cabezas, H., Pawlowski, C. W., Mayer, A. L., & Hoagland, N. T. (2005). Sustainable systems theory: Ecological and other aspects. *Journal of Cleaner Production, 13*(5), 455–467.

Campbell, D. T. (1965). Variations and selective retention in socio-cultural evolution. In H. R. Barringer, G. I. Blanksten, & R. W. Mack (Eds.), *Social change in developing areas: A reinterpretation of evolutionary theory* (pp. 19–49). Cambridge, MA: Schenkman.

Capps, C. J., & Hazen, S. E. (2002). Applying general systems theory to the strategic scanning of the environment from 2015 to 2050. *International Journal of Management, 19*(2), 308–315.

CBS News (2005, November 3). Brown: 'Can I go home?' Retrieved June 11, 2007, from http://www.cbsnews.com/stories/2005/11/03/national/main1009209.shtml

Daneke, G. A. (2005). The reluctant resurrection: New complexity methods and old systems theories. *Journal of Public Administration, 28,* 89–106.

D'Aprix, R. (1982). *Communicating for productivity.* New York: Harper & Row.

Dessler, G. (1980). *Organization theory: Integrating structure and behavior.* Englewood Cliffs, NJ: Prentice Hall.

Eisenberg, E. M. (1984). Ambiguity as a strategy in organizational communication. *Communication Monographs, 51,* 227–242.

Eisenberg, E. M., & Goodall, H. L., Jr. (1993). *Organizational communication: Balancing creativity and constraint.* New York: St. Martin's.

Farace, R. V., Monge, P. R., & Russell, H. M. (1977). *Communicating and organizing.* Reading, MA: Addison-Wesley.

Gould, S. J. (1978). Review of *On human nature* by E. O. Wilson. *Human Nature, 1,* 20–28.

Hendry, J., & Seidl, D. (2003). The structure and significance of strategic episodes: Social systems theory and the routine practices of strategic change. *Journal of Management Studies, 40*(1), 175–196.

Huse, E. F., & Bowditch, J. L. (1973). *Behavior in organizations: A systems approach to managing.* Reading, MA: Addison-Wesley.

Katz, D., & Kahn, R. (1966). *The social psychology of organizations.* New York: John Wiley & Sons.

Konopaske, R., Robie, C., & Ivancevich, J. M. (2005). A preliminary model of spouse influence on managerial global assignment willingness. *International Journal of Human Resource Management, 16*(3), 405–426.

Kreps, G. L. (1990). *Organizational communication: Theory and practice* (2nd ed.). New York: Longman.

Lawrence, P., & Lorsch, J. (1969). *Organization and environment: Managing differentiation and integration.* Homewood, IL: Irwin.

Lee, J., & Jablin, F. M. (1995). Maintenance communication in superior-subordinate work relationships. *Human Communication Research, 22,* 220–257.

Lewontin, R. (1977). Biological determinism as an ideological weapon. *Science for People, 9,* 36–38.

Liska, J. (1990). Dominance-seeking strategies in primates: An evolutionary perspective. *Human Evolution, 5,* 75–90.

Littlejohn, S. W. (1992). *Theories of human communication* (4th ed.). Belmont, CA: Wadsworth.

Luhmann, N. (1986). The autopoiesis of social systems. In G. Geyer & J. Van den Zeuwen (Eds.), *Sociocybernetic paradoxes: Observation, control and evolution of self-steering systems* (pp. 172–192). London: Sage.

Luhmann, N. (1989). Law as a social system. *Northwestern University Law Review, 83,* 136–150.

Luhmann, N. (1995). *Social systems.* Stanford, CA: Stanford University Press.

March, J., & Simon, H. (1958). *Organizations.* New York: John Wiley & Sons.

Markoczy, L., & Goldberg, J. (2004). Yabba-dabba-doo! A response to unfair accusations. *Human Relations, 57*(8), 1037–1046.

McGrew, W. C. (1994). Tools compared: The material of culture. In R. W. Wrangham, W. C. McGrew, F. B. M. de Waal, & P. G. Heltne (Eds.), *Chimpanzee culture* (pp. 25–40). Cambridge, MA: Harvard University Press.

McPhee, R., & Zaug, P. (2000). *The communicative constitution of organizations: A framework for explanation.* Paper presented to the annual conference of the Western States Communication Association, Sacramento, CA, April 2000.

Mee, J. (1964). Matrix organizations. *Business Horizons, 7,* 70–72.

Miele, F. (2005). Evolutionary psychology is here to stay: A response to Buller. *Skeptic, 12*(1), 57–61.

Miller, P. (1995, December). Crusading for chimps and humans . . . Jane Goodall. *National Geographic, 188,* 102–128.

Monge, P. R. (1982). System theory and research in the study of organizational communication: The correspondence problem. *Human Communication Research, 8,* 245–261.

Monge, P. R., Farace, R. L., Eisenberg, E. M., Miller, K. I., & White, L. L. (1984). The process of studying process in organizational communication. *Journal of Communication, 34,* 22–43.

Nielsen, F. (1994). Sociobiology and sociology. *Annual Review of Sociology, 20,* 267–303.

Pearce, W. B., & Cronen, V. (1980). *Communication, action, and meaning.* New York: Praeger.

Pinker, S. (2002). *The blank slate: The modern denial of human nature.* New York: Penguin.

Richardson, K. A. (2004). Systems theory and complexity: Part 1. *E:CO, 6,* 75–79.

Schoeneborn, D. (2005). *Organizations as communications: Examining the value of Luhmann's social systems theory for organizational communication research.* Paper presented at the annual meeting of the International Communication Association, New York, NY, May 2005.

Sewell, G. (2004). Yabba-dabba-doo! Evolutionary psychology and the rise of Flintstone psychological thinking in organization and management studies. *Human Relations, 57*(8), 923–955.

Spoor, J. R., & Kelly, R. (2004). The evolutionary significance of affect in groups: Communication and group bonding. *Group Processes & Intergroup Relations, 7*(4), 398–412.

Studd, M. V., & Gattiker, U. E. (1991). The evolutionary psychology of sexual harassment in organizations. *Ethology and Sociobiology, 12,* 249–290.

Teboul, J. C. B., & Cole, T. (2005). Relationship development and workplace integration: An evolutionary perspective. *Communication Theory, 15*(4), 389–413.

Tooby, J., & Cosmides, L. (1989). Evolutionary psychology and the generation of culture, Part I: Theoretical considerations. *Ethology and Sociobiology, 10,* 29–49.

Udry, J. R. (1995). Sociology and biology: What biology do sociologists need to know? *Social Forces, 37,* 1267–1278.

Weick, K. (1979). *The social psychology of organizing* (2nd ed.). Reading, MA: Addison-Wesley.

Woodward, J. (1958). *Management and technology.* London: Her Majesty's Stationery Office.

CHAPTER 6

Organization Theory

Communication and Culture

Chapter Outline

COMMUNICATION AND CULTURE: A WAY TO UNDERSTAND ORGANIZATIONS
    Traditionalist Perspective
    Interpretivist Perspective
    Critical-Interpretivist Perspective
    Merging Perspectives

APPROACHES TO UNDERSTANDING ORGANIZATIONAL CULTURE
    Language and Worldview
    Knowledge Structures
    Consensual and Contested Meanings
    Multiple Cultures Perspective
    Metaphors
    Narratives
    Rites and Ceremonies
    Reflexive Comments
    Fantasy Themes

DESCRIBING ORGANIZATIONAL CULTURE: THE CASE OF BEN & JERRY'S

Although the study of culture is a longstanding tradition in the field of anthropology, the concept of **organizational culture** is a relatively recent development. Many scholars and practitioners have become intrigued with the idea that organizations have cultural features. Some even assert that an organization literally is a culture and that organizational communication is a *performance* of this culture (Pacanowsky & O'Donnell-Trujillo, 1984). One very popular cultural perspective of organizations is presented in Deal and Kennedy's (1982)

Corporate Cultures. Wright's (1979) *On a Clear Day, You Can See General Motors*, Maccoby's (1976) *The Gamesmen*, and Kanter's (1977) *Men and Women of the Corporation* also have been called studies of organizational culture. What comes to mind when you think about the word culture? Do you think of the history, values, beliefs, language, and modes of expression as part of the culture of a particular people or nation? Or do you think of culture as their customs, folklore, and artifacts? If you associate any of these elements with culture, you have at least some sense of the concepts that have been used to study and understand cultures. In this chapter, we describe the concept of organizational culture, traditionalist, interpretivist, and critical-interpretivist perspectives of culture, and some communication-based approaches to understanding organizational culture.

COMMUNICATION AND CULTURE: A WAY TO UNDERSTAND ORGANIZATIONS

Viewing organizations as cultures may be considered a perspective on par with our other theory chapters. In order to justify this stance, let us return to the work of George Herbert Mead (1934) and Berger and Luckmann (1966) that we reviewed in Chapter 2. The symbolic interaction perspective (Mead, 1934) and the social construction perspective (Berger & Luckmann, 1966) underlie much of the organizational culture literature. By incorporating these perspectives into an understanding of organizational cultures, we align ourselves with Denison (1996), who observed that the individual "cannot be analytically separated from the environment and that the members of social systems are best regarded as agents and subjects simultaneously" (p. 635). Thus, when attempting to understand a given social context, we must recognize that social context is both the medium and the outcome of communication among system members. So, instead of arguing that an organizational system affects its members, cultural theorists claim we must focus on the recursive dynamics between the individual and the system (Denison, 1996). In other words, through communication organization, members create and recreate the system that becomes their social context. This context influences how they interpret their experiences and how they carry out actions. However, just as communication creates a given social context, members may change that context through communication (Giddens, 1979; Lave & Wenger, 1990; Riley, 1983).

By embedding our understanding of organizational culture within symbolic interactionist and social constructivist frameworks, we gain insight into how social processes evolve over time. Through communication over time organization members simultaneously create meaning and social structure. This communication establishes interaction patterns that evolve into systems of normative control that guide member actions.

In a fundamental sense, a culture exists when people come to share a common frame of reference for interpreting and acting toward one another and the world in which they live. This common frame of reference includes language, values, beliefs, and interpretations of experience. It is reflected in customs, folkways, communication, and other observable features of the community, including rites, rituals, celebrations, legends, myths, and heroic sagas (Bormann, Howell, Nichols, & Shapiro, 1982).

For many years, anthropologists have used the concept of culture to study nations, communities, and even tribal groups, but the discipline of anthropology has never settled on a uniform definition of culture. The term is used in several different ways. The same problem occurs in organizational studies. Although there is consensus among scholars in various fields that the concept of culture can be applied to organizations, there are different ways of defining organizational culture.

Eisenberg and Goodall (1993), two organizational communication scholars, define culture primarily in terms of practices rather than values. Claiming that anthropologists have rejected the idea of culture as shared meaning, they say, "nothing in the culture metaphor requires that values be shared" (p. 152). In contrast, anthropologist W. A. Haviland (1993) says, "Culture consists of the abstract values, beliefs, and perceptions that lie behind people's behavior. . . . They are shared by members of a society, and when acted on, produce behavior considered to be acceptable within that society" (p. 29).

Haviland's definition of culture differs sharply from the conception presented by Eisenberg and Goodall, but these positions are not as contradictory as they might appear to be at first glance. Just as shared meaning is essential to communication, Haviland makes it clear that shared values are essential to culture. The claim that anthropologists have rejected this idea may be overstated. Even so, the presence of enough commonality in meaning and values to sustain communication and culture still leaves plenty of room for ambiguity, conflict, pluralistic ignorance, and false consensus between many different organizational groups and constituencies. Organizational culture arises from a dynamic tension and interplay among these groups. Culture may depend on shared values, but it is also an ongoing dialogue among diverse subcultures (Clifford, 1983; Eisenberg & Goodall, 1993).

The concept of subcultures is particularly important to consider when describing an organization's culture. The stance we adopt here is that an organization's culture is not a monolithic form controlled from above by managers and owners. Although managers and corporate owners play an important role in shaping or influencing an organization's culture, it is also necessary to examine the role employees play in creating and sustaining culture through their interactions with one another at work. In order to clarify the stance we take here, let's consider one of Clifford Geertz's (1973) observations in the book *The Interpretation of Cultures*. Geertz argued that "man is an animal suspended in webs of significance he himself has spun . . . culture [is] those webs" (p. 5). As webs, cultures are spun continuously as people within a social system interact with one another and create their own rules and norms. Interestingly, the webs spun by cultural members are both confining and mobilizing. Just as a web confines a spider's movement to the area traversed by the web, an organization's culture restricts worker actions to those considered acceptable by the norms and rules within the system. However, webs are not only confining, they also make movement for the spider possible. This is also true of the webs spun by employees interacting with one another at work. The webs spun within an organization empower employees to act in ways legitimized by their collectively created culture. Finally, webs are places of struggle where spiders attack their prey. Likewise, when organization members spin their cultural webs, there may be struggles over meaning and the construction of one type of culture rather than another.

We would like to extend Geertz's metaphor by describing an organization's culture as a collection of interconnected webs. These interconnected webs represent subcultures within the organization. Each subculture is somewhat unique because of the particular workers it comprises; however, because the subcultures are interconnected and embedded within a single organization, they also share certain characteristic features and commonly held meanings or interpretations.

Viewing subcultures from a social construction framework raises interesting questions about organizational politics and ideology. For example, when multiple subcultures exist within an organization, what group "controls" the organizational social context? Denison (1996) explains:

> [I]t is far less clear who is in "control" of the organizational context. Top management? Labor? Bioengineers? New executives from the consumer goods industry? The Dutch? Men? Women? Blacks? Whites? New Yorkers? Californians? In short, with social construction as an organizing framework, competing cultural influences are engaged in a power struggle to define the organizational culture. (p. 640)

Recognizing the many subcultures that exist in any large organization, we need to consider the fact that organizational culture is actually a "contested reality" (Jermier, 1991). Once we accept this position, subcultures may be of as much interest as attempting to describe overarching organizational cultures is. In order to understand and describe these individual subcultures, we must conduct research at a level that allows us to understand individual meaning and organizational symbolism (Denison, 1996). Geertz (1973) refers to this process as *thick description* or "an elaborate venture in" (p. 25). Focusing on the act of "winking," Geertz describes how to distinguish winking as an involuntary twitch from a social gesture with a specific meaning. In order to do this

> We must move beyond the action to both the particular social understanding of the *winking* as a gesture, the state of mind of the winker, his/her audience, and how they construe the meaning of the winking action itself. *Thin description* is the winking. *Thick* is the meaning behind it and its symbolic import in society or between communicators. (p. 27)

Traditionalist, interpretivist, and critical-interpretivist scholars have written about and produced studies of organizational culture, but these three groups understand organizational culture in very different ways. To the traditionalist, a culture is something that an organization has—a set of characteristics that the organization possesses. The interpretivist and the critical-interpretivist see culture as what the organization *is*—the essence of organizational life. However, whereas the pure interpretivist is content to describe an organization's culture, the critical-interpretivist describes and evaluates cultures by focusing on power struggles among competing groups. The basic differences among the three approaches to organizational culture are summarized in Table 6.1.

TABLE 6.1   Comparison of Traditionalist, Interpretivist, and Critical-Interpretivist Orientations to Organizational Culture

	Traditionalism	*Interpretivism*	*Critical-Interpretivism*
Goals	Develop and change organizational culture to produce organizational effectiveness	Describe organizational culture according to the meanings that it makes possible to members	Describe and critique organizational culture according to meanings generated by members to uncover sources of oppression in systems of language, meaning, and organizational structure, and identify paths to member emancipation
Definition of Culture	Artifacts of organizational life such as stories, myths, legends, rituals, documents, and symbols	Common interpretive frame of reference; a network of shared meanings	Sites of power struggle revealed through discourse and organizational structure and focused on the interests of managers, employees, and external constituents
Activities	Promote managerial control over cultural artifacts through management of symbolism	Study meanings and themes in members' organizational sense making, as revealed in symbolic discourse	Critique the power struggles among managers, employees, and external constituents for the purpose of revealing paths to emancipation for the oppressed

Traditionalist Perspective

According to Smircich (1981), traditionalism (also called functionalism) has always been concerned with the actions that organizations can take to ensure their "continued survival in an essentially competitive situation" (p. 3). This translates into discovering the right combinations of organizational variables that promote effectiveness. Consequently, traditionalist research is characterized by studies of variables such as structure, size, technology, leadership, and communication. Eventually, traditionalists added cultural variables to those that they typically study in recognition that organizations produce not only goods and services, but also "cultural artifacts, e.g., stories, myths, legends, rituals, that are distinctive" (p. 3).

The kinds of artifacts that Smircich identified are, in effect, the concrete, objective features of a culture. Traditionalists study these artifacts in much the same way that they would study any other observable feature of organizational behavior. In line with their traditional concern for regulation of organizational processes, traditionalists usually want to know how to develop and change an organizational culture in order to make the organization more effective. Strategies for change usually emphasize managerial control over the observable features of culture (e.g., goals, practices, language, rites, rituals, sagas, and the content of orientation and indoctrination programs).

Deal and Kennedy's *Corporate Cultures* (1982), a very popular book in business circles during the early 1980s, provides an interesting example of the traditionalist viewpoint. Deal and Kennedy regard organizational culture as a kind of identity for a corporation. Management is supposed to develop and foster commitment to this identity by propagating desired beliefs and informal rules that influence behavior, by celebrating desired organizational values through rites and rituals, and by creating legends through sagas that glorify the adventures, exploits, and successes of organizational heroes and heroines.

According to Deal and Kennedy, corporate executives should try to build a "strong" culture for two reasons. First, organizational effectiveness can be increased simply by letting employees know what is expected of them. A strong culture provides this information both formally and informally. Second, a strong culture "enables people to feel better about what they do, so they are more likely to work harder" (p. 16). For example, the use of rites, rituals, and sagas helps to legitimize and justify various forms of organizational behavior by answering such questions as: Who are we? What do we do? Why are we here? (Bormann et al., 1982).

What is a strong culture? For Deal and Kennedy, strong culture means a highly cohesive organization in which members are fully committed to organizational goals. In their words, a strong culture exists only when "everyone knows the goals . . . and they are working for them" (1982, p. 4). It follows then, in Deal and Kennedy's view, that organizations characterized by competing values and divided loyalties have "weak" and fragmented cultures.

Interpretivist Perspective

Like the traditionalist, the interpretivist also is concerned with uncovering the frame of reference shared by organization members, but the interpretivist understands this frame of reference in a different way. Smircich (1981) describes the difference between traditionalist and interpretivist ideas about organizational culture:

> Social action becomes possible because of consensually determined meanings for experiences that to an external observer may have the appearance of an independent rule like existence. What looks like an objective and real world to the [traditionalist] researcher is seen by the interpretivist researcher to be a product of interaction processes whereby meanings for experience are negotiated and then continually sustained through the course of interaction. (pp. 5–6)

In other words, the observable, tangible world of social action (i.e., behavior) is based on organization members' sharing of subjective meanings. To the interpretivist, organizational culture is understood only as a network of shared meanings. Consequently, the interpretivist describes organizational culture according to the meanings that it makes possible for its members and the ways in which the culture itself is enacted or "performed" through communication (Pacanowsky & O'Donnell-Trujillo, 1982).

Interpretive studies of organizational culture are characterized by an explicit focus on symbols and themes that are revealed in symbolic discourse (communication). According to Smircich, these themes "show the ways the symbols are linked into meaningful relationships . . . they specify the links between values, beliefs, and actions" (1981, p. 7). Presumably, the interpretive researcher is primarily concerned with revealing these linkages rather than with connecting organizational culture with traditionalist concerns for organizational efficiency and effectiveness.

Critical-Interpretivist Perspective

The most recent development in understanding and studying organizational culture has been to combine the theories and methods associated with the interpretive and critical perspectives (see, e.g., Barker, 1993; Barker & Cheney, 1994; Papa, Auwal, & Singhal, 1995, 1997). Critical-interpretive researchers start with the premise that organizations are places where members develop shared and conflicting meanings to accomplish individual and organizational goals. Of course, this stance is not radically different than that advocated by many interpretivists. What separates the two interpretive approaches is that critical-interpretivists also view organizations as places of struggle over competing meaning systems. In this power struggle, certain groups (e.g., managers and owners) are privileged, meaning they receive the majority of the benefits associated with organizational membership. Other groups (e.g., nonmanagement personnel) are disadvantaged, meaning they receive fewer benefits while absorbing a higher level of the costs associated with organizational membership.

In order to clarify the approach taken by critical-interpretivists, let's consider an example. A group of managers within a large manufacturing company have become worried over a downturn in sales during the past year. These managers and their subordinates meet to decide how to address the problem of diminishing sales. During this meeting, the two groups decide mutually that in order to remain competitive in their industry and meet the demands of consumers, worker performance must increase in terms of quantity and quality of output. The managers are happy to receive the agreement of their workers on this issue, and the workers accept the fact that they must work more diligently in order to receive positive performance evaluations and contribute to organizational goals. However, whose interests are being served best by this decision? The increase in task performance does not bring with it an increase in pay because that would increase the organization's overhead costs.

Furthermore, not only are these workers required to work more diligently, there is an expectation that they work overtime (without increased pay) in order to meet performance goals. Contrasting this expectation for higher worker output, managers do not increase their level of task performance. Their job is to oversee the workers to ensure that performance goals are met. The critical-interpretive researcher would draw attention to the imbalances created by the new work rules.

One question this researcher would pose is: Why don't managers and workers share equally in the burden of increased performance? Another question is: Who receives most of the economic benefits of increased production? If the organization generates more income from increased worker performance, shouldn't workers receive a share of this added income? Of course workers must surrender some of their individual goals in order to receive the benefits (e.g., salary, prestige, power, etc.) of organizational membership; however, at what point are the benefits of membership outweighed by the costs of continued participation? By addressing such questions and making employees aware of alternative interpretations of the rules and norms they create and sustain for one another, potential paths to empowerment and emancipation may be identified. For example, how can new technological equipment increase task performance without requiring workers to work overtime? How can manager contributions to increased performance expectations reduce the pressure placed on their subordinates? Thus, through focusing on worker conversations and interpreting their experiences, stories, and metaphors, the critical-interpretivist identifies sources of struggle between opposing groups and opportunities for change and empowerment for the oppressed.

Merging Perspectives

The more researchers attempt to describe organizational culture, the more they recognize that a combination of forces accounts for the emergence and evolution of culture over time. This combination of forces can perhaps best be accounted for by turning to the work of traditionalists *and* critical-interpretivists. This view is not a new one. In one of the first articles written about organizational culture in the field of communication, Pacanowsky and O'Donnell-Trujillo (1982) argued that a quantitative assessment of employee perceptions about aspects of organizational communication could be combined with in-depth examinations of employee interpretations of organizational rites, rituals, stories, myths, and metaphors. The quantitative assessment of employee perceptions of communication factors is more consistent with the traditionalist approach, whereas the qualitative assessment of employee interpretations is more consistent with the interpretive approach.

One compelling reason for combining traditionalist and critical-interpretivist approaches to organizational culture analysis is to improve the accuracy of the overall cultural assessment that is offered. Traditionalists often use survey questionnaires with objective items to tap employee perceptions of communication in their organizations. These questionnaires can be completed relatively quickly by employees and they do not require a great amount of time to administer and score. Because of the ease associated with survey administration and scoring, hundreds or thousands of surveys can be distributed and examined. The results obtained from these surveys can then be used to guide the observations and questions subsequently asked by the critical-interpretive researcher. Also, critical-interpretive researchers can use the results obtained from survey questionnaires to guide their selection of certain groups of employees for in-depth interviews. The purpose of these in-depth interviews is to gain a more complete understanding of the struggles over competing meaning systems that are present within the organization.

In-depth interviews and detailed observations of employees at work take a substantial amount of time, thereby limiting the number of employees that can be included in any critical cultural analysis. Indeed, it is rare for a critical-interpretive researcher to interview as many as 100 employees. This raises an important question: How can the critical-interpretive researcher feel confident in the questions he or she asks and in the particular employees chosen for interviews? By relying on results obtained from survey questionnaires, critical-interpretive researchers can feel more confident in the decisions they make in the field.

In advancing our argument for merging perspectives, we purposefully exclude *pure* interpretivists from consideration. We do so because a comparison of interpretivism with critical-interpretivism shows that both approaches use similar methods of communication analysis and both take the stance that culture is the essence of organizational life. What separates the two approaches is the critical-interpretivists' belief that competing meaning systems create power struggles within organizations. Because we believe that power struggles exist in all organizations (an issue explained more fully in Chapter 11), we turn to the more embracing approach to cultural analysis that the critical-interpretivists provide. So, in order to understand how researchers from these two perspectives can make important contributions to our understanding of organizational culture, let us return briefly to the premises linked to each one.

As explained earlier, traditionalists are usually concerned with how to develop and change an organization's culture in order to make the organization more effective. Strategies for development and change emphasize managerial control over the observable features of a culture such as rites, rituals, stories, metaphors, and work practices. The stance we advocate here is that this approach yields important insights into an organization's culture. Clearly, managers or owners of an organization have an incentive for creating and sustaining a culture that preserves their interests for profit and organizational survival. For example, Shockley-Zalabak and Morley (1994) point out that the founders of an organization "create a set of personal values that results in the development of the initial organizational rules specifying the way organizations should and should not be" (p. 353). Among the many important concerns of founders is how to create a productive work culture that allows the organization to survive and earn profits. Of course, such concerns are not exclusively negative for employees. The founders could decide that on-site daycare facilities meet the needs of working mothers and fathers and reduce worker lateness and absenteeism linked to child-care needs. Such decisions and actions are a central part of an organization's culture and can be examined from the traditionalist perspective.

Critical-interpretivists, on the other hand, believe that organizational culture emerges primarily through the practices and interactions of people at work. As employees talk with one another, they form and sustain interpersonal relationships that influence how they view working for an organization. Some of these conversations may focus on rules and norms created by company founders or particular managers, whereas other conversations deal with performing specific work tasks. During the course of the workday, employees also talk about social matters, personal problems, and after-work activities. Importantly, all of these conversations shape worker experiences, and excluding them from consideration would result in an incomplete picture of any organization's culture. As employees talk with one another, they figure out how to cope with company rules, they learn to enjoy or despise their coworkers, and they form judgments about the value of continuing their organizational membership. Thus, critical-interpretivists provide us with information that is vital to understanding how workers understand organizational culture.

Critical-interpretivists also draw our attention to the struggles that exist between different groups and organization members. Organizations are places where resources, rewards, and punishments are distributed differentially depending on one's place within the system. Company owners and managers receive more of the monetary rewards and are more likely to have favorable working conditions. Nonmanagement employees compete over what rewards remain after managers and owners have received their share, and they have to accept directives received from management in order to receive rewards and advance within the company. The critical-interpretivist draws attention to the fact that the distribution of resources, rewards, and punishments creates struggles between organization members and groups. Some members and groups are more likely to receive benefits, whereas others are more likely to absorb costs. The struggles that occur between these members and groups constitute a central feature of organizational life that cannot be ignored. On the basis of the preceding observations, we argue that any holistic description of an organization's culture needs to draw on the theories and methods linked to traditionalism and critical-interpretivism.

Barker and Tompkins (1994) provide us with an excellent example of a study that merges the traditional and critical-interpretive perspectives. They examined characteristics of worker identification (e.g., loyalty) with self-managed work teams. Working within the traditionalist framework, the authors administered a 33-item questionnaire to 68 employees of a small manufacturing company. This questionnaire tapped worker levels of identification with their work teams and with their organization.

In addition to administering their questionnaire, Barker and Tompkins integrated observations and interviews with employees that took place over a 2-1/2 year period. The approach they took is referred to as ethnographic data collection. Before continuing to describe their study, let's take a moment to describe the practice of ethnography. This form of data collection and assessment involves a written representation of selected aspects of an organization's culture based primarily on field study (see, e.g., Patton, 1990; Van Maanen, 1988). When studying employee behavior in the field, researchers engage in what is called participant observation. As participant observers, researchers attempt to interpret cultural members' experiences from their frame of reference rather than offering objective or detached assessments of those experiences. Also, participant observers recognize that their presence within an organization can alter members' perceptions of their surroundings and can influence their behavior. Keeping these challenges in mind, ethnographers try to offer interpretations that reflect how employees perceive their organizational experiences. How do ethnographers accomplish this goal? Ethnographers offer detailed observations of employee behavior in task and social settings. They focus on employee stories, accounts, and metaphors, and they examine their rites and rituals as they are performed. In addition, ethnographers involve themselves in conversations with organization members and conduct in-depth interviews to gain insight into member perceptions and experiences.

In the Barker and Tompkins (1994) study, Barker was primarily responsible for ethnographic data collection. Over a 2-1/2 year period, he spent a total of 275 hours at the small manufacturing company that was the focus of the study. He conducted 37 in-depth interviews that ranged from as short as 45 minutes to as long as 2 hours. Barker also observed and recorded team and company meetings, and examined company memos, flyers, newsletters, and in-house surveys. On the basis of this extensive process of data collection and analysis, Barker and Tompkins drew three conclusions: (a) workers identify more strongly with their work teams than with their company, (b) long-term workers identify more strongly with both their team and their company than short-term workers do, and (c) team-based systems of worker surveillance and concertive control are more powerful than bureaucratic systems of control. What Barker and Tompkins mean by concertive control is a control system designed and enforced by nonmanagement employees working in concert with one another.

APPROACHES TO UNDERSTANDING ORGANIZATIONAL CULTURE

Although the methods of traditionalism and interpretivism can be combined in studying organizational communication (see, e.g., Barker & Tompkins, 1994; Faules, 1982; Gioia & Pitre, 1990; Papa et al, 1995; Shockley-Zalabak & Morley, 1994), many of the ideas associated with the study of organizational culture are new to traditionalism. Traditionalism is usually concerned with developing general knowledge about relationships among organizational communication variables with data drawn from many types of organizations (e.g., the relationship between openness and job satisfaction in superior-subordinate communication or the effects of different problem-solving methods on group effectiveness). The methods usually are quantitative and statistical. There are some qualitative traditionalist studies of organizational culture, but these studies are scientific classifications of observable cultural variables. So, how can traditionalists attempt to describe central aspects of an organization's culture?

Chiles and Zorn (1995) published a study that combined quantitative and qualitative data collection techniques within a traditionalist framework to describe one aspect of an organization's culture, namely, employee perceptions of empowerment. The authors administered a six-item empowerment questionnaire to 40 employees of a large manufacturing company. The degree to which employees felt empowered was tapped quantitatively by items such as (a) I have the authority to make decisions that need to be made; (b) management trusts me to make decisions that need to be made; and (c) I have the opportunity to use my judgment for problem solving. In addition to these questionnaires, Chiles and Zorn conducted in-depth interviews with the same 40 employees to gain a more complete understanding of worker definitions and experiences with workplace empowerment. The qualitative component of their study was to analyze the content of the interview responses to identify factors that employees perceived as important in empowerment. The authors found that employees' feelings of empowerment were influenced strongly by their perception of the organization's overall culture. Specifically, the more they felt hindered by the culture to act on the basis of their own expertise, the less likely they were to feel empowered. Also, the more positive verbal recognition employees received from their supervisors, the higher their feelings of empowerment tended to be.

Despite the fact that traditionalists can derive important insights about an organization's culture, there are limitations associated with this approach. Studies of organizational culture are intended to reveal the meanings and interpretations of organizational life made possible by a cultural frame of reference or to understand the process by which culture is created, transmitted, and changed through communication. Given this focus, interpretivist or critical-interpretivist methods are more appropriate for examining organizational culture.

Before turning to a description of the methods used by interpretivists and critical-interpretivists, a final note on studying organizational culture seems in order. The studies conducted by Barker and Tompkins (1994) and Chiles and Zorn (1995) show some of the complexities associated with describing and evaluating an organization's culture. Both studies involved hundreds of hours of observations, interviews, conversations, and data analysis. The time and effort expended by these researchers were necessary to gain accurate insights into employee perceptions of organizational culture. However, logging hundreds of hours of data collection and analysis may not yield cultural descriptions that are reflective of every employee's interpretations. This is true for two primary reasons.

First, as discussed earlier, within any large organization there are likely to be many subcultures. For example, in a huge multinational corporation such as General Motors with plants and offices located across the world, can there be a single corporate culture? Certain common cultural features may be found in many of the plants and locations, but each separate facility also exhibits cultural features that are unique to the particular collection of people working there. Cultural researchers need to take this fact into consideration before attempting to provide an overarching description of an organization's culture.

Second, although organization members collectively create organizational culture, individuals interpret these cultures. For example, let's consider two employees (Jim and Mary) who work in the collections department of a large retail store. Mary has several close friendships with her coworkers. In addition, Mary has a congenial working relationship with her supervisor. Jim, on the other hand, is an isolate who rarely interacts with coworkers. Furthermore, Jim has a history of conflict with his supervisor. Although Jim and Mary work in the same department, their interpretations of departmental and organizational culture may be quite different because they have different experiences at work. This example does not negate the value of conducting an organizational cultural analysis; rather, it shows the complexities associated with the process and the restrictions researchers must recognize when drawing their conclusions.

Now that we have considered the difficulties associated with cultural analysis, let's turn to some of the major approaches to understanding culture from the interpretive and critical-interpretive perspectives. First, we will describe the ways four approaches influence our thinking about how communication constructs culture: language and worldview, knowledge structures, consensual and contested meanings, and a multiple cultures perspective. Second, we examine different types of communication that contribute to the construction of culture: metaphors, narratives, rites and ceremonies, reflexive comments, and fantasy themes.

Language and Worldview

One approach to understanding organizational culture focuses on how a group's use of language influences their worldview. In order to understand this approach, let's turn to the Sapir-Whorf hypothesis (Sapir, 1921, 1958; Whorf, 1940, 1956). According to Sapir and Whorf, the language we use influences the way in which we view and think about the world around us. In the extreme version of this perspective, language actually determines thought.

This is referred to as *strong determinism*. By contrast, *weak determinism* is more accepted today. From the standpoint of weak determinism, thought is merely affected by or influenced by our language. One frequently used example that speaks to this principle is to compare how different groups experience and describe their understanding of snow. An American living in Indiana encounters snow for a limited amount of time during any given year. This limited experience will produce few variations in terms of how they describe snow. An Eskimo living in Northern Canada, however, encounters snow during much of the year, and the diversity of his or her experience will be reflected in nuanced descriptions. For example, Eskimos use different words to distinguish among types of snow particles (e.g., snowflakes, frost, fine snow/rain particles, drifting particles, clinging particles). In addition, fallen snow may be soft and deep on the ground, crusted on top, or floating on the water. Next, snow formations are distinguished by snow banks, carved snow blocks, or cornice formations about to collapse. Finally, Eskimos use different words to distinguish between typical blizzards and severe blizzards (Jacobson, 1984). Thus, Eskimos use their language to divide their reality into compartments that characterize their experience.

In an interesting study focusing on language strategies used by Israeli and Indian businesspeople, Zaidman (2001) offers insight into the problems that may surface when people communicate using different discourse systems. She starts by explaining that a *utilitarian discourse system* dominates communication in business, government, and academe. Utilitarian discourse values clarity, brevity, and simplicity. So a speaker or writer should focus on conveying information with no attempt to influence the receiver of the message. One should also avoid set phrases, metaphors, proverbs, and clichés. Rather, message senders should strive to make statements that are fresh and original.

Although both Israelis and Indians are aware of the characteristics of utilitarian discourse, they are socialized differently in their exposure to this system. Specifically, "the ideological principles of utilitarian discourse, such as the belief in the creative, free, and equal individual, are transmitted to children in Israel in their primary socialization" (Zaidman, 2001, p. 414). By contrast, Indians are introduced to utilitarian ideology only through secondary socialization in high schools and universities.

The impact of this difference in socialization comes through in how Israelis and Indians use language in business. Dugri speech is a major style of communication among Israelis. This form of speech emphasizes truthfulness, informativeness, and clarity. Speakers display a high level of directness and are impatient with verbal polish or circumlocution (Katriel, 1986).

The discourse system in Indian English (spoken by the educated class in India) is formal and poetic and includes elegant forms derived from long-established literary traditions (Mehrotra, 1995). So Indian English consists of long sentences with complicated structures. Often the point a speaker intends to make is only expressed at the end of the statement. Also, politeness depends on the length of the sentence and a lack of directness. This means that the more indirect the speaker is, the more polite he or she is. Finally, Indian speakers prefer hyperbole and exaggerated forms. For example, "I am bubbling with zeal and enthusiasm to serve as a research assistant" (Mehrotra, 1982, p. 164).

When communication takes place between Israelis and Indians in business settings, problems may arise because of how they use language differently. Israelis expect clarity, directness, and brevity. Indians expect indirectness, complicated structure, and politeness. Zaidman provides an example of the problems this may create in the following exchange between an Israeli and an Indian. The first statement was from a fax sent by the owner of Rom, an Israeli firm. The second statement is from the Indian businessman who received the fax:

> The project will be executed only after down payment will be paid for the feasibility study. Please don't ask me for any information regarding market potentiality and technology before the above is done. I am sure you can, by now, represent Rom and explain our experience and abilities. I would stress the part that we are a commercial company and not a charity company.

The reply was as follows:

> I am quite upset to receive your fax especially with the line "I would stress the part that we are a commercial company and not a charity company." You must appreciate we are trying to sell Rom for the various . . . technologies. We are already seriously talking of three projects. Any new entrepreneur would like to have a brief information on the project before he makes up his mind for making advance payment. Nobody is here for charity. Our time, our efforts, and our image has a value. If we ask for information & if you don't have it, you can politely refuse rather than conveying such sarcastic remarks. . . . Please send a brief profile to help A. Industries to enter into a memorandum of understanding with Gotam. (Zaidman, 2001, p. 428)

For both speakers, their worldview is expressed through the language that they use. The dugri code used by the Israeli business owner faithfully projects the speaker's feelings in a forceful and confrontational tone. He acts like a "tough talker" because he wants to preserve his own face in these negotiations. On the other hand, the Indian manager expects business communication between professionals to display humility, respect, and politeness. Although these two businessmen may eventually resolve their dispute, they may each need to alter they way they use language to establish common ground for future exchanges.

Knowledge Structures

A starting point for understanding knowledge structures is to consider the meaning of *schema*. A *schema* is a knowledge structure that is formed by people through communication when they share an experience in a given group or organizational environment. Social actors then impose this schema on a given context to construct and interpret its form and meaning (Bachrach, Bamberger, & Sonnenstuhl, 1996; Kuhn & Corman, 2003). *Schemata* (plural of schema) provide direction for our attention and facilitate our encoding of information. When we apply a schema to a situation it helps us to produce information and to interpret an experience. We may then use that information and interpretation in making a decision about how to act (Fiske & Taylor, 1991; Neisser, 1967; Walsh, 1995).

Schemata are cognitive structures that are causally connected. What this means is that in any organizational environment multiple schemata are related and connected in a way that informs our experience and our ability to understand the world around us. For example, in a conflict between department members, there may be causal connections among constructs such as aggressiveness, understanding, and clarity that may give us insight into understanding that conflict and what it means for this particular organizational culture. Importantly, we form schemata through interaction with others and through the macro discourses that take place in organizations. Thus, knowledge structures are inherently communicative (Kuhn & Corman, 2003).

When we take a social cognitive perspective on communication, organizations are framed "as ongoing, dynamic bodies of thought and action comprised of distributed knowledge actors" (Kuhn & Corman, 2003). So, schemata change as organization members interact with one another in response to myriad everyday experiences. If we attempt to examine schemata in an organizational setting, we can learn how knowledge is dispersed among members. We can also learn how collective knowledge is created through the construction and reconstruction of conceptual systems as organization members engage in joint activity (Giddens, 1979; Harris, 1994; Wenger, 1998). Finally, schemata may be considered collectively to represent an organizational structure.

Although the concept of schemata implies homogeneity, there may also be heterogeneity in knowledge structures within organizations. In fact, a recent study by Kuhn and Corman (2003) found both homogeneity and heterogeneity in knowledge structures during a planned change at an organization called DPC. The change studied involved a change in the workflow process. Specifically, DPC is a division of city government in the "Oasis" community that is responsible for guiding, approving, and supervising new construction projects. The advising and processing of applications is a multistage process. A new director of DPC believed that there was a more efficient way to organize the process, so he instituted a new workflow process shortly after assuming his duties. Although all organization members were affected by this change, different knowledge structures surfaced in assigning meaning to the change. For example, in the following comment by a technical worker, the workflow change affected internal issues related to technical details in DPC's routine procedures:

> The whole goal of the reengineering thing is to find fatal flaws and technical issues further up front in the process rather than letting it go on. . . . in the reengineering, we've really bumping up what is required of [applicants] up front. And we think it's going to help. . . . it's adding a screening for us. It's adding a step in the process. My question will be, if this process works, and it helps us get better submittals, and it helps to coordinate because the coordinators are identifying problems better, and all this is happening before the designers are very far in their plans so that they're willing to make changes, then that's great, you know. (personal interview reported in Kuhn & Corman, 2003, pp. 213, 215)

Although administrators at DPC also recognized internal issues in the workflow change, they focused much more on the impact on external constituents. In doing so the meaning they attached to the change was structured much more around external issues related to site development, research, and applicant concerns. One administrator stated:

> What made [the reengineering] necessary was the crunch time that the Coordinators were having to write reports and do everything, was so cramped that they were having problems getting them done. . . . They've bought themselves some time in the beginning by reengineering it so that they don't cash the check from the developer until they see if the case is really ready to go forward. And I think Roy was the guy to do it, I mean, he's the one to pull it all together, and I don't think anyone else could have. (personal interview reported in Kuhn & Corman, 2003, p. 215)

The findings of Kuhn and Corman (2003) do not challenge the existence of knowledge structures in organizations; rather, they add complexity to our understanding of such structures. Specifically, when employees experience a common event they may communicate in ways that give rise to multiple knowledge structures rather than a single structure.

Consensual and Contested Meanings

The preceding discussion of heterogeneous knowledge structures raises the question of the degree to which organizational cultures are places that generate consensual or contested meanings. This is not a simple question to answer. Perhaps the safest response is to argue that organizations are sites of both consensual and contested meanings.

An organization could not survive without some level of consensus over meaning regarding the purpose of the organization or over what is acceptable and unacceptable personal behavior. However, is absolute consensus likely in a large organization? There may always be a small number of employees at the fringes who do not buy into meanings that are accepted by the vast majority.

Rather than attempting to describe the level of meaning consensus that exists in an organization, it may be more important to gain an understanding of the contested meanings that create struggles for employees. Consider an organization in which employees regularly say, "We're like one, big happy family." The meanings associated with this expression may be fiercely contested within that organization. One type of struggle may be between employees who feel connected with others in ways similar to familial connections and employees who feel disrespected and isolated. Other struggles may exist between and among organization members who have very different perspectives of the meaning of family. Some people are part of families that are fragmented and full of conflict. A family metaphor at work may not resonate with such a person. Other employees may feel co-opted by the family metaphor. Specifically, some may feel that organizations connect themselves to a family metaphor so employees will display unquestioned dedication to the workplace, perhaps even forgoing time with "real" family members to solve work-related problems.

Meanings may also be contested when a counterculture surfaces in an organization. "A counterculture is one whose constitutive and regulative rules directly confront those of the dominant culture" (Rose, 1988, p. 165). When a counterculture gains support, its members may even contest the right of the dominant culture to exercise power. Author Michael Papa encountered a counterculture at a university where he served as a consultant several years ago. In this university, faculty were unionized. In one department, a powerful counterculture developed that challenged the dominant culture in place in the other academic departments.

The dominant culture in place at this institution was one in which faculty members helped to move the mission of the university forward by participating on committees related to university governance, offering help to students outside of the classroom, developing new curriculum, and keeping current in the discipline. In this one department, however, faculty members reached the conclusion that they were being taken advantage of by a miserly board of trustees that did not pay them a competitive wage and overworked them by adding meaningless tasks to the role of faculty member. They became experts in union bylaws and in the faculty contract. Rather than contribute to the university's mission, they fought every request that was made of them. Most did not participate on any university committees, and faculty members kept only virtual office hours (answering e-mail and phone calls without being present in their offices). The same courses were taught year after year, and few made any attempt to keep current in the discipline. They did not fear reprisal because they were all tenured. They felt empowered because their jobs were much easier and they had much more free time than faculty members who bought into the dominant culture and supported the university's mission. Arguments surfaced frequently between administrators at this university and this department's faculty. When pushed, the faculty members would threaten lawsuits and grievances, and the administration would back down. Although this was not a terribly productive cultural struggle, it does show how powerfully organization members may contest dominant meaning systems.

Multiple Cultures Perspective

Our earlier observations concerning organizational subcultures and the preceding section focusing on contested meanings and countercultures indicate that organizations often contain multiple cultures. A number of studies provide insight into this phenomenon. For example, Smircich (1983) described two distinct subcultures in her study of top executives in an insurance company. She observed an "inside" group of longstanding organization members and an "outside" group that was brought in from other companies in the insurance industry.

Smircich's observations about distinct subcultures in an insurance company point to one of the main reasons multiple cultures surface in organizations. Specifically, when a large organization recruits and imports new employees from other organizations, these new employees often bring with them interaction patterns and cultural frameworks they have experienced elsewhere. The introduction of new technology may also spark multiple cultures as different employees incorporate that technology into their work in various ways. In addition, if an organization expands and needs new professional and occupation groups, these new categories of employees may act in ways that are unique to their roles (Rose, 1988). Finally, mergers and takeovers result in a blending of distinct cultures that both creates a new cultural form and sustains elements of the former separate cultures.

Although changes in organizational membership and the introduction of new procedures and technologies may give rise to new subcultures, the existence of multiple cultures is prompted by more fundamental communication processes. Cultures develop because of regularized patterns of interaction among employees that create specific socially created realities. As Linda Putnam (1983) noted

Although behavior is voluntaristic, people enact regularized sets of relationships that reflect back on everyday interactions. The processes they create become accepted practices that impact on everyday interactions. . . . Thus, in the interpretive view, process and structure merge together over time. (pp. 44–45)

At the core of Putnam's observation is recognition of the reflexive relationship between structures as regularized patterns and the communication processes that create them. So, if a group of departmental employees communicate most frequently with fellow departmental members, they are likely to create a culture that is unique to the regularized patterns they establish. Other departments with different interactions patterns and separate network connections will create different cultures.

On a final note, it is important to recognize that there are different frameworks that give rise to multiple cultures in organizations. Consider the observations of Rose (1988):

On the one hand the phrase [multiple cultures] might refer to a loose constellation of unique cultures (in terms of meanings, values, structures or linkages between meanings/values) not connected to an overarching core culture. On the other hand, the phrase could be defined as an array of distinct cultures that exist in relationship to a core or umbrella culture. In this usage, subcultures would consist of pockets or enclaves of individuals, within a broader culture, that generally shared values, meanings, and structures. (p. 143)

Whether subcultures are unique or connected to an umbrella culture, organizational size and complexity is a key determinant in the emergence of multiple cultures. Small organizations may be able to sustain a single culture. Once an organization reaches a certain size, however, cultures will be created within pockets or enclaves where there is frequent and regulated patterns of interaction that are repeated over time.

Metaphors

Susan Koch and Stan Deetz (1981) believe that metaphors are at the heart of an interpretive process "that continually structures the organization's reality" (p. 16). Familiar phrases such as "the game of life," "hard as a rock," "working at a snail's pace," and "running like a well-oiled machine" are all metaphorical statements. The game, the rock, the snail's pace, and the machine are metaphors for other things.

Koch and Deetz argue that metaphors literally anchor our understandings of experience. When we speak metaphorically of life as a game and organizations as machines, these metaphors reflect our interpretations of life and of organizations. Because interpretation depends not only on language but on many other factors as well, metaphors may not be as powerful as Koch and Deetz suggest. Cohen (1977) summarized a number of studies suggesting that some forms of interpretation and thinking can occur without any particular reference to language. If this is the case, the metaphors that people use sometimes may be little more than convenient figures of speech. Nevertheless, common metaphors that occur in organizational communication could provide important clues to the meanings that members hold for their experiences.

Metaphor analysis begins by recording the talk of organization members in interviews and discussions. Data also may be obtained from written records. Interview questions should be free of any metaphors that might bias results. For example, "Tell me what it's like to be *part* of this organization" might prompt the interviewee to answer with "machine" metaphors.

The next step is to isolate metaphors by examining all of the statements in the data. This process is complicated and depends on the researcher's familiarity with different types of metaphors and on the researcher's ability to recognize them in statements. Metaphors may be created in several ways, but four of the most common rely on **spatial orientation, activities, substances**, and **entities**. For example, "I have authority *over* this matter" relates the idea of authority to a spatial orientation, *over.* "We're breathing new life into the company" relates an organizational process to a well-known biblical metaphor for the activity of creation, *and* it relates the organization to the substance of a living organism. "We're just one big, happy *family* at Burger Queen" relates the organization to the entity, *family.*

After metaphors are identified, they are worked through progressively until it is possible to identify all of the main or "root" metaphors used in the organization. In many cases, subcultural divisions yield more than one main metaphor. We observed this condition first-hand in a large research laboratory in which conflicts between a technical training department and a human resource development department seemed to be related to differences in root metaphors. The technical training group understood itself as a family, whereas the human resource development group characterized itself as a small business. The technical trainers spoke in terms of being a good neighbor to others in the laboratory "community." The supervisor was regarded literally as the head of a household. The human resource group described its function as "marketing services" to "client" groups in the laboratory. The supervisor was "the boss," who controlled and coordinated the business. The business group regarded the family group as unprofessional. The family group regarded the business group as rigid, competitive, and cold. Simply identifying these metaphors did not resolve the conflicts between the two departments, but it did seem to help members to make more sense of the conflicts.

One good example of the scholarly application of metaphor analysis is a study by Smith and Eisenberg (1987) of labor-management conflict at Disneyland. Late in 1984, the conflict culminated in a 22-day strike by unionized employees. This is an interesting work because, as Smith and Eisenberg put it, "Disneyland occupies a special place in the American psyche" (p. 367). Moreover, the Disney Corporation has used its success and strong public image as a foundation for becoming a consultant to other companies on management methods and employee relations. Yet, the study by Smith and Eisenberg revealed a somewhat troubled state of affairs in Fantasyland. Smith and Eisenberg began their study in 1983 through eight interviews with Disneyland managers. Later, in 1985, they conducted intensive audiotaped interviews of 35 hourly employees, who were men and women of various ages and lengths of employment and who represented six different divisions of Disneyland operations. In order to analyze the interviews, they applied what they describe as a "semantic sorting process in which coherent patterns or clusters of meaning emerged around specific metaphorical expressions" (p. 371). In effect, this means that they examined all of the metaphorical expressions in the interview transcripts for shared understandings that could be characterized with a root metaphor. Smith and Eisenberg provide an example of this process:

Expressions [used by interviewees]:

"The cast members"

"The show"

"Our costumes"

"The Disney image"

"The Disney role"

Shared understanding:

Disneyland has actors, costumes, stories to be enacted on stage and an audience to be entertained.

Organizational entailment:

Disneyland puts on a show.

Root metaphor:

Disneyland is a drama.

Smith and Eisenberg (1987) found two root metaphors, namely, *drama* and *family*, that characterized employees' experiences at Disneyland. They applied both of these metaphors to interpret various aspects of the labor-management conflict. Disney himself played a primary role in shaping the drama metaphor and supporting it with the image of Disneyland as an oasis for friendly family entertainment. This vision was adopted thoroughly by employees. After his death, the management philosophy began to shift, at least as it was perceived by employees. In response, employees cast themselves as defenders and caretakers of Disney's founding vision, but they revised their interpretation of that vision by extending the concept of family to Disney employees. Friendliness not only referred to employee-customer relationships (the original intention), but it also referred to relationships among employees themselves (the new interpretation). In short, Disneyland not only provided family entertainment, it was a family itself. This new interpretation was one that even Disney himself "may not have fully endorsed [and it] led ultimately to conflict with management" (p. 373).

As explained by Smith and Eisenberg (1987), the family metaphor was accepted uncritically by most employees and by many managers. It was believed to characterize employee relationships and the management-employee relationship. But with increasing competition from other theme parks, takeover attempts, high-level corporate resignations, and greater operating costs, management gradually placed a rather un-family-like emphasis on the bottom line, including a wage freeze and elimination of benefits in its efforts to operate at a profit. Management tried to redefine the family metaphor (e.g., family life sometimes is hard and families sometimes have to make sacrifices), but employees rejected management's new idea of family. Management's bottom-line view "was perceived by many as constituting a breach of Disney's caring philosophy" (p. 374).

Another very important feature of this particular study occurs in the way in which Smith and Eisenberg (1987) draw conclusions from their analysis. You may recall from Chapter 1 that interpretive approaches to organizational communication regard the organization as a negotiated order composed of pluralistic interests. These approaches generally attempt to avoid the managerial bias of functionalism and the worker-oriented bias of critical theory. The interpretive point of view clearly is reflected in Smith and Eisenberg's efforts to find a way for management and labor groups at Disneyland to share a common understanding of their organization:

> A conscious reconsideration of the drama metaphor might help reconcile manage-ment with employees, and past with present. An appeal of the drama metaphor lies in its ability to subsume some of the interpretations of both management and employees; it simultaneously retains the image of the park as family entertainment and permits a business orientation. (p. 378)

Although a specific metaphor may be used regularly within an organization, workers and researchers need to exercise care in interpreting the meaning that metaphor has for the organizational as a whole. Gibson and Zellmer-Bruhn (2001) examined the teamwork metaphor across organizational cultures in different countries. They discovered that the metaphor of teamwork was embedded in five different categories: military, family, sports, associates (cliques, crews), and community. The category a particular group used depended on their values, orientations, and practices. For example, if the national con-text is individualistic, sports or associates metaphors are more likely. Alternatively, if the organization emphasizes tight control, then a military or family metaphor is more likely. So, the key to understanding how metaphors structure reality in an organization is to dig deeply to uncover the resonant meanings employees attach to these terms or expressions.

Narratives

One generic approach to examining organizational stories or narratives is provided by Walter Fisher (1978, 1984, 1985, 1987). Fisher believes that human reasoning is a process of using symbols to guide thinking. Furthermore, he argues that a person's reasoning is displayed in the narratives or stories that he or she tells.

Fisher (1984) contends that storytelling is central to the human experience. In other words, we make sense of the world around us by translating our experiences into stories or narratives that we share with others. In organizations, employees justify decisions and offer reasons for their actions by telling stories to coworkers. Also, a person's values can be detected in the stories they tell (Meyer, 1995). Indeed, a number of researchers have sug-gested that employees tell stories to indicate how others should act or not act within an organization (Brown, 1990; Kirkwood, 1992; Mitroff & Kilmann, 1976). In order to show how narratives can play a central role in shaping an organization's culture, let's turn to a story told by a Grameen Bank field worker in Bangladesh. This story was reported to Rahnuma Shehabuddin (1992), and it focuses on how a group of female loan recipients empowered themselves against a moneylender (a powerful village resident who charges poor people exorbitant interest rates for loans):

> A moneylender threatened to break the legs of a [Grameen] bank worker who walked along the path in front of the former's house every week on his way to the centre meeting. When they heard about this, the thirty loan recipients at the centre showed up at the moneylender's house. They told him that he could threaten the bank worker only if he himself was prepared to lend them the money they needed on the same terms as the Grameen Bank did. The moneylender, of course, was not willing to give up his exorbitant interest rates, but he promised to stop harassing the bank workers as well as the members who no longer came to him for money. So you see, there is power in numbers: Thirty landless women can intimidate a wealthy man if they join forces. (Shehabuddin, 1992, p. 83)

This story has been told many times by employees and loan recipients of the Grameen Bank, and it serves two central purposes. First, it is unlikely that the 30 women mentioned above would have ever confronted the powerful moneylender prior to their affiliation with the Grameen Bank. Their membership in the Grameen empowered them to feel confident in their strength to collectively oppose an oppressive force, and in sharing the story they remind each other of what they can accomplish by working together. Second, field workers share this story with one another to show how their efforts can help transform the lives of the poor so they are no longer taken advantage of by powerful village citizens. Thus, the workers' commitment to helping the poor is strengthened by a story that shows how their efforts make a real difference in people's lives.

John Meyer (1995) provides us with further insight into organizational storytelling. Meyer attempted to discern the values that were embedded in stories told by 19 employees of a day-care center. A total of 555 stories were told in these interviews, showing how prevalent storytelling is in some organizations. Also, on analyzing the content of the stories, Meyer uncovered 10 different organizational values. This finding underscores how many different types of messages or themes can be detected through listening to the stories employees tell. The 10 organizational values Meyer discovered were (a) people should show concern for others' needs and feelings; (b) people should plan for work tasks and activities in advance; (c) people should communicate information as quickly or as appropriately as possible; (d) there should be opportunities to influence events and make decisions; (e) conflict should be handled by talk among the persons involved; (f) people should be personal and easy to get along with; (g) messages should be sent clearly and repeated to ensure accuracy; (h) people should derive intrinsic rewards from their work, doing more than should be expected for their jobs; (i) people should be given flexibility and independence on the job; and (j) people should respect and follow directives of those above them in the decision hierarchy.

Stories told in organizations may also serve a powerful control function, informing new employees about how they are expected to act. Gibson and Papa (2000) interviewed employees at Industry International (II), a medium-sized manufacturing organization in the Midwest. Many of the stories workers in this organization told were meant to paint a clear picture of the expected work ethic. One employee with 29 years of experience at II relayed a story he frequently tells younger workers:

> When I was younger and working here, I got sick one day. I had the flu and wanted to go home. I knew I'd be losing money for me and the company if I left.

This old-timer came up to me and said, "You've got to tough it out." So, I got a bucket and put it next to my machine. I just kept pukin' and workin' all day, but I didn't leave. (Gibson & Papa, 2000, p. 83)

The moral of this story is that completing the workday is to be valued over succumbing to personal discomfort and illness. A worker who leaves because he is sick is letting down the company and his family. You display your commitment to your employer and family by "toughing it out" and finishing your job. Gibson and Papa (2000) also interpret this story from the perspective of organizational identification. They contend that because the workers identify so strongly with the organization and their workgroup, they do whatever it takes to work productively. The stories the workers then share with one another help to sustain this identification.

All organizational stories present the listener with the narrator's version of a particular experience. So, by asking employees to recount those stories that have been influential in their affiliation with an organization, we can gain insight into what they view as an important encounter, how they make sense of their membership, and how they want others to understand their experiences.

Rites and Ceremonies

Harrison Trice (1985) has been largely responsible for drawing our attention to the importance of rites and ceremonies in describing organizational culture. A rite brings together a number of discrete cultural forms (e.g., customary language, metaphors, stories, ritualized behavior, settings) into "an integrated, unified public performance" (Trice & Beyer, 1984, p. 654). Ceremonies connect several rites into a single occasion or event. In order to clarify this perspective, let's consider an example.

In a large computer manufacturing company, sales representatives compete for an award that is given twice a year to the top seller. Because this award has been given 20 times during the past 10 years, it has become a ritualized event. When the award is made, all of the sales representatives in the company gather together to congratulate the top performer. During the award ceremony, the national sales manager praises the sales representative's performance, encourages other sales representatives to follow his or her example, and presents the award winner with a bonus check. Furthermore, stories are told about the diligent work necessary to receive this award, and metaphors are used comparing the winners to tireless warriors who refuse to be beaten by competitors. Such an event can be considered an organizational rite because it connects a number of cultural forms such as stories, metaphors, and symbols (e.g., bonus checks) to a single event.

Trice and Beyer (1984) identified six different rites that can be linked to organizational ceremonies: (a) rites of passage, (b) rites of degradation, (c) rites of enhancement, (d) rites of renewal, (e) rites of conflict reduction, and (f) rites of integration. A rite of passage occurs when employees move into roles that are new to them. An example would be successfully completing the basic training program of the U.S. Army. Rites of degradation dissolve the power associated with an organizational identity such as occurs when a person is fired from his or her job, or demoted or sanctioned in some way. Rites of enhancement provide public recognition for an employee's accomplishments as shown by our sales representative example. Rites of renewal refurbish social structures by improving their functioning. For example, a developmental program that trains managers to be more effective administrators could be considered a rite of renewal. Rites of conflict reduction reestablish equilibrium in an organization beset by destructive arguments between certain members or groups. A collective bargaining session would exemplify this type of rite. Finally, rites of integration "revive common feelings that bind members together and commit them to a social system" (Trice & Beyer, 1984, p. 657). An annual reward and recognition dinner or event would be representative of an integration rite.

Trice and Beyer (1984) argue that an examination of organizational rites and ceremonials is a comprehensive form of cultural analysis because the researcher focuses on events that bring a number of different cultural forms together. Rather than focus on stories or metaphors individual employees tell about many varied experiences, the researcher who observes an organizational ceremony is exposed to how different cultural forms are used in a given setting for a particular purpose. They also argue that this type of cultural analysis is very efficient because "identifying, observing, and even participating in them does not require sustained access over time" (Trice & Beyer, 1984, p. 664). In order to show the usefulness of this approach to cultural analysis, let's consider an example.

As part of their field study of the Grameen Bank in Bangladesh, Papa et al. (1995) observed local branch office meetings attended by bank field workers and loan recipients. These meetings can be viewed as ceremonies that bring together a number of different rites. One of the first items of business addressed in these meetings is loan repayment. The members either repay their loans or explain to the field worker why they could not repay. Because weekly repayment is considered the norm, failure to repay is considered a failure. A rite of degradation is linked to the failure to repay as members are criticized by the bank worker for not meeting their financial obligations. Furthermore, because the loans of other center members are jeopardized when one member does not repay, the loan defaulter also receives criticism from his or her fellow members. Rites of enhancement can also occur during these meetings. For example, if a loan recipient builds a new house with a loan received from the bank, the other center members will visit the house and compliment the owner for working so diligently to afford it. Rites of conflict reduction can take place when the field worker attempts to manage conflicts among loan recipients concerning failed business ventures. Finally, rites of integration are performed. For example, the members perform physical exercise drills as part of these meetings and they shout slogans that reaffirm their commitment to the bank's programs. This rite of integration is linked to the belief that members must act together so they can move forward together out of poverty and toward financial independence.

Papa et al. (1995) derived three important insights from their examination of the weekly loan meetings. First, the potential for public criticism served as a powerful motivating force for loan recipients to repay their loans in a timely manner. Second, both loan recipients and bank field workers displayed high levels of organizational commitment. Third, genuine camaraderie was shown among loan recipients and workers who shared in one another's successes.

Reflexive Comments

Analysis of reflexive comments is a technique originally described by Harre and Secord (1972). It has been applied in organizational communication studies by Tompkins and

Cheney (1983), Cheney (1983), and Geist and Chandler (1984). Like other interpretive methods, this technique focuses on language and discourse in order to reveal meanings and understand human behavior.

What is a **reflexive comment**? To begin with, we human beings generally not only are aware of our actions in social situations, but we also know that we are aware. We are both actors and observers of our own actions. This is reflexiveness. It allows us to make comments in the form of explanations, justifications, criticisms, and so forth about our own behavior. If we make a comment about an anticipated action, it is a **plan**. If it is about ongoing action in the present, it is a **commentary**. If it is a statement made after the occurrence of an event or action in a way that justifies or gives reasons for the occurrence, it is an **account**. According to Tompkins and Cheney (1983), these comments reveal "the meanings and interpretations actors assign to items in their environment and the rules . . . that they follow in monitoring their social behavior" (p. 129).

Analysis of reflexive comments may be conducted in various ways. Cheney (1983) used analysis of accounts (after-the-fact comments) in a study of the relationship between identification and decision-making processes. He began with the assumption that identification as "the process by which individuals link themselves to elements in the social scene" (p. 342) is acted out in organizational decision making. For example, decisions or evaluations of alternatives might be based on identification with the entire organization, a department, or even a specific individual. Cheney's procedures were developed to explore the extent to which identification helps to explain decision-making processes. Cheney collected accounts through moderately scheduled interviews (i.e., interviews in which major questions are preplanned, but follow-up questions intended to probe interviewee answers are generated spontaneously in the interview). Questioning proceeded through five steps:

1. The employee's role(s) in the organization (i.e., duties, decision making, responsibilities).

2. "Accounts" for specific decisions.

3. "Accounts" for decision-making practice (especially useful when an employee does not isolate specific episodes).

4. The employee's identifications.

5. Actions by the company that either foster or discourage identification with the organization (p. 349).

The accounts obtained from interviews were analyzed in order to identify decision premises (the reasons or factors taken into account that influence a decision), the sources of decision premises (person, group, or other authority from which premises are acquired), and targets of identification (people, groups, or organizational units with which an employee identifies). Cheney used this information to answer questions about the relevance of organizational values and goals in employees' evaluations of decision alternatives, about overlap between identification targets and sources of decision premises, about changes in identification and decision making as length of employment increases, and about the influence of organizational policy on identification and decision making.

Geist and Chandler (1984) used reflexive comments to study the exercise of influence in group decision making, although the major purpose of their investigation involved a test of five claims made by Tompkins and Cheney regarding the value of account analysis:

1. Accounts express decisional premises or rules.

2. Accounts point to the sources of rules.

3. Accounts enumerate social units for whom the decision maker was prepared to give accounts at the time of making the decision.

4. Accounts reveal identification targets.

5. Accounts help to explain the nature of the identification process (pp. 136–139).

In their investigation, Geist and Chandler videotaped weekly staff meetings of a psychiatric healthcare team, then transcribed the tapes in order to analyze decisions related to the care and treatment of patients. Instead of soliciting accounts through interviews with organization members, Geist and Chandler attempted to locate reflexive comments in a record of *ongoing group interaction*. They did this by examining any statement that a group member made that revealed the member's values or targets of identification. Consequently, their data appeared to include not only accounts but also plans and commentaries. They concluded that analysis of reflexive comments will serve all five of the functions that Tompkins and Cheney claimed.

Fantasy Themes

Fantasy themes are based on Ernest Bormann's symbolic convergence theory of communication. Symbolic convergence occurs when groups create rhetorical visions of their social world and what it is like to be in that world. As applied to organizations, a rhetorical vision is a view held by organization members "of the organization and its relationship to the external environment, of the various subdivision and units of the organization, and of their place in the scheme of things" (Bormann, 1981, p. 6). For example, consider the vision that GM's Saturn division creates with the motto "Saturn: A different kind of car, a different kind of company."

Rhetorical visions arise from shared fantasies involving creative interpretation of events and fantasy types, that is, common themes that reflect beliefs, goals, and values. How does one identify fantasies and rhetorical visions in an organization's life? Bormann has devised a system of fantasy theme analysis to address this question. Bormann et al. (1982) said, "A good way to discover the symbolic world of a group is by collecting dramatic messages, stories, histories, and anecdotes that they tell and retell" (p. 83). This may be done by observing and listening to members interact with one another, by interviewing organization members, by examining the organization's official written record (mission statements, official memos, reports, and newsletters), and even by using the unofficial written record (underground newsletter, songs, or graffiti).

Once the materials are gathered, they are subjected to a script analysis in which organizational life is treated as a drama with characters acting in scenes. The messages, stories, and other materials are examined to identify the following features:

1. Heroes, heroines, villains, and their goals and values.

2. The action line, including the things that characters do to achieve their goals.

3. The scene where the action takes place and the forces that are presumed to control the action.

After analyzing a number of stories and messages in this way, the researcher should be able to identify common themes that, like the moral of a story, reflect shared fantasies and rhetorical visions within the organization. One may then be able to understand the values that prevail within the organization or within its various groups and the realities of organizational life as members construct and understand them.

One example of the application of fantasy theme analysis to organizational communication is a study conducted by Bormann, Pratt, and Putnam (1978) of male response to female leadership in a female-dominated organization. Actually, the case was a laboratory company operated by college students—nine males and 13 females. Conflicts over authority and power in the company led to a restructuring of its formal system, but the "real" organization ultimately was enacted through an informal communication network that was dominated by the women. Only two of the nine men fully accepted the situation. Two others actively attempted to achieve leadership positions, but were blocked by the women. The other men withdrew as much as possible from active participation. They disconnected from the network and did as little work as possible. As Bormann et al. put it, "They were goldbricking" (p. 150).

When Bormann et al. analyzed the discourse and dialogue of company members, they found fantasy themes that seem to explain what had occurred in the male response to female leadership and in the female response to challenges. First and foremost, they identified "the recurrence of fantasy themes which linked leadership with male potency" (p. 154), portraying and dramatizing males under female domination as symbolically castrated. These themes were related to dramatization of a double-bind theme among the men: A male who challenges female leadership is a chauvinist pig, whereas a male who accepts female leadership is a castrated eunuch. Most of the men in the company opted for withdrawal as the only plausible response to this paradox. Others took up a portrayal of the women as mother. Those men "who merged with the group accepted dependency on the mother and on the female leadership" (p. 155).

DESCRIBING ORGANIZATIONAL CULTURE: THE CASE OF BEN & JERRY'S

Ben & Jerry's is a Vermont-based ice cream manufacturing company that has attracted considerable attention and interest because of its high-quality ice cream and unique corporate culture. Company founders Ben Cohen and Jerry Greenfield started their business because they were dissatisfied with traditional employment opportunities and were both antagonistic toward authority. As their business grew, two fundamental and interrelated traits characterized this organization's culture: (a) a casual, carefree, employee-focused atmosphere and (b) a commitment to social values. Interestingly, the culture at Ben & Jerry's is not just something that the employees experience, it has helped build customer loyalty as well as attract, retain, and motivate employees (D'Souza, 2006).

Jerry Greenfield is famous for his motto, "If it's not fun, why do it?" This expression largely characterizes the corporate culture at Ben & Jerry's. A casual and relaxed environment pervades the company's manufacturing plant in Waterbury, Vermont. When there were concerns that corporate growth would create stress that would challenge this culture, management created "Joy Gangs." Each gang is given the time and resources to plan ways for employees to have fun including the organization of birthday parties, team sports, and concerts.

When author Michael Papa visited the plant, he found that employees typically dressed in jeans, T-shirts, and tennis shoes. Although workers were busy performing tasks, they also talked and joked with one another. Importantly, worker commitment to this organization is not prompted solely by the working climate; the company also offers a "living wage" and a generous benefits package that includes health and child-care services and free health-club memberships.

The corporation's social mission emphasizes the initiation of innovative ways to improve the quality of life locally, nationally, and internationally. The company accomplishes this in a variety of ways. First, they strive to create economic opportunities for those who have been typically denied them. This is accomplished through hiring the poor and buying products from small family farms. Second, they minimize the waste they create through the manufacturing process. Third, they support safe methods of food production from suppliers that do not use toxic chemicals to grow crops. Fourth, they support nonviolent ways to achieve peace and justice. For instance, at company headquarters and on their Web site they advocate "50 Ways to Promote Peace." This program describes peace-promoting ideas and activities that cover a flexible range of topics and commitment levels from the simple to the powerfully provocative. Examples of activities include attending a peace rally, making friends with someone of another race, driving with patience and tolerance, volunteering on a peace project, and teaching young people skills for nonviolent conflict resolution (Ben & Jerry's, 2006).

A central part of Ben & Jerry's social mission is motivating their employees to participate actively in a broad range of social causes. Specifically, employees are oriented to social activism as part of their everyday work through paid participation in Community Action Teams (CATs). For example, employees at the company's Springfield, Vermont, plant worked to build a baseball field for local children and planted trees at a historic home site. In another instance, a production line worker helped to spearhead a campaign to oppose the James Bay hydroelectric plant in Quebec because of its negative impact on the environment (D'Souza, 2006).

Although Ben & Jerry's social mission has been a prominent part of their culture, there are concerns about the survival of that culture with the sale of the company to Unilever, an Anglo-Dutch conglomerate, in 1999. Ben and Jerry helped to assuage those concerns by incorporating specific terms into the sale. For example, in addition to the $326 million offer, Unilever contributed $5 million to Ben & Jerry's Foundation, $5 million for a venture capital fund for ethical business start-ups, and a minimum of $1.1 million a year for social change groups (Henery, 2005). More recently, the company has moved into organic ice cream, and they are using only "fair trade" vanilla, coffee, and chocolate so that farmers in developing countries are paid higher prices. In addition, to confront global warming they have reduced carbon monoxide output by investing in new refrigeration technology (Kiger, 2005). Finally, the company started running commercials in the fall of 2005 taking on the decline in family-owned farms in the United States. In these commercials, consumers are encouraged to buy locally grown produce to help out smaller, local farms (Riven, 2005).

Although there are clear signs that Ben & Jerry's is sustaining its employee friendly and socially conscious culture, there are critics who doubt their ability to sustain this culture over time. As Henery (2005) observes, Ben & Jerry's is still trying to "demonstrate the feel of a small quirky company, but the reality is that they are owned by a huge conglomerate and the product is mass marketed" (p. 2). On the other hand, large companies such as Unilever have started to recognize that any newly acquired company will retain its consumer base only if it retains its reputation. What do you think? Will Ben & Jerry's be able to sustain their unique corporate culture? What will need to be done to sustain this culture? What will the major challenges be to sustaining this culture?

SUMMARY

In a fundamental sense, a culture exists when people come to share a common frame of reference for interpreting and acting toward one another and the world in which they live. This common frame of reference includes language, values, beliefs, and interpretations of experience. It is reflected in customs, folkways, artifacts, communication, and other observable features of the community, including rites, rituals, celebrations, legends, myths, and heroic sagas.

Although there is consensus among scholars in various fields that the concept of culture can be applied to organizations, there are different ways of understanding organizational culture. Traditionalists study cultural artifacts in much the same way that they would study any other observable feature of organizational behavior. In line with their historic concern for regulation of organizational processes, traditionalists usually want to know how to develop and change an organizational culture in order to make the organization more effective. To the interpretivist, organizational culture is understood as a network of shared meanings. Consequently, the interpretivist describes organizational culture according to the meanings that it makes possible for its members and the ways in which the culture itself is created and recreated through communication. Critical-interpretivists also describe culture according to the meanings it makes possible for members; however, their focus is on the struggles that occur over competing meaning systems. In these struggles, there are certain groups more likely to receive the rewards or benefits from organizational membership, whereas other groups are more likely to absorb the costs.

There are many approaches that may be taken to understand organizational culture. A focus on language draws our attention to how language shapes our worldview. When we describe knowledge structures, we gain an understanding of how schemata provide direction for our attention and facilitate our encoding of information. Of course, any complex understanding of culture requires us to recognize that there may be consensus over certain meanings and contests over other meanings. The contests over meaning that result in struggles among employees may reflect the fact that there are multiple cultures and even countercultures within large, complex organizations.

In this chapter, we considered different types of communication that may give us insight into understanding an organization's culture. Specifically, we looked at metaphors, narratives, rites and ceremonies, reflexive comments, and fantasy themes. Metaphor analysis assumes that metaphors literally anchor our understandings of experience. Metaphor analysis begins by recording the talk of organization members in interviews and discussions. The next step is to isolate metaphors by examining all of the statements in the data. Three of the most common types of metaphors rely on spatial orientation, activities, or substances and entities.

Narrative analysis focuses on the stories told by organization members. These stories are told for a variety of reasons. Employees justify their decisions or actions through stories as well as give insight into their values. Stories are also told to indicate how members should act or not act within an organization. Finally, organizational stories provide researchers with insight into how employees make sense of their membership and how they want others to understand their experiences.

Rites and ceremonials are activities that bring together a number of different cultural forms (e.g., customary language, metaphors, stories, ritualized behavior) in a single setting. Trice and Beyer identified six different rites that can be linked to organizational ceremonies: rites of passage, rites of degradation, rites of enhancement, rites of renewal, rites of conflict reduction, and rites of integration. This form of analysis is valuable in terms of its efficiency and its insight into member perceptions of organizational culture because it allows researchers to observe a single event that displays a number of different cultural forms.

Reflexive comments are statements of explanation, justification, criticism, and so forth that we make about our own action. According to Tompkins and Cheney (1983), these comments reveal "the meanings and interpretations actors assign to items in their environment and the rules . . . that they follow in monitoring their social behavior" (p. 129). Organizational communication researchers have gathered reflexive comments through use of moderately scheduled interviews with organization members and by taping and transcribing comments from group meetings.

Bormann defines a fantasy as a "creative and imaginative interpretation of events" that includes both real and imagined elements. He believes that symbolic convergence occurs through sharing of fantasies within groups. Group fantasies provide the basis for and reinforce common beliefs, goals, values, and wishes within a group.

Fantasy themes are identified through a script analysis in which organizational life is treated as a drama with characters acting in scenes. Messages, stories, and other materials including written records, jokes, songs, and even graffiti are examined to identify heroes, heroines, and villains; the action line, including the things that characters do to achieve their goals; the scene where the action takes place; and the forces that are presumed to control the action.

Although interpretive or critical-interpretive methods appear to be best suited for the study of organizational culture, the traditionalist concept of managerially planned cultural change has gained great popularity. The idea of controlling and changing organizational culture through unilateral management direction is controversial because many different forces influence an organizational culture. In particular, diversity of the workforce is changing organizational cultures whether managers intend it or not. Thus, in Chapter 8 we will deal specifically with the issues of cultural control, cultural change, and workforce diversity.

DISCUSSION QUESTIONS/ACTIVITIES

1. Write a brief characterization of the culture at your college. Identify some of the major rites, rituals, myths, legends, and other symbolic artifacts of this culture. What do these artifacts reveal about the meaning that members of the college community have for their experiences?

2. What are some of the essential differences among the traditionalist, interpretivist, and critical-interpretive perspectives of organizational culture? Are the goals of the three perspectives compatible or incompatible?

3. Studying culture sounds like a problem for an anthropologist. Why should the field of organizational communication be interested in organizational culture?

4. The television show *The Apprentice* has aired on NBC for several seasons. Donald Trump, the show's creator, sustains a very specific type of group or organizational culture through the competitions that pit one team against another. Sometimes these teams are divided by gender; other times each team comprises both men and women. How would you describe the culture that is reflected in the communicative actions of team members? How do the group cultures differ when the teams are composed of one gender versus when the teams are composed of men and women?

REFERENCES

Bachrach, S. B., Bamberger, P., & Sonnenstuhl, W. J. (1996). The organizational transformation process: The micropolitics of dissonance reduction and the alignment of logics of action. *Administrative Science Quarterly, 41,* 477–506.

Barker, J. R. (1993). Tightening the iron cage: Concertive control in self-managing teams. *Administrative Science Quarterly, 38,* 408–437.

Barker, J. R., & Cheney, G. (1994). The concepts and practices of discipline in contemporary organizational life. *Communication Monographs, 61,* 19–43.

Barker, J. R., & Tompkins, P. K. (1994). Identification in the self-managing organization: Characteristics of target and tenure. *Human Communication Research, 21,* 223–240.

Ben & Jerry's. (2006). Ben & Jerry's home. Retrieved March 26, 2006, from http://www.benjerry.com/our_company/our_mission/index.cfm

Berger, P., & Luckmann, T. (1966). *The social construction of reality.* New York: Penguin.

Bormann, E. G. (1981). *The application of symbolic convergence communication theory to organizations.* Paper presented at the SCA/ICA Conference on Interpretive Approaches to the Study of Organizational Communication, Alta, UT, August 1981.

Bormann, E. G., Howell, W. S., Nichols, R. G., & Shapiro, G. L. (1982). *Interpersonal communication in the modern organization* (2nd ed.). Englewood Cliffs, NJ: Prentice Hall.

Bormann, E. G., Pratt, J., & Putnam, L. (1978). Power, authority, and sex: Male response to female leadership. *Communication Monographs, 45,* 119–155.

Brown, M. H. (1990). Defining stories in organizations: Characteristics and functions. In J. Anderson (Ed.), *Communication yearbook 13* (pp. 162–190). Newbury Park, CA: Sage.

Cheney, G. (1983). On the various and changing meanings of organizational membership: A field study of organizational identification. *Communication Monographs, 50,* 342–362.

Chiles, A, M., & Zorn, T. E. (1995). Empowerment in organizations: Employees' perceptions of the influences on empowerment. *Journal of Applied Communication Research, 23,* 1–25.

Clifford, J. (1983). On ethnographic authority. *Representations, 1,* 118–146.

Cohen, G. (1977). *The psychology of cognition.* London: Academic Press.

D'Souza, S. (2006). *Ben and Jerry - Case Study.* Retrieved March 26, 2006, from http://www.geocities.com/dsouzsj/articles/benjerrycasestudy.html

Deal, T. E., & Kennedy, A. A. (1982). *Corporate cultures: The rites and rituals of corporate life.* Reading, MA: Addison-Wesley.

Denison, D. R. (1996). What is the difference between organizational culture and organizational climate? A native's point of view on a decade of paradigm wars. *Academy of Management Review, 21,* 619–654.

Eisenberg, E. M., & Goodall, H. L., Jr. (1993). *Organizational communication: Balancing creativity and constraint.* New York: St. Martin's.

Farace, R. V., Monge, P. R., & Russell, H. M. (1977). *Communicating and organizing.* Reading, MA: Addison-Wesley.

Faules, D. (1982). The use of multi-methods in the organizational setting. *Western Journal of Speech Communication, 46,* 150–161.

Fisher, W. R. (1978). Toward a logic of good reasons. *Quarterly Journal of Speech, 64,* 376–384.

Fisher, W. R. (1984). Narration as a human communication paradigm: The case of public moral argument. *Communication Monographs, 51,* 1–22.

Fisher, W. R. (1985). The narrative paradigm: An elaboration. *Communication Monographs, 52,* 347–367.

Fisher, W. R. (1987). *Human communication as narration: Toward a philosophy of reason, value, and action.* Columbia: University of South Carolina Press.

Fiske, S. T., & Taylor, S. F. (1991). *Social cognition* (2nd ed.). New York: McGraw-Hill.

Geertz, C. (1973). *The interpretation of cultures.* New York: Basic Books.

Geist, P., & Chandler, T. (1984). Account analysis of influence in group decision making. *Communication Monographs, 51,* 67–78.

Gibson, C. B., & Zellmer-Bruhn, M. E. (2001). Metaphors and meaning: An intercultural analysis of the concept of teamwork. *Administrative Science Quarterly, 46,* 274–303.

Gibson, M. K., & Papa, M. J. (2000). The mud, the blood, and the beer guys: Organizational osmosis in blue-collar work groups. *Journal of Applied Communication Research, 28,* 68–88.

Giddens, A. (1979). *Central problems in social theory.* Berkeley: University of California Press.

Gioia, D. A., & Pitre, E. (1990). Multiparadigm perspectives on theory building. *Academy of Management Review, 15,* 584–602.

Harre, R., & Secord, P. F. (1972). *The explanation of social behavior.* Totawa, NJ: Littlefield, Adams.

Harris, S. G. (1994). Organizational culture and individual sensemaking. *Organization Science, 5,* 309–321.

Haviland, W. A. (1993). *Cultural anthropology* (7th ed). Fort Worth, TX: Harcourt, Brace, Jovanovich.

Henery, M. (2005). How many small firms can sell while avoiding selling out? *The Times* [online edition]. Retrieved March 26, 2006, from http://business.timesonline.co.uk/article/0,,8213–1617835_1,00.html

Jacobson, S. A. (1984). *The Yup'Ik Eskimo Dictionary.* Fairbanks: Alaska Native Language Center.

Jermier, J. (1991). Reflections on street corner society. In P. Frost, L. Moore, M. Louis, C. Lundberg, & J. Martin (Eds.), *Reframing organizational culture* (pp. 223–233). Newbury Park, CA: Sage.

Kanter, R. M. (1977). *Men and women of the corporation.* New York: Basic Books.

Katriel, T. (1986). *Talking straight: Dugri speech in Israeli sabra culture.* Cambridge, UK: Cambridge University Press.

Kiger, P. J. (2005, April). The original Ben and Jerry have taken up other causes. *Workforce Management, 17*(3), 37–38.

Kirkwood, W. G. (1992). Narrative and the rhetoric of possibility. *Communication Monographs, 59,* 30–47.

Koch, S., & Deetz, S. A. (1981). *Metaphor analysis of social reality in organizations.* Paper presented at the SCA/ICA Conference on Interpretive Approaches to Organizational Communication, Alta, UT, August 1981.

Kuhn, T., & Corman, S. R. (2003). The emergence of homogeneity and heterogeneity in knowledge structures during planned organizational change. *Communication Monographs, 70,* 198–229).

Lave, J., & Wenger, S. (1990). *Situated learning.* Cambridge, UK: Cambridge University Press.

Maccoby, M. (1976). *The gamesmen: The new corporate leaders.* New York: Simon & Schuster.

Mead, G. (1934). *Mind, self, and society.* Chicago: University of Chicago Press.

Mehrotra, R. R. (1982). Indian English: A sociolinguistic profile. In J. Pride (Ed.), *New Englishes* (pp. 151–173). Rowley, MA: Newbury House Publishers.

Mehrotra, R. R. (1995). How to be polite in Indian English. *International Journal of the Sociology of Language, 116,* 99–110.

Meyer, J. C. (1995). Tell me a story: Eliciting organizational values from narratives. *Communication Quarterly, 43,* 210–224.

Mitroff, I. I., & Kilmann, R. H. (1976). On organization stories: An approach to the design and analysis of organizations through myths and stories. In R. H. Kilmann, L. R. Pondy, & D. P. Slevin (Eds.), *The management of organization design, strategies, and implementation* (pp. 189–207). New York: Elsevier North-Holland.

Neisser, U. (1967). *Cognitive psychology.* Englewood Cliffs, NJ: Prentice Hall.

Pacanowsky, M. E., & O'Donnell-Trujillo, N. (1982). Communication and organizational cultures. *Western Journal of Speech Communication, 46,* 115–130.

Pacanowsky, M. E., & O'Donnell-Trujillo, N. (1984). Organizational communication as cultural performance. *Communication Monographs, 50,* 126–147.

Papa, M. J., Auwal, M. A., & Singhal, A. (1995). Dialectic of control and emancipation in organizing for social change: A multitheoretic study of the Grameen Bank in Bangladesh. *Communication Theory, 5,* 189–223.

Papa, M. J., Auwal, M. A., & Singhal, A. (1997). Organizing for social change within concertive control systems: Member identification, discursive empowerment, and the masking of discipline. *Communication Monographs, 64,* 219–251.

Patton, M. Q. (1990). *Qualitative evaluation methods.* London: Sage.

Putnam, L. L. (1983). The interpretive perspective: An alternative to functionalism. In L. L. Putnam & M. E. Pacanowsky (Eds.), *Communication and organizations: An interpretive approach* (pp. 31–54). Beverly Hills, CA: Sage.

Riley, P. (1983). A structurationist account of political cultures. *Administrative Science Quarterly, 28,* 414–437.

Riven, R. (2005). *Supporting local farms.* Retrieved March 26, 2006, from http://66.232.56.61/ee/index.php?/fist/more/supporting_local_farms?/

Rose, R. A. (1988). Organizations as multiple cultures: A rules theory analysis. *Human Relations, 41,* 139–170.

Sapir, E. (1921). *Language.* New York: Harcourt, Brace & Co.

Sapir, E. (1958). The status of linguistics as a science. In E. Sapir (Ed.) *Culture, language and personality* (pp. 160–166). Berkeley: University of California Press.

Shehabuddin, R. (1992). *The impact of Grameen Bank in Bangladesh.* Dhaka, Bangladesh: Grameen Bank.

Shockley-Zalabak, P., & Morley, D. D. (1994). Creating a culture: A longitudinal examination of the influence of management and employee values on communication rule stability and emergence. *Human Communication Research, 20,* 334–355.

Smircich, L. (1981). *The concept of culture and organizational analysis.* Paper presented at the SCA/ICA Conference on Interpretive Approaches to Organizational Communication, Alta, UT, August 1981.

Smircich, L. (1983). Concepts of culture and organizational analysis. *Administrative Science Quarterly, 28,* 339–358.

Smith, R. C., & Eisenberg, E. M. (1987). Conflict at Disneyland: A root-metaphor analysis. *Communication Monographs, 54,* 367–380.

Tompkins, P. K., & Cheney, G. (1983). The uses of account analysis: A study of organizational decision making and identification. In L. L. Putnam & M. E. Pacanowsky (Eds.), *Communication and organizations: An interpretive approach* (pp. 123–146). Beverly Hills, CA: Sage.

Trice, H. M. (1985). Rites and ceremonials in organizational cultures. *Research in the Sociology of Organizations, 4,* 221–270.

Trice, H. M., & Beyer, J. M. (1984). Studying organizational cultures through rites and ceremonials. *Academy of Management Review, 9,* 653–669.

Van Maanen, J. (1988). *Tales of the field: On writing ethnography.* Chicago: The University of Chicago Press.

Walsh, J. P. (1995). Managerial and organizational cognition: Notes from a trip down memory lane. *Organization Science, 6,* 280–321.

Wenger, E. (1998). *Communities of practice: Learning, meaning, and identity.* Cambridge, UK: Cambridge University Press.

Whorf, B. L. (1940). Science and linguistics. *Technology Review, 42*(6), 229–231, 247–248.

Whorf, B. L. (1956). Language, mind and reality. In J. B. Carroll (Ed.), *Language, thought and reality* (pp. 246–270). Cambridge, MA: MIT Press.

Wright, J. P. (1979). *On a clear day, you can see General Motors.* Grosse Pointe, MI: Wright Enterprises.

Zaidman, N. (2001). Cultural codes and language strategies in business communication: Interactions between Israeli and Indian businesspeople. *Management Communication Quarterly, 14,* 408–441.

Information Technology

Put the words "information technology ubiquity" into Google, and that engine will return an overwhelming number of hits in less than a second. Commentary about the ubiquity of electronic, computer-based information technology in organizational and social life has become the first great cliché of the 21st century. Information technology is everywhere, and all of us already know this. The wireless phone, PDA, Blackberry, PC, Mac, and other hardware devices as well as the e-mail, word, database, search, voice, and other applications that run on these machines are ordinary features of everyday life. The Internet and satellite communications systems provide global connectedness, and the World Wide Web offers a vast repository of data and information on immediate demand. If you grew up with all of these technologies in your life, you might wonder why we are writing about something that is so familiar to you. What will a chapter on information technology do to enhance your knowledge about this subject and about its relevance to organizational communication? We are writing about information technology mainly because computer literacy and individual skill in the use of technology do not translate automatically into real information technology fluency in organizational life.

Computer literacy refers merely to skills with tools such as word processing, e-mail, and Web browsers. The National Research Council's Computer Science and Telecommunications Board noted in 1999 that such skills are "necessary but not sufficient for individuals to prosper in the information age" (p. 6). According to the NRC board, the new era requires *fluency* in information technology, including abilities to use technology productively in work and everyday life, to adapt to technological change, to understand when technology can assist or impede achievement of a goal, and to evaluate information technology's effects on society. We aim for the chapter to help you with this kind of information technology fluency.

We are reviewing most of the basic themes of information technology in organizational communication under the traditional perspective. We are considering particular issues of information technology in organizational sense making under the interpretive perspective and organizational control through information technology primarily under the critical perspective. We do not mean to imply that the interpretive and critical perspectives are unconcerned with the topics that we are covering under the traditional perspective, but sense making and control are the focal points for interpretive and critical treatments of information technology in organizational communication. We are beginning, however, with one topic that cuts across all three perspectives and provides a frame of reference for the entire chapter. This topic is information technology and change.

INFORMATION TECHNOLOGY AND CHANGE

To say that information technology is pervasive in today's world certainly does not mean that it is new. In a sense, Western civilization had an earlier "information age" when Johannes Gutenberg introduced the first movable-type printing press in 1450. The Protestant Reformation, Renaissance, and Scientific Revolution transformed Western civilization. Various forces either drove or set the stage for these developments, including *Yersinia pestis*, that deadly microorganism known as the plague that we mentioned in

Chapter 4. Even so, James Dewar (1998) of the Rand Corporation made a case that the Gutenberg press was the indispensable "breakthrough technology" that enabled them. Dewar contended that the wave of change in today's shift from the industrial age to the information age will be every bit as profound and transformative as the wave of change that swept away medieval society.

Some scholars regard information technology quite literally as a force that causes organizational and social change (e.g., Rogers, 1988). This position, known as technological determinism, is rejected by others (e.g., Olson, 1982) who argue that change is produced through choices made by human beings in their uses of technology, not as a result of the technology itself. We cannot resolve that debate in this chapter, but we are suggesting, in agreement with Mendonca (2004), that information technology enables change. Even if it does not cause change directly, information technology is, at the very least, a catalyst for change; it influences the kinds of changes that can occur and how quickly they can occur. This is not a phenomenon that somehow just arose at the end of the 20th century. For example, Yates (1989) has described how advances in information technologies between 1850 and 1920 led to revolutionary changes in the organizational communication in that era.

Either way, whether one regards the shift as a literal change of ages from industrial to information or just a next step in an ongoing process of change over many decades, the pervasiveness of information technology is enabling organizational conditions and dynamics in the 21st century that are fundamentally different from those of the 19th and 20th centuries. Some of these new conditions are fairly obvious: for example, the emergence of virtual organizations that are unbounded by time, place, and even membership (Pang, 2001) and a global economy supported by a global Internet (Prestowitz, 2005). Other conditions are more subtle, such as new inequalities resulting from the so-called digital divide between those with and without access to technology (National Telecommunications and Information Administration, 1999) and relentless pressure in a culture of expectations for 24/7 accessibility where, in one example described by CBS News (2006), the CEO of a major corporation is so obsessed with on-demand availability to his customers that he networked his entire home to check e-mail and answer the phone from any location . . . including the bathroom and the shower.

Information technology is an important topic to address in organizational communication not only because technological fluency is so important in the information age, but also because technology both enables and constrains systems of organizational communication and human interaction. The theme of information technology and change draws out differences between the traditional, interpretive, and critical perspectives, but not to the extent that one might expect. One does not have to be a critical studies scholar to be uneasy about the consequences of the digital divide and a 24/7 culture.

TRADITIONAL PERSPECTIVE

The traditional perspective of information technology in organizational communication typically is concerned with the potential of technology to enhance efficiency, effectiveness, and ultimately productivity. It is also concerned with barriers to these objectives that may arise in difficulties with adaptation to technological change, including the disruptive influences of technology itself. As we will show in this section, the traditional perspective also does have concerns about the negative consequences of technology in organizational life.

Purposes of Information Technology

Organizations adopt information technologies ostensibly for reasons of organizational efficiency and effectiveness, but Pfaffenberger (2004) has pointed out that these technologies also are developed and deployed for reasons that have nothing to do with efficiency and effectiveness. For example, as early as 1980, Kling summarized studies of technology adoption decisions in government agencies indicating that politics, personal agendas, and private rationales often dominated these decisions. In some cases, the mere appearance of improvement through use of information technology rather than achievement of any actual efficiencies was enough to sustain systems that were "otherwise relatively useless" (p. 73). Put another way, it was more important in those agencies to look good than to actually be good, and having new technology in place certainly looked good.

We know from our own experiences in large institutions that Pfaffenberger and Kling are right about political and personal motives figuring into organizational decisions to adopt and use information technology, but personal and political agendas influence all kinds of organizational decisions, and such motives are only part of the information technology story. Among other functional reasons, organizations invest in information technology for productivity, knowledge management, and control.

Productivity

Between 1970 and 1990, computing power in the United States increased by more than 200% with no discernible impact on productivity in the economy (Brynjolfsson, 1993). For corporations and institutions that had realigned resources in order to make major investments in information technology, the result was "disillusionment and frustration" (Brynjolfsson, p. 67). That state of affairs provided the incentive for a flurry of research studies to unravel the "productivity paradox." Brynjolfsson reviewed and summarized the findings of these studies to test four potential answers to the question, "Why haven't computers measurably improved productivity?" Two of the answers involve the practices of the organizations using the technology, and the other two answers concern the ways in which productivity was being assessed.

The two issues in organizational practices are redistribution and mismanagement. Information technology sometimes appears to merely redistribute work rather than make work more efficient, so the technology does not add to total output. Another possible explanation is mismanagement, i.e., managers tend to misallocate information and consume information in excess.

Brynjolfsson's review of research on the subject suggested that redistribution and mismanagement do not really account for the productivity paradox. The primary problems are mismeasurement and timing of measurement. Simply put, we might be trying to measure the productivity outputs of information technology in the wrong way, and we might be trying to measure them too soon because there can be a substantial lag between the point of investment in technology and the point of payoff on that investment.

Whatever the correct answer to the productivity question might be, the picture of the connection between information technology and productivity clearly had changed by 2000. Prompted by a Federal Reserve study indicating that information technology contributed more than 70% of the total gain in U.S. business productivity over the preceding five years, *Information Week* declared that the productivity paradox was resolved, in part because economists had "finally figured out how to calculate IT's contribution to productivity" and in part because "investments made in IT are realizing their greatest return now" (McGee, 2000, p. 1).

Brynjolfsson's suspicions about mismeasurement and timing of measurement appear to have been right, but McGee's *Information Week* article also pointed to another insightful conclusion: "It's not just IT but the reengineering of business practices in conjunction with IT that produces the biggest boosts in productivity" (p. 1). This point was reinforced later by McKinsey and Company, a major technology research and consulting firm, in their own finding that "IT only contributes to productivity growth when accompanied by business process innovation [and] IT applications have to be tailored to sector-specific business processes" (Baily, 2003, p. 9).

The imperative to connect information technology with process innovation and to tailor technology to the unique needs of a particular business or service points to the need for information technology fluency as opposed to mere literacy. Productivity is not achieved by knowing how to use a word processor, a spreadsheet, or a Web browser. It is achieved by knowing how to apply technology in tandem with innovation. Ability to multitask with a wireless phone in one hand and a computer mouse in the other while watching CNBC on a tube across the room also does not equate to productivity. Productivity is achieved when the activities that are being multitasked add value to the enterprise.

Knowledge Management

The preceding section on the connection between information technology and productivity may seem as if it should be in a business book rather than an organizational communication book, but the connection between technology and productivity is linked to another theme that is central to the study of organizational communication: information management or, more properly from today's point of view, the problem of *knowledge* management (Wiig, 1997).

Drucker (1998) defined information as data organized for a particular purpose. In this sense, data are "simply 'facts' and 'figures'" (Blair, 2002, p. 1019). They become informative when they are placed in a useful context. Knowledge certainly requires information, but information in and of itself is not knowledge, and a management information system is not the same thing as a knowledge management system.

In its early years, the electronic computer was little more than a highly efficient calculator. When commercial versions moved into business and other organizational environments, uses quickly expanded to include data processing, storage, and retrieval for many kinds of organizational activities. The next step was to unify data from various organizational subsystems and functions into integrated systems. These integrated systems evolved into management information systems that provided reports tailored for management use in planning, controlling, and evaluating organizational activities (Thierauf, 1978). These systems exist in their current form today as so-called enterprise applications that organize mountains of data to make them accessible and usable across many functional areas of a complex organization in "a single, integrated software program that runs off a single database so that the various departments can more easily share information and communicate with each other" (Koch, 2006).

With today's technology, the problem of finding, storing, and retrieving information as Drucker defined it is easy. So easy, as Blair (2002) noted, that all but the smallest organizations have such capabilities, so the technology, at least among those who have it, is now just one more cost of doing business that otherwise provides "no real advantage to its users" (p. 1023). This recognition has driven organizations to think about what they can leverage above and beyond information technology, and the answer in many cases is knowledge.

Knowledge and knowledge management are more complex concepts than information and information management. Davenport and Prusak (1998) described knowledge as "a mix of framed experience, values, contextual information, and expert insight that provides a framework for evaluating and incorporating new experiences and information" (p. 5). In this sense, knowledge is not just the information in one's possession, but also one's understanding of that information, i.e., how to interpret and act on information as well as where and how to find it. Without a system to manage it, organizational knowledge walks out the door every day at closing time.

We do not know exactly when, where, and with whom the knowledge management concept originated, but academic articles and books on the subject appeared in the late 1980s, and several large consulting firms were selling knowledge management services by the mid-1990s. The *Journal of Knowledge Management* was launched by the Knowledge Research Institute in 1997 (Wiig, 1997). The concept has been characterized by some as little more than the next management fad, but the idea at least seems to frame a new way of thinking about a current organizational problem (Rowley, 1999; Sieloff, 1999).

Knowledge management, according to Galagan (1997), generally includes some or all of the following activities:

- Generating new knowledge.
- Representing knowledge in documents and databases.
- Embedding knowledge in products, services, and organizational processes.
- Diffusing or transferring knowledge within the organization.
- Using accessible knowledge in decision making.
- Providing incentives and a culture to facilitate knowledge growth.
- Measuring the value of knowledge as an organizational asset.

How does one create, capture, embed, and transfer organizational knowledge?

A knowledge management system requires a lot of information technology, but Kankanhalli, Tanudidjaja, Sutanto, and Tan (2003) found in a study of 12 major corporations known for successful knowledge management programs that the organizations varied in the way they deployed information technology to support knowledge management. The use of technology depends on the type of organization and the stability of the organization's environment.

In some situations, information technology is used mainly to create electronic knowledge repositories (codification). In others, it is used mainly to help people find and communicate with one another (personalization). The idea in codification is to turn knowledge into a commodity and put it where everyone can find it. Personalization focuses on people and the transactions among people as sources of knowledge, so the objective is to connect the people. In general, Kankanhalli et al. found that service-based organizations in a low-volatility environment rely heavily on codification. Those in a high-volatility environment use personalization. Product-based organizations in a low-volatility environment rely heavily on personalization, but they also make moderate use of codification, and product-based organizations in a high-volatility environment rely heavily on both strategies.

Ironically, much of the impetus for organizations to move into knowledge management came not only from a degree of parity that reduced the competitive advantage of information technology for one organization over another, but also from the disruptive influence of information technology itself, mostly as a result of extreme information overload (Sieloff, 1999). It may seem strange to think of information technology as disruptive, but "it is arguably the most disruptive force for organizations in the past half century" (Mendonca, 2004, p. 244). Greengard (2000) reminds us, "Computers were supposed to make it easier to manage information, and the Internet was supposed to make it easier to find it [yet] most of us have found ourselves completely overwhelmed" (p. 22). Technology does make it easier to find and manage information, but it also gives all of us the ability to produce it and disseminate it at quantities and rates that are greater than we can process. Hence, according to Edmunds and Morris (2000), the glut of information, rather than enabling people to do their jobs better, "threatens to engulf and diminish [their] control over the situation" (p. 18).

Hewlett-Packard, a corporate icon in the high-technology industry and also one of the 12 corporations in the study by Kankanhalli et al., provides a good illustration of technology as both problem and solution. HP moved to develop knowledge management systems in the 1980s when rapid growth began to break down its cherished culture of small, autonomous business units, open office environments, and emphasis on face-to-face communication. In an environment of large, geographically distributed operations and a complex web of relationships and networks, HP executive John Doyle expressed the company's new challenge in these words: "If only HP knew what HP knows" (Sieloff, 1999, p. 50).

HP's problem was no longer one of storing, retrieving, and shaping information for managerial decisions. It was the gulf between the company's wealth of absolute knowledge and the distribution of that knowledge within a complex organization in a highly volatile environment. But the tipping point for the move into knowledge management, according to Charles Sieloff, an HP program manager, was the "disruptive technology of the Internet and the World Wide Web" (p. 51). With the new reality, "that information vital to your job and your company could be just a few clicks away on the Web . . . information overload went from a theoretical concept to a visceral everyday reality" (p. 51). According to Kankanhalli et al., Hewlett Packard is now one of those product-based companies in a highly volatile environment that relies heavily on codification and personalization in deployment of information technology to support knowledge management.

Control

As Edmunds and Morris suggest in their reference to concerns about information overload causing loss of control, the use of information technology also entails the purpose of control. For some technology enthusiasts, the idea of control means personal control, i.e., liberation and empowerment for the individual human user, controlling one's own choices and circumstances through better access to information and to other people (Communications News, 1994). In a larger and darker sense, it may imply hegemony and even global control where the liberating effects of technology for the common citizen are an illusion, and empowerment is realized mostly by those who have power already. We will deal with this darker point of view in our discussion of the critical perspective later in the chapter.

In the traditional perspective of organizational communication, control through information technology is tied to objectives of efficiency, effectiveness, and productivity. As we have indicated elsewhere in this book, the function of communication in coordination and control of complex organizations is a well-established subject in the traditional perspective, and advances in information technology historically have affected that function (Yates, 1989). The traditional perspective is concerned with the issue primarily from a managerial point of view, but the concerns in this point of view are multifaceted. They include not only issues of direct, managerial use of technology for control, but also attention to paradoxical consequences of technology for control such as the disruptive influences of technology and the locus and diffusion of organizational control.

We just described the first paradox in the section on knowledge management. Contemporary information technology is supposed to improve control over information environments for the organization in general and the individual in particular, but it also can overwhelm organization members, demolishing any sense of control that one has over that environment. Hence, it is both indispensable and disruptive.

The second paradox of locus and diffusion of control involves the potential for information technology to have both centralizing and decentralizing effects on organizational structure as well as to control consequences for organizational processes and work. The same technology that enables those at the top echelons of the organization also enables people in many other areas and levels of the organization as well. Subsequent sections of this chapter cover all of these issues.

The Digital Divide and Information Technology Fluency

If information technology empowers the individual, it is clear that the blessings of empowerment through information technology are not bestowed in equal measure on all who might want to receive them. One might assume that this issue belongs only to critical and feminist scholars, but concerns about the problems of a digital divide and information technology fluency have received a good deal of attention in recent years within the traditional perspective (National Telecommunications and Information Administration, 1999).

The Digital Divide

The label "digital divide" arose in the late 1990s as a way of characterizing the differences between those with and those without access to computers and the Internet (Robinson, 2003). The divide has been associated variously with differences in race, gender, ethnicity, economic status, educational level, and geography. Generally, minorities, the poor, the less educated, and the rural were less likely to have access to information technology, a situation that would only reinforce second-class citizenry in the information age. Hence, discussions of the digital divide have focused on how to reduce or eliminate it. The concept later was extended to characterize the relative technological standing of whole countries (developed vs. developing vs. undeveloped) and even to differences between organizations in their ability to acquire, implement, and leverage information technology for competitive advantage (Vegh, 2003).

The necessity of access to information technology as one condition for prosperity in the information age is not in dispute, but many billions of dollars have been expended nationally and internationally to close the divide on the assumption that access and computer skills somehow will ensure upward mobility for economically disadvantaged people. Tufekci (2005) noted that "pronouncements to the power of these skills for providing upward mobility are made as if these were self-evident facts" (p. 1), yet she found that a computer skills training program for economically disadvantaged persons in Austin, Texas (a technology center in the southwest), did little to enhance their prospects for employment. Keniston (2002) described similarly ineffective efforts for disadvantaged groups in India. Although India, according to Keniston, is a world leader in "technologies for reaching ordinary people" (p. 2), he also noted that, "the transfer of wealth from the information technology industry to ordinary people is not automatic" (p. 11). These studies and others suggest that information technology alone is not a "magic bullet" for alleviating poverty and inequality.

In cases of digital divides along national and organizational lines, the issue is not just access to computers and the Internet, nor even basic skills in using software, but also access to and facility with large-scale enterprise systems for managing information and business processes. Wal-Mart can afford not only the highly sophisticated, state-of-the-art emergency operations center that we described in Chapter 1, but also the people who know how to use that center to manage a crisis. Could a smaller enterprise or even a city such as New Orleans ever afford this kind of investment?

At the international level, divides still exist. Chen and Wellman found in 2003 that divides within developed countries are diminishing, but the divide between developed and developing countries is still substantial, and divides within developing countries actually are worsening. These divides are produced by existing social inequalities, and the divides, in turn, reinforce these inequalities. Those most likely to be on the wrong side of the divide are less educated, less well off, older, and, in some countries, female.

Although digital divides are continuing to occur, information technology has become global. Even the references that we used for this chapter point to increasing globalization. Several are from Asia, Australia, India, and the European Union. Some underdeveloped nations are still on the technologically impoverished side of the digital divide, but even where stereotypes might invoke such an expectation, there are stark and unsettling surprises. For example, consider Akin, a 14-year-old Nigerian boy in the city of Lagos who works up to 70 hours a week along with dozens of other teenagers, laboring for a person who keeps 80% of their earnings. Your first mental image may be of child labor in a factory sweatshop, but Akin's sweatshop is more like an office than a factory, and he makes enough money there to support the rest of his family, own a Rolex watch (a real one), and put two pounds of gold bling around his neck. What do Akin and his fellow adolescent coworkers do? According to *Fortune Magazine* (Lawal, 2006), they design and run Internet identity theft and business scams from computer stations in a cybercafé, a vocation that Akin calls his "God-given talent." The digital divide is not necessarily where one might expect to find it and not necessarily what one might expect it to be.

Information Technology Fluency

The so-called digital divide, insofar as it is conceived as a problem of access to information technology, provides an incomplete picture of the uneven distribution of technology's benefits. The difference between simply having access to information technology and actually getting results from the use of technology is connected in part to the distinction drawn by the National Research Council's Computer Science and Telecommunications Board between computer literacy and information technology fluency. Knowing how to write formulas in a spreadsheet, construct a relational database, or create a PowerPoint slide is, by today's standards, just basic computer literacy. Producing knowledge management, innovation, or other value-added outcomes with these skills is something else.

Because computer literacy does involve some sophisticated skills, the idea that literacy is not fluency is a little confusing, but a similar distinction applies in other domains of human endeavor. To draw one analogy, just as knowing how to hammer a nail, read a bubble level, and saw a piece of lumber does not make one into a carpenter who can build a house, neither does computer literacy make one into a creative and competent user of information technology. Here is the list of competencies that collectively constitute information technology fluency as defined by the Computer Science and Telecommunications Board. Some of them may seem surprising, but they make sense if you consider them in light of the purposes for which information technology is used in organizations.

- *Engage in sustained reasoning.* Be able to understand exactly what problem is to be solved and when it has been solved.

- *Manage complexity.* Be able to deal with the complexity of problems to which information technology is applied, the resources provided by the technology, and the interdependencies of technology-based systems.

- *Test a solution.* Be able to determine that both the design and implementation of a solution are correct.

- *Manage problems in faulty solutions.* Be able to diagnose and correct problems when technological tools fail . . . (unless, of course, you would rather spend your life calling the Help Desk).

- *Organize and navigate information structures and evaluate information.* Be able to find information, make judgments about its reliability and validity, and structure it to make it useful and meaningful.

- *Collaborate.* Know how to collaborate within and between groups and also how technology changes the way in which collaboration takes place.

- *Communicate to other audiences.* Be able to understand audiences and adapt messages and information as well as technological tools to the audience.

- *Expect the unexpected.* Be able to anticipate and adjust to unexpected or unintended consequences of technological systems.

- *Anticipate changing technologies.* Know when it is appropriate to use an information technology tool, how many features to learn, and when to upgrade or adopt new technology.

- *Think about information technology abstractly.* Be able to transfer principles of technological solutions from one situation to another and understand the policy and social implications of technology.

Organizational Impact of Information Technology

When we think about most of the tools that we use to accomplish work in organizations, we certainly think about them in terms of their potential for efficiency and effectiveness, but how often do we think about their potential to shape the organization itself? When the tool is information technology, that question is almost automatic. Nadler, Gerstein, and Shaw (1992) said that the evolution of information technology may very well be the largest single influence on organizational design. Information technology is not just another tool for accomplishing work; it actually influences the ways in which we organize. As we noted at the beginning of this chapter, information technology is a catalyst for changes in organizational structure, function, and communication.

Many scholars use the word "impact" to talk about information technology's influence in organizations (e.g., Mahmood & Mann, 1993; Mendonca, 2004; Nunamaker & Briggs, 1997; Roberts, 1996; VonKortzfleisch, 2003; Whisler, 1970). The use of that word sounds like technological determinism, but it is intended to reinforce the point that the use of information technology has important organizational consequences. Again, we are not inclined to take sides in the technological determinism debate, but it does seem quite clear that information technology, at least in the ways that we humans have used it, does have "organizational impact."

Concern over the organizational impact of information technology developed right along with the advent of large-scale computerization in organizations. In 1970, Whisler produced a complete book on studies of the organizational effects of computerization, reporting findings such as functional reorganization, centralization of control and decision making, and decreased face-to-face communication. Other scholars in the 1980s predicted continuing developments with information technology that would lead to creation of new jobs, elimination of old jobs, changes in management functions, a paradoxical mix of centralization and decentralization in flatter organizations, higher levels of stress, and changes in the ways we carry out and manage complex human interaction (Gratz & Salem, 1984; Olson, 1982). Nunamaker and Briggs (1997) noted that many of these predictions from the 1970s and 1980s had become realities by the mid-1990s. For example, "Many organizations have flattened, eliminating many middle-management positions . . . The Internet and World Wide Web have connected people in ways that challenge the very concept of the traditional organization" (p. 3).

Organizing and communicating in organizational contexts today are very different from the 20th century versions of these activities. But these new conditions are now just part of the organizational landscape with which today's students are well familiar, so why are scholars still concerned about the organizational impact of information technology? The short answer is that information technology and choices we make about its use are continuing to change the organizational landscape. McFarlan indicated in 2002 that change in information technology is occurring at a rate of 35% to 50% per year, and that rate of change is expected to continue through 2025. Mendonca (2004) summarized three major areas of current and continuing impact: organizational structure, organizational processes, and work and workers.

Organizational Structure

As early as 1958, Leavitt and Whisler predicted that organizations in the 1980s would have few middle managers, greater centralization of decision making, and new organizational forms as a result of advances in information technology. Questions about the structural consequences of information technology have persisted ever since with mixed results in research. More recently, so-called new-form organizational theory has asserted that technology either drives or enables structural changes with pressure toward greater flexibility, decentralization, and shifts in authority relationships, but studies do not always support these claims (Schwarz, 2002). Two areas of continuing interest involve centralization of control and decisions and the emergence of new organizational forms.

Centralization Versus Decentralization. The locus of control and decision making in organizations is an inherently interesting and provocative issue, and the degree to which information technology serves to accomplish such arrangements is intriguing. Malone (1999) concluded from a review of relevant research, "In some cases, information technology (IT) appears to have led to more centralization, in others to more decentralization, and in still others, it appears to have no effect at all. . . . there appears to be no clear answer to the question of how IT affects centralization and decentralization of organizations" (p. 142).

Malone suggested that part of the reason for lack of clarity on this issue has to do with the conditions that some scholars accept as evidence of decentralization, i.e., changes that involve small degrees of autonomy and shifts of power within a more general structure that is nonetheless conventional, hierarchical, and centralized. But it may also be that information technology is paradoxical in this respect; it can have both centralizing and decentralizing consequences, even within the same organization. How is this possible?

Integrated, real-time management information systems and enterprise applications provide access for executives to what is happening across various levels and functional areas of the organization. Instead of relying on indirect access through middle management reporting, the executive potentially can have direct access. Direct access provides greater potential for direct control. Even when executives do not really understand how the technology works and do not directly use it themselves, they shape the design and implementation of systems to reinforce managerial control (Schwarz, 2002).

The force toward centralization, i.e., the tendency of executives and managers to use information technology for control of decisions, processes, and information, is perhaps always present in organizations. So when decentralization does occur in an organization, is it only because executives will it to be so? To answer this question, consider the problem from the following point of view.

We said earlier in the chapter that today's information technology provided integrated management information systems, enterprise applications, and automation of routine decisions that led to fewer levels of hierarchy and a smaller, less powerful cadre of middle managers in many organizations (Nunamaker & Briggs, 1997). It also brought greatly increased volumes of information through the Internet along with relatively unbounded flexibility of communication in systems such as e-mail.

The tsunami of information rushing into the middle management vacuum has obliged a transition from workers with lesser skills to knowledge workers "capable of collecting, analyzing, and integrating information" and also handling "complex transactions and queries that require integrated skills and which cannot be easily automated" (Mendonca, 2004, p. 246). These sophisticated workers have e-mail and other communication tools, i.e., tools that are very ordinary. But these ordinary communication systems are nonetheless powerful because they are not constrained by formal hierarchy and chains of command. The combination of sophisticated knowledge workers with powerful communication tools may not lead inevitably to decentralization, but it does have "the potential to allow various strategic and political manipulations of information . . . affecting the organization's structure in terms of power and control" (Ducheneaut & Watts, 2005, p. 33). This is a somewhat complicated way of saying that top managers and executives are not the only people in an organization who have the knowledge and the tools to operate with some degree of autonomy and organizational influence, and there are potentially decentralizing forces at work in organizations as well.

One flaw in our argument about the power of flexible communication systems is that e-mail can be and often is subject to surveillance, at least in large and midsized organizations. We have more information about this issue later in the chapter, but we note here that people have lost their jobs for writing e-mails that challenged management (Kierkegaard, 2005). Even so, it appears at this point that managerial efforts to control e-mail usage have done very little to diminish cross-functional and cross-organizational use of this tool (Ducheneaut & Watts, 2005), and such usage is decentralizing whether or not executives intend it.

Virtual Organizations. Organizational structure also has been influenced through use of information technology to introduce new organizational forms, notably so-called virtual organizations. Pang (2001) notes that there are many definitions of virtual organization. In general, the idea of the virtual organization involves an information technology dependent linkage among persons or organizations sharing knowledge and skills or collaborating in nontraditional ways.

A virtual organization could be as simple as a team of individuals who "collaborate from remote locations using e-mail, groupware" and other information technologies or as complex as a cooperative arrangement of companies or institutions to deliver "a product or service on the basis of a common business understanding . . . and present themselves as a unified organization" (Pang, 2001, pp. 1–2). Alexander (1997) noted that the term "virtual organization" really is used in a least two senses that he calls "physically virtual organizations. . . . [and] virtual ownership organizations" (pp. 122–123).

The physically virtual organization may be the kind that first comes to mind for most of us. These are organizations that carry out their activities "without requiring the physical proximity that is normally regarded as necessary" (p. 122). This kind of organization is made possible through space-time independent communication, i.e., interaction over the Internet and other electronic networks and use of group support software systems that allow us to coordinate our activities as an organization without being in the same location at the same time.

Virtual teams are simple instances of physically virtual organizations, for example, geographically distributed persons within the same larger organization who come together with information technology to manage a particular project or crisis and disband when their task is completed. Pang describes more complicated versions such as a U.S. Department of Agriculture initiative to merge 11 units of its inspection services into one organization. Instead of moving 250 distributed staff to one central office, staff in the new organization remained in their original locations. According to Pang (2001), "90 percent of interaction is done via teleconferencing, e-mail, and video conferencing" (p. 4), and some members have never met face-to-face.

The virtual ownership organization is a somewhat more complicated concept, but it also has become an easier kind of organization to enact with current information technologies. Virtual ownership organizations operate with little direct ownership of the assets and resources that are required to accomplish their work. As Alexander (1997) puts it, these organizations rely on getting things done, but not by doing things themselves.

A typical tool (although by no means the only tool) in the arsenal of the virtual ownership organization is outsourcing. One example Pang notes is Dell Computers. The company that we think of as Dell assembles, markets, and provides customer support for computers, but just about everything that goes into a Dell computer is made by other companies. The kind of supply-chain management that Dell requires to support this enterprise would be impossible without today's information technology. Alexander notes that some airline companies are even more virtual in this sense. They lease their planes and outsource for engineering, maintenance, ground support, and sometimes even for cabin crews and pilots. Consider the level of coordination that is required to make such an arrangement work, and the importance of current information and communications technologies becomes quite clear.

In whatever form it occurs, virtual organizing is becoming common. Malone (1999) reported that organizations are carrying on ever-increasing volumes of work outside traditional boundaries. Large companies are outsourcing noncore activities, small companies are gaining more importance, and work that previously might have been performed by a single, large institution is now carried out in virtual and networked environments among "shifting alliances of people and organizations" (p. 143).

Organizational Processes

Mendonca (2004) also noted that information technology alters organizational processes. The preceding discussion of virtual organizations probably makes this point a bit obvious. Mendonca is speaking here about reengineering or redesigning organizational processes in ways that take advantage of IT. This kind of redesign sometimes is concerned mainly with gaining efficiencies through elimination of unnecessary processes, but it can involve radical change. As we noted in the discussion of productivity as a purpose for adopting information technology, there is an emerging consensus that information technology contributes to productivity only insofar as it is linked to innovation in business processes or, as it is more commonly known, business process reengineering.

In business process reengineering, organizational processes are scrutinized in an effort to eliminate those that do not add value to the enterprise, to automate wherever feasible, to simplify workflow and procedures, and to improve just about anything that can be improved. These efforts may be part of a total quality management program or similar initiative, and they are not exclusively information technology activities, but information technology serves as a major enabler for this kind of transformation (Gunasekaran & Nath, 1997; Mendonca, 2004).

Gunasekaran and Nath contend that information technology and process reengineering operate together as an integral system to improve performance of organizational processes. Consider processes such as logistics, operations, sales, and customer service in terms of performance criteria such as quality, cost, speed, and innovation. One would look at the potential for information technology to improve any given processes on such performance criteria.

One illustration of the use of information technology both as a tool and a solution in business process reengineering is provided by the Social Security Administration. In the mid-1990s, one study among private-sector firms with call centers indicated that they considered an average wait time of 8 minutes to secure a representative on the phone to be an acceptable standard of customer service (Pang, 2001). The Social Security Administration reengineered its own system of 36 sites across the United States into a single virtual system optimized with communications technology to level out workloads while minimizing the busy signal rate. In 2000, their system wait time was down to a mean of 2 minutes.

Work and Workers

We already have noted specifically or at least alluded to many ways in which contemporary information technology affects work and workers in organizations, but it seems worthwhile to reiterate Mendonca's point that this is one of the major ways in which information technology is a transformative agent. Simply stated, information technology can influence "what tasks workers perform, where and when they perform them, who does the work, and what kinds of skills are needed" (Mendonca, 2004, p. 246).

Certainly the thinning out of middle management ranks in many organizations and the advent of the knowledge worker is one major way in which this transformation has occurred. Although this may conjure up images of a warehouse of cubicles populated by Dilbert-like characters who labor at mind-numbing information processing tasks, that image belies underlying levels of intensive communication and collaborative work. To illustrate the point that Mendonca is making, consider two basic technologies, e-mail and group support software.

E-mail. In the early 1990s, e-mail was just beginning to be adopted as a tool in many organizations and institutions. At the time, even scholars who studied it assumed that e-mail would just be another "communication medium with well defined properties, leading to predictable effects" (Ducheneaut & Watts, 2005, p. 20). That expectation turned out to be short-sighted. We already mentioned the great flexibility of e-mail and its relative freedom from the constraints of hierarchy and chains of command, so it is not especially surprising that professionals and knowledge workers in today's organizations struggle with an overload of e-mail (Bellotti, Ducheneaut, Howard, Smith, & Grinter, 2005). E-mail has become the preferred medium of communication for most purposes. For many knowledge workers, it is also the main tool that they use "to support project management and informal workflow" (p. 91).

E-mail contributes to load in one sense only insofar as it requires a person to put effort into the construction of messages or to do something in response to messages. Approximately 35% of the messages in the study by Bellotti et al. involved little more than announcements, but elimination of those messages along with spam still left most of the traffic with some kind of task implication for message recipients. Approximately 20% of the time that study participants spent on e-mail was used just to find or organize messages and attachments. Managing the quantity of e-mail is only one part of the overload issue. The other is quality or, more precisely, complexity of the requirements in the messages. E-mail messages concerning interdependent tasks that require a lot of coordination with others "contribute heavily to a sense of overload and are difficult to manage with current e-mail clients [software]" (Bellotti et al., 2005, p. 135).

The picture that emerges from Bellotti et al.'s research is compounded by the use of e-mail for strategically ambiguous communication. Viewed in terms of information richness theory (Daft & Lengel, 1984), e-mail is at the extreme low end of the richness scale. In theory, e-mail is not an appropriate medium for highly equivocal or ambiguous communications, but researchers have found nonetheless that managers rely heavily on e-mail for precisely this kind of use (Ducheneaut & Watts, 2005). Thus, the management of e-mail is bound up with the management of uncertainty, consensus seeking, clarification of authority, use of power and influence, and other organizational issues that oblige considerable mental effort and stress.

An additional issue that is not entirely new, but certainly has received more attention with widespread organizational use of e-mail, is the privacy of one's communications as an employee. As we indicated earlier, e-mail in organizations frequently is subject to surveillance. According to Kierkegaard (2005), an American Management Association survey in 2004 found that 60% of surveyed companies monitor e-mail entering and leaving the company, and 27% also monitor internal e-mail messages.

Kierkegaard argues that United States law provides very little privacy protection for employee communications. The Electronic Communications Privacy Act of 1986 prohibits interception of messages while they are being transmitted, but "employers are permitted to monitor networks for business purposes" (Kierkegaard, 2005, p. 233). The U.S. Third Circuit Court of Appeals also has ruled that retrieval of e-mail archived on a company server does not constitute "interception" because it already has been transmitted and processed. In another case involving the Pillsbury Company, a court ruled that an employee had no reasonable expectation of privacy for messages sent over an e-mail system owned by an employer. Privacy of employee communications receives better protection in the European Union, but even in the E.U., employers can monitor e-mail legally if employees are forewarned and informed of the purpose.

We do not want to overstate the extent of employee communications surveillance, but if you as an employee put something into an e-mail system owned by an employer, you should not assume that the communication enjoys any privacy protection.

Group Support Software. Group support software, also known simply as groupware or, in more sophisticated forms, as group decision support systems, has been around since the 1980s. We assume that most if not all of our readers know about and use e-mail, but group support software may be less familiar to many, so we will start with a description.

In its basic form, groupware combines e-mail with tools such as scheduling, note taking, conferencing, posting, and project tracking (Wheeler, Dennis, & Press, 1999). As described by Barnes and Greller (1994), groupware is the basic instrument for enabling virtual teams:

> With groupware, each computer screen becomes the participant's blackboard or the flipchart located at the staff conference. Simply put, groupware simulates the experience of a group working in the same room, but the group participants are in different geographic locations. Moreover, unlike the blackboard or flip-chart, the collaborative work product produced with groupware can be printed, stored, copied, re-read, or forwarded to and from other people. (p. 136)

Working on a project through groupware involves more than mere teleconferencing or videoconferencing. In teleconferencing or videoconferencing, remotely separate participants can hear and/or see each other, but groupware adds computer-based tools to facilitate collaboration and to document the work product. Moreover, although Barnes and Greller's description suggests that group members are working at the same time (synchronous interaction), such systems generally allow for asynchronous communication as well.

In its most sophisticated form, groupware provides group decision support systems (GDSSs). According to Cil, Alpturk, and Yazgan (2005), the main difference between collaborative groupware and GDSSs is that collaborative systems document the process used by a group to arrive at a decision, whereas GDSSs actually structure the decision-making process. As described by Jensen and Chilberg (1991), GDSS software for group conferencing provides tools not only for creating, exchanging, and printing computer messages, but also for decision-making and voting procedures. A GDSS may provide users with a choice among different models or protocols for decision making or problem solving, typically from a menu of options. The software guides the group through each step of the selected procedure.

Although a GDSS may offer a choice of methods for making a decision, Cil et al. (2005) contend that most GDSS software products are based on a common, underlying phase model built around problem identification, development of alternative solutions, analysis of alternatives, and choice of one alternative for implementation. A newer approach relies on development of multiple perspectives of a problem, then synthesis of these perspectives as a basis for generating possible solutions and defining actions.

The team of Cil, Alpturk, and Yazgan (two engineering professors at Sakarya University and a business consultant in Adapazari, Turkey) adopted this newer multiple perspectives approach to create a system called InteliTeam, but they did it with an essentially collaborative model as opposed to a GDSS model by incorporating several multiple-criteria decision methods to allow both model-driven and data-driven problem solving. According to its inventors, InteliTeam is designed to help groups achieve consensus among different perspectives, so it is better suited to address complex problems with multiple issues and multiple points of view.

We do not know if InteliTeam works better than other groupware systems, and we suspect that the basic phase model in most systems does not automatically preclude identification of multiple perspectives and consensus decisions, but this is not really the point of describing InteliTeam. In part, the example illustrates not only that information technology is global, but also that its development is now global as well, in this case, in Turkey.

We also suspect that our description of InteliTeam sounds complicated, and this complexity speaks again to skill and knowledge demands placed on those who have to work in these systems. Simply using a GDSS will not produce good decisions or effective solutions to problems. Indeed, one major finding from more than 150 research studies by a University of Arizona research center on use of group support systems is that a GDSS "can make a well-planned meeting better, and it can make a poorly planned meeting worse" (Nunamaker, Briggs, Mittleman, Vogel, & Balthazard, 1997, p. 171).

Wherever groupware systems are in use, organization members should expect to work not only in teams, but possibly in virtual teams. Organization members will have to understand team collaboration and how technology alters it. They will need to know theories and models of group communication, decision making, and problem solving in order to even understand how a high-end GDSS works and how to use it effectively.

INTERPRETIVE PERSPECTIVE

The interpretive perspective of information technology is concerned with sense making in at least two respects. First, how does information technology itself influence sense-making processes in organizations? Second, how are understandings and uses of technology constructed in sense-making processes?

Technology's Influence on Sense Making

Prior to widespread Internet access, much of the attention to the consequences of information technology for sense making was centered in concerns that human-computer interaction would displace human-human interaction. For example, Gratz and Salem (1984) noted that the advent of contemporary information technology had the "potential to do great harm to human relationships" (p. 100) not only by diminishing relational skills, but also by altering the processes through which self-concepts and identities are formed in a culture of restricted communication among humans. Managing emotion, ambiguity, paradox, and multiple levels of abstraction would become impossible in "the completely logical world of the computer" (p. 101). The prospect of telecommuting and home offices raised concerns about pervasive alienation, the demise of negotiated order, and even the end of "schmoozing" as a means of "achieving a sense of companionship and togetherness among workers as they chat about their lives and gripe about common problems" (Renfro, 1982, p. 44). Concern with the alienating effects of technology has shifted to the critical perspective, but interpretive work still addresses the particular consequences of technology for sense making. In a general review of interpretive work on computer-mediated communication, Gephart (2004) summarized four basic ways in which sense making is altered in computer-mediated environments. We are not convinced that these effects are unique to the use of computers, but they may occur to a greater degree in computer-mediated environments.

First, people sustain reciprocity in ordinary interaction, but computer mediation "requires users to actively find evidence that they share meanings with others in the communication" (Gephart, 2004, p. 482). For example, the manager of a company support unit producing an event for another department dashed off a quick, one-line e-mail indicating that the event "cannot happen" until she has an account number to charge against for expenses. The head of that department, relatively new to the organization and apparently unaware that the support unit is supposed to charge other departments for its services, fired off a responding e-mail demanding to know why the support unit was "threatening to cancel" the event. The next step was a phone call (not an e-mail) to clarify and resolve the misunderstanding in a personal conversation.

Second, people use "normal-form" terms and utterances in ordinary interaction to describe their environment and experiences. As a normal part of the work environment, the computer and its software applications have entered into the domain of normal-form workplace terms and utterances. This consequence probably is obvious. For example, until just a few years ago, nobody had ever Googled anything. The name of a search engine morphed into a verb for its use. A vocabulary and a discourse about the devices, operations, and problems of information technology are insinuated thoroughly into organizational life.

Third, much of the knowledge that supports ordinary interaction is tacit and not explicit, and utterances are incomplete, vague, and ambiguous. We assume that others can and will fill in the right meanings or that meanings will be clarified in the ongoing conversation. In computer-mediated communication, one must "actively seek additional information to interpret events [and] wait for this information to emerge" (Gephart, 2004, p. 482). The previous example of the support unit manager and department head seems to illustrate this difference as well.

Finally, in ordinary interaction, participants expect each other to "look beyond the surface meanings of words" for understanding. Various aspects of context enable us to do this, e.g., knowledge about the other person, the situation, or the setting. Computer-mediated communication brings its own kind of demand for this ability "to comprehend computer displays and communications by using contextual information" (p. 483). For example, a popular software package for displaying and managing documents includes a camera icon on the horizontal toolbar. If you move your mouse to position the cursor over the icon, a box will open to indicate that this is the snapshot tool. If you are clueless about the meaning, you can get details in the help feature, but if you think about the context of document management, you may realize intuitively that this tool allows you to drag a box around an area of the document such as a table and copy that area to the clipboard. Even reading and understanding the example requires one to grasp information technology language, context, and meanings.

Social Construction of Information Technology

Interpretive studies also are concerned with the ways in which information technology itself is socially constructed, i.e., understanding the meanings that technology has for its users and how these meanings are constituted through communication. One of the major concepts demonstrated in this line of work is interpretive flexibility, i.e., the emergence of multiple understandings for the same technology. For example, there is longstanding recognition of the divergence (some would call it a chasm) between the technologist who designs, implements, and/or supports the technology and the ordinary user who applies that technology to tasks and problems (Gephart, 2004). The technologist often does not understand the nuances of the user's needs, and the user seldom understands the nuances of the technology itself.

Interpretive flexibility also involves variations in users' understandings as well. Zorn (2003) found that implementation of a nationwide database system in a New Zealand agency was greeted with considerable ambivalence. Any given member might experience both positive and negative feelings about the change, being open to it on the one hand, but harboring reservations about it on the other. Hence, members were open to influence and, indeed, members attempted to influence one another toward particular understandings of the technology and its consequences for the agency.

On a somewhat grander scale, Zoonen (2002) has suggested interpretive flexibility extends to the entire Internet in the sense that it is "a contested medium as far as its social cultural meanings and significance are concerned" (p. 5). She focused on gender in particular, arguing that gender and the Internet are mutually influential; each is shaping the other. Zoonen noted that the Internet began as a masculine technology in the military-industrial complex and that men still constitute the great majority of technical actors behind the Internet today. In recent years, feminist scholars began to characterize the Internet as a "woman's medium" suited to collective networking and "an ethic of community, consensus, and communication" (p. 9). More recently, a movement known as cyberfeminism has begun to lay claim to the Internet as a vehicle for contesting the idea of gender itself. So, in cyberspace, we now find various forms of "grrl" groups engaged in degendering, transgendering, and other challenges to gender as they "construct a new particular cyberculture of womanhood" (p. 13).

Zoonen's own study of Internet use and negotiation suggests that masculine, feminine, and cyberfeminine conceptions of the Internet all fail to capture what actually occurs in everyday life. She found that the involvement of gender in understandings of the Internet is even more multidimensional, although she did this in the households of young, childless, heterosexual Dutch couples rather than in work organizations. According to Zoonen, these households reflected four different information technology cultures: traditional, deliberative, individualized, and reversed.

In the traditional arrangement, the Internet and computer are coded at a symbolic level by both partners as "male territory in the household" (p. 17). In the reversed culture, the territory is female. Separate domains are established in the individualized culture, e.g., with multiple computers in the household; she has hers, he has his. Partners actively negotiate use of the computer and Internet in the deliberative culture, and talk surrounding the technology actually becomes "instrumental in constructing [the partners'] sense of togetherness" (p. 18).

We close this section by noting that the social construction of information and communication technology is not just an interest of the interpretive perspective. Some scholars have appropriated interpretive concepts and subjected them to traditional methods of social science in order to explain how users constitute meanings for technology. One prominent example is a social influence theory developed by Janet Fulk (1993) and various collaborators. Fulk acknowledges interpretive flexibility by noting that technologies can be interpreted in multiple and conflicting ways, so they are equivocal. Information and communication technologies pose "unusual problems in sense-making because they are often poorly understood [and] continuously redesigned and reinterpreted in the process of implementation and accommodation" (p. 922). Following a theme that dates back to the Hawthorne Studies, Fulk turns to workgroups and social networks as sources of influence on individual attitudes and as sites of reality construction. Various studies under this theoretical framework have found influences such as similarity within personal communication networks in attitudes toward and uses of technology and moderating factors such as greater social influence when individuals are highly attracted to their workgroups.

CRITICAL PERSPECTIVE

Issues of social and organizational control through the use of information technology figure prominently in the critical perspective. Interests here are highly varied, but they range from use of information technology to reinforce managerial authority in any given organization, support neoliberal hegemony in Western societies, and enable global control by transnational corporations. Use of information technology in resistance to such forces also is a topic in this perspective.

Technology and Managerial Authority

Schwarz (2002) noted that new-form organization theory assumes that information technology drives or enables organizational change. In particular, innovations in information technology lead to greater flexibility, decentralization, new networks, altered authority relationships, and less specialization in jobs and members' organizational roles. Schwarz contested these assumptions, arguing that information technology innovations tend to reinforce rather than change existing organizational structures and systems of authority.

In a study of two Australian organizations implementing major information technology initiatives, Schwarz found that the new systems did not lead to structural transformations and did not alter the existing systems of hierarchy and authority. In one of the organizations, management announced at the outset of the initiative that it would fundamentally alter the organization, but as soon as the first phase of implementation was completed, the same management group began to nudge it back into conformity with their preexisting values. Instead of enabling decentralization, management used the system for closer supervision and scrutiny, and "individual roles and formalization . . . remained much the same" (p. 166). One high-level manager justified the outcome by suggesting that the new system always was supposed to be fundamentally a *management* information system.

The second organization also used its new system to reinforce centralization of authority. Insofar as the system itself might have allowed for greater autonomy at lower levels, it was controlled with new rules, e.g., a requirement for management approval. As one lower level employee observed, "No one can really make a low-level decision . . . [it] still has to go to management" (p. 168). In this organization, the information technology change was even used to reduce employee independence by automating processes that formerly had required human interpretations and decisions.

The really interesting feature in Schwarz's discussion is the role of nonexecutive or nonmanagerial information technology users. Schwarz attributes little or no autonomy to these organization members in constructing their own understandings of the technology. When lower level workers use the technology, "they draw on the technological and structural properties guided by management's power over, knowledge, assumptions, and expectations about the technology and its intended use" (p. 174). In other words, the way that nonmanagers use technology actually sustains managerial control because the nonmanagement users are "socialized to hierarchy" (p. 177).

Technology and Neoliberal Hegemony

McKenna (2004) asserts that "neo-liberal hegemony in Western culture is very close to absolute" (p. 17). The concept of neoliberalism itself is rather elaborate because it is a moral and political philosophy as well as an economic philosophy, but the essence of it is a revival and transformation of the economic liberalism that flourished in the United States until the Great Depression in the 1930s. Economic liberalism was predicated on free enterprise and free trade with little or no government intervention in the form of controls, barriers, and restrictions. In the wake of the Depression, this kind of thinking was replaced by the basic premise of political liberalism that government control and intervention are warranted and necessary insofar as government's purpose is to promote the common good. Neoliberalism is a return to basic principles of economic liberalism, but with a new twist involving belief in the primacy of market forces. This belief is no longer based on the production of goods and services. The market is an end in itself. Every human transaction is a market transaction, potentially competing with and influencing every other transaction.

Because the market is the standard and the guide for all human action, it supplants any other system of ethics and beliefs. This notion is not necessarily a late 20th century invention. Mark Twain's 19th century Tom Sawyer embraced this principle when he made the idea of whitewashing Aunt Polly's fence so appealing to his friends that he got them not only to do it in his place, but also to pay him for the privilege. One might make a case that neoliberalism was the philosophy imparted to Enron by CEO Jeff Skilling . . . a philosophy readily exploited by CFO Andy Fastow's fraudulent financing schemes. Now how is this connected with technology?

The neoliberal position envisions a global, economic order in which traditional bureaucratic organization and hierarchy are outmoded. This kind of thinking is reflected in new-form organization theory. Organizations are boundaryless and do not require centralized systems of authority. The new order is one of flexibility and adaptability to take advantage of the opportunities that the market presents. In other words, the new order is a virtual order that, of course, is enabled by technology and also obliges a virtual consciousness. Thorne (2005) describes virtual consciousness as a pervasive worldview in which "globalization is an inevitable historical framework . . . where virtual organizations are the only viable organizational form" (p. 596).

In Thorne's analysis, virtual consciousness involves neoliberal and postmodernist fantasies in which the "the iron cage of the rational, hierarchical, authoritarian organization . . . is replaced by the new, benign, boundary-less, flexible, networked, information and technology-driven, empowering, virtual organization" (p. 581). The fantasies of virtual consciousness are not benign from a critical standpoint. Among other criticisms, Thorne contends that the literature of business restructuring, infused with this consciousness, ignores analysis of technology's negative consequences and presents us instead with "a technological immanence where a future, with its specific set of social changes, is already upon us and cannot be stopped" (p. 587). We are to accept the notion that this transformation is not only good, but also inevitable. In other words, resistance is pointless.

Moreover, according to Thorne, virtual consciousness obscures the capitalist forces that drive the virtual enterprise, reinforce inequalities in wealth and power, and make individuals dispensable. It also ignores the fact that even terrorist and criminal organizations have many characteristics of virtual organizations, "including mastery of cyberspace and the global, digital domain" (p. 596).

Technology and Global Control

If virtual consciousness is pushed beyond the bounds of Western culture, the implication is not just for a global economy, but also for a condition of global control. Although the term "globalization" may be relatively new and generally invoked along with ominous visions of outsourced jobs and trade deficits, Peter McMahon (2002) argues that global control with the aid of information technology has been a de facto state of world affairs since 1845, and recent history can be divided into three periods in which information technologies with global reach have either helped or hindered these systems of control.

McMahon describes the period from 1845 to 1914 as a "liberal-international world order" controlled by a few very powerful financiers with the aid of the telegraph. That period ended with World War I, an event described by Harvard historian Niall Ferguson (2006) as "an avoidable political error" (p. 40) that many knew could happen, but few believed would happen. Hence, the financial markets and the controlling interests were caught largely by surprise. In the next period from 1914 to the late 1960s, global control shifted to a few nation-states with corporate and military-industrial complexes supported by the technology of mass media. In the third period, the present day, McMahon sees the new technologies that might seem to be liberating and empowering for the individual, as tools that once again have shifted the balance of global power to a cadre of financiers and major multinational corporate executives.

McMahon is concerned mainly about control of corporations and financial institutions over telematics and transnational data flows that enable them to locate the means of production anywhere and control it from anywhere. How can a labor union or even a national government negotiate with a multinational enterprise when that enterprise can move jobs to another country? Vegh (2003) also provides illustrations of the differences in influence and effectiveness between large corporate and institutional concerns with the resources to leverage technology in support of their goals and less well-to-do nonprofit or nongovernmental organizations that lack this capability. According to Vegh, "As the corporate world continues to colonize cyberspace the inequalities of resources online are still fairly evident" (p. 89).

The vestiges of the nation-state era certainly are still with us, as evidenced by the continuing global influence of the United States, Japan, and the European Union, but also consider the rapid emergence of China and India as global economic powers. Although it is tempting to point to their abundant supplies of inexpensive labor as an explanation for Chinese and Indian success, Clyde Prestowitz, president of the Washington, D.C. Economic Strategy Institute, notes that information technology also is an important factor. According to Prestowitz (2005), global access to high-speed Internet communications and sophisticated supply-chain management for express delivery have invalidated the classic assumptions of international economic theory:

> The classic assumptions hold that technology, capital, and labor are immobile and that low-wage countries focus on labor-intensive production, while developed countries focus on innovation and capital-intensive production. In fact, all these factors are not only mobile, but instantly so. As a result, globalization is no longer a matter of Americanization; globalization is going truly global at the speed of light. India and China have become not only the world's fastest growing economies, but are also destined to become the world's largest–surpassing both Japan and the United States.

Those who agree with McMahon's thesis of global control might be quick to point out that China and India have their own cadres of super-rich elites, with 33 billionaires in China (including Hong Kong) and 23 in India (Kroll & Fass, 2006), but both countries also have an economic middle class numbering in the hundreds of millions (Hasan, 2006). How much control can a few dozen billionaires really exert over "three billion new [Chinese and Indian] capitalists" (Prestowitz, 2005)?

Technology and Resistance

Critical theory is concerned not only with the problems of power and control, but also with resistance to systems of domination. In the area of information technology, one example of this interest is Taylor's (2005) study of hacktivism.

Hacktivism is a movement that combines oppositional political activism with the methods and techniques of computer hacking. It is in some respects similar to other resistance groups that act by disrupting the processes of dominant systems. Given claims in critical theory that the cumulative effect of information and communication technology is to produce total disillusionment, Taylor contends, "hacktivism at least offers some hope that a critical, proactive dimension can be restored to the predominantly passive nature of our usual reception of the media" (p. 627).

Taylor considers the case of Electronic Disturbance Theater (EDT) and its alliance with the antigovernment Zapatista movement in Mexico. EDT has on various occasions coordinated Web sit-ins for the Zapatistas and used a software system known as Floodnet to disrupt the Web sites of corporations and financial institutions. The effectiveness of Floodnet depends on how many Web browsers simultaneously use it on a given Web site, so its strength from EDT's standpoint is demonstration of "the solidarity of simultaneous collective action" in electronic civil disobedience (p. 635).

EDT is interesting because its tactics have been criticized from the right and left of the political spectrum. Certainly the corporations and institutions targeted in cyber attacks and sit-ins would loathe hacktivism, but EDT also has been challenged for engaging in a form of censorship by interfering with others' access to the Internet. EDT responds in its own legitimizing discourse with an analogy to the Agora in Plato's *Republic*, the place where the privileged and powerful were entitled to engage in rational discourse. As EDT develops its analogy, the Agora was disturbed by the Demos, the people who did not use the rational discourse, did not have access to the rules of logos, and disrupted the discourse of power with a different language. EDT views itself as enabling the contemporary Demos (e.g., the Zapatistas) to disrupt the contemporary Agora by squatting on the Internet lanes of the Virtual Republic.

Because many critical scholars are so focused on the oppressive effects of technology, they are not quite sure how to address uses of the technology in resistance because they have not adequately conceptualized its benefits. In this case, the use of the technology for electronic civil disobedience provides hacktivism with a way of "getting inside the palace of power" (Taylor, 2005, p. 636). The cyberfeminist grrl groups noted in Zoonen's work represent another manifestation of resistance on the Internet. So, whereas some critical theorists worry over capitalism's extension beyond production into communication itself and the corporate colonization of the Internet, others see the Internet as contested terrain not just in terms of its meanings, but also in terms of its uses. Taylor concludes that "electronic culture facilitates the emergence of global groups of like-minded radicals" (p. 638). Whether such facilitation is good or bad may depend on what kind of radical one has in mind: the Zapatista-supporting hacktivist described by Taylor or the terrorist described by Thorne.

The Technologized Life

As we have suggested throughout this chapter, information technology, perhaps more than any other tool or technology, influences organizing and organizational communication in important and compelling ways. For good or ill, Baby Boomers such as your authors, who experienced the transition into the information age and remember a time before the technology, now regard it as indispensable to daily life and work. We would be lost without our laptops, PDAs, and wireless phones. Gen-Xers and Millennials, having grown up with the technology, may take it for granted, but they might be even more lost without it.

Perhaps the phenomenon is not altogether new, but 21st century life for many of us is more thoroughly technologized than ever before. So we end this chapter on a cautionary note. The traditionalist, interpretivist, and critical theorist would agree at least that information technology disconnects the organization from the bonds of space and time, and it disconnects the work as well. As Mendonca (2004) observed, this situation presents "several major negatives for workers" (p. 246). The line between work life and personal life is being obliterated by the extension of work into leisure time and home life. The pace of technological change obliges continuous adaptation and upgrading of skills. And once an infrastructure is in place for virtual work, it can be accomplished anytime, anywhere, by anyone with the requisite skill sets. This means that global competition not only among organizations and institutions, but also among workers may be a given for many years to come. This is the consequence of neoliberalism and the "virtual consciousness" that worries Thorne (2005).

SUMMARY

Information technology is ubiquitous, so it is easy to take it for granted, but it has compelling consequences for organizations and organizational communication. Mere computer literacy is not enough for organization members today. Real information technology fluency is necessary.

Whether one believes that technology determines social and organizational change or merely enables it, it is clear that information technology is at the very least a catalyst for change. It has led to organizational conditions and dynamics in the 21st century that are fundamentally different from those of the 19th and 20th centuries. Just as the Gutenberg press helped to bring on the Reformation, Renaissance, and Scientific Revolution, sweeping away medieval society, today's information technology may have equally profound consequences in the information age.

The traditional perspective of information technology in organizational communication typically is concerned with the potential of technology to enhance efficiency, effectiveness, and ultimately productivity. It examines barriers to these objectives that may arise in difficulties with adaptation to technological change, including the disruptive influences of technology itself, and it does raise concerns about the negative consequences of technology.

Information technology is adopted in organizations for many reasons, but three major purposes are productivity, knowledge management, and control. Tying productivity to information technology historically has been a problem, but recent trends seem to support the connection. In part, failures to find associations in the past may be a result of mismeasurement and the fact that the benefits of technology do not materialize until well after adoption. Information technology links most closely to productivity when it also is connected with innovation.

Knowledge management is regarded by some as a passing fad, but the idea of getting beyond information management to identify, capture, embed, and transmit organizational knowledge is a response to complex environments. Knowledge management requires sophisticated information technology, yet the disruptive influence of information technology itself, especially information overload from the Internet and Web, has led to knowledge management initiatives.

Adoption and use of information technology involve control. The function of communication in coordination and control of complex organizations is a well-established subject in the traditional perspective, and advances in information technology historically have affected that function. The traditional perspective is concerned with the issue primarily from a managerial point of view, but the concerns are multifaceted, including not only issues of direct, managerial use of technology for control, but also attention to paradoxical consequences of technology for control such as the disruptive influences of technology and the locus and diffusion of organizational control.

It is generally agreed that access to information technology is essential today, so the digital divide has received a great deal of attention and a great deal of money has been directed to alleviate it. But the digital divides can be viewed in terms of race, economic class, gender, and geography, and even between organizations and nations. There is doubt that mere access to information technology will provide upward mobility for the disadvantaged. Even so, information technology is becoming truly globalized, and many countries are bridging the digital divide and improving their globally competitive positions in the process. Hence, mere computer literacy is inadequate for prosperity, and real information technology fluency appears to be the new standard of competence. Fluency with information technology includes reasoning ability, adaptability, and knowledge about problem solving, collaboration, and communication as well as an understanding of the organizational and societal implications of technology.

Information technology has consequences for organizing and organizational communication, and many scholars use the word "impact" to talk about the influence of information technology on organizations. In particular, influences on organizational structure, organizational processes, and work and workers are worth some attention.

Interest in the structural effects of information technology has been around ever since Leavitt and Whisler made predictions in 1958 about the shape of organizations in the 1980s, including more centralization, fewer middle managers, and flatter organizations. By the 1990s, it was clear that many predictions were turning out to be correct, but claims of new-form organization theory that information technology will drive greater flexibility, decentralization, and realignments of authority are not always supported in research.

The effect of technology on organizational structure seems to be a paradox. Sometimes it is linked to centralization, at other times to decentralization. Although managerial concern for control may always be a force for centralization, today's combinations of sophisticated and highly trained knowledge workers with highly flexible communication tools such as e-mail that defy hierarchical channels also have the potential to shift power and control in decentralizing ways.

Virtual organizations also have received much attention as new organization forms. Information technology allows space-time independence in organizing. Members of virtual teams can do their work and collaborate without being in the same place or even in the same time. Virtual organizations may even include large collectives of different organizations that band together for a common purpose. We also may view virtual organizations in terms of virtual physicality and virtual ownership. The latter include organizations that rely heavily on outsourcing for most of their work, or, as Alexander (1997) described them, organizations that rely on getting things done, but not by doing things themselves.

Change in organizational processes is connected mainly with the concept of business process reengineering or redesign. In business process reengineering, organizational processes are scrutinized in an effort to eliminate those that do not add value to the enterprise, to automate wherever feasible, to simplify workflow and procedures, and to improve just about anything that can be improved. This is not exclusively an information technology activity, but information technology serves as a major enabler for this kind of transformation

The effects of information technology on work and workers involve who is doing the work, what kind of work is being done, and where it is being done. One can see the consequences today in use of two systems, e-mail and group support software. E-mail originally was treated as little more than a basic communication tool, i.e., for sending and receiving messages, but e-mail overload is the order of the day in organizations. E-mail not only has become the preferred communication medium for most purposes, but also serves as the primary tool for project management and workflow. E-mail affords little assurance of private communication, however. Most large and midsized organizations engage in some level of e-mail surveillance.

Groupware has enabled virtual organizing. It may be as simple as a group support system or as complex as a multiple-criteria group decision support system. Groupware adds conferencing and work product documentation to messaging. Decision support adds options for executing a decision-making or problem-solving process and guides users through each step in the process. Where groupware is used, organization members should expect to work in teams and possibly even virtual teams. In order to use these systems effectively, members need to understand theories and models of group communication, decision making, and problem solving.

The interpretive perspective of information technology in organizational communication is concerned with the consequences of technology for sense-making processes and also with the way in which technology itself is socially constructed and understood. Technology in the form of computer-mediated communication obliges participants to actively seek evidence that they share meanings and to more actively seek additional information to interpret events. The normal-form systems, operations, and problems of technology also are now insinuated in the language of organizations. The technology also brings its own demands for contextual understanding of information in computer displays.

The meanings of technology itself are socially constructed. One of the major concepts demonstrated in this line of work is interpretive flexibility, i.e., the emergence of multiple understandings for the same technology. It is reflected in the divergent understandings of technologists and users, ambivalence of users toward technological innovations and mutual influence attempts to shape understandings of technology, and even in varying constructions of the gender of the Internet. Social information theory, which uses interpretive concepts with traditional research methods, has shown that workgroup and personal communication network dynamics do influence member understandings of and attitudes toward technology.

The critical perspective is concerned in various ways with the theme of technology and control. Critical studies have challenged new-form organization theory's assumptions about the decentralizing effects of technology, suggesting instead that managers shape new systems to reinforce their own authority and nonmanagers take up these managerial perspectives in their own uses of technology. Even where systems are supposed to diffuse authority, executive and managerial ideology is a powerful centralizing force.

Critical studies also have focused attention on the role of technology in neoliberal hegemony and a pervasive virtual consciousness. Here, the neoliberal, new-form, postmodernist notions of organizational transformation from traditional bureaucratic systems to boundaryless, flexible, technology-driven, empowering, virtual organizations are regarded as fantasies of virtual consciousness that are not benign from a critical standpoint. Virtual consciousness ignores technology's negative consequences, obscures the capitalist foundation that reinforces inequalities, and presents transformation as not only good, but also inevitable. Extended beyond its place in Western societies, neoliberal virtual consciousness also suggests conditions of global control to critical scholars, even to the point of one argument that global control already has been an established fact since the mid-19th century. What has changed is a shift from control by nation-states to control by multinational corporations.

Although the critical perspective tends to see technology primarily in terms of oppression, critical studies also examine and celebrate the use of information technology in resistance. The relatively recent emergence of hacktivism, a movement that combines oppositional political action with computer hacking techniques, provides one example. One common tactic is use of Web or cyber sit-ins, in which large numbers of participants flood and crash Web sites of targeted corporations and financial institutions. Another example is the emergence of cyberfeminism and extensive use of the Internet and Web by grrl groups for networking and advocacy.

Regardless of perspective, it seems clear in the information age that life is more thoroughly technologized than ever before. The line between work and leisure or home life is being obliterated. New skills and continuous upgrading of skills are necessary. Virtual organizing and infrastructure mean that work can be done anytime, anywhere, by anyone with the requisite skill sets, so global competition among organizations and among workers may be assured for years to come.

DISCUSSION QUESTIONS/ACTIVITIES

1. In what ways do you already use information technology and how has does it influence your life? Is there anything in this chapter about information technology in organizations that surprises or maybe even alarms you? What do you think you need to do, if anything, to be better prepared for a technologized organization and a technologized life?

2. Has Thorne (2005) hit on a disturbing issue in his critique of virtual consciousness? Do you think there is a prevailing virtual consciousness? If so, what does it mean for your future?

3. The role of information technology in globalization has all kinds of implications. What are some of the more important issues in your mind? Relate some of this discussion to the material in this chapter on economic growth in India and China, the development of InteliTeam in Turkey, and Akin, the 14-year-old Internet scam artist in Nigeria.

4. If your college or university has groupware features in a course support system that you have not used, the next time that you have to do a team project, be sure to attempt the project with the support of this system. Better yet, get your group to use one of many free groupware applications available on the Web. Just Google "free groupware."

REFERENCES

Alexander, M. (1997). Getting to grips with the virtual organization. *Long Range Planning, 30*(1), 122–124.

Baily, M. N. (2003, January). Information technology and productivity: Recent findings. Presentation at the AEA (American Economic Association) meetings, Washington, DC [Electronic version]. Retrieved on May 17, 2006, from http://www.iie.com/publications/papers/baily0103.pdf

Barnes, S., & Greller, L. M. (1994). Computer mediated communication in the organization. *Communication Education, 43,* 129–142.

Bellotti, V., Ducheneaut, N. Howard, M., Smith, I., & Grinter, R. E. (2005). Quality vs. quantity: E-mail-centric task management and its relation with overload. *Human-Computer Interaction, 20,* 89–138.

Blair, D. C. (2002). Knowledge management: Hype, hope, or help? *Journal of the American Society for Information Science and Technology, 53*(12), 1019–1028.

Brynjolfsson, E. (1993). The productivity paradox of information technology. *Communications of the ACM, 36*(12), 67–77.

CBS News *Sixty Minutes* (2006, April 2). Working 24/7 [Electronic version]. Retrieved May 17, 2006, from http://www.cbsnews.com/stories/2006/03/31/60minutes/main1460246.shtml

Chen, W., & Wellman, B. (2003). Charting and bridging digital divides: Comparing socio-economic, gender, life stage, and rural-urban Internet access and use in eight countries. Paper presented to the AMD Global Consumer Advisory Council, October 27.

Cil, I., Alpturk, O., & Yazgan, H. R. (2005). A new collaborative system framework based on a multiple perspective approach: InteliTeam. *Decision Support Systems, 39,* 619–641.

Communications control shifts to workgroups, individuals. (1994) *Communications News, 31*(10), 11–14.

Daft, R. L., & Lengel, R. H. (1984). Information richness: A new approach to managerial information processing and organization design. In B. Staw & L. Cummings (Eds.), *Research in organizational behavior* (pp. 191–233). Greenwich, CT: JAI.

Davenport, T. H., & Prusak, L. (1998). *Working knowledge: How organizations manage what they know.* Boston: Harvard Business School Press.

Dewar, J. A. (1998). *The information age and the printing press: Looking backward to see ahead* (Rand Paper P-8014). Santa Monica, CA: Rand Distribution Services.

Drucker, P. (1998). *The coming of the new organization.* Cambridge, MA: Harvard Business School Press.

Ducheneaut, N., & Watts, L. A. (2005). In search of coherence: A review of e-mail research. *Human-Computer Interaction, 20,* 11–48.

Edmunds, A., & Morris, A. (2000). The problem of information overload in business organizations: A review of the literature. *International Journal of Information Management, 20,* 17–28.

Ferguson, N. (2006). Political risk and the international bond market between the 1848 revolution and the outbreak of the first world war. *Economic History Review, 66(2),* 70–112.

Fulk, J. (1993). Social construction of communication technology. *Academy of Management Journal, 36*(5), 921–950.

Galagan, P. (1997). Smart companies (knowledge management). *Training and Development, 51*(12), 20–25.

Gephart, R. P. (2004, December). Sensemaking and new media at work. *American Behavioral Scientist, 48*(4), 479–495.

Gratz, R. D., & Salem, P. J. (1984). Technology and the crisis of self. *Communication Quarterly, 32,* 98–103.

Greengard, S. (2000, November). Taming the information glut. *Workforce,* pp. 22–24.

Gunasekaran, A., & Nath, B. (1997, June). The role of information technology in business process reengineering. *International Journal of Production Economics, 50*(2–3), 91–104.

Hasan, S. R. (2006, February 8). China, India lead consumer confidence survey. *Asia Times Online.* [Electronic version]. Retrieved May 17, 2006, from http://www.atimes.com/atimes/China_Business/HB08Cb06.html

Jensen, A. D., & Chilberg, J. C. (1991). *Small group communication: Theory and application.* Belmont, CA: Wadsworth.

Kankanhalli, A., Tanudidjaja, F., Sutanto, J., & Tan, B. C. Y. (2003). The role of IT in successful knowledge management initiatives. *Communications of the ACM, 46*(9), 69–73.

Keniston, K. (2002). IT for the common man: Lessons from India. A M. N. Srinivas Memorial Lecture published as *NIAS Special Publication SP7-02.* National Institute of Advanced Studies, Indian Institute of Science.

Kierkegaard, S. (2005). Privacy in electronic communication. Watch your e-mail: Your boss is snooping! *Computer Law & Security Report, 21,* 226–236.

Kling, R. (1980). Social analyses of computing: Theoretical perspectives in recent empirical research. *Computing Surveys, 12*(1), 61–110.

Koch, C. (2006). The ABCs of ERP. CIO.Com Enterprise Resource Planning Research Center [Electronic version]. Retrieved May 17, 2006, from http://www.cio.com/research/erp/edit/erpbasics.html

Kroll, L., & Fass, A. (Eds.) (2006, March 9). The world's billionaires. *Forbes*. [Electronic version]. Retrieved May 17, 2006, from http://www.forbes.com/billionaires?boxes=custom

Lawal, L. (2006, May 22). On-line scams create "Yahoo! millionaires." *Fortune*. [Electronic version at CNN.Money.com]. Retrieved May 23, 2006, from http://money.cnn.com/magazines/fortune/fortune_archive/2006/05/29/8378124/index.htm?cnn=yes

Leavitt, H., & Whisler, T. (1958, November–December). Management in the 1980's. *Harvard Business Review*, pp. 41–48.

Mahmood, M. A., & Mann, G. J. (1993). Measuring the organizational impact of information technology investment: An exploratory study. *Journal of Management Information Systems, 10*(1), 97–122.

Malone, T. W. (1999, October). Is "empowerment" just a fad? Control, decision-making, and information technology. *BT Technology Journal, 17*(4), 141–144. Excerpt reprinted from full article in *Sloan Management Review, 38*(2), 23–35, 1997, by permission of MIT.

McFarlan, F. W. (2002, March). Technology: Turning organizations inside out. *Association Management, 54*(3), 46–51.

McGee, M. K. (2000, April 17). It's official: IT adds up. *Information Week Online* [Electronic version]. Retrieved May 17, 2006, from http://www.informationweek.com/782/productivity.htm

McKenna, B. (2004). Critical discourse studies: Where to from here? *Critical Discourse Studies, 1*(1), 9–39.

McMahon, P. (2002). *Global control: Information technology and globalization since 1845*. Northampton, MA: Edward Elgar.

Mendonca, J. (2004, October). Organizational impact of information technology: A leadership course for IT. *Proceedings of the 5th Conference on Information Technology Education* (pp. 244–247). New York: ACM Press.

Nadler, D. A., Gerstein, M. S., & Shaw, R. B. (1992). *Organizational architecture: Designs for changing organizations*. San Francisco, CA: Jossey-Bass.

The National Research Council's Computer Science and Telecommunications Board. (1999). *Being fluent with information technology*. Washington, DC: National Academies Press.

National Telecommunications and Information Administration. (1999). *Falling through the net, etc., defining the digital divide*. Washington, DC: U.S. Department of Commerce.

Nunamaker, J., & Briggs, R. O. (1997). Special issues: Information technology and its organizational impact. *Journal of Management Information Systems, 13*(3), 3–6.

Nunamaker, J. F., Jr., Briggs, R, O., Mittleman, D. D., Vogel, D. R., & Balthazard, P. A. (1997). Lessons from a dozen years of group support systems research: A discussion of lab and field findings. *Journal of Management Information Systems, 13*(3), 163–207.

Olson, M. H. (1982, December). New information technology and organizational culture. *MIS Quarterly*, pp. 21–30.

Pang, L. (2001). Understanding virtual organizations. *Information Systems Control Journal, 6*, 1–8 [Electronic version]. Retrieved May 17, 2006, from http://www.isaca.org/Template.cfm?Section=Archives&template=/TaggedPage/TaggedPageDisplay.cfm&TPLID=7&UserDefinedDate1=11/01/2001

Pfaffenberger, B. (2004). Book review: Global control: Information technology and globalization since 1845. *Technology and Culture, 45,* 214–216.

Prestowitz, C. (2005). China-India entente shifts global balance. *Yale Global Online*. Yale Center for the Study of Globalization [Electronic version]. Retrieved May 17, 2005, from http://yaleglobal.yale.edu/display.article?id=5578

Renfro, W. L. (1982, June). Second thoughts on moving the home office. *The Futurist*, pp. 43–48.

Roberts, C. B. (1996). The impact of information technology on the management of system design. *Technology in Society, 18*(3), 333–355.

Robinson, J. P. (2003). Introduction to issues 4 and 5, digital divides: Past, present and future. *IT & Society, 1*(5), i–xiv.

Rogers, E. M. (1988). Information technologies: How organizations are changing. In G. M. Goldhaber & G. A. Barnett (Eds), *Handbook of organizational communication* (pp. 437–452). Norwood, NJ: Ablex.

Rowley, J. (1999). What is knowledge management? *Library Management, 20*(8), 416–419.

Schwarz, G. M. (2002). Organizational hierarchy adaptation and information technology. *Information and Organization, 12,* 153–182.

Sieloff, C. G. (1999). If only HP knew what HP knows. *Journal of Knowledge Management, 3*(1), 47–53.

Taylor, P. A. (2005). From hackers to hacktivists: Speed bumps on the global superhighway? *New Media & Society, 7*(5), 625–646.

Thierauf, R. J. (1978). *Distributed processing systems.* Englewood Cliffs, NJ: Prentice Hall.

Thorne, K. (2005). Designing virtual organizations? Themes and trends in political and organizational discourses. *Journal of Management Development, 24*(7), 580–607.

Tufekci, Z. (2005). Digital divide and social mobility: How much hope and how much hype? Paper presented at the annual meeting of the International Communication Association, New York, NY, May 2005.

Vegh, S. (2003). Classifying forms of online activism: The case of cyberprotests against the World Bank. In M. McCaughey & M. D. Ayers (Eds.), *Cyberactivism: Online activism in theory and practice* (pp. 71–96). New York: Routledge.

VonKortzfleisch, H. F. O. (2003). Organizational impact of information technology (IT) in the context of e-business: Development of a general framework for balancing the tensions between opportunities and risks. Proceedings of the 36th Hawaii International Conference on System Sciences [Electronic version]. Retrieved on May 17, 2006, from http://csd12.computer.org/comp/proceedings/hicss/2003/1874/08/187480263a.pdf

Wheeler, B. C., Dennis, A. R., & Press, L. I. (1999). Groupware comes to the Internet: Charting a new world. *The Data Base for Advances in Information Systems, 30*(3–4), 8–21.

Whisler, T. (1970). *The impact of computers on organizations.* New York: Praeger.

Wiig, K. M. (1997). Knowledge management: An introduction and perspective. *The Journal of Knowledge Management, 1*(1), 6–14.

Yates, J. (1989). *Control through communication: The rise of system in American management.* Baltimore: The Johns Hopkins University Press.

Zoonen, L. v. (2002). Gendering the Internet: Claims, controversies, and cultures. *European Journal of Communication, 17*(1), 5–23.

Zorn, T. (2003). *Feeling the hardware: The emotionality of technology-based organizational change.* Paper presented at the International Communication Association conference, San Diego, CA, May 2003.

Cultural Control, Diversity, and Change

In Chapter 6, we defined the concept of organizational culture and considered how it is studied in the field of organizational communication. Among the issues raised in Chapter 6 was management's interest in promoting a productive work culture in which employees labor in pursuit of organizational goals such as survival and profit. Also, we drew attention to the existence of subcultures within organizations. Management's interests in controlling culture and the needs and concerns of various subcultural groups form the essence of this chapter. Our purpose in this chapter is to focus on the struggles for cultural control that exist among various groups in organizations and some of the major factors in workplace diversity that influence these struggles.

CULTURAL CONTROL

It should certainly be clear from Chapter 6 that organizational culture involves much more than simply defining the work process and roles of the organization. Consequently, many different forces and constituencies attempt to shape culture, sometimes by design, sometimes by accident. One aspect of this struggle is management's attempt to create and sustain a productive work culture. Another aspect of this struggle relates to the increasing diversity of the workforce in the United States. Over the last 20 years, women, racial and ethnic minorities, and the physically challenged have joined organizations in increasing numbers. The increased presence of these various group members has brought with it an increase in struggles for power within organizations. An important part of this power struggle is creating and sustaining a workplace culture that meets the needs of diverse members. Each group wants to be recognized, respected, and empowered to accomplish individual and organizational goals. Each group also has interests and views that can influence the overall culture of the organization. Given these observations, this chapter will proceed as follows. First, we will examine the concept of cultural control. Cultural control will be viewed both from the perspective of management's interests as well as the interests of various employee groups. Second, we will examine the issue of workplace diversity from the traditional, interpretive, and critical perspectives. In these sections, we consider the status of Affirmative Action programs, the impact of diversity on organizational culture, and the needs and concerns of people based on their placement in different demographic categories. Specifically, we will focus on gender, sexual orientation, race and ethnicity, socioeconomic class, physical abilities, and age. Finally, we consider the ethics of diversity from the standpoint of providing support to people who belong to diverse groups.

Limits of Managerial Action

There are a number of ways to address the issue of cultural control. One way is to focus on management's attempts to control organizational culture. Indeed, when the traditionalist concept of organizational culture was first popularized, it was so novel and attractive that it quickly became the newest cure-all in corporate America's search for excellence. Many management and communication consultants began to talk to their clients about "changing corporate culture" with an emphasis on managerial control of the culture's objective features. However well intentioned this idea may be, the concept of cultural change through management direction has been questioned. For example, the October 17, 1983, issue of *Fortune* magazine carried this revealing cover headline: "The Culture Vultures: Can They Help Your Company?" The cover story inside pointed out that change in organizational culture involves many factors that are *not* controlled by unilateral management decisions (Uttal, 1983). As the "vulture" metaphor implies, the article took an uncharitable view of consultants who are telling executives to attempt large-scale change in organizational culture.

Eisenberg and Goodall (1993) also provide us with insight into the traditionalist perspective on changing organizational culture. They make reference to a financial firm in Boston that "bought" a culture from a consulting firm. Managers within this firm were provided with slogan buttons and award plaques to distribute to employees at appropriate times. A new policy of casual dress at work was also instituted. The employees were forced to comply with this culture, even though many considered it a corporate joke. Eventually, the new culture was abandoned, "but not until after it had seriously damaged the organization through turnover and ill-will among employees toward the managers" (Eisenberg & Goodall, 1993, p. 150).

The preceding example shows what can happen when culture is treated as a commodity—something that can be bought and sold to naïve workers. However, managers can pursue a number of different options in their attempt to influence or control an organization's culture. For example, in Chapter 6 we explained that systems of concertive control emerge within organizations when management produces a value-based corporate vision that guides member behavior and decision making (e.g., Saturn Corporation's founding). The value and factual premises linked to this vision statement are accepted by employees in exchange for incentives such as continued employment, wages, and salary (Papa, Auwal, & Singhal, 1997). Workers then exhibit their identification with this corporate vision when, in making a decision, they perceive the organization's values and interests as relevant in evaluating the alternatives of choice (Tompkins & Cheney, 1983).

Deal and Kennedy's (1982) ideal of a strong culture certainly has intuitive appeal; however, it is important to realize that the culture of an organization arises from and can be changed by many complex economic, technological, and social forces. Today, such forces are reshaping organizational cultures. Although managers and, for that matter, all organization members should plan for these changes, the changes will occur whether or not management wants them.

A more encompassing view of cultural control is articulated by Dennis Mumby (1988, 1989). According to Mumby, the social construction of meaning in organizations does not occur separately from the power relations that exist between the different social groups that constitute it. Referring to Geertz's (1973) metaphor of the web, Mumby (1989) argues that the analysis of a cultural web should "be concerned not only with how it is constructed, but also with whose interests are served by virtue of that particular construction" (p. 292). Importantly, it is through communication that cultural meaning systems are created (Berger & Luckmann, 1966). Given the centrality of communication to the social construction of culture, what can managers do to exert their influence? Let's turn to the views of Linda Smircich (1983) to understand how managers can communicate in ways that control culture:

They may attempt to define interpretations and meanings that can become widely understood and shared by organization members so that actions are guided by a common definition of the situation. Those with power are able to influence the course of organizational development through control over valued resources and through use of symbols by which organization members mediate their experience. (p. 161)

Mumby (1989) extends this perspective by arguing that as employees talk with one another, relations of domination are produced and reproduced. For example, a group of workers respond positively to a directive from their manager because they accept the fact that their cooperation is part of what it means to be a good employee. However, this does not mean that culture always encourages the smooth functioning of an organization. The construction of culture through communication "involves a struggle over dominant interpretations of the myriad of discourses that make up a culture" (Mumby, 1989, p. 293). In other words, just because group A (e.g., management) wants group B (e.g., workers) to accept a given interpretation of a rule does not mean that group B will passively accept that interpretation. Indeed, they may offer a counterinterpretation that creates a struggle for power within the organization. The example presented by Eisenberg and Goodall (1993) in which employees forced management to abandon their "purchased culture" shows just how such a power struggle can take place.

Of course, managers and corporate owners are often able to influence the interpretations and meanings formed by their subordinates. As Mumby (1989) explains, "certain dominant groups are able to frame the interests of competing groups within their own particular worldview" (p. 293). For example, to protect their own financial interests, corporate owners may advocate a culture of "protecting the bottom line at all costs." This culture sustains multiple tensions for employees who then must confront ethical issues in making decisions to save money and deal with angry customers who want higher levels of service. Van Maanen and Kunda (1989) also advocate this view. They explain that senior managers often influence work culture in the following ways: codification of values and beliefs, promotion of interaction and close ties among employees, taking care of newcomers through socialization activities, and carefully monitoring the extent to which corporate values, norms, and practices are received and put into use by employees. It is in this context that ideology plays a key role in the meaning formations that emerge within organizations, so let's take a look at what is meant by this term.

Ideology

The concept of *ideology* refers to the body of ideas that reflect the social needs or worldview of an individual, group, or culture. There are two approaches to understanding ideology: *interest theory* and *strain theory*. From the perspective of interest theory, ideologies emerge "against the background of a continuous struggle between various groups who vie for power in society; the most powerful group is the one which is able to institutionalize its own particular worldview or ideology" (Mumby, 1989, p. 294). Obviously, managers are often able to institutionalize their ideologies because of their control over rewards and punishments that are meaningful to employees. Strain theory takes the perspective that people accept a particular ideology because it provides them with the means of dealing with the strains associated with a social role. So, a subordinate may accept a manager's interpretation of a work rule because it both meets the manager's expectation of what "good performance" is (thereby enhancing the manager's evaluation of the subordinate) and prevents a troublesome conflict from surfacing between the two organization members.

When managers attempt to persuade workers to adopt certain values, norms, and ideas about what is good, important, and praiseworthy within an organization, they are engaging in a form of ideological control (Alvesson, 1993). The ideologies advocated by management justify certain principles, actions, and feelings and discourage others (Alvesson, 1987; Czarniawska-Joerges, 1988). For example, managers within an organization may persuade workers to internalize a commitment to producing products of high quality. They are persuaded to do so because the production of high-quality products helps ensure organizational survival, increases corporate profits, and results in positive employee performance evaluations.

Although managers are often able to influence ideology formation within organizations, resistant meanings can also surface. As Giddens (1979) argues, all power relations are reciprocal. He uses the term *dialectic of control* to account for this phenomenon. What Giddens means by this is that every social actor within a system has the capacity to exercise power and control to some extent. Even if managers within an organization dominate ideology formation, counter-meanings can surface to challenge their dominance. One group cannot impose an ideology on another without expecting some sort of challenge. As Mumby (1989) argues, alternative, resistant interpretations are always possible.

Organizational Socialization and Assimilation

Another way of looking at how culture may be controlled or manipulated is to focus on how workers are socialized into organizations and how they manage the assimilation process in which they negotiate changes in how they function within organizations. Jablin's (2001) essay in *The New Handbook of Organizational Communication* provides an excellent description of these processes. According to Jablin, socialization processes begin well before an employee enters an organization. For example, children learn about how they should act in organizations on the basis of conversations they have with family members, or by listening to dinner-table talk when their parents talk about their jobs. Further information about what to expect in organizations is gleaned from lessons at school that describe work in different types of jobs and companies. Peers and friends, as well as the media, may also influence our thinking. Finally, part-time employment provides insights into what to expect when performing work tasks and interacting with coworkers and managers.

These preparatory experiences are described as the *anticipatory socialization* stage. Our expectations become shaped by what we hear, the conversations we have, the media we see, and the work experiences we have over time. This stage may serve to control our expectations on the basis of information we encounter. If we primarily hear about managers wielding power and workers accepting orders passively, we may believe that is all we may expect in organizations. Conversely, if we are exposed to information about many different types of organizational environments and management-worker relationships we may form opinions about what type of organization would most meet our needs.

The next stage Jablin describes is the *organizational anticipatory socialization* stage. During this stage, workers receive information on the basis of formal or informal recruitment strategies used by organizations such as advertisements and articles in trade publications or through initial contacts with organizational representatives. When a potential worker participates in a selection interview, he or she is also exposed to information about the organization. From a control perspective, the problems associated with this stage are linked to being exposed to primarily or exclusively positive information. The employee thus receives a distorted view of what working for the organization will actually be like. Also, the employee may also be exposed to messages that start to give insight into the culture of the organization and "the way things are done around here." Such messages may shape employee perceptions and subsequent behavior in ways that limit choices for thinking and acting rather than encouraging creativity and independence.

The subsequent stage is *organizational entry and assimilation.* Most employees begin their employment with one or more orientation sessions that describe what their jobs will be like and what they may expect from the organization. They may even be presented with a description of what the culture of the organization is like. For example, in the early years of the Saturn Corporation, each employee participated in no less than 15 hours of training, much of which was culture based. Of course, more specific job-oriented training activities may also occur. During these training activities, the employee will be given instruction in how he or she is to perform a specific job. Then, once they begin working, employees may be exposed to formal or informal socialization strategies. When experienced workers or managers attempt to guide a new worker's socialization, they may do so in ways that restrict what that worker thinks is possible in terms of thinking about issues, performing tasks, and engaging in political actions or power relations.

Formal or informal mentoring may also be part of a worker's early experiences in an organization. In a mentoring relationship, a new employee learns from the experiences of a more seasoned employee or manager. On the one hand, the information an employee receives from a mentor may limit what he or she thinks is possible to do in the organization. On the other hand, an employee may be connected to a mentor who recommends challenging the system through creative action.

New employees are not merely passive receivers of information; they also may actively seek out information about how to perform their jobs, advance in their career, learn about how the organization operates, and negotiate organizational politics (Gibson & Papa, 2000). Depending on the person, some new employees may seek out information that helps them work within the system so they may internalize "how things are done around here." Others may seek information that gives them insight into how they may carve out space for individual control and personal empowerment.

The assimilation process moves away from control and toward independence and empowerment when the new employee attempts to change the organization on the basis of his or her personal views, experiences, and abilities. In order to accomplish this, he or she may share information about his or her views with others to see how they are received. He or she may even talk about how previous work experiences have provided insight into different ways of structuring work or managing and motivating workers. In order to build support for such ideas, the new worker may seek relationships with like-minded workers. Finally, the worker may consider what he or she has learned and what feedback he or she has received to negotiate a role that is based on his or her personal views. Through role negotiation the worker separates himself or herself from the mechanisms of control and carves out space for individuality and empowerment.

The final stage of Jablin's model is organizational exit. Although an employee may leave an organization for reasons other than being controlled or manipulated by its culture (e.g., retirement, a more lucrative offer, etc.), exit may characterize an employee's dissatisfaction with having his or her needs met. For example, exit may be preferable to accepting and internalizing an organization's control or rule system. Alternatively, other organizations may offer more opportunities for independence and empowerment.

ORGANIZATIONAL CULTURE AND DIVERSITY

The emergence of alternative, resistant ideologies is more likely to occur when an organization employs members who have different perspectives or worldviews. This is where the issue of *workplace diversity* comes into play. The commonly held interpretation of workplace diversity is that diversity exists when an organization employs members of different demographic characteristics. The demographic characteristics most often linked to programs of workplace diversity are gender, race and ethnicity, age, and physical ability. So, a diverse organization is one that employs (a) men and women, (b) people with varied sexual orientations, (c) members of African, Asian, European, and Latin American descent, (d) people from different socioeconomic classes, (e) young, middle-aged, and older workers, and (f) people with a range of physical abilities and challenges. However, we would like to add a component to the definition of diversity, i.e., the fact that diversity involves not only variation in demographics, but also variation in modes of thinking, feeling, and acting.

We certainly believe that all people should have equal access to organizations. Indeed, many of those who champion workplace diversity point to the historical discrimination that made it difficult for women, members of racial and ethnic minorities, older workers, and physically challenged people to find meaningful employment. Responding to this discrimination, many organizations have opened up employment access to people formerly denied entry, thereby creating more diverse workplaces.

As we mentioned in Chapter 1, contemporary organizations operate in an increasingly complex global environment. In order to succeed in this environment, organizations need creative thinkers who approach issues or problems from multiple perspectives. Diversity is not just about different demographic characteristics; it is about differences in thinking and behavior that can help firms to compete in a global economy (Conrad, 1994; Cox, 1993; Gardner, Peluchette, & Clinebell, 1994). An organization that employs people from different demographic backgrounds does not experience the benefits of diversity if all these diverse members think and behave the same way. Differences in worldviews and differences in approaches to problem solving are what organizations need to thrive in a rapidly changing world. Of course, an organization is more likely to experience the benefits of diversity if it employs people with different demographic characteristics. But what needs to be promoted within corporate walls is differences in thinking and behavior. Now that we have provided our views of what workplace diversity is, let's turn to a discussion of how workplace diversity can influence and change organizational culture.

The agents of change in organizational culture include not only top management, but also middle- and lower-level management, various labor groups, the divisions and departments of the organization, occupational groups, political coalitions, the community, and the environment in which the organization functions. These agents sometimes work in harmony, sometimes conflict sharply, and generally coexist in a dynamic tension and interplay that shapes the culture of the organization. To say that the culture of an organization is based on a commonly held frame of reference for interpreting and acting toward one another does not mean that everyone in the organization is the same or that members have the same values and commitments. This point is especially important because the most undeniable source of change at the moment is the increasing diversity of people who make up the workplace. Many leaders in business, industry, education, and government began for the first time to pay serious attention to this issue with the 1987 publication of *Workforce 2000*, a study that predicted radical changes in the composition of the 21st century American workplace due primarily to the entry of vast numbers of women and minorities into the labor market. The predictions made in this report started to occur in the 1990s and continue today. Accommodating the concerns of these new members and dealing with problems that arise from differences between new and old members, as well as among different groups of new members, has transformed the problem of "changing corporate culture" from cultural engineering to diversity management and **learning how to value diversity**. A review of some of the key issues brought on by diversity of gender, race, ethnicity, class, physical ability, and age in the workplace illustrates just how complex the process of valuing and managing diversity will be and how attention to communication will figure into the process. We start with a discussion of cultural control, diversity, and change from the traditional perspective.

TRADITIONAL PERSPECTIVES ON CULTURAL CONTROL, DIVERSITY, AND CHANGE

There are different ways of viewing cultural control, diversity, and change from the traditional perspective. One view is that management may control a diverse corporate culture in ways that promote efficiency and productivity. Whether or not this is possible, management may operate under the assumption that diversity may be harnessed to benefit the organization. Traditionalists may focus on the impact of diversity in other ways as well. For instance, to the extent that the presence of diverse worldviews increases the pool of creative ideas in an organization, diversity may improve the quality of group decision making (White, 1999). So, rather than management controlling a diverse culture, diverse employees are hired specifically for the purpose of promoting positive organizational outcomes. Finally, traditionalists would be concerned with pursuing diversity in ways consistent with federal mandates and the guidelines set forth by the Equal Employment Opportunity Commission. From this standpoint, diversity is not necessarily viewed as something that is beneficial, but rather as something that is required to avoid litigation.

Affirmative Action and Its Misconceptions

One of the greatest controversies surrounding the hiring, development, and advancement of racial and ethnic minorities in U.S. companies is the issue of *affirmative action.* The term "affirmative action" was coined by President Lyndon B. Johnson in 1965 when he issued Executive Order 11246. This order prohibited federal agencies from contracting with firms that were not committed to affirmative action. What was meant by this term was that companies must engage in "vigorous efforts to bring people of color into jobs from which they had previously been excluded" (American Civil Liberties Union, 1995, p. 1).

The American Civil Liberties Union (ACLU) has discussed four major misconceptions that have been associated with affirmative action over the years. First, affirmative action is often linked to quota systems. In fact, quotas are illegal. However, in some organizations biased hiring and promotion practices have been so pronounced that courts have had to exercise their power under the Civil Rights Act of 1964. Hiring goals and timetables have been included among the enforced remedies. These goals and timetables estimate the number of women and minority group members who would be hired if there were no discrimination. Although some affirmative action critics insist on calling these mechanisms "quotas," such a stance cannot be justified. Hiring goals and timetables are "flexible, remedial instruments of *inclusion,* while quotas were used historically to *ex*clude members of some ethnic groups from workplaces and educational institutions" (American Civil Liberties Union, 1995, p. 2).

Another misconception associated with affirmative action is that it promotes preferential treatment. It is true that preference programs have been created for affirmative action purposes. Berkman (1995) discusses a Library of Congress study that yielded a 32-page list of laws and regulations granting preferences based on race, gender, national origin, or ethnicity. Some preference programs, e.g., a gender preference policy used by the Federal Communications Commission in awarding radio station licenses, are being overturned by courts (Veraldi, 1993). But one may question whether such programs really are preferential in the usual sense of the word. The ACLU says that affirmative action is "an equalizer that accommodates people whose gender and color have long been viewed as proxies for incompetence" (American Civil Liberties Union, 1995, p. 2). In order to clarify this point, let's consider an example.

Two job candidates, one black and the other white, apply for the same position. On paper their credentials are identical; however, they have earned those credentials through very different life experiences. From birth, the black person has had to contend with various forms of racial discrimination. Conversely, the white person was raised in a society that favors whites, giving him or her a built-in advantage from birth. Arguing that these two candidates have the same credentials glosses over the fact that the black applicant traveled a much harder road to get where he or she is. These applicants are also different in the way they are perceived by those who will interview them. Indeed, many black applicants are often given less interview time than white applicants with similar credentials (American Civil Liberties Union, 1995). Also, when equally qualified applicants are sent on job interviews, and are coached to display similar levels of enthusiasm and articulateness, white applicants receive 45% more job offers than black applicants (American Civil Liberties Union, 2000).

Also, approximately 80% of executives get their jobs through networking, and approximately 86% of available jobs are not listed in classified advertisements (Blumrosen, 1995). Unfortunately, people of color have been excluded from these networks because they comprise mostly white men. As a result, the black applicant confronts a hiring process that privileges whites, and one that does not test the full range of skills he or she may possess. Thus, affirmative action policies attempt to balance a scale that is tipped sharply in favor of the white candidate.

A third misconception associated with affirmative action programs is that they force employers to hire and admit unqualified people just because they are nonwhite or female. In fact, affirmative action has never been about hiring people *solely* because of their color or sex without concern for their abilities. Rather, affirmative action guidelines require employers to make a conscientious effort to find and train *qualified* people, based on job-related standards (American Civil Liberties Union, 2000).

A final misconception associated with affirmative action is that reverse discrimination penalizes white males. There are two responses to this misconception. First, "restructuring a discriminatory status quo to create a nondiscriminatory environment isn't reverse discrimination, but it may feel that way because something is being lost: White people are losing the favoritism they have enjoyed for so long" (American Civil Liberties Union, 1995, p. 2). Second, affirmative action abuses are relatively rare. One study conducted from 1990 to 1994 found that the problem of reverse discrimination is not widespread and that when it does occur, the courts have provided relief (Blumrosen, 1995). Furthermore, the courts have found that many people claiming reverse discrimination were actually disappointed job applicants who were less qualified for the job than the chosen female or minority applicant (Blumrosen, 1995).

A somewhat sarcastic treatment of the issue of reverse discrimination was provided by Bruning (1995). He stated:

> White people love to torture themselves with the belief that when a black presents himself at an employment office, the cheering begins. Bosses tremble with excitement, kick white applicants out the door, take the honored new arrival to lunch at a four-star restaurant, enroll him in the executive health club and eagerly inquire as to his starting date. Of course, the black individual is allowed to set his salary and dictate the terms of his benefit package. Then someone runs out and leases him a BMW, and, bingo, the guy is on his way to wealth and power, and all because he has had the incredible good fortune to be born black in America! (Bruning, 1995, p. 9)

Sarcasm aside, racism in the United States is real and it must be handled in a variety of ways including some form of affirmative action. In 1995, the U.S. Supreme Court argued that the federal government must narrowly tailor its programs to survive strict judicial scrutiny. What this means is that courts will now look carefully at an organization's past history of discrimination and how precisely its affirmative action efforts are targeted. This prevents employers from enacting programs that automatically advantage or disadvantage individuals because of their race or gender. As Susan Estrich (1995) recently argued, if we can look at affirmative action as a matter of narrowly remedying past injustices and helping those who need a helping hand, there is at least a possibility that more Americans will support these programs.

The most recent Supreme Court cases that provide insight into the type of affirmative action program that will receive judicial support are *Gratz v. Bollinger* (2003) and *Grutter v. Bollinger* (2003). Interestingly, both cases involved affirmative action programs at the University of Michigan. The *Gratz* case focused on the College of Literature, Science, and the Arts (LSA) at University of Michigan (UM) whereas the *Grutter* case focused on the law school at UM (Lehmuller & Gregory, 2005). The LSA program was found to be improper because the admissions department "automatically awarded 20 points (out of a possible 100) to every underrepresented minority applicant solely because of race" (*Gratz v. Bollinger* 2003, 539 US 244, 270). More specifically, this program was not found to be narrowly tailored because it did not consider applicants as individuals; rather, people were awarded points simply because they belonged to a particular racial category. As Justice O'Connor wrote, "even the most outstanding national high school leader could never receive more than five points for his or her accomplishments, merely a quarter of what a minority applicant received based solely on race" (*Gratz v. Bollinger* 2003, 539 US 244, 279).

Although the LSA program was found to be improper, the University of Michigan Law School program was supported. Justice O'Connor's support was based on the program's "holistic and individualized assessment where admissions officers and law school deans count race as one of many relevant factors as they select a law school class" (Guinier, 2003, p.1). The Supreme Court also supported the argument that diversity may be considered a "compelling government interest" and that "educational institutions have the authority to decide that diversity is essential to their missions" (Lehmuller & Gregory, 2005, p. 450). Justice O'Connor also noted that the "hallmark of [the Law School's] policy is its focus on academic ability coupled with a flexible assessment of the applicants' talents, experiences, and potential to contribute to the learning of those around them" (*Grutter v. Bollinger,* 2003, 539 US 306, 315). Finally, the Supreme Court supported the law school because diversity "is not defined solely on the basis of race or ethnicity . . . the policy sought to guide admissions officers in producing diverse and academically outstanding classes" (Lehmuller & Gregory, 2005).

Importantly, affirmative action represents only one part of the process of integrating racial and ethnic minorities into the workplace. Other efforts are also needed for organizations to receive the benefits of having a diverse workforce. For example, in order to successfully manage diversity, groups must be willing to share power (Allen, 1995). This means that people who have historically had access to power (e.g., white males) must be willing to relinquish some control to others. Also, those groups historically excluded from positions of power (e.g., those of African, Asian, and Latin American descent) must refrain from actions that simply reverse the power imbalances that formerly existed. Once an organization is able to sustain a cultural environment in which all members have equal access to power, the advantages of workplace diversity will surface clearly. Instead of focusing on how the organization can socialize the individual to fit within a preexisting culture, minority group members can be encouraged to innovate their work roles by engaging in behaviors that are more consistent with their cultural heritage (Allen, 1995; Van Maanen & Schein, 1979). In such a cultural environment, diversity is truly valued.

One way that organizations have attempted to grapple with the challenges of an increasingly diverse workforce is to institute programs that value diversity. These programs, usually organized by human resource departments, emphasize that people who are differ-ent should be able to maintain their cultural and ethnic identities in a pluralistic society. For example, Black and Mendenhall (1990) argue that employees need three broad skill dimen-sions to interact effectively with members of different racial and ethnic backgrounds: (a) skills related to the maintenance of self, mental health, psychological well-being, stress reduction, and feelings of self-confidence; (b) skills related to the fostering of relationships with people of different cultural backgrounds; and (c) cognitive skills that promote a cor-rect perception of the other culture.

On the more specific issue of race relations training, Foeman (1991) contends that inter-personal processes must be emphasized to create a productive work culture in which diver-sity is valued. In her review of race relations training programs, she found that successful programs tend to espouse five interpersonal objectives. First, trainees need to discuss race-related issues in order to clear up misunderstandings and myths linked to positions on controversial subjects. Second, each racial group needs to articulate its views on issues that concern them about the workplace. Third, these views need to be examined carefully by all members. Fourth, each racial group needs to find validity in the perspectives advanced by members of other racial groups. Finally, the perspectives advanced by each racial group must be valued and used so that all organization members can work more effectively toward common goals.

Although many race relations training programs are improving the nature of interracial communication within organizations, further research is necessary to help promote under-standing and racial harmony in the workplace. As Kim and Sharkey (1995) noted, people from different racial and cultural backgrounds "bring different meanings, value assump-tions, and discourse styles into the workplace conversation" (p. 33). These differences can lead to communication breakdowns and can threaten a common orientation to organiza-tional goals (Fine, 1991). Workers must learn to become more open-minded and accepting of other people's viewpoints. Also, workers need to manage conversations with diverse members more sensitively by taking the time to listen and ask questions to check for under-standing (Martin, Hecht, & Larkey, 1994). This is where additional research by organizational communication scholars is necessary. Specifically, research is needed to test and evaluate the effectiveness of diversity training programs within organizations.

There are two key issues that must be addressed in order to effectively integrate and value the contributions of racial and ethnic minorities in the workplace. First, people from different racial and ethnic backgrounds have life experiences that influence the way they think, talk, and behave. In order for people from these different backgrounds to work pro-ductively together, instructional programs are needed to increase each group's understand-ing of the other groups' behaviors and worldviews. Second, once intergroup understanding exists, the key to profiting from diversity is to value it. This means integrating the perspec-tives and behaviors of racial and ethnic minorities into the workplace so no single ideology silences the voices of those who can make important and meaningful contributions. Also, valuing diversity means that minority group members are a part of the organization's lead-ership team. When minority group members are fully integrated and empowered in orga-nizations, the advantages of their membership will be felt more clearly. Merging different worldviews together can help to promote creativity in decision making. Tapping diverse national and international markets requires employing organization members who understand the needs that exist within these markets. So, although organizations will undergo changes in integrating and empowering minority group members, there are many benefits associated with these changes.

Managing the Diverse Organization

As will be seen as this chapter unfolds, the workplace will only continue to become more diverse. This is true in the United States and across the world. Importantly, diversity in any country is a product of both internal and external forces. Internal forces that lead to a more diverse workforce occur when groups of people who have lived in a country for many years gain access to employment opportunities once denied to them by prejudice and discrimination. External forces involve the global migration of workers across national borders. These workers are both competing for opportunities and responding to demand for particular skill and ability sets that are in short supply in certain nations. Both of these forces are creating more diverse workforces across the globe than was imagined possible a generation ago.

Managing the diverse workforce brings new challenges to organizations. Models of assimilation and socialization assume that workers will adjust to systems of management and organizational cultures that were based on much more homogenous membership. Not only are these models losing their relevance, their continued use may prevent diverse workers from having their greatest impact on organizations. Diverse workers bring into organizations new ways of seeing the world, different ways of communicating, and unique ways of organizing tasks. Furthermore, researchers have shown that diverse organizations display higher creativity, innovation, and problem-solving ability (Adler, 1991; Morgan, 1989; White, 1999).

Adler (1991, 1992, 2002) has written extensively on managing the diverse workforce. Although her work speaks primarily to the globally diverse workforce, her ideas may also be applied to organizations that become more diverse as a product of hiring more women, racial/ethnic minorities, and other disenfranchised groups within a country's borders. In order to be successful in a diverse world, organizations must hire managers who are competent working with and supervising diverse workers. The first dimension of competence is exhibiting a *global perspective*. This means understanding business from the perspective of different cultural groups and groups traditionally excluded from power (e.g., women, workers of different physical abilities, etc). In order to become competent, managers must seek opportunities to learn about people representing these diverse groups, including their perspectives, tastes, trends, technologies, and approaches to business and communication. Managers also need to learn to work with multiple cultures simultaneously because of the rapid increase in the number of diverse workers in the 21st century. The second dimension of competence is *transition and adaptation*. In order to transition to an increasingly diverse workforce, managers need to develop specific knowledge of various diverse groups and learn how to adapt their thinking and behavior to respond and work effectively with these new workers. The third dimension is *lived cultural experience*. Ultimately, managers must be comfortable living among workers representing diverse groups. This may be as simple as a man learning to work cooperatively on a day-to-day basis within a department otherwise composed exclusively of women. Alternatively, if a department increasingly attracts Malaysian workers, a manager may benefit from taking an assignment in an organization's overseas affiliate in Malaysia to learn more about the culture of Malaysian people.

The human resource system must also respond to diversity. Adler's (1992) diverse human resource system includes three components: diverse scope, diverse representation, and diverse process. Diverse scope means that the human resources department emphasizes learning and adopting a "frame of mind" that is inclusive of the worldviews and perspectives of diverse members. Diverse representation means that the management and executive levels of the organization should also be diverse. Finally, diverse process means including representatives and ideas from many groups in all organizational planning and decision-making processes.

INTERPRETIVE PERSPECTIVES ON CULTURAL CONTROL, DIVERSITY, AND CHANGE

The social construction of reality is very different in diverse versus nondiverse organizations. When all employees in an organization come from the same demographic group, there will be limited differences in the worldviews or perspectives that are represented. In such an environment, one may expect a great deal of agreement about how to perceive the world. When there is a great deal of diversity in an organization, however, there will be many differences in the worldviews that are represented. This will result in a more complex and diverse social construction of reality. First, some employees may be exposed to perspectives they have never encountered before. This exposure may open some employees' minds to a new way of thinking. Alternatively, some employees may be very critical of these new perspectives and fight against their being considered by others. Second, in some instances employees from diverse groups may merge their different perspectives in ways that create a more complex, encompassing point of view. Third, the presence of diverse perspectives may set the stage for frequent conflict that may or may not be resolved. In such a setting, power relations may emerge in ways that support one perspective over another or that shift support for different perspectives depending on who holds power at a particular time. Thus, from the interpretive perspective, diversity results in a much more complex and multilayered process of socially constructing reality in organizations.

How Diversity Affects Organizational Culture

When an organization commits itself to diversity, both challenges and opportunities must be anticipated. When a group of people has been historically excluded from participation in an organization, their entry will not be easy. The reason for that group's prior exclusion is often linked to prejudices. Some experienced organization members may devalue the potential contributions of new group members and do everything they can to make adjustment difficult for them. For diverse workers, this creates a culture dominated by struggle. Of course, actions that oppose the inclusion of diverse workers are ultimately counterproductive and organizational productivity suffers.

Another challenge related to increasing diversity in organizations is the inevitability of increased conflict. The reason for increases in conflict is related to broadening the worldviews present within an organization as more diverse members join the ranks. Organizations that are less diverse are more likely to be dominated by a single, dominant worldview (e.g., European American male perspective). When people from different racial and ethnic backgrounds, gender identities, classes, physical abilities, and ages are working in the same organization, there will be very different ways of viewing issues and problems. As these different worldviews clash, not only will more conflicts surface, but the ones that do will also be more complex to manage. More time will need to be spent clarifying how different types of people define and understand an issue. Relations of power will also need to be negotiated as each group may view the legitimacy of certain power dynamics differently. On the negative side, the increase in the number and complexity of conflicts may make for a contentious culture, and worker productivity may decline.

There are also positive effects related to diversity that we believe outweigh the negatives. Increases in the number and complexity of conflicts may result in a more sophisticated understanding of problems and yield more productive solutions. This positive impact may be related to overall decision making in organizations as well. Specifically, the presence of multiple worldviews will assist organizational groups in addressing any issue or problem. The reason for this is that creativity is often inspired by the blending or juxtaposition of differences to produce a new way of seeing a problem. This is perhaps the greatest impact that diversity has on overall organizational culture and on the performance of employees.

Another positive effect is linked to what diversity says about an organization and how that affects employees' views about working for that organization. When an organization employs people from many diverse groups, a statement is being made about how that organization respects, celebrates, and values differences among people. This affects how employees from diverse groups feel about working for a company. Specifically, if there are many diverse employees working in an organization, no member may feel that he or she is just a token. Also, organization members from dominant groups may feel positive about working for an organization that supports and respects people from many different groups.

Taken collectively, gender, race, ethnicity, class, ability, and age differences in the workplace of the 21st century present an almost overwhelming array of issues, questions, and novel conditions not only for management, but also for all organization members. It will be difficult to work through and resolve some of the issues, but diversity is not just a condition to be treated as a management problem. It is also a management opportunity. Moreover, diversity management is not just an activity to be carried out by management. All organization members will have to learn in a real sense how to manage and value diversity. Responses to some issues will be dictated by legislation and court rulings, others by the construction of management policy. We hope most will be worked out through the sort of dialogue that Mary Parker Follett envisioned among all organizational constituencies.

Age

In this section, we separate age from the other demographic categories addressed in the critical perspectives section. In doing so, we are not denying the existence of age discrimination, because older workers have faced prejudice and illegal treatment. The nature of the challenges facing older workers is changing, however, as Baby Boomers are remaining healthy into their later years, and organizations are recognizing the value of their experiences and continued contributions. So, here we position our discussion of age within the interpretive perspective by looking at clashing values and worldviews brought together in organizations that employ people ranging in age from their 20s through their 80s and beyond.

Age differences among employees will add to cultural diversity because of unique values and worldviews embedded in varied age groups. Specifically, the workplace of the next decade or so will be inhabited by four basic age groups: Traditionals, Baby Boomers, Generation X, and Millennials (Bradford & Raines, 1992; Howe & Strauss, 2000). The values and needs of these four groups are not especially compatible, and organizations will need creative reconstructions of the workplace and of work processes in order to maximize the effectiveness of each group and achieve reasonable levels of mutual tolerance.

Descriptions of the four groups suggest to us that many of the potential age difficulties reside in the groups' attitudes toward one another. Traditionals, born between 1925 and 1945, are influenced by the history of catastrophic events such as the Great Depression and World War II. They tend to regard Baby Boomers as disrespectful, too blunt, yet also too "warm and fuzzy." They regard Generation X as impatient and unethical and Millennials as too distracted by technology. Traditionals include people such as World War II veteran and former president George Bush and Massachusetts Senator Ted Kennedy.

Baby Boomers, born between 1946 and 1964, make up the enormous post-World War II generation that created, or in the case of younger Boomers, grew up under the influence of the 1960s counterculture. They tend to see Traditionals as too cautious, too conservative, and inflexible. They regard Generation X as selfish and manipulative, and Millennials as lacking focus. Bill and Hillary Clinton, as well as Rush Limbaugh, are members of this generation.

Generation X, born between 1965 and 1976, are in numbers a much smaller generation than the Boomer generation that preceded them. Solomon (1992a) says that Generation X is "not a monolithic group that can be defined by one set of principles: they're different in significant ways from the generations that came before them" (p. 52). Generation X tends to bring a new set of concerns to the workplace, especially an emphasis on quality of work life, including the work environment and the nature of the work itself. Members of this age group are also more likely to view work as a means to support their current lifestyle interests (skiing, kayaking, travel) versus viewing work as a means to support retirement activities. They see Traditionals as rigid, old, and over-the-hill, regard Boomers as disgustingly "New Age" workaholics, and see Millennials as too optimistic and insufficiently rule-governed. Google founders Larry Page and Sergey Brin and actress Drew Barrymore are members of this generation.

Although they are children of the counterculture, Boomers nonetheless tacitly accepted many conventions that Traditionals hold as bedrock principles of work life. Generation X is much less likely to accept these conventions, so the arrival of this generation of workers in the workplace presents a new set of management issues and opportunities. According to Thielfoldt and Scheef (2004), Generation X is turned off by inflexible time schedules, workaholism, and close supervision. They like to learn new things, expect praise, and want work to be fun. They also want to be encouraged to display creativity and initiative to find new ways to get tasks done. Rather than pressuring Generation X to convert to Traditionalist behavior, many organizations are trying to figure out how to creatively meet their needs.

Millennials were born between 1977 and 1998. They celebrate diversity in all forms and they are both optimistic and realistic in their worldview. Millennials pride themselves on being self-inventive and individualistic. Rather than following or rejecting rules, they seek to rewrite the rules that will govern their lives. They have grown up in an environment in which change is rapid, and they believe that organizing will be much more spontaneous in the future. As a result, they do not so much reject institutions as see them as increasingly irrelevant (e.g., they believe that the federal government was incapable of dealing with the Katrina disaster). For Millennials, technology is not something to be used (as it is for Generation X); it is what life is all about. In short, they assume a technology-dominated world. They do not merely multitask, they multitask fast. Finally, because their parents nurtured them, they expect nurturing organizations. Race car driver Danica Patrick and England's Prince William are members of the Millennial generation.

CRITICAL PERSPECTIVES ON CULTURAL CONTROL, DIVERSITY, AND CHANGE

One way of viewing cultural control, diversity, and change from a critical perspective is to argue that powerful groups (e.g., European American men) will sustain power no matter how much diversity is present in an organization. This may occur because those groups with historical access to power have more resources and experience at manipulating power relations and holding on to control. Another way of viewing diversity is that greater diversity promotes increased conflict in organizations. As these conflicts are played out there will be winners and losers where certain organization members will have access to greater resources and be able to exhibit more control than others. So, the group with historical access to power may not win this struggle. However, whatever group does win creates a pattern of dominance and control similar to the one it replaced.

Critical perspectives on cultural control, diversity, and change also offer positive outcomes. If diversity is genuinely celebrated in an organization, groups historically excluded from participation and power relations become equal participants who are empowered. In such an environment, a person's skills, abilities, and contributions determine their success rather than their demographic classification. There would also be recognition that groups historically excluded from power would need developmental experiences to prepare them for leadership positions. Although it may take many years to construct organizations that truly celebrate diversity in ways that maximize success for all groups, this road will be paved by innovative organizations during the 21st century. In the following subsections, let's consider the opportunities and struggles likely to occur for workers on the basis of gender, sexual orientation, race/ethnicity, class, and physical abilities.

Gender

As college students, we can remember seeking summer employment in companies where it was, however illegally, still tacitly understood that "only able-bodied men need apply." Those days are over forever. In 2005, women constituted 46% of the total American labor force, and by 2012 they are projected to constitute 47% of the total labor force (U.S. Department of Labor, 2006). The transformation of the workplace from a predominantly male to a mixed-gender environment has compelled organizations to address and make decisions about issues such as company-sponsored daycare, redesign of benefits, and creative work scheduling. Three of the most important issues are the prevalence of sexual harassment, the "glass ceiling," and the contentious question of differences between women and men in styles of leadership and communication.

Sexual Harassment

We can cite the numerous studies on sexual harassment, but the results are generally consistent. Sexual harassment is pervasive in the American workplace, and women usually are the victims. Wagner (1992) summarizes several surveys in which 70% to 90% of working women report having experienced conditions that constitute sexual harassment according to the Equal Employment Opportunity Commission (EEOC) definition. Although there is no recent single nationwide survey of the percentage of women experiencing sexual harassment in the workplace, the evidence is still strong that the problem is pervasive. For example, the American Association of University Women reported that in 2005 nearly two-thirds of all female college students experience sexual harassment at some point during college (American Association of University Women, 2006). Furthermore, in fiscal year 2005 the U.S. EEOC reported 12,859 charges of sexual harassment that resulted in $47.9 million in settlements for the charging parties (U.S. Equal Employment Opportunity Commission, 2006).

Under the EEOC definition, illegal sexual harassment takes two forms: *quid pro quo* and hostile environment (Wagner, 1992). *Quid pro quo* (this for that) harassment occurs when employment conditions such as raises, promotions, or job security are contingent upon sexual favors. *Quid pro quo* may be overtly coercive ("If you want to keep your job, you'd better put out") or covertly suggestive ("Let's fly to Vegas for the weekend and discuss your future with the company").

Harassment in the form of a sexually hostile environment is more complicated. It may include behavior such as sexual propositions, sexual jokes, lewd comments, displays of pornographic materials, fondling, and even nonsexual actions directed at a person because of that person's sex, but it must be unwelcome and constitute an environment that a *reasonable person* would regard as offensive. Moreover, whereas one instance of *quid pro quo* may be enough to sustain an allegation of sexual harassment, hostile environment usually requires repetition or the establishment of a general pattern of behavior.

When does a hostile environment exist? In 1986, the U.S. Supreme Court adopted the standard of offensiveness to that of a "reasonable person." In recent years, this standard has been changed to "reasonable woman" by some lower courts. Women tend to differ from men in their interpretation of harassment situations, and the intent of the "reasonable woman" standard is to privilege the female interpretation over the male interpretation (Wagner, 1992). Thus, the behavior alone does not constitute harassment. Harassment is defined by a combination of behavior, the circumstances under which it occurs, and its effect on women. If the sexualized condition of the workplace is unwelcome (i.e., neither solicited nor desired) and a reasonable woman would be offended by it, it probably constitutes a hostile environment.

Sexually hostile environment so defined casts a broad net, and one study of sexual harassment court cases occurring after 1986 found that 75% involved hostile environment claims. At least one case, *Robinson v. Jacksonville Shipyards,* 760 F. Supp. 1486 (M.D. Fla. 1991) has generated heated debate over whether this net has become too broad. Jacksonville Shipyards apparently had every condition that might conceivably be construed as sexually hostile: everything from sex-oriented conversations, pornographic literature, and display of nude pinups to sexual taunting and hazing. Some of this behavior was specifically targeted at the six female employees in the 850-person company. Some of it was not, but all of it contributed to the environment. When the women complained about that environment, the situation actually got worse. So one of the women, Lois Robinson, took legal action.

The sexual taunting that was directed toward Robinson was so outrageous that we will not print it in this text. We can tell you that the most explicit lyrics in songs by controversial rock and rap music artists just about match some of the comments to which Robinson was subjected. In ruling on Robinson's case, however, the court not only responded to actions targeted at Robinson, but also ordered fundamental changes in other areas of male behavior at the shipyard, including tight restrictions on the kinds of photographic and reading materials that could be brought into the workplace.

The American Civil Liberties Union (ACLU) initially argued that the court's application of the "reasonable woman" standard in *Robinson* was so sweeping in its restrictions that the remedies violated First Amendment rights. *Glamour* magazine ("Porn at work: Is it Legal?," April, 1992) reported that the Florida ACLU, led by Robyn Blumner, sought to overturn the decision in *Robinson*. Nadine Strossen, ACLU's national president, told the 1992 convention of the Speech Communication Association that the national ACLU opposes some aspects of the *Robinson* decision, but accepts others. At that time, the national ACLU and its Florida chapter apparently agreed that mere offensiveness does not warrant prohibition of behavior; behavior must be *targeted* at the offended party in order to qualify as sexual harassment. In April 1993, however, the national ACLU board voted after a heated and divisive debate to abandon the targeted-behavior concept in favor of a broader definition of harassment and, according to *The New York Times,* took the position that "Courts should make it easier for women to bring harassment complaints" (Lewis, 1993, p. 12). A court test of the ACLU position was needed to clarify what does—or does not—constitute sexual harassment. Such a test was provided when the Supreme Court heard *Harris vs. Forklift Systems,* 510 U.S. 17 (1993), in which a lower court ruled that sexual jokes were not harassment because they caused neither harm nor interference with job performance. In delivering the opinion of the court, Justice Sandra Day O'Connor stated that the plaintiff was not required to prove psychological trauma in order to have a valid claim of harassment. The two standards the court used to determine sexual harassment in this case were the "reasonable person" standard and the victim's feeling that he or she was abused. Under the "reasonable person" standard, if a reasonable person would find the conduct severe or pervasive enough to create a hostile or abusive environment, sexual harassment has taken place. The second standard to be met is that the victim must feel that the environment is abusive.

The cost of violating a worker's rights through engaging in sexual harassment may be significant. Chakravorty (2006) reported that a Toyota Motor Corporation employee filed a $190 million lawsuit charging that the company's top U.S. executive sexually harassed her and that other executives failed to act on her multiple complaints. The plaintiff charged that Chief Executive Hideaki Otaka made repeated sexual advances toward her in 2005. Among the specific claims were repeatedly asking the plaintiff to accompany Otaka to lunches, on walks in

Central Park (New York), and on business trips during which he tried to engage in sexual relations with her. Toyota settled with the plaintiff in August 2006, although the specific terms of the agreement were not disclosed. Otaka denied any wrongdoing; however, he left his U.S. post and returned to Japan earlier than planned (O'Donnell & Woodyard, 2006).

What practical advice may be given to a person who experiences sexual harassment? The Tidewater Florida Chapter of the National Organization for Women offers eight specific strategies (Sunshine for Women, 2006). First, you should tell your harasser to stop the offensive behavior and make clear that you do not want sexual attention from him or her. If the person persists, you should write a letter telling the harasser to stop and you should make a copy of that letter for your records. Second, when you are harassed you should write down exactly what happened, whether it is inappropriate language or touch. The time, date, and place of the occurrence should be recorded as well as the names of any witnesses. These notes should be kept at home. Importantly, if the unacceptable actions continue, these notes may be useful if you decide to take legal action against the company. Third, you should seek out support from friends, family, and coworkers. This support may help you to deal with the psychological depression and physical problems (e.g., ulcers, headaches, nausea) that are caused by the harassment. You should also talk to other women to see if they have experienced similar problems. If so, you may join with them to confront the harassment. Fourth, if you are a member of a union, you should talk to your union representatives about your options. Fifth, you should talk to your employer because all organizations should have written policies against sexual harassment. There should also be clearly specified procedures for making a complaint. If the manager you speak to is uncooperative, talk to staff in personnel or in your equal employment opportunity office. Sixth, you should keep an accurate record of your work performance including performance evaluations and any informal statements (e.g., e-mails, memos) that speak to the quantity or quality of your work. These records may prove useful if the harasser attempts to criticize your job performance in order to defend his actions. Seventh, recognize that you have the right to file a charge with the EEOC, a federal agency created for your protection. The EEOC may be contacted toll free at 1-800-669-EEOC. Finally, find out more about your legal rights by talking with a lawyer who specializes in sex discrimination. Although you do not need a lawyer to file a charge with the EEOC, a lawyer may help you decide what further actions to take. In order to find a lawyer who is a specialist in sexual discrimination and harassment, you should contact your state's bar association or the women's bar association in your area.

Glass Ceiling

Women not only constituted 46% of the workforce in 2005, but also held half of all management and professional positions (Bureau of Labor Statistics, 2006). Yet, whereas half of all entry-level managers are female, the number of women in top corporate positions remains small in comparison to men. Catalyst, a nonprofit research and advisory organization working to advance women in business and professions, provided the most recent information we found. Researchers at Catalyst reported that in 2005 only eight women were CEOs in the Fortune 500; an additional nine were CEOs in Fortune 501–1000 companies. Furthermore, women account for only 14.7% of all Fortune 500 board seats and only 7.9% of positions with the title of Chairman, Vice Chairman, CEO, President, Chief Operating

Officer, Senior Executive Vice-President, and Executive Vice-President (Catalyst, 2006). Thus, women can see the top, but they are still excluded from positions there—a condition known as the "glass ceiling."

Is the glass ceiling a result of *de facto* sex discrimination or a condition that exists only because large numbers of women are still in the process of gaining the experiences that ultimately will bring promotions and parity in senior management? Opinions vary. Marion Sandler, president of Golden West Financial Corp., says, "It's the power structure that doesn't allow women entry" (Catalyst, 2006, p. 3). But Carleton Fiorina, a vice president with AT&T, responds, "I've never felt that my sex has been a disadvantage to me. . . . No one can expect to be handed power" (Catalyst, 2006, p. 3). Both women probably are reflecting accurately their personal experiences. In either case, the coming decades should tell us how top decision makers in organizations perceive women. That is to say, if the lack of parity really is attributable to factors other than sex discrimination, then we should see many more women assuming senior positions over the next few years. This should occur because a critical mass of women in many organizations will have the experience and accomplishments generally expected for admission to the top echelons of business, industry, government, and education. If a substantial change in female representation at senior management levels does not occur within the next few years, *de facto* sex discrimination will be the only plausible explanation.

As the situation stands at the moment, many women executives are frustrated with the glass ceiling. A Catalyst survey of women executives in 2003 found that 47% believed that a lack of significant general management and line experience continues to restrict women's advancement to top management, 41% point to exclusion from informal networks of communication, and 33% cite stereotyping and preconceptions of women's roles and abilities (Catalyst, 2006). Finally, in examining trends of women's participation on corporate boards from 1995 to 2005, Catalyst President Ilene H. Lang reports, "Our research reveals that if we continue at this pace, it could take 70 years for women to reach parity with men on corporate boards" (Catalyst, 2006, p. 5).

Feminine Styles of Leadership and Communication

Are there general characteristics that can be said to define feminine styles of leadership and communication that one would expect to be more consistently exhibited by women than by men? If so, then such a difference between men and women suggests a more provocative question. Are these feminine styles more conducive than masculine styles to the effective management of organizations?

Whatever the behavioral similarities between men and women may be, there is one difference "on which virtually every expert and study agree: Men are more aggressive than women. It shows up in 2-year-olds . . . persists into adulthood. . . . And there is little doubt that it is rooted in biology" (McLoughlin, 1988, p. 56). It is this difference that prompts questions about the possibility of gender differences in leadership and communication styles.

Sally Helgesen (1990) not only contends that women differ from men in their ways of leadership, but also calls this difference *the female advantage*. Helgesen is neither the first nor the only scholar to advance this argument. During the 1980s, feminist theorists relied on the presumption of a "feminine difference" to promote an agenda for nonhierarchical, democratic, collective life in organizations (e.g., Ferguson, 1984). As early as 1979, Baird and Bradley found that employees perceived the communication styles of female managers to be more open and receptive than those of male managers and suggested that the findings for females are more consistent with the requirements of modern management methods. Burrell, Buzzanell, and McMillan (1992) also cite some studies of gender differences in conflict management in which women are found to be less competitive, more accommodating, and more willing than men to share power and discuss diverse viewpoints.

If these findings point to a "feminine" style of leadership and communication, its elements would be more consistent than a competitive, aggressive "masculine" style with the human resource development ideal of participative management. Most studies, however, report either no differences between men and women in leadership positions or that gender has a trivial, almost nonexistent influence on that behavior. For example, in a comprehensive review of quantitative studies on this question, Wilkins and Andersen (1991) stated, "It can be safely concluded that *there is no meaningful difference in the behavior of male and female managers*" (p. 27).

How does one explain the inconsistency of research findings on the question of gender differences in styles of leadership and communication? Burrell et al. suggest that quantitative studies of conflict management may simply fail to reveal important differences or that women may be obliged to subordinate their preferred feminine style to requirements of aggressive, male-dominated situations. This second explanation has been advanced by a number of feminist writers (Marshall, 1984, 1993; Natalle, Papa, & Graham, 1994; Sheppard, 1989). As Judi Marshall (1993) explains, male behaviors represent the norm to which organization members must adapt. Women copy the behaviors of men in order to gain acceptance and succeed in their careers. If this is indeed the case, organizations are losing out on the benefits of gender diversity in the workplace. As we argued earlier, the benefits of diversity are experienced only when diverse members are encouraged to think and behave according to their own unique perspectives.

The prevalence of sexual harassment, women's resentment about the glass ceiling, and a potentially divisive debate over which sex is best equipped for management make gender alone a confounding problem in the management of diversity. Sexual harassment must be addressed by active programs of prevention, investigation, and, where warranted, disciplinary action against offenders. Dialogue between women and men about the conditions and effects of harassment might also be appropriate, but such a dialogue would require that women's interpretations cannot automatically be privileged over men's interpretations in defining harassment. Breaking the glass ceiling requires the same commitment to development of female management talent that has been devoted to male management talent followed by equitable treatment in promotion practices. Importantly, developmental efforts targeted at women managers must recognize, value, and promote the thoughts and behaviors that distinguish women from men. As for differences between women and men in communication, we need to create and sustain organizational cultures that value differences rather than suppress them.

Women, Feminist Philosophy, and Cultural Change

Classifying values as "masculine" or "feminine" may involve a certain degree of stereotyping, and members of either gender may internalize values attributed to the other, but feminist writers have argued that there are characteristic value differences between men and women. For example, three central values of feminist organization theory are cooperative enactment, integrative thinking, and connectedness (see Chapter 14). Here, we focus on feminist theory to illustrate how diversity of ideas and values can enhance organizational cultures.

Marshall (1993) explains that masculine values are characterized by "self-assertion, separation, independence, control, competition, focused perception, rationality, analysis, clarity, discrimination and activity" (p. 124). The underlying themes linked to male values include a self-assertive tendency, a desire to control the environment, and a focus on personal and interpersonal processes. Feminine values are characterized by "interdependence, cooperation, receptivity, merging, acceptance, awareness of patterns, wholes and contexts, emotional tone, personalistic perception, being, intuition, and synthesizing" (p. 124). The underlying themes linked to these values are openness to the environment, interconnection, and mutual development. Buzzanell (1993), another feminist scholar, argues that four feminist themes are relevant to organizational communication: cooperation, caring and concern for relationships and community, viewing humans as significant holistic beings, and recognizing the value of pursuing possibilities and alternatives.

When such themes are considered in light of the moral and ethical teachings of major religious movements such as Judaism, Islam, Christianity, and Buddhism, it is obvious that the supporting values of caring, respect, human dignity, and cooperation are hardly unique to 21st century feminist theory. Yet institutionalized religions often seem to function as cold bureaucracies. The point of feminist theory is to escape from the entrapments of a bureaucratic life-world that feminists regard as male-constructed. So, how would an organization that embraced feminine values be different than an organization that espoused only masculine values? Also, what are the potential advantages to embracing feminine values?

By focusing on the values and themes identified by Marshall (1993) and Buzzanell (1993, 1994), we can gain some insights into what working for a "feminist" organization would be like. First, workers would be encouraged to cooperate with one another to reach individual and organizational goals rather than to compete against one another for limited rewards. In order to encourage such a cooperative environment, organization members may need to think of structures other than pyramids with multilayered hierarchical forms of control (see description of Casa de Esperanza in Chapter 14). For example, Peters (1987) has proposed organizational structures that resemble circles with permeable boundaries and self-designing functional linkages. Alternatively, Weick and Browning (1991) discuss the possibility of self-organizing forms that evolve as the environment changes. Finally, Buzzanell (1994) recommends engaging in consensus processes for negotiating decisions where there is minimal rule use, little differentiation among members, and value-based rather than reward-based incentives.

Part of creating a cooperative environment within an organization is placing an emphasis on interconnections between people and groups. Most feminists believe that people are more likely to accomplish their goals through working cooperatively with others. Thus, people from different departments may be encouraged to work collaboratively on a problem because each member has some specific expertise or a unique perspective on how the problem should be addressed. The concept of mutual development can also be linked to cooperation and interconnectedness. Feminists posit that workers can grow and develop together if a supportive environment is created in which they are encouraged to combine their talents with others to reach mutual goals. This perspective is in stark contrast to the ethic of "competitive individualism" that dominates most bureaucracies. As Buzzanell (1994) explains, "at the heart of the competitive orientation is the need to excel over others, to stand out against the performance of others, and to distinguish oneself publicly by seeing others fail" (p. 345).

In order for a cooperative environment to exist within an organization, all members must exhibit care and concern for relationships with others. This means sustaining an organizational culture in which members care about one another's needs and concerns and provide help for each other. In this cooperative culture, workers recognize that their professional development and their satisfaction with the organization is tied to establishing and sustaining helpful and caring relationships with others.

The sort of cooperative workplace culture envisioned by many feminists is not one that privileges any particular ideology over any other. So, conflict between members is an expected reality (an issue discussed more extensively in Chapter 12). Rather than suppress conflict because it interferes with "getting the job done," feminist researchers advocate bringing conflict out into the open and reevaluating issues in a search for common ground (Putnam, 1990). Furthermore, for conflict to be managed successfully, organization members need to learn threat-reducing strategies, integrative decision making, and nondefensive conflict-reduction techniques (Pearson, 1981). However, the emphasis on reducing threats and engaging in nondefensive communication does not mean suppressing emotions in the workplace. On the contrary, emotions play a powerful role in how we interpret the world. As Ferguson (1984) explains, "we need the connection to the world that emotion allows in order to reflect on and evaluate the world" (p. 199). Thus, feminist theorists emphasize the importance of sustaining organizational environments in which members can express their emotions in a cooperative and constructive way (Mumby & Putnam, 1992).

Another aspect of feminist philosophy that has implications for organizational communication theory is viewing human beings as significant, holistic beings. For example, women recognize that the boundaries between work life and personal life are fluid. This means that the workplace is an arena for work and personal relationships and that members must have time to balance family and personal needs with work needs (Chester & Grossman, 1990). For example, in the attempt to help professors balance work and family roles, Harvard University has recently implemented two policies. First, faculty members in the Arts and Sciences may request up to six months of relief from teaching with full pay for each child they have (up to two children). In addition, for each child they have, faculty members can put off the review for their next promotion for a year (Wilson, 1995).

Care and concern for the community and the environment are also linked to feminist philosophy. Devoting resources (e.g., personnel and money) for community development projects, homeless shelters, child abuse programs, and battered women's shelters are some of the ways that organizations can help improve the communities in which they operate. Also, feminists advocate paying careful attention to the potentially damaging effects of organizational operations on the environment. For example, many feminists argue that science that neglects social responsibility is unacceptable (Schiebinger, 1987). Given this stance, it would be considered unacceptable for a timber company to harvest an old-growth forest without considering the impact of their efforts on local wildlife. Also, if the timber company were to perform environmentally sound harvesting, it would be considered imperative to replace the trees that were harvested with seedlings to promote new growth in the forest.

Finally, one of the greatest strengths of feminist theory is its emphasis on enlarging what is considered possible within organizations and encouraging creative thinking about alternatives (Buzzanell, 1993). This aspect of feminist theory links up with our earlier observation about diversity in thinking and behavior. The diverse organization embraces differences rather than rejects them. Every employee should be encouraged to submit new ideas and approaches for accomplishing tasks. Discussions that challenge the very nature of what the organization is and what goals it should pursue need to occur on an ongoing basis. Only through considering all possibilities and alternatives can organizations remain responsive to their environment and change to meet new demands.

In this general overview of key aspects of feminist theory, one can see the possibilities for organizational change as women's voices are allowed to resonate more clearly within corporations. One of the key problems confronting women and organizational communication researchers is how to "surface repressed voices and how to enable them to express themselves in the face of dominant groups embedded within current power structures" (Poole, 1994, p. 272). Now that we have considered the possibilities for cultural change that are linked to women's participation and integration of feminist theory into the workplace, let's turn to a discussion of sexual orientation.

Sexual Orientation

The dominance of heterosexuality in society has historically created difficulties for people of diverse sexual orientation including gay, lesbian, bisexual, and transgendered individuals. The types of difficulties faced by people of diverse sexual orientation are wide ranging: exclusion from groups, derogatory jokes, discrimination, hateful language, and violence.

What are the issues pertaining to sexual orientation in the workplace? First, sexual orientation discrimination is not covered by the federal laws that generally prohibit discrimination on the basis of race, color, sex, religion, national origin, age, and disability for private employers (Workplace Fairness, 2006). There are policies in place, however, in different parts of the federal government and in various state governments. For example, many federal government employees are covered by provisions in the Civil Service Reform Act of 1978 that prohibit sexual orientation discrimination (Workplace Fairness, 2006). In addition, in 1998, President Clinton issued Executive Order 13087, reaffirming the Executive Branch's longstanding internal policy that prohibits discrimination based on sexual orientation within the Executive Branch for civilian employees (U.S. Office of Personnel Management, 1999). Finally, several hundred municipalities (counties and cities) and 16 states have laws that prohibit discrimination based on sexual orientation (Workplace Fairness, 2006).

Sexual orientation discrimination is similar in form to any other type of discrimination. Simply stated, it means treating a person differently or harassing him or her because he or she belongs to a minority or disempowered group. So, if a gay, lesbian, bisexual, or transgendered person is not hired, not promoted, or fired because of his or her sexual orientation, he or she has been discriminated against. Of course, differential treatment may also be subtler and come from anyone in the organization. Subtle forms of differential treatment may mean exclusion from specific task or social groups or derogatory looks cast at the picture of a gay worker's partner. Discrimination may also take the form of harassment, similar in kind to the sexual harassment described earlier. On the *Workplace Fairness* Web site, sexual orientation harassment is described as being forced to "experience comments about your mannerisms or sexual activity, sexual jokes, requests for sexual favors, pressure for dates, touching or grabbing, leering, gestures, hostile comments, pictures or drawings negatively portraying lesbian and gay people, or sexual assault or rape" (Workplace Fairness, 2006, p. 1). Finally, sexual orientation discrimination may take the form of benefits discrimination. Specifically, a company pays health insurance and other benefits to the spouse and families of heterosexual employees but not to same-sex partners of homosexual workers (Workplace Fairness, 2006).

Some employers have mistakenly interpreted the protections afforded to people of diverse sexual orientations in ways that restrict everyday social interaction. For example, are jokes related to sexuality against the law? Consider the following statement from the Workplace Fairness organization:

> Federal law and the laws of most states do not prohibit simple teasing, offhand comments, or isolated incidents that are not extremely serious. The conduct must be sufficiently frequent or severe to create a hostile work environment or result in a tangible employment action such as hiring, promotion, demotion, [or termination]. (Workplace Fairness, 2006, pp. 2–3)

To this point we have focused on the protections that workers may receive against sexual orientation discrimination. What happens in organizations where employees are not protected? The answer is linked to the recognition that private-sector employees are "at will" employees. This means that an employer has the right to terminate a worker's employment at any time, for no reason at all or for any reason (even a bad one). As long as the reason for dismissal is not illegal, an employer may terminate an employment contract. This places the worker of diverse sexual orientation in a difficult situation. If he or she suspects that other workers or administrators in the organization hold discriminatory views toward different sexual orientations, he or she may need to hide any behavior or action that reveals that sexuality.

One widely discussed example of an organization that requires workers to hide any evidence or display of their sexuality is the U.S. military with their "don't ask, don't tell" policy. Lenora Billings-Harris believes that this is an unrealistic and unfair policy for any person to endure. She explains:

> If you are straight, imagine how much energy it would take to work for eight or more hours a day when you are compelled to hide your sexuality. That is what this rule requires. As busy as everyone is at work, people do not sit around talking about their social life, however the subject does come up occasionally. Think about what you would say when someone asks, "What did you do for Memorial Day?" If you had to live by the "don't ask, don't tell" rule, you would not be able to refer to your loved one as your wife, husband, boyfriend, or girlfriend. You might feel compelled to avoid answering the question, or lie. Neither are good

alternatives when talking to people with whom you need to develop a trusting working relationship. (Billings-Harris, 2006)

Absent laws protecting the rights of people belonging to diverse sexual orientation, employers need to consider what is humane to do *and* what benefits the organization. Sexual orientation places a person in a demographic category no different from any other category. Simply stated, there is no justifiable reason to discriminate against a person because of his or her sexual orientation. But humane treatment means more than a nondiscriminatory environment; it means *inclusion.* Creating an environment of inclusion means using language in ways that makes every person feel like he or she is part of the group or organization. Inclusion also means encouraging and seeking participation from a person in work and social activities.

A final reason to provide protection for persons of diverse sexual orientation is the benefits provided to the organization. First, consider the observation that creativity increases when you bring together people who view the world in different ways. People of diverse sexual orientation have ways of viewing the world that are linked to the relationships they have established in their lives. When confronting complex problems, it is always advantageous to draw upon differences in experience and worldviews. Furthermore, sustaining an environment that does not tolerate hateful talk about sexuality may contribute to worker productivity. As Billings-Harris explains

When GLBT (gay, lesbian, bisexual, and transgendered) jokes, gestures, and rumors are tolerated at work, it creates an environment that negatively affects productivity even if there are no GLBT's present. Such behavior can also be offensive to heterosexuals who are not biased in this way, because many workers have friends and relatives who are GLBT. (Billings-Harris, 2006)

Although public discussion of the rights of people of diverse sexual orientation has occurred only recently, it is important that organizations consider how to create supportive environments for this group of workers. All employees deserve to be treated respectfully and supportively. When people are evaluated for their actions, it should not be for their personal choices but for actions that are linked exclusively to their performance of their jobs and how they contribute to the goals of their department and the organization.

Race and Ethnicity

If women are concerned about breaking through the glass ceiling, members of racial and ethnic minority groups are worried about getting through the door. The condition of minorities is reflected rather ironically in the fact that 97% of all *women* managers are white. Only 1.5% of women managers are African American, and 1.5% are members of other minorities (Bureau of Labor Statistics, 2006). In many ways, African Americans as a group actually are worse off today than at any other time since the 1960s. Although affirmative action programs have helped millions of African Americans to enter the mainstream economy, millions more have been left behind. The situation is so serious that 34% of all African American children live in poverty (National Center for Children in Poverty, 2006) and 28.5%

of African American men are likely to be incarcerated in their lifetime (Joint Center for Political and Economic Studies, 2003). On the positive side, African American representation in the workforce continues to increase. Total workforce participation for African Americans was 15.3 million in 2005 (Bureau of Labor Statistics, 2006). The numbers of Asians and Hispanics in the workforce were 6.2 million and 18.6 million, respectively (Bureau of Labor Statistics, 2006). So, collectively, these three groups accounted for 40.1 million workers in 2005.

Employment projections for Native Americans do not even appear in any of the data that we have seen. Although 2 million people in this country are legally identified as Native Americans, they are treated in many respects as America's invisible people. We did find out that approximately 197,300 business firms in this country are owned by Native Americans, compared to more than 1.6 million by Hispanics, 1.2 million by African Americans, 1.1 million by Asians, and more than 6.5 million by women (U.S. Census Bureau, 2006). Even when the relatively small size of the Native American population is taken into account, Native Americans are far worse off than other minorities and women in business ownership, and we suspect that the same may be said for Native American employment in general.

As for those minorities who are not invisible, there is a real possibility that they will confront insidious forms of racism, hostility, and even hatred as their numbers increase in the workplace. In 1992, Marge Schott, Cincinnati Reds owner, was suspended from Major League Baseball for a year and fined $25,000 for using slurs against African Americans, Jews, and Asians (Sports People: Baseball; Schott's Chance to Talk, 1993). Although everyone would like to think that the kind of racism that embroiled the Cincinnati Reds' owner in controversy is no longer typical in America, in fact it is. Former baseball commissioner Fay Vincent reportedly said that the Schott incident proves that baseball reflects the racism that exists throughout our society. It was convenient in the 1960s and 1970s to see racism only as a southern problem, but racially motivated murders in the East and race riots in the West belie that myth. From New York to Cincinnati to Los Angeles, bigotry tears at the community fabric in every region of the nation.

A report by Charlene Solomon (1992c) on hatred in the workplace paints a despicable picture of the treatment that often is accorded to racial and ethnic minorities and to people of diverse sexual orientation. The behaviors range from racial slurs (not only in conversations but also in hate mail, graffiti, and even hate faxes) to sabotage of computer files or work projects, and even outright physical assaults.

All three authors of this text have observed personally these kinds of behaviors in organizations. For example, one of us was involved in a consulting project with a nationally prominent insurance company when a group of white managers joked in the office lunchroom on Martin Luther King Day. One manager said to his two colleagues that instead of celebrating Martin Luther King Day, they should be celebrating James Earl Ray Day (Ray was King's assassin). This comment was said loudly enough to be clearly overheard by some African American employees, who responded by laughing nervously. The unfortunate pervasiveness of such clear bigotry has lead many researchers to paint a rather bleak picture of workplace culture in the United States. Indeed, Howard Erlich of the National Institute Against Prejudice and Violence says, "The workplace probably is going to be the major site of ethnoviolent conflict" (Solomon, 1992c, p. 30).

Solomon offers four basic recommendations that organizations can implement in order to prevent or at least reduce racial and ethnic hatred in the workplace:

1. Have clear standards for acceptable behavior and monitor the culture for unacceptable behaviors that require intervention, especially those with the potential to escalate into violence.

2. Have a management team that supervisors can call on for help. This team might consist of human resources, security, and employee assistance staff.

3. Have a consulting psychologist available.

4. Provide counseling or additional training for "toxic" supervisors who provoke high levels of frustration and hostility among employees.

On a more personal level, what can an employee do if confronted with racist behavior? In order to address this question we would like to borrow and reframe the recommendations presented earlier concerning sexual harassment from The Tidewater Florida Chapter of the National Organizational for Women (Sunshine for Women, 2006).

First, inform the person making the racist statement or engaging in the racist action that you consider the statement or action unacceptable. If it happens again, send a letter telling the person to stop, and keep a personal copy. Second, write down what happened including the date, time, place, and exactly what the person said to you and/or what he or she did to you. Third, seek out support from friends, family, and coworkers, especially if you start to suffer from physical or psychological problems as a result of the racist behavior. Fourth, talk to your union representative, if a union represents you. Fifth, talk to your employer because all organizations should have a written policy against racist statements and actions and a procedure for making a complaint. Sixth, keep a record of your work including copies of performance evaluations and memos that show that you do a good job at work. Seventh, recognize that you have a right to file a charge. The EEOC was created to protect you. Finally, find out more about your legal rights by talking with a lawyer who specializes in race discrimination. The state bar association in your area can refer you to lawyers.

Controversies and Possible Solutions

Ethnic and racial minority group members in the United States have reported a number of significant problems in workplace culture that need to be addressed by managers, consultants, and researchers. For example, one African American executive in the transportation industry reported that his new boss greeted him at their first meeting with the statement, "The South should have won the war" (Leinster, 1988, p. 118). More pervasive, however, is dealing with the assumption that minority group members cannot perform as well as their white colleagues or, if they do perform at high levels, it is considered surprising. H. Naylor Fitzhugh, former PepsiCo vice president, provided an excellent example of dealing with these assumptions. He recalled a business colleague congratulating him for his ideas and then "just as often saying, 'It's hard to remember you're black.' Now that's hardly a compliment" (Leinster, 1988, p. 118).

Other minority group members focus on the pressure of being under constant observation. For example, consider the comments of Gary Jefferson, the African American vice-president of the Midwest Region of United Airlines. He stated: "It's always catastrophic when a black fails. Individual blacks have got to be allowed to fail without everybody thinking that all blacks screwed up. Whites are allowed that" (Leinster, 1988, p. 118).

Part of the rage felt by many minority group members is related directly to their experiences in U.S. organizations. Cose (1993) recently interviewed an African-American corporate attorney who shared a story reflective of his workplace experiences. Despite having brought millions of dollars into the firm the year before, he felt he was not receiving his due. To make his point he referred to an experience that happened a few days earlier. When he arrived at work early one morning, he entered the elevator with a white junior staff attorney. When the two attorneys exited the elevator on the same floor, the white attorney turned around and blocked the path of the African American, saying, "May I help you?" He tried to pass only to be stopped again with the same question, only this time in a louder voice. The African American spat out his name and identified himself as a partner in the firm, and the junior staff attorney quickly stepped aside. Sadly, this successful African American attorney no longer expects praise, honor, or acceptance from his white colleagues. Rather, he concluded, "Just make sure my money is at the top of the line. I can go to my own people for acceptance" (Cose, 1993, p. 56).

Although African Americans have been burdened by particularly humiliating experiences in U.S. organizations, other groups have suffered as well. In newly diversified organizations, many problems can arise that influence different racial and ethnic groups, and women as well. In an ethnography entitled, "It's Like a Prison in There," Zak (1994) addresses the communication problems that can occur in newly diversified organizations. Zak includes an example from the vehicle maintenance unit of a large company. This unit had recently become more demographically diverse by hiring people from different racial and ethnic groups and class levels as well as integrating more women. Unfortunately, leading veteran employees (mostly white males) asserted their power through horseplay and shoptalk that was traditionally used to maintain hierarchy and control in this workplace. In response to the conflicts that surfaced between the newcomers and the veterans, management increased their surveillance of the workers and enforced punitive policies that lead to a fragmented and dysfunctional organization. Zak attributed this outcome to management's failure to promote "communication processes through which shared or negotiated meaning and agreed-upon language and behaviors appropriate to the new workplace could be constructed" (p. 282). Indeed, in this study Zak found that worker race, ethnicity, and gender accounted for differences in language and behaviors among the employees. Until these workers figure out how to understand their differences and similarities, their problems will likely continue.

More recently in 2005, the claims administrator in the *Gonzalez v. Abercrombie & Fitch* (No. 3:03-cv-02817, U.S. District Court, Northern District of California) discrimination lawsuit sent award checks totaling $40 million to more than 10,000 present and former employees of Abercrombie & Fitch (A&F) who were discriminated against for their race or ethnicity. Specifically, the claims administrator found evidence that the company purposefully targeted white employees for both entry-level employment and advancement opportunities in the company. In fact, A&F was found to target fraternities, sororities, and specific colleges for recruitment purposes. This method of recruitment purposefully excluded Latino, African-American, and Asian applicants. Among the provisions in the settlement of this case are (a) "benchmarks" for hiring and promoting Latinos, African Americans, and Asian Americans[1]; (b) advertising of available positions in publications targeting minorities; (c) a new Office and Vice President of Diversity, responsible for reporting to the CEO on A&F's progress toward fair employment practices; (d) Equal Employment Opportunity (EEO) and diversity training for all employees with hiring authority; (e) revision of performance evaluations for managers, making progress toward diversity goals a factor in their bonuses and compensations; and (f) a new internal complaint procedure (Lieff, Cabraser, Heimann, & Bernstein, 2006).

In dealing with problems and controversies such as those described above, managers need to keep in mind the many reasons to support workplace diversity programs. Companies need to diversify their workforce "to best utilize the country's labor pool and to lure a changing consumer base" (Lowery, 1995, p. 150). Concerning the consumer base, Lowery is alluding to the purchasing power of U.S. racial minority groups, which is enormous. So, it would simply be bad business to alienate them. In fact, the Selig Center for Economic Growth predicts that in 2007 purchasing power will reach the following levels for the three major racial minority groups in the U.S.: African Americans, $847 billion; Hispanic Americans, $863 billion; and Asian Americans, $420 billion (Selig Center for Economic Growth, 2006). Thus, workplace diversity is not only a moral issue; it is a strategic issue. Simply stated, diversity in the workplace will help American organizations compete successfully in a global economy.

Class

Large organizations frequently employ people belonging to widely divergent socioeconomic classes. Often the simplest, most repetitive, and most laborious jobs are performed by people belonging to the lowest socioeconomic classes. Work tasks that require college degrees usually employ workers of middle to upper middle class. Finally, at the top of the organization's hierarchy we frequently find people from the highest social and economic class categories.

Problems related to class diversity are not due inherently to the presence of different classes but to how people belonging to particular classes perceive their treatment. Very often problems occur when people performing mundane tasks for low pay experience mistreatment or disrespect by employers or employees who are paid much higher salaries. For example, avoiding eye contact or not talking to employees belonging to lower social or economic classes may show disrespect. Alternatively, an upper middle class employer may talk to a janitor but only to give that person an order in a condescending tone.

The resentment felt by the worker of a lower socioeconomic class is a product of two factors. One factor is pay. Too many workers in the United States and in other countries are not paid a living wage for full-time work. As Barbara Ehrenreich (2001) explains in her best-selling book *Nickel and Dimed: On (Not) Getting by in America,* millions of Americans work full-time, year-round for poverty-level wages. These workers labor as wait staff, cleaning people, nursing home aides, and department store sales clerks. There is no justification for paying people wages for full-time work that do not allow them to be self-sufficient above the poverty level. Unfortunately, too many workers cannot be self-sufficient because of their wages, which forms the basis for a significant amount of class conflict between those who languish in poverty and their much wealthier managers and employers.

The second reason for resentment among lower socioeconomic class workers is how they perceive their treatment by others. Every person deserves to be treated with respect no matter what job he or she works. People who clean offices deserve the same sort of friendly greeting that any other employee would receive. When asking a person to perform a task, there is no reason to bark an order or use a condescending tone. The same sort of pleasantries that characterize conversations between workers who have equal status should characterize discussions between blue-collar and white-collar workers.

The issue of resentment extends beyond those occupying lower socioeconomic classes, however. Consider an upper middle class businessman (Rich) who enters a fast-food restaurant in a suit while talking on a cell phone. The worker behind the register (Jim) may be a high-school dropout in his 20s who resents everything that this wealthy businessman stands for. Likewise, Rich looks at the shabbily dressed Jim behind the register and prejudges him to be a lazy, uneducated troublemaker. When Rich gives his order to Jim, he doesn't look him in they eye and he uses a condescending tone. This short exchange confirms everything that Jim thinks about Rich. Jim knows that Rich despises him for who he is, a poor, undereducated worker who does little to contribute to society. In order to restore some of his dignity, Jim purposefully delays filling the order by making a mistake with the register, requiring intervention from the manager. When Jim gives Rich the order he says nothing and doesn't look Rich in the eyes. Rich walks away in a huff (adapted from "Fast-Food Purchase Seething With Unspoken Class Conflict," 2001).

In the United States, the sort of interaction described between Rich and Jim plays itself out millions of times each day. The United States is a country where there are vast differences between the wealthiest and the poorest workers. People at the extremes (high versus low) are most likely to resent the other, and this resentment shows in how they communicate to one another. There is no way to condone the behavior of either group. The starting point to resolve such conflicts is for each person to treat the other humanely and respectfully.

Class conflict will also occur in organizations when a higher level group makes decisions without the input of the lower level group. Such action sends the signal that the views of the lower level group do not matter. For example, consider Gibson and Schullery's (2000) description of a blue-collar worker philanthropy program. The organization that was the focus of their study experienced an economic crisis that required them to consider dismissing employees. Rather than resort to this tactic, however, they came up with a solution that involved partnering with nonprofit organizations in the area that required additional workers. By enacting a policy of "loaned labor," employees were able to work in local nonprofit organizations rather than the factory for a period of up to three months. These workers received the same level of pay and benefits that they did at the factory. Despite the fact that they were employed rather than unemployed, not all of the workers were happy. Consider the following comment by one worker:

> I was mad because at first it sounded like we would be doing construction work like at Habitat for Humanity and I know how much construction workers make and I knew we wouldn't be getting paid for that so I wasn't going to work for half of what construction workers made. (Gibson & Schullery, 2000, pp. 210–211)

Gibson and Schullery (2000) explain this reaction may have been prompted by the manner in which the "loan labor" decision was communicated. The workers were told what solution was going to be implemented to deal with the economic crisis. They were not consulted and they believed they were faced with an ultimatum: work elsewhere or don't get paid. They were also fearful that they would be required to perform work that they were not trained for. Ultimately, this conflict between two different class groups could have been prevented if management had been more inclusive in talking with employees about what options could have been pursued to prevent mass layoffs.

Physical Abilities

There are at least 54 million Americans with disabilities (The White House, 2006). Until 1992, many were effectively kept out of employment because employers had done very little to accommodate the workplace to their needs (Solomon, 1992b). The federal government changed this situation with the implementation of the Americans with Disabilities Act (ADA), "the most sweeping civil rights legislation since 1964" (Solomon, 1992b, p. 70). The ADA requires employers to make "reasonable accommodations" for the workplace needs of the disabled and prohibits discrimination against the disabled "in regard to *all* employment practices" (Barlow & Hane, 1992, p. 53). Importantly, this will become even more of an issue as thousands of veterans of the Iraq War return with a range of physical disabilities and a desire to work jobs that maximize their contributions to organizations and to society at large.

Defining "reasonable accommodation" is, like defining sexual harassment, a process that probably will be worked out in the courts, but it is generally clear that making these accommodations will require close attention to job descriptions, supervisors' responsibilities, employee etiquette, and training programs not only for the people with disabilities, but also for those who need to know what kinds of accommodations to make and how to make them.

Patricia Morrissey, vice president of Employment Advisory Services, has observed rather astutely that effectiveness in complying with the ADA will center on the quality of interaction that occurs between disabled employees and those who are receiving them into the workplace (Solomon, 1992b). Morrissey emphasizes courtesy in interviews, provision of appropriate orientation, adapting one's communicative behavior to the nature of the disability, and ensuring that the people with disabilities have appropriate access to information, tools needed for work, and physical facilities.

We would add to Morrissey's list that organization members in general could provide acceptance and support for the people with disabilities (or, for that matter, toward any other historically excluded group) as they assimilate into the workplace. The disabled endure much derision in our society, and the physically abled often react to the presence of people with disabilities with great discomfort, so sensitivity and respect will be required by all in the workplace if the people with disabilities are to realize the promise of the ADA.

Despite the existence of the ADA, much progress needs to be made in integrating people with disabilities into the workforce. The national graduation rate for students receiving special education and related services is approximately 27%, in comparison to a rate of 75% for students not relying on special education. Furthermore, the unemployment rate for working-age adults with disabilities is approximately 70%. Finally, computer use and

Internet access for people with disabilities are approximately half of that for people without disabilities (The White House, 2006). Thus, much progress needs to be made in more fully integrating the disabled into the social and economic life of the United States.

THE ETHICS OF DIVERSITY

Organizational commitment to diversity means more than opening the doors for entry into an organization. From an ethical standpoint, organizations must also provide support for people who belong to diverse groups. When people representing diverse experiences and worldviews are brought together in the same place, misunderstandings and conflicts are inevitable. Many of these problems are the result of minimal contact between certain groups of people, so mistaken assumptions and prejudices can cloud thinking. One responsibility that human resource personnel and training staff must consider is how to anticipate these conflicts and prepare employees for them so they will learn how to work together rather than fight against one another. Importantly, two types of training and development activities are warranted. Cultural education and information sharing will be needed, as well as training in productive conflict management.

When people from diverse groups are brought into an organization, they will bring ways of thinking and acting with them that may separate them from others. Although they may need to make some personal adjustments, the organization may miss valuable contributions if they encourage diverse workers to "check their diversity at the door." As long as a person's diverse views are not potentially damaging to the organization, they need to be encouraged and supported in their display of diverse thinking and behavior.

In the rapidly changing global environment of the 21st century, creative thinking and actions will be necessary for organizational survival. Doing business the way it has always been done is a sure recipe for disaster. If diverse ways of thinking and acting are truly valued, these diverse views and actions should be present in every part of the organization. What this means is that a given demographic group should not be limited to one type of job or function within the organization. Also, support should be shown in promoting diverse members on the basis of their contributions to the organization. Indeed, evidence of an ethical approach to diversity will be demonstrated when corporate leadership contains as much diversity as entry-level positions.

SUMMARY

The influx of women, people of diverse sexual orientation, racial and ethnic minorities, different class groups and ages, and the physically challenged into the workplace continues to affect the nature of corporate culture in the United States. In this chapter, we addressed the challenges faced by different demographic groups, the contributions each group can make to organizational success, and the ways these different groups can change organizational culture by their presence and empowerment. For example, women face challenges such as sexual harassment and the glass ceiling, whereas racial and ethnic minorities continue to face entry and advancement barriers in many companies. Also, acts of hatred are still targeted at different minority group members while they are at work. People of diverse sexual orientation face derision and discrimination. The physically challenged face problems of access and accommodation in many companies, but the Americans with Disabilities Act seems to be opening many doors that were formerly closed to this group. Age differences among employees also pose challenges when people of different ages must work together on projects.

In order for companies to reap the benefits of diversity, the members of different demographic groups must be valued and empowered. This means valuing and empowering women and men, people of different sexual orientations, racial and ethnic minority group members, the physically challenged, and workers of different classes and ages. What corporate leaders and managers need to recognize is that the members of these various groups have different ways of viewing issues, problems, and work procedures based on their particular worldviews. These differences offer limitless possibilities for creativity and innovation in the workplace as the members of different groups are empowered and encouraged to work together. Also, the globalization of the economy requires hiring people who represent the varied markets companies are attempting to tap. There is no better way to find out about the needs and concerns of different market groups than to hire people from these groups and rely upon their expertise and experience. Organizations that value diversity by employing and empowering members of different demographic groups will experience significant challenges and changes in corporate culture as different worldviews are integrated into companies formerly dominated by a single perspective. However, the payoff for this diversity will eventually become clear. Remember the statement we quoted earlier from J. T. Childs, Jr., director of workforce diversity at IBM: "It [workplace diversity] may have been a moral issue 30 years ago. Today it is a strategic issue" (Lowery, 1995, p. 150).

DISCUSSION QUESTIONS/ACTIVITIES

1. What kinds of cultural diversity issues have you encountered in your own experience? Were these issues handled effectively by everyone involved? What do you think organizations can do to address the problems and opportunities of diversity?

2. To what extent do you think leaders and executives can really control and direct organizational cultures? In your own organizational experiences, what are some of the important factors that have shaped the organizational culture?

3. How would you assess the prospects for constructing or reconstructing organizations according to feminist principles? Will this be easier to do in some kinds of organizations than in others? What are some of the factors that might influence the effectiveness of feminizing organizations?

4. On the basis of the descriptions of the four different age groups provided in the chapter (Traditionals, Boomers, Generation X, and Millenials) what sort of problems do you anticipate occurring as these different groups interact in the workplace? What sort of advantages or opportunities exist in combining people from these different groups in one department?

NOTE

1. These benchmarks are goals, rather than quotas, and A&F is required to report on its progress toward these goals at regular intervals.

REFERENCES

Adler, N. J. (1991). *International dimensions of organizational behavior.* Boston: PWS-Kent.

Adler, N. J. (1992). Managing globally competent people. *The Academy of Management Executive, 6*(3), 52–65.

Adler, N. J. (2002). Global companies, global society: There is a better way. *Journal of Management Inquiry, 11*(3), 255–260.

Allen, B. J. (1995). "Diversity" and organizational communication. *Journal of Applied Communication Research, 23,* 143–155.

Alvesson, M. (1987). *Organization theory and technocratic consciousness.* Berlin: de Gruyter.

Alvesson, M. (1993). Cultural-ideological modes of management control: A theory and a case study of a professional service company. In S. Deetz (Ed.), *Communication yearbook 16* (pp. 3–42). Newbury Park, CA: Sage.

American Association of University Women. (2006). Drawing the line: Sexual harassment on campus. Retrieved May 21, 2006, from http://www.aauw.org/research/dtl.cfm

American Civil Liberties Union. (1995). *Affirmative action: Still effective, still needed in the pursuit of equal opportunity in the '90s.* New York: American Civil Liberties Union Press.

American Civil Liberties Union. (2000). *Affirmative action.* New York: American Civil Liberties Union Press.

Baird, J. E., Jr., & Bradley, P. H. (1979). Styles of management and communication: A comparative study of men and women. *Communication Monographs, 46,* 101–111.

Barlow, W. E., & Hane, E. Z. (1992, June). A practical guide to the Americans with Disabilities Act. *Personnel Journal,* pp. 53–60.

Berger, P., & Luckmann, T. (1966). *The social construction of reality.* New York: Doubleday.

Berkman, H. (1995). Many "tentacles" to race-based federal policies. *National Law Review, 17,* A1, A29.

Billings-Harris, L. (2006). Sexual orientation in the workplace. Retrieved May 24, 2006, from http://www.sideroad.com/Diversity_in_the_Workplace/sexual-orientation-in-the-workplace.html

Black, J. S., & Mendenhall, M. (1990). Cross-cultural training effectiveness: A review and theoretical framework for future research. *Academy of Management Review, 15,* 113–136.

Blumrosen, A. A. (1995). *Affirmative action programs and claims of reverse discrimination.* New York: American Civil Liberties Union.

Bradford, L. J., & Raines, C. (1992). *Twentysomething: Managing and motivating today's new work force.* New York: Master Media, Ltd.

Bruning, F. (1995, March 20). In defence of affirmative action. *Maclean's,* p. 9.

Bureau of Labor Statistics. (2006). Labor force statistics from the current population survey. Retrieved May 25, 2006, from ftp://ftp.bls.gov/pub/special.requests/lf/aat9.txt

Burrell, N. A., Buzzanell, P. M., & McMillan, J. J. (1992). Feminine tensions in conflict situations as revealed by metaphoric analyses. *Management Communication Quarterly, 6,* 115–149.

Buzzanell, P. M. (1993). Feminist approaches to organizational communication instruction. In C. Berryman-Fink, D. Ballard-Reisch, & L. H. Newman (Eds.), *Communication and sex-role socialization* (pp. 525–553). New York: Garland.

Buzzanell, P. M. (1994). Gaining a voice: Feminist organizational communication theorizing. *Management Communication Quarterly, 7,* 339–383.

Catalyst. (2006). *2005 Catalyst census of women board of directors of the Fortune 500.* New York: Author.

Chakravorty, J. (2006). Toyota hit with $190 million sexual harassment suit. Retrieved May 5, 2006, from http://today.reuters.com/business/newsArticle.aspx

Chester, N. L., & Grossman, H. Y. (1990). Introduction: Learning about women and their work through their own accounts. In H. Y. Grossman & N. L. Chester (Eds.), *The experience and meaning of work in women's lives* (pp. 1–19). Hillsdale, NJ: Lawrence Erlbaum.

Conrad, C. (1994). *Strategic communication: Toward the twenty-first century* (3rd ed.). Fort Worth, TX: Harcourt, Brace, Jovanovich.

Cose, E. (1993, November 15). Rage of the privileged. *Newsweek,* pp. 56–63.

Cox, T., Jr. (1993). *Cultural diversity in organizations: Theory, research and practice.* San Francisco: Berret-Koehler.

Czarniawska-Joerges, B. (1988). *Ideological control in nonideological organizations.* New York: Praeger.

Deal, T. E., & Kennedy, A. A. (1982). *Corporate cultures: The rites and rituals of corporate life.* Reading, MA: Addison-Wesley.

Ehrenreich, B. (2001). *Nickel and dimed: On (not) getting by in America.* New York: Henry Holt and Company.

Eisenberg, E. M., & Goodall, H. L., Jr. (1993). *Organizational communication: Balancing creativity and constraint.* New York: St. Martin's.

Estrich, S. (1995, May 9). *Counterpoints: An apt compromise on affirmative action. USA Today,* p. 9A.

Fast-food purchase seething with unspoken class conflict. (2001). Retrieved May 25, 2006, from http://www.theonion.com/content/node/28290

Ferguson, K. E. (1984). *The feminist case against bureaucracy.* Philadelphia: Temple University Press.

Fine, M. G. (1991). New voices in the workplace: Research directions in multicultural communication. *Journal of Business Communication, 28,* 259–275.

Foeman, A. K. (1991). Managing multiracial institutions: Goals and approaches for race-relations training. *Communication Education, 40,* 255–265.

Gardner, W. L., Peluchette, J. V. E., & Clinebell, S. K. (1994). Valuing women in management: An impression management perspective of gender diversity. *Management Communication Quarterly, 8,* 115–164.

Geertz, C. (1973). *The interpretation of cultures.* New York: Basic Books.

Gibson, M., & Papa, M. J. (2000). The mud, the blood, the beer guys: Organizational osmosis in blue collar work groups. *Journal of Applied Communication Research, 28,* 68–88.

Gibson, M. K., & Schullery, N. M. (2000). Shifting meanings in a blue-collar worker philanthropy program: Emergent tensions in traditional and feminist organizing. *Management Communication Quarterly, 14*(2), 189–236.

Giddens, A. (1979). *Central problems in social theory.* Berkeley: University of California Press.

Guinier, L. (2003, July 2–8). Saving affirmative action [Electronic version]. *Village Voice, 64,* 17–18.

Helgesen, S. (1990). *The female advantage: Women's ways of leadership.* New York: Doubleday.

Howe, N., & Strauss, W. (2000). *Millennials rising: The next great generation.* New York: Vintage.

Jablin, F. M. (2001). Organizational entry, assimilation, and disengagement/exit. In F. M. Jablin & L. L. Putnam (Eds.), *The new handbook of organizational communication* (pp. 732–818). Thousand Oaks, CA: Sage.

Joint Center for Political and Economic Studies. (2003). Chance of going to prison during the rest of life. Retrieved May 25, 2006, from http://www.jointcenter.org/DB/table/databank/crime/Corrections/Jail%200r%20Prison/Lifetime%20Likelihood/during%20rest%200f%201ife/byage.txt

Kim, M. S., & Sharkey, W. F. (1995). Independent and interdependent construals of self: Explaining cultural patterns of interpersonal communication in multi-cultural organizational settings. *Communication Quarterly, 43,* 20–38.

Lehmuller, P., & Gregory, D. E. (2005). Affirmative action: From before Bakke to after Grutter, *NASPA Journal, 42*(4), 430–459.

Leinster, C. (1988, January 18). Black executives: How they're doing. *Fortune,* pp. 109–120.

Lewis, N. A. (1993, April 4). At A.C.L.U., free speech balancing act. *The New York Times,* Sec. 1, p. 12.

Lieff, Cabraser, Heimann, & Bernstein, LLP. (2006). $40 million paid to class members in December 2005 in Abercrombie & Fitch discrimination lawsuit settlement. Retrieved May 25, 2006, from http://www .afjustice.com/

Lowery, M. (1995, February). The war on equal opportunity. *Black Enterprise,* pp. 148–154.

Marshall, J. (1984). *Women managers: Travellers in a male world.* Chichester, England: John Wiley.

Marshall, J. (1993). Viewing organizational communication from a feminist perspective: A critique and some offerings. In S. Deetz (Ed.), *Communication yearbook 16* (pp. 122–143). Newbury Park, CA: Sage.

Martin, J. N., Hecht, M. L., & Larkey, L. K. (1994). Conversational improvement strategies for interethnic communication: African American and European American perspectives. *Communication Monographs, 61,* 236–255.

McLoughlin, M. (1988, August 8). Men vs. women. *U.S. News & World Report,* pp. 50–56.

Morgan, G. (1989). Endangered species: New ideas. *Business Month, 133*(4), 75–77.

Mumby, D. K. (1988). *Communication and power in organizations: Discourse, ideology and domination.* Norwood, NJ: Ablex.

Mumby, D. K. (1989). Ideology & the social construction of meaning: A communication perspective. *Communication Quarterly, 37,* 291–304.

Mumby, D. K., & Putnam, L. L. (1992). The politics of emotion: A feminist reading of bounded rationality. *Academy of Management Review, 17,* 465–486.

Myers, S., & Lambert, J. (1990). *Managing cultural diversity: A trainer's guide.* Solana Beach, CA: Intercultural Development.

Natalle, E. J., Papa, M. J., & Graham, E. E. (1994). Feminist philosophy and the transformation of organizational communication. In B. Kovacic (Ed.), *New approaches to organizational communication* (pp. 245–270). Albany, NY: State University of New York Press.

National Center for Children in Poverty. (2006). United States: Demographics of poor children. Retrieved May 25, 2006, from http://www.nccp.org/state_detail_demographic_poor_US.html

O'Donnell, J., & Woodyard, C. (2006, August 7). Toyota's sex-harassment lawsuit could set standard. *USA Today* [Electronic version]. Retrieved June 20, 2007, from http://www.usatoday.com/money/companies/management/ 2006-08-07-toyota-settle-usat_x.htm

Papa, M. J., Auwal, M. A., & Singhal, A. (1997). Organizing for social change within concertive control systems: Member identification, empowerment, and the masking of discipline. *Communication Monographs, 64,* 219–249.

Pearson, S. S. (1981). Rhetoric and organizational change: New applications of feminine style. In B. L. Forisha & B. H. Goldman (Eds.), *Outsiders on the inside: Women & Organizations* (pp. 55–74). Englewood Cliffs, NJ: Prentice Hall.

Peters, T. (1987). *Thriving on chaos: Handbook for a management revolution.* New York: Knopf.

Poole, M. S. (1994). Afterword. In B. Kovacic (Ed.), *New approaches to organizational communication* (pp. 271–277). Albany, NY: State University of New York Press.

Porn at work: Is it legal? (1992, April). *Glamour,* p. 130.

Putnam, L. L. (1990, April). *Feminist theories, dispute processes, and organizational communication.* Paper presented at the Arizona State University Conference on Organizational Communication: Perspectives for the 90s, Tempe, AZ.

Schiebinger, L. (1987). The history and philosophy of women in science: A review essay. In S. Harding & J. E. O'Barr (Eds.), *Sex and scientific inquiry* (pp. 7–34). Chicago: University of Chicago Press.

Selig Center for Economic Growth. (2006). The multicultural economy: Minority buying power in 2006. Retrieved October 28, 2006, from http://www.terry.uga.edu/news/releases/2006/buying_power_ study.html

Sheppard, D. L. (1989). Organizations, power and sexuality: The image and self-image of women managers. In J. Hearn, D. L. Sheppard, P. Tancred-Sheriff, & G. Burrell (Eds.), *The sexuality of organization* (pp. 139–157). London: Sage.

Smircich, L. (1983). Studying organizations as cultures. In G. Morgan (Ed.), *Beyond method: Strategies for social research* (pp. 160–172). Beverly Hills, CA: Sage.

Solomon, C. M. (1992a, March). Managing the baby busters. *Personnel Journal,* pp. 52–58.

Solomon, C. M. (1992b, June). What the ADA means to the disabled. *Personnel Journal,* pp. 70–72.

Solomon, C. M. (1992c, July). Keeping hate out of the workplace. *Personnel Journal,* pp. 30–35.

Sports people: Baseball; Schott's chance to talk. (1993, February 24). *The New York Times* [Electronic version]. Retrieved June 20, 2007, from http://query.nytimes.com/gst/fullpage.html?res=9F0CE5DC163DF937 A15751C0A965958260&n=Top%2fReference%2fTimes%20Topics%2fPeople%2fS%2fSchott%2c%20M arge

Strossen, N. (1992, October 31). *The first amendment in the communication century.* Speech presented at the Speech Communication Association convention, Chicago, IL.

Sunshine for Women. (2006). Sexual harassment: NOW or never. Retrieved May 24, 2006, from http://www.pinn.net/ ~ sunshine/now-news/harass2.html

Thielfoldt, D., & Scheef, D. (2004, August). Generation X and the Millennials: What you need to know about mentoring the new generations. *Law Practice Today* [Electronic version]. Retrieved June 18, 2007, from http://www.abanet.org/lpm/lpt/articles/mgt08044.html

Tompkins, P. K., & Cheney, G. (1983). The uses of account analysis: A study of organizational decision making and identification. In L. L. Putnam & M. E. Pacanowsky (Eds.), *Communication and organizations: An interpretive approach* (pp. 123–146). Beverly Hills, CA: Sage.

U.S. Census Bureau. (2006). Data on business owners. Retrieved September 26, 2006, from http://ask.census.gov/cgibin/askcensus.cfg/php/enduser/std_adp.php?p_faqid=811&p_created=1107440229& p_sid=V7yst08i&p_lva=&p_sp=cF9zcmNoPTEmcF9zb3J0X2J5PSZwX2dyaWRzb3J0PSZwX3Jvd19jbnQ9M TM1JnBfcHJvZHM9JnBfY2F0cz0mcF9wdj0mcF9jdj0mcF9wYWdlPTEmcF9zZWFyY2hfdGV4dD1idXNpbnb VzcyBvd25lcg**&p_li=&p_topview=1

U.S. Department of Labor. (2006). *Women's bureau: Quick statistics 2004.* Retrieved May 5, 2006, from http://www.dol.gov/wb/stats/main.htm

U.S. Equal Employment Opportunity Commission. (2006). Sexual harassment. Retrieved May 24, 2006, from http://www.eeoc.gov/types/sexual_harassment.html

U.S. Office of Personnel Management. (1999). Addressing sexual orientation discrimination in federal civilian employment: A guide to employee's rights. Washington, DC: Author.

Uttal, B. (1983, October 17). The corporate culture vultures. *Fortune,* pp. 66–72.

Van Maanen, J., & Kunda, G. (1989). Real feelings: Emotional expression and organizational culture. In B. M. Staw & L. L. Cummings (Eds.), *Research in organizational behavior* (Vol. 11, pp. 87–113). Greenwich, CT: JAI.

Van Maanen, J., & Schein, E. H. (1979). Toward a theory of organizational socialization. *Research in Organizational Behavior, 1,* 209–264.

Veraldi, L. (1993). Gender preferences. *Federal Communications Law Journal, 45,* 219–245.

Wagner, E. J. (1992). *Sexual harassment in the workplace.* New York: AMACOM-American Management Association.

Weick, K. E., & Browning, L. D. (1991). Fixing with the voice: A research agenda for applied communication. *Journal of Applied Communication Research, 1,* 1–19.

The White House. (2006). Fulfilling America's promise to Americans with disabilities. Retrieved May 25, 2006, from http://www.whitehouse.gov/news/freedominitiative/freedominitiative.html

White, R. D. (1999). The imperative for a new multicultural paradigm. *Public Administration & Management: An Interactive Journal, 4*(4), 469–493.

Wilkins, B. M., & Andersen, P. A. (1991). Gender differences and similarities in management communication: A meta-analysis. *Management Communication Quarterly, 5,* 6–35.

Wilson, R. (1995, November 17). Colleges help professors balance work and family. *Chronicle of Higher Education, 62*(12), A24.

Workforce 2000—Work and Workers for the 21st Century. (1987). Indianapolis: The Hudson Institute.

Workplace Fairness. (2006). Sexual orientation discrimination. Retrieved May 24, 2006, from http://www .workplacefairness.org/index.php?page=sexualorientation

Zak, M. W. (1994). It's like a prison in there. *Journal of Business and Technical Communication, 8,* 282–298.

Group Relationships

Chapter Outline

TRADITIONAL PERSPECTIVE ON GROUP RELATIONSHIPS
   Communication Skills: Communication Competence in Groups
   Groups as Organizational Subsystems
      Quality Circles
      Focus Groups
      Task Forces
   Group Decision Making and Problem Solving
      Group Decisions Versus Individual Decisions
      Effective Group Decision Making and Task Performance
      Group Decision Development
   Roles and Role Categories in Groups

INTERPRETIVE PERSPECTIVE ON GROUP RELATIONSHIPS
   The Bona Fide Group Perspective
   Norms and Conformity
   Values and Sense Making
   Decision Making and Culture

CRITICAL PERSPECTIVE ON GROUP RELATIONSHIPS
   Giddens's Structuration Theory and the Creation of Social Structure

$\mathbf{A}$s we take you through the subject matter of this book, we talk about organizational culture, diversity, power, conflict, technology, and organizational change as important subjects in organizational communication, but communication always occurs within and, at the same time, creates a relational context. As Goldhaber, Dennis, Richetto, and Wiio (1979) wrote, "the relationship level is where most of the work of the organization is accomplished, where most of the communication difficulties are encountered, and where the survival potential of the organization is qualitatively judged" (p. 104).

Our approach to understanding organizational communication within relational contexts focuses on group processes and leader-member or superior-subordinate relationships. In this chapter, we will examine traditional, interpretive, and critical perspectives on group relations. Although one of the more prominent group roles is reflected in leadership behavior, there are too many important ideas about leadership and leader-member relations for us to put everything in this chapter. So, the topics of leadership and leader-member relations are covered in the next chapter.

Some scholars, such as Herbert Simon (1957), literally regard an organization as a group of groups. Organizations comprise many types of groups: special project teams, management teams, committees, functional work groups and departments, social groups, groups derived from occupational and professional communities, and coalitions of special interests that arise from organizational politics. Much of the problem solving, decision making, day-to-day work, and social activity of organizations occurs in groups. Consequently, communication processes within and between groups exert substantial influence on organizational performance and the quality of organization life.

Most of the research on group communication in organizations seems to focus on group decision-making and problem-solving processes, including models of effective decision making, the phases or steps that characterize group decision making, and factors that distinguish effective from ineffective decision-making groups (Littlejohn, 1992). But groups are more than mere decision-making mechanisms. Group membership often is a critical factor in the individual members' sense of identity and self-concept. Groups exercise power in order to gain and control resources. Groups provide values, justifications, and frames of reference from which individual members make sense of their organizational experiences.

The traditional, interpretive, and critical perspectives on group relationships structure our commentary in this chapter. Starting with the traditional perspective we describe the central importance of communication competence as a skill for group members to have. Second, we turn to aspects of structure by describing different types of organizational groups: quality circles, focus groups, and task forces. Third, we take a look at group decision-making and problem-solving processes followed by a description of roles and role categories in groups. From the standpoint of the interpretive perspective, we examine the bona fide group perspective to draw attention to the fact that organizational groups are not unchanging containers for members, rather membership changes frequently in groups. Also, members' linkages to other groups impact any given group substantively, including group cultural dynamics. From the interpretive perspective, we also look at norms and conformity, values and sense making, and decision making and culture. Finally, from the critical perspective, we focus on Giddens's structuration theory and the creation of social structure.

TRADITIONAL PERSPECTIVE ON GROUP RELATIONSHIPS

A substantial amount of group research has been done from the traditional perspective. Early group communication research and corporate trainers up to the present day have spent considerable time identifying and describing the communication skills that are necessary to be an effective group member and the various roles that group members may fulfill. Much contemporary research and training activities have also examined the decision-making and problem-solving processes that lead to high-quality group decisions. These efforts have been directed both at the behaviors or skills that tend to lead to effective group decisions and the sequencing of actions that promote decision quality. Finally, communicative actions and processes that promote productive conflict management have been examined in considerable detail. What unifies most of the group research and training activities from a traditional group perspective is a focus on internal communication skills and processes that promote positive group outcomes. Although much work has been done from the traditional perspective, we still need continued insight into internal group processes as organizational groups confront a range of problems from the simple to the complex.

Communication Skills: Communication Competence in Groups

Among the most important skills for group members is **communication competence**. The simplest way to describe communication competence is the ability to select and perform a communication behavior that is both *appropriate* and *effective* in a given situation (Rothwell, 2004). Behaving in an appropriate manner means that you do not violate a relational or situational rule. Effective behavior allows you to accomplish your goals through communication. Spitzberg and Cupach (1984) developed the model most often used to describe competence. Their model includes three components: (a) knowledge, (b) skill, and (c) motivation. Knowledge refers to knowing what behavior is best suited for a particular situation. Skill is having the ability to perform that behavior. Motivation refers to the desire to communicate in a competent manner.

In groups within organizations, communication competence is a vitally important skill to possess to accomplish individual goals within the group, promote group productivity, and sustain good interpersonal relationships within the group. Without effectiveness in communicating your ideas, you cannot accomplish any of your personal goals within a group. So, the ability to communicate your ideas logically and persuasively is important, as is your ability to establish alliances and coalitions to build support for your ideas. At a group level, effective communication is important because it allows each member to offer his or her best contributions to solving group problems. Accomplishing personal and group goals is only part of what competence is, however. Group members also need to communicate in ways that are relationally or situationally appropriate. Every group develops rules that determine what is appropriate communication and what is not. Sometimes these rules are explicitly stated: "There will be no personal attacks when arguing over an issue." Other times the rules will be established subtly through interaction. For example, over a period of several months in a newly formed quality circle, no group member raises his or her voice when arguing with another member. This rule is internalized through repeated interaction within the group. If a member violates this rule, he or she will likely receive negative verbal or nonverbal reactions from other group members even though the rule was never explicitly stated. So, behaving in appropriate ways helps to sustain good relationships within the group. Appropriate communication also contributes to the development of a group culture in which members want to continue their association with one another.

Groups as Organizational Subsystems

When Simon argued that an organization is a group of groups, he seemed to be saying that groups are the most obvious subsystems of an organization. Groups affect and are affected by the organizational system. Homans (1950) noted that certain types of activities, member interactions, and "sentiments" (members' feelings) are required for group survival. These required conditions, according to Homans, are imposed on the group by the larger organizational system. He referred to these imposed conditions as the **external system**. Other activities, interactions, and sentiments arise within the group that are different from and even at odds with the requirements of the external system. Homans called this emergent set of group behaviors the **internal system**. He argued that the emergent internal system is influenced by and, in turn, influences the external system. In particular, the internal system shapes the actions of individual group members and protects the group from outside interference.

Suppose that a special project team is assembled to reposition a company product that has leveled off in sales. The members are Ted, Sally, Juan, Bob, and Jessie, and they are from different departments. They all know one another, but they have never really worked together before. The group's objective is imposed by the larger system. In order to reposition the product, the group has to determine why its sales have declined, then figure out how to recover the old market or find a new market. In order to solve these problems, the group members are required to interact in certain ways. Moreover, the external system demands some feeling of commitment to the project.

The conditions of the external system seem clear, but as the group develops, "it elaborates itself, complicates itself, beyond the demands of the original situation" (Homans, 1950). Ted believes that the product has outlived its usefulness to the company and should simply be discontinued. He resents top management's insistence that it be repositioned in the market. Sally, a "radical feminist," and Bob, a "male chauvinist," quickly develop a severe interpersonal conflict. Juan, an accountant with no marketing background, can contribute little to the task. Jessie, the team leader, is a rigid authoritarian who wants unilateral control over all group decisions.

As the group members approach their task, they not only cope with the demands of the external system, but they also adapt to individual idiosyncrasies. The internal system that emerges from this coping and adaptation could have several features. For example, members do not ridicule Juan's inability to contribute to the task because it turns out that he is very adept at mediating conflicts and relieving tension in the group—a critical skill in light of Ted's opinion about the product, Sally and Bob's dislike for each other, and Jessie's aggressiveness. Jessie's need for control has to be reconciled with the other members' desire for a democratic approach to leadership. The group discards Ted's concerns about the product, establishing a shared expectation that some sort of solution will be developed. Yet, Ted's continued objections serve a purpose by stimulating the group to develop justifications for the project. The gender-related conflict between Bob and Sally creates many uneasy moments and occasional male versus female coalitions in the group, but Juan defuses these situations with humor. The group develops a pattern of conflict followed by humorous tension relief, although it never really resolves the conflict between Sally and Bob.

Any given organization may comprise a number of identifiable groups. In open systems, these subsystems interact for a variety of purposes. In some cases, the interaction and interdependence may be minimal. In other cases, interdependence of groups is essential to the organization's mission and functions.

The environment of contemporary organizations often is turbulent. Despite the optimism of the 1990s, the past few decades have taught us that we cannot count on stability in markets, technology, government regulations, energy costs, tax revenues, societal needs, and a host of other factors that affect organizations. A turbulent environment seems to promote or even require high levels of intergroup dependence and cooperation (Lippitt, 1982). But which types of organizations are the most adaptive and flexible in the face of environmental change? Those characterized by high levels of coordination and interdependence among subsystems, or relatively awkward and uncoordinated loosely coupled systems? Weick (1976) argued that loosely coupled systems are more flexible and have a better chance of long-term survival. Lippitt (1982) also suggests that high levels of interdependence among organizational subsystems reduce adaptiveness. Yet, interdependence, coordination, and integration of subsystems is precisely what many scholars call for as a response to turbulent environments.

As we saw in the discussion of horizontal communication in Chapter 3, many organizations, unaccustomed to the flexibility of communication required for cooperative effort, are finding it difficult to develop effective intergroup relationships. Even in organizations in which group subsystems are relatively independent and loosely coupled, these subsystems still may affect one another. As Beckhard (1969) pointed out, "By the very nature of organizations, there are bound to be conditions where, if one department achieves its goals, it frustrates the achievement of some other group's goals" (p. 33). When subsystems are coupled (loosely or otherwise), cooperation and conflict within and between groups is a daily part of organizational life. Consequently, an understanding of intragroup and intergroup communication is essential to an understanding of organizations.

Several concepts are important in developing an understanding of communication processes at the group level of organizations. Groups are characterized by **norms** that regulate the behavior of individual members. Members can generate pressure on one another to **conform** to these norms. Groups function as **sense-making** systems for members and also as vehicles for **decision making** and **problem solving**. All of this is accomplished through group members' enactment of roles. Finally, even though group action is more or less a cooperative venture, interaction within and between groups often is characterized by conflict as well as cooperation and by differences between members and between groups in their potential to exercise power. The concepts of conflict and power, like leadership, are so important that they get their own chapters in this book. Although we will not discuss leadership, power, and conflict in this chapter, you should keep in mind that they are especially important in understanding group processes.

Each of these elements in group dynamics affects and is affected by communication processes, but the significance of communication in group dynamics runs a bit deeper than most treatments of group dynamics suggest. Social psychologists traditionally have regarded factors such as norms, roles, and power relationships as the causative or "driving" forces in group behavior. People behave as they do in groups because of normative expectations, role requirements, or compliance in the face of power. Now, there is no doubt that groups do develop normative expectations, role requirements, and differences in power. However, explaining group dynamics in these terms reduces communication to the status of just one more variable among many in group dynamics—a position that does not coincide with the beliefs of the communication theorists.

Blumer (1969) argued that a group cannot be understood without the concept of joint action among members. Joint action does not necessarily depend on mutual agreement in interpretation, but it does depend on some level of mutual understanding of one another's interpretations. This mutual understanding arises only through communication. Hence, all group dynamics, whether they take the form of cooperation, games, sense making, and even conflict, hinge on communication.

In large organizations, there are many departments that fulfill different functions: production, marketing, human resources, accounting, and so forth. Departments are only one type of organizational group, however. In the following sections let's consider other types of organizational groups or subsystems. Specifically, we look at quality circles, focus groups, and task forces.

Quality Circles

Although we addressed the concept of quality circles in Chapter 3, there are a few additional issues that are relevant to discuss here. First, why is the recommended size of quality circles between 5 and 15 members? Fewer than 5 members decrease the pool of creative ideas that may surface. Groups larger than 15 may encourage social loafing and less-than-enthusiastic participation on the part of some members. Second, what accounts for the success of quality circles? The success of quality circles is linked to the fact that workers performing a particular job know the most about how that job should be performed and what can be done to improve performance. Also, people are often more willing to do their jobs and change their performance when their opinions are taken into account (Wilson, 2002). Recommended frequency of meeting is usually once a week for approximately an hour. In order to facilitate success, employees may be offered training in group communication principles and practices such as group relationships, cohesiveness, roles, consensus, decision making, problem solving, and conflict management (Beebe & Masterson, 2003). In addition, the leaders of quality circles may benefit from training in how to lead groups and facilitate discussion and effective decision making. Importantly, by training quality circle members and leaders you enhance the likelihood that the employees will have the skills to make high-quality decisions. Finally, how do quality circles form? A quality circle may form spontaneously when a group of interested workers decides to meet to focus on work-related issues and problems. Alternatively, a supervisor may delegate the authority to make decisions to a group of subordinates. However the group is formed, members must participate voluntarily or their motivation to contribute will wane.

Focus Groups

Organizations convene focus groups for the purpose of gathering information about a particular topic so management can gain a better understanding of how people view these topics (Beebe & Masterson, 2003). The conversation of the focus group is relatively unstructured because the group is encouraged to discuss the issue or problem in any way they choose. The role of the focus group facilitator is to introduce the topic and give no further direction, although he or she may ask questions of a general, follow-up, or probing nature (Adams & Galanes, 2003). Focus group discussions often reveal the participants' interests and values concerning the topic that is considered. These discussions might also provide insight into what the participants perceive to be the important issues regarding the problem it is facing.

There are many issues or problems that would prompt an organization to turn to focus group input. Often the advertising industry will seek input into consumer opinions about products or services an organization provides. For example, an apparel manufacturer may seek input about a new line of skiwear it intends to market. A public relations department of an oil company could rely on a focus group to determine how a company should address the public following an oil spill. A human resources department may enlist a focus group to understand problems of sexual harassment within an organization.

The purpose of focus groups is to obtain depth and detail concerning the topic or problem under discussion. Participants should be encouraged to spark off of one another. When a particularly spirited discussion ensues, the participants may uncover dimensions or nuances of the topic or problem that any one individual might not have thought of (Rubin, 2005).

When focus groups are convened for purposes that are critically important to an organization's strategic interests, steps may be taken to ensure that the most accurate conclusions are drawn. The greatest possible insights are derived from focus groups when the facilitator tape-records the entire discussion. Written transcripts should then be produced and subjected to detailed qualitative analysis. This analysis might yield a list of underlying themes that captures the most important dimensions of the topic or problem that is discussed. The information produced from the analysis may also prove helpful when decisions need to be made by the organization that sponsored the focus group. Given the expense of this analysis procedure, however, it should be used only in limited circumstances.

Task Forces

A task force is a committee authorized by management to study a specific subject or problem for a specified period of time (also referred to by other names such as ad hoc groups or product development teams). The end product the task force produces might be a formal report of findings or recommended solutions. For example, an organization could convene a task force to study evaluations of several plans that consider different sites for a new factory. Task forces could also be created to develop suggestions to increase product sales or cut operational costs. When the task force produces its report, it is usually delivered in writing and orally to the person or department who called for the special committee. Once the end product is produced the task force disbands.

An organization will not find a task force's report or proposed recommendations useful if that report is not of high quality. To help ensure a quality report, task force members should be selected because they have the knowledge and skills to do a good job. The task force should also be given the resources it needs to do a thorough job. For example, economic support might be needed for travel or to compensate members for their time. The level of resource support that is given should be commensurate with the value or risk associated with tasks confronting the group. So, if a task force is convened to determine which site will be best for construction of a $50 million plant, sufficient resources should be dedicated for site visits and compensating experts for the time they spend in selecting the recommended site. When experts are given the resources to do a job well, task forces can confront problems of the highest level. In fact, U.S. presidents have created task forces to "investigate and make recommendations on such national concerns as illegal drug traffic, acid rain, the condition of national parks, health care, waste in government expenditures, and disease epidemics" (Adams & Galanes, 2003, p. 117). Given the prevalence of task forces to confront organizational problems, the average professional worker will likely serve on many task forces during a lifetime of work.

Group Decision Making and Problem Solving

Many organizational groups exist primarily for decision-making and problem-solving purposes. Project teams, task forces, and committees typically serve such functions. Sometimes groups are created temporarily to deal with one special contingency. The members of such ad hoc groups work through to the solution of a particular problem, then disband and move on to other projects. The importance of group decision making to organizations has led researchers in small-group communication to study these processes almost to the exclusion of any attention to other aspects of communication in group action (Littlejohn, 1992).

Group decision making is a rule-bound process, but members often seem to be aware only tacitly of the norms, roles, and regularities that they enact in the process. Status and power factors are accepted implicitly without reflection or examination. Members often note the presence of conflict, but they do not seem to understand its nature. Certain patterns of interaction and ways of doing things are simply taken for granted. Thus, as Schein argued, groups are not always aware of their own processes for problem solving and decision making, even when these processes are inefficient and ineffective. Schein (1969) pointed out that groups typically make decisions in one of six ways, even though members may not recognize that their groups are operating in these ways.

1. *Lack of response.* This method is evident in a group when ideas are introduced, then immediately dropped without discussion. In effect, the ideas are vetoed by silence.

2. *Authority rule.* In this case, the power structure in the group places final authority for decision making with one person, usually the leader. The group may discuss an issue, share information, and suggest ideas, but the authority figure has the last word.

3. *Minority coalition.* Schein describes this method as a process of "railroading" decisions through a group by a vocal minority, especially a minority with a powerful member. When other members remain silent in the face of strong minority support for an idea, it can create the impression that the group has reached a consensus. In fact, most members may be opposed to the idea, but no one voices an objection for fear of disrupting what appears to be a consensus.

4. *Majority rule.* This is a familiar system of decision making through voting. Majority rule is typical of highly formal decision-making procedures. An issue or problem is discussed, then a policy or proposal is adopted or rejected on the basis of the percentage of members who favor it.

5. *Consensus.* When the members of a group are prepared to accept an idea, even though they may have some reservations about it, a group has a consensus. Schein is careful to point

out that consensus does not necessarily mean that the group unanimously and enthusiastically endorses an idea. Consensus only implies that discussion of the problem has been open and all points of view have been considered. Although group members may not be in complete agreement, the solution or proposal falls within their range of acceptability.

6. *Unanimity.* This rare but ideal mode of decision making occurs when all of the members in a group are in full agreement on a point of view, proposal, policy, or problem solution.

Schein (1969) regards consensus and unanimity as preferred modes of arriving at decisions. Although the processes required to achieve consensus can be inefficient and time-consuming, the result is more effective implementation of the decision. More recent research by Renz (2006) supports and extends this view. Specifically, she discovered that groups' use of consensus decision making allowed the members to balance three goals: making an appropriate decision, meeting members' needs, and maintaining the group's well-being. Although decisions that are made by authority, minority coalition, and majority rule may be arrived at quickly, those members with other viewpoints may feel frustrated and have little incentive to support the decision. Why are some groups able to achieve consensus-based decision making, whereas others are not? The answer may have something to do in part with culture, an issue we will discuss later in the chapter.

Group Decisions Versus Individual Decisions

Group decision making is not always the preferred approach to decision making in organizations. Clearly, there are many situations in which group decision making produces higher quality decisions than an individual making a decision in isolation. There are also situations, however, when an individual should make a decision without input from others. In what types of situations will groups likely produce higher quality decisions than individuals? There are four conditions under which groups will probably outperform individuals, all attributable to *synergy,* or the ability of people working together to produce a result that is greater than the sum of their individual capabilities. (Forsyth, 1990; Pavitt & Curtis, 1994; Rothwell, 2004). First, a group will tend to produce a superior decision when the task requires a wide range and variety of information and skills. Groups outperform individuals in such situations because the members pool their knowledge. This has implications for group construction. Specifically, groups should comprise members who may pool non-overlapping areas of knowledge (Stasson & Bradshaw, 1995). Second, groups usually outperform individuals when neither the group nor the individual compared possess expertise on the task. In support of this contention, Stasson and Bradshaw (1995) found that when no individual member of a group knew the answer to a test question, the group as a whole selected the correct answer 28% of the time. Individual members working alone selected the correct answer only 4% of the time. Third, groups generally outperform individuals when the task is particularly complex even when both the group and the individual compared have expertise. Because a group may choose to share the load among members, a better decision is usually produced than one overburdened expert attempting to do it all. In fact, Michaelson (1989) found that expert groups outperform their best members 97% of the time when confronting a complex task. Fourth, when comparing a group of nonexperts to an individual with special expertise, the group may sometimes produce a superior decision. The explanation for this outcome is that effective group functioning often results in the performance of *error correction* (Hastie, Penrod, & Pennington, 1983). As Rothwell (2004) explains: "Assumptions are challenged and alternatives are offered that an individual might overlook. In addition, the collective energy and chemistry of the group may produce a synergistic result" (p. 74).

In what types of situations will individuals likely produce higher quality decisions than groups? There are five conditions under which individuals will probably outperform groups (Rothwell, 2004). First, groups comprising uninformed members will not usually outperform a person with special expertise in the problem being confronted. For example, a mechanical engineer is more likely to produce a high-quality solution to a problem related to power plant design than a group of human resource professionals. Second, individuals may outperform groups when groups establish norms of mediocrity. In such a situation, an individual working to full capacity and with high motivation may be able to produce a more effective decision than a group that is satisfied with low performance. Third, when groups become too large (in excess of 10 members), individuals may outperform groups. The reason for this outcome is that groups much larger than 10 confront problems with task coordination and efficiency (Rothwell, 2004). Also, in groups much larger than 10 it is more likely that one or more members will engage in **social loafing** because they know someone else in the group will take up the slack and their own nonperformance will probably not be noticed. Fourth, when the task is a simple one groups do not produce superior decisions than individuals. Importantly, with simple tasks a manager must recognize the waste of resources associated with group decision making. Why involve five people in the solution of a simple problem when one person may solve the problem alone? Finally, when time is a critical factor, individuals usually perform more effectively than groups. For example, in a crisis situation one person acting alone often performs better than a group because groups tend to be slow in deciding what needs to be done.

Effective Group Decision Making and Task Performance

What distinguishes effective decision-making groups from ineffective groups? Social scientists have been interested in this question for several decades, but much of the research has been more concerned with comparing group performance to individual performance. These studies indicate that groups generally produce more and better ideas than individuals working alone, but the evaluative judgments of groups are not as good as those of the very best individuals.

Research on the characteristics of interaction in decision-making groups has not yet provided a comprehensive picture of the differences between effective and ineffective groups, but several studies during the 1980s and 1990s have at least provided many of the pieces for this particular puzzle. Randy Hirokawa and his colleagues have conducted a series of group effectiveness studies. In one of his early investigations (1980), he assembled groups to study a problem for which experts already had devised a correct solution. All of the group interactions were recorded. Hirokawa distinguished between effective and ineffective groups on the basis of agreement between their solutions and the expert solution, then compared their recorded interactions. Surprisingly, Hirokawa found many more similarities than differences between effective and ineffective groups. Only one major difference occurred in the communicative behaviors and interaction patterns: *effective groups were much more attentive to the procedures used to solve the problem.* Specifically, one member would make a statement of procedural direction (e.g., "Why don't we set up some evaluation criteria?"), and the others would adopt this direction.

Hirokawa became concerned that he might not be finding differences between effective and ineffective groups because he was focusing on behaviors that might be irrelevant to group tasks and effective decisions. He tried to correct this problem in a 1983 study by examining only group communication acts that served one of five functions: (a) *establishing operating procedures,* (b) *analyzing the problem,* (c) *establishing evaluation criteria,* (d) *generating alternative solutions,* and (e) *evaluating solutions.* Results of the study indicated a positive relationship between the effectiveness of a group's decision and the group's efforts to analyze the problem, but the relationship between effectiveness and attempts to establish operating procedures was *negative.* Moreover, there was no association between effectiveness and attempts to establish evaluation criteria, to generate alternative solutions, or to evaluate solutions.

In spite of these mixed findings, Hirokawa continued his work and gradually developed the idea that group interaction affects group decisions by shaping critical thinking. Hirokawa's position and others like it are known as **vigilant interaction theory.** This theory claims that the quality of group decisions depends on the group's vigilance [attentiveness] in interaction concerning four questions:

1. *Problem analysis:* Is there something about the current state of affairs that requires change?

2. *Objectives:* What do we want to achieve or accomplish in deciding what to do about the problem?

3. *Choices:* What are the choices available to us?

4. *Evaluation:* What are the positive and negative aspects of those choices? (Hirokawa & Rost, 1992, p. 269)

Over the years, Hirokawa and his colleagues gradually have accumulated extensive evidence to support the theory. One study by Hirokawa and Rost (1992) is particularly important because it involved groups from a large utility company. Many group decision-making studies are laboratory experiments, but this study shows clearly that vigilant interaction theory applies to groups in real organizations. In the utility company groups, interaction that facilitated problem analysis and evaluation of both positive and negative features of choices led to high-quality decisions. Interaction that inhibited problem analysis, development of standards to assess choices, and evaluation of positive features of choices led to low-quality decisions.

Hirokawa recently has extended his studies of group effectiveness beyond decision making and problem solving to focus on the more general problem of work team performance. He and Joann Keyton (1995) studied work teams implementing drug abuse prevention programs in schools to identify factors perceived by team members to facilitate or inhibit team progress and to determine whether these factors actually had anything to do with team effectiveness. Hirokawa and Keyton found a dozen factors, some facilitative, some inhibitive, that distinguished between effective and ineffective teams. As you might suspect, team members reported that facilitating factors occurred more often in effective teams, whereas inhibiting factors occurred more often in ineffective teams. Fortunately, the one dozen factors can be reduced to four basic conditions that Hirokawa and Keyton say are necessary for team effectiveness:

1. Motivated team members.

2. Adequate time and informational resources for the task.

3. Competent leadership.

4. Direct organizational assistance (e.g., training).

Group Decision Development

In addition to Hirokawa's work on the differences between effective and ineffective group decision making, another important line of research has addressed the stages or phases of decision development within groups. One of the most complete treatments of this topic was developed by B. Aubrey Fisher (1970), who identified four stages in group decision-making processes: **orientation**, **conflict**, **emergence**, and **reinforcement**.

The orientation phase begins as the members of a group meet for the first time. The members experience uncertainty; they are not sure what to expect. Behavior is based on members' understanding of social norms regarding politeness and initiation of relationships. These norms are brought into the situation because the group has evolved no rules of its own.

Politeness norms become less important as members acquire some familiarity with one another, and the group moves into a conflict phase characterized by disputes, disagreements, and hostility. The group gradually works through conflict, entering an emergence stage in which increased tolerance for ambiguity in opinions is reflected. Ambiguity at this point allows for face-saving and reconciliation of conflicts. Finally, the group moves to a reinforcement stage in which the members develop and endorse a decision. The idea of reinforcement implies that group members engage in a mutual process of justifying and committing themselves to the decision. For example, they might say, "This is the right decision because . . ." or "This solution is better than the other possibilities."

Many studies of group development, including Fisher's own studies, have examined the processes of groups during a relatively limited time frame (e.g., over several meetings or even in only one meeting). The results of these studies suggest that group development occurs in an orderly, linear fashion, proceeding from one step to the next. Fisher points out, however, that a phase model may not apply to all task-oriented groups. A series of studies by Marshall Scott Poole (1981, 1983a, 1983b) reinforces the limitations of phase models like Fisher's. Poole found that the stages of decision development in small groups may follow any one of several possible sequences. He concluded that a "logical" or unitary sequence of problem-solving steps may provide normative expectancies that influence the group, but the group's actual course of action emerges from many complicated factors. In other words, groups in different situations act in different ways. Even when group decision making fits a phase model, the specific types and cycles of interaction within any given phase differ substantially from group to group.

Roles and Role Categories in Groups

Group action, whether it is effective or ineffective, is produced through the members' enactment of roles. George Kelly (1955) defined role as "an ongoing pattern of behavior that follows from a person's understanding [or misunderstanding] of how others who are associated with him or her in his or her task think (p. 97). Simply stated, the enactment of a role depends on a person's interpretations of a given situation. It does not necessarily follow from others' expectations for what a person in the role is supposed to do.

Wofford, Gerloff, and Cummins (1979) attempted to clarify the idea of role by distinguishing between perceived, expected, and enacted roles:

> The *perceived role* is the set of behaviors that the occupant of the position believes he or she should perform. The *expected role* is the set of behaviors that others believe he or she should perform. The *enacted role* is the actual set of performed behaviors. (p. 39)

There may be a high level of agreement between perceived, expected, and enacted roles, but the three frequently differ. Suppose that the members of a work group expect a supervisor to be a democratic leader, providing guidance and encouraging participation. The supervisor's perception of the leadership role, based on a belief in autocratic methods such as controlling decisions, dictating orders, and using punishment to gain compliance, is quite different from the members' expectations. Moreover, the supervisor's actual behavior—the enacted role—turns out to be a laissez-faire approach of "cool your heels on the desk and leave things alone," in which the supervisor actually relinquishes much of the leadership responsibility. As we shall see later, disparities between expected, perceived, and enacted roles can be significant sources of conflict in groups.

Any role is enacted. It is not only defined by others' expectations for appropriate behavior, but it is also defined by the perceptions, capabilities, and choices of the person who enacts it. Even so, there do seem to be some types of roles that frequently occur in task groups. A classic description of typical task group roles that Benne and Sheats developed in 1948 is still widely accepted today. Their description includes:

Task Roles

Initiator: defines problem, contributes ideas and suggestions, proposes solutions or decisions, offers new ideas.

Information seeker: asks for clarification, promotes participation by others, solicits facts and evidence.

Energizer: prods members into action.

Orienter: keeps group on track, guides discussion.

Secretary: keeps track of group progress, remembers past actions.

Maintenance Roles

Encourager: provides support, praise, acceptance for others.

Harmonizer: resolves conflict, reduces tension.

Comedian: provides humor, relaxes others.

Gatekeeper: controls communication channels, promotes evenness of participation.

Follower: accepts others' ideas, goes along with others.

Self-Centered Roles

Blocker: interferes with progress of group by consistently making negative responses to others.

Aggressor: attacks other members in an effort to promote his or her own status.

Dominator: monopolizes group time with long, drawn-out monologues.

Deserter: withdraws from group discussion by refusing to participate, engages in irrelevant conversations.

Special-interest pleader: brings irrelevant information into discussion, argues incessantly for his or her own point of view.

As you read the descriptions, most may have seemed familiar to you from your own experience in group activities. It is very likely that you have seen some, if not all, of these roles enacted in task groups. Sometimes a particular individual consistently will enact one of these roles, but Benne and Sheats do not mean to imply that any given member has only one role. Generally, the actions of a given member will reflect some of these roles but show little or no evidence of others, and more than one member may enact any given role.

Among the roles that may occur in groups, organizational groups generally are characterized by leadership roles that are exercised in relation to member (follower) roles. The subjects of leadership, leader-member relations, and hierarchical superior-subordinate relationships are addressed in the next chapter.

INTERPRETIVE PERSPECTIVE ON GROUP RELATIONSHIPS

Group research and training activities representing the interpretive perspective have emerged since the 1970s. Consistent with this perspective, focus is given to how groups socially create the reality that structures and informs their experiences. Importantly, the social construction of reality occurs at the small-group level in the same way as it does at the larger organizational level. Also important to consider is the powerful impact that a group's particular social construction has on members. Most employees spend the majority of their work time in a single or, at most, a few primary groups. A culture of personal and professional support may be created, as well as a culture of opposition and underhanded competition. On a day-to-day basis, the culture of the group is played out through member actions that support a particular social structure. More specifically, through using language in a certain way, relying on particular metaphors, and abiding by group rules and norms the group displays its culture in ways that both enable and constrain member actions.

In this chapter, we have introduced aspects of the interpretive perspective in two different ways. First, the bona fide group perspective acknowledges that the group's cultural context establishes norms and values for members. Interpretivists would be interested in understanding how these norms and rules are developed and supported through member actions and how and why they change. Also important to recognize is the fact that group membership changes with some members leaving and others joining the group. These changes in membership may influence the norms and rules that are supported and introduce new ones. Second, we considered how individualistic and collectivistic cultures establish particular expectations for member communication, including the rules and norms that group members follow. Interpretive researchers would be interested in exploring how members sustain a particular cultural framework through their communicative actions and how that framework enables and constrains member actions.

Author Michael Papa grew up in New York City where many of his friends became New York City police officers. In keeping touch with these friends over the years, he visited one police precinct in the Bronx (46th precinct) where a number of them worked. During the 8:00 A.M. to 4:00 P.M. shift, a total of eight police officers formed a closely-knit work group. During the mid-1990s, when Papa visited on several occasions he developed a number of insights about this work group. This group of eight police officers had worked together for six years. They supported one another not only in dealing with the tension of police activities and fighting crime, but in their personal lives as well. If one officer had a sick child or spouse, other officers would help with food shopping or transporting children to different activities around the neighborhood. The officers often socialized together after work and went on family vacations with one another. They shared common stories, and before and after their shifts they would engage in good-natured ribbing and laugh at different experiences they had shared. Viewing the work experiences of these officers from an interpretive perspective, they created a cultural framework of close personal support and camaraderie. They knew they could count on one another at work and in their personal lives. They wanted to help one another, and they enjoyed being with one another. Although the work they performed was often difficult, they knew they would receive help in any situation that required it. As one officer put it, "I always know my back is covered with these guys whether it is on the street, dealing with precinct politics, or at a bar on the weekends. We are like brothers. That's the way it should be."

The Bona Fide Group Perspective

Putnam and Stohl have described the bona fide group perspective in a number of articles and essays (Putnam, 1994; Putnam & Stohl, 1990, 1996; Stohl & Putnam, 1994). This perspective offers us an alternative to the "container model" of groups. When a group is viewed as a container, it is "considered to be a relatively closed entity with fixed boundaries and borders that define who is and is not a member" (Frey, 2003, p. 3). When researchers study groups from a container perspective, they examine internal communication processes as the members engage in problem solving, make decisions, and provide one another with social support. What is lacking when one views groups as containers is the impact that environment or context has on group life. The bona fide group perspective directly challenges the assumptions of the container metaphor by drawing attention to two interrelated characteristics that are central parts of the group experience: (a) stable yet permeable group boundaries, and (b) interdependence with their relevant contexts.

What does it mean to say that groups have stable yet permeable boundaries? First, the bona fide group perspective acknowledges that all groups have stable boundaries that are defined and firm. Clearly, a group cannot be said to exist without boundaries that differentiate it from other entities. Importantly, communication within the group both creates and reinforces that differentiation. Simultaneously, however, group boundaries are permeable, meaning that they are dynamic and fluid. In order to explain why group boundaries are permeable, Putnam and Stohl (1996) describe four features that characterize bona fide groups. The first feature of such groups is that people are simultaneously members of many different groups. For example, all of us are part of family, work, and friendship groups. This is important to recognize because these multiple memberships potentially influence how we act or are expected to act in our various groups. So, a person who plays a peace-making role in one group may expect to play a similar role in another group. Of course, this may create conflict if this person does not want to recreate their peace-making role in a new group. The second feature speaks to the impact of being a member of different groups in terms of the expectations that are placed on you as a member. The only woman on a task force may be asked to represent a "woman's point of view" when the topic of discussion turns to an area in which men feel they lack expertise. The third feature recognizes that the membership of bona fide groups changes, with some members leaving and others joining the group. Importantly, these changes in membership impact the internal dynamics of the group because of the particular behaviors that exiting members take with them and new members add to group discussions. The fourth feature acknowledges that group members vary in their degree of loyalty or commitment to their various groups. So, a group member may exhibit more allegiance to one group than another. This not only impacts the identity that a group holds for a given member, members displaying different levels of allegiance impact the entire culture of a group.

The second characteristic of bona fide groups is that such groups are interdependent with their relevant contexts. Specifically, there is a reciprocal relationship between a group and the environments within which it is embedded (Frey, 2003). These environments or contexts influence what happens within a group, and what happens within a group influences those environments or contexts. There are many possible contexts that influence groups. For example, the historical context within which a group is created and develops is an influential context. The economic context within which a group is funded may be important to consider. Also, the cultural context that establishes norms and values for members is relevant to understand. Putnam and Stohl (1996) argue that the interdependence of a group with its relevant contexts is a result of "(a) inter-group communication, (b) coordinated actions among groups, (c) negotiation of jurisdiction or autonomy, and (d) interpretations or frames for making sense of inter-group relationships" (p. 153). The first feature recognizes that individual group members and groups as a unit communicate frequently with other groups and their members. The communication that occurs is both formal and informal. The second feature acknowledges that certain tasks require groups to coordinate their actions together. This is especially true with complex tasks. The third feature focuses on the need for groups to negotiate their boundaries. Specifically, what should the group accept as its mission, and what activities are outside their purview. The fourth feature speaks to the fact that individual members and the group as a whole make sense of the intergroup relationships that exist for them.

Small-group researchers have paid considerable attention to what occurs within groups (e.g., decision making, problem solving, conflict management, and so on). Although such work is important, it neglects the fact that the environment and various contextual constraints impact all groups significantly. The bona fide group perspective moves these environmental influences to the foreground (Poole, 1999).

Norms and Conformity

Many scholars and professionals have suggested that organizations do not like uncertainty. Indeed, we depend on some degree of regularity and predictability to structure our interactions with others. In group communication, many of these regularities are derived from norms. As defined by Secord and Backman (1964), "A norm is a standard of behavioral expectations shared by group members against which the validity of perceptions is judged and the appropriateness of feelings and behavior is evaluated" (p. 323).

Norms—shared expectations for behavior, thought, and feeling—may be developed within the group or imported (brought in) from the larger system of which the group is a part (e.g., standards prevailing in the larger organization or mutual expectations acquired through prior experience in other groups). Importation is apparently what occurs in the orientation phase of Fisher's decision-development model. The internal development of norms occurs as the group negotiates and tests certain rules for interaction (e.g., think back to our earlier example of not raising one's voice when arguing with another group member). Some of the characteristics in Homans's concept of internal systems are developed through such negotiation and testing.

Norms also may be explicitly stated or implicitly understood. Explicit normative standards could include policies, written rules, and verbally communicated procedures and standards. Implicit norms and other rules are not explicitly articulated, but the individual group member can observe and learn about their functions. Sometimes, new members of groups discover implicit norms only when they inadvertently violate such norms. This type of violation is illustrated in an example that one of the authors encountered several years ago at a luncheon meeting of an industrial project group.

The group often met over lunch in order to discuss problems associated with its project. However, on this particular day, the initial topic of conversation involved a recent string of losses by the local professional football team. Later, there was some specific discussion of work-related matters but nothing directly relevant to the project itself. Finally, during a lull in the conversation, a new member, who had been with the group for less than one week, made a remark about the unusually brutal November temperatures, then said, "I sure hope it clears up some. I hate for my kids to walk home in this kind of weather."

The comment seemed perfectly harmless, but there was no reply from the other members—only downcast eyes and sullen expressions. The new member was quite embarrassed by this response. When the author later asked some of the other members about their reaction to the comment, they testily replied that luncheons are "business meetings where personal topics like families and children are off-limits." Apparently, however, discussion of the football team's win/loss record was not regarded as inconsistent with the purpose of a "business meeting." In fact, the catalyst that triggered this uncomfortable situation may well have been gender. The new member was a woman. All the rest were men. As long as she talked about football like "one of the boys," everything was fine, but the mention of children may have provoked the men's stereotype of a "female" topic.

This example illustrates one of the ways in which groups exert pressure for conformity to norms. Methods for producing this pressure include the following:

1. Delay action toward the deviant, allowing for self-correction.

2. Joke humorously with the deviant about the violation.

3. Ridicule and deride the violation.

4. Seriously try to persuade the deviant to conform.

5. Engage in heated argument with the deviant.

6. Reject or isolate the deviant.

Bormann (1969) indicated that these methods actually reflect several stages of pressure toward conformity. If conformity does not occur after delaying action, the group might engage in humor. Should deviance still continue, the group would move to ridicule. As pressure toward conformity progresses through these steps, the amount of communicative action directed at the deviant increases until, at stage six, attempts to communicate cease.

Rules and norms are essential to group action for at least two reasons. First, they help to reduce uncertainty. When we understand the norms and rules in a situation, we can have more confidence about the appropriateness of our own actions and in our expectations of others. Second, some predictability is required for joint action and cooperation. In order to collaborate at all, we must have some shared expectations for one another's behavior. But norms also have some unfortunate effects as well. As Baird and Weinberg (1981) noted, norms can hamper group creativity and protect inefficient and archaic practices (e.g., changes in policy can only occur if there is consensus support for the change). Such practices may take the form of certain traditions or so-called sacred cows. Norms also enforce inequities within and between groups. They can be used as instruments of repression that primarily serve the interests of a privileged few (e.g., only upper level managers may take advantage of the flexible work hours policy). Nevertheless, norms and rules are ever-present in group interaction.

Values and Sense Making

In Chapter 4, we talked about the emergence of the human relations movement from the Hawthorne Studies. Evidence from the Hawthorne Studies suggested that workgroup relationships provide the primary context from which individual values and attitudes toward work and the organization are derived. One of the most important functions of group communication may be to provide the basic frames of reference from which individual members understand, enact, and justify the organization and its mission. This idea is getting renewed attention at least in part because of the interpretive movement in the study of organizational communication. As we noted in Chapter 1, the interpretive perspective of organizational communication is concerned especially with the social construction of organizational reality through collective discourse. This topic received much more attention in Chapter 6 on organizational culture. The point here is that the group, as *the* unit of social life" (Jensen & Chilberg, 1991, p. 5), provides the basic "petri dish" for culturing the negotiated order of meanings and values. We know, for example, from Van Mannen's work on occupational communities (in Chapter 3) that these shadowy structures not only cut across formal organizational structure, but also give rise to and sustain powerful work values.

Decision Making and Culture

The contrast between different methods of arriving at decisions is easy to see when one compares the methods of traditional Western organizations to those of Japanese organizations. As Ryutard Nomura, chairman of Japan's Triyo Industries, pointed out, the "bottom-up," consensus-based decision methods of Japanese organizations are painfully slow and cumbersome, but most decisions are implemented effectively because support has been developed among all essential participants during the decision-making process. In contrast, decisions are made quickly with traditional Western methods such as reliance on centralized authority, but implementation is slow and uncertain. According to Nomura (1981), "Opposition and misunderstanding which inevitably arise emerge after the decision has been announced" (p. 43). One only has to examine the American political system to see that losing factions often are more interested in regaining power, winning the next decision, and stalling unwanted decisions than in cooperating with the winner.

Differences between cultures in their methods of group decision making can be explained in part by the degree to which a given culture is *individualistic* or *collectivistic*. As Hofstede and Bond (1984) explain, people in individualistic cultures "are supposed to look after themselves and their immediate family only," whereas those in collectivistic cultures "belong to in-groups or collectivities which are supposed to look after them in exchange for loyalty" (p. 419). When Hofstede and Bond talk about in-groups, they are referring to people such as coworkers, colleagues, and classmates. Out-groups include strangers or anyone who is not specifically a member of an in-group.

Gudykunst, Yoon, and Nishida (1987) argued that in-group relationships are more intimate in collectivistic cultures than in individualistic cultures. Consequently, in-group communication should be more personalized, better coordinated, and less difficult in collectivistic cultures than in individualistic cultures. Results from their study of in-group communication among students from South Korea (highly collectivistic), Japan (moderately collectivistic) and the United States (highly individualistic) supported this hypothesis. In-group communication was more personalized, better coordinated, and less difficult for the South Koreans than for the Japanese, and more personalized, better coordinated, and less difficult for the Japanese than for the Americans.

These results do not necessarily mean that we should make American society more collectivistic. Individualistic values may offer some communicative advantages. Gudykunst, Yoon, and Nishida also found that American students had somewhat better experiences than the Japanese and Koreans with out-group communication. Interaction with strangers was easier and better coordinated (though less personal) for American students. Infante and Gorden (1987) also have claimed that independent-mindedness of organization members, a condition that can be troublesome in group interaction, is essential to productivity in American organizations.

There are two additional observations that are important to make before concluding this section on decision making and culture. First, nationalistic cultures are not monolithic. Some organizations in nations like Korea and Japan may display individualistic features, just as organizations in the United States may display collectivistic features. Second, there are aspects of culture that influence decision making beyond individualism and collectivism. For example, an organization may be guided by a "customer is always right" culture. In such a culture, the needs and concerns of employees will always be subordinate to customers, and all organizational decisions will be guided by customers' views. Alternatively, an organization may be guided by a "protect the bottom line" culture. In such an organization, all decisions will be framed by options that protect the financial interests of the organization.

CRITICAL PERSPECTIVES ON GROUP RELATIONSHIPS

Although there are many different critical perspectives that can be applied to group relationships, group members create the structures that guide their actions through producing and reproducing those structures in their everyday interaction (Giddens, 1979; 2003). In producing and reproducing structures, group members may create work environments that are oppressive or empowering. In order to illustrate, let's consider an example from an academic department in a university on the east coast of the United States. Elizabeth, a professor in this department, became pregnant with her second child. At the time she was teaching four classes per semester. Her overall job included course preparation, teaching, grading, conducting research, office hours, and other service responsibilities. Elizabeth worked 60 hours in an average week. When she approached her supervisor about her maternity leave, she heard the first of many stories that showed how women may communicate in ways to control one another's choices.

Elizabeth's supervisor was a woman who told a story about her last maternity leave, which she restricted to three weeks so she would not miss teaching her classes and meeting other professional responsibilities. When Elizabeth responded to this story by saying that she would like to take the full six weeks that the faculty contract allowed, the supervisor suggested that Elizabeth rearrange her teaching schedule and double the time she taught each week for the four weeks prior to the birth of her child. Given a teaching load of 16 hours per week, this solution proved impractical in terms of time, room availability, and student schedules. The supervisor then agreed reluctantly to find other instructors to cover her classes for the remaining weeks.

Over the course of the next several weeks, several other women (university professors) in the department talked to Elizabeth about what they did during their maternity leaves. One colleague explained that two weeks of maternity leave was reasonable because it does not disrupt classes. Another professor talked about taking only three weeks of maternity leave as she felt pressure from the faculty to continue to "pull her weight" in terms of teaching, service, and research. Then, one of Elizabeth's closest friends in the department talked about limiting her leave to four weeks and bringing a breast pump, so she could bring home breast milk for her baby. When Elizabeth reflected on these stories, she realized that the underlying message was that a woman's professionalism would be compromised, and her job evaluations may suffer, if she took a full six weeks of maternity leave.

Elizabeth carefully considered her options. Her annual contract was coming up for renewal. She was worried about the tone of the stories shared by her fellow women colleagues in the department, including her supervisor. Elizabeth felt that the standards set by these women restricted her choices, and she decided to take only two weeks of maternity leave.

The preceding story shows how a group of women limited one another's choices in ways that were clearly oppressive. They all worked for an organization that granted all full-time employees a full six weeks of maternity leave. The choice was theirs to limit the length of their leave. Of course, they were also embedded in a department of 15 faculty members where these stories were produced and reproduced in ways that created a powerful system of control. This is not the end of the story, however. Three years later Elizabeth became a tenured faculty member in the department. She began to tell her story in the classes she taught. Students not only talked with one another, they talked to faculty members in Elizabeth's department about the unfair way that women were treated. Elizabeth also joined a women's forum at the university. Thirty women from departments all over campus participated in this forum. They discussed many issues including the ways in which they sometimes limited one another's choices rather than argue assertively for fair treatment. An article was published in the campus newspaper that focused on the maternity leave issue, among others. Elizabeth was amazed by the response to the article. People across campus were discussing the maternity issue and other issues related to women's disempowerment. The next fall one of Elizabeth's departmental colleagues (Cathy) announced her pregnancy at a faculty meeting. This time there were no stories of shortened maternity leaves. The department chair asked Cathy to come to her office so they could discuss when her maternity leave would begin. When Cathy specified the approximate date, she was told that she would receive six weeks of paid maternity leave and that she would receive an additional six weeks of unpaid leave if she wanted it. Cathy was also told that her husband Richard, also a faculty member in the department, could take six weeks of paid paternity leave and an additional six weeks of unpaid leave. Interestingly, these policies had been in place for years.

In the first part of the story, women's communication contributed to an oppressive environment in which women limited one another's choices. In the second part of the story, women's communication led to empowerment. By telling stories to students in classes, meeting with one another at the women's forum, and writing an article in the university newspaper, women were able to gain what was rightfully theirs. The rules concerning maternity leave had always been in place. It was the way those rules were discussed that determined whether women were oppressed or empowered. Giddens (1979) uses the term *dialectic of control* to refer to such actions. What he means by this is that every social actor within a system has the capacity to exercise power and control. In the department and in the university in which Elizabeth worked, women engaged in communication that resisted the dominant meanings that limited their choices.

Giddens's Structuration Theory and the Creation of Social Structure

At the core of Giddens's structuration theory is the cyclical relationship between social structure and human action. Specifically, Giddens argues that social structure is a product of human action. These social structures both enable humans to act and to constrain their subsequent actions. According to Giddens, the weakness in functional and structural approaches to social theories is that they do not adequately recognize the power of human action to create social structure. Structuration theory responds to this weakness in social theory by explaining that human action creates social structures by producing and reproducing them (e.g., our earlier example of not raising one's voice in a group meeting). This is called the duality of structure. As Giddens (1993) writes in *New Rules for Sociological Method*:

> . . . let me first of all explain why I developed the concept of the duality of structure. I did so in order to contest two main types of dualism. One is that found among pre-existing theoretical perspectives. Interpretive sociologists . . . are "strong on action but weak on structure." They see human beings as purposive agents, who are aware of themselves as such and have reasons for what they do, but they have little means of coping with issues which quite rightly bulk large in functionalist and structural approaches—problems of constraint, power and large scale social organization. The second group of approaches, on the other hand, while "strong on structure," has been "weak on action." Agents are treated as if they were inert and inept—the playthings of forces larger than themselves. In breaking away from such a dualism of theoretical perspectives, the analysis in *New Rules* also rejects the dualism of "the individual" and "society." (p. 4)

Structuration theory has clear implications for understanding group communication and group relationships. Essentially, group members create the structures that guide their actions through producing and reproducing those structures in their everyday interaction. Group members are not prisoners of the structures they create, however. Rather, we have the capability of changing the meanings we give to events or experiences. When we change the meanings we give to our experiences, we change the very structure that guides our communication with one another. Although this is not a simple process, it is possible. Think back to our example in Chapter 2 regarding Far End Design. The owner and the workers created a structure that established a pattern of workers producing designs that did not meet the expectations of the owner and he responded by berating them. This structure was produced and reproduced many times as the workers tried to be independent or to guess what type of design the owner wanted. When they inevitably failed, they accepted his anger as an unavoidable by-product of their actions. The workers and the owner may choose, however, to confront this structure directly by talking about it. For example, the workers and owner may decide to work collaboratively on designs so the designs match the owner's vision. Alternatively, the workers may decide to match the owner's anger with their own anger over being given an impossible task. Finally, the workers may choose to walk away from the owner when he gets angry or to leave the organization entirely. There are implications to each of these alternatives. Some may lead to productive problem solving that makes this a better work group. Other solutions may result in people leaving the organization. Importantly, each of these alternatives shows how group members do not have to be prisoners to the structures they have created. Rather, we have the power to change those structures through our own actions. We may also make a link here to our earlier discussion of norms. Specifically, norms are structures created by group members. As such, they restrain communicative choices, but those same group members may also change them.

SUMMARY

Groups constitute the most obvious and, perhaps, most important organizational subsystems. Communication within and between groups can be channeled toward cooperation or conflict. In either case, group action must be understood as joint action. A group not only serves the functions of a larger system, but it also strives to survive within that system. Hence, the goals of different organizational groups are not always consistent with one another or with the goals of the larger system. Groups, like living organisms, appear to move through stages of development. In some cases, the stages seem orderly and sequenced, but activities of many groups take on cyclical characteristics. Interaction in groups is a rule-bound process based on normative expectations and role enactment. Group members are accorded varying levels of power and status within the group. Most communication research on small-group processes has been conducted from the traditional perspective and concerned with decision making. Hirokawa's studies are fairly typical of research in this area. Few consistently reliable differences have been found between effective and ineffective groups, although recent studies suggest that communicative behaviors involving evaluation of opinions, evaluation of alternatives, decisional premises, and the styles of influential group members may explain some of the differences.

Group activity is carried out through the enactment of member roles. There are many different kinds of roles, and different members may enact them at different times. Some of the more important categories of roles include task roles, maintenance roles, and self-centered roles.

More recently, research, training, and human resources discussions about group relationships have focused on the interpretive and critical perspectives. Interpretive work concentrates on how groups socially create a reality that becomes the context for communication and relationships within the group. In fact, one of the most important functions of group communication may be to provide the basic frames of reference from which individual members understand, enact, and justify the organization and its mission. Interpretive research especially has created renewed interest in this aspect of group communication. In this chapter, we developed our views on the interpretive perspective by focusing on studies about the bona fide group perspective, norms and conformity, values and sense making, and the impact of decision making on group culture.

Social reality is not static; it may change over time. For social reality to change, however, members must negotiate and support those changes through their interaction with one another. Critical work is concerned with the communicative construction of structures that are oppressive for workers. Alternatively, as Giddens informs us, group members may also enact a dialectic of control by engaging in resistance that challenges dominant meanings. When this is done, group members may empower one another.

DISCUSSION QUESTIONS/ACTIVITIES

1. Observe a group in a decision-making process. What kinds of communicative behaviors seem to influence the group's effectiveness? Can the group's decision-making process be characterized by any of the models or procedures described in this chapter?

2. Do you think that group memberships within an organization play an important role in shaping individual members' values? Can you provide some examples to support your conclusion?

3. Some organizational scholars have argued prescriptive models of group decision making are undesirable and should be avoided. Do you agree with this position? Why or why not?

REFERENCES

Adams, K., & Galanes, G. J. (2003). *Communicating in groups: Applications and skills* (5th ed.). New York: McGraw-Hill.

Baird, J. E., Jr., & Weinberg, S. B. (1981). *Group communication: The essence of synergy* (2nd ed.). Dubuque, IA: Wm. C. Brown.

Beckhard, R. (1969). *Organization development: Strategies and models.* Reading, MA: Addison-Wesley.

Beebe, S. A., & Masterson, J. T. (2003). *Communicating in small groups: Principles and practices* (7th ed.). Boston: Allyn & Bacon.

Benne, K. D., & Sheats, P. (1948). Functional roles of group members. *Journal of Social Issues, 4,* 41–49.

Blumer, H. (1969). *Symbolic interactionism: Perspective and method.* Englewood Cliffs, NJ: Prentice Hall.

Bormann, E. (1969). *Discussion and group methods.* New York: Harper & Row.

Fisher, B. A. (1970). Decision emergence: Phases in group decision making. *Speech Monographs, 37,* 53–66.

Forsyth, D. (1990). *Group dynamics.* Pacific Grove, CA: Brooks/Cole Publishing Co.

Frey, L. R. (Ed.). (2003). *Group communication in context: Studies of bona fide groups* (2nd ed.). Mahwah, NJ: Lawrence Erlbaum.

Giddens, A. (1979). *Central problems in social theory.* London: Macmillan.

Giddens, A. (2003). *New rules for sociological methods* (2nd ed.). Palo Alto, CA: Stanford University Press.

Goldhaber, G. M., Dennis, H. S., III, Richetto, G. M., & Wiio, O. (1979). *Information strategies: New pathways to corporate power.* Englewood Cliffs, NJ: Prentice Hall.

Gudykunst, W. B., Yoon, Y., & Nishida, T. (1987). The influence of individualism-collectivism on perceptions of communication in in-group and out-group relationships. *Communication Monographs, 54,* 295–306.

Hastie, R., Penrod, S., & Pennington, N. (1983). *Inside the jury.* Cambridge, MA: Harvard University Press.

Hirokawa, R. Y. (1980). A comparative analysis of communication patterns within effective and ineffective decision-making groups. *Communication Monographs, 47,* 312–321.

Hirokawa, R. Y. (1983). Group communication and problem-solving effectiveness II: An exploratory investigation of procedural functions. *Western Journal of Speech Communication, 47,* 59–74.

Hirokawa, R. Y., & Keyton, J. (1995). Perceived facilitators and inhibitors of effectiveness in organizational work teams. *Management Communication Quarterly, 8,* 424–446.

Hirokawa, R. Y., & Rost, K. M. (1992). Effective group decision making in organizations: Field test of the vigilant interaction theory. *Management Communication Quarterly, 5,* 267–288.

Hofstede, G., & Bond, M. (1984). Hofstede's culture dimensions: An independent validation suing Rokeach's value survey. *Journal of Cross-Cultural Psychology, 15,* 417–433.

Homans, G. C. (1950). *The human group.* New York: Harcourt Brace Jovanovich.

Infante, D. A., & Gordon, W. I. (1987). Superior and subordinate communication profiles: Implications for independent-mindedness and upward effectiveness. *Central States Speech Journal, 38,* 73–80.

Jensen, A. D., & Chilberg, J. C. (1991). *Small group communication: Theory and application.* Belmont, CA: Wadsworth.

Kelly, G. A. (1955). *The psychology of personal constructs* (Vol. 1). New York: Norton.

Lippitt, G. L. (1982). *Organization renewal: A holistic approach to organization development* (2nd ed.). Englewood Cliffs, NJ: Prentice Hall.

Littlejohn, S. W. (1992). *Theories of human communication* (4th ed.). Belmont, CA: Wadsworth.

Michaelson, L. (1989). A realistic test of individual versus group consensus decision-making. *Journal of Applied Psychology, 74,* 834–839.

Nomura, R. (1981). *West learns Japanese ways, executives wear workclothes.* Nihon Keizai Shimbun. Tokyo: Translation Service Center, the Asia Foundation.

Pavitt, C., & Curtis, E. (1994). *Small group discussion.* Scottsdale, AZ: Gorsuch Scarisbuck.

Poole, M. S. (1981). Decision development in small groups I: A comparison of two models. *Communication Monographs, 48,* 1–24.

Poole, M. S. (1983a). Decision development in small groups II: A study of multiple sequences in decision making. *Communication Monographs, 50,* 206–232.

Poole, M. S. (1983b). Decision development in small groups III: A multiple sequence model of group decision development. *Communication Monographs, 50,* 321–341.

Poole, M. S. (1999). Group communication theory. In L. R. Frey (Ed.), D. S. Gouran, & M. S. Poole (Assoc. Eds.), *The handbook of group communication theory & research* (pp. 37–70). Thousand Oaks, CA: Sage.

Putnam, L. L. (1994). Revitalizing small group communication: Lessons learned from a bona fide group perspective. *Communication Studies, 45,* 97–102.

Putnam, L. L., & Stohl, C. (1990). Bona fide groups: A reconceptualization of groups in context. *Communication Studies, 41,* 248–265.

Putnam, L. L., & Stohl, C. (1996). Bona fide groups: An alternative perspective for communication and small group decision-making. In R.Y. Hirokawa & M.S. Poole (Eds.), *Communication and small group decision-making* (2nd ed., pp. 147–178). Thousand Oaks, CA: Sage.

Renz, M. A. (2006). Paving consensus: Enacting, challenging, and revising the consensus process in a cohousing community. *Journal of Applied Communication Research, 34*(2), 163–190.

Rothwell, J. D. (2004). *In mixed company: Communicating in small groups and teams* (5th ed.). Belmont, CA: Wadsworth.

Rubin, H. J. (2005). *Qualitative interviewing: The art of hearing data.* Thousand Oaks, CA: Sage.

Schein, E. (1969). *Process consultation: Its role in organization development.* Reading, MA: Addison-Wesley.

Secord, P. F., & Backman, C. W. (1964). *Social psychology.* New York: McGraw-Hill.

Simon, H. A. (1957). *Administrative behavior.* New York: Free Press.

Spitzberg, B., & Cupach, W. (1984). A component model of relational competence. *Human Communication Research, 10,* 575–599.

Stasson, M., & Bradshaw, S. (1995). Explanations of individual-group performance differences: What sort of bonus can be gained through group interaction? *Small Group Research, 26,* 296–308.

Stohl, C., & Putnam, L. L. (1994). Group communication in context: Implications for the study of bona fide groups. In L.R. Frey (Ed.), *Group communication in context: Studies of natural groups* (pp. 284–292). Hillsdale, NJ: Lawrence Erlbaum.

Weick, K. W. (1976). Educational organizations as loosely coupled systems. *Administrative Science Quarterly, 21,* 1–19.

Wilson, G. L. (2002). *Groups in context: Leadership and participation in small groups* (6th ed.). Boston: McGraw-Hill Irwin.

Wofford, J. C., Gerloff, E. A., & Cummins, R. C. (1979). Group behavior and the communication process. In R. S. Cathcart & L. A. Samovar (Eds.), *Small group communication: A reader* (3rd ed.). Dubuque, IA: Wm. C. Brown.

Leader-Member Relationships

Most organizational theorists believe that leadership is a central factor in the effectiveness of groups as well as organizations. In both the United States and Europe, belief in "the central importance of leadership has been accepted and institutionalized," and intensive interest in the subject "is an international phenomenon" (Storey, 2005, p. 91). We assume that leadership is required in order to initiate structure, to coordinate activities, and to direct others toward the accomplishment of group goals. The preoccupation with leadership is driven in part by a longstanding desire to identify the means of achieving organizational effectiveness through managerial control, but it also is marked today by "an increasing tendency to assume and assert that leadership is the answer to a whole array of intractable problems" (p. 92).

Attention to the quality of leader-member relationships came about to some extent through the human relations assumptions that managers gain compliance from employees by promoting interpersonal relationships and satisfaction of social needs. Later on, in the 1960s and 1970s, emphasis shifted to the basic theme in human resource development theory that the role of leaders is to create the proper climate for the development of members' abilities and to facilitate that development. In either case, *the study of leader-member relations, at least from a traditional point of view, has been preoccupied with a quest to identify the essence of effective leadership and with understanding effective leadership mainly in terms of influence* (Storey, 2005; Yukl, 2006).

Interpretive scholarship on leadership and leader-member communication also addresses themes that are similar to those in the traditional perspective, but much of this work in recent years really has shifted into the domain of critical scholarship. The very idea of organization implies not only coordinated action, including divisions of labor and role specialization, but also a hierarchy of authority in which those who occupy higher positions are accorded more status, privilege, and power than those who occupy lower positions. In Chapter 14, we will describe some emerging alternatives to traditional systems of hierarchy, but it is still generally true in the organizational world that a person at any given level of the organization is subordinate to another. Given this condition, McKenna (2004) aptly summarizes the critical perspective on leader-member relations: "Critical management theorists are not duped by this libertarian spin . . . that describes the postmodern organization as 'having no centrally organized system of authority.' . . . power does centralize in definable clusters" (p. 22).

LIMITATIONS OF LEADERSHIP THEORY AND RESEARCH

Our discussion of leader-member relations is based on two general conditions of leadership research. First, leadership research historically has concerned leader behavior at middle and lower levels of organizations (Storey, 2005). Second, most leadership research has focused on the vertically linked, leader-member dyad (Yukl, 2006). This history is convenient for our purposes in this chapter, but it also has three limitations that we are obliged to address as well. If these limitations are evident in leadership theory and research, we suggest by comparison that they are absolutely rampant in trade literature and practice.

Executive Leadership

The first limitation concerns the issue of top management or executive-level leadership. Zaccaro and Horn (2003) concluded that less than 5% of the leadership research literature in the last half of the 20th century actually concerned *executive* leadership. Scholars began to shift more attention to executive leadership in the 1980s, but the subject poses some interesting challenges. Although executives enjoy high status and value, it is not clear that executive leadership actually has much direct influence on organizational effectiveness (Barker, 1997). This is not to say that executive leadership is unimportant. Higher level leadership is not so much a technical activity as it is an aesthetic activity (Ackoff, 1998). This kind of leadership involves values, symbolism, and creativity, i.e., "the production of solutions that are *not* expected" (p. 29). At the risk of oversimplifying Ackoff's aesthetic analysis with an old cliché, executive leadership is more art than science. Hence, Storey (2005) described executive leadership as an essential, but *intangible,* organizational asset:

> Being seen to have a competent leader, and indeed *being seen to be attending to* the task of building a constantly replenishing 'leadership pool' is virtually *de rigueur* [a social requirement] for any self-respecting organization. The symbolic presence of these attributes is arguably of even more importance than whether there is any evidence of their impact on organizational outcomes. (p. 96)

Leadership in the Dyad

The second limitation involves the focus on the dyad. We certainly talk about leadership of groups and teams and leadership as a determinant of organizational effectiveness, but we often examine leader behavior and its consequences at the level of the dyad. As Tjosvold (1985) noted, communication in vertically linked relationships "is central to organizational work" (p. 281), but focusing on this vertically linked dyad directs one's attention to leader influence over organization members as individuals rather than leader influence in group or organizational processes (Yukl, 1999). This focus not only misses the point of Yukl's concern about the consequences of leadership for group and organizational processes; it also ignores the influence that group and organizational characteristics exert on leader behavior (Storey, 2005). As we will note at various points in this chapter, leadership occurs in a larger social context, and this social context influences leader behavior and leadership effectiveness (Hogg et al., 2005).

The Leader as Individual

The third limitation rarely is identified as such in leadership literature, but it should be just as evident as the others. As implied by leader-follower and leader-member terminology, leadership theory and research conceives of leaders as individuals engaged in the direction of one or more other organization members. This conception of leadership certainly figures prominently in the beliefs, language, and practices of society at large. We look to leaders as the individuals with the traits and abilities required to direct or guide the rest of us, and this tendency, according to Barker (1997), "serves two important social functions: hope for salvation and blame for failure" (p. 348). The chief executive officer receives lavish compensation when the corporation profits and the head coach gets fired when the team has a losing season because leaders are presumed to be the agents of (and accountable for) success and failure. Our concern here may seem at odds with the first limitation that we noted regarding executive leadership, but some scholars really have begun to challenge the leader-as-individual bias in leadership theory.

Gemmill and Oakley (1992) suggested that leadership emerges out of a social process of collaboration. Gastil (1994) noted that leadership functions within groups actually may be performed by many group members. In one case study of major strategic change at a large hospital, Denis, Langley, and Cazale (1996) found that the execution of strategic change actually "requires collaborative leadership involving constellations of actors playing distinct but tightly-knit roles" (p. 673). From this point of view, the locus of leadership is in collective action, not just in the behavior of leaders as individuals.

Barker (1997) identified this point of view as an emerging paradigm that "provides for examination of beliefs and assumptions behind leadership theories" (p. 355). He also noted that it is not a theory of leadership, and it does not necessarily require rejection of traditional assumptions that may be entirely appropriate in some situations. But Barker does point to a possibility that we also have suspected for a long time. Much of the leadership that results in success or failure occurs in micro practices distributed throughout an organization, and it is enacted by and transacted among many members.

We cannot strip the lower level, dyadic, and leader-as-individual framework out of our coverage in a survey text. The literature is what it is. To the extent that this framework obscures or diverts attention from alternative conceptions, we certainly want to call attention to its biases.

TRADITIONAL PERSPECTIVE

Theories of Leadership Behavior

Despite the overwhelming belief in the importance of leadership in organizations, no one has been able to develop a uniformly accepted theory of leadership behavior (Barker, 1997). Over the years, scholars have attempted to distinguish leaders from nonleaders on the basis of personality traits, to identify and describe ideal styles of leadership, and to determine the kinds of situations under which any given type of leadership behavior is likely to be effective or ineffective. Some have even argued that "leadership" and "management" involve two different and sometimes inconsistent forms of behavior (Bennis, 1976a, 1976b).

Leadership as Trait

The earliest theories of leadership attempted to distinguish leaders from nonleaders on the basis of certain personality traits. The list of distinguishing traits such as intelligence, responsibility, character, and others like them typically sounds as if it came from the pages of the Boy Scout or Girl Scout Handbook. Despite many efforts to identify a clear and consistent set of characteristics of leaders, results of the trait approach are mixed. Jennings (1961) argued many years ago that the trait school was simply failing to identify any personality traits that would consistently distinguish leaders from followers. On the other hand, Koehler, Anatol, and Applbaum (1981) concluded that at least three specific traits are associated with effective leaders across a broad range of situations: *intelligence, adjustment,* and *deviancy.* The potential relevance of intelligence and adjustment may seem self-evident, but what about deviancy? The idea here is that good leaders need an intuitive understanding of when to break the rules, to innovate, and to change.

Despite the argument made by Koehler et al., years of trait research have not produced any agreement about their relevance to leadership (Barker, 1997), and trait theory inspires much more interest today in trade literature and among practitioners than it inspires among academic scholars. Even so, trait-based studies still show up on occasion in social science research. For example, Barlow, Jordan, and Hendrix (2003) found that advanced Air Force officers scored higher than midlevel officers on the character traits of selflessness and spiritual appreciation. In turn, midlevel officers scored higher than early career officers on both of these characteristics and also on integrity. Barlow et al. concluded that these character traits undergo development and growth among officers as they advance in their careers. In a study of Norwegian middle managers, Kornor and Nordvik (2004) found that self-reports of personality characteristics predicted self-reports of leadership style. Those with conscientious traits reported themselves to be production-oriented leaders, extraverts opted for change-oriented leadership, and managers with agreeable personalities preferred employee-oriented leadership.

Leadership as Style

The stylistic approach to leadership behavior developed, in part, out of frustration with the earlier trait approach. As Koehler et al. pointed out, "Unlike the trait approach to leadership, the stylistic approach is concerned with what leaders do rather than the personal characteristics they possess"" (p. 228). Three widely used models of leadership style include an early model developed by White and Lippitt (1960); the Blake and McCanse (1991) Leadership Grid, an extension of earlier work by Blake and Mouton (1964, 1985); and transformational leadership theory, particularly a version elaborated by Bernie Bass (1985, 1996).

Early Style Theory. One early and classic version of stylistic theory was developed by White and Lippitt (1960). They identified three basic styles of leadership that they labeled as laissez-faire, authoritarian, and democratic.

Laissez-faire leaders relinquish virtually all control of decisions and group processes to members. Such leaders may remain available for consultation or problem solving, but they generally delegate all authority for tasks to members and avoid decisions and responsibilities. You might say with good reason that the idea of a "laissez-faire leader" is an oxymoron, a contradiction in terms, because this leader's style is nonleadership.

Authoritarian leaders exercise strong command and control over decisions and tasks. They issue and enforce orders to ensure that their plans are executed in an acceptable manner. They closely monitor and supervise the work of members. They demand respect for and compliance with their authority as leaders.

Democratic leaders are more oriented toward guiding and coaching members rather than completely controlling their activities. They share authority with members and seek member input in decision making. They delegate responsibilities, provide recognition, and promote development for their members.

The characteristics of democratic leadership style are similar to those of participative management practices under the human resource development model that we described in Chapter 4. Not surprisingly, democratic leadership, like participative management, has enjoyed favor in organizational communication theory and scholarship for many years as a generally preferred style.

The Leadership Grid. A second and more widely used stylistic approach to leadership is presented in Blake and McCanse's (1991) Leadership Grid. Extending from earlier work by Blake and Mouton (1964, 1985), Blake and McCanse argued that eight basic managerial (i.e., leadership) styles can be identified according to their degree of concern for production and concern for people. Five of these styles can be located in the Blake and McCanse Leadership Grid, in which the two dimensions of concern form axes. The remaining three are not displayed graphically in the grid. As the phrase "concern for," implies, Blake and McCanse's concept of style is more *attitudinal* than behavioral.

The 1,1, or impoverished leader, is theoretically the least effective. Given low concern for both production and people, the impoverished leader exercises no initiative and abdicates any responsibility for group outcomes. According to Blake and McCanse, the 9,1 authority-obedience and 1,9 country club leaders are not much more effective. The authority-obedience leader basically regards people concerns as obstacles to production accomplishment. This leader may use punitive and even abusive strategies to subordinate people concerns to the all-important goal of production accomplishment. In contrast, the country club leader thinks of nothing but people concerns. This leader strives primarily to maintain morale, satisfaction, and harmony among group members, even if production has to suffer in order to accomplish maintenance functions.

The 5,5, or middle-of-the-road leader, attempts to compromise and balance production and people concerns. The middle-of-the-road manager may believe that production and people concerns are competing and contradictory aspects of group behavior. In order to cope with the contradiction, the middle-of-the-road leader settles for moderately harmonious group relationships and adequate but not outstanding task performance.

The ideal style for leadership effectiveness presumably is the 9,9 or team leader. Whereas the 5,5 leader sees production and people concerns as competing, the team leader believes that group effectiveness depends on integration of people needs with production objectives. The 9,9 team leader personifies the ideals of human resource development theory as described in Chapter 4. Specifically, group effectiveness is presumed to depend on the extent to which individual members are able to develop, assume responsibility, and function as a team. The team leader concentrates on bringing about this form of development.

Some writers (e.g., Hersey & Blanchard, 1982) have claimed that the Leadership Grid is based on earlier studies of leadership behavior at the Institute for Social Research (ISR) in Michigan and at Ohio State University (OSU). The ISR studies identified two basic styles of leadership, job-centered and employee-centered. The OSU studies found two similar leadership variables—initiating structure and consideration. The OSU model regarded *both* variables as potential factors in a leader's behavior, whereas the ISR model viewed them as different styles. In either case, the job-centered and initiating structure factors represent a task dimension of leadership style, whereas employee-centered or consideration behavior represents a maintenance dimension. Despite the similarity of terms in all of these models, there are some important differences. The OSU and ISR models specifically are behavioral, whereas the Leadership Grid, as we noted earlier, is attitudinal. Moreover, Scientific Methods, Inc., the corporation holding the rights to the Leadership Grid, contends, "Blake and Mouton's research and writings are not based on either the ISR or the OSU studies" (Knause, 1990).

Transformational Leadership. Transformational leadership theory is classified appropriately as a theory of leadership style (Kirkbride, 2006), but this theory differs from earlier stylistic theories and models in some of its key assumptions. The first scholar to lay groundwork for the concept of transformational leadership may have been Burns (1978), who distinguished between transacting and transforming leadership (Rafferty & Griffin, 2004). Bernie Bass (1985, 1996) elaborated this idea into a coherent theory that not only generates intensive academic interest, but also enjoys widespread popularity among practitioners today (Kirkbride, 2006; Yukl, 1999).

To begin with Burns's distinction, transactional leaders work on exchange principles, i.e., by providing rewards that are contingent on accomplishing goals and complying with leadership. Transformational leaders actually change members' values. More to the point, they motivate members to perform beyond expectations (Bass, 1985). Bass, along with Avolio (Avolio, 1999; Bass & Avolio, 1998), developed a model of eight leadership styles that differs from earlier stylistic models in at least three respects. First, the styles are assumed to operate on a continuum of performance effectiveness (Kirkbride, 2006). Second, any given manager or leader may exhibit any or all of the styles (Bass & Avolio, 1998). Finally, whereas traditional leadership theories rely on concepts of rational processes, transformational theory is concerned with emotions, values, symbolic behavior, and "the role of the leader in making events meaningful for followers" (Yukl, 1999, p. 286).

The first (and least effective) style is *laissez-faire,* i.e., the nonleader leadership style much as White and Lippett defined it, where members are without direction and often in conflict with one another. The second and third styles are passive and active *management-by-exception* (MBE). MBE is still basically laissez-faire, but the MBE leader does pay attention to deviations from normal conditions (i.e., errors and problems) in order to correct the deviations and return to normal conditions. Expressed in terms of system theory, MBE aims for homeostasis and operates on negative feedback. In the passive form, the leader is roused into action only when problems become obvious. In the active form, the leader is vigilant, relying on elaborate systems to monitor and control activity. MBE is presumed at best to lead to marginal performance.

The fourth style, *contingent reward*, fits the basic definition of transactional leadership as an exchange process. The contingent reward or transactional leader understands the objectives, acquires and coordinates the resources that members need to accomplish objectives, supports their efforts, and rewards accomplishment. According to Kirkbride (2006), "If done successfully, this style will produce performance at the required levels" (p. 26).

Moving member performance beyond "required levels" presumably requires something more than transactional leadership. The next four styles, in theory, lead progressively to performance beyond expectations, and each of the four is a form of transformational leadership. These styles are *individualized consideration, intellectual stimulation, inspirational motivation,* and *idealized influence.*

Individualized consideration involves leader recognition of individual differences, management of work in light of those differences, open communication, and member development. Intellectual stimulation involves the leader more actively as a facilitator, advisor, and catalyst for problem solving by members. Some of the attributes in these two styles also appear in descriptions of democratic and team leadership as well as participative management in human resource development.

The last two styles clearly move into the symbolic domain and involve member identification with leaders. The leader with an inspirationally motivating style has a vision for the future and is able to communicate about that vision in a clear, compelling, and engaging way so that members adopt that vision and pursue it. Finally, in idealized influence, the summit of transformational leadership, the leader is virtually iconic, i.e., a person who is perceived as the personification of the best organizational values and regarded as a model to emulate.

As we noted earlier, Bass's version of transformational leadership has inspired many research studies, and there is evidence to support the performance continuum suggested in the theory (Kirkbride, 2006). Specifically, transformational leadership correlates more highly than transactional leadership with leadership effectiveness. In turn, transactional leadership is more effective than MBE, and MBE is more effective than laissez-faire. Yukl also stated that studies have shown a link between transformational leadership and organizational effectiveness across different levels of management, types of organizations, and countries, but he also noted that possible situational influences have not been adequately tested. That observation leads us to the next section on situational theory of leadership.

Situational Theory

Just as trait theories have been criticized for failing to produce clear distinctions between leaders and nonleaders, stylistic theory has been criticized for assuming that any one style of leadership can be effective in all situations. Situational or contingency theories of leadership argue that no one leadership style is ideal and that the circumstances of leadership will determine whether a particular style will be effective or ineffective.

Frederick Fiedler (1967) devised one early and popular contingency theory. Fiedler argued that the effectiveness of a leadership style will be influenced by three factors:

1. Leader-member relations, or the degree of confidence and trust that members have in the leader.

2. Task structure, or the degree of certainty and routine as opposed to ambiguity and unpredictability in the task.

3. Position power, or the influence inherent in the leadership role (legitimate authority and ability to reward or punish).

Fiedler conducted a number of studies on directive and permissive styles of leadership under varying combinations of the three key situational factors. Results of these studies led him to propose a model of situational conditions under which each style would be most effective. Fiedler's model is presented in Table 10.1.

The group and task characteristics identified by Fiedler probably are not the only factors that influence the effectiveness of a given leadership style. Eblen (1987) found that the relationship between leadership style and employee commitment varied across organizational contexts. Given the two basic leadership variables from the OSU studies, initiating structure and consideration, her study indicated that consideration was positively related to employee commitment in hospitals, whereas initiating structure was positively related to commitment among employees in city government departments.

Hogg et al. (2005) found that salience of group identity for group members also affects the relationship between leadership style and leadership effectiveness in studies of service and manufacturing companies located in Wales and India. A personalized style was more effective in low-salience groups, whereas a depersonalized style was more effective in high-salience groups. In other words, when group members do not identify strongly with the group as an entity, a personalized relationship with the leader is more important for leadership effectiveness. When group identification is strong, it is more important for the leader to be perceived as "group prototypical" (p. 993) and act toward members as group members rather than individuals.

The issue of situational influences on leadership and organizational effectiveness is especially interesting in the case of transformational leadership theory because of its widespread

TABLE 10.1 Fiedler's Situational Model

	Group Situation			
Condition	Leader-Member Relations	Task Structure	Position Power	Leadership Style Correlated w/Productivity
1	Good	Structured	Strong	Directive
2	Good	Structured	Weak	Directive
3	Good	Unstructured	Strong	Directive
4	Good	Unstructured	Weak	Permissive
5	Moderately Poor	Structured	Strong	Permissive
6	Moderately Poor	Structured	Weak	No Data
7	Moderately Poor	Unstructured	Strong	No Relationship
8	Moderately Poor	Unstructured	Weak	Directive

SOURCE: From A *Theory of Leadership Effectiveness*, by Frederick Fiedler, 1967. New York: McGraw-Hill. © Fred Fiedler. Reprinted with permission from author.

popularity. Even advocates for transformational leadership have suggested that it is best suited for organizations dealing with rapid change in turbulent environments (Kirkbride, 2006). Pawar and Eastman (1997) developed a theory that environmental stability, dominant organizational functions, organizational structure, and mode of organizational governance will determine the effectiveness of transformational leadership. Specifically, they hypothesized that transformational leadership is less likely to work in relatively stable, bureaucratic organizations with strong, technical core functions that can operate in relative isolation from the environment.

We are not aware of any studies that specifically test Pawar and Eastman's theory, but some studies have pointed to other situational limitations with transformational leadership. Ozaralli (2003) found in a small study of eight companies in Turkey that transformational leadership as well as organization members' sense of empowerment contributed substantially to the effectiveness of teams, but transformational leadership and empowerment themselves were not highly correlated. So what contributes to member empowerment? Ozaralli concluded that "*transactional* [emphasis added] leadership behaviors may also have a share in employee [member] empowerment" (p. 342).

Rafferty and Griffin (2004) reframed the basic transformational style in five dimensions (vision, inspirational communication, supportive leadership, intellectual stimulation, and personal recognition). They found in a study of nearly 1,400 public employees in Australia that the dimensions had different consequences for organizational outcomes including member commitment, self-efficacy (confidence to carry out tasks beyond prescribed requirements), and helping others. Leadership vision and personal recognition actually had negative relationships with members' commitment to stay with the organization. Supportive leadership, which generally is associated with organization members' satisfaction, was unrelated to commitment, self-efficacy, and helping others. Intellectual stimulation was related positively to commitment, but inspirational communication was the only one of the five dimensions to correlate positively with commitment, self-efficacy, and helping others.

Leader-Member Exchange Theory

Situational, as well as stylistic, theories of leadership also have one other very important limitation. They assume that leaders behave in a consistent manner toward all of the members within a group, exhibiting something like an "average leadership style" (ALS model). Graen (1976) challenged this assumption with a leader-member exchange (LMX) model, arguing that leaders discriminate significantly in their behavior toward members.

Fairhurst and Chandler (1989) examined the LMX model in a qualitative study of interaction between the manager and three employees in the warehouse division of a large manufacturing company. One member was an "in-group" member (worked under conditions of mutual trust, influence, and support with the manager), one was an "out-group" member (worked under conditions involving low trust and support along with exercise of the manager's formal authority), and the third was a "middle group" member, which fell between the conditions of the other two. Fairhurst and Chandler found both consistency and inconsistency in the manager's relationship with these three employees.

The manager used indirect and ambiguous communication to exercise unobtrusive control with all three employees. As described by Fairhurst and Chandler, he was "a control-based manager who tries to appear noncontrolling and participative" (p. 230). At the same time, the manager's behavior and the patterns of interaction between the manager and employees clearly differed across in-group, middle-group, and out-group relationships. Both parties frequently challenged and disagreed with each other in the in-group relationship. The manager was somewhat more dominant in the middle-group relationship and exercised direct authority with the out-group member. Interestingly, the out-group member went to great lengths to maintain his out-group status with communicative behaviors that created social distance between the manager and himself.

Waldron (1991) reported results that are only partially consistent with Fairhurst and Chandler's findings. In Waldron's study, in-group members were able to communicate informally with their leaders about subjects that had no relationship to the work. In Albrecht and Ropp's (1984) terms, we might say that these members had multiplex linkages with the supervisors, "a kind of latitude not available to out-group members" (p. 301). But some of the differences between in-groups and out-groups were so small that Waldron concluded that members in neither group exercise much control in defining their relationships with their leaders and that leaders maintain power over in-group members as well as out-group members.

Fairhurst (1993) has continued to find marked differences in leader-member communication among in-groups, middle-groups, and out-groups. In a much larger study than the original Fairhurst and Chandler work, Fairhurst found that in-group communication emphasized supportiveness, collegiality, and similarity. Out-group leader-member exchange involved face threats and competitive conflict, implying "an openly contentious and adversarial relationship" (p. 345). Middle groups reflected both accommodating and polarizing interactions.

One explanation for the inconsistency between the Waldron and Fairhurst studies may be that differences in relationship quality have more influence on members' behavior than on leaders' behavior. Lee and Jablin (1995) found evidence of this when they were studying what leaders and members do to maintain their relationships under stressful circumstances, for example, when the relationship is deteriorating or when one party wants to escalate the relationship to a level that is too close for the other party's comfort.

Lee and Jablin found that leaders' perceptions of the leader-member exchange quality (i.e., in-group vs. out-group) had no effect on the relationship maintenance strategies that they used with members in any situation. This is consistent with ALS theory and with the results in Waldron's study. On the other hand, the quality of the leader-member exchange was very important to choices made by members in communicating with their leaders. Where relationship stress was caused by escalation, out-group members were more likely than in-group members to avoid communication. Where deterioration was occurring, out-group members were more likely than in-group members to use both direct *and* deceptive strategies to deal with the situation. You probably are asking, "How can that be?" It is a matter of timing. Because out-group members' relations with leaders are rule-driven and formal, they can call attention directly and openly to any deviation from the rules. If this does not solve the problem with the leader, the out-group member may turn to deception and distortion. This certainly looks like the kind of LMX in-group/out-group difference that Fairhurst has seen in her studies.

Given some of these research findings, it might not be surprising that more recent studies have begun to attach value to LMX by distinguishing between "good" and "bad" LMX (Morrow, Suzuki, Crum, Ruben, & Pautsch, 2005). In effect, some recent LMX research has taken a prescriptive turn, suggesting that LMX can range from high to low in quality, and "the level of exchange quality predicts a variety of positive outcomes" (Hochwarter, 2005, p. 506). In particular, members of in-groups (the *de facto* higher quality condition) are more satisfied, more committed, and less likely to leave the organization. Lee (1999) also concluded from a review of LMX studies that "LMX quality *does* affect communication behaviors and attitudes between leaders and members" (p. 417).

In one study of employees in several different kinds of organizations, Lee (1999) found that LMX quality appears to have self-perpetuating consequences for members' communication expectations. Members in high-quality conditions expected positive communication with leaders and motivated themselves to fulfill these expectations. Members in low-quality conditions had little expectation for positive communication with leaders and behaved in ways that served to confirm this expectation, "thereby recreating the state or quality of their low LMX" (p. 425).

In another study, also with employees drawn from a variety of organizations, Lee (2001) found that leaders "may build unfairness into work relationships with subordinates" under low LMX conditions, and he argued in light of this result that "leaders must offer opportunities for subordinates to improve the quality of LMXs" (p. 585). Should leaders themselves undertake an obligation to create high-quality exchange for all members? According to Sparrowe and Liden (1997), "An unresolved issue in LMX research is whether leaders should or should not differentiate among their members. . . . Our understanding of the differentiation process indicates that this is not a simple question" (p. 545).

As Lee's studies and others suggest, too much differentiation disenfranchises out-group members in low-quality LMX conditions. On the other hand, providing high-quality LMX to everyone can overburden the leader. Moreover, Sparrowe and Liden remind us of one hard condition that permeates organizational life: We do not all perform at the same level, and "organizational effectiveness may be dependent upon internal selection processes and competition for promotions in which the differentiation process plays a crucial role" (p. 545).

In addition to the idea that differentiation might be something like a necessary evil in organizational life, it is not entirely clear that high-quality LMX consistently translates into desirable outcomes. Morrow et al. found that employee turnover was lowest under what they described as moderate LMX conditions, with higher turnover under both low- and high-quality LMX. Given the purpose of their study, the choice of a study population was interesting. They surveyed over-the-road truck drivers, i.e., employees who might have relatively little direct contact with their leaders for extended periods of time.

Hochwarter (2005) conducted a study of the relationship between LMX and members' experience of job tension with results that might surprise many people, although Hochwarter actually predicted them. Hochwarter classified organization members' affective dispositions on negative and positive scales. Negative and positive affective dispositions as studied by Hochwarter are not polar opposites. Negative affect involves nervousness and distress. Positive affect involves interest and attentiveness. Potentially, a person could have both or neither, e.g., the apathetic member who is not distressed and definitely not interested. Organization members with high negative affect experienced their greatest job tension under conditions of moderate LMX quality. Job tension for low negative affect members did not change much over LMX conditions. Both high and low positive affect members experienced less job stress as LMX improved, but tension for low positive affect members went up again under high LMX conditions.

Again, these results were, for the most part, just what Hochwarter predicted, and he had elaborate theoretical arguments for these predictions. Before your eyes glaze over at the prospect of reading them, you may be comforted by the fact that we do not have enough space in the chapter to cover them. It is complicated, and that is our point here. Should leaders differentiate among their members? To reiterate Sparrowe and Liden's response, this is not a simple question. Indeed, given studies such as the one conducted by Hogg et al. (2005), in which personalized leadership (a kind of differentiation) worked well in low-salience groups and depersonalized leadership (undifferentiated) worked best in high-salience groups, claims regarding the consequences of high-quality LMX may be subject to all of the cautions that we described under situational theories of leadership.

Leadership as Development

In many organizational and professional settings, integration and development of new members, especially in management, professional, and certain trade occupations, occurs in mentor-protégé relationships. These relationships may be formal, but often are informal. In the traditional conception of the relationship, the new member becomes a protégé to an older or more established member who functions as a mentor (Higgins & Kram, 2001). We know of no leadership theory that specifically includes mentoring as a dimension of leadership, although Sparrowe and Liden (1997) used LMX as a framework for theorizing about sponsorship, an activity often associated with mentoring. We are identifying mentoring with leadership here because mentors lead protégés in a developmental sense. The mentor role entails teaching, guidance, counseling, appraisal, and other developmental activities, including sponsorship and promotion of the protégé's career advancement (Bolton, 1980; Shelton, 1981).

Although a mentor may also be a protégé's immediate superior, the mentor frequently occupies another role (e.g., a higher level manager or a more experienced peer at the same level of the organization). Moreover, the mentor role is inherently different from the definition of the conventional role of an immediate superior, in which the relationship is based on task rather than the objectives of career development.

Early studies of mentor-protégé relationships focused primarily on determining how common they are in the work world and whether protégé participation in such relationships actually leads to career advancement (e.g., McLane, 1980; Shelton & Curry, 1981). One investigation by Daniels and Logan (1983) specifically analyzed the communicative features of mentor-protégé relationships. They restricted their study to female managers and professionals, comparing those who participated as protégés in career development (mentor-protégé) relationships with others who only had experience as subordinates in conventional vertically linked relationships. Daniels and Logan found that levels of supportiveness, influence, satisfaction, and overall communicative activity were perceived to be much higher in career development relationships than in conventional vertically linked relationships. They also found that the mentor's supportiveness and upward influence were both important to protégés' satisfaction with the relationship.

We pointed out at the beginning of the chapter that leadership theory and research has focused mainly on the vertically linked dyad. This tendency is especially pronounced in transformational leadership theory (Yukl, 1999) and in LMX theory (Sparrowe & Liden, 1997). Similarly, the single dyadic relationship has gotten most of the attention in studies of mentor-protégé relationships. In 1985, Kathy Kram pointed out that people commonly rely on multiple relationships for career development support, not only from those in vertically linked relationships, but also from peers, professional colleagues, community members, and even family. In effect, they may have multiple career development relationships that Kram called "relationship constellations" (Higgins & Kram, 2001, p. 264). Higgins and Kram suggested that the traditional mentor-protégé perspective is much less relevant today for four reasons:

1. The contract between organization members and their employers has changed substantially, especially in terms of limited (if any) job security.

2. The rapid pace of technology change, as we noted in Chapter 7, has increased the value of knowledge workers who are not only adaptive, but also continuous learners.

3. Organizational structures have changed with virtual organizations, frequent restructuring, and more boundary spanning.

4. Organizations are increasingly diverse in terms of gender, race, ethnicity, and nationality.

In some ways, these conditions increase the desirability of career development relationships, and they may make some kinds of development relationships more relevant than others. They constrain opportunities for some, yet also create new opportunities for others.

The consequences of these organizational changes involve not only a shift in focus from the single relationship concept to a multiple relationship concept, but also a need for more attention to *developmental networks* (Higgins & Kram, 2001). Career development support from this point of view can be occurring simultaneously in multiple relationships at multiple levels both inside and outside the organization and in the context of social networks where the developmental apparatus may be much like a support group.

Motivation and Control

It is almost impossible in American culture to talk about the effectiveness of leadership without addressing motivation and control because the function of leaders is the direction of others' activities toward organizational goals. Many theories of leadership are concerned at least implicitly with the problem of motivating members. Even LMX theory, which begins with the premise that a leader's behavior is not the same with all members, values the power of "transformative leadership" in high-quality LMX conditions in which members "move beyond self-interest" (Fairhurst, 1993, p. 321).

Some of the early work on the problem of motivation and control was driven by traditional human relations values and beliefs in the linkage between communication and effective supervision. In organizational communication, one important source of these values and beliefs is a series of graduate research projects directed by W. Charles Redding at Purdue University. These studies classified supervisors as effective or ineffective on the basis of ratings by higher level managers, then examined the supervisors' communicative dispositions. Redding (1972) drew five major conclusions from these studies:

1. The best supervisors tend to be more "communication-minded." For example, they enjoy talking and speaking in meetings, they are able to explain instructions and policies, and they enjoy conversing with subordinates.

2. The best supervisors tend to be willing, empathic listeners; they respond understandingly to so-called silly questions from employees; they are approachable; and they will listen to suggestions and complaints with an attitude of fair consideration and willingness to take appropriate action.

3. The best supervisors tend (with some notable exceptions) to "ask" or "persuade," in preference to "telling" or "demanding."

4. The best supervisors tend to be sensitive to the feelings of others. For example, they are careful to reprimand in private rather than in public.

5. The best supervisors tend to be more open in their passing along of information; they are in favor of giving advance notice of impending changes and of explaining the reasons behind policies and regulations. (p. 433)

Although the Purdue studies were not directly concerned with the effect of leaders' communicative behavior on member satisfaction and morale, the tone of Redding's conclusions bears a strong resemblance to the prescription that earlier human relations theorists offered: Management promotes compliance by promoting morale and satisfaction. Morale and satisfaction depend on effective interpersonal relations: namely, empathy, sensitivity to social needs, receptivity, and two-way communication—essentially the same communicative behaviors that the Purdue studies link with "effective supervision."

Satisfaction and Communication Climate

In a classic investigation closely related to the ideal of the Purdue studies, Jack Gibb (1961) made a more direct connection between leader communication and member satisfaction by distinguishing between climates of supportive and defensive interpersonal communication. According to Gibb, a supportive climate leads to member satisfaction and accuracy in communication, whereas a defensive climate leads to dissatisfaction and distortion of communication. He identified the communicative behaviors that trigger the development of these climates. The resulting model is summarized in Table 10.2.

The influence of the Purdue studies, Gibb's model, and other studies such as those on communication openness continued through the 1980s in many investigations of factors

---

TABLE 10.2   Descriptions of Gibb's Defensive and Supportive Communication Climates

Defensive

1. *Evaluation:* To pass judgment on another; to blame or praise; make moral assessments of another or question his [or her] motives; to question the other's standards.
2. *Control:* To try to do something to another; to attempt to change behavior or attitudes of others; implicit in attempts to change others is the assumption that they are inadequate.
3. *Strategy:* To manipulate another or make him or her think that he or she was making his or her own decisions; to engage in multiple and/or ambiguous motivations; to treat the other as a guinea pig.
4. *Neutrality:* To express a lack of concern for the other; the clinical, person-as-an-object-of-study attitude.
5. *Superiority:* To communicate that you are superior in position, wealth, intelligence, etc.; to arouse feelings of inadequacy in others; to express that you are not willing to enter into joint problem solving.
6. *Certainty:* Dogmatic; wanting to win an argument rather than solve a problem; seeing one's ideas as truths to be defended.

Supportive

1. *Description:* Nonjudgmental; to ask questions which are perceived as requests for information; to present feelings, emotions, events which do not ask the other to change his or her behavior.
2. *Problem Orientation:* To convey a desire to collaborate on mutual problem solving; to allow the other to set goals and solve problems; to imply that you do not desire to impose your solution.
3. *Spontaneity:* To express naturalness; free of deception; a "clean id"; straightforwardness; uncomplicated motives.
4. *Empathy:* To respect the other person and show it; to take his [or her] role; to identify with his [or her] problems; to share his [or her] feelings.
5. *Equality:* To be willing to enter into participative planning with mutual trust and respect; to attach little importance to differences in ability, worth, status, etc.
6. *Provisionalism:* To be willing to experiment with your own behavior; to investigate issues rather than taking sides; to solve problems, not debate.

SOURCE: From Gibb (1961). Used by permission.

in organization members' satisfaction with their jobs, leaders, and organizations. Most of these studies concern the relationship between some aspect of the leader's communicative behavior and member satisfaction. Generally, these studies affirm the claim that supportive, "people-oriented" styles of communication promote satisfaction.

Motivational Limits of Leadership and Supervision

The quality of communication between leaders and members, whether understood in the context of supervision or the context of leadership, is important, but we do not want to leave the impression that morale and satisfaction are completely dependent on the behavior of leaders and supervisors. Some researchers have tried to build a more comprehensive picture of the factors that influence satisfaction. An excellent example of this kind of work is a study by Eileen Ray and Katherine Miller (1991), who found that employee job satisfaction depends on a complex set of relationships among several factors. In their study, job satisfaction was negatively related to role ambiguity and positively related to fatigue that employees experienced. As role ambiguity increased, satisfaction went down, but to some extent, fatigue led to higher satisfaction. Apparently, satisfying work is tiring work. In turn, fatigue was related to perceived workload. Role ambiguity was positively related to perceived workload and negatively related to supportiveness of one's coworkers and supervisor. Interestingly, coworker support was more important than supervisor support in lowering role ambiguity, and employee perceptions of their coworkers' supportiveness depended on the strength of the network links that they had with those coworkers.

Some motivational theories in the human resource development era of the 1960s, 1970s, and 1980s also pointed to limits in the quality of leader-member relations to influence motivation and, thus, performance. The best example of this is Frederick Herzberg's (1966) motivator-hygiene theory. Like a number of other motivational theories of the 1960s, motivator-hygiene theory is based on Abraham Maslow's (1954) need hierarchy, but Herzberg added two novel and unique features to his theory:

1. Satisfaction and dissatisfaction are *not* opposite conditions. The opposite of satisfaction is simply the absence of satisfaction.

2. The factors that lead to job satisfaction and, therefore, to motivation are different from the factors that lead to job dissatisfaction.

Herzberg observed in his studies of organizations that six factors seemed to contribute to job satisfaction and motivations for high levels of performance. A different set of 10 factors was related to job dissatisfaction. The satisfiers, called *motivators*, and the dissatisfiers, called *hygiene factors*, are as follows: motivators include achievement, recognition, advancement, the work itself, responsibility, and potential for personal growth; hygiene factors include policy and administration, technical supervision, relationships with supervisor, relationships with peers, relationships with subordinates, salary, job security, personal life, work conditions, and status.

According to Herzberg, failure to provide for organization members' hygiene needs will lead to job dissatisfaction and poor performance, but merely meeting these needs does not produce motivation to improve performance. In Herzberg's view, positive relationships between leaders and members may prevent dissatisfaction, but relationship quality will not lead to better performance. Better performance depends on incorporating the six motivators into the work environment. Thus, as Wayne Pace (1983) explains:

> A supervisor who does a good job of creating positive relationships with employees will be disappointed if he or she thinks that those employees will be motivated to work harder as a result . . . To motivate employees, the supervisor will need to find ways to give employees greater freedom and more responsibility for doing their work, or at least give them more recognition for work done well. (p. 89)

Member Behavior Toward Leaders

Feedback and Distortion

So far in this chapter we have focused on the way in which leaders behave toward members, but organization members also act toward their leaders in ways that affect the relationship and its outcomes. Historically, much of this research addressed two themes, upward distortion and feedback. We have not seen a study in many years that has attempted to describe or explain member feedback to leaders, but Jablin (1979) reviewed and summarized some studies of this type. The studies indicated generally that members provide more responsive feedback to leaders when the members have role clarity, and leaders tend to improve their own performance after receiving feedback from members.

Although most studies of upward distortion also occurred prior to Jablin's review, researchers in the 1980s continued to show some interest in this topic. Early studies of upward distortion indicated that members' mobility aspirations (desire for promotion and advancement) are *negatively* related to accuracy in upward communication, whereas trust in leaders is *positively* related (Read, 1962). As mobility aspirations go up, accuracy goes down. Increased trust is associated with increased accuracy. Other studies suggest that distortion is more likely to occur in rigid, machinelike organizational climates than in open, "organic" climates (Young, 1978).

Studies in the 1980s extended earlier research by attempting to identify other variables that influence distortion of upward communication. For example, Krivonos (1982) reviewed studies suggesting that members are more likely to distort information when that information reflects unfavorably on them. When he extended this research by distinguishing between task and nontask situations, he found that members are more likely to distort unfavorable information in a task situation but actually seem to relay unfavorable information more accurately than favorable information in a nontask situation. According to Krivonos, distortion of unfavorable information occurs in task situations because leaders exercise more power over members in such situations. The possible consequences of a "bad report" in a task situation are more ominous than they might be in a nontask situation. Because the nontask situation is less risky, members might capitalize on "pratfall effect" by accurately reporting unfavorable information. Pratfall effect occurs when a person's admission of errors or mistakes actually increases his or her credibility with others.

Upward Influence

More recently, scholars have turned their attention away from traditional topics such as feedback and upward distortion in order to explore new themes about member behaviors in communicating with leaders. One newer theme concerns members' use of influence tactics in upward communication. Put another way, we know that leaders are trying to manage members, but how does the member manage the leader? As a result of the same organizational changes that Higgins and Kram noted in their reframing of the mentor-protégé concept, the opportunities for exerting influence also have changed. Hence, the issue of upward influence has generated dozens of research investigations and theoretical models through the 1980s and 1990s. Much of this work is summarized in an extensive monograph by Waldron (1999).

Waldron reviewed studies of a dozen different contextual factors under the general categories of relationship factors, individual differences, and situational factors. We will note only a few that either relate directly to other topics in this chapter or otherwise seem to us to be particularly important.

One contextual factor of interest to several researchers is LMX. We already have described LMX mainly from the standpoint of leader behaviors, but LMX also sets a context for members' communication with leaders. Krone (1992) found that members in high-quality LMX conditions used open, logic-based tactics rather than covert, deceptive tactics in the attempts to influence leaders. Deluga and Perry (1991) got similar results, specifically, limited use of hard tactics such as coercion in high-quality LMX. One benefit for leaders in fostering undifferentiated, high-quality LMX may be that members are likely to be more honest, direct, and reasonable with attempts at influencing those leaders.

High-quality LMX may amount to a kind of leadership style, but Waldron treats leadership style as a different contextual factor. Here, again, studies have indicated a link between leadership style and members' use of upward influence tactics. Ansari and Kapoor (1987) found that followers working under participative styles of leadership tended to use reasoning tactics in upward influence attempts. Where leadership style is low in both initiation and consideration (i.e., laissez-faire), Chacko (1990) found that members use so-called hard tactics.

One additional factor worth considering is power, or, more to the point, the degree of power difference between leader and member. Generally speaking, research on upward influence assumes at least implicitly that upward influence is a different process from downward influence simply because of power inequalities. Many tactics used in upward influence might be similar to the tactics used in downward influence, but that does not mean that the less powerful party uses them in the same way that the more powerful party uses them. More powerful members appear to use a greater variety of influence tactics with leaders and to use them more frequently than less powerful members do (Ferris & Judge, 1991). Waldron and Hunt (1992) also found that upward influence tactics are associated with members' position in the organizational hierarchy. Higher level members are more likely to use direct tactics in their attempts to influence leaders.

INTERPRETIVE PERSPECTIVE

The idea that leadership is largely symbolic seems to fit easily into the interpretive viewpoint, but the interpretive perspective is still concerned mainly with the collective, pluralistic construction of social reality and negotiated order rather than the leader's solo act of influencing members. Most of the research and writing on transformational leadership theory, which explicitly emphasizes symbolism, actually has been done within the traditional perspective, although a new book by Gail T. Fairhurst (2007) on the topic of discursive leadership is likely to set the stage for extensive interpretive inquiry in this area. Moreover, most of the contemporary work that applies interpretive methods to leader-member communication does so from a critical point of view as described in the next section. Except for a large number of rhetorical studies on major political or social movement leaders, there seem to be relatively few truly interpretive studies of leadership communication per se. The examples that we include here are concerned with the symbolic power of leader discourse and its relationship to other processes that, as Yukl put it, make events meaningful for members.

Leadership, Structure, and Meaning

Vallaster and de Chernatony (2006) studied how organization members align their actions with the identity of the organization in a corporate context. These two European researchers use the term "brand" to refer to corporate identify and use "internal brand building" to refer to the alignment process. They also do something that might alarm most interpretive scholars: They state some beliefs about what they expected to find in their study.

Vallaster and de Chernatony note that the literature of corporate branding points mainly to structural aspects of organizations that express identity as drivers for internal brand building. Drawing on Giddens's structuration theory, they describe how structures of interpretive schemes, norms, and resources constrain and enable organization members. Members do not create these systems, but they do reproduce and transform them. But why do some instances of such reproduction succeed in becoming institutionalized whereas others fail? Vallaster and de Chernatony contend that structuration theory cannot answer this question, and they refer to other critics of structuration theory to support this claim. They believe that leadership is an additional and crucial ingredient in aligning individual action with brand identity.

Their study involved extensive interviews with persons from multiple levels of management in nine Austrian and German corporations as well as close examination of corporate documents. After extracting what they called "distinct categories of meaning" from the texts of interviews and documents, they organized them into "theoretical memos" from which they derived relationships among corporate structures, individual action, and leadership.

The result of their work suggested that correspondence between the formal corporate identity and the culture of the organization "was widely acknowledged as a key component of the firm's overall corporate branding strategy" (p. 767). In other words, alignment of individual members actions with the brand depends on consistency between the desired corporate identity and the actual corporate culture. They also found that corporate design (graphics, logo, and brand-related language) supported member identification with the brand. Salary and incentive systems generally were not tailored specifically to reward identification and alignment, mainly out of concern that such reward systems are too controlling.

What about leadership? Vallaster and de Chernatony concluded from their study that "successful leaders are those who consistently and repeatedly communicate messages to employees about the brand identity and commitment to living the brand's promise" (p. 772). They noted that the symbolism of leader discourse does not ensure alignment of individual action with the corporate identity, but it does provide a significant statement of values and priorities. In addition, by showing their own commitment to the brand values and identity, successful leaders "act as facilitators between structures and individuals, creating a framework that encourages brand supporting employee behaviours" (p. 773).

Leadership and Ethics

Another area in which interpretive approaches have been applied to leadership communication is the area of leaders' ethical responsibilities. Seeger and Ulmer (2003) used the case of Enron Corporation to show how ethical failures in leadership can lead to catastrophe. Their study is based mainly on works of other journalists and scholars who covered or studied Enron rather than on direct examination of leader discourse, but they relied on some basic interpretive assumptions to guide their study.

Seeger and Ulmer begin with the proposition that "leadership is inherently a communication-based process involving clarifying goals and methods, motivating and persuading followers, resolving conflict, and framing meaning" (p. 63). Working from this proposition, they identified three basic, communication-based leader responsibilities in the literature of ethics and leadership. These responsibilities are "(a) communicating appropriate values to create a moral climate; (b) maintaining adequate communication to be informed of organizational operations; and (c) maintaining openness to signs of problems" (p. 63). Then, they proceeded to show through examination of reports about leader discourse and behavior how Enron's senior executives, especially Ken Lay and Jeff Skilling, not only failed in these responsibilities, but also acted in ways that were antithetical to them.

Enron Corporation developed from humble beginnings as a gas pipeline company. It was transformed under Ken Lay's leadership into a multinational enterprise regarded widely by many business and government leaders as America's premier energy company. In 2001, the company collapsed in a wave of accounting and financial scandals and the realization by investors that the idea of Enron as a highly profitable leader in innovation was an illusion built on fraud and irrational business models.

On the surface, Enron had the appearance of an ethically responsible company, right down to its 1996 Statement of Human Rights emphasizing respect, integrity, communication, and excellence (also known in the company as RICE). Although all employees were required to sign a RICE compliance agreement, RICE in practice was not taken seriously because executives fostered and rewarded a very different set of values.

Lay actually emphasized an entrepreneurial vision of aggressive and radical innovation. Seeger and Ulmer show how this vision, under Skilling, was "driven to new levels of excess and eventually corrupted into a self-serving ethic of greed" (p. 71). In spite of the lip service given to RICE, Lay and Skilling actually modeled values of privilege, wealth, arrogance, and the acceptability of power abuse and rule breaking when it suits one's ends to do so. Others ranging from Andy Fastow, the chief financial officer who concocted schemes to hide Enron's debt, to Enron energy traders, who manipulated electricity supplies to spike prices in California, flourished in this culture of corruption.

Rather than assuming a responsibility to be informed, Enron executives also engaged in what one Securities and Exchange Commission officer described as "willful blindness" (p. 73). Enron was a decentralized organization made even more so when Skilling eliminated several levels from the formal organizational structure. The resulting four-level system was very flexible and very fast. Relatively autonomous units could act on opportunities, seeking approval only at the final stages of deal making or sometimes not at all. As you have seen at other points in the book, this kind of decentralization and flexibility is associated with the idea of member empowerment, but Seeger and Ulmer suggest that Lay and Skilling actually did not want to know details of operations because being unaware of them created plausible deniability if anything went wrong. The result was an environment with "little oversight or control and few reviews of decisions" (p. 73).

Willful blindness also extended to ignoring or avoiding signs of problems rather than being open to them. As we noted in Chapter 3, distortion or shaping of upward communication by members to fit what they believe leaders want to hear is a well-known phenomenon. According to Seeger and Ulmer, instead of creating a system that encouraged identification and attention to problems, "Enron executives created the opposite" (p. 74). Lay and Skilling were obsessed with the value of the company's stock, and negative information that might affect that value was unwelcome. The culture of discouraging bad news was sufficiently pervasive that Sherron Watkins, the first inside whistle-blower to go to Lay with concerns about the potential disaster of accounting scandals, concealed her identity with an anonymous memo. At least some of what Watkins knew had been deciphered by financial analysts, and questions had been raised about the company in the *Wall Street Journal*, but Andy Fastow was not fired until banks literally refused to do business with Enron. Fastow himself instilled fear of reporting bad news in outside financial firms by threatening them with the loss of Enron's lucrative investment banking business if their analysts produced unfavorable reports about the company.

CRITICAL PERSPECTIVE

The critical perspective has inspired entire books on the subject of leadership (e.g., Maxcy, 1991). As we note elsewhere in this book, power is a central theme in the critical perspective, especially where, through manipulation of symbols and discourse, "the interests of those with power are disguised as universal interests serving all members of the organization" (Frost, 1987, p. 506). Drawing on earlier work by Conrad (1983) and Conrad and Ryan (1985), Brenton (1993) described power as "a dynamic process of signification and legitimation involving interactions between leaders and followers" (p. 228), so the arena of leader-member relations is rich territory for critical scholars. In arguing for his collectivist vision of leadership, Barker (1997) characterized leadership as a social construction that has distorted the concept into an essentially manipulative enterprise. He suggested, for example, that Burns's original concept of transformational leadership emphasized a relational context, but Bass and others reinterpreted it to fit the traditional influence paradigm "as simply an extension of their old views" (p. 350). Gemmill and Oakley (1992) went even further, characterizing this traditional paradigm as a myth that serves mainly to preserve existing systems.

Critical scholarship on leader-member communication addresses a range of issues, but most of this work covers three basic topics:

- The discourse of individual leaders in their efforts to influence members.
- The consequences of discursive practices of leadership and management groups in general.
- The discourse of resistance to leadership.

Leader as Individual Agent

Although the critical point of view actually challenges the value of viewing leadership as the activity of an individual, one way to understand the dynamic of power in leader-member relations is to examine the discourse of individual leaders as they attempt to influence members. Harrison and Young (2005) provide an example of this approach in a study of the government agency that administers Canada's system of socialized health care. The agency was subjected to a major reorganization, including formation of an entirely new and large branch over a four-month period in 2000. Harrison and Young studied the discourse of the person who was appointed to lead the new branch in an effort to understand "how [a leader's] concealed messages contribute to the success or failure of discursive events, specifically at a time of organizational transformation" (p. 42). In this case, Harrison and Young focused on two specific messages. One was an informal speech delivered by the leader during his first meeting with his team of senior managers. The other was a memorandum distributed six weeks later by e-mail to all employees in the new branch.

The leader was a veteran of many years of service in traditional bureaucratic systems, and he was comfortable with directive, command-and-control leadership. At the same time, he was sensitive to "new capitalist" (neoliberal) trends toward globalization, market economies, technology, and innovation in which value is placed on transformational leadership and worker empowerment, i.e., a vision of the leader "not as a commander, but as a coach, mentor, facilitator, and motivator" (p. 47). According to Harrison and Young, the differences between the speech to the senior managers and the e-mail to all employees reflect a tension between these two visions of leadership.

The speech had two basic aims. The first was forging unity and social cohesion in the ranks of senior management through a discourse of internal identification and characterization of outside forces and agents that pose threats to the group. The second was motivating and inspiring management to meet the deadline for making the new branch fully operational by invoking a sense of challenge and opportunity along with moral obligation on the part of management to act.

In the e-mail message to all employees, the leader espoused values of transparency, consultation, and open communication, but he also established "a subtle separation" (p. 63) between management and the employees. For example, he encouraged all employees to contact members of his staff (referring to senior management) and talk to their managers about concerns. The memorandum described plans for the branch as well as actions already taken with the implication that certain decisions were made already and not open to question. Moreover, the leader used a concealment strategy regarding "hot issues" involved in the reorganization by depersonalizing decisions about those issues. The discourse described purposes, goals, and challenges without any reference to how they were defined and who was doing the defining.

According to Harrison and Young, the consequences of the two messages also were quite different. The speech to senior management, a new capitalist exercise in the discourse of transformational leadership, fostered management team spirit and subsequent cooperation with the leader. The memorandum to employees, intended on the surface to be inclusive, was undercut by the values of traditional, bureaucratic management. The leader's offer at the outset of a seemingly participatory system was interpreted as a sham, and people "knew they were being moved around like pawns on a chessboard" (p. 67). Harrison and Young seem to attribute the difference to the leader's own internal conflicts about the two styles of management, but the difference also could be quite deliberate and strategic, although the result for the employees was disappointment and cynicism about the change.

Leadership Discourse in General

One portal into the subject of leadership discourse in general is the language of management. Fairclough (2004) contends that "the language of management has colonized public institutions and organizations" (p. 105). It dominates organizational discourse and shapes our understanding of organizational experience. One variation of this managerial language is managerial pseudojargon as described in a study by Watson (2004).

According to Watson, "Managerial pseudojargon is a form of language widely used in corporate settings" (p. 67). The form is not really the kind of specialized language used within a community of experts such as physicians, lawyers, or engineers, but it appears on the surface to be such a language.

Managerial pseudojargon is based on terms and phrases that one does not generally hear in ordinary language outside corporations and institutions, although some of it may be quite familiar to you. It includes words and phrases such as thinking outside the box, tasked with, repurposed, strategic vision, customer focused, rightsizing, driving forward the mission, value added, performance metrics, and seamless process.

The list provides just a few examples. Watson collected many other examples of and stories about managerial pseudojargon to understand how it functions from a critical standpoint.

Watson identified two distinct categories of pseudojargon. One involves use of metaphors to make abstract aspects of organizational life seem to be concrete. He noted that sports metaphors, e.g., hit a home run, scoring inside the red zone, and playing hurt, are especially prominent in this category. Such metaphors may very well offer a kind of shorthand expression with meanings that are intuitively obvious to many organization members, but consider a statement such as, "You must think outside the box." In one sense, all of us may know what this means, i.e., a concrete, visual metaphor for the abstract process of escaping constraints on creative problem solving. In another sense, the phrase is little more than a cliché, and it does nothing to illuminate just how one is supposed to get out of the box.

Reading Watson's study reminded your authors of another example that all three of us have heard in corporate and government organizations. The phrase "steep learning curve" is used to describe a task that is difficult to master. In fact, as Atherton (2003) noted, the underlying concepts of a learning curve are just the opposite; steep curves are easy, shallow curves are hard, and the person who characterizes something difficult as a steep learning curve unwittingly reveals a misunderstanding of the concept. Not surprisingly, many participants in one survey examined by Watson admitted that they use managerial pseudojargon without knowing what it really means.

The second category of pseudojargon identified by Watson has an ideological function. It is not used merely to make abstract ideas more concrete. It is used instead to reinforce and legitimize the power of leadership and management. Here the language becomes or at least takes on the appearance of being instrumental and technical. Consider an executive officer speaking to other organization members about "selecting the right metrics to assess effective leveraging of resources in an integrated process to realize the strategic vision." Such a statement certainly sounds authoritative, emanating from expertise or maybe even profound insight. According to Watson, "The language demands respect from non-experts" (p. 79), obliging the member to place trust in the leader. At the same time, the language actually mystifies the work of management and leadership. How is a metric selected or a resource leveraged or a process integrated? It all sounds rather complex. Moreover, the language emphasizes technical means while obscuring the ends served by these means. As Watson explains it, "Outcomes are emphasized as important, but they are utterly nonspecific in terms of human values" (p. 79).

Managerial pseudojargon also seems to have an international reach. Watson's study was conducted in Britain, and some of his examples, such as sports metaphors, are situated specifically in British culture, so we used American equivalents here. But most of Watson's examples, especially those with ideological functions, are examples that we also see frequently in American usage.

The Discourse of Resistance

A third area of interest in critical studies of leadership is resistance. Critical theory tends to see ordinary organization members as somewhat unaware of oppression insofar as they have internalized management interests as their own. As Frost (1987) puts it, because power is a "real but unperceived part of the interpretive framework of actors, it is virtually impossible for some of the actors to recognize that their interests are not being met" (p. 506). But even assuming this condition to be true for at least some actors, critical theory also seems to recognize that this is not the case for all actors. Members do resist the efforts of leaders to influence and control them.

Recognition of resistance in organizational settings certainly is not new, and it is not a unique insight in the critical perspective. The Hawthorne Studies of the 1920s, described in Chapter 4, revealed the power of informal workgroup norms to prevail over management plans. Scholars in traditional and interpretive perspectives also have studied resistance in organizational communication, but the traditional aim is to overcome or at least manage resistance, and the interpretive aim is to understand how it plays out in the negotiation of organization order. The critical perspective is concerned with the contribution of resistance to workplace emancipation and democratization, concepts that we discuss in more detail in Chapter 14.

Resistance studies often are focused mostly on the communicative actions of members. One investigation by Brenton (1993) actually explores the legitimizing discourse of leaders against the delegitimizing discourse of member resistance in a case where leaders ultimately lost the battle for legitimacy.

Brenton's study focused on conflict that developed over a 10-year period within a church congregation. The church elders, as the formal leaders of the congregation, had exercised absolute authority over church affairs. They controlled all of the church's formal systems of communication and decision making. According to Brenton, this authority largely was accepted and unquestioned by most, but not all, of the members. Three members of the congregation ultimately came together as plaintiffs in a lawsuit against the elders. The plaintiffs obtained a court order for the elders to release certain church documents. When the elders refused, one plaintiff and an elder got into a physical confrontation that was featured in local media. The confrontation led to two discursive events that Brenton examined to show how the discourse of resistance overcame the discourse of legitimacy.

In the first event, the plaintiff who had gotten into the physical confrontation with the elder spoke out during a regular ritual of public confession in the morning church service to apologize and ask forgiveness for his role in the confrontation, but he also took advantage of the occasion to directly challenge the authority of the elders and point out that the elders, by refusing to comply with the court order, were placing themselves above the law. Brenton called this discourse tactic "defamiliarizing the context of utterance" (p. 236). This particular ritual has very clear expectations for how it is to be performed (familiarity). The disgruntled church member used the ritual in a way that conformed to those expectations in one sense, but also violated them in another (defamiliarizing). Breaking the cultural rules in this way might have been risky, but the effect, according to Brenton, was a "potent symbolic action" (p. 236). In any case, the elders responded with a statement of their own on the evening of the same day.

This second event, the elders' release of their own statement, was an "attempt to reproduce the legitimacy of their authority" (p. 231). Their statement offered no apology or assumption of responsibility for the confrontation. They suggested instead that the plaintiffs were trying to exceed the scope of the court order by demanding records that were confidential and not covered by that order; that their refusal to turn over the records was a rational choice in a situation with few options. But the elders also faced a dilemma in this response. On one hand, they were portraying themselves as victims. On the other hand, they needed to show strength, which they did in the message by identifying the elders as distinct from the rest of the congregation.

Although the court order to release church records ultimately was overturned on appeal, the elders were forced in the process to make previously implicit claims of absolute authority over the church much more explicit. For most of the congregation, this was a turning point. Brenton concludes, "Members of the congregation who would never have questioned the implicit ideology . . . would not accept the explicit claims that elders made about the extent of their authority" (p. 239). The elders won the battle over the records, but lost the war over legitimacy of their authority in the church.

SUMMARY

Leadership generally is regarded as essential to group and organizational effectiveness. Leadership and supervision by superiors are presumed to be necessary in order to initiate structure and direct members toward organizational goals. The study of leader-member relations in our culture has been preoccupied with a quest to identify the essence of effective leadership and with understanding effective leadership mainly in terms of influence. The literature of leadership theory and research tends to focus on lower levels of organizations, on the dyadic (especially vertically linked) relationship, and on an individualized conception of leaders.

Leadership itself has been studied as a trait and as a style in an effort to identify ideal leadership behaviors, but situational theorists suggest that no one approach to leadership is right for all situations. Trait-based research has produced no agreement among scholars on a consistent set of traits that either distinguishes leaders from nonleaders or relates to leadership effectiveness. Stylistic theories have identified clear forms of leadership behavior. Models such as the Leadership Grid suggest that team leadership is an ideal arrangement, and transformational leadership theory suggests that transformational leadership is more effective than transactional leadership and that transactional forms are more effective than laissez-faire forms. However, situational constraints including task structure, group characteristics, and traits of members may influence the effectiveness of a given style.

Advocates of leader-member exchange theory also have shown that leaders do not act in a consistent way toward all members, but treat different members in different ways. Studies suggesting that LMX can be relatively good or bad also imply prescriptions for leadership effectiveness that appear to be subject to situational constraints.

Leadership also may be viewed as a developmental activity in the context of mentor-protégé relationships. New conditions in organizational environments, however, suggest that a shift from mentor-protégé to developmental network concepts is now a more appropriate way to understand career development support.

One pervasive issue in the study of leadership and supervision centers on motivation and control, i.e., the means by which superiors are able to direct subordinates. Early human relations theory emphasized especially the connection between subordinates' satisfaction and subordinates' compliance with superiors, stressing especially the quality of supervisory communication in promoting satisfaction. The Purdue studies of effective supervision and Gibb's model of defensive and supportive communication both are testaments to human relations principles, providing support for the argument that effective supervision is related to positive, open, and receptive communication behaviors. It is not clear whether any of these factors is connected with task performance, and human resource development theories of motivation such as Herzberg's motivator-hygiene theory challenge the idea that the quality of leader-member relationships will motivate subordinates to perform better.

Although a climate of open, supportive, and trust-based communication may be the ideal in leader-member relationships, leaders' claims that they have adopted these ideals may be based more on wishful thinking than on fact. Studies of leaders' communicative behaviors in attempts of compliance gaining, influence, and conflict management with members suggest that coercive, threatening, autocratic, and punitive tactics are still quite common. Factors such as low self-esteem and confidence in one's supervisory abilities, external locus of control, and mistrust of members continue to promote defensive styles of communication.

Members' behaviors toward superiors also are far removed from a picture-perfect representation of openness and supportiveness. Studies continue to show that distortion is a common occurrence in upward communication and that various situational factors may contribute to this phenomenon. Moreover, although members generally are in a less powerful position in the leader-member relationship, they certainly are not powerless. They can and do attempt to influence their leaders. Situational constraints including LMX, leadership style, and degree of power difference also shape upward influence attempts.

True interpretive studies of leader-member relations are relatively uncommon, in part because much of this work has moved in a critical direction. Interpretive studies have suggested that leaders are important figures in mediating the relationship between organizational structures and the actions of organization members and in shaping meanings of organizational experience for members. Interpretive work also has addressed the potentially serious consequences of ethical failures in leadership.

Since power involves signification and legitimation in interactions between leaders and members, the arena of leader-member relations is rich territory for critical scholars. Critical scholarship on leader-member communication addresses a range of issues, but most of this work covers the discourse of individual leaders in their efforts to influence members, the consequences of discursive practices of leadership and management groups in general, and the discourse of resistance to leadership. Critical scholarship has provided insights on the ways in which leaders' concealed messages influence organization members; the degree to which the language of management and leadership "colonizes" organizations, legitimizes leadership, and mystifies leadership; and the ways in which the delegitimizing discourse of resistance can overcome the legitimizing discourse of leadership.

DISCUSSION QUESTIONS/ACTIVITIES

1. Some scholars believe that the leader-member relationship is the most important level at which organizational communication occurs. What is the basis for this belief? Do you agree or disagree? Why?

2. Identify some of the reasons for researchers' preoccupation with the study of leader-member relationships and superior-subordinate communication.

3. After studying the chapter discussion, write a summary of what we think we know about leadership and superior-subordinate communication. Are there any problems with some of the conclusions that we have drawn? Discuss your summary with others in your class.

4. What is the connection, if any, between effective leadership or supervision and performance of organization members?

REFERENCES

Ackoff, R. L. (1998). A systemic view of transformational leadership. *Systemic Practice and Action Research, 11*(1), 23–36.

Albrecht, T. L., & Ropp, V. A. (1984). Communicating about innovation in networks of three U.S. organizations. *Journal of Communication, 34,* 78–91.

Ansari, M. A., & Kapoor, A. (1987). Organizational context and upward influence tactics. *Organizational Behavior and Human Decision Processes, 40,* 39–49.

Atherton, J. S. (2003) *Learning and teaching: Learning curve* [On-line] UK. Retrieved January 28, 2007, from http://www.learningandteaching.info/learning/lerncrv.htm

Avolio, B. J. (1999). Full leadership development: Building the vital forces in organizations. Thousand Oaks, CA: Sage.

Barker, R. A. (1997). How can we train leaders if we do not know what leadership is? *Human Relations, 50*(4), 343–362.

Barlow, C. B., Jordan, M., & Hendrix, W. H. (2003). Character assessment: An examination of leadership levels. *The Journal of Business and Psychology, 17*(4), 563–584.

Bass, B. M. (1985). *Leadership and performance beyond expectations.* New York: Free Press.

Bass, B. M. (1996). *A new paradigm of leadership: An inquiry into transformational leadership.* Alexandria, VA: U.S. Army Research Institute for the Behavioral and Social Sciences.

Bass, B. M., & Avolio, B. J. (1998). Improving organizational effectiveness through transformational leadership. Introduction. In G. R. Hickman (Ed.), *Leading organizations: Perspectives for a new era* (pp. 135–140). Thousand Oaks: Sage.

Bennis, W. (1976a). Leadership—A beleaguered species. *Organizational Dynamics, 5,* 3–16.

Bennis, W. (1976b). *The unconscious conspiracy: why leaders can't lead.* New York: American Management Association.

Blake, R. R., & McCanse, A. A. (1991). *Leadership dilemmas—Grid solutions.* Houston: Gulf.

Blake, R. R., & Mouton, J. S. (1964). *The managerial grid.* Houston: Gulf.

Blake, R. R., & Mouton, J. S. (1985). *The managerial grid III: The key to leadership excellence.* Houston: Gulf.

Bolton, E. (1980). A conceptual analysis of the mentor relationship in the career development of women. *Adult Education, 30,* 195–207.

Brenton, A. L. (1993). Demystifying the magic of language: Critical linguistic case analysis of legitimation of authority. *Journal of Applied Communication Research, 21*(3), 227–244.

Burns, J. M. (1978). *Leadership.* New York: Harper & Row.

Chacko, H. E. (1990). Methods of upward influence, motivational needs, and administrators' perceptions of their supervisors' leadership styles. *Group and Organizational Studies, 15,* 253–265.

Conrad C. (1983). Organizational power: Faces and symbolic forms. In L. L. Putnam and M. E. Pacanowski (Eds.), *Communication and organizations: An interpretive perspective* (pp. 172–194). Beverly Hills, CA: Sage.

Conrad, C., & Ryan, M. (1985). Power, praxis, and self in organizational communication theorey. In R. D. McPhee & P. K. Tompkins (Eds.), *Organizational communication: Traditional themes and new directions* (pp. 233–258). Beverly Hills, CA: Sage.

Daniels, T. D., & Logan, L. L. (1983). Communication in women's career development relationships. In R. N. Bostrom (Ed.), *Communication yearbook 7* (pp. 532–553). Beverly Hills, CA: Sage.

Deluga, R. J., & Perry, J. T. (1991). The relationship of upward-influencing behavior, satisfaction, and perceived superior effectiveness with leader-member exchanges. *Journal of Occupational Psychology, 64,* 239–252.

Denis, J.-L., Langley, A., & Cazale, L. (1996). Leadership and strategic change under ambiguity. *Organizational Studies, 17*(4), 673–699.

Eblen, A. L. (1987). Communication, leadership, and organizational commitment. *Central States Speech Journal, 38,* 181–195.

Fairclough, N. (2004). Critical discourse analysis in researching language in the new capitalism: Overdetermination, transdisciplinarity, and textual analysis. In L. Young & C. Harrison (Eds.), *Systemic functional linguistics and critical discourse analysis: Studies in social change* (pp. 103–122). London: Continuum.

Fairhurst, G. T. (1993). The leader-member exchange patterns of women leaders in industry: A discourse analysis. *Communication Monographs, 60,* 321–351.

Fairhurst, G. T. (2007). *Discursive leadership: In conversation with leadership psychology.* Thousand Oaks, CA: Sage.

Fairhurst, G. T., & Chandler, T. A. (1989). Social structure in leader-member interaction. *Communication Monographs, 56,* 215–239.

Ferris, G. R., & Judge, T. A. (1991). Personnel/human resources management: A political influence perspective. *Journal of Management, 17,* 447–488.

Fiedler, F. (1967). *A theory of leadership effectiveness.* New York: McGraw-Hill.

Frost, P. J. (1987). Power, politics, and influence. In F. M. Jablin, L. L. Putnam, K. H. Roberts, & L. W. Porter (Eds.), *Handbook of organizational communication: An interdisciplinary perspective* (pp. 502–548). Newbury Park, CA: Sage.

Gastil, J. (1994). A definition and illustration of democratic leadership. *Human Relations, 47,* 953–975.

Gemmill, G., & Oakley, J. (1992). Leadership: An alienating social myth? *Human Relations, 45,* 113–129.

Gibb, J. (1961). Defensive communication. *Journal of Communication, 11,* 141–148.

Graen, G. (1976). Role-making processes within complex organizations. In M. D. Dunnette (Ed.), *Handbook of industrial and organizational psychology* (pp. 1201–1245). Chicago: Rand McNally.

Harrison, C., & Young, L. (2005). Leadership discourse in action: A textual study of organizational change in a government of Canada department. *Journal of Business and Technical Communication, 19*(1), 42–77.

Hersey, P., & Blanchard, K. (1982). *Management of organizational behavior: Utilizing human resources* (4th ed.). Englewood Cliffs, NJ: Prentice Hall.

Herzberg, F. (1966). *Work and the nature of man.* New York: Collins.

Higgins, M. C., & Kram, K. E. (2001). Reconceptualizing mentoring at work: A developmental network perspective. *Academy of Management Review, 26*(2), 264–288.

Hochwarter, W. (2005). LMX and job tension: Linear and non-linear effects and affectivity. *Journal of Business and Psychology, 19*(4), 505–520.

Hogg, M. A., Martin, R., Epitropaki, O., Mankad, A., Svensson, A., & Weeden, K. (2005). Effective leadership in salient groups: Revisiting leader-member exchange theory from the perspective of the social identity theory of leadership. *Personality and Social Psychology Bulletin, 31*(7), 991–1004.

Jablin, F. M. (1979). Superior-subordinate communication: The state of the art. *Psychological Bulletin, 86,* 1201–1222.

Jennings, E. (1961). The anatomy of leadership. *Management of Personnel Quarterly, 11,* 2.

Kirkbride, P. (2006). Developing transformation leaders: The full range leadership model in action. *Industrial and Commercial Training, 36*(1), 23–32.

Knause, C. (1990, March). Letter stating the position of Scientific Methods, Inc., on the origin of the managerial grid.

Koehler, J. W., Anatol, K. W. E., & Applbaum, R. L. (1981). *Organizational communication: Behavioral perspectives* (2nd ed.). New York: Holt, Rinehart & Winston.

Kornor, H., & Nordvik, H. (2004). Personality traits in leadership behavior. *The Scandinavian Journal of Psychology, 45,* 49–54.

Kram, K. E. (1985). *Mentoring at work.* Glenview, IL: Scott, Foresman.

Krivonos, P. D. (1982). Distortion of subordinate to superior communication in organizational settings. *Central States Speech Journal, 33,* 345–352.

Krone, K. J. (1992). A comparison of organizational, structural, and relationship effects on subordinates' upward influence choices. *Communication Quarterly, 40,* 1–15.

Lee, J. (1999). Leader-member exchange, gender, and members' communication expectations with leaders. *Communication Quarterly, 47*(4), 415–429.

Lee, J. (2001). Leader-member exchange, perceived organizational justice, and cooperative communication. *Management Communication Quarterly, 14*(4), 574–589.

Lee, J., & Jablin, F. M. (1995). Maintenance communication in superior-subordinate relationships. *Human Communication Research, 22,* 220–257.

Maslow, A. H. (1954). *Motivation and personality.* New York: Harper & Row.

Maxcy, S. J. (1991). *Educational leadership: A critical pragmatic perspective.* Westport, CT: Greenwood.

McKenna, B. (2004). Critical discourse studies: Where to from here? *Critical Discourse Studies, 1*(1), 9–39.

McLane, H. J. (1980). *Selecting, developing, and retaining women executives.* New York: Van Nostrand Reinhold.

Morrow, P. C., Suzuki, Y., Crum, M. R., Ruben, R., & Pautsch, G. (2005). The role of leader-member exchange in high turnover work environments. *Journal of Managerial Psychology, 20*(8), 681–694.

Ozaralli, N. (2003). Effects of transformational leadership on empowerment and team effectiveness. *Leadership and Organization Development Journal, 24*(6), 335–344.

Pace, R. W. (1983). *Organizational communication: Foundations for human resource development.* Englewood Cliffs, NJ: Prentice Hall.

Pawar, B. S., & Eastman, K. K. (1997). The nature and implications of contextual influences on transformational leadership: A conceptual examination. *Academy of Management Review, 22*(1), 80–109.

Rafferty, A. E., & Griffin, M. A. (2004). Dimensions of transformational leadership: Conceptual and empirical extensions. *The Leadership Quarterly, 15,* 329–354.

Ray, E. B., & Miller, K. I. (1991). The influence of communication structure and social support on job stress and burnout. *Management Communication Quarterly, 4,* 506–527.

Read, W. H. (1962). Upward communication in industrial hierarchies. *Human Relations, 15,* 3–15.

Redding, W. C. (1972). *Communication within the organization: An interpretive review of theory and research.* New York: Industrial Communication Council.

Seeger, M. W., & Ulmer, R. R. (2003). Explaining Enron: Communication and responsible leadership. *Management Communication Quarterly, 17*(1), 58–84.

Shelton, C. (1981, July). Mentoring programs: Do they make a difference? *National Association of Banking Women Journal,* p. 25.

Shelton, C., & Curry, J. (1981, July). Mentoring at Security Pacific. *National Association of Banking Women Journal,* p. 25.

Sparrowe, R. T., & Liden, R. C. (1997). Process and structure in leader-member exchange. *Academy of Management Review, 22*(2), 522–553.

Storey, J. (2005). What next for strategic-level leadership research? *Leadership, 1*(1), 89–104.

Tjosvold, D. (1985). Power and social context in superior-subordinate interaction. *Organizational Behavior and Human Decision Processes, 35,* 381–293.

Vallaster, C., & de Chernatony, L. (2006). Internal brand building and structuration: The role of leadership. *European Journal of Marketing, 40*(7/8), 761–784.

Waldron, V. R. (1991). Achieving communication goals in superior-subordinate relationships: The multi-functionality of upward maintenance tactics. *Communication Monographs, 58,* 289–306.

Waldron, V. R. (1999). Communication practices of followers, members, protégés: The case of upward influence tactics. In M. E. Roloff (Ed.), *Communication yearbook 22* (pp. 251–299). Thousand Oaks, CA: Sage.

Waldron, V. R., & Hunt, M. D. (1992). Hierarchical level, length, and quality of supervisory relationship as predictors of subordinates' use of maintenance tactics. *Communication Reports, 5,* 82–89.

Watson, T. J. (2004). Managers, managism, and the tower of babble: Making sense of managerial pseudojargon. *International Journal of the Sociology of Language, 166,* 67–82.

White, R., & Lippitt, R. (1960). *Autocracy and democracy.* New York: Harper & Row.

Young, J. W. (1978). The subordinate's exposure of organizational vulnerability to the superior: Sex and organizational effects. *Academy of Management Journal, 21,* 113–122.

Yukl, G. (1999). An evaluation of conceptual weaknesses in transformational hand charismatic leadership theories. *Leadership Quarterly, 10*(2), 285–305.

Yukl, G. (2006). *Leadership in organizations* (6th ed.). Upper Saddle River, NJ: Prentice Hall.

Zaccaro, S., & Horn, Z. (2003). Leadership theory and practice: Fostering an effective symbiosis. *Leadership Quarterly, 14,* 769–806.

Power

We began this text with the simple observation that organizations are constituted through communication. The constitutive function of communication, however, depends on the manner in which it is used to exercise one of the most pervasive phenomenon in organizational life—power. Russell (1983) claims that power is the fundamental concept in the social sciences, analogous to the place of energy in physics. W. Charles Redding (1985) expressed the importance of power in organizational life quite neatly, though somewhat grimly, during some informal comments to members of the International Communication Association's organizational communication division. "We must not forget," said Redding, "that organizations run on subservience." Subservience means being submissive or acting as a servant. Consequently, organizational power is tied to status.

TRADITIONAL VIEWS OF STATUS AND POWER

In hierarchically structured organizations, differences in members' status and power are a simple fact of life. These differences, in large part, create the "top to bottom" character of contemporary organizations. Even within groups, different members are accorded varying degrees of power and status. Just as some members of a group have more power and status than others, some groups within an organization have more prestige and are better able to exert influence than other groups.

Status refers essentially to the rank or importance of one's position in a group. Traditionally, power has been regarded as any means or resource that one person may employ to gain compliance and cooperation from others (Secord & Backman, 1964). As Dahl (1957) expressed it, power is the capacity of actor A to get actor B to do what actor B would not otherwise do. Traditional views of power also recognize that it involves the ability to control the agenda or plan of action in a situation and to suppress issues in discussions and decision making that would pose a challenge or create controversy (Bachrach & Baratz, 1962). Status and power should not be regarded as traits that are inherent in a particular position. Generally, it is more appropriate to think of status and power as conditions that other members of the group accord to a person in a given position. The two conditions are closely related. The ability to exercise power enhances status; status enhances the ability to exercise power.

Types of Power

Status distinctions facilitate the use of power by people in higher positions to secure compliance from those in lower positions. In part, the power that actor A has over actor B is determined by B's dependence on A (Emerson, 1962). Status distinctions create barriers that reduce the dependency of those in higher positions on those in lower positions. Such barriers help to maintain a power difference that favors the higher position.

French and Raven (1959) provided an analysis of social power that has become a classic model for classifying the forms of power applied in organizational relationships. They described five basic types of power: reward, coercive, referent, expert, and legitimate.

Reward and coercive power are closely related. The former involves the ability to control and apply rewards, either directly or indirectly, whereas the latter involves the ability to control and apply punishments. One's reward or coercive power over others depends on at least two factors. First, those things that can be controlled or mediated (e.g., salary increases, promotions, work assignments, demotions, suspensions, terminations) must be perceived as rewards or punishments by others. Second, a person has these forms of power only to the extent that he or she is perceived as being willing and able to apply or at least mediate rewards and punishments. As Secord and Backman (1964) observed, "If a supervisor has seldom rewarded or punished an employee, either directly or indirectly, his reward and coercive power is likely to be weak" (p. 275).

Referent power depends on identification. Identification sometimes is defined as the desire to be like another person. In this sense, actor A has referent power with actor B to the extent that B wishes to be like A. The concepts of identification and referent power, however, are somewhat more complex. According to Kelman (1961), identification involves a desirable, satisfying, and self-defining relationship with another person or group. Consequently, a given individual or group has referent power with a person to the extent that this person engages in certain behaviors because these behaviors maintain the relationship or the definition of self that is anchored in the relationship. One form of identification occurs when one person literally models another's behavior. A second form involves different but complementary behaviors. Identification also occurs when a person adopts the attitudes and values of a self-defining group.

Expert power is based on the perception that a person possesses some special knowledge that is required to solve a problem, perform a task, or decide on a course of action. A person wields expert power with others if they follow his or her course of action in the belief that the individual knows more than they do about what should be done in the situation.

Legitimate power is based on acceptance of internal norms and values regarding authority and the right to exercise authority. People accept influence from someone in a certain position because they believe this person has the right to exercise the authority accorded to that position. For example, a company president might create a team leader position for a project group and decree that the position has certain status and powers. Functionally, however, status and power depend on group members' acceptance. In other words, the team leader exercises legitimate power only to the extent that team members accept the leader's authority to exercise controls over the members' behavior.

Dimensions of Power

The work of Max Weber is central to any study of power in organizations. Weber (1978) focused on describing and analyzing the system of rationality that is such an obvious part of Western industrial society. More specifically, he examined the system of rationality that operates within bureaucracies. As Mumby (2001) explained

> Weber . . . left us with both a structural and ideological legacy: a bureaucratic system of rules and regulations constitutive of authority, along with an ideology of rationality that shapes and constrains the behavior of actors in organizational contexts. (p. 587)

Although Weber viewed bureaucratic rationality as a key feature of Western society, he expressed concerns with its practice and its potential to overshadow other forms of rationality such as the charismatic, which he viewed "as an essential, magical feature of human collective action" (Mumby, 2001, p. 587). In his description of Western society, Weber presented us with an "ideal type" of rational legal authority. He saw the ideal type of authority as firmly linked to technical criteria and expertise. In other words, authority structures human action with clear rules so employees know exactly how to act in any situation. The problem with this system, however, is as it reproduces itself through communication among organization members it may create an "iron cage" that traps those it was intended to empower.

As scholars debated Weber's views from the 1950s through the 1970s, they attempted to gain an understanding of the structure and distribution of power in organizations. In what was termed the "community power debate," two camps developed: the pluralists (Dahl, 1957, 1958, 1961; Wolfinger, 1971) and the elitists (Bachrach & Baratz, 1962, 1963; Hunter, 1953; Mills, 1956). The pluralists believed that power was distributed equitably in society and that there was no "ruling elite" who controlled decision-making processes. Elitists, on the other hand, believed that power was concentrated in the hands of the privileged.

Dahl's (1957) one-dimensional model of power focuses on the rational, causal, and behavioral aspects of power as they relate to decision making. As he stated, "A has the power over B to the extent that he [or she] can get B to do something that B would not otherwise do" (pp. 202–203). By defining power in this way, Dahl concentrates on the "manifest *exercise* of power, and not on power as a potential or dispositional quality of actors" (Mumby, 2001, p. 588). Also central to his perspective is the belief that power is exercised only in decision-making situations in which parties hold opposing views.

Bachrach and Baratz (1962) did not disagree with Dahl's view that power was displayed in decision-making situations; however, they believed that power had another face. Specifically, they argued that power is also displayed when certain individuals are able to control communication so the political process is restricted to issues that serve only to reinforce their power. As Bachrach and Baratz (1962) explain, "To the extent that A succeeds in doing this, B is prevented, for all practical purposes, from bringing to the fore any issues that might in their resolution be seriously detrimental to A's set of preferences" (p. 948).

Lukes's (1974) three-dimensional model of power identifies shortcomings with both Dahl's one-dimensional model and Bachrach and Baratz's two-dimensional model. Lukes's criticism is that both models focus on power only in decision making or conflict situations; instead, he argues that power may be displayed in the absence of decision making or conflict. In this sense, power resides in the "socially structured and culturally patterned behavior of groups and practices of institution" (Lukes, 1974, p. 22). From the traditional viewpoint, power may be the ability of actor A to get actor B to do what B otherwise would not do. But, in Lukes's model, there is nothing quite so powerful as the assumption within a group that things are or should be a particular way. As Lukes observed, it is "the supreme exercise of power to get another or others to have the desires you want them to have . . . to secure their compliance by controlling their thoughts and desires" (p. 23).

The community power debate that we outlined in this section shows how scholars have wrestled with understanding how power functions in organizational settings. This debate provided us with insight into "how to move beyond individual and relationally focused conceptions of power" (Mumby, 2001, p. 589).

Resource Dependency

In their coalition model of power, Pfeffer and Salancik focus on the extent to which organizational subunits are dependent on resources provided by other social actors (Pfeffer, 1981; Pfeffer & Salancik, 1974, 1978; Salancik & Pfeffer, 1974, 1977). From their perspective, organizational decision making is a political process that can be understood by examining the relative power of the various subunits in the organization. This is more than a matter of who gets what resources. Rather, the key issue is how dependent is a given unit on the resources provided by other actors or units. There are many different types of resources that organizational subunits need; some of the most important are money, prestige, legitimacy, rewards and sanctions, expertise, and the ability to deal with uncertainty (Mumby, 2001).

The more dependent a unit is on resources provided by others, the more important communication is with those resource providers. Specifically, to obtain needed resources a subunit within the organization must engage in transactions with other subunits. The nature of the transaction will vary on the basis of the reason for requesting the resource. Among the most common types of transactions will be simple requests, justifications for needed resources, and offers of resource exchange. In explaining how we may use communication to enhance power and gain resources, Pfeffer (1981) explains:

> The view developed here . . . is that language and symbolism are important in the *exercise* of power. It is helpful for social actors with power to use appropriate political language and symbols to legitimate and develop support for the decisions that are reached on the basis of power. However, in this formulation, language and the ability to use political symbols contributes only marginally to the development of the power of various organizational participants; rather, power derives from the conditions of resource control and resource interdependence. (p. 184, emphasis in original)

Pfeffer's perspective clearly considers the role of communication in gaining needed resources, but he falls short of giving communication a central role. Instead, communication plays a secondary or supplemental role. This is substantially different from the interpretive and critical views of power that we will consider shortly in which communication constitutes power relations. Simply stated, Pfeffer views communication as serving the purpose of reproducing and legitimizing already-existing power relations within the organization.

INTERPRETIVE PERSPECTIVES ON POWER

The starting point in taking an interpretive perspective on power is recognizing that communication is constitutive of organizing (Pacanowsky & O'Donnell-Trujillo, 1982; Putnam, 1983; Smith & Eisenberg, 1987). What this means is that organization members collectively construct a shared reality through communication (Mumby, 2001). In order to create this shared reality, we need to understand the notion of *intersubjectivity*, which requires us to break from the Cartesian model of subject-object separation. Specifically, Descartes believed that knowledge is the mind's discovery of a preexisting reality. The shift to an interpretive perspective requires that we view "communication [as] the process of creating an intersubjectively meaningful reality" (Mumby, 2001, p. 593). And, as Gadamer (1960/1989) explains, it is through language that we create the self, meaning, and the world as we know it. So, the displays of power we see and the power relations that are present in all organizations are created through communication among organization members. Importantly, changes in how people communicate with one another will also affect the nature of power dynamics within an organization.

The interpretive approach on power focuses on the relationships that exist among communication, power, and meaning (Fowler, Hodge, Kress, & Trew, 1979). For example,

Grameen Bank field workers do not only act in the organization's interests, they develop a sense of identity through committing themselves to the organization and its goals, even if it means working 12–14 hours a day, seven days a week (Papa, Auwal, & Singhal, 1995, 1997). The identifications and commitments of the field workers are not developed without problems, however. In fact, there are struggles over meaning. For example, some field workers question how much sacrifice is too much, and some administrators of the bank disapprove when field workers work alongside loan recipients whose businesses are struggling. At the same time, these administrators pressure the field workers to keep their loan repayment levels high. Such struggles do not prevent the construction of a shared reality; rather, they point to the difficulties organization members face when creating an intersubjectively meaningful reality.

Farmer (1999) studied the culture of a mining community in southwestern Virginia by asking community members to describe events surrounding a 1989 miner's strike. One dimension of power relations that was revealed in this study was how "replacement workers" were viewed and described in the community. Replacement worker was the term used by the Pittston Mining Corporation to refer to workers who crossed the picket line to replace the unionized miners during the strike. One of Farmer's interviewees talked about how these workers were described in the community:

> I did not feel sorry for the quote unquote replacement workers, but let's call them what they are, scabs. Scabs. And in this area, someone can call you the vilest of obscenities, and you'll pretty much take it and go on, but someone calls you a scab, you don't get any lower than that. Because a scab not only takes your job, your livelihood, they're taking food out of your family. It's despicable. And that's what a quote unquote replacement worker is, the lowest, the very lowest. (Farmer, 1999, p. 184)

In this mining community, a single word separated the reviled from the accepted member. A person who crossed the picket line, even if his excuse was to feed his own family, was the lowest of all human beings. Being called a scab marked that person permanently. Such a person could never return to a position of respect and acceptance in the community. Thus, with a single word a person's place in the community is identified and they are completely disempowered.

POWER IN THE VIEW OF CRITICAL THEORY

Traditional theories of power have tried to describe the forms of power that occur in social processes and have emphasized social exchange explanations for the operation of power. The result is an appealing—but somewhat sterile—view of power that fails to account for the connection between power and communication and ignores the dark side of the subservience to which Redding called attention.

Peter J. Frost (1987), a prominent professor of industrial relations at the University of British Columbia, has advanced four propositions about power that are not explicit in traditional treatments of the concept:

1. Organizational life is significantly influenced by the quest for and exercise of power by organizational actors, which constitute the political activity of organization.

2. Power exists both on the surface level of organizational activity and deep within the very structure of organizations.

3. Communication plays a vital role in the development of power relations and the exercise of power.

4. The manipulation and exercise of power is expressed, in the sense both of actions and relations, as organizational games. (p. 504)

Frost points out that communication provides the means for the development and exercise of power. In turn, power creates and shapes communication structure and rules. With respect to power and politics, "the communication medium is never neutral" (p. 507).

Critical theory focuses explicitly on a communicative and symbolic approach to power. For the critical theorist, power is inextricably tied to domination and oppression—conditions in the structure of society and in organizations that scholars should reveal and criticize. But critical theory does something that goes beyond mere complaining about societal oppression. As Dennis Mumby (1987) explained, it attempts to show how symbolism can "potentially legitimate dominant forms of organizational reality . . . restricting the interpretations and meanings that can be attached to organizational activity" (p. 113).

Power and Legitimation

Critical theory has its roots in the works of Marx, but real development and articulation of modern critical theory began in Germany during the 1930s at the University of Frankfurt's Institute for Social Research, known more simply as "The Frankfurt School" (Farrell & Aune, 1979). Whatever Marx's original notions about history and society, Soviet-style communism had refined Marxist theory into a purely materialistic philosophy. Like the early machine metaphor of traditionalism, materialism reduced explanations for social process to machinelike causal relations that were divorced from questions of human consciousness and values. The Frankfurt School aimed at creating a form of neo-Marxism that addressed dominance and oppression in terms of values and morals (McGaan, 1983). Since the 1960s, this effort has been best reflected in the works of Jürgen Habermas (1968, 1976/1979). Lee McGann (1983) clearly explains the difference between traditional Marxism and Habermas's brand of neo-Marxism:

> The traditional Marxist argument is that the West will fall as a result of economic collapse brought on by an uncontrollable cycle of inflation and recession. This will lead to class consciousness by workers and bring the revolution. Habermas has shown that . . . the real source of difficulty for capitalistic societies involves problems of **legitimation** [emphasis added] . . . the crisis faced by institutions in the West comes from challenges to the legitimacy of power and function of capitalistic structures. . . .
>
> What Habermas did in developing the concept of a legitimation crisis was to shift the traditional Marxist critique of society from the positivistic and material to

the conceptual and moral. Critical theory in this light looks not at the economic relations undergirding social institutions. Instead, it focuses on the conceptual structures that justify the existence of institutions and the relation of those legitimations to real human interests. (p. 5)

In fact, because Western capitalism has managed to remain more or less intact despite the doomsaying of traditional Marxist theory, one of the more interesting issues addressed in modern critical theory concerns why this has happened. Although dominance can be achieved through force and coercion, and force and coercion are not unusual in organizations, the maintenance of power in capitalist organizations depends in large part on its legitimation (i.e., the manner in which its use is justified and accepted). Thus, as Robert McPhee (1985) pointed out, some of the most prominent examples of modern critical research "concentrate on a single question: how is it, given the alienated and exploitative nature of work in capitalist organizations, that workers cooperate with management, labor at their jobs, and forego resistant stances, without the constant presence of coercion and threat?" (p. 1).

Power and Organizational Structure

In an effort to answer this question, critical theory focuses on the intricate relationships between power and organizational structure. The idea of organizational structure in critical theory is not quite the same thing as the traditionalist concepts that we presented in Chapter 3. There, we considered structure in terms of formally designated lines of authority and divisions of labor and in terms of communication networks. But you may also remember the basic definition of a *system* that we presented in Chapter 5; namely, it is a set of elements and the *rules* that define the relationships among those elements. Structure is realized through these rules, and this is the concept of structure with which critical theory is concerned.

What is the relationship between structure and power? As explained by Stewart Clegg (1975), power arises from the **deep structure rules** of organization and is achieved by controlling those rules. Deep structure rules include shared, unquestioned assumptions that guide our social actions. The organizational rule system provides what Clegg characterizes as a "mode of rationality" by shaping and directing the ways in which we think and act. When we internalize this mode of rationality, we act only in ways that support the organizational rule system because we believe that "that's the way things are around here."

Mumby and Stohl (1991) also address the issue of power structures, but their approach is somewhat different than Clegg's. They argue that within organizations there are struggles between different interest groups "to create a meaning system in which certain views of the world are privileged over others" (p. 318). The dominant group is the one that is best able to create and sustain a meaning system that serves its own interests. More specifically, Mumby and Stohl claim that discourse (e.g., conversations, written interaction) functions to structure systems of *presence* and *absence* within the organization, meaning that certain views of what is acceptable within the organization are organized into everyday practices, whereas other alternative views are organized out (or absented). For example, in most organizations members are expected to make decisions according to rational procedures intended to produce optimal outcomes. Within such organizations, "rationality is given primacy (made present) over emotionality (absented) as a legitimate model of organizational experience" (Mumby & Stohl, 1991, p. 319; also see Mumby & Putnam, 1992).

Power, Symbols, and Systematic Distortion

Obviously, different rule systems provide us with different ways of organizing our behavior. In Chapter 2, we described how domination occurs in organizations by focusing on the concepts of **hegemony** and **systemically distorted communication**. By returning to these two concepts and extending our analysis of them, we can gain further insight into how power relations are sustained through symbols and distorted communication.

In organizations, hegemony may be legitimized through systematically distorted communication in various ways, but systematic distortion in its most basic form can be found in the political functions of organizational **ideology**. As we explained earlier, an ideology is a set of assumptions and beliefs that constitute a system of thought. Ideology provides the structure for an organization's mode of rationality. In other words, ideology is central to an organization's deep structure. Giddens (1979) contends that ideology functions politically in three ways to privilege the interests of one group over another. A concise summary of Giddens's claims is adapted from Mumby (1987):

1. *Representing sectional interests as universal.* Although the real organization may consist of competing constituencies and conflicting interests (e.g., management versus labor, staff versus line), ideology can tell us "We're all in this together" (i.e., that the interests of one group really are the interests of all).

2. *Denying or transmuting contradictions.* From the vantage point of critical theory, capitalist society and organizations within capitalist society are fraught with fundamental contradictions. The ownership of the means for producing goods and services is private, yet, in organizations, the production is accomplished through a social process. Ideology can obscure the fundamental nature of these contradictions by making them appear to be nothing more than social conflict. Thus, ideology tells us that decision making is purely rational, when, in fact, it is political, or that we are "all equal here," when, in fact, we are not.

3. *Naturalizing the present through reification.* In effect, reification means that we make a socially constructed reality appear to be concrete (i.e., objective, fixed, and immutable). Ideology reifies meaning by telling us, "This is the way things are." As we pointed out in earlier chapters, the most obvious example of this probably is the concept of organizational hierarchy itself. It is taken to be concrete and is literally the natural order of things, but it has its existence only in shared meanings which shape our actions to fit the idea.

Mumby has added a fourth function, *control,* to Giddens's list of three. Perhaps the control function already is implied in Giddens's list, but Mumby wants to make it clear that ideological control is not so much a matter of one group's domination over another as it is the ability of a group or class to make the interests of other groups appear to be consistent with its own. We think it is also important to specifically connect Mumby's idea of control with systematically distorted communication. *Members of dominated groups participate in their own oppression through self-deception by identifying with and actively consenting to the system of hegemony.* When this occurs, we have, as Gramsci (1971) suggested, the condition under which hegemony works best.

One of us was involved in a consulting project with a large accounting and investment firm in which we were able to observe firsthand how employees can participate in their own oppression through self-deception. In this firm, there were three women who had reached the rank of partner (out of 21 total partners). Two of the women, who had young children at home, realized that they could no longer meet the demands of heavy workloads that often resulted in 60-hour workweeks. They felt that their children's needs were being sacrificed so the firm could continue to make money. After presenting their concerns to the other partners, they struck a deal in which the women were able to reduce their workweek to an average of 30 hours. Of course, with the reduction in hours came a 40% reduction in their share of the firm's profits. At first glance, it may seem that these women had struck a good deal. But did they really? Another way of interpreting their actions is to argue that they accepted without question the fact that partners must work 60 hours a week in order to retain full partner status. Couldn't the women have posed other questions, such as "Why do we have to work 60 hours a week to retain partner status?" or "Can't we promote more accountants or investment analysts to partner status so we can reduce the workload for all of us?" Unfortunately, these women struck a deal that was based on their unquestioned acceptance of what a fair workload is for partners. If they had questioned these beliefs about a fair workload, perhaps they could have negotiated a 40-hour workweek, retained full partner status, and spent more time with their children.

Communication Distortion in Organizational Hierarchies

Communication distortion may occur in organizations in ways that preserve power for certain groups and reduce the power available to other groups. One way of looking at communication distortion is considering how it is used at different levels of an organization's hierarchy. There may be incentives for subordinates to distort messages that reveal negative information about individual or departmental performance. The reason the message is distorted is to prevent or delay criticism or punishment from management for poor performance. For example, let's say that a sales manager for a retail store experienced a quarterly decline in sales for a particular line of clothing. The honest explanation for the decline was an error in inventory management. Specifically, the sales manager did not stock an adequate inventory of this line of clothing. When asked to account for the decline in sales, however, the sales manager cites increased competition from other retailers in the area and a slight increase in the county's unemployment rate, which decreased consumer's disposable income. If upper management accepts the explanation, the store manager avoids criticism or punishment for a mistake that he made. A number of years ago, Sussman (1973) wrote an article describing this general phenomenon as "you can fool some of the supervisors some of the time."

Upper management may also choose to distort communication to preserve power for itself and restrict power from subordinates. *Wal-Mart: The High Cost of Low Price* (2005), a documentary film produced and directed by Robert Greenwald, explains the retail giant's use of communication distortion in great detail. For example, Wal-Mart pays its sales associates in the United States so poorly that many full-time workers need to seek social welfare assistance to pay for food and access healthcare and low-cost subsidized housing. In fact, applying Wal-Mart's reported percentages of workers and children enrolled in Medicaid and other state-supported health programs implies that Wal-Mart workers and children cost taxpayers $456 million nationally through their use of public health programs (Jacobs & Dube, 2004). This is just one part of the cost to U.S. taxpayers, however. There are also costs associated with offering free or reduced-price lunches to children of Wal-Mart employees, housing assistance, tax cuts for low-income families, and low-income energy assistance. When all of these costs are added together, Wal-Mart costs U.S. taxpayers approximately $1.5 billion per year (Miller, 2004).

One type of information distortion that Wal-Mart employs with its sales associates is to broadcast on closed-circuit television in employee break rooms a program that describes the disadvantages of unionization. Employees are told that all that unions do is take money out of workers' paychecks for dues without increasing wages or improving benefits. This programming serves to discourage employees from forming unions. Of course, the company fails to inform their employees that Wal-Mart stores are unionized in Germany, where employees are paid a living wage, provided with a free healthcare program, and given 30 days of vacation a year. By distorting information on the closed-circuit telecast in U.S. stores concerning unionization, Wal-Mart saves more than $19 billion a year in additional payroll costs. This estimate comes from comparisons between the average wage of unionized workers in the United States ($760 per week) and the average wage of Wal-Mart workers ($263 per week) (Miller, 2004). Clearly, information distortion pays huge dividends for this corporation.

Limits of Ideological Manipulation

Advocates of the theory of hegemony as we have described it so far contend that power in organizations works through *ideological manipulation* (Witten, 1993). What this means is that the dominant group manipulates and structures the interests of the oppressed group. This manipulation is accomplished through convincing the oppressed group that their interests can best be served by adhering to the values and behaviors the dominant group advocates.

Although the concept of ideological manipulation is linked to some critical theorists, other theorists criticize this perspective. Specifically, Abercrombie, Hill, and Turner (1980) observe that ideological manipulation is predicated on the Marxist notion of *false consciousness*. False consciousness refers to a condition in which the less powerful members of a social system ignorantly subscribe to the dominant control of more powerful members. The less powerful members accept this control because they uncritically accept the positions advocated by the dominant group as being in their best interests.

One good reason for discomfort with the notion of false consciousness is its contradiction of Giddens's (1979) description of the *dialectic of control*. As you'll remember from Chapter 9, Giddens argued that every social actor within a system has the capacity to exercise power and control. Hancox and Papa (1996) and Gibson and Papa (2000) reported an interesting example of the dialectic of control in action. They conducted their studies in a manufacturing organization that uses a monetary incentive system to reward employees for high levels of performance. The "bonus pay" high performers receive comes out of annual company profits. The positive side of this incentive system is that the employees are paid at rates three times higher than the average for workers in U.S. manufacturing companies.

The negative side of this system is that the employees sometimes have to work six or seven days a week to meet production goals. The pressure to produce at high levels also creates equipment hazards that have resulted in severed fingers, burns, and eye injuries.

Given the preceding description, how do employees within this manufacturing organization exhibit control over management? Recently, the company operated at a financial loss because of poor performance from subsidiaries located in Europe. Certain managers within the company began to float the rumor that bonuses would not be paid because of the financial loss. Worker reaction to this rumor was emotional and forceful. For example, many employees indicated that violence would erupt if the bonus was not paid and that the majority of the laborers would quit their jobs. As one employee with 30 years' experience stated, "People think that maybe somebody's gonna come in here with a gun if he doesn't like what he hears [on bonus day]" (Hancox & Papa, 1996, p. 22). Echoing this sentiment, an employee with 29 years' experience explained that too many of the employees rely on the bonus to pay their everyday bills. So, if a particular employee does not receive the bonus he expects, "this might break this guy and he's likely to come in with a autoloader on bonus day and wipe everybody out" (p. 23). Finally, dealing with the issue of a massive walkout, an employee with 26 years' experience explained, "The average worker would walk out because they would find it very difficult to justify their presence there. They would probably lose 40% of their employees immediately" (p. 22).

What was management's response to these worker statements? Well, despite the fact that bonuses had never before been paid when the company lost money, the owners borrowed $50 million in 1993 so they could still provide performance bonuses to qualifying employees. Of course it is difficult to prove that management's decision to take out the loan was due solely to worker statements. However, a case can be made that these statements had their intended impact. As one worker with 29 years' experience put it, "That bonus keeps all your good workers here, and keeps people from leaving. That is the reason they borrow money to pay the bonus" (Hancox & Papa, 1996, p. 24).

As the above example shows, employees have the ability to empower themselves even in organizations in which managers attempt to engage in ideological manipulation. Does this mean that workers are always aware of management's attempts to manipulate them? Of course, this claim cannot be made either. Sometimes management is successful in its attempts to manipulate workers, and other times workers realize what is going on and empower themselves. In still other instances, workers recognize that they are being manipulated but decide that the rewards associated with continued organizational membership outweigh the costs of continued manipulation. So, within organizations power and structure are related but the nature of that relationship is sometimes more complex than it seems at first glance.

Critical Theory in Organizational Communication Research

Critical theory has produced some outstanding studies of power in work and organizational settings (e.g., Burawoy, 1979; Clegg, 1975; Edwards, 1979), but it has begun only recently to exert influence in the study of organizational communication. One good example of this kind of research is a study by Mumby on the political use of *narratives*, literally, the use of storytelling in organizations. Mumby examined a story that purportedly was widely disseminated in IBM Corporation and that was told and retold by many members of this company. The story concerns an incident between IBM's chairman, Thomas Watson, Jr., and an IBM employee named Lucille Burger. Although the exact form and content of the story might vary somewhat from one telling to another, the basic form published by Martin, Feldman, Hatch, and Sitkin (1983) goes this way:

> Lucille Burger, a twenty-two-year-old bride weighing ninety pounds, whose husband had been sent overseas, had been given a job until his return. The young woman was obliged to make certain that people entering security areas wore the correct clear identification. Surrounded by his usual entourage of white-shirted men, Watson approached the doorway to an area where she was on guard, wearing an orange badge acceptable elsewhere in the plant, but not a green badge, which alone permitted entrance at her door. "I was trembling in my uniform, which was far too big," she recalled. "It hid my shakes, but not my voice. 'I'm sorry,' I said to him. I knew who he was alright. 'You cannot enter. Your admittance is not recognized.' That's what we were supposed to say." The men accompanying Watson were stricken; the moment held unpredictable possibilities. "Don't you know who he is?" someone hissed. Watson raised his hand for silence, while one of the party strode off and returned with the appropriate badge. (pp. 439–440)

Mumby demonstrates how this story can plausibly accomplish all of the political functions of ideology—how the story is, in effect, an instance of systematically distorted communication. Although every statement in the story may be factually correct, the story nonetheless obscures and mystifies the actual conditions of organizational life at IBM.

As interpreted by Mumby (1987), the story implies that sectional interests are transcended by rules that are designed for the benefit of all, but it obscures the fact that the rules are "created *by* the corporate elite (of which Watson is head) to protect their own interests" (p. 121). The rules at issue in this story "are in place for the benefit of people like Watson, and not for people like Lucille Burger" (p. 121). Moreover, the story denies a fundamental contradiction and is, itself, a contradiction. It portrays Watson as an ordinary person who must obey Burger in her official capacity as an enforcer of the rules, yet also makes him "a larger-than-life figure about whom fables are told" (p. 122). More to the point, it is the fact that Watson really *is* an exception that makes the story compelling. Watson wisely used the occasion to make a dramatic statement about corporate rules by deferring to a relatively low-echelon employee. In fact, he could have walked right by Burger without any consequences at all.

Mumby argues that this story provides a very good instance of reification simply because it can be recounted over and over again as a statement not only about rules, but also about the rationale for enforcing them, not to mention latent statements about sex roles and status differences. In particular, Mumby says, "The story serves to reify ideologically the organizational rule system itself. . . . Lucille Burger's single-minded adherence to the rules reflects not so much a heightened sense of corporate loyalty, but rather an enforcing of the rules *because they exist*" (p. 123). Finally, the story serves the control function because it is recounted not only by high-level executives, but throughout the company as "an example of 'intellectual and moral leadership'" (p. 123). The story itself is actively recounted by employees, and they actively take up and adopt its ideology. Its illustration of Burger's commitment to the system is identified and equated with the legitimacy and appropriateness of that system.

Mumby's study of the Watson-Burger story suggests three goals for critical scholarship, which are adapted from Deetz (1982):

1. *Richer understanding of naturally occurring events.* Deep structure elements of meaning are largely taken for granted. They shape our actions without much conscious reflection, examination, or questioning. Critical research attempts to produce insights not only for scholars, but also for organization members themselves by calling attention to the deep structure of meaning systems. This is similar to the idea of "consciousness-raising."

2. *Criticism of false consensus.* When we deceive ourselves through systematically distorted communication, the result is false consensus. As Deetz expresses it, false consensus "is reached by the power of definition rather than open discussion" (p. 140). If illusions and the conditions that make them necessary can be overcome, it is possible to have open dialogue among different organizational groups and constituencies. Returning to Habermas, the task of the critical theorist is to identify and criticize strategic action in order to move toward communicative action in society.

3. *Expansion of the conceptual base from which organization members think and work.* Organization members need to learn how to engage in communicative action in order to have a better understanding of organizational life and to expand their concepts and languages in order to grapple creatively with the problems that confront them.

In Chapter 6, we described systems of concertive control in organizations. Studies focusing on such systems have yielded interesting insights into the nature of power in organizations (Barker, 1993; Barker & Cheney, 1994; Papa et al., 1995, 1997). In order to understand how power operates within concertive control systems, we need to return to two concepts we discussed in Chapter 6: *identification* and *discipline*. As you will remember, workers exhibit their identification with an organization when, in making a decision, they perceive the organization's values or interests as relevant in evaluating the alternatives of choice (Tompkins & Cheney, 1983). Such worker perceptions lead to the conclusion, "What's good for the organization is also good for me." In addition, in systems of concertive control, workers show their identification with the organization and their work team by establishing and sustaining disciplinary techniques that allow workers to accomplish goals that they have created for themselves. These disciplinary techniques act as a powerful social force that governs and regulates worker behavior. In order to clarify how discipline acts as a powerful social force in organizations, let's turn to an example Papa et al. (1995) report in their study of Grameen Bank workers:

> Atiquar Rahman is a Grameen bank field worker who works on the outskirts of Dhaka [Bangladesh]. He told us about the pressure he feels from fellow field workers to retain a high loan recovery rate. When he experienced problems with loan recovery in a particular center (four members had ceased loan repayment), he felt personally responsible to solve the problem. The four members had taken out a loan for a rickshaw repair business. However, they soon discovered that they

could not compete with the more established repair businesses in Dhaka. Rahman met with the non-paying members and attempted to persuade them to resume loan repayment. When that did not work he offered to help them move their business to an area where they could compete. Rahman eventually wound up working on rickshaw repairs himself to help the loan recipients keep their business functioning. (pp. 208–209)

In interpreting this story, Papa et al. noted that the loan repayment records of Rahman's centers were posted on a wall behind his desk for all the other field workers to see. Rahman felt incredible guilt when he returned to the branch office at the end of a long day without having received any loan repayments from the delinquent borrowers. He felt that he was failing as a field worker, and he became most upset when he compared his loan recovery record to the posted records of his coworkers. He even considered quitting his job because he felt incapable of meeting the high standards his coworkers had established.

Why did Rahman identify so strongly with the standards his coworkers established? First of all, he was part of establishing the standards. Second, sustaining these high standards allows the Grameen Bank to sustain its position as one of the most successful social and economic development organizations in the world. Rahman felt that he was part of this success until experiencing problems with loan recovery in one of his bank centers. Third, discipline acts as a social force in the Grameen Bank because of the carefully designed system of monitoring and evaluating worker performance. Papa et al. (1997) explain this system as follows:

The monitoring and evaluation of worker performance became particularly clear to us in the branch offices when field workers returned from their village centers. Although exhausted from a long day's work, bank workers would begin counting and recording loan repayments as soon as they sat down at their desks. Each member counted the money in full view of the other branch members and the branch manager. The pace of the counting and recording operations is fast and clearly stressful. As we learned in talking with a number of field workers, the stress they feel is linked to the immediacy of the evaluation they receive. Lagging performance is quickly discovered and corrected, and good performance is quickly rewarded. (p. 20)

Papa et al. note that the counting of loan repayments at the end of the day is similar to Foucault's (1975/1979) threefold disciplinary mechanism: *examination, hierarchical observation,* and *normalizing judgment.* The public counting of loan repayments is a form of daily examination for the workers. Hierarchical observation occurs as the counting of the money is performed in full view of the manager. The manager and the coworkers then offer a normalizing judgment in the feedback given to the worker about his or her performance. Workers who collect all outstanding loan repayments are praised. Those who fail to recoup all outstanding loan repayments are criticized and made to feel unworthy to be a teammate. Thus, the punishment workers receive is essentially communicative in form. Field workers criticize each other and make reference to the loan repayment records posted behind workers' desks. In order to avoid this criticism and prove their strong identification with the bank's continued success, the workers labor long hours and forgo vacations to ensure that members continue their loan repayments. Finally, Papa et al. (1997) explain that the workers accept these forms of discipline because of their strong identification with the bank.

As one Grameen Bank worker, Shamsul Hoque, put it: "I feel like the engine of change. An engine that gets its fuel from the vision of Muhammad Yunus [Grameen's Managing Director] and water from the dreams of the poor and the landless" (p. 19).

Thus, in concertive control systems power is embedded within a system of interaction among workers who identify strongly with an organization and its goals. What this means is that workers communicate with one another in ways that sustain the disciplinary system so continued goal attainment is possible. Instead of a form of power in which a dominant group (e.g., management) enforces discipline upon workers, a concertive control system empowers workers to be their own enforcers. Because the workers themselves create the system of control, they are committed to sustaining it despite the personal sacrifices entailed in continued organizational participation.

Reconceptualizing Power

In the first decade of the 21st century, we continue to struggle with our understanding of power relations in organizations and how communication intersects with power. Although there are many emerging perspectives that inform our current thinking, two stand out in particular: feminisms and poststructuralism.

Feminisms

In viewing power from a broad range of feminist perspectives (see Chapter 14), the first recognition that seems important is seeing organizations as "gendered" structures. Acker (1990) advocates this position when observing that "advantage and disadvantage, exploitation and control, action and emotion, meaning and identity, are patterned through and in terms of a distinction between male and female, masculine and feminine" (p. 146). In terms of understanding everyday actions within organizations, feminism draws our attention to the "institutional character of women's economic, political, and ideological subordination" (Mumby, 2001, p. 609).

In Chapter 4, we discussed Mary Parker Follett's distinction between power *over* others and power *with* others in organizational relationships and her use of "power with" as the basis for her concept of participation. Feminists have an interest similar to Follett's in distinguishing between power as a means of domination and power as "the ability to accomplish goals" (Iannello, 1992, p. 43). Specifically, feminists advocate the substitution of **empowerment** for power. As Kathleen Iannello explains:

> Power is associated with the notion of controlling others, while empowerment is associated with the notion of controlling oneself. Therefore, within organizations based on empowerment, members monitor themselves. In organizations based on power, there must be an administrative oversight function. (pp. 44–45)

When describing the differences in how men and women access power, the notion of power over others is associated more with men, and the notion of empowerment is linked more to women. Both neo-Marxist theory and poststructuralists examine the relationships that exist among capitalism, patriarchy, organization, and gendered communication practices as a way of understanding notions of power over others and empowerment. When social actors seek to exhibit power over others, power becomes a force of domination.

Alternatively, empowerment may be viewed as a force or resistance. For example, feminist neo-Marxist research considers opportunities for collective resistance and change and "examines the ways in which community and egalitarianism can emerge within hierarchical and patriarchal structures" (Mumby, 2001, p. 611).

In the feminist critique of modern organizations, the exercise of power as a means of domination over others is realized through hierarchy, and hierarchy is a fundamental instrument of patriarchal order. According to Kathy Ferguson (1984), "Social relations between classes, races, and sexes are fundamentally unequal. Bureaucracy [hierarchy] . . . serves as a filter for these other forms of domination, projecting them into an institutional arena that both rationalizes and maintains them" (p. 8).

Eliminating domination requires replacement of hierarchy with a collectivist, cooperative structure. In a **collectivist** as opposed to hierarchical organization, decisions and actions would be developed through participative dialogue to achieve action through consensus rather than action through top-down communication of orders from a central authority. Thus, feminist theorists such as Iannello (1992) speak of "decisions without hierarchy" (p. xi). The reformation of organizations into collectivist systems is a goal that appears to be common to most versions of feminist theory, but the attainment of this goal does pose a dilemma. As Hester Eisenstein (1991) expresses the problem:

> A fundamental issue [is] unresolved for feminists, and that is how we get from the values we hold dear—of collective, non-hierarchical, democratic behavior—to the outcome we seek, of a peaceful world safe for women and others now subject to discrimination, victimization, and oppression, without sacrificing these values in the rush to seize and use power on behalf of feminist ends. (p. 3)

Achieving organizational reformation seems to depend implicitly in many feminist writings on the hope that women somehow will do a better job than men have done with the use of power. The potential difficulty in fulfilling this hope is reflected in Albrecht and Hall's (1991) study of innovation networks that we discussed in Chapter 3. They found that core groups of elite insiders dominated the networks. Although two-thirds of the outsiders—the disenfranchised—in Albrecht and Hall's study were women, women were also 75% of the elites—groups that manipulated the system to reinforce "their own relational positions of privilege, power, and influence" (p. 557). If the quality of organizational life is to be made better for everyone, women and men alike must find an answer to the dilemma Eisenstein poses.

Marshall (1989) discusses an alternative to hierarchy that addresses Eisenstein's concerns. Specifically, she argues that organizations can structure themselves in *heterarchies* (also discussed in Chapter 3) rather than hierarchies. As she explains, "A heterarchy has no one person or principle in command. Rather temporary pyramids of authority form as and when appropriate in a system of mutual constraints and influences." (Marshall, 1989, p. 289) An example of a heterarchy was observed by Wyatt (1988) in an ethnographic account of a weaver's guild. In this guild, there was a system of shared leadership and all opinions expressed by members were respected. Two forms of leadership were present within the guild. First, there was a leader who focused on the overall operation of the guild. Second, task leaders were associated with specific weaving projects. This resulted in a pyramid of authority among the eight women of the guild. They shared leadership of the entire group and rotated responsibility for tasks while sustaining flexibility in goals and values. In an evaluation of Wyatt's study, Mumby and Putnam (1992) observed, "Nestled in an environment of caring, members balance the demands of differing values, goals and relationships to make the group a place where all members feel comfortable and achieve their individual aims" (p. 475). In such an organizational environment, the opportunities for worker empowerment are clear and meaningful.

Although feminism places emphasis on empowerment, this does not mean that differences among organization members are suppressed under a single structure that empowers everyone in the same way. Consider the experiences of author Michael Papa in participating in community suppers orchestrated by the Good Works organization. When we first discussed the Friday Night Suppers in Chapter 2, we drew attention to the fact that participants in the suppers experienced a dialogic struggle between unity and fragmentation. Specifically, despite many cooperative activities and the building of fellowship among participants, there were people who felt disconnected and fragmented from those around them. Consider the words of Keith Wasserman, Managing Director of Good Works. His commentary provides some insights about transcending dialogic struggle between fragmentation and unity:

> Helping homeless people who have been hurt and abused is impossible outside the context of community. It is in the formation of community that we can bear one another's burdens, share vital information, and hand off to one another the most difficult people who need our assistance and love . . . It is in community that we help one another to heal the emotional pain experienced by our homeless neighbors. It is in community that we can do the most loving things toward those who need the most help. It is in community that we can model dignity and responsibility. It is in the context of community that we learn to prevent burn out. What we are suggesting ultimately is that we must intentionally join hands and deliberately attach ourselves to others and organize in a way to maximize our energy so we can all move forward together. (Papa, Papa, Kandath, Worrell, & Muthuswamy, 2005, p. 265)

In order to sustain a feminist perspective on empowerment, we must be careful in interpreting Wasserman's ideas concerning community. Wasserman's insights are potentially illuminating concerning feminist empowerment, but only if we describe community as a product of forces that both unify and fragment. When we promote unity only among the poor, or between the poor and other social classes, we risk perpetuating the status quo rather than interrogating it. Status quo attitudes have created the problem of homelessness, and changes in how we form communities may be necessary so that voices of dissent are not suppressed. Ultimately, we may need to transform our cultural conversation about the problem of homelessness through dialogue. Importantly, this dialogue must manage carefully the tension between unity and fragmentation. Dialogue helps us to discover the bonds that unify us. Just as important, however, dialogue can fragment us in ways that highlight differences that may be impossible to overcome. These tensions do not deny the existence of community. Rather, the dialogic tensions make for a vibrant community (Papa et al., 2006).

In forming and sustaining organizations structured by feminist principles, there are important lessons to be learned from the Good Works community suppers. What is empowering for one person is not empowering for another. No single structure, set of practices, or form of communication will be empowering for everyone. Power or empowerment from a feminist perspective means sustaining multiple and competing structures that may potentially create empowerment opportunities for all members while also recognizing that there will be moments when certain members struggle over what empowerment means to them. Organization members must also be willing to sustain dialogue over how empowerment opportunities may be made available for all members even if that means juggling multiple systems of organizing and communicating. Finally, organization members need to recognize that despite all efforts certain members within the system may not experience empowerment. This frustrating reality is simply a part of organizational life. From a feminist perspective, however, concentrated effort will be expended in sustaining structures and communicating in ways that provide opportunities for empowerment for many different people in the organization.

Poststructural Perspectives

Poststructuralism focuses on the multiple meanings that may be assigned to texts. Before proceeding to describe the implications that this perspective has for power, it is important to note that texts may be written documents, visual or aural images (such as film), or human action or communication. In Barthes's (1968/1977) essay, "The Death of the Author," he argues that the birth of the reader must be at the cost of the author. In making this argument, Barthes gives the reader or observer of a text a greater role in the creation of meaning. In a subsequent work, Barthes (1971/1996) contends that although a text may contain meanings that may be traced to the author (closed reading), a text is actually something that remains open. What he means by this is that different readers or observers may assign different readings or interpretation of the text. Barthes (1971/1996) coined the term *intertextuality* to express the idea that meaning is brought to the text by the audience.

Barthes's ideas have clear implications for understanding power in organizations. Specifically, an employee may act in a way to assert power by demanding that his supervisor justify a recent decision. Independent of the intention of the author of that action, the person to whom the act is directed (the supervisor) may assign a different meaning: this employee is just blowing off steam. This interpretation then justifies the supervisor's nonresponse. Furthermore, to the extent that multiple people observe a given action, there are multiple possible meanings that will be assigned to that action. So, when people communicate in ways to display or enact power relations, the nature of how that communication will be interpreted depends on who observes or experiences it.

Foucault (1966/1973) has also made significant contributions to poststructuralism. For Foucault, the statements that a person produces are not meaningful in and of themselves. Rather, statements create a network of rules that determine what is meaningful. These rules are the preconditions for statements or utterances to have meaning. According to Foucault, all statements are produced within certain societal conditions and exist within a *field of discourse*. When he uses the term field of discourse, Foucault means the total field within which social actors communicate with one another. This encompasses all statements or utterances that are made in a given societal context. This enormous field of statements is called *discursive formations*.

When Foucault attempts to describe the meanings that statements may have, he brackets out issues of truth and meaning. What this means is that he does not look for a deeper meaning that underlies discourse. Rather, he examines the conditions of existence for meaning. Meaning is produced against the backdrop of particular societal conditions during a given time period. More specifically, meaning production takes place within various discursive formations that influence how we view a given text or human action.

If Foucault were to assign a single meaning to discourse, it would position him as a structuralist. What makes Foucault a poststructuralist is the fact that he focuses on differences in meaning that are assigned to particular texts or actions. He is also interested in documenting the different meanings that may develop over time as people consider and reconsider varied interpretations. Finally, he recognizes that a given discursive formation continually generates new statements that may produce new discursive formations. When such changes occur, different meanings are assigned to texts.

Foucault extends Barthes's thinking about power by providing us with a richer understanding of how context influences the meanings that people assign to texts or actions. In an organization, the total communication environment created by people interacting with one another forms discursive formations that influence the meaning that is given to human actions in which power is displayed. Of course different interpretations may be possible in a large organization where people's discursive formations may be influenced by a dominant or exclusive communication network. In other words, more than one discursive formation may be present in a single organization. Furthermore, continued interaction among organization members may produce new discursive formations that produce new interpretations of a given action.

Let's return to the example of the employee who demands that a supervisor justify a recent decision. One context for understanding this action is that it is a legitimate request for accountability from an organization member concerned with the operations of a department. Another context is that this employee wants to discredit the supervisor because of a prior grievance he has with her. Alternatively, the employee makes the demand to draw attention away from his own misbehavior. Or, this employee acts to advocate the interests of another departmental member whose favor he seeks. All of these contexts may operate simultaneously, or individual organization members may accept one as reflective of their understanding of the action. Foucault would also argue that continued interaction among organization members might alter the interpretation they give to the action. These changes occur as organization members redefine their understanding of power dynamics in the department.

Derrida (1967/1976) also advocates opening texts to a broad range of meanings and interpretations. His approach is to take binary oppositions within a text and show how they are not so clear-cut as seems at first glance. For example, let's consider the binary opposition of good and evil. From Derrida's perspective, a reader or observer may view a particular text and recognize that the opposing concepts (good and evil) are in fact fluid. The implication of this recognition is that the text's meaning then becomes fluid. The process of showing this fluidity in texts is *deconstruction*. The process of deconstruction involve "a double movement of overturning these binary oppositions (thus destabilizing the dominant term) and engaging in a process of 'metaphorization,' by which the opposing terms are shown to implicate and define one another in an endless display of signifiers" (Mumby, 2001, p. 607; see also Cooper, 1989, p. 483). When we apply this perspective to the opposing concepts of good and evil, we need to recognize not only that understanding "good" requires an understanding of evil, but that good is in fact defined by evil.

Returning once more to our example of the employee demand for supervisor accountability, Derrida might observe that the action is both good (legitimate request for decision justification) and evil (purposefully manipulative). From one perspective, the request is legitimate (good) because the interests of the department are served by the demand. Supervisors should be held accountable for decisions that significantly affect a department. This action, however, serves the simultaneous purpose of discrediting the supervisor to meet the subordinate's desire to administer punishment (evil), whether or not it is deserved. Alternatively, the act of manipulation on the part of the employee (evil) may serve to draw attention to dysfunctional power dynamics in the department (good) involving the employee who demands accountability and others with whom he is allied. So, choosing whether the act of the employee is good or evil is not as important as understanding that good and evil define each other in the series of actions and interpretations that evolve from the act.

Derrida's significant contribution to poststructuralism is explaining how the meaning of texts or human actions may be shown through deconstruction. As an example, Mumby and Putnam (1992) offered a deconstruction of the concept of "bounded rationality." The term "bounded rationality" was developed by Simon (1976) to acknowledge that there are limitations associated with decision-making rationality in organizations. Specifically, organization members rarely make optimal choices with full recognition of all the relevant facts or information. Rather, "rules of thumb" and minimal information processing characterizes most decisions. In their deconstruction of the term, Mumby and Putnam (1992) juxtapose it with the notion of "bounded emotionality." This poststructural feminist deconstruction does not privilege the feminist (emotionality) over the patriarchal (rationality). Rather, Mumby and Putnam play one term against the other by considering the "rationality of emotions" and the "emotionality of the rational." In offering this deconstruction, they offer us alternative ways of viewing organizing processes. With respect to power relations in organizations, this means that power does not reside in either rationality or emotionality but in both.

POWER AND CONFLICT: CONNECTED AND SEPARATE PHENOMENA

Power and conflict are often connected in the traditional management and conflict literature. Pfeffer's (1981) work is representative of this literature. According to Pfeffer, "power follows from situations in which there is conflict" (p. 96). Why are power and conflict so closely intertwined? Well, when organization members are interdependent, and those members have competing goals in an environment in which rewards and resources are scarce, each member views the other as an obstacle to goal attainment. Hocker and Wilmot (1995), two conflict researchers, make this very point in their definition of interpersonal conflict: "Conflict is an expressed struggle between at least two interdependent parties who perceive incompatible goals, scarce rewards and interference from others in achieving their goals" (p. 21). So, when one person views another as an obstacle to goal attainment or the procurement of rewards, he or she will exercise power to try to get his or her way.

Are power and conflict always related? Well, it is difficult to envision a struggle between organization members over scarce rewards or competing goals in which power would not be present. As people present their interpretation of a dispute and express their personal needs, they are clearly acting in an empowering manner. Empowerment, however, can exist without conflict. For example, Eisenberg (1994) discusses a form of employee empowerment that is linked to the promotion of *dialogue*. In establishing dialogue, all organization members must have equal opportunities to present their ideas and opinions on important issues. Second, members must display empathy for differing ideas, opinions, and worldviews. Finally, the personal feelings and experiences of organization members must be considered legitimate in making decisions. According to Eisenberg (1994), dialogue both "limits defensiveness by reducing attacking communication and, more important, gives people insight into the ways in which others frame their opinions and behavior—the personal and cultural context that can help others seem different, yet sensible" (p. 282). It is certainly reasonable to assume that dialogue (as a form of empowerment) can exist in certain instances without the emergence of conflict.

Given the preceding observations, we feel comfortable with the following two conclusions about the relationship between power and conflict. When a conflict exists in which employees are struggling over scarce rewards and competing goals, there will be displays of power as each side tries to maximize their outcomes. However, there are forms of empowerment (such as dialogue) in which the expression of different viewpoints on an issue will not necessarily promote conflict. The reason for this is that when dialogue is promoted, the different parties to the discussion do not view one another as obstacles to goal attainment; rather, organization members exchange different perspectives on an issue until a potential decision emerges that meets the needs of *all* members. As the discussion evolves, members recognize that their commitment to and respect for one another will prevent a destructive conflict from surfacing in which one side tries to defeat the other. So, a conversation can be sustained in which members help one another to reach goals that are mutually defined and important to all involved. Now that we have explained how power and conflict can be viewed as connected and separate phenomena, we will turn to a more developed description of conflict in organizations in the next chapter.

SUMMARY

The function of communication in constituting organizations depends on the manner in which it is used to exercise power, one of the most pervasive phenomena in organizational life. In hierarchically structured organizations, differences in members' status and power are a simple fact of life. Status refers essentially to the rank or importance of one's position in a group. Traditionally, power has been regarded as any means or resource that one person may employ to gain compliance and cooperation from others.

French and Raven (1959) provided an analysis of social power that has become a classic model for classifying the forms of power applied in organizational relationships. They described five basic types of power: reward, coercive, referent, expert, and legitimate.

Traditional theories of power have tried to describe the forms of power that occur in social processes and have emphasized social exchange explanations for the operation of power. The result is an appealing, but somewhat sterile, account of power that fails to account for the connection between power and communication and somehow seems to ignore the dark side of organizational subservience.

The work of Max Weber inspired the community power debate during the 1950s through the 1970s. This debate moved thinking beyond individual and relationally focused conceptions of power by examining the different dimensions in which power relations were displayed. In his three-dimensional view of power, Lukes (1974) observed that power may be displayed in situations other than decision making or conflict because power resides in the socially constructed and culturally patterned behavior of organization members.

Interpretive perspectives on power emphasize that communication is constitutive of organizing because organization members collectively construct a shared reality through communication. Interpretivists focus on the relationships that exist among communication, power, and meaning. In doing so, interpretivists give us insight into how communication among organization members creates meaning systems that create and sustain relations of power.

In view of modern critical theory, power is inextricably tied to domination and oppression—conditions in the structure of society and in organizations that scholars should reveal and criticize. Critical theory also attempts to show how symbols are used to legitimate dominant forms of organizational reality, thereby restricting the interpretations and meanings that members can attach to organizational actions. In the process, critical theory relies heavily on showing how ideological manipulation and systematically distorted communication sustain hegemony.

Feminist theory has contributed to the critique of power and domination by arguing for "empowerment" as a substitute for traditional concepts of power. Feminist theory calls for reforming organizations from hierarchical systems to collectivities or heterarchies that achieve action through consensus.

Poststructuralists focus on the multiple meanings that may be assigned to texts. One poststructuralist view is that human action needs to be interpreted from the standpoint of the multiple people who observe that action. This perspective also draws our attention to how context influences the meanings people assign to actions.

Finally, we looked at power and conflict as connected and separate phenomena. Power and conflict are connected when workers view one another as obstacles to goal attainment. The two phenomena can exist separately when workers mutually empower one another through dialogue. When dialogue is promoted, workers recognize how goals can be obtained through cooperation rather than by defeating their opposition. We will return to the issues of power and conflict at the beginning of the next chapter.

DISCUSSION QUESTIONS/ACTIVITIES

1. In what ways does the critical perspective of power differ from the traditional treatment of power?

2. Does the fact that our democratic society protects individual rights limit the application of critical theory to organizational communication? Why or why not?

3. What are the challenges of promoting dialogue in the workplace? Can you envision a problem-solving situation in which the promotion of dialogue would prevent a destructive conflict from surfacing? Have you ever had a conversation with another person that you would classify as a dialogue? If so, what happened in this conversation?

REFERENCES

Abercrombie, N., Hill, S., & Turner, B. S. (1980). *The dominant ideology thesis.* London: Allen and Unwin.

Acker, J. (1990). Hierarchies, jobs, bodies: A theory of gendered organizations. *Gender & Society, 4,* 139–158.

Albrecht, T. L., & Hall, B. (1991). Relational and content differences between elites and outsiders in innovation networks. *Human Communication Research, 17,* 535–561.

Bachrach, P., & Baratz, M. (1962). Two faces of power. *American Political Science Review, 56,* 947–952.

Bachrach, P., & Baratz, M. (1963). Decisions and nondecisions: An analytical framework. *American Political Science Review, 57,* 641–651.

Barker, J. R. (1993). Tightening the iron cage: Concertive control in self-managing teams. *Administrative Science Quarterly, 38,* 408–437.

Barker, J. R., & Cheney, G. (1994). The concepts and practices of discipline in contemporary organizational life. *Communication Monographs, 61,* 19–43.

Barthes, R. (1977). The death of the author. In S. Heath (Ed. and Trans.), *Image, music, text* (pp. 142–148). New York: Hill. (Original work published 1968.)

Barthes, R. (1996). From work to text. In P. Rice & P. Waugh (Eds.), *Modern literary theory* (pp.166–171). New York: Arnold. (Original work published 1971)

Burawoy, M. (1979). *Manufacturing consent.* Chicago: University of Chicago Press.

Clegg, S. (1975). *Power, rule, and domination.* London: Routledge & Kegan Paul.

Cooper, R. (1989). Modernism, postmodernism and organizational analysis 3: The contribution of Jacques Derrida. *Organization Studies, 10,* 479–502.

Dahl, R. (1957). The concept of power. *Behavioral Science, 2,* 201–215.

Dahl, R. (1958). A critique of the ruling elite model. *American Political Science Review, 52,* 463–469.

Dahl, R. (1961). *Who governs? Democracy and power in an American city.* New Haven, CT: Yale University Press.

Deetz, S. A. (1982). Critical interpretive research in organizational communication. *Western Journal of Speech Communication, 46,* 131–149.

Derrida, J. (1976). *Of grammatology* (G. Spivak, Trans.). Baltimore: Johns Hopkins. (Original work published 1967)

Edwards, R. (1979). *Contested terrain.* New York: Basic Books.

Eisenberg, E. M. (1994). Dialogue as democratic discourse: Affirming Harrison. In S. A. Deetz (Ed.), *Communication Yearbook 17* (pp. 275–284). Thousand Oaks, CA: Sage.

Eisenstein, H. (1991). *Gender shock.* Boston: Beacon.

Emerson, R. M. (1962). Power-dependence relations. *American Sociological Review, 27,* 31–41.

Farmer, J. D. (1999). If you don't have your heart in it, get your hind end out of it: Discursive practices, identification, and power in the Sandy Valley Basin. (Doctoral dissertation, Ohio University, 1999). *Dissertation Abstracts International-A, 60/04,* p. 938.

Farrell, T. B., & Aune, J. A. (1979). Critical theory and communication: A selective literature review. *Quarterly Journal of Speech, 65,* 93–120.

Ferguson, K. E. (1984). *The feminist case against bureaucracy.* Philadelphia: Temple University Press.

Foucault, M. (1973). *The order of things: An archaeology of the human sciences* (R. Sawyer, Trans.). New York: Vintage. (Original work published 1966)

Foucault, M. (1979). *Discipline and punish: The birth of the prison* (A. S. Smith, Trans.). New York: Random House. (Original work published 1975)

Fowler, R., Hodge, B., Kress, G., & Trew, T. (1979). *Language and control.* London: Routledge and Kegan Paul.

French, J. R. P., Jr., & Raven, B. H. (1959). The bases of social power. In D. Cartwright (Ed.), *Studies in social power* (pp. 150–167). Ann Arbor: University of Michigan Press.

Frost, P. J. (1987). Power, politics, and influence. In F. M. Jablin, L. L. Putnam, K. H. Roberts, & L. W. Porter (Eds.), *Handbook of organizational communication: An interdisciplinary perspective* (pp. 503–548). Newbury Park, CA: Sage.

Gadamer, H. G. (1989). *Truth and method* (2nd ed., J. Weinsheimer & D.G. Marshall, Trans.). New York: Continuum. (Original work published 1960)

Gibson, M., & Papa, M. J. (2000). The mud, the blood, the beer guys: Organizational osmosis in blue collar work groups. *Journal of Applied Communication Research, 28,* 68–88.

Giddens, A. (1979). *Central problems in social theory.* Berkeley: University of California Press.

Gramsci, A. (1971). *Selections from the prison notebooks* (Q. Hoeare & G. Nowell Smith, Trans.). New York: International Publishers.

Greenwald, R. (Director). (2005). *Wal-Mart: The high cost of low price* [Motion picture]. Los Angeles: Brave New Films.

Habermas, J. (1968). *Knowledge and human interests* (J. Shapiro, Trans.). Boston: Beacon Press.

Habermas, J. (1979). *Communication and the evolution of society* (T. McCarthy, Trans.). Boston: Beacon Press. (Original work published 1976.)

Hancox, M., & Papa, M. J. (1996). *Employee struggles with autonomy and dependence: Examining the dialectic of control through a structurational account of power.* Paper presented at the annual meeting of the International Communication Association, Chicago, May 1996.

Hocker, J. L., & Wilmot, W. W. (1995). *Interpersonal conflict* (4th ed.). Dubuque, IA: Wm. C. Brown.

Hunter, F. (1953). *Community power structure.* Chapel Hill: University of North Carolina Press.

Iannello, K. P. (1992). *Decisions without hierarchy: Feminist interventions in organization theory and practice.* New York: Routledge.

Jacobs, K., & Dube, A. (2004). *Hidden costs of Wal-Mart jobs.* Berkeley: University of California Labor Center.

Kelman, H. C. (1961). Processes of opinion change. *Public Opinion Quarterly, 25,* 57–78.

Lukes, S. (1974). *Power: A radical view.* London: Macmillan.

Marshall, J. (1989). Revisioning career concepts: A feminist invitation. In M. B. Arthurs, D. T. Hall, & B. S. Lawrence (Eds.), *A handbook of career theory* (pp. 275–291). Cambridge: Cambridge University Press.

Martin, J., Feldman, M., Hatch, M. J., & Sitkin, S. B. (1983). The uniqueness paradox in organizational stories. *Administrative Science Quarterly, 28,* 438–453.

McGaan, L. (1983). *Critical theory and communicative action: An introduction to the work of Jürgen Habermas.* Paper presented to the Humanities Colloquium, Wabash College, October 1983.

McPhee, R. (1985). *Four critical approaches to workplace power/control in organizational communication.* Paper presented at the annual meeting of the International Communication Association, Chicago, May 1985.

Miller, G. (2004, February 16). *Everyday low wages: The hidden price we all pay for Wal-Mart.* Washington, DC: Democratic Staff of the Committee on Education and the Workforce.

Mills, C. W. (1956). *The power elite.* Oxford, UK: Oxford University Press.

Mumby, D. K. (1987). The political function of narrative in organizations. *Communication Monographs, 54,* 113–127.

Mumby, D. K. (2001). Power and politics. In F. M. Jablin & L. L. Putnam (Eds.), *The new handbook of organizational communication: Advances in theory, research, and methods* (pp. 585–623). Thousand Oaks, CA: Sage.

Mumby, D. K., & Putnam, L. L. (1992). The politics of emotion: A feminist reading of bounded rationality. *Academy of Management Review, 17,* 465–486.

Mumby, D. K., & Stohl, C. (1991). Power and discourse in organization studies: Absence and the dialectic of control. *Discourse & Society, 2,* 313–332.

Pacanowsky, M., & O'Donnell-Trujillo, N. (1982). Communication and organizational cultures. *Western Journal of Speech Communication, 46,* 115–130.

Papa, M. J., Auwal, M. A., & Singhal, A. (1995). Dialectic of control and emancipation in organizing for social change: A multitheoretic study of the Grameen Bank in Bangladesh. *Communication Theory, 5,* 189–223.

Papa, M. J., Auwal, M. A., & Singhal, A. (1997). Organizing for social change within concertive control systems: Member identification, empowerment, and the masking of discipline. *Communication Monographs, 64,* 219–251.

Papa, W. H., Papa, M. J., Kandath, K. P., Worrell, T., & Muthuswamy, N. (2005). Dialectic of unity and fragmentation in feeding the homeless: Promoting social justice through communication. *Atlantic Journal of Communication, 13,* 242–271.

Pfeffer, J. (1981). *Power in organizations.* Marshfield, MA: Pitman.

Pfeffer, J., & Salancik, G. (1974). Organizational decision-making as a political process: The case of a university budget. *Administrative Science Quarterly, 19,* 135–1251.

Pfeffer, J., & Salancik, G. (1978). *The external control of organizations: A resource dependence perspective.* New York: Harper & Row.

Putnam, L. L. (1983). The interpretive perspective: An alternative to functionalism. In L. L. Putnam & M. E. Pacanowsky (Eds.), *Communication and organizations: An interpretive approach* (pp. 31–54). Beverly Hills, CA: Sage.

Redding, W. C. (1985). Rocking boats, blowing whistles, and teaching speech communication. *Communication Education, 34,* 245–258.

Russell, B. (1983). *Power: A social analysis.* New York: Norton.

Salancik, G., & Pfeffer, J. (1974). The bases and uses of power in organizational decision-making: The case of a university. *Administrative Science Quarterly, 19,* 453–473.

Salancik, G., & Pfeffer, J. (1977). Who gets power and how they hold on to it: A strategic contingency model of power. *Organizational Dynamics, 5*(3), 3–21.

Secord, P. F., & Backman, C. W. (1964). *Social psychology.* New York: McGraw-Hill.

Simon, H. (1976). *Administrative behavior* (3rd ed.). Glencoe, IL: Free Press.

Smith, R., & Eisenberg, E. (1987). Conflict at Disneyland: A root metaphor analysis. *Communication Monographs, 54,* 367–380.

Sussman, L. (1973). Perceived message distortion in organizational hierarchies, or you can fool some of the supervisors some of the time. *Personnel Journal, 53,* 679–682.

Tompkins, P. K., & Cheney, G. (1983). The uses of account analysis: A study of organizational decision making and identification. In L. L. Putnam & M. E. Pacanowsky (Eds.), *Communication and organizations: An interpretive approach* (pp. 123–146). Beverly Hills, CA: Sage.

Weber, M. (1978). Bureaucracy. In H. H. Gerth & C. Wright Mills (Eds.), *From Max Weber: Essays in sociology* (pp. 196–244). New York: Oxford.

Williams, R. (1977). *Marxism and literature.* New York: Oxford University Press.

Witten, M. (1993). Narrative and the culture of obedience at the workplace. In D. K. Mumby (Ed.), *Narrative and social control: Critical perspectives* (pp. 97–118). Newbury Park, CA: Sage.

Wolfinger, R. E. (1971). Nondecisions and the study of local politics. *American Political Science Review, 65,* 1063–1080.

Wyatt, N. (1988). Shared leadership in the weaver's guild. In B. Bate & A. Taylor (Eds.), *Women communicating: Studies of women's talk* (pp. 147–175). Norwood, NJ: Ablex.

Conflict

The forms of conflict with which we are primarily concerned in this chapter are those that fit Putnam and Poole's (1987) definition of conflict as "the interaction of interdependent people who perceive opposition of goals, aims, and values, and who see the other party as potentially interfering with the realization of these goals" (p. 552). Understanding conflict is critically important because it is an intrinsic part of organizational life (Putnam & Poole, 1987). Also, as we argued in the last chapter, conflict and power are inextricably related. Whereas organizational action depends on the exercise of power, the exercise of power often leads to conflict (one exception being those situations in which employees mutually empower one another). In turn, conflict situations, by definition, involve interdependent actors who have the power to constrain or interfere with each other's goals. In a sense, conflict entails the exercise of power.

Conflict offers both advantages and disadvantages or opportunities and challenges for organizations. On the positive side, contemporary organizational theorists stress the point that conflict is an inevitable and even necessary aspect of group and organizational processes (Jameson, 1999; Janis, 1972; Robbins, 1977). Thus, conflict should not be suppressed and avoided but confronted, managed, and resolved. Furthermore, conflict can bring to the surface issues that require resolution, relieve tensions, and lead to the development of new channels of communication (Koehler, Anatol, & Applbaum, 1981). On the other hand, no one would deny that uncontrolled conflict is harmful within groups and organizations. Richard Beckhard (1969) argued, "one of the major problems affecting organization effectiveness is the amount of dysfunctional energy expended in inappropriate competition and fighting between groups that should be collaborating" (p. 33). Another type of problem occurs when conflicts are avoided or suppressed. Avoidance or suppression of conflict leaves underlying issues unresolved. These issues, like Schein's (1969) personal emotional needs, will continue to reemerge in forms that hamper the group's task efforts. Even when conflict is successfully suppressed, the effect may be poor decisions and solutions based on badly distorted conceptions of problems and situations.

TRADITIONAL PERSPECTIVES ON CONFLICT

Much of the research and organizational training on conflict uses the traditional perspective. Specifically, researchers and corporate trainers focus on the strategies, styles, communication choices, and processes that produce high-quality conflict resolution and effective decisions. In this section of the chapter, we focus on mainstream work representing this perspective. First, we look at how interpersonal conflicts may be managed productively by selecting particular conflict styles. Second, we discuss a competence-based model that shows how conflicting parties can be both appropriate and effective during conflict to produce outcomes such as high-quality decisions, relational satisfaction, and trust. Third, we examine how groupthink may suppress conflict in unproductive ways and how to overcome this problem. Fourth, we present a model for managing conflict. Finally, we consider work that has been done in bargaining and negotiation that follows a traditional perspective, including principled negotiation.

Scholarly studies conducted from the traditional perspective and organizational training programs provide us with insight into the strategies and sequences of actions that produce effective and ineffective decisions. Although work representing the traditional perspective is important for us to understand how to manage conflicts more effectively, it represents only one way of understanding conflict. Later in the chapter we look at the interpretive and critical perspectives on conflict to provide a more complete overview of how conflict is experienced in organizations.

Interpersonal Conflict

Putnam and Poole (1987) note that most work on interpersonal conflict in organizations has centered on **conflict styles** in superior-subordinate relationships. Conflict style refers to "a person's characteristic manner or habitual way of handling a dispute" (p. 556). Models of conflict style vary somewhat, but most are consistent with an early model proposed by Blake and Mouton (1964) and revised by Hall (1969). The model is based on two dimensions: concern for your personal goals in the conflict and the importance of your relationship with the other person in the conflict. Both are rated on a 1–9 scale (low to high). Your "style" of conflict presumably can be located by the coordinate of your ratings on these two dimensions. Although there are 81 possible coordinates, each coordinate falls into one of five basic style categories.

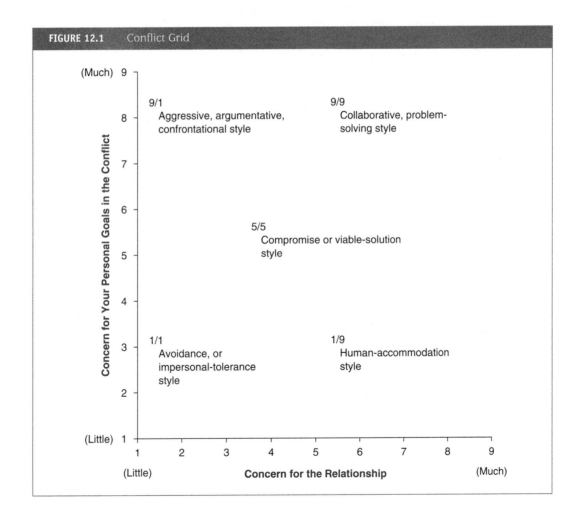

FIGURE 12.1 Conflict Grid

1/1 Avoiding Style. This style is based on low concern for personal goals and for the relationship. The avoider refrains from arguing, withdraws from the situation, or otherwise tries to remain disconnected from the conflict.

9/1 Forcing Style. The forcer has high concern for personal goals in the conflict but low concern for the relationship. Consequently, the forcer is aggressive, competitive, and confrontational in an effort to get his or her way.

1/9 Accommodating Style. When high concern for the relationship is coupled with low concern for personal goals, the result is an accommodating style. The accommodator glosses over differences or downplays disagreements in an effort to maintain the relationship.

9/9 Collaborating Style. The collaborator has high concern for personal goals and for the relationship. The collaborator faces the conflict directly and works toward an integrative solution. An integrative, or "win-win," solution embraces the goals of both parties in the conflict. Hence, the collaborating style often is viewed as the ideal in conflict management. Because this approach addresses the conflict directly, it is sometimes referred to as the confronting style.

5/5 Compromising Style. Given a moderate concern for personal goals in the conflict and a moderate concern for the relationship, the compromiser is willing to "split the difference" with the other party in the conflict, where each party gets something, but the end result probably is less than ideal for either. This is sometimes called the *viable solution* approach to conflict.

In considering the types of conflict styles reported in the literature, Putnam and Wilson (1982) expressed concern that there was an inadequate focus on concrete communication behaviors so they set out to develop the Organizational Communication Conflict Instrument (OCCI). The OCCI identifies three communicative strategies that employees use in conflict: *nonconfrontation strategies, solution-oriented strategies,* and *control strategies.* Nonconfrontation strategies avoid disagreements and downplay controversies by approaching conflict indirectly. These strategies reflect a combination of what Blake and Mouton (1964) would call avoidance or accommodation. Solution-oriented strategies move toward the opposition by using compromise as well as a search for innovation. Finally, control strategies involve arguing persistently for positions and using nonverbal behavior to emphasize demands. By using these strategies, one moves against the opposition.

Different conflict strategy schemes draw our attention to specific features of conflict behavior. One question that has attracted the interest of many researchers is how employees make decisions about what strategy to use in a specific situation. Generally, research suggests that several factors in the *relationship* between conflicting parties influences choice of conflict strategy. Superiors most often rely on forcing as a method of handling conflicts with their subordinates, although first-line supervisors are more likely than either middle or upper level managers to exhibit a collaborative style (Putnam & Wilson, 1982). Perhaps not surprisingly, subordinates tend to adopt avoiding, compromising, or accommodating styles in conflicts with superiors. Burke (1970) found that subordinates preferred for superiors to use a collaborative or confronting style, but superiors regarded collaborating as effective only when the issues are negotiable and conflicts of interest are low. According to Robbins (1978), forcing was regarded as the most effective strategy under conditions of incompatible goals or organizational endorsement of a particular solution. In this case, "organizational endorsement" probably is a euphemism for top-management insistence. Lawrence and Lorsch (1967) found that accommodating and compromising were acceptable strategies to subordinates, but superiors regarded these strategies as counterproductive. Organization members in general have reported that the avoiding style is neither desirable nor effective (Burke, 1970).

Some studies, in particular Putnam and Wilson (1982), suggest that organization members adapt the conflict styles across different types of relationships. Although the concept of conflict style assumes that a person typically engages in a particular mode of action, one's actions in handling a conflict clearly depend on the relationship within which the conflict occurs.

Conflict style also appears to be influenced by *conflict issues.* When conflict involves incompatible values, forcing is likely to occur. Compromising and accommodating are more likely when the conflict involves personality differences or competition for scarce resources. Putnam and Poole (1987) concluded that personality traits and contextual variables, such as organizational climate, leadership style, and communication climate, do not influence the selection of conflict strategies, although high levels of member commitment to the organization are positively associated with collaborative styles of conflict management.

The selection of conflict strategies also may be influenced to some extent by sex or gender, but the effect is unclear. Burrell, Buzzanell, and McMillan (1992) reviewed studies suggesting that women tend to assume noncompetitive and accommodating styles of conflict. In their own investigation, however, they found that although women do not prefer a destructive approach to conflict, they might engage in it because they have no other option. Similarly, Conrad (1991) found that women try longer than men to maintain prosocial strategies in handling conflict situations, but if the conflict wears on, both sexes ultimately turn to coercion in order to exact compliance from others. Finally, Papa and Natalle (1989) found that the key to discovering similarities and differences in the conflict behavior of men and women is to examine how their behaviors change over the course of a dispute. Specifically, they found that male-male conflict dyads used reason and assertiveness consistently over time, whereas female-female dyads shifted from high levels of assertiveness and reason to bargaining. Also, they found that when males and females were paired together, reason and bargaining were used throughout the interactions.

Researchers have begun to extend the study of interpersonal conflict in organizations beyond the narrow boundaries of conflict style in superior-subordinate relationships. One example of such work is a study by Papa and Pood (1988) on coorientational accuracy and differentiation in conflict management within coworker dyads and superior-subordinate dyads in a large insurance company. Coorientational accuracy refers to knowing where another person stands on an issue and what conflict tactics he or she prefers. For example, a person displays coorientational accuracy when he or she says, "I know from our previous discussions of this issue that you oppose the work for incentives plan. I also know that to convince you otherwise I will need clear statistical evidence from several other companies like ours that similar plans have worked in improving worker performance." Differentiation is the process of clarifying differences in interactants' positions and pursuing the reasons behind those positions. For example, differentiation would be displayed in the following statements: "You oppose Jim's candidacy for the supervisor's position because you believe he is too accommodating in meeting worker needs. You hold this point of view because you believe it results in workers being treated unequally. I support Jim's candidacy because the workers in his department are loyal to him and that loyalty will translate into high performance." Papa and Pood found that dyads entering a conflict with low coorientational accuracy spent much more time in differentiation than did high-accuracy dyads. The finding is important because adequate differentiation is necessary in order to move conflict into an integration stage. According to Papa and Pood, workers entering a conflict with low coorientational accuracy find it difficult to reach the integration phase.

Weider-Hatfield and Hatfield (1995, 1996) conducted two studies that offer insight into how the selection of particular conflict styles influences perceptions of interpersonal conflict in organizations and the outcomes that conflicting parties reach. In their 1995 study, they discovered that when subordinates used a high-obliging or accommodating style with supervisors, they experienced more intrapersonal conflict. They also reported that when supervisors used a high-integrating style with subordinates, they experienced more intrapersonal and intragroup conflict, and when supervisors used low-dominating styles, they experienced greater intragroup conflict. On the positive side, when subordinates used the integrating style frequently with supervisors, they experienced less intrapersonal, intragroup, and intergroup conflict than subordinates who did not use this style as frequently. Finally, Weider-Hatfield and Hatfield (1995) found that there was a strong relationship between the use of the integrating style to manage conflict and six organizational outcomes: job satisfaction, perceptions of workplace equity, system outcomes, job and performance outcomes, and interpersonal outcomes. In their 1996 study, the authors focused on the relationship between superiors' conflict management strategies and two subordinate outcomes, interpersonal and performance rewards. Interpersonal rewards referred to recognition for good work, job friendships, status, appreciation, and a feeling of belonging. Performance rewards included perceptions of accomplishment, competence, achievement, confidence, and personal worth. Results of the study showed significant positive relationships between managers' use of collaborating strategies and subordinates' experiencing interpersonal and performance rewards. The study showed significant negative relationships between managers' forcing strategies and those same outcomes (Weider-Hatfield & Hatfield, 1996).

A Competence-Based Approach to Interpersonal Conflict

One development in conflict theory and research is a competence-based approach to describe how people can manage their disputes (Canary, Cupach, & Serpe, 2001; Canary & Spitzberg, 1987, 1989; Spitzberg & Canary, 1985). Although this approach has typically been associated with personal relationships outside the organizational arena (e.g., marriages, friendships), recent work has shown its relevance to relationships within organizations (Gross, Guerrero, & Alberts, 2004; Papa & Canary, 1995; Papa & Papa, 1996). On the basis of research supporting this approach to conflict management and our own experience as organizational consultants, we present this model as one that can help employees to successfully manage workplace conflict.

A competence model of conflict specifies how "various styles of conflict differ in terms of their effectiveness and appropriateness with more competent styles leading to positive outcomes" (Gross et al., 2004). There is a variety of different strategic options that conflicting parties may use during a conflict. One way to characterize these strategic choices is to describe them as integrative, distributive, or avoidant. Integrative strategies focus on collaborating and solving problems. Distributive strategies attempt to control or dominate the discussion. Avoidant strategies remove a participant from involvement in the conflict through physical exit or topical avoidance. Research has shown consistently that integrative strategies are perceived as more competent than either distributive or avoidant strategies (Canary & Cupach, 1988; Canary et al., 2001; Canary & Spitzberg, 1987, 1989, 1990; Gross et al., 2004). Integrative strategies during conflict have also been associated with more effective decision making (Kuhn & Poole, 2000). In order to understand the nature of the relationships among perceptions of conflict strategies, communication competence, and positive conflict outcomes, let's consider a competence model of conflict.

The first feature of a competence-based approach to conflict management is to focus on the **impressions** of a person's communication behavior, not just on the behavior itself. In other words, in conflict it is important to know how each person's behavior is perceived because any single behavior can be interpreted in a number of different ways. For instance, a threat can be perceived as inappropriate in certain instances but appropriate in others (e.g., "If you do not complete this project by the deadline, your performance appraisal will suffer.").

The second feature of a competence-based approach is its focus on two behavioral criteria that are linked to communication quality: **appropriateness** and **effectiveness**. "Appropriateness refers to communication that avoids violation of relationally or situationally sanctioned rules, whereas effectiveness refers to communication that achieves the valued objectives of the interactant" (Papa & Canary, 1995, pp. 154–155). So, the more appropriate and effective an interactant is, the more competent he or she is likely to be perceived. Importantly, "when two employees successfully manage a conflict in terms of appropriateness and effectiveness, not only is the immediate conflict issue resolved, the relationship between them is also preserved" (p. 157). Because relational preservation is necessary for people to work together productively, it is vital for organization members to manage their conflicts in ways that are effective at the individual level and appropriate at the relationship level.

In order to explain how their competence-based approach is relevant to organization members, Papa and Canary (1995) linked their discussion of competence to a **phase** model of conflict. Phase models describe the sequence of behaviors that people produce over time. Papa and Canary described three conflict phases: **differentiation**, **mutual problem description**, and **integration**.

Differentiation refers to the process of people coming to terms with their differences in conflict. Sustaining this behavior during a conflict can be quite difficult. For example, during differentiation, emotional statements are likely as participants commit to positions (Apfelbaum, 1964). Also, differentiation can create uncertainty about the outcomes of the conflict and result in a heightened awareness of the consequences of not reaching a solution (Folger, Poole, & Stutman, 1993; Holsti, 1971; Smart & Vertinsky, 1977). So, how can the pitfalls of differentiation be overcome? Papa and Canary (1995) argue that the key lies in **information sharing** (explaining your position on the issue of dispute) and **information seeking** (soliciting the other person's perspective). Information sharing is important so each party to a conflict can understand the perspective advanced by his or her partner. Information seeking is important because it allows interactants to confirm the accuracy of their perceptions of a partner's views on the conflict issue (Papa & Papa, 1996). Also, without information seeking it may be difficult for each person to reach a clear understanding of his or her partner's views on the conflict.

In order to move from differentiation to integration, Papa and Canary (1995) argue that a middle phase must be enacted, namely, mutual problem description. In describing a conflict in mutual terms, each party accepts responsibility for the conditions of the conflict and socially constructs the conflict in understandable terms. What this means is that each party accepts his or her role in creating and sustaining the conflict and the conflict problem is described clearly so each party understands what issues need to be negotiated. Mutual problem description also requires that the conflict problem be described as one requiring the efforts of each party to reach a mutually satisfying solution.

The final phase of conflict management is the integration phase, during which the parties remain focused on the problem and commit themselves to a solution that meets the goals of each party. According to Papa and Canary, six communication behaviors are linked to successful integration: (1) recognizing and postponing attributions, (2) maintaining cooperative tactics, (3) generating alternative solutions, (4) evaluating the positive and negative aspects of each proposed solution, (5) selecting and clarifying the solution to be implemented, and (6) establishing a monitoring system to determine if the solution is being implemented correctly. Let's take a brief look at each of these six behaviors.

Recognizing attributions refers to the fact that many people harbor biases regarding their attributions for causes of events (Bradbury & Fincham, 1990). For example, in dissatisfying conflicts, both parties "tend to attribute the causes of negative events to internal and stable features of the partner" (Papa & Canary, 1995, p. 166). A comment reflecting such a bias would be, "We are behind schedule because *he* is a slow worker." On the other hand, in satisfying conflicts the interactants are less likely to make such attributions. A statement reflecting this position would be, "We are having financial problems because the cost of doing business has increased." So, a first step in the integration phase is recognizing that "both parties to a conflict tend to think that the partner causes negative events, while (self-serving) biases preserve each person's own view of the self in conflict" (Papa & Canary, 1995, p. 167).

Maintaining cooperative tactics, the second part of Papa and Canary's integration phase, means enacting behaviors such as seeking a mutually beneficial solution, reasoning in a give-and-take manner, and compromising. Generating alternative solutions, the next integration step, is important for two reasons. First, it prevents disputants from identifying a solution too early in the process. Indeed, as Graham, Papa, & McPherson (1997) note, it is important to withhold the advancement of solutions until both parties agree on the nature of the problem. Second, when a number of solution alternatives are generated, it is more likely that a workable, mutually satisfying one will be identified. Once alternative solutions are identified, the disputants need to evaluate the positive and negative ramifications of each solution so the best one can be selected. Finally, a monitoring mechanism needs to be implemented. A monitoring mechanism is necessary to "prevent conflicting parties from undermining a solution by reverting to prior destructive behaviors" (Papa & Canary, 1995, p. 172).

Although the testing of this competence-based model in organizational settings is only in its early stages, there are some promising preliminary findings. Specifically, Papa and colleagues have found that their competence-based model can be applied to each of the four major arenas of organizational conflict, namely, interpersonal, bargaining and negotiation, intergroup, and interorganizational. For example, in examining videotaped interactions of superiors and subordinates managing conflicts, Papa and Papa (1996) found that the competence-based model provided insight into how the disputes were managed successfully through each of three phases (differentiation, mutual problem description, and integration). They were also able to show how the successful collective bargaining agreement negotiated by players and owners of NBA teams in 1983 followed the competence-based model. This collective bargaining agreement resulted in the first player-owner partnership in professional sports.

A more recent study of perceptions of conflict strategies and communication competence in task-oriented dyads also provided support for a competence-based model of conflict in organizations. Gross et al. (2004) found that people generally perceive the solution-oriented strategy as both appropriate and effective and more likely to promote positive outcomes such as relational satisfaction and trust. Conversely, nonconfrontational or avoidant strategies were perceived as incompetent. Finally, when a controlling strategy was used it was perceived as inappropriate by the person subject to the strategy; however, the user of the strategy rated himself or herself as effective.

Groupthink

Underlying the competence model of conflict is the requirement that conflicting parties actively engage one another in discussing the problem that confronts them. This is not always the case, however, when people in organizations recognize problems. Irving Janis (1972) identified a phenomenon known as "groupthink" in which extreme efforts are made to suppress conflict and stop the input of any information that contradicts an established or dominant view. Individual group members surrender their own beliefs and begin to see things only from the group perspective. The group develops a dogmatic commitment to the "moral rightness" of its position and may even believe that it is being persecuted by enemies. Janis argued that the ill-fated Bay of Pigs invasion during John F. Kennedy's presidential administration was a product of groupthink. Virtually anyone outside Kennedy's cloistered group of advisors would have said that the concept of invasion to oust Cuba's Fidel Castro was misguided and unworkable, but suppression of competing views, avoidance of conflict, and a quest to gain consensus merely for its own sake resulted in a disastrous decision. Actions by members of the Nixon administration during the Watergate era, Jimmy Carter's ill-fated decision to attempt a military rescue of American hostages in Iran, Bill Clinton's decision to bomb a weapons plant that turned out to be a pharmaceutical manufacturing company in Sudan, and George W. Bush's decision to invade Iraq may also have been products of groupthink.

Janis also illustrated how the phenomenon figures into corporate decisions to continue marketing inferior or hazardous products. In a film on the development of groupthink, Janis showed how a pharmaceutical company arrived at a decision to market a drug with some extremely dangerous side effects by downplaying the importance and validity of studies demonstrating the hazards. The management team justified its decision by highlighting the benefits of the product and suggesting that those who had qualms about the drug were "not being team players." The group even developed a vision of itself as a heroic paragon of moral virtue in standing behind the product.

Janis (1982) made six suggestions that may be followed to avoid groupthink. First, the leader should assign the role of critical evaluator to each group member. This alerts group members that part of their role is to critically evaluate all solutions that are suggested. Second, the leader should avoid stating preferences and expectations at the outset so he or she does not influence how the discussion proceeds. Third, each member of the group should discuss the group's deliberations with a trusted colleague (organization member but not a group member) and report the colleague's reactions back to the group. Fourth, one or more experts should be invited to each meeting on a staggered basis. These outside experts should be encouraged to challenge the views of the group members. Fifth, at least one articulate and knowledgeable group member should be assigned the role of devil's advocate. This person needs to question assumptions and plans that surface during the group's deliberations. Finally, the leader should set aside a significant block of time to survey warning signals from rivals. The leader and the group should then construct alternative scenarios of their rivals' intentions.

Managing Conflict

Although a number of frameworks have been proposed to describe the process of managing conflict in organizations (Costantino & Merhant, 1996; Elangovan, 1995, 1998; Ewing, 1989), we would like to focus on Jameson's (1999) model because it concentrates on key communication processes and structures. Her model is based on three components: conflict dimensions, conflict management strategies, and desired outcomes (see Figure 12.2).

Concerning conflict dimensions, Jameson (1999) considers the *content, relational*, and *situational* features. With respect to content dimensions, conflict may be objective or subjective, task or relational, or a matter of policy interpretation or policy change. Objective conflicts are about tangible resources or disputed facts, whereas subjective conflicts are over

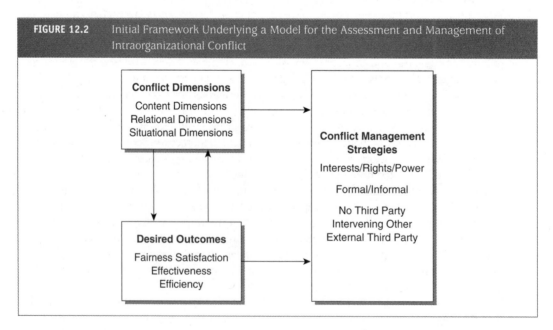

FIGURE 12.2   Initial Framework Underlying a Model for the Assessment and Management of Intraorganizational Conflict

SOURCE: Jameson, 1999.

differences in perceptions, interpretations, or values. Task conflict is concerned with issues such as resource allocation or the content of tasks being performed by employees. This may include differences in viewpoints or opinions about tasks. Relationship conflicts deal with interpersonal incompatibilities among group members. Tension, animosity, and annoyance among members are common in relationship conflicts. Finally, conflicts may surface over the development of a new policy or how to interpret an existing policy.

When looking at the relational features of conflict, a number of issues are relevant. First, the extent to which the parties are interdependent or independent will influence the degree to which the parties will need to work together to manage their differences. Parties in an interdependent relationship need to reach a solution that maximizes all of their interests. Parties that are relatively independent may work around one another and not confront their differences as directly. Second, parties of equal status confront different options for action than parties of unequal status. For example, an employee may find it easier to refuse a demand from a coworker than from a supervisor. Third, if there is high trust between parties, conflicts unfold more productively than if there is low trust. Fourth, a good record of success in managing conflict creates a more productive environment for discussion than a low record of success. Finally, dyadic conflicts are different from multiparty conflicts because the addition of multiple parties usually adds complexity to the discussion process.

Situational features are also important to consider in any conflict. The first situational feature is high versus low time pressure in managing the conflict. The greater the time pressure, the more anxious group members may be to reach a decision. Second, conflicts that have a broad range of impact are considered with greater care and concern than conflicts with a narrower range of impact. Third, conflicts with low escalation potential cause less apprehension than those with high escalation potential. Finally, conflicting parties are confronted with a certain range of conflict management options. This factor deals with the norms or cultural constraints that guide parties' behavior. Is there a narrow range of options for how employees may act in a conflict or is there a broad range of choices?

Jameson (1999) identifies four features of desired outcomes: *fairness, satisfaction, effectiveness,* and *efficiency.* Outcomes that are fair institute better rules and procedures or set a precedent that guides future action. A satisfactory outcome is reached if the solution is fully acceptable to all parties, maintains privacy, makes the dispute public, or results in vindication. Effective outcomes may improve the relationship between parties, prevent repetition of the conflict, teach the parties to manage future conflict, create more clarity between parties, or result in a high-quality decision. Finally, effectiveness is measured by the timeliness of the settlement process or by a solution that minimizes costs and the use of organizational resources.

The third component of Jameson's (1999) model comprises conflict management strategies. Three types of strategies are considered: *interest-based, rights-based,* and *power-based.* Interest-based strategies focus on attempts to reconcile disputants' underlying interests in a conflict. When interest-based conflicts surface, the disputants themselves may confront the problem. In this situation, the parties negotiate informally with one another and try to reach an agreement on their own. If these parties cannot resolve their dispute, a third party may intervene. The third party may be an intervening manager, a peer, or a human resources practitioner. The communicative options that may be used by the third party include advising, facilitating, and mediating. The third party acts as a counselor when using the advising role. The adviser may speak to a single party, act as a go-between, or facilitate conversations between the disputants to help them see one another's point of view.

When acting as a facilitator, the third party takes on a problem-solving role. In this capacity, the third party emphasizes problem identification and problem-solving procedures. The facilitator may also encourage the open sharing of information to settle conflicts in a way that promotes understanding and prevents recurrence of the conflict. Finally, the third party may act as a mediator. In a mediating role, the third party guides the discussion process but allows the disputants control over the outcome. As Jameson (1999) explains, the mediator may "provide information concerning relevant legal issues, help parties engage in perspective taking, guide parties toward a realistic settlement, help improve the relationship between participants, or engage in some combination of these tactics" (p. 282).

Rights-based conflicts focus on determining which party is right in accordance with some accepted guidelines for behavior. An organization may follow informal or formal management strategies during rights-based conflicts. Let's consider informal strategies first. *Adversarial intervention* is a courtroom-style procedure in which the disputants present their case and a manager determines the appropriate solution. *Inquisitorial intervention* is similar, but the manager assumes more control over the process. Specifically, the manager asks the disputants questions rather than allowing them full control over how they present their cases. Then the manager acts as the judge.

Another informal rights-based strategy is *advisory alternative dispute resolution* (ADR). Here an external third party may set up systems of private judging, mini-trials, summary jury trials, and advisory arbitration. In each of these methods there is some type of presentation of arguments and evidence to a third party, who makes a finding. The disputing parties then decide how to proceed on the basis of that finding (agree to mediation or pursue formal legal action).

Rights-based conflicts may also follow formal management strategies. First, a fact-finding investigation may be performed, although the third-party investigator has no power to impose a solution. Rather, the investigator listens to the employees' problems, conducts an investigation, and then determines the most appropriate course of action. Second, a process of internal adjudication may be followed. Typically, the adjudicator is a senior executive or a review board composed of managers and lower level employees. The adjudicators are then only given the power to interpret right or wrong. They may not change policy or offer alternative solutions to the dispute. Finally, an organization may seek binding arbitration. Here the arbitrator is an external third party who makes binding decisions concerning an organization's internal policies. The arbitrator's job is to make an interpretation of the organization's policy, not to judge its fairness or offer a creative solution.

Power-based strategies attempt to resolve conflict on the basis of who has the most power. First, disputants may use power-based approaches without the involvement of a third party. For example, a disputant may use threats to coerce another party to submit to their demands. This option may be selected when one disputant has higher status than the other. Coalition building may also be exercised as an option. This alternative works if a disputant builds his or her power base by connecting with allies who strengthen his or her position. Strikes or lockouts are also examples of power-based strategies, although these options are typically selected in unionized workplaces. Importantly, when a strike or lockout occurs, it is often necessary for an external third party to mediate or arbitrate the conflict.

When third parties use power-based strategies, there are three major options. First, the intervening party may act autocratically by imposing a solution. Second, a third party may restructure the work assignments of the disputing parties to minimize their interdependence. Finally, third parties may use the strategy of providing impetus by threatening to punish or promising a reward. By offering the impetus, the intervening party hopes to coerce the disputants to solve the conflict on their own.

Before proceeding to discuss bargaining and negotiation, we feel it is important to advance one more option for productive conflict management. We have found in our personal work experiences that even when conflicting parties realize it is in their best interests to negotiate a mutually beneficial outcome, deadlocks occur over problem description. For example, in a typical management-labor dispute over wages, the following problem interpretations are likely. Management views the demand for higher wages as potentially threatening to organizational survival. Managers justify this stance because higher wages drive up production costs. Higher production costs both reduce profits and potentially require higher prices (reducing the competitiveness of the firm). Workers, on the other hand, view the problem as one of management greed. Managers, from the workers' perspective, receive an unfair percentage of the firm's profits. The workers believe that their wages should be increased because of the vital role they play in producing high-quality products. One way to remove such deadlocks is to restructure the problem. As Sycara (1991) observes, "problem restructuring is the process of dynamically changing the structure of the conflict problem to achieve momentum toward agreement" (p. 1248). The first step in problem restructuring is for each side to put their desired outcome goals (both short-term and long-term) on the table. Once these goals are on the conflict table, the parties can search for relations among the goals that indicate a dovetailing of interests. According to Sycara, "by having access to information concerning goals and relations among them, [conflicting parties] can produce promising problem reformulations" (p. 1249).

How does problem restructuring work? Let's return to the example presented above. Management and labor can restructure the problem as one of production efficiency and innovation. If labor is willing to work with management on reducing the costs of production (through increases in efficiency and worker-recommended innovations), then higher wages can be paid without reducing corporate profits or increasing product prices. In order for such a solution to be reached, however, both management and labor must be willing to work together to figure out how their interests coincide with one another.

Bargaining and Negotiation

Bargaining and negotiation involve a special case of organizational conflict. As Putnam and Poole (1987) state:

> Bargaining constitutes a unique form of conflict management in that participants negotiated mutually shared rules and then cooperate within these rules to gain a competitive advantage over their opponent. . . . Bargaining, then, differs from other forms of conflict in its emphasis on proposal exchanges as a basis for reaching a joint settlement in cooperative-competitive situations. (p. 563)

In Chapter 4, we mentioned Mary Parker Follett's work on redefining traditional ideas of power and authority in order to achieve integration of competing interests. Follett's ideas directly influenced the development of classic bargaining theory. In particular, Walton and McKersie (1965) expanded on Follett's work to classify bargaining processes in four categories: distributive, integrative, attitudinal structuring, and intraorganizational bargaining. Putnam and Jones (1982) narrowed the focus to distributive and integrative bargaining for purposes of communication research.

Putnam and Poole (1987) also suggest that much of the research on bargaining processes can be understood in terms of the distinction between distributive and integrative processes. A **distributive** bargaining situation "is one characterized by the existence or the appearance of fixed-sum (zero-sum) alternatives; one party must win and the other party must lose" (p. 172). In contrast, **integrative** bargaining "refers to situations where the potential outcomes can be expanded; inconsistent goals are combined to create a new alternative, one where neither side sacrifices his or her ultimate aims" (p. 172).

Distributive bargaining is characterized by deception, withholding of information, or the use of "disinformation" activities (i.e., directly disclosing information that obscures the negotiator's true objective). Bluffs, exaggerated demands, threats, and ambiguous cues are common in distributive bargaining. Negotiators conceal the strength of their positions, the outcomes that they really want, and the points that they are prepared to concede. Integrative bargaining is based on open communication, accurate disclosure of objectives, and sharing of information. Information is used for purposes of fact-finding, problem definition, and generation of alternative solutions (Putnam & Poole, 1987).

How does one know the difference between accurate disclosure in an integrative situation and the misinformation of the distributive situation? In some cases, the circumstances themselves—the bargaining issue, the parties involved, and the resources at stake—will define the situation as distributive or integrative. For example, a local school board faced with a severe decline in tax revenues due to plant closings in the community enters negotiations with a teachers' union. The board, having exhausted all other possible options to reduce costs, must eliminate some teaching positions in order to balance its budget, but the union is absolutely committed to a "no lay off" clause in the new contract. The resulting environment is tense and distributive. In another school district on the other side of the state, the community is enjoying a strong period of economic expansion. Here, the issues between the board and the union are entirely different and both parties are seeking the best ways in which to use the abundant resources available to them.

But bargaining situations often are "mixed" rather than purely distributive or integrative. Moreover, Putnam and Jones (1982) contend that many bargaining situations are defined inappropriately as distributive. The situation is treated as a win-lose dilemma when, in fact, it is possible to achieve an integrative, win-win settlement. Integrative strategies often do not appear until negotiators have gone through a lengthy period of distributive bargaining. In these situations, reciprocity is a critical factor in moving from distributive to integrative bargaining (e.g., when one party makes a concession and the other reciprocates). As we saw earlier in the study by Papa and Pood (1988), differentiation also is critical for movement into integration stages of conflict, and differentiation appears to depend on coorientational accuracy. As Putnam and Poole (1987) point out, "integrative solutions emerge only after differences in perceptions of the problem are openly discussed" (p. 569).

Rather than look at bargaining and negotiation sessions as characterized primarily as distributive or integrative, some researchers contend that it is the sequence of strategies that are used that affects outcomes. For example, Olekalns and Smith (2003) examined the relationship between negotiation strategies and the quality of negotiated outcomes using a simulated employment contract negotiation. They discovered that the frequency and sequencing of strategies were related to negotiation outcomes. Specifically, impasse negotiations included frequent use of contention (threats and promises; attributing bad faith to the opponent; denying the relevance of the opponent's position; personal insults). In addition, impasse negotiations were characterized by sequences that paired similar (either cooperative or competitive) strategies. In negotiations producing settlements, there was a lower level of contention and use of sequences that paired dissimilar strategies (cooperative-competitive pairings). Finally, increasing joint gain was associated with the introduction of priority information (proposing a new way of proceeding; suggesting a range of trade-offs or options; requesting or providing information about the values of issues) and conciliation (proposing modifications to an opponents offer; offering an opponent a concession).

Principled Negotiation

In the classic text, *Getting to Yes: Negotiating Agreement Without Giving In* (1981), Roger Fisher and William Ury describe four principles for effective negotiation. According to Fisher and Ury, good agreements reached through bargaining (a) are fair and efficient, (b) improve the parties' relationship, (c) satisfy the parties' interests, and (d) are fair and lasting. Many negotiations do not yield good agreements because the parties argue from positions rather than from their real underlying interests. Specifically, in positional bargaining, each party opens with a position on an issue. The bargaining process then unfolds with each side bargaining from its opening positions to agree on one position. Fisher and Ury argue that positional bargaining does not produce good agreements because the agreements tend to neglect the parties' real underlying interests. As an alternative to positional bargaining, Fisher and Ury offer principled negotiation, a process based on four principles:

1. Separate the people from the problem.
2. Focus on interests rather than positions.
3. Generate a variety of options before selecting an agreement.
4. Insist that the agreement be based on objective criteria.

The first principle Fisher and Ury (1981) discuss is to separate people from the problem. This separation is necessary because negotiators often become personally involved with the issues they are discussing and with their group's positions. When this occurs, a negotiator will perceive a response to his or her positions as a personal attack. This ensures a quick downward spiral in the ensuing discussions, with each side perceiving that they are being attacked personally and then responding in kind. Conversely, when you effectively separate people from the issues under discussion you may address the issues without damaging the relationship between sides. Simply stated, the focus of the negotiation session should be on the problem and how to solve it.

The second principle is to focus on interests rather than positions. As Fisher and Ury (1981) explain, "Your position is something you have decided upon. Your interests are what caused you to so decide" (p. 42). When parties define a problem in terms of positions, it sets up the outcome that at least one party will "lose" the dispute. However, when the problem is defined in terms of the underlying interests of the parties, it is more likely that they will find a solution satisfactory to both parties' interests.

The third principle is to generate a variety of options before selecting an agreement. Too often parties rush to reach agreement and, in doing so, fail to consider alternatives. According to Fisher and Ury, parties should work creatively by dedicating themselves to an invention process in producing alternative solutions. Brainstorming is often an effective preliminary technique in which wild and creative proposals are presented. Eventually the sides may reduce the available options to a few alternatives. Importantly, the alternatives to be considered should focus on the shared interests of the parties so all sides win with the negotiated agreement.

The final principle is insistence that the agreement be based on objective criteria. In order to accomplish this, the parties must spend time developing objective criteria that they may judge their agreement against. By doing so, they will be able to explain clearly why their selected agreement is in fact a good one. Scientific findings, professional standards, or legal precedent are possible sources of objective criteria (Glaser, 1988). The sides may then test for objectivity by seeing if both sides would be willing to be bound by these standards.

INTERPRETIVE PERSPECTIVES ON CONFLICT

An interpretive perspective on conflict requires us to concentrate on the subjective meanings that organization members develop on the basis of their experiences in engaging in conflicts. Given Putnam and Poole's (1987) opening observation that conflict is an "intrinsic part of organizational life" (p. 550), most employees have many experiences to draw on in giving meaning to the conflicts they have experienced in different work settings. Researchers and consultants attempting to understand conflict from an interpretive perspective would seek to gain insight into the various subjective meanings that employees had developed about conflict in a given organization; they would also want to trace the process of how socially constructed meanings had been created.

Interpretivists recognize that organizational cultures often sustain patterns of behavior through repetition. Sometimes we repeat behaviors in conflict that are productive; sometimes they are destructive. Whatever the patterns are, they play a large role in shaping the cultural environment in which employees work. Think back to the example we shared in Chapter 2 of the company called Far End Design. Although the owner of the company wanted the designers to be independent, he yelled at them if they did not produce the designs that he wanted. Then, if they asked for direction, he berated them for not being autonomous and violating the organizational culture. Despite the fact that the workers were very upset over the conflicts that were produced over their designs, they did not see a way out of the cycle. The unproductive conflict cycle continued because that was the way they did things at Far End Design. They socially created a system that defined what conflict was for them, and they repeated the sequence of behaviors that was part of that system despite its negative impact on them personally and as workers.

Repeated patterns of conflict management need not be negative. Author Michael Papa worked as a technical advisor and consultant to the Conflict Resolution Program (CRP) at The Carter Center (TCC) in Atlanta, Georgia, from 2003 to 2006. During that time, he focused on examining the activities of President Carter and TCC staff in bringing peace to Sudan and Uganda. In several visits to TCC and in interviews with President Carter, TCC administrators, and staff, the culture of the center with respect to conflict management has become very clear. Although TCC has involved itself in some of the most intractable conflicts across the world over the past 20 years, their mission is to "wage peace across the world." This dedication to waging peace by confronting conflict is present throughout the organization. There are plaques and signs as well as messages that appear on television screens throughout the center that state, "Waging Peace." When you ask staff members and administrators who are part of the conflict resolution program what they do, they say, "We wage peace across the world." This notion of waging peace is at the center of how they think about conflict management, and it influences their actions and integrates the various programs throughout the center. Consider the following statement from The Carter Center's Web site:

Peace is more than the absence of conflict. And peace making is more than stopping war. It encompasses democratic ideals and protection of human rights. Not only does the lack of peace often lead to poverty, it is as well one of poverty's many symptoms. Waging peace and promoting democracy prevents conflict and instability, improves governance, and strengthens the rule of law. When citizens are empowered, they use their voices to influence policy, protect human rights, and hold their governments accountable.

Whether working on anticorruption efforts in Latin America, on conflict resolution in Sudan, on a national development strategy in Mali, or with civil society groups in Guyana or Mozambique, the end result is the empowerment of people. The Center's work creates long-term effects by laying and strengthening frameworks within a country's institutions, whether it's through the electoral commission, judicial court, or nongovernmental organizations seeking a voice in the national agenda (Peace Programs Overview: Waging Peace, 2007).

In an interview that Michael Papa conducted with Dr. Ben Hoffman, Director of Conflict Resolution at The Carter Center from 2000 to 2003, the notion of waging peace came through strongly as the core of the center's conflict resolution strategies. Although Dr. Hoffman realized that standard mediation techniques require mediators to be neutral, he realized that such an approach does not work when you are dealing with violent conflict. As he stated in an interview reported in Papa and Mapendere (2005),

When I was in war zones [in Sudan] it occurred to me that I *am* partial. I'm partial to peace. I am deeply invested in peace and I'm highly directive [as a mediator]. I began to realize that you have to wage peace; that you have to be in peace advocacy. You have to advocate peace. You have to design processes [as a mediator] and sell them that way. (personal interview, August 2005)

At The Carter Center, the notion of waging peace is embedded in the actions of practitioners as they intervene in international conflicts and civil wars throughout the world. From an interpretive perspective, administrators and staff at the center have socially constructed the practice of waging peace through their daily conversations about peace making, through conferences held at the center, and through mediation work conducted in many countries.

Cultural Context: Gender, Race, and Nationality

Nicotera and Dorsey (2006) recently reviewed and critiqued studies focusing on individual and interactive processes in organizational conflict. In doing so, they drew attention to certain cultural contexts that influence how people communicate in organizational conflict situations. In particular, they focused on gender and race. With respect to gender, a study by Burrell et al. (1992) focused on how metaphor analysis offers a means of deconstructing women's multilayered realities with respect to conflict. Interestingly, the women participating in their study overwhelmingly used war or destruction metaphors to depict their experiences with conflict in organizations. Consistent with these metaphors, conflict was viewed as adversarial, with clear winners and losers. Furthermore, the metaphors the women selected portrayed conflict as an ongoing process that did not necessarily lead to any clear resolution or end points. Concerning the impact of conflict on their self-image, there were reports of emotional distress, helplessness, and vulnerability. Looking at these findings holistically, Burrell et al. (1992) concluded that although war or destruction metaphors were dominant, the passivity, powerlessness, and feelings of impotence "indicated that these women abhorred this confrontational approach" (p. 140).

Shuter and Turner (1997) combined gender and race by studying conflict narratives used by African American and European American women in managerial and nonmanagerial roles. They discovered that African American women value more direct approaches to conflict than European American women do. Shuter and Turner also asked their respondents to describe their perception of workplace conflict behaviors for African American women, for European American women, and for themselves personally. The women were asked to focus their responses on four behaviors: avoidance, maintenance, reduction, and escalation. They found that European American women were viewed as more likely to avoid conflict than were African American women. Also, in comparison to European American women, African American women viewed all women as more likely to choose escalation, were more likely to see themselves as reducing conflict, and were less likely to see European Americans as maintaining conflict. These findings show clearly that race influences women's perceptions of conflict.

The cultural environment in which one lives influences the type of social construction that unfolds with respect to particular communication processes such as conflict management. For example, Kim and Leung (2000) note that American culture promotes individualism that results in the desirability of direct confrontation in conflict. Conversely, in many Asian countries where collectivism is cultivated, avoidance is used regularly to preserve relational harmony and to save others' face. Interestingly, Kim and Leung also found that bicultural individuals are likely to internalize both individualistic and collectivist constructions and are thus able to display more flexible conflict behaviors in which both direct confrontation and avoidance are used.

Although living in individualistic versus collectivistic cultures may influence how people act during conflict, it is important that we do not oversimplify this observation. For example,

Oetzel (1998) examined whether self-construal (independent or interdependent) or ethnicity predicted individual self-reported conflict styles in the small-group context. Respondents included Latinos (collectivistic) and European Americans (individualistic). Oetzel discovered that self-image is a better predictor of conflict styles than ethnicity is. Specifically, an independent self-construal is positively related to a dominating conflict style, whereas an interdependent self-construal is related positively to avoiding, obliging, and compromising conflict styles. These findings point to the importance of not overgeneralizing the impact of national culture on an individual's communication behavior in specific settings.

Dialogic Culture

The wide variety of individuals and groups that make up contemporary organizations creates a pluralistic environment in which interests both dovetail and collide. One way of managing conflicts in such an environment is to foster a culture in which dialogue is the primary means of managing conflict while sustaining community. This culture of dialogue stands in stark opposition to an oppositional culture in which competitive arguments and power dynamics dominate conflict. Barge (2006) explains that there are several commitments that characterize a dialogic culture that emphasizes collective thinking and respectful relationships. First is the recognition that multiple voices, perspectives, and points of view will characterize any large organization. Given this reality in contemporary organizations, dialogue provides a space for multivocality to be heard and respected. Second, a dialogic culture values otherness. This means that different people and groups within an organization are honored and engaged, particularly if they articulate positions that are opposed by the majority. Also, a persistent commitment to seek understanding of diverse positions dominates a dialogic culture. Third, through dialogue, organization members pursue a richer understanding of the complexity of a situation, an issue, or a problem. Specifically, dialogue facilitates the process of seeing the connections that exist among differing positions and interests. Fourth, dialogue generates new possibilities for meaning and action by allowing for the emergence of new possibilities that may be entirely different from the original ideas that surfaced before dialogic interaction. Finally, dialogue transcends polarization by moving beyond hostile discourse to seek the commonalities that link people together. As Barge (2006) concludes, dialogue provides "a way of being and living together that recognizes the differences that exist among members of community and highlights possibilities for collaboration" (pp. 520–521).

CRITICAL PERSPECTIVES ON CONFLICT

A critical perspective on conflict focuses on how power relations within an organization may create an oppressive environment for certain workers and interfere with their ability to manage conflicts productively. This oppressive environment may exist because the needs of certain employees are privileged over others. Oppression may also be embedded in systems of language and meaning. For example, ways of talking about women may be disempowering and may restrict their opportunities for equitable resolution of conflicts. Finally, workers may organize their interaction around a particular rule system that restricts their options in managing conflict.

One of us is a friend to a faculty member in a small theater department at a college in the southeastern United States. The department had nine faculty members (one of whom was chairperson) and three design staff. The conflicts that surfaced in this department were attributable primarily to a very abrasive and angry department chairperson (Randy) who "ruled the department with an iron fist." Although Randy possessed a good sense of humor and faculty and staff often laughed at his jokes at faculty meetings, he had very narrow and specific views on how everyone should do his or her job. When a person did not perform as he thought appropriate, Randy yelled at and berated him or her. Sometimes at faculty meetings, he would publicly discuss an individual's performance, identify a shortcoming or mistake he thought had occurred, and wait for the person to defend himself or herself. Of course, no explanation met his satisfaction, and he would not stop his criticism until the person agreed to work the way Randy thought was correct. When asked to justify yelling at an untenured faculty member who was not on enough university committees (from his perspective), he responded, "She needed to be kicked in the ass." Randy yelled at a scene designer on stage because he did not design a set to Randy's liking, although the designer had explicitly followed his orders regarding how the set should look. This particular instance was disturbing because the microphones were on and the entire cast of students listened backstage in shock as the designer was subjected to merciless personal attacks that bellowed throughout the theater. One faculty member who was subjected to frequent public criticism at faculty meetings said, "I feel like he is a sniper, looking for his spot to nail you in public." Another faculty member described the approach that everyone took toward conflicts with the chairperson: "Do what it takes to make Randy happy." In fact, that single statement represents the rule system that the entire department was organized around.

Why did these faculty members and staff tolerate Randy's behavior? Sadly, jobs in the arts are difficult to find. So, choosing to leave an intolerable situation may result in a long period of unemployment. This college was also located in a community with a good school system, a favorable climate, and many entertainment activities to enjoy. When the recommendation was made to confront Randy, no one was willing to take the risk. Randy had been with this college and department for over 15 years. No one had ever been successful in confronting him. Those who could not tolerate his abuse simply left. Everyone feared that confrontation was not worth the risk. Because he was a tenured faculty member it was very difficult to fire him, so the fear was that confrontation would result only in an angrier chairperson who would do everything he could to make everyone's life miserable.

The conflicts Randy initiated created an oppressive environment for all of his colleagues. His viewpoints were privileged, and everyone else's views were irrelevant. Doing what it takes to make Randy happy was the single rule that dominated the department. No one saw an alternative. Do you?

Looking at conflict from a feminist perspective allows us not only to look critically at conflict, but also to gain insight into how conflict may lead to emancipation. Papa, Singhal, and Papa (2006) described a conflict experienced by women dairy farmers in India that yielded insights into the dynamics of power and resistance. Women dairy farmers in the village of Lutsaan in India's Uttar Pradesh state were organized into an all-women cooperative. India's National Dairy Development board was giving a special subsidy to such cooperatives in an attempt to encourage their formation to empower rural women. Although this cooperative (on paper) was an all-women's cooperative, it was administered by two men who pocketed all of the proceeds from the milk sales in addition to the special subsidy. The women attempted to argue with the men who took over the center, but their arguments were met with anger and a refusal to return leadership responsibilities to the women. Given the strong patriarchal system dominant in rural India, the women felt they had no choice but to back down. So, these women dairy farmers were participating in their own oppression by allowing the men to administer a cooperative that was rightly theirs to manage. However, these same women devised a separate strategy to earn money and empower themselves. Through democratic decision making, they agreed to join hands and establish a business to make *ghee* (clarified butter) from surplus milk. They sold this ghee locally and in the neighboring township through private vendors. So, although they did not confront the men directly, the women found a way to work around the men by holding back some of the milk their cows produced so they could earn money in a separate enterprise. Also, given the premium price that was paid for *ghee*, they more than made up for the money lost through allowing the men to run the cooperative. This story shows how power relations in conflict may involve processes of both domination and resistance—that is, processes that are oppressive and empowering simultaneously.

Contradictions Between Capitalism and Democracy

In order to understand the contradictions that exist between capitalism and democracy, we must look at the actions taken by the leaders of national governments who engage in economic competition with one another. For example, John Dryzek (1996) writes that the structural economic pressures embedded in capitalism force nations to act in certain ways regardless of what their populations want or think. Specifically, whereas the ideological forces linked to capitalism limit the range of political debate, government and market together promote aggressive individualism. As aggressive individualists, people feel compelled to compete as consumers and "profit maximizers" rather than to relate to one another as citizens.

The globalization of the economy also creates contradictions between capitalism and democracy. Kellner (2005) explains that globalization significantly increases the supremacy of big corporations and big government. In fact, one of the trends of globalization is depoliticization of publics, the decline of the nation-state, and the end of traditional politics (Boggs, 2000). Globalization is promoted by tremendously powerful economic forces that often undermine democratic movements and decision making. What ultimately happens is growing centralization and organization of power and wealth in the hands of the few. Consider, for instance, our description of Wal-Mart's employment practices in Chapter 11. Wal-Mart operates in the United States, a political democracy founded on the principle of protecting each citizen's rights to life, liberty, and the pursuit of happiness. The corporation is also incredibly profitable, maximizing its earnings in a global economy structured by capitalistic forces. Yet, Wal-Mart's actions toward their employees in the United States clearly value profit maximization over fair economic treatment. As we noted in Chapter 11, despite record profits, Wal-Mart pays most of its workers wages so low that they cannot adequately feed their families or afford healthcare.

McCloskey and Zaller (1984) offer extended commentary on the contradictions between capitalism and democracy in their book *The American Ethos: Public Attitudes Toward Capitalism and Democracy.* In their view, modern industrial capitalism has created great concentrations of wealth, which threaten such democratic values as social and political equality. Although the centers of wealth and power are difficult to fight, Americans do offer resistance. For example, at various points in history American citizens, through their elected representatives, have demanded that federal and state governments enact various regulations that impinge significantly on the workings of the free market. McCloskey and Zaller (1984) say that the conflict "manifests itself mainly in the form of disagreements over incremental adjustments in existing practice—greater or less regulation of business, higher or lower pay for workers, more power or less power for labor unions" (p. 185). Still, there is an inherent conflict between the idea that democracy promotes equality for all and the fact that capitalism often results in gross inequalities of opportunity.

Coalitions and Intergroup Conflict

The large, complex organization provides a rich medium for the development of coalitions and the occurrence of intergroup conflict (i.e., conflict between different groups or units within the same organization). As Putnam and Poole (1987) point out, "When complexity increases, communication networks fragment and lead to different perspectives within units. If this condition is combined with high interdependence, conflict between units increases" (p. 575).

Intergroup conflict is affected by many contextual and structural factors in the organization. Factors as simple as physical separation of groups (e.g., different departments on different floors of a building or distances between field offices) may escalate conflict by making communication more difficult. Status distinctions between different groups also may lead to intergroup conflict (Dalton, 1959). As we previously mentioned, competition for resources or ambiguous conditions in policy or authority may become sources of conflict. Zald (1981) found that groups in intergroup conflict increase their concern for equitable resource distribution in an effort to control their own destinies. Putnam and Poole (1987) also point out that "'destabilizing' incidents, such as the departure of an executive or a financial crisis, often trigger struggles over the redistribution of power" (p. 576).

Not surprisingly, one of the major factors in intergroup conflict is the perception that groups have of their relationship. Those who see their relationship as competitive engage in misrepresentation, withholding of information, minimization of intergroup agreements accompanied by maximization of differences, discourse slanted favorably toward in-group positions and unfavorably toward out-group positions, and even charges of disloyalty against in-group members who support the out-group's positions (Blake & Mouton, 1964; Walton, Dutton, & Cafferty, 1969).

On the positive side, Thalhofer (1993) notes that intergroup conflict can be managed successfully if two conditions are present: **separateness** and **equal valuation**. The condition of separateness promotes the existence of separate, positive group identities. In other words, it is important to recognize that organization members are likely to group together on the basis of such factors as demographic (e.g., race, gender, ethnicity, age) or attitudinal similarities (e.g., comparable positions on issues). These various separate groups need to feel that their presence and contributions are respected within the organization. Also, in order for conflict to be managed successfully, an environment must be created in which different group members recognize that their positions are equally valued in the intergroup environment. Thalhofer (1993) concludes that the conditions of separateness and equal valuation are particularly important for an organization to reap the benefits of an ethnically and racially diverse membership.

In reviewing research on intergroup conflict, we discovered that much of it is concerned with formal intact groups. Many of the more interesting conflicts in organizations, however, involve **coalitions** that exist independently of the formal organizational structure. We touched briefly on the concept of organizational coalitions in Chapter 3, saving the more detailed discussion for this chapter because coalitions are, by virtue of their very existence, agents of conflict. A coalition occurs when individuals band together in order to wield influence within the organization. Coalitional activity in large organizations seems to be as inevitable as the ebb and flow of the ocean tides, although the tides, unlike coalitions, are quite predictable. Stevenson, Pearce, and Porter (1985) say that a coalition has eight essential characteristics:

Interacting Group. Coalitions consist of members who communicate with one another about coalition issues and potential coalition action.

Deliberately Constructed. Coalitions are explicitly constructed for a purpose, and they can be distinguished from other informal groups by their self-conscious formation and design.

Independent of Formal Organization's Structure. A coalition is independent of formally designated groups such as departments, committees, or task forces.

Lack of Formal Internal Structure. Coalitions lack formal structures such as hierarchy and formal, legitimate authority. They are much more dependent on attempts at informal influence among members.

Mutual Perception of Membership. Coalitions often have fuzzy boundaries. Nevertheless, there is some reasonable consensus about who is a member and whose commitment is questionable.

Issue Oriented. Coalitions are formed to advance the purposes of their members. When their members cease to interact around these issues, the group no longer exists as a coalition.

External Focus. Coalitions form to influence some external agent. This means that a coalition does not form merely so that its members may debate or argue some issue among themselves. Rather, coalitions are created to get other organization members or groups to yield to its purposes through persuasion, coercion, or other means of influence.

Concerted Member Action. Coalitions must act as a group, either through a group action or through orchestrated member action.

Stevenson et al. also point out that many of the factors associated with intergroup conflict in general also may be linked with the formation of coalitions. They argue that coalitions are more likely to form in an organization when there is a major change in the allocation of resources or when some organization members believe that comparable others are receiving more favorable treatment. They also argue that coalition formation is more likely when there are opportunities for frequent interaction among organization members and organization members have discretion in carrying out their job responsibilities. As the coalition itself becomes more visible, the issues it pursues also become more visible, and the likelihood increases that a "countercoalition" will form in order to block the aims of that coalition. Two examples of organizational coalitions that we have observed or read about will illustrate, however, that the forms, motives, and methods of coalitions may be very diverse.

The first example concerns the accounting department of a large manufacturing firm that has always had a male manager. Historically, all of the professional accountants in the department had also been men, although the clerks and bookkeepers had been women. During the past few years, however, more women had entered the department as accountants. Now, approximately one-third of the accountants are female, and more than one-half of the department employees are women. Apparently, the manager had a long history of sexual harassment, but the female clerks and bookkeepers had always been reluctant to take any action because they were in vulnerable positions and harassment was "just something you put up with." But the new professional women in higher status accounting positions were not so willing to put up with the situation, particularly given new laws that allow for action against sexual harassment in organizations that allow it to occur. Under these new conditions, the women soon coalesced in order to support each other and pursue sexual harassment charges against the manager.

Eventually, the department manager was fired, but another male who was promoted from within the department replaced him. Although most of the women were relieved by the change, two of the more influential female accountants were incensed that yet another man was given the manager's position. The two began to engage in a series of covert actions designed to redirect the coalition toward the replacement of the new manager with a female. Among other things, they initiated a biweekly "Women's Night Out," when all of the female members of the department met for dinner to discuss their work-related problems, but the primary purpose was to encourage all of the women to create problems for the new manager (e.g., taking maximum sick leave, making difficult requests for resources or work schedules, asking the manager continually to repeat or clarify directives, etc.) and, during managerial performance reviews, to turn in negative subordinate evaluations of their superior. The strategy worked. Frustrated and angry, the new manager resigned after less then 12 months in the position. He was replaced by one of the two coalition leaders.

The second example concerns the increase during the last two decades of public health issues surrounding the hazards of cigarette smoking. These expanded because of the concern for the dangers to smokers, which included the health risks to nonsmokers exposed to secondary smoke. Many companies were required to handle the problem of developing policies on smoking in the workplace. In some cases, top-level executives or personnel managers surveyed employees to determine their opinions toward various options (e.g., open smoking, smoking only in restricted areas, or a complete smoking ban), then implemented policies that seemed to have the broadest support in the surveys. In other cases, policies developed only as a response to coalitional action among nonsmoking employees. These coalitions were visible only through the efforts of a few core members who were very vocal on the issue, but who were given more force by the tacit support of the "silent majority" of nonsmokers who outnumbered smokers by two to one. A coalition of this type can be very loose in the sense that most of its "members" engage in little or no direct interaction about the issue and may not even know each other. Yet, efforts to ban or restrict smoking in public areas and in the workplace have been so effective that Philip Morris Corp., a major producer of tobacco products, has undertaken an active effort to promote "smokers' rights" groups throughout the country and to encourage countercoalitions to combat the actions of antismoking coalitions in organizations. *Philip Morris Magazine* even publishes what it calls a "Hall of Shame" list of companies that have imposed restrictions on workplace smoking.

In the first case, the coalition is small, is localized in a specific organizational unit, and works toward its objectives over a long period of time, sometimes overtly, sometimes covertly, with the concerted efforts of its members. In the second example, the coalition is large, with fuzzy boundaries. Status as a nonsmoker is the only specific defining characteristic of its members. Many of them may not really be "members" of the coalition, yet their presence in the organization and the policymakers' realization that they are nonsmokers tacitly lend force to the efforts of vocal core members.

Feminist Bureaucracy as Organized Dissonance

Like Thalhofer (1993), Ashcraft (2001) recognizes the benefits of conflict among organization members; however, she describes conflict from a unique feminist standpoint. Specifically, she argues in favor of feminist bureaucracy through *organized dissonance*. The concept of organized dissonance opposes the assumption of rational organization and shakes faith in unity of direction or in "one head with one plan." Rather, Ashcraft believes that irony and paradox within and among organizational groups should be promoted rather than avoided. Motivated by strategic incongruity, the dissonance model reflects organizations that employ incompatible forms to meet conflicting objectives and demands. The shift in perspective this model promotes allows one to "engage contradiction as *deliberate* dialectic tension" (Ashcraft, 2001, p. 1318). Interestingly, Mary Parker Follett presented a similar view when she described the benefits of conflict:

> Instead of condemning it, we should set it to work for us. . . . The music of the violin we get by friction. . . . So in business, too, we have to know when to try to eliminate friction and when to try to capitalize it. . . . Integration involves invention, and the clever thing is to recognize this and not to let one's thinking stay within the boundaries of two alternatives which are mutually exclusive. (cited in Graham, 1995, pp. 68, 70).

As an example of how organized dissonance works in organizations, Ashcraft studied SAFE, a nonprofit organization providing battered women with support, shelter, and advocacy. One of the observations that brought to the surface how contradiction reveals deliberate dialectic tension was labeled *parodies of power.* Ashcraft observed that SAFE members would regularly satirize familiar relations of dominance and submission in the organization. For example, when an intern asked repeatedly for directions from the shelter director, the director mimicked the slow, clear voice of an elementary school teacher. Everyone, including the intern, laughed vigorously, but the intern did not ask another question. Ashcraft explains that the use of humor lightened the mood of the meetings. The humor also served to both mark and minimize inequalities. Also, the person displaying power (the director) is absolved of responsibility by masking her criticism with humor. Underlying the power parody is the message, "I'm not really dominating/submitting because if we're laughing it must be OK" (Ashcraft, 2001, p. 1319). Humor thus manages the inequality/equality or dominance/submission dialectic through absolving members from liability for their actions.

ETHICS IN CONFLICT

At the core of ethics in conflict is the competitive environment in which organizational disputes occur. When conflicts are over valued resources and a win-lose approach to resolution is taken, competing sides may be tempted to do anything to win. As Wilmot and Hocker (2007) observed in *Interpersonal Conflict,* losing "does not build character, it builds frustration, aggression, or apathy" (p. 85). Furthermore, as Rothwell (2004) observed, "when much is at stake and few can be winners, cheating and dishonesty flourish in a hypercompetitive environment" (p. 94).

The ethical violation most tempting to conflicting parties is lying to gain a strategic advantage. If we refer back to our descriptions of our competence-based approach to conflict and Fisher and Ury's principled negotiation, the problems of lying during conflict become clear. According to our competence model, central to communication during conflict is the need to engage in appropriate discourse. As Papa and Canary (1995) observed, engaging in appropriate (truthful) communication mediates between interactant perceptions of the conflict strategies that are used and relational outcomes such as trust and satisfaction. Lying would not be considered appropriate because it violates a relational and situational rule during conflict to produce optimal outcomes for all parties. Lying would be characterized as such a rule violation because it is a purposeful attempt to manipulate an outcome to the favor of one party. From the perspective of principled negotiation, lying would be considered an ethical violation because it would misrepresent the underlying interests of one party to the conflict. Because of such misrepresentation, it would be impossible for adversaries to identify the underlying interests that would produce an outcome most beneficial to all concerned.

The harms caused by lying extend beyond an agreement that is more favorable to one party. If the lie were uncovered at a subsequent point, trust between the parties would be difficult to reestablish. Should the parties be required to renegotiate a new agreement? How can both sides be sure that lying and manipulation will not be introduced into the new agreement? Why should the party that was the recipient of the lie trust that his or her partner is telling the truth now? Will the party that lied initially perceive that his or her partner may be tempted to lie in a new negotiation to regain a lost advantage? These questions must be addressed, but the problems embedded in them are difficult to resolve. Once a significant lie is uncovered, it will take a long time before trust can be rebuilt. That is why lying is an ethical violation that must be discussed in great detail within organizations. Simply stated, the price of lying is too high to ignore if an organization wants to function effectively.

SUMMARY

Conflict is a common yet widely misunderstood phenomenon in group processes and intergroup relations. Classical theorists regarded conflict as an anomaly—an abnormal occurrence that was not supposed to happen. Contemporary organizational theorists stress the point that conflict is an inevitable and even necessary aspect of the group and organizational experience. Conflict should not be suppressed and avoided; instead it should be confronted, managed, and resolved.

Conflict arises from many sources within groups and organizations, including various forms of role conflict, competition for limited resources, and interpersonal conflict among workers and between superiors and subordinates. A traditional perspective on conflict examines the communicative actions, strategies, and structures that produce productive and destructive outcomes. From this perspective, much work on interpersonal conflict in organizations has centered on conflict styles in superior-subordinate relationships. Conflict style refers to a characteristic mode or habitual way that a person handles a dispute. Researchers have also looked at the strategic communication choices that employees make in conflicts by focusing on nonconfrontational, solution-oriented and control strategies. A more recent development in studying interpersonal conflict in organizations looks at ways to sustain competent communication during conflict episodes. The competence perspective emphasizes how workers may display relationally appropriate behaviors while also remaining effective in pursuing individual goals.

When looking at the process of managing conflict, traditionalists have identified a number of frameworks. Jameson's (1999) framework examined conflict dimensions, conflict management strategies, and desired outcomes. Conflict dimensions referred to content, relational, and situational factors that influence the dispute. Conflict management strategies focused on interests, rights, and power; whether a formal or informal conflict process was needed; and whether the disputants could manage the conflict themselves or an intervening or third party was needed.

Traditionalists also focus extensively on bargaining and negotiation in organizations. Bargaining and negotiation involves a special case of organizational conflict. Communication research on bargaining processes usually is based on a distinction between distributive and integrative processes. Distributive bargaining involves the existence or the appearance of a fixed-sum, win-lose situation that may deteriorate into a lose-lose outcome in which the relationship between parties is permanently damaged. Integrative bargaining involves situations in which the potential outcomes can be expanded or inconsistent goals combined in win-win outcomes. Distributive bargaining is characterized by deception, withholding of information, or the use of disinformation. Integrative bargaining is based on open communication, accurate disclosure of objectives, and sharing of information. Information is used for purposes of fact-finding, problem definition, and generation of alternative solutions. We also looked at Fisher and Ury's (1981) framework of principled negotiation that is based on four principles: separate the people from the problem, focus on interests rather than positions, generate a variety of options before selecting an agreement, and insist that the agreement be based on objective criteria.

Interpretivists concentrate on how conflict is socially constructed. They also draw attention to how different cultural environments produce different social constructions. From the interpretive perspective, we focused on cultural context by examining the conflict experiences of workers in organizations based on gender, race, and country of national origin. A number of insights surfaced. First, women are likely to see conflict through the lens of war and destruction and as an activity that is ongoing without any clear resolution. Second, African American women value more direct approaches to conflict and were less likely than European American women to avoid conflict. Third, we observed that workers from individualistic cultures are more likely to engage in direct confrontation, whereas those from collectivistic cultures use avoidance to preserve relational harmony and save others' face.

Interpretivists are also interested in how the promotion of a dialogic culture influences conflict in organizations. An emphasis on dialogue ensures that employees hear and respect multiple voices, value otherness, pursue richer understandings of complex situations, and transcend polarization by seeking the commonalities that link people together. Ultimately, a dialogic culture is one that recognizes differences among people while searching deliberatively for possible collaboration.

A critical perspective draws our attention to how conflicts may create an oppressive environment for workers where the views of a select few are privileged and people organize around rule systems that are disempowering. We described a critical perspective on conflict in a few ways. First, we pointed to the contradictions between democracy and capitalism. These contradictions are often managed in ways that sustain gross inequalities of opportunities by concentrating wealth and threatening democratic values such as social and political equality. Second, we examined coalitions and intergroup conflict. Much of the research on intergroup conflict is concerned with formal, intact groups, but many of the more interesting conflicts in organizations may involve coalitions that exist independently of the formal organizational structure. At the center of many conflicts between groups or coalitions are struggles over redistribution of power or fights for equal treatment. Finally, we looked at feminist bureaucracy as organized dissonance. From this perspective, conflict reveals contradictions and deliberate dialectic tensions that preserve the struggles between forces such as dominance and submission and empowerment and disempowerment.

Finally, when considering the ethics of conflict, we focused on how competitiveness may tempt parties to considering lying to gain a strategic advantage. However, lies prevent the emergence of solutions that are to the mutual benefit of all parties. Furthermore, relationship trust may be irrevocably damaged when a lie is discovered.

DISCUSSION QUESTIONS/ACTIVITIES

1. In what ways are power and conflict intertwined in organizations?

2. Are there any problems with a stylistic approach to the study of interpersonal conflict? Is one conflict style more preferable than others? Why or why not?

3. Given the political nature of coalitions, under what conditions would it be ethically acceptable to form and work through coalitions in organizations? Are there circumstances under which coalitions might be unethical?

4. Assuming that integrative bargaining is superior to distributive bargaining, how does one move toward or encourage an integrative approach in the bargaining process? Can you think of any conditions under which distributive bargaining might be more effective than integrative bargaining?

5. What are some productive ways to manage the conflicts Randy created in the theater department? Are there any possible suggestions that may be derived from The Carter Center or the women's dairy cooperative examples?

REFERENCES

Apfelbaum, E. (1964). On conflicts and bargaining. In L. Berkowitz (Ed.), *Advances in experimental social psychology* (pp. 134–162). New York: Academic Press.

Ashcraft, K. L. (2001). Organized dissonance: Feminist bureaucracy as hybrid form. *Academy of Management Journal, 44*(6), 1301–1322.

Barge, J. K. (2006). Dialogue, conflict, and community. In J. G. Oetzel & S. Ting-Toomey (Eds.), *The Sage handbook of conflict communication: Integrating theory, research, and practice* (pp. 517–544). Thousand Oaks, CA: Sage.

Beckhard, R. (1969). *Organization development: Strategies and models.* Reading, MA: Addison-Wesley.

Blake, R. R., & Mouton, J. S. (1964). *The managerial grid.* Houston: Gulf.

Boggs, C. (2000). *The end of politics.* New York: Guilford.

Bradbury, T. N., & Fincham, F. D. (1990). Attributions in marriage: Review and critique. *Psychological Bulletin, 107,* 3–33.

Burke, R. J. (1970). Methods of resolving superior-subordinate conflict: The constructive use of subordinate differences and disagreements. *Organizational Behavior and Human Performance, 5,* 393–411.

Burrell, N. A., Buzzanell, P. M., & McMillan, J. J. (1992). Feminine tensions in conflict situations as revealed by metaphoric analyses. *Management Communication Quarterly, 6,* 115–149.

Canary, D. J., & Cupach, W. R. (1988). Relational and episodic characteristics associated with conflict tactics. *Journal of Social and Personal Relationships, 5,* 305–325.

Canary, D. J., Cupach, W. R., & Serpe, R. T. (2001). A competence-based approach to examining interpersonal conflict: Test of a longitudinal model. *Communication Research, 28,* 79–104.

Canary, D. J., & Spitzberg, B. H. (1987). Appropriateness and effectiveness perceptions of conflict strategies. *Human Communication Research, 14,* 93–118.

Canary, D. J., & Spitzberg, B. H. (1989). A model of the perceived competence of conflict strategies. *Human Communication Research, 15,* 630–649.

Canary, D. J., & Spitzberg, B. H. (1990). Attribution biases and associations between conflict strategies and competence outcomes. *Communication Monographs, 57,* 139–151.

Conrad, C. (1991). Communication in conflict: Style-strategy relationships. *Communication Monographs, 58,* 135–155.

Costantino, C. A., & Merchant, C. S. (1996). *Designing conflict management systems.* San Francisco: Jossey-Bass.

Dalton, M. (1959). Conflicts between staff and line managerial officers. *American Sociological Review, 15,* 342–351.

Dryzek, J. (1996). *Democracy in capitalist times: Ideals, limits, and struggles.* Oxford, UK: Oxford University Press.

Elangovan, A. R. (1995). Managerial third-party dispute intervention: A prescriptive model for strategy selection. *Academy of Management Review, 20,* 800–830.

Elangovan, A. R. (1998). Managerial intervention in organizational disputes: Testing a prescriptive model of strategy selection. *International Journal of Conflict Management, 9,* 301–335.

Ewing, D. W. (1989). *Justice on the job: Resolving grievances in the nonunion workplace.* Boston: Harvard Business School Press.

Fisher, R., & Ury, W. (1981). *Getting to yes: Negotiating agreement without giving in.* New York: Penguin.

Folger, J. P., Poole, M. S., & Stutman, R. K. (1993). *Working through conflict* (2nd ed.). New York: HarperCollins.

Glaser, T. (1998). *Conflict research consortium: Getting to yes: Negotiating agreement without giving in.* Retrieved December 10, 2005, from http://www.colorado.edu/conflict/peace/example/fish7513.htm

Graham, E. E., Papa, M. J., & McPherson, M. B. (1997). An applied test of the functional communication perspective of small group decision making. *Southern Communication Journal, 63,* 114–132.

Graham, P. (Ed.). (1995). *Mary Parker Follett: Prophet of management.* Boston: Harvard Business School Press.

Gross, M. A., Guerrero, L. K., & Alberts, J. K. (2004). Perceptions of conflict strategies and communication competence in task-oriented dyads. *Journal of Applied Communication Research, 32*(3), 249–270.

Hall, J. (1969). *Conflict management survey: A survey of one's characteristic reaction to and handling of conflicts between himself and others.* Monroe, TX: Telemetrics International.

Holsti, O. R. (1971). Crisis, stress, and decision-making. *International Social Science Journal, 23,* 53–67.

Jameson, J. K. (1999). Toward a comprehensive model for the assessment and management of intraorganizational conflict: Developing the framework. *The International Journal of Conflict Management, 10*(3), 268–294.

Janis, I. L. (1972). *Victims of groupthink.* Boston: Houghton Mifflin.

Janis, I. L. (1982). *Groupthink: A psychological study of policy decisions and fiascoes.* Boston: Houghton.

Kellner, D. (2005). *Theorizing globalization.* Retrieved December 10, 2005, from http://www.gseis.ucla.edu/faculty/kellner/essays/theorizingglobalization.pdf

Kim, M. S., & Leung, T. (2000). A multicultural view of conflict management styles: Review and critical synthesis. In M. E. Roloff (Ed.), *Communication yearbook 23* (pp. 227–269). Thousand Oaks, CA: Sage.

Koehler, J. W., Anatol, K. W. E., & Applbaum, R. L. (1981). *Organizational communication: Behavioral perspectives* (2nd ed.). New York: Holt, Rinehart & Winston.

Kuhn, T., & Poole, M. S. (2000). Do conflict management styles affect group decision making? *Human Communication Research, 26,* 558–590.

Lawrence, P. R., & Lorsch, J. W. (1967). *Organization and environment.* Boston: Division of Research, Graduate School of Business Administration, Harvard University.

McCloskey, H., & Zaller, J. (1984). *The American ethos: Public attitudes toward capitalism and democracy.* Cambridge, MA: Harvard University Press.

Nicotera, A. M., & Dorsey, L. K. (2006). Individual and interactive processes in organizational conflict. In J. G. Oetzel & S. Ting-Toomey (Eds.), *The Sage handbook of conflict communication: Integrating theory, research, and practice* (pp. 293–325). Thousand Oaks, CA: Sage.

Oetzel, J. G. (1998). The effects of self-construal and ethnicity on self-reported conflict styles. *Communication Reports, 11,* 133–144.

Olekalns, M., & Smith, P. L. (2003). Social motives in negotiation: The relationship between dyad composition, negotiation processes and outcomes. *International Journal of Conflict Management, 14,* 233–254.

Papa, M. J., & Canary, D. J. (1995). Conflict in organizations: A competence-based approach. In A. M. Nicotera (Ed.), *Conflict and organizations* (pp. 153–179). Albany: State University of New York Press.

Papa, M. J., & Mapendere, J. (2005, October). *Using programmatic evaluation to stimulate new thinking about peace initiatives.* Paper presented at the joint conference of the American Evaluation Association and the Canadian Evaluation Society, Toronto, Ontario, Canada.

Papa, M. J., & Natalle, E. J. (1989). Gender, strategy selection and discussion satisfaction in interpersonal conflict. *Western Journal of Speech Communication, 53,* 260–272.

Papa, M. J., & Papa, W. H. (1996). Competence in organizational conflicts. In W. R. Cupach & D. J. Canary (Eds.), *Competence in interpersonal conflict* (pp. 214–242). New York: McGraw-Hill.

Papa, M. J., & Pood, E. A. (1988). Coorientational accuracy and differentiation in the management of conflict. *Communication Research, 15,* 400–425.

Papa, M. J., Singhal, A., & Papa, W. H. (2006). *Organizing for social change: A dialectic journey of theory and praxis.* New Delhi, India: Sage.

Peace programs overview: Waging peace. (2007). Retrieved June 26, 2007, from http://www.cartercenter.org/peace/index.html

Putnam, L. L., & Jones, T. S. (1982). Reciprocity in negotiations: An analysis of bargaining interaction. *Communication Monographs, 49,* 171–191.

Putnam, L. L., & Poole, M. S. (1987). Conflict and negotiation. In F. M. Jablin, L. L. Putnam, K. H. Roberts, & L. W. Porter (Eds.), *Handbook of organizational communication: An interdisciplinary perspective* (pp. 549–599). Newbury Park, CA: Sage.

Putnam, L. L., & Wilson, S. R. (1982). Communicative strategies in organizational conflicts: Reliability and validity of a measurement scale. In M. Burgoon (Ed.), *Communication yearbook 6* (pp. 629–652). Beverly Hills, CA: Sage.

Robbins, S. P. (1977). Managing organizational conflict. In J. Schnee, E. K. Warren, & H. Lazarus (Eds.), *The progress of management* (pp. 248–279). Englewood Cliffs, NJ: Prentice Hall.

Robbins, S. P. (1978). "Conflict management" and "conflict resolution" are not synonymous terms. *California Management Review, 21,* 67–75.

Rothwell, J. D. (2004). *In mixed company: Communication in small groups and teams* (5th ed.). Belmont, CA: Wadsworth.

Schein, E. (1969). *Process consultation: Its role in organization development.* Reading, MA: Addison-Wesley.

Shuter, R., & Turner, L. H. (1997). African American and European American women in the workplace. *Management Communication Quarterly, 11,* 74–96.

Smart, C., & Vertinsky, I. (1977). Designs for crisis decision units. *Administrative Science Quarterly, 22,* 640–657.

Spitzberg, B. H., & Canary, D. J. (1985). Loneliness and relationally competent communication. *Journal of Social and Personal Relationships, 2,* 387–402.

Stevenson, W. B., Pearce, J. L., & Porter, L. W. (1985). The concept of "coalition" in organization theory and research. *Academy of Management Review, 10,* 256–268.

Sycara, K. P. (1991). Problem restructuring in negotiation. *Management Science, 37,* 1248–1268.

Thalhofer, N. N. (1993). Intergroup differentiation and reduction of intergroup conflict. *Small Group Research, 24*(1), 28–43.

Walton, R. E., Dutton, J. M., & Cafferty, T. P. (1969) Organizational context and interdepartmental conflict. *Administrative Science Quarterly, 14,* 73–84.

Walton, R. E., & McKersie, R. B. (1965). *A behavioral theory of labor negotiations: An analysis of a social inter-action system.* New York: McGraw-Hill.

Weider-Hatfield, D., & Hatfield, J. D. (1995). Relationships among conflict management styles, levels of conflict, and reactions to work. *The Journal of Social Psychology, 135*(6), 687–698.

Weider-Hatfield, D., & Hatfield, J. D. (1996). Superiors' conflict management strategies and subordinate outcomes. *Management Communication Quarterly, 10*(2), 189–208.

Wilmot, W. W., & Hocker, J. L. (2007). *Interpersonal conflict* (7th ed.). New York: McGraw-Hill.

Zald, M. (1981). Political economy: A framework for comparative analysis. In M. Zey-Ferrell & M. Aiken (Eds.), *Complex organizations: Critical perspectives* (pp. 237–262). Glenview, IL: Scott, Foresman.

Strategic Communication

> THE CRITICAL PERSPECTIVE
> Strategy and Hegemony
> Coping With Power
> Transformation and Strategic Communication

This chapter concerns communication that supports and advances organizational strategy. Strategy usually is understood to be a top management function, but the field of management seems to have no consensus on exactly what it involves. Chaffee noted in 1985 that "virtually everyone writing on strategy agrees that no consensus on its definition exists" (p. 89). Fifteen years later, this situation apparently had not changed. According to Hendry (2000), "The distinction between strategy and the functional areas of management, though widely recognized, turns out to be quite difficult to draw in terms of actions" (p. 970).

Some scholars have carried out elaborate studies of strategic communication without even attempting to define the concept (Segars & Kohut, 2001). Aside from connecting the idea of strategy to planning (usually managerial planning), they are otherwise silent about the definition of strategic communication, apparently assuming that we all know exactly what strategy means and how it differs from other related concepts such as tactics and operations.

Conrad and Poole (2005) regard all organizational communication as strategic in the sense that societies and organizations act strategically through communication to constrain member behavior, and organization members (not just top managers, but everyone else as well) are obliged to communicate strategically in order to navigate their way through organizational life. Our own idea of strategic communication is not as expansive as Conrad and Poole's. We are writing about strategic communication primarily as an executive function, but communicating about the results of managerial planning is just one aspect of this function.

CHARACTERISTICS OF STRATEGIC COMMUNICATION

In this section, we describe the basic characteristics of strategic communication beginning with the concept of strategy itself. As we have done with other concepts in this book, we will consider strategic communication from traditional, interpretive, and critical perspectives. Ellen Chaffee (1985) framed the concept of strategy with three models that can be understood easily from these points of view.

Models of Strategy

Chaffee identified the three basic models of strategy as linear, adaptive, and interpretive. Each model has implications for strategic communication. The linear and adaptive models of strategy are closely related to the traditional perspective of organizational communication. As the label suggests, the interpretive model of strategy lines up with the interpretive perspective of organizational communication.

In the linear model, "strategy consists of integrated decisions, actions, or plans that will set and achieve viable organizational goals" (p. 90). This model reflects the most conventional and traditional understanding of strategy in which top managers engage in a sequential, long-term planning process with rational decision making aimed at producing and controlling organizational change. As Chaffee described the process, managers identify goals, generate alternatives for achieving those goals, and weigh the likelihood of success for each alternative, then decide which alternatives to implement. The linear model is based on the older, machinelike notion of rational control in the traditional perspective. Under this model, strategic communication is concerned with presentation of managerial plans to stakeholders and with stakeholder acceptance of those plans.

The adaptive model shifts the focus of strategy from sequential planning and decisions about organizational goals to continuous adjustment of the relationship between the organization and its larger environment. The organization is an open system in a dynamic environment where "the 'goal' is represented by coalignment of the organization with its environment" (p. 91). Coalignment refers to matching up opportunities and risks in the environment with the capabilities and resources of the organization. Although the adaptive model, as described by Chaffee, is less centralized, less integrated, and more multifaceted than the linear model, it is nonetheless in the domain of top management responsibility. The adaptive model is based on the organismic metaphor of system theory. Under this model, strategic communication is more than just messages aimed at informing and persuading stakeholders. It includes all of the communication processes involved in adaptation, i.e., the information exchange and feedback processes within the organization and interactions between the organization and its environment. Much of the contemporary interest in knowledge management as we described it in Chapter 7 is linked to this model of strategy.

The interpretive model is concerned with the social construction of reality. According to Chaffee, this model is based on a social contract view that "portrays the organization as a collection of cooperative agreements entered into by individuals with free will" (p. 93). In this model, strategy is concerned with the management of meaning and with symbol construction aimed at legitimizing the organization by providing "orienting metaphors or frames of reference that allow the organization and its environment to be understood by organizational stakeholders" (p. 93). Strategy is embedded in those metaphors and frames of reference, and strategic communication is all about negotiating and shaping stakeholders' understandings of what the organization is and what it does. Once again, presumably, top management is leading most of the shaping, orienting, and meaning management.

As defined, these three models of strategy certainly appear to be very different from each other, but Chaffee argued that they are interrelated and even interdependent and that multiple models may be operating in a given organization at any one time. The models may also function in a hierarchy of complexity with organizations evolving from linear to adaptive to interpretive modes of strategizing.

Chaffee's models of strategy cover the major perspectives that we are using for organizational communication with exception of the critical perspective. The omission of the critical perspective from Chaffee's discussion is not just an oversight inasmuch as she was characterizing an organizational activity carried out by top management, and she was not working from a point of view that might be oppositional to top management. As an executive function, however, strategic communication certainly can be approached from an oppositional standpoint (e.g., Manheim, 1991). At the very least, the quest for managerial control implicated in the linear model and the assumptions of freely willed cooperation and use of symbols to legitimize the organization in the interpretive model provide an open invitation for critical response, and we will address this point of view in the chapter as well.

Strategic Communication as Public Communication

Discussions of strategic communication among academics and practitioners alike are often about public communication, i.e., the effort of a source or agent to communicate with an audience in a public context. We are not suggesting that strategic and public communication are the same thing, but strategic communication generally is intended for relevant audiences. The relevant audiences for strategic communication are organizational stakeholders (Chaffee, 1985). Stakeholders include shareholders (owners), employees or members, and customers or clients, but Lim, Ahn, and Lee (2005) noted that the stakeholder concept extends to any important organizational constituency that can affect or be affected by the organization. For many organizations, especially large, complex organizations, this means that the relevant audiences in strategic communication include not only shareholders, employees, and customers, but also government, media, activist groups, special interest coalitions, communities, and maybe even citizen-journalist Web bloggers.

As a form of public communication, strategic organizational communication can require a substantial commitment of resources: production facilities for Web sites, newsletters, company magazines, and video programs; advertising space in print and electronic media; time, space, and materials for special events; and salaries for the professionals who write, edit, and produce the messages, programs, and events. Whether such resources are procured through outsourcing or owned, top-level executives and managers ultimately control their use, and executives and managers can deploy such resources for strategic purposes in framing the organizational mission and directing the organization toward that mission. Although the content of strategic communication programs may be influenced by stakeholders, those who control the resources also have more power to control the agenda for strategic communication. Public communication often is described as a process of one communicating with many (Wiseman & Barker, 1967). One person, who functions as a message source, creates and transmits a message to many others, who function as receivers. This definition of public communication may seem intuitively obvious, but it oversimplifies the idea of a "source" in strategic organizational communication activities and also fails to recognize the transactional character of communication. Consider the following illustration from a case reported by Barrett (2002).

Barrett's case involves a very large, global energy company (65,000 members) that acquired a much smaller refining and marketing company. She referred to the larger company as GEC and the smaller company as RMC to conceal their identities. RMC was in serious financial trouble and beset by problems that previous organizational restructurings had failed to solve, and GEC executives had to figure out how to turn the smaller company around. They devised a strategic plan that included a new vision, identification of opportunities, organization development initiatives, a new performance management system, and other features.

Next, the executives created a strategic communication team of 15 staff, including two communication professionals and 13 members from various levels and areas of RMC to develop a communication program for the change effort with RMC's 5,000 employees. Barrett, who worked with this team, said, "We ended up with . . . sub-teams on vision/strategy, media, message/materials, training, and assessment" (p. 229). These subteams conducted interviews with more than 200 other employees throughout RMC, and the strategic communication team used the results along with other inputs to develop and test messages and materials for a "change communication program" (p. 228). The team also developed and presented a report to senior management with recommendations to ensure success for the program.

Senior management and professional communication staff implemented the program, and a few members from the original strategic communication team continued their involvement as "extra help for the communication staff" (p. 230). RMC accomplished the turnaround, with one senior executive noting, "The change program was a success by all measures . . . and the change communication program helped make it happen" (p. 228). With this illustration in mind, we will now consider the concepts of source and transaction.

The Source in Strategic Communication

Conventional definitions of public communication treat the message source as a specific individual or agency (e.g., senior management). Although this may apply in some situations, messages intended for strategic communication in organizations often are originated and produced by organizational subsystems composed of many individuals. Who is the message source in the GEC-RMC case? Executives made the initial decision to attempt a turnaround at RMC, and they devised the key elements of the strategic plan for this change. But they delegated development of messages, materials, and other aspects of supporting communication to a team. The team, in turn, sought input through interviews with many other organization members in order to develop its communication program. In one sense, this could be described as an exercise in audience adaptation, but the audience, in another sense, influenced the design of the messages that it ultimately would receive.

And in still another sense, although professional communication staff and others collaborated with top management on design and implementation of the communication program, senior management reserved final judgment on recommendations from the strategic communication team, so it was nonetheless management's message that the internal employee public ultimately received. The communication professionals served as a staff arm of top management in producing and executing the change communication program. As the example indicates, strategic communication can be a complex process in which a number of units and individuals contribute to the design and dissemination of messages.

Strategic Communication as Transaction

Strategic communication, like other forms of public communication, is often regarded as a linear process. Most of us seem to understand public communication in terms of a source-oriented view of presenting messages in ways designed to secure a desired response. Because top management's purpose in strategic communication often involves persuasion and gaining acceptance for management plans, the image of the successful program is one in which management has found some guaranteed formula for achieving this objective. Even if they do not say so explicitly, practitioners often imply that failure of strategic initiatives is a result of ineffective communication; that there is a clear method for achieving effective communication, and that "it can be the ticket that allows a company to move onto that short list of successful change programs" (Barrett, p. 231). Sources do gain compliance from receivers, but acceptance of an idea is an act that arises from the receivers' choices. No universal formula in public communication exists for guaranteeing that receivers' choices will be consistent with the intentions of the source.

Strategic communication programs such as the one at GEC-RMC arise out of executive objectives derived through a linear model, but even in cases such as this one, strategic communication may be more appropriately characterized as a transactional process that merely takes on a deceptively linear appearance. The design of the change strategy for RMC does not appear to have been in any way participatory; it was determined by top management at GEC. But the design of the communication program to support the strategy was participatory, cutting across various levels and areas of RMC. Even though the "source" and "receiver" roles in any given episode of strategic communication may be relatively fixed, the people in these roles are participants who influence one another simultaneously.

THE TRADITIONAL PERSPECTIVE

The traditional perspective on strategic communication is concerned mainly with the problem of effective forms of public communication. These forms may be classified generally as internal or external. Internal strategic communication is management's effort to provide information to and exert influence with organizational membership in general. External strategic communication traditionally has included public relations and issues management efforts designed to influence consumers, communities, special-interest groups, voters, regulators, legislators, and other nonmembers. We use the distinction here with some hesitation because the boundary between inside and outside often is permeable and, in some cases, practically nonexistent for strategic purposes (Roberts, 2006).

Internal Communication

Management often engages in efforts to disseminate messages and information through the entire structure of an organization to employees or other specific groups within the organization. This is *internal communication* or, as it is often called, *employee communication*. A 1978 survey of chief executive officers in major United States and Canadian corporations found that the majority regarded employee communication as an important feature of their management plan and a contributor to organizational effectiveness and productivity (Williams, 1978). We have no evidence that this belief has changed over the years, but Barrett (2002) claimed that at least some companies still do not appreciate the strategic value of effective employee communication, i.e., they may have a deep understanding of financial and operational components in strategy, but "they do not apply the same analytical rigor to employee communications" (p. 219).

Compared to many other topics in organizational communication, employee communication has also attracted relatively little interest among academic scholars. According to Freitag and Picherit-Duthler (2004), the importance of employee communication is accepted generally, but "research offering frameworks, models and constructs to help guide such programs is scarce" (p. 476). In fact, we cite more material from trade literature in this section than we cite from academic literature. Stories and case studies from practitioners and industry-sponsored research projects can be very useful, but these sources of information are not substitutes for academic scholarship, which is subjected to rigorous review before it is published.

Organizational efforts at internal communication occur for many reasons. These reasons often are managerially biased in the sense that they represent management views and objectives. Whether this bias is appropriate or not, managerial bias influences the choice of topics and the content of messages involved in internal communication. Many of the conventional internal communication topics can be grouped under four functional areas: orientation and indoctrination, morale and satisfaction, compensation and benefits, and organizational change and development.

Orientation and Indoctrination

Imagine that you are a new employee in a large organization. You have just been hired for a job in which you are well trained. Even so, you may arrive with a number of unanswered questions that range from "What is the company philosophy?" and "How does my job relate to the total organization?" to "When do I receive my first paycheck?" and "Where do I park my car?"

Many organizations provide answers to such questions through some type of formal orientation program. An orientation program may include topics that pertain to the organization as a whole (policies, procedures, operating philosophy, and structure), your specific position (scope of authority, job duties, work procedures), and other personal concerns.

Completion of orientation does not mean that you will never again be exposed to messages on organizational matters or your role within the organization. The maintenance and integration functions of communication that we described in Chapter 2 are often carried out in part through a continuous program of public communication aimed at indoctrination and socialization of organization members. Such programs are often intended to build an organizational image with the internal employee public and to present and reinforce specific values, beliefs, and practices. Interpretive scholars certainly would note that management is not the only voice in the discourse that constructs the social reality of an organization, but that very realization provides a motivation for executives to invest resources in this effort and to control it insofar as possible (e.g., see Howard & Geist, 1995; Whittington & Whipp, 1992).

Morale and Satisfaction

A second functional area in internal communication is the promotion of morale and satisfaction among organization members. Barrett (2002) suggested that an effective employee communication program in and of itself contributes to morale, and messages concerned with any area of internal communication may serve this purpose, but the specific aim of promoting morale and satisfaction includes many types of messages that are unrelated to these other areas. Messages that serve maintenance and human functions often fall into this group. For example, an employee-of-the-month column in a company magazine, notes about departmental accomplishments in the newsletter, and the discourse at special celebratory events are instances of messages that have as their primary objectives the improvement of members' self-concepts, interpersonal relationships, and attitudes toward the organization.

As we noted in Chapter 10, satisfaction among organization members is linked to the quality of relationships with peers and immediate supervisors, role ambiguity, stress, compensation, and other organizational conditions, yet some practitioners clearly believe that maintenance use of employee communications is a potent force for satisfaction. For example, The Confidence Center's manual, *Fire Up Your Staff on a Shoestring Budget,* advertised as "the only source you'll ever need for raising morale" (Meyerson, 2006), offers ideas for celebrations, other special events, newsletters, and personal development activities.

A more sophisticated variation of the assumed linkage between employee communications and morale takes the point of view Barrett suggested, i.e., that all functions of employee communications figure into the promotion of morale. For example, Lippincott Mercer, a large brand and identity management consulting firm, also advises its clients on the value of strategically integrated employee communications in promoting morale. Noting that employee loyalty and support depend on active and honest employee communications, Kenneth J. Roberts, Lippincott Mercer Chairman and CEO, expressed surprise at "how often this tenet is brushed aside in the executive suite" (2006, p. 1).

Compensation and Benefits

Whether or not work organizations wish to implement and maintain employee benefits, communication programs concerning any benefits that they do offer are mandatory. The Employee Retirement Income Security Act (ERISA), which became federal law in 1974, requires organizations to make full and understandable disclosure of employee benefit programs.

Benefit programs in large organizations can be very elaborate and very expensive. According to a study by the U.S. Chamber of Commerce (2006), benefit programs constituted more than 40% of payroll expenses in 2004. In 2005, 70% of employees in private industry had access to medical plans, and 60% had access to retirement plans. In addition to basic health protection and retirement plans, these programs also may include life insurance, disability insurance, credit union participation, use of company recreation facilities, child-care services, family and personal counseling services, and profit-sharing plans.

Although one might assume that benefits communication under ERISA requirements is just a matter of clear and accurate provision of information, benefits communication is also used to promote wellness programs and preventative care. A more diverse and multicultural workforce complicates the benefits communication process because expectations for and beliefs regarding benefit use and lifestyle choices differ along gender, ethnic, and primary language lines (Wojcik, 2005).

Over the past 30 years, ERISA has spawned an entire industry of benefits management and communication companies ranging from small regional service providers to national companies such as AON, Mercer, and Wells Fargo, and even the ERISA Industry Committee, a large ERISA trade association for organizations that provide comprehensive benefit plans that employ at least 5,000 people. Given costs of benefit programs as well as the legal and regulatory complexities surrounding them, the employee benefits arena is a very big business, not only in terms of benefits provision, but also in terms of benefits communication and exertion of influence on government regulation of benefits programs.

Organizational Change and Development

If declarations about the ubiquity of information technology reflect the first great cliché of the 21st century, as we suggested in Chapter 7, perhaps the last great cliché of the 20th century was that of the inevitability of change. Change is a stressful process even when it is desirable. This is especially true for organization members who do not participate in the basic decisions on such matters. When organizations undergo substantial change, many of the members may be very uncertain about the impact that the change will have on the organization and their positions within it. Members may need a great deal of new information in order to understand the purposes and effects of major change.

The kinds of changes that we have in mind here are, of course, generally strategic in nature, including merger of different organizations in one entity, acquisition of one organization by another, major new ventures, restructuring, downsizing, or radical reengineering of core organizational processes and functions. These are the kinds of changes that authors such as Barrett and Roberts have in mind when they are writing about the purposes and functions of employee communication programs. Such changes are stressful enough in and of themselves, but the subject of organizational change also is greeted with skepticism and cynicism because it results too often from "any number of flavors-of-the-day management fads" (Barrett, 2002, p. 219).

As one might imagine, there is an abundance of trade and practitioner literature on effective design and implementation of communication programs to support organizational change initiatives, but the task of major organizational change and the communication processes associated with change are generally not neat and simple. An employee communication program is only one element of a change program. According to Miller (1997), successful strategic change depends on *backing* from those who authorize change, *accessibility* in the sense that managers understand what they are working toward, *specificity* in terms of the detailed planning, and *cultural receptivity,* i.e., those affected by change are receptive enough to facilitate it. As Miller's research suggests, successful change also depends on *propitiousness.* Simply stated, accomplishing major change also requires some luck. And all of this assumes that the organization has the experience, resources, structure, and flexibility to manage the implementation.

Effective Employee Communications

Although effectiveness is a key concern in the traditional perspective, limited academic attention to the area of employee communication also means that research on this issue is limited as well. Barrett did carry out one study of best practices in employee communication. She found several practices common to effective programs that we have consolidated and summarized in five points.

1. Management is supportive. Top and middle management are directly involved in and responsible for communication.

2. Professional communication staff members are well positioned, i.e., close to the issues and included in the strategic planning. Communication is integrated into other business processes and part of the business plan.

3. Communication reinforces strategic objectives to all employees. Targeted messages are adapted to relevant audiences, but they also are consistent.

4. Communication uses all appropriate media, but it privileges face-to-face communication over print and electronic media.

5. The effectiveness of the communication program is assessed formally and frequently.

On the basis of studies conducted by his company, Lippincott Mercer, Roberts offers a different list of criteria for effective programs, but several elements are the same as or very similar to Barrett's.

1. Executive involvement is the most critical factor. The CEO must be responsive to employee communication. Incorporate a cascading communication system that involves all levels of management.

2. Give employee communication the respect it deserves. Make it a core function of management.

3. Focus messages to support the company's purpose and goals and make messages direct, relevant, and consistent.

4. Use a full range of media and methods (meetings, magazines, newsletters, video, web, etc.), but remember that message content is more important than the medium.

5. Coordinate internal and external communication programs to support the same goals.

The two lists do not agree completely, but they do suggest generally a basic model for effective employee communications. We hasten to repeat our earlier caution about the quest for tried-and-true formulas for effectiveness. Perhaps the kinds of communication practices described by Barrett and Roberts are necessary for successful strategic initiatives, but this does not mean that they are sufficient.

External Communication

J. W. Hill (1977) argued that every private-sector corporation in contemporary America is faced with two tests: maintaining profitability and meeting the expectations and demands of society. A similar admonition can be offered to public-sector and nonprofit organizations by changing "maintaining profitability" to "providing services within budget." In either case, contemporary organizations are faced with the problem of meeting societal demands as well as the needs of the organization itself as a community.

Public disenchantment with large corporations and institutions is not a new phenomenon. Gallup surveys were pointing to this problem in 1979. Hill believed that this problem developed, in part, because of public dependence on large organizations—dependence that brings about public frustration when such organizations fail to meet legitimate public needs and expectations. In recent years, cases of executive fraud that bankrupted major corporations such as Enron, Tyco, and WorldCom; multilevel ineptitude of government disaster response during and after Hurricane Katrina; an intractable war in Iraq; and other institutional failures have undermined public confidence in these systems. External communication is a means through which organizations can understand and respond to public expectations in ways that allow an organization to meet its other tests.

External communication occurs in at least three major forms: (1) advertising and promoting products and services, (2) creating a desirable public image for the organization, and (3) shaping public opinion on issues that are important to the organization. In this text, we are concerned with the second and third functions. Traditionally, communication concerned with image building has been the responsibility of public relations practitioners. During the past 20 years, however, many organizations have expanded the concept of strategic communication to include a new function—the management of public issues and public affairs. In fact, some types of organizations exist largely if not entirely for the purpose of advocating and gaining acceptance of positions on public issues.

For example, virtually everyone has at least some familiarity with organizations such as the American Association of Retired Persons, Business Roundtable, Common Cause, Greenpeace, National Consumers League, the National Organization for Women, the Sierra Club, the U.S. Chamber of Commerce, and the U.S. Public Interest Research Group. Fountain (2004) lists Web links for more than 250 active advocacy groups with national reach in more than 40 general categories of public issues. Frequently, public-interest organizations and special-interest groups challenge business and government policies when these policies adversely affect the environment, consumers, minorities, and communities. Some corporations have attempted to cope with these challenges by shifting away from image building to identifying and tracking public issues that concern the organization. An organization may try to change in order to respond to public criticism or it may try to influence public opinion on important issues by advocating its own position in the public arena (Sethi, 1982).

Public Relations and Image Building

Gerald Goldhaber (1993) described image building as a process of creating the identity an organization wants its relevant publics to perceive. Image building involves an organization's attempt to cultivate a public impression that a set of positively valued features defines the essential character of the organization.

Corporate and business concerns over image building date back to at least the mid-1950s, when the *Harvard Business Review* published a landmark article on business image (Gardner & Rainwater, 1955) and many major companies made definite efforts to change their corporate images (Finn, 1962). Typically, such changes are accomplished by developing and publicizing specific organizational characteristics and behaviors that are consistent with the image being cultivated. The art of image building usually is associated with the field of public relations. Clearly, it is inappropriate to equate the whole field of public relations with nothing more than image-building activity. As Heath and Nelson (1986) indicated, the field of public relations typically includes activities such as media relations, marketing, publicity, and internal communication, but the process of image building is a major feature of public relations practice. For example, public relations has been defined as "the management function which evaluates public attitudes, identifies the policies and procedures of an individual or an organization with the public interest, and executes a program of action to earn public understanding and acceptance" (Cutlip & Center, 1964, p. 4).

The second part of this definition, identifying an individual or organization with the public interest, lies at the heart of the image-building process. Hence, Scott Cutlip and Allen

Center, whose text on public relations is a classic in the field, argued in 1964 that farsighted, contemporary public relations practice is concerned with developing public appreciation of good organizational performance. Presumably, this appreciation is the public image of what the organization is or does. Image building continued through the 1990s to be a major concern in many types of organizations (Benoit, 1997; Fombrun, 1996).

Big corporations are not the only organizations that worry about image. For example, American labor unions, struggling with dramatic losses of membership that began during the 1970s, are still attempting to redefine their relevance to workers. Labor historian Robert Korstad, commenting on the Service Employees International Union's withdrawal from the AFL-CIO in 2005, said that the union must successfully construct an image that gives dignity, status, and respect to service work in order to revitalize the labor movement (Todd, 2005). The American Red Cross, caught up in public squabbling and disagreements with FEMA over the role of each agency under the government's National Response Plan, was scrambling at the beginning of the 2006 hurricane season to present an image of reconciliation and resolution of disagreements.

Issues Management

Since the mid-1970s, several types of organizations, especially large corporations, trade and professional associations, and public interest organizations, have moved beyond the traditional image-building functions of public relations in order to deal more effectively with social and political issues that affect organizations and their relationships with various publics (Gaunt & Ollenburger, 1995). This newer concern often is identified by the label *issues management*. Coates, Coates, Jarratt, and Heinz (1986) defined issues management as "the organized activity of identifying emerging trends, concerns, or issues likely to affect an organization in the next few years and developing a wider and more positive range of organizational responses" (p. ix). Issues management is related to risk management and crisis management, two additional concepts that we will link to strategic communication later in this chapter, but it is distinguishable from both (Gaunt & Ollenburger). As early as 1982, 91% of Fortune 500 companies had implemented issues management programs (Buchholz, 1982).

Organizations become involved in public affairs and issues management for various reasons. In the case of a public-interest or special-interest group, the principal purpose of the organization is to create public awareness of issues and to influence local, state, or federal government policies on these issues. Issues management in business emerged largely as a response to the activism of public interest and special interest groups and as a means of identifying, understanding, tracking, and acting on issues before they are subjected to public policy deliberations and decision making (Jones & Chase, 1979).

Such attempts to influence the development and public policy disposition of issues arise not only from conflicts between business and public-interest groups, but also from conflicts among entire industries. Industry versus industry confrontations occurred several times in recent years. For example, when introduction of MP3 technology and file-sharing software in the late 1990s threatened the music recording industry's control over its products, the Recording Industry Association of America launched concerted advocacy and legal challenges against the upstart MP3 and music download businesses. Although one RIAA suit against the maker of the Rio MP3 player was tossed out of court, RIAA also went after

Napster, the first provider of peer-to-peer file sharing, contending that the company was "trying to build a business on the backs of artists and copyright owners. . . . Napster has created, and is operating, a haven for music piracy on an unprecedented scale" (Recording Industry Association of America, 1999). As the RIAA's copyright infringement lawsuit against Napster worked its way through the courts, recording artists themselves took sides in the dispute, and the attendant publicity drew millions of new users to Napster's service. Napster lost the suit and shut down in July 2001. It was acquired by Roxio, Inc., in 2002 and eventually reopened with restructured services.

A more recent example involves Wal-Mart's application in 2006 to create an industrial loan corporation (ILC) in Utah. The ILC would process the store's credit card, debit card, and other electronic transactions, eliminating all of the processing fees that Wal-Mart now pays to other financial institutions to handle these transactions. An ILC does not offer checking accounts, but it can accept deposits and make loans, so it is like a bank. The banking industry is lined up solidly in opposition to Wal-Mart's plan, arguing that it would destroy a long-standing separation of banking from commerce. At the same time, the banking industry itself is trying to get around this very distinction in order to enter the commercial business of real estate brokerage. In turn, the real estate industry, represented by the National Association of Realtors, is opposing the banking industry with the same argument the bankers are using to oppose Wal-Mart (Wallison, 2006).

These examples of industry versus industry conflicts involve legal regulation. Heavily regulated industries and trade groups traditionally have relied on legislative lobbying to influence the regulatory process. The basic idea in lobbying is to obtain passage of laws that favor your industry or group and to ensure the failure of unfavorable legislation. But influencing legislative and regulatory processes poses two problems for industries and trade groups. First, many public issues do not become the objects of legislative action until they have grown, developed, and become politicized. In this case, lobbying is a reactive approach to a matter on which public opinion may already be frozen (i.e., not easily changed). Second, many organizations have used political and legislative influence strategies in ways that are almost exclusively self-serving, without regard for the real public interest in a situation.

Public issues often represent adversity to executives and managers precisely because they raise challenges to the organization's established traditions and modes of operation. It is not surprising that managers avoid such issues until an effect on the organization seems inevitable. As Jones and Chase (1979) argued, "The most significant explanation of the failure of business to gain respect for its positions on public issues is that corporate leadership either does not recognize or ignores, the discernible trends which always precede issues" (p. 3). James E. Post (1978) has developed a model of corporate responses to public issues that helps to explain how such failures occur.

Post characterizes organizational responses in light of two factors: (1) the organization's stake in maintaining the status quo (i.e., in continuing its current practices) and (2) the perceived legitimacy of public complaints against the status quo. According to Post's model in Figure 13.1, organizations will avoid a public issue if both the stakes and perceived legitimacy are low. If the stakes are high and perceived legitimacy is low, organizations tend to "stonewall" with cover-ups, distortions, and other methods. Where stakes are low and perceived legitimacy is high, the organization attempts to accommodate critics through some

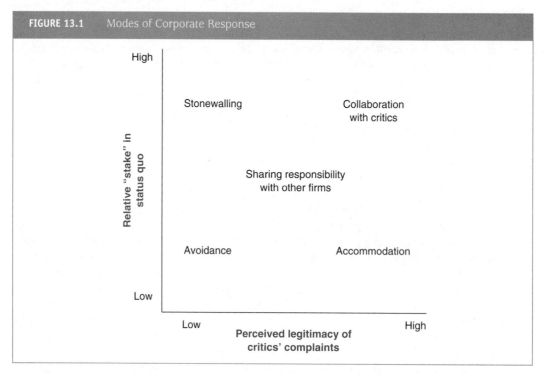

FIGURE 13.1 Modes of Corporate Response

SOURCE: From *Corporate Behavior and Social Change,* by J. E. Post, 1978, Reston, VA: Reston Publishing. Adapted by permission of John Wiley & Sons from "Conflict and conflict management," by K. Thomas, 1976, in M. Dunnette (Ed.), *Handbook of Industrial and Organizational Psychology,* Chicago: Rand-McNally.

form of change. If both the stakes and perceived legitimacy are high, the organization attempts to collaborate with critics.

Avoidance and stonewalling are based on a perception that the legitimacy of complaints arising from a public issue is low, but executives' perceptions of legitimacy may have little to do with the actual impact that a public issue may have on an organization. The only way to assess the importance of a public issue and to develop an appropriate response to the issue is through some means of tracking and monitoring the issue as it develops. This process is the central feature of issues management (Jones & Chase, 1979).

Raymond P. Ewing (1979) pointed out that issues management is concerned with "emerging issues whose definition and contending positions are evolving in the public arena and legislation or regulation is likely in a moving time frame of 18 to 36 months" (p. 15). He described several techniques that organizations can use to track and predict the development of such issues. Some of the more common techniques include the following:

1. *Trend extrapolation.* A factor or variable is measured over time and statistical forecasting techniques are used to project a trend from these measurements.

2. *Trend impact analysis.* This technique is a variation on trend extrapolation. After a trend is extrapolated, experts identify future events that would affect the extrapolation and the trend is modified in light of these events.

3. *Scanning.* This is a relatively simple technique in which issues that might affect an organization are identified and monitored by use of volunteers who regularly scan print and electronic media for useful information.

4. *Monitoring.* This method may be used in conjunction with scanning. Scanning identifies potential issues, whereas monitoring tracks these issues through systematic analysis of data. Monitoring may include public opinion polling and other forms of social science research.

5. *Scenario writing.* This technique begins by asking the question, "What would happen if X came to pass?" Given an assumption that X occurs, a chronological projection into the future is written. According to Ewing, some large organizations hire novelists and playwrights to develop and write such scenarios.

The kinds of tools that Ewing described help organizations to gather and interpret information on emerging public issues. However, developing an information base and an understanding of a public issue is only one component of an issues management project. The other important component involves the use of this information in decision-making processes that lead to organizational action on the issue. This action typically takes one of two forms: issues management and organizational change or issues management and issue advocacy.

Issues Management and Organizational Change. Fox (1983) reported that many executives engage in issues management to address regulation (i.e., to resist or shape regulation), but also devote issues management attention to social responsibility programs. Such efforts are grounded in Chaffee's adaptive model of strategy, i.e., with a working assumption of interaction and interdependency between the organization and its environment. Under this model, the next step after issues management is some form of adaptive change to accommodate the organization to the environment. Consider the case of General Electric and its "ecomagination" project. Characterized in the media as GE's effort to "go green," ecomagination also has been called a "bold move" by Joel Makower, a prominent sustainable business and clean technology consultant, and an "act of courage" by Eileen Claussen, president of the Pew Center for Climate Change (Schneider, 2005). The core elements of the program include a commitment to increase GE's research investment in clean technologies to $1.5 billion per year by 2010, to realize more than half of its revenue from clean technology products by 2015, and to turn a projected 40% increase in its production of greenhouse gases into a net decrease of 1% by 2012.

General Electric is in business to make a profit, and ecomagination is a strategic business decision to pursue a global market for clean technology products and energy efficient technologies that may experience astonishing growth by 2015. GE supports action on global warming, developing alternative fuels, and providing market-based incentives for businesses to reduce pollution. The company even agreed to pay for removal of PCB-contaminated sediments from the Upper Hudson River, a project that will cost tens of millions of dollars (U.S. Environmental Protection Agency, 2007). But GE's position is a product of carefully calculated expectations for future trends. This company studied the relevant issues, markets, and technologies; identified products and programs to put on a strategic platform; created the ecomagination theme as an identity for that platform; and backed it with strong executive commitment. In effect, rather than denying that climate change is occurring, General Electric is adapting in order to make money on it.

Issues Management and Issues Advocacy. Whereas organizational change is sometimes a response to public issues, another form of action is advocacy of the organization's positions on these issues. Public communication programs based on issues advocacy are quite different from the traditional image-building activities of public relations. As described by Prakesh Sethi (1982), traditional image building is "usually rather general in scope and bland in character," whereas issues advocacy "addresses itself to specific controversial issues, presenting facts and arguments that project the sponsor's viewpoint . . . to try to influence political decisions by molding public opinion" (p. 162).

Some issues advocacy campaigns focus on a single issue that is salient to an organization. For example, Pfizer, a major pharmaceutical company, appears only on occasion to engage in advocacy and does so indirectly. Pfizer advertised its Access program to help uninsured persons obtain free prescription drugs when politicians were debating the addition of drug coverage to Medicare, an action Pfizer opposed. According to the Annenberg Public Policy Center (2003), the message was an image ad in appearance, but it functioned as an advocacy ad by implying that the Medicare drug program was unnecessary.

Other issues advocacy campaigns are quite complex. ExxonMobil, America's top-ranked corporation in revenue and in profits for 2005 (CNNMoney.com, 2006), engages in issues advocacy on a range of issues in a dozen different categories, although most are energy related, e.g., climate change, energy policy, and energy prices. For example, whereas General Electric talks about the global warming problem without taking a specific position on the human activity hypothesis, ExxonMobil's advocacy campaign on climate change simultaneously acknowledges global warming, then sows a seed of doubt about the human activity hypothesis, not by outright denial, but through references to scientific uncertainty, the "interplay of the climate's natural variability," and a need for more research (Tillerson, 2006).

ExxonMobil does run some social responsibility campaigns, including one special advocacy program directed at saving tigers. A cartoon tiger was a longtime Exxon symbol, so the company maintains something like an official corporate affection for the animal. Otherwise, ExxonMobil's issues advocacy is crafted carefully to serve its strategic objectives.

Organizations also actually shift through a range of activities from advocacy to accommodation in managing an issue. Shin, Jin, Cheng, and Cameron (2003) identified this tendency in a study of public issues conflicts involving Enron, Napster, Philip Morris, McDonald's, Monsanto, Boy Scouts of America, and the Catholic Church along with their oppositional publics. The major finding in the study was evidence that public conflict resolution processes move both the organizations and their opposing publics "on a continuum from advocacy to accommodation and back over time" (pp. 19–20). The organizations and their publics did tend toward advocacy, and more advocacy by one fueled more advocacy by the other. The two nonprofit organizations (Boy Scouts and the Catholic Church) engaged in less advocacy than the for-profit companies, but all exhibited movement between advocacy and accommodation in the process.

Risk and Crisis Communication

Risk communication and crisis communication are closely related yet distinguishable activities. As we indicated earlier, the distinction that we have made between internal and external communication can be fuzzy at best. This seems to be especially true for risk and crisis communication. In the wake of terrorist attacks, major natural disasters, corporate scandals, and the threat of a global flu pandemic all occurring within the first few years of the 21st century, risk and crisis seem to figure prominently in contemporary public consciousness, but risk and crisis management and communication were woven into the fabric of organizational life well before the turn of the century. We write about risk and crisis communication not because risks and crises are more numerous or larger today than in the past, but because they pose challenges for organizational strategy. Risk complicates strategy and crisis disrupts strategy, yet both demand coherent strategic response (Ulmer, Sellnow, & Seeger, 2006).

Leiss (2004) defined the concept of risk in very simple terms as "the chance of loss (or gain)" (p. 399). He said that he put "gain" in parentheses because most of us intuitively associate risk with the potential for loss or harm. In ordinary language, people also use the term risk to refer to a convergence of the thing that can cause a loss, its anticipated likelihood of occurrence, and the potential magnitude of the loss. Crisis in one sense is a set of circumstances that creates a turning point or tipping point for a radical change. More commonly, we think of crisis as an urgent situation with the potential for an undesirable outcome, i.e., loss or harm. Viewed in this way, a crisis is an event or episode produced by a risk. Natural disasters, acts of terrorism, workplace violence, serious accidents, financial collapse, and other major threats to organizations are managed as crises when they occur and as risks before they occur.

Risk Communication

Risk management is concerned with identifying an organization's exposure to potential losses, preventing or reducing their likelihood of occurrence, and mitigating potential loss. The domain of risk management can include anything from theft, fraud, and basic workplace safety to catastrophic events caused by nature, by humans, or, in the case of Hurricane Katrina, by both. Leiss (2004) defined the related activity of risk communication as "the process of communicating responsibly and effectively about the risk factors associated with industrial technologies, natural hazards, and human activities" (p. 401).

The definition of risk communication may be simple, but risk communication is quite complex because it involves tensions in society and organizations and division between risk experts and nonexpert publics in their understanding of and discourse about risk. Leiss (2004) argued that these tensions and divisions are fundamental and permanent. According to Leiss, risk communication is not about managing risks per se: it is about managing the divide between the expert and the nonexpert to achieve an informed understanding of risks and benefits.

Because risk concerns not only the likelihood of loss but also the likelihood of gain, risk assessment and risk management involve tradeoffs. Risk-taking behavior generally is a prerequisite for gain, and we accept some level of risk just to negotiate the demands of everyday life. There is tension in this paradox. How much risk are we prepared to accept in order to realize an objective or a gain? How much are we prepared to spend for protection against risk? Risk experts are inclined to address such questions directly in terms of cost-benefit ratios. Nonexperts make such judgments as well, but more implicitly. Experts focus on quantitative assessments, whereas nonexperts make qualitative judgments, and nonexperts are more inclined to attach significance to involuntary risks even when the consequence of a voluntary risk may be much larger.

Leiss argued that the basic responsibility of risk communication practitioners is promotion of "reasoned dialogue among stakeholders on the nature of the relevant risk factors and on acceptable risk management strategies" (p. 402). In order to fulfill this purpose, practitioners must understand how risks are perceived by relevant publics, be able to present expert risk assessments in ways that nonexperts can understand, and help interested parties reach a shared understanding of risk. This position is a rational-ideal model of risk communication processes and intended outcomes. It fits within a traditional perspective on organizational communication. It hints at some features of an interpretive approach, but the assumption of rationality does not fit well within the social constructionist notions of interpretive theory.

Risk communication as an area of scholarly attention and an area of practice has experienced rapid and substantial growth. Gurabardhi, Gutteling, and Kuttschreuter (2004) reported the existence of various university centers for risk communication studies, offerings of risk communication services by numerous consulting firms, inclusion of risk communication in academic degree programs, and nearly 350 scholarly journal articles on the subject published between 1988 and 2000. They cited historical evidence that communication has been an aspect of risk management for centuries, but they also noted that the formal idea of risk communication did not emerge until the 1980s.

Leiss (1996) traced the history of risk communication to 1975 in order to discuss its development in three phases. The first, from 1975 to 1984, emphasized a scientific-technical approach to risk management. It assumes that risk assessment is carried out with imperfect but rigorous and exacting scientific analysis, and that the technical experts who carry out this science arrive at the best, objective understanding of true risk. Not surprisingly, a prescriptive risk communication practice emerged from this approach that can be characterized metaphorically as carrying the light to the heathen. As could also have been predicted, it was a failure in the arena of public discourse.

The second phase from 1985 to 1994 was a response to the first. It borrowed from the field of marketing, emphasized audience analysis and the legitimacy of audience perceptions, and recast risk communication as a kind of marketing communication. Effective risk communication was all about persuasion. According to Leiss, this approach also ran into "severe difficulties" (p. 89). Specifically, it did little to overcome public distrust of technical and expert risk analysis. It also carried a risk of its own, i.e., practitioner emphasis on style over substance and audience attention to style rather than substance.

The third phase, described as the current phase in Leiss's (1996) article, began to shift the assumptions of risk communication away from instrumental methods and techniques of persuasion to an understanding of the social context for risk communication, i.e., to the relationships among "the players in the game of risk management" (p. 90). This phase provides the basis for the rational-ideal model of risk communication that we described above. Here, the focus is on stakeholder interaction and consensus building. The aim is to develop commitment to responsible risk management and communication by major organizational actors, which will influence others to act responsibly as well. This kind of reasoning is reflected in expressions of hope that General Electric's ecomagination strategy and similar efforts by some other major corporations will pull others along with them.

Crisis Communication

The concepts and examples of strategic communication that we have considered thus far in strategic communication presume that organizations have time to think through and carefully plan their strategies and messages. What happens when an organization must mount a major communication effort in the midst of a crisis?

Crises pose both dangers and opportunities for organizations (Keown-McMullen, 1997). Strictly speaking, a crisis is a turning point with the potential for undesirable or desirable outcomes, and things could go either way. The prevailing ordinary language of crisis, however, is negative. Barton (1993) defined crisis as "a major, unpredictable event that has potentially negative results [and] may significantly damage the organization" (p. 5). Because a crisis can have devastating consequences for an organization, Williams and Treadaway (1992) add three other characteristics: urgency, observation by the media, and interruption of normal operations. The concept of crisis in this sense certainly is nothing new to corporations, institutions, and other types of organizational entities. Imagine the shock and horror that must have afflicted officials of the White Star Line when they heard on April 15, 1912, that their "unsinkable" passenger ship, *Titanic,* had gone to the bottom of the Atlantic Ocean with some 1,500 souls aboard or the panic that must have swept over bank executives and stock exchange officers on Tuesday, October 29, 1929, the date of the stock market crash that signaled the beginning of the Great Depression. The purpose of crisis communication is to respond appropriately in such situations to minimize damage and maintain public confidence.

Egelhoff and Sen (1991) estimated from surveys that a typical, large organization confronts an average of 10 crises per year. Although most crises do not rise to the level of public scrutiny and concern accorded to events such as the fall of Enron Corporation, Hurricane Katrina, or the December 2004 tsunami that devastated coastal regions in South Asia, the Institute for Crisis Management reported that newsworthy organizational crisis events in the United States were occurring at a pace of more then 6,000 per year during the 1990s (Irvine & Millar, 1996).

Crisis and Stakeholder Relationships. Crisis communication in situations that affect the organization's relationships with stakeholders, especially those that draw mass media attention, requires management of those relationships. A simple but compelling reason is presented by Bud Englehart, a public relations officer who has worked for companies such as Kraft Foods, Lockheed, and Mellon Bank. As Englehart (1995) explained it, if you begin with the value of an organization and subtract from it the organization's material assets, "what you have left is the value that *perception* creates . . . You can lose that value in a nano-second in a crisis" (p. 27).

Much of the literature on crisis communication actually is concerned first and foremost with this issue. A good example is Benoit's (1995, 1997) theory of image restoration discourse in crisis situations.

Benoit's theory is concerned with crisis situations in which relevant audiences believe an organization to be responsible for an offensive act. For Benoit, the important point is not whether the organization in fact is responsible, but whether it is believed to be responsible. Benoit developed a typology of message options for responding to such situations under five basic strategies: denying responsibility, evading responsibility, reducing offensiveness of the act, taking corrective action, and apologizing for the act. He described specific cases in crisis situations where each strategy has been used, then referred to these cases to consider the circumstances under which any given strategy may be effective. The theory has inspired many studies of image restoration and adaptations of Benoit's ideas by other scholars (Burns & Bruner, 2000).

Factors in Crisis Communication. Sturges (1994) said that discussions of crisis management usually focus on three issues: (1) planning and preparation for crisis events, (2) behavior of the organization during the crisis, and (3) communication to important publics during the crisis.

We may think of these issues as elements to which organizations must attend in crisis management. Although Sturges considers communication as a separate element, planning and preparation as well as organizational behavior during the crisis clearly are relevant to what is communicated and how it is communicated.

The idea of planning for a crisis may seem like a contradiction in terms, but such planning seems to be a central concern to most people who write about or have to engage in crisis communication and management (Ulmer et al., 2006). Crisis is unpredictable in the sense that the time, place, and kind of a specific, future event are unknown. When a crisis does occur, the ensuing uncertainty and chaos can demand a great deal of adaptability in the response. Even so, one assumes that such events will occur, and one plans accordingly. Englehart (1995) recommended four basic steps in the planning process.

First, one should identify potential crises. What could potentially go wrong? Second, one must evaluate the potential impact of a crisis, not only in terms of the physical event, but also in terms of public response. One tool for accomplishing these first two steps is the "worst case scenario" technique (Barton, 1993). The label alone should provide you with a good idea of how this technique works. Third, one must assign specific responsibility for execution of the crisis management strategy. Who does what and when? According to Englehart (1995), the number of actors should be limited: "*If you manage crisis by committee, you are doomed to failure. . . .* There needs to be a chain of command and agreement on who's going to do the speaking" (p. 28). Finally, the plan must be put in writing, although it is not a good idea to put too much in writing. How does one know when there is enough in writing? The answer to this question resides in a point that Englehart could have identified as a fifth critical step, namely, rehearsal. The plan should be tried out with drills.

Most of the advice about planning for crisis management is very useful, but it seems to carry with it an assumption that planning and preparation in and of themselves will take care of issues two and three, organizational actions during a crisis and communication with relevant publics. The problem with this kind of thinking, according to Sturges (1994), is that communication especially is "only alluded to in preparation discussions and rarely is the focus of specific conjecture or study" (p. 299). In other words, crisis management plans often lack a coherent and well-thought-out strategy of public communication. If a strategy exists at all, it may be based on assumptions that all crisis communication has the same objective and all relevant publics can be approached with the same strategy.

Sturges challenged the first of these two assumptions by arguing that the communication objective should depend on the stage of the crisis. In cases when communication programs can actually begin before a crisis occurs, messages should provide internalizing information to build positive public opinion toward the organization. When it appears that a crisis is imminent, the strategy should shift from internalizing messages to instructing messages that tell the public how to respond to the crisis. Instructing communication should increase greatly at the breakout stage of the crisis so that affected publics know what they are to do. As the crisis subsides, communication may shift to adjusting messages intended to help people cope with the effects of the crisis. Finally, as the crisis abates, the organization can return to an internalizing strategy.

Public Bias in Crisis Communication. Sturges obviously is concerned almost entirely with public communication. As we noted earlier, this is true for much of the crisis communication literature, but the scope of crisis communication goes beyond dissemination of messages to publics. Crisis management is concerned with preventing or minimizing imminent loss, protecting or rescuing assets and people, and maintaining or recovering core functions. Consequently, crisis communication in a broader sense also includes the communication systems and processes necessary for coordinated action among those who respond to the crisis. Rasberry (2006) makes this point clearly in a study of organizational failures in the Katrina disaster. He concluded, "At the heart of Katrina were massive information gaps and broken communication networks" (abstract), not only in terms of ineffective public communication, but also in terms of planning failures and the inability of agencies to function and to coordinate with one another during the crisis.

Focusing on communication only in terms of messages to and interactions with publics and stakeholders obscures the importance of communication process issues in all aspects of crisis planning and management. As we will see in the next section on interpretive perspectives on strategic communication, a crisis creates an environment of uncertainty and unpredictability where the ordinary routines of communicating and organizing often fail. Understanding how to circumvent such failures through novel and nonroutine processes is a vital aspect of crisis planning and management.

THE INTERPRETIVE PERSPECTIVE

The interpretive perspective examines strategic communication in terms of the social construction of reality and organizational sense-making processes. Chaffee's interpretive model of strategy frames one such approach. This approach is concerned mainly with management's symbolic efforts to shape the negotiated order for organizational strategy and with stakeholder responses to such efforts. In effect, such an approach concentrates on the construction of strategy in the management-stakeholder relationship. There are other ways to study strategic communication from an interpretive point of view. For example, rather than focusing on the management-stakeholder relationship, one might take a more systematic or collectivist view. Rather than addressing sense making in the construction of strategy, one might examine sense making in the execution of strategy.

Although interpretive studies involve essentially the same forms of strategic communication that we used to organize our discussion of the traditional perspective, repeating the same scheme for the interpretive discussion is not especially informative. Instead, we will consider some of the major lessons about strategic communication that can be drawn from interpretive work. Three of these are the limitations of the effectiveness model, the transactional character of strategic communication, and the constraints of prior experience during crisis.

Limits of the Effectiveness Model

One lesson that can be drawn from the body of interpretive work on strategic communication is the limitation of an effectiveness model. Effectiveness advocates tend to attribute failure of strategic initiatives to ineffective communication and contend that there are, in fact, "best practices" for effective strategic communication. Such practices may be useful, but they do not assure success for strategic initiatives. One example of this limitation is the study by Smith and Eisenberg (1987) of labor-management conflict at Disneyland that we described in Chapter 6.

You may recall from the earlier discussion that Smith and Eisenberg were looking for root metaphors that characterized employees' experiences at Disneyland. One of these was a family metaphor that Walt Disney himself initiated with the image of Disneyland as an oasis for friendly family entertainment. This vision was adopted so thoroughly by employees that they cast themselves as defenders and caretakers of Disney's founding vision when management philosophy began to shift after Disney's death. Employees, however, had revised this vision by extending the concept of family to themselves. Disneyland not only provided family entertainment, it was a family itself. This new interpretation was one that even Disney himself "may not have fully endorsed [and it] led ultimately to conflict with management" (p. 373).

Smith and Eisenberg noted that the family metaphor was accepted uncritically by most employees and even by many managers as a characterization of employee relationships and the management-employee relationship. As operating costs and competition from other theme parks increased, management gradually placed greater emphasis on cost containment, including a wage freeze and elimination of benefits, in its efforts to operate at a profit. Moreover, management attempted to redefine the family metaphor (e.g., family life sometimes is hard and families sometimes have to make sacrifices) to support the strategy, but employees rejected management's new idea of family. Management's bottom-line view "was perceived by many as constituting a breach of Disney's caring philosophy" (p. 374), a situation that culminated in a 22-day strike by unionized employees.

Transactional Strategic Communication

A second lesson from interpretive scholarship concerns the transactional aspects of strategic communication. Especially when one assumes a linear perspective of strategy, it is easy to forget that communication is a transactional process. Rapert, Velliquette, and Garretson (2002) demonstrate this point in a study of strategic consensus.

Strategic consensus, as Rapert et al. use the term, is a "shared understanding of middle management and those at the operational level to [sic] the top management team's strategic goals" (p. 303). They concluded from a large study of hospital administrators that such a consensus is critical for successful implementation of strategy. Strategic consensus does not necessarily mean that members are in total agreement with and entirely committed to the strategy. It does mean that members have constructed a common understanding of what it is. Rapert et al. concluded, "Communication, then, becomes a vital part of strategy implementation in . . . a process through which they [organization members] converge on commonly shared meanings" (p. 303). This involves not only the message of top management to others in the organization, but others' transactions among themselves.

The transactional character of strategic communication also is revealed in Hendry's treatment of strategic decision making as discourse. Hendry (2000) pointed out that most organizational practices involve doing things, but strategy as a practice is talking about things more than doing things, and "the output of the strategy process typically takes the form of communications" (p. 970). Hendry contended that strategic decision making is not just a prelude in a linear sequence leading to organizational change, but also an ongoing change process. Hendry reminds us in his conclusion:

> Speech is ephemeral and in an organizational context even texts are short-lived, so a decision must not only be effectively communicated, but also recommunicated [and] it must also be continually refined and adapted through dialogue so as to meet the specific and ever changing needs of different actors and different circumstances. (p. 973)

Constraint and Crisis

A third lesson that can be drawn from interpretive work is the potentially constraining effect of previous experience on communication and action in crisis events. This lesson is drawn from a case study of the 1997 Red River flood in Minnesota and North Dakota (Sellnow, Seeger, & Ulmer, 2002). We referred briefly to this study in Chapter 1, but we present it here in more detail because its central lesson is well established in crisis management literature, yet somehow lost in practice. Some of the major problems in the Red River event returned to haunt crisis management on a much larger scale during Hurricane Katrina.

Sellnow et al. used the Red River flood case to show how chaos theory can be applied to crisis events. Their work is not strictly an interpretive study like Smith and Eisenberg's Disneyland study in which an interpretive method is applied to analyze discourse, but they do use interpretive principles to explain their findings. The study used several concepts from chaos theory; the two key concepts for our purpose here are the cosmology episode and self-organizing. A cosmology episode occurs "when the crisis situation creates an overwhelming sensation on the part of observers. . . . where all existing forms of sense-making fail to account for experiences" (p. 271). Self-organizing is a "process whereby order re-emerges out of a random and chaotic state" with new forms, structures, and procedures, "often at a high level of order and complexity" (p. 272).

Nobody expected a cosmology episode at the outset of Red River crisis. Severe spring flooding is common in that region, and flood planning that year already had been underway for three months. Forecasting flood levels depended on a system of gauges along the Red River that had worked well in the past for predicting the usual spring flood water levels. With more than twice the normal amount of snow on the ground, 1997 was different, but nobody seemed to realize how this would challenge the region's flood management routines. According to Sellnow et al., officials were "locked into a 'certainty seeking' mode [and] insisted on obtaining their information, as they always had done, from the National Weather Service's gauge estimates" (p. 279).

The initial prediction was a flood crest of 38 feet, but it was not long before the predictions began to change, first higher, then lower, then still higher again. The April 17 forecast was for a crest of 50.5 feet at Grand Forks, where the dikes were built up to withstand 52 feet. The actual crest turned out to be 54 feet. On the night of April 18, water topped the dikes, and the entire city of 50,000 people had to be evacuated. To make matters worse, a fire broke out and spread through several blocks of the downtown area. At this point, the occurrence of the cosmology episode for Grand Forks residents and flood management officials was summed up by one relief worker: "It was just beyond belief" (p. 281).

The mayor of Grand Forks characterized the weather service forecast as something that city officials were told in absolute terms and argued that the disaster could have been prevented if the city had known that the crest would top the dikes. The National Weather Service responded that it had never told Grand Forks it could rely absolutely on the forecast, although it could have done more to emphasize uncertainty in the prediction. But Sellnow et al. said that all of the officials, from local to federal, were excessively confident about the forecast, and they communicated with others accordingly.

Sellnow et. al concluded "that preexisting sensemaking structures favoring rationalized, traditional views of a complex system led officials to make inappropriately unequivocal predictions and ultimately diminished the effectiveness of the region's crisis communication and planning" (p. 269). Perhaps we can summarize succinctly just how this lesson seems to be lost in practice by repeating George Bush's famous comment to former FEMA director, Michael Brown, during the Katrina crisis: "Brownie, you're doing a heck of a job."

There is more to the Red River case study, and it concerns the concept of self-organization. Sellnow et al. also devoted attention to the manner in which the region began to recover from the crisis. They noted the emergence of novel systems of interagency cooperation that actually began during the crisis itself, especially in the cities of Fargo and Moorhead, and Fargo's move ultimately to supersede the county emergency services operation and have the city itself designated as an emergency operations center for the state. And they found that stories about the crisis, told and retold, interpreted and reinterpreted, led residents of particular communities to a larger, regional perspective of the area.

One more important point that emerged from the study concerns the nonroutine and novel use of communication systems during the crisis, e.g., radio programs normally in a talk/call-in format that became community bulletin boards. Such uses should serve as a reminder to crisis managers that flexible and resilient systems of communication should be a priority.

THE CRITICAL PERSPECTIVE

The critical perspective on strategic communication essentially starts with an interpretive frame of reference on symbols and discourse, then transforms it into critical engagement with power and authority (Sewell, 2004). Examples of critical studies and cases in strategic communication are numerous because the fundamental subject matter for the critical perspective of organizational communication is, in one sense, strategic communication. Given the goals of critical scholarship, much of the discourse of interest is in a domain of communication that is generally presumed to be controlled and directed by top management.

The lessons from critical scholarship about strategic communication mainly concern the manner in which symbols and discourse are manipulated and distorted to serve elite and privileged interests or the ways in which those who are subject to such hegemonic control use communication to cope with their plight. We will review one example of each. We also will describe one somewhat atypical use of the critical perspective that reveals the transformative power of strategic communication.

Strategy and Hegemony

A good, but also fairly typical example of the critical approach to strategic communication is a study of TransAtlantic Business Dialogue by Zoller (2004). The basic idea for the TransAtlantic Business Dialogue (TABD) was developed in the 1990s by U.S. Secretary of Commerce Ron Brown under the Clinton administration. The TABD promotes close commercial ties between the United States and the European Union. TABD claims to do this through a dialogue system of input from public and civil society to foster a more integrated transatlantic marketplace. Presumably, this input from public and civil sources shapes TABD policy recommendations. In addition to the TABD, there are separate dialogues for consumers, labor, and environment, literally the TACD, TALD, TAED, but Zoller contends that these three are much less influential than the TABD.

Zoller points out that the TABD is a corporate coalition that advises the E.U. and U.S. governments about business regulation and global trade. Increased economic and political tension between the European Union and the United States in recent years pushed the TABD into "a dual rhetorical challenge: promoting its success to business and government participants to further the process while encountering a small but growing activist community protesting TABD's influence as an example of corporate hegemony" (p. 205). On the one hand, TABD is less successful now than it was in the 1990s in gaining government adoption of its recommendations. On the other hand, critics contend that TABD policies undermine economic, environmental, and health regulations. Hence, the TABD faces challenges to its legitimacy on two fronts.

Zoller studied TABD's public communication on issues management "to understand how the organization constitutes and justifies its role in global policy making to legitimize and forward its goals in the face of potential conflicts, and the implications of that discourse for public participation in regulatory and trade policy making" (p. 208). In part, TABD is an important subject for communication study because it uses the concept of dialogue strategically to mask "monologic goals" (p. 209). In other words, Zoller is suggesting that TABD manipulates dialogue to accomplish its own ends. How does it do this?

According to Zoller's analysis, TABD uses the language of the two-way symmetrical model of public relations, but it exploits this model by manipulating the multiple meanings of dialogue. For example, TABD promotes dialogue in terms of conflict prevention. The quest is for unitary agreement rather than pluralistic points of view, so the system is used to obscure conflicts. TABD links dialogue with the public good and denies any aims to weaken regulations on business, yet deregulatory goals are apparent in its public communication. TABD represents dialogue as civil participation and its own role as advisory and nongovernmental, but its goal is incorporation of its expert group recommendations into government policy.

Zoller concludes that the effect of TABD's strategy actually is to exclude multiple viewpoints from dialogue on trade and business policies: "Rather than contributing to increased public debate, the process forwards only business interests and only one version of those interests" (p. 233).

Coping With Power

The complexity of power is well illustrated in a study of change discourse from the point of view of organization members during a corporate merger (Howard & Geist, 1995).

Howard and Geist studied a 4,200-employee public utility company that they identified with the pseudonym California Gas and Power (CGP). CGP was engaged in a merger with a larger utility company, an effort supported by a strategic plan and a transition program. The state public utilities commission ultimately rejected the merger, but there was no way at the time that CGP employees could know that this would be the outcome.

Howard and Geist pointed out that organizations have to maintain stability even as they promote acceptance of organizational change, whereas organization members have to deal with the paradox of this dilemma and the inherent contradiction between stability and change. As members attempt to manage the paradox and rationalize the choices they make in response to change, they develop interpretations and discourses that are ideological. In effect, they engage in "ideological positioning" to cope with "the dominant power structures and sectional interests of the organization" (p. 112). Howard and Geist's study concerned the primary and secondary organizational contradictions embedded in the CGP merger and the ideological positions that emerged in response to these contradictions.

CGP's identity and culture were based on espoused values of empowerment, openness, and participation. It also was a relatively small, secure, and family- and community-oriented company. The merger decision set up a primary contradiction between the desires of shareholders for increased profitability and the needs of the organization as a community of people, especially because the merger decision was essentially centralized. This primary contradiction involving control was accompanied by secondary contradictions between change and stability (especially over the issue of job security), empowerment and powerlessness (the tradeoff of the espoused value of participation against the nonparticipatory merger decision), and identification and estrangement (a company once promoting organizational identification and commitment, but now offering severance packages for people who go away).

Howard and Geist found that organization members developed four distinct ideological discourses to deal with the contradictions: invincibility, diplomacy, betrayal, and defection. Those who engaged in a discourse of invincibility represented themselves not only as accepting the merger, but also as immune from any negative consequences. The discourse of diplomacy simultaneously embraced the value of change while questioning the benefits of this specific merger, going along with the transition, hoping to remain in the merged organization, yet unwilling to renounce the values and culture of the unmerged CGP. Betrayal probably needs no explanation. Those who adopted this ideological position engaged in a discourse of powerlessness, lost identity, and estrangement from the organization. Finally, there was a discourse of defection, the meaning also self-evident, but it obliges explanation inasmuch as this was a discourse recounted by remaining members about those who opted out, took the severance package or just rejected the change and left.

There may be a number of lessons about change communication programs to be drawn from Howard and Geist's study of CGP, but two seem especially notable. First, despite strategic planning and implementation of a transition program by CGP executives, there was no glossing over the fundamental contradictions of control in this organization, and the emergence of four distinct discourses and ideological positions suggests that management could not achieve anything like the kind of strategic consensus envisioned by Rapert et. al. (2002) as a condition for change. Second, Howard and Geist noted that ideological positioning not only serves a sense-making function for organization members, but also serves to "enhance or inhibit autonomy, identification, empowerment, and change" (p. 129). In other words, organization members do use ideological positioning to serve their own interests, and this is yet another constraint on the effectiveness model of employee communication.

Transformation and Strategic Communication

Executives who frame strategy certainly hope for it to have transformative effects in terms that they define, but strategic communication can be transformative for the organization in ways that may not be obvious. Transformation in this sense involves more than executives getting compliance and acceptance out of stakeholders. Executives also may be caught up in the transformation. Livesey (2002) points out this lesson in a study of Shell Oil's discourse on sustainable development.

Roper and Toledano (2005) say that the traditional and dominant view of issues management "is closely linked to public policy development, with the aim of strategically influencing legislation that might impose restrictions upon organizational practices" (p. 480). They suggest that an "anthropocentric world view" drives certain kinds of global problems such as climate change with an imperative to use resources for immediate benefits. The alternative view of long-term harmony with the planet is marginalized. Issues management should be reframed or recontextualized by shifting to an imperative for organizational legitimacy, where legitimacy is understood in terms of responsiveness to the needs of the organization's environment, in particular, by favoring "a precautionary approach to sustainability" (p. 481). Livesey's study involves a major case where such a shift may be occurring.

Livesey (2002) examined Shell's first corporate social report issued in 1998, "Profits and Principles: Does There Have to Be a Choice?" Shell had made a strategic decision to embrace the concept of sustainable development. The report, also characterized by Shell in part as a "dialogue" or, at least, an invitation to dialogue, was a presentation of the strategic change. Shell began by answering the question in the report's title with a negative, contending that profits and principles and the interests of business and society are compatible. The corporation went on in the report to describe in detail how it intended to accomplish its new objectives with sustainable development and the issues and challenges that it would face in the process.

Livesey subjected the report to an intensive and complex form of critical analysis, but she drew some conclusions that seem to be unusual for critical scholarship. She noted that

Shell's report could be read from a fairly typically critical standpoint, i.e., "simply as a corporate attempt to reestablish discursive regularity and hegemonic control in the wake of challenges by environmentalists and human rights activists" (p. 314). But Livesey found instead that the corporation's discourse on sustainable development had transforming effects on the company and on the idea of sustainability.

In particular, Livesey noted that the constitutive effects of strategic discourse do not necessarily unfold in accordance with corporate direction and control. Talk can be an obstacle to change, but it also may be the vehicle for change; realization of alternatives happens in talk about alternatives, and Livesey cites other examples where "the accidental effects of talk have been shown to foster corporate greening" (p. 338). Finally, Livesey asserts that "words have effects [and] Shell's words, highlighted here, embodied commitments to actions, at least some of which are tangible and radical" (p. 343).

SUMMARY

Strategic communication in organizations is a complex process. Despite its linear appearance, it has the transactional characteristics of other communication contexts. Strategic communication emerges from the efforts of various individuals and organizational units, although much of the communication agenda is regulated by management through control over the resources that are required for communication programs.

Strategic communication programs should be concerned not only with transmission of messages in order to influence various publics, but also with ways in which publics seek out and use information. Much strategic communication activity also is concerned with responding to or attempting to shape public policy regulation.

An organization's strategic communication efforts can be classified generally as internal or external. Traditional perspectives generally rely on this distinction, although it is not very useful in many instances of strategic communication.

Internal communication, sometimes referred to as employee communication, usually involves management efforts to exert influence with organization members in general. Some of the most common uses of internal communication include orientation and indoctrination, provision of information on compensation and benefits, explanation and facilitation of organizational change, and promotion of member morale. Effective employee communication presumably requires upper management backing, integration of employee communication with strategy and business plans, and adaptive but consistent messages.

External communication is a means through which organizations adapt to and influence relevant publics, including customers, voters, communities, regulators, and legislators. Traditionally, external communication has been dominated by public relations image-building strategists. Image building is a process of developing and publicizing specific organizational characteristics and behaviors that are consistent with the image being cultivated.

More recently, many organizations have turned their strategic resources to issues management activities that differ from traditional image building. Issues management involves a process of identifying and tracking public issues that may affect an organization. In some cases, organizations respond to issues by changing and communicating with relevant publics about the change. In other cases, organizations couple issues management with issues advocacy—a strategic attempt to shape public opinion on issues before political action on these issues results in legislation or regulation that affects the organization.

Risk communication and crisis communication are related but distinguishable activities. Risk communication has evolved into a position that can be described as a rational-ideal model. The model envisions risk communicators as professionals who facilitate interaction between scientific-technical risk experts and nonexpert publics and foster responsible and effective communication about risks involving industrial technologies, natural hazards, and human activities. The model does have limitations, and this area of strategic communication in particular warrants questions from the critical scholarship point of view.

Crisis communication, especially where media have interests in pursuing a story about the crisis, is more complicated than most of the forms of public communication that we review in this chapter. Generally, experts in crisis communication suggest that organizations must plan and rehearse plans for responding to crisis situations. In particular, they must understand that a crisis progresses through stages and that crisis communication requires different objectives and different kinds of messages at different stages. Messages in crisis communication also must be adapted to accommodate the expectations of multiple publics. There is a public communication bias in much of the crisis communication literature that may obscure the importance of communication processes in all aspects of crisis management.

The interpretive perspective of strategic communication offers its own lessons. Three of these lessons involve the limitations of effectiveness models of strategic communication, the transactional character of strategic communication, and the constraining influence of a preexisting system of meaning in crisis management. Studies of conflict at Disneyland, strategic consensus among hospital administrators, and the crisis management failures in the 1997 Red River floods illustrated these lessons.

In one sense, strategic communication is the fundamental subject matter for the critical perspective of organizational communication. The lessons from critical scholarship about strategic communication mainly concern the manner in which symbols and discourse are manipulated and distorted to serve elite and privileged interests or the ways in which those who are subject to such hegemonic control use communication to cope with their plight. We considered a study of the TransAtlantic Business Dialogue as a typical example of the first type and a study of employee responses to a California energy company merger for the second. We also reviewed one somewhat atypical use of the critical perspective that reveals the transformative power of strategic communication at Shell Oil.

DISCUSSION QUESTIONS/ACTIVITIES

1. Find some examples of internal communication. What kinds of topics and problems are addressed in these examples? What do you think the main purpose of internal communication seems to be?

2. Find some examples of external communication concerned with *organizational* (not product or service) image building. What are the organizations behind these messages trying to accomplish? How?

3. Watch some segments of television programs such as "Face the Nation" and "Meet the Press." Can you identify some examples of issues advocacy in the advertisements on these programs?

4. Who controls the agenda for strategic communication? What are the ethical and philosophical issues involved in such control? How would most strategic communication initiatives be described from traditional, interpretive, and critical points of view?

REFERENCES

Annenberg Public Policy Center. (2003). Issue ads @ aapc: An online tracking of inside the beltway legislative issue advocacy for 2001–2002 [Electronic version]. Retrieved June 12, 2006, from http://www.annenberg publicpolicycenter.org/ISSUEADS/issues.htm

Barrett, D. J. (2002). Change communication: Using strategic employee communication to facilitate major change. *Corporate Communications: An International Journal, 7*(4), 219–231.

Barton, L. (1993). *Crisis in organizations: Managing and communicating in the heat of crisis.* Cincinnati, OH: SouthWestern.

Benoit, W. L. (1995). *Apologies, excuses, and accounts: A theory of image restoration strategies.* Albany: State University of New York Press.

Benoit, W. L. (1997). Image repair discourse and crisis communication. *Public Relations Review, 23*(2), 177–186.

Buchholz, R. (1982). Education for public issues management: Key insights from a survey of top practitioners. *Public Affairs Review, 3,* 65–76.

Burns, J. P., & Bruner, M. S. (2000). Revisiting the theory of image restoration strategies. *Communication Quarterly, 48*(1), 27–39.

Chaffee, E. E. (1985). Three models of strategy. *The Academy of Management Review, 10*(1), 89–98.

CNNMoney.com. (2006). Fortune 500 annual rankings of America's largest corps 2006 for 2005. Retrieved June 8, 2006, from http://money.cnn.com/magazines/fortune/fortune500/performers/companies/profits

Coates, J., Coates, V., Jarratt, J., & Heinz, L. (1986). *Issues management: How you can plan, organize, and manage for the future.* Mt. Airy, MD: Lomond.

Conrad, C., & Poole, M. S. (2005). *Strategic organizational communication in a global economy* (6th ed.). Belmont, CA: Wadsworth/Thompson.

Cutlip, S. M., & Center, A. H. (1964). *Effective public relations* (3rd ed.). Englewood Cliffs, NJ: Prentice Hall.

Egelhoff, W. G., & Sen, F. (1991). Six years and counting: Learning from crisis management at Bhopal. *Public Relations Review, 17,* 69–83.

Englehart, B. (1995). Crisis communication: Communicating under fire. *The Journal of Management Advocacy Communication, 1,* 23–28.

Ewing, R. P. (1979, Winter). The uses of futurist techniques in issues management. *Public Relations Quarterly,* pp. 15–18.

Finn, D. (1962, June). Stop worrying about your image. *Harper's Magazine,* p. 225.

Fombrun, C. J. (1996). *Reputation: Realizing value from the corporate image.* Boston: Harvard Business School Press.

Fountain, K. C. (2004, May 4). Public advocacy groups: A directory of United States lobbyists [Electronic version]. Retrieved June 12, 2006, from http://www.csuchico.edu/~kcfount

Fox, J. (1983). Communication on public issues: The CEO's changing role. *Public Relations Review, 9*(1), 11–23.

Freitag, A. R., & Picherit-Duthler, G. (2004). Employee benefits communication: Proposing a PR-HR cooperative approach. *Public Relations Review, 30,* 475–482.

Gallup Public Opinion Index, June 1979.

Gardner, B. B., & Rainwater, L. (1955). The mass image of big business. *Harvard Business Review, 33,* 61–66.

Gaunt, P., & Ollenburger, J. (1995). Issues management revisited: A tool that deserves another look. *Public Relations Review, 21*(3), 199–210.

Goldhaber, G. M. (1993). *Organizational communication* (6th ed.). Dubuque, IA: Brown & Benchmark.

Gurabardhi, Z., Gutteling, J. M., & Kuttschreuter, M. (2004). The development of risk communication: An empirical analysis of the literature in the field. *Science Communication, 25*(4), 323–349.

Heath, R. L., & Nelson, R. A. (1986). *Issues management: Corporate public policymaking in an information society.* Beverly Hills, CA: Sage.

Hendry, J. (2000). Strategic decision making, discourse, and strategy as social practice. *Journal of Management Studies, 37*(7), 955–978.

Hill, J. W. (1977). Corporations: The sitting ducks. *Public Relations Quarterly, 22,* 8–10.

Howard, L. A., & Geist, P. (1995). Ideological positioning in organizational change: The dialectic of control in a merging organization. *Communication Monographs, 62,* 110–131.

Irvine, R. B., & Millar, D. P. (1996). Debunking the stereotypes of crisis management: The nature of business crisis in the 1990s. Institute for Crisis Management. Retrieved October 13, 2006, from http://www.crisis experts.com/debunking_main.htm.

Jones, B. L., & Chase, W. H. (1979). Managing public policy issues. *Public Relations Review, 5,* 3–23.

Keown-McMullen, C. (1997). Crisis: When does a molehill become a mountain? *Disaster Prevention and Management, 6*(1), 4–10.

Leiss, W. (1996, May). Three phases in the evolution of risk communication practice. *Annals, AAPSS, 545,* 85–94.

Leiss, W. (2004). Effective risk communication practice. *Toxicology Letters, 149,* 399–404.

Lim, G., Ahn, H., & Lee, H. (2005). Formulating strategies for stakeholder management: A case-based reasoning approach. *Expert Systems with Applications, 28,* 831–840.

Livesey, S. M. (2002). The discourse of the middle ground: Citizen Shell commits to sustainable development. *Management Communication Quarterly, 15*(3), 313–349.

Manheim, J. B. (1991). *All of the people, all the time: Strategic communication and American politics.* Armonk, NY: M. E. Sharpe.

Meyerson, H. (2006). *Fire up your staff on a shoestring budget.* Dallas, TX: The Confidence Center [Electronic version]. Retrieved June 26, 2007, from http://www.confidencecenter.com/index.html

Miller, S. (1997). Implementing strategic decisions: Four key success factors, *Organization Studies, 18,* 577–602.

Post, J. E. (1978). Corporate response models and public affairs management. *Public Relations Quarterly, 24,* 27–32.

Rapert, M. I., Velliquette, A., & Garretson, J. A. (2002). The strategic implementation process: Evoking strategic consensus through communication. *Journal of Business Research, 55,* 301–310.

Rasberry, R. (2006, October). *Katrina's crisis communication lessons.* Paper presented at the annual conference of the Association for Business Communication, San Antonio, Texas.

Recording Industry Association of America. (1999, December 7). Recording industry sues Napster for copyright infringement. *RIAA Press Room* [Electronic version]. Retrieved June 14, 2006, from http://www .riaa.com/news/newsletter/press1999/120799.asp

Roberts, K. J. (2006). Employee communications can affect a CEO's health: Informed employees are good for business. Lippincott Mercer Publications [Electronic version]. Retrieved June 9, 2006, from http://www .lippincottmercer.com/insights/a_roberts02.shtml

Roper, J., & Toledano, M. (2005). Taking in the view from the edge: Issues management recontextualized, *Public Relations Review, 31*(4), 479–485.

Schneider, G. (2005, May 10). GE determined to show more "ecomagination": Program sets pollution reduction targets. *The Washington Post* [Electronic version]. Retrieved June 12, 2006, from http://www.washing tonpost.com/wp-dyn/content/article/2005/05/09/AR2005050901169.html

Segars, A. H., & Kohut, G. F. (2001). Strategic communication through the world wide web: An empirical model of effectiveness in the CEO's letter to shareholders. *Journal of Management Studies, 38*(4), 535–556.

Sellnow, T. L., Seeger, M. W., & Ulmer, R. R. (2002). Chaos theory, informational needs, and natural disasters. *Journal of Applied Communication Research, 30*(4), 269–292.

Sethi, S. P. (1982). *Up against the corporate wall: Modern corporations and social issues of the eighties* (4th ed.). Englewood Cliffs, NJ: Prentice Hall.

Sewell, G. (2004). Exploring the moral consequences of management communication theory and practice. *Management Communication Quarterly, 18*(1), 97–114.

Shin, J.-H., Jin, Y., Cheng, I.-H., & Cameron, G. (2003). *Tracking messy organization-public conflicts: Exploring the natural history of conflict management through the news coverage of unfolding cases.* Paper presented at the annual meeting of the International Communication Association, San Diego, CA, May 2003.

Smith, R. C., & Eisenberg, E. M. (1987). Conflict at Disneyland: A root-metaphor analysis. *Communication Monographs, 54,* 367–380.

Sturges, D. L. (1994). Communicating through crisis: A strategy for organizational survival. *Management Communication Quarterly, 7,* 297–316.

Tillerson, R. W. (2006, April 20). Economic and environmental solutions in the global energy system. Comments at EFR Business Week, Rotterdam, The Netherlands [Electronic version]. Retrieved June 12, 2006, from http://exxonmobil.com/Corporate/Newsroom/SpchsIntvws/Corp_NR_SpchIntrvw_RWT_200406.asp

Todd, J. (2005, July 25). To revitalize labor movement, breakaway unions must focus on public image of service workers. *Duke University News & Communications* [Electronic version]. Retrieved June 11, 2006, from http://www.dukenews.edu/2005/07/afl_cio_split_print.htm

Ulmer, R. R., Sellnow, T. L., & Seeger, M. W. (2006). *Effective crisis communication: Moving from crisis to opportunity.* Thousand Oaks, CA: Sage.

U.S. Chamber of Commerce. (2006, April 25). U.S. Chamber study finds employee benefit costs consume 40 percent of payroll expenses. Press Release [Electronic version]. Retrieved June 11, 2006, from http://www.uschamber.com/press/releases/2006/April/06-72.htm

U.S. Environmental Protection Agency. (2007). Hudson River PCBs. Retrieved June 26, 2007, from http://www.epa.gov/hudson

Wallison, P. J. (2006, May 9). The Wal-Bank principle. *On the Issues, AEI Online* [Electronic version]. Retrieved June 13, 2006, from http://www.aei.org/publications/pubID.24350/pub_detail.asp

Whittington, R., & Whipp, R. (1992). Professional ideology and marketing implementation. *European Journal of Marketing, 26*(1), 52–63.

Williams, D. E., & Treadaway, G. (1992). Exxon and the Valdez accident: A failure in crisis communication. *Communication Studies, 43,* 56–64.

Williams, L. C., Jr. (1978). What 50 presidents and CEO's think about employee communications. *Public Relations Quarterly, 23,* 6–11.

Wiseman, G., & Barker, L. (1967). *Speech—Interpersonal communication.* Chicago: Chandler.

Wojcik, J. (2005, February 21). Benefit communications redesigned for diverse workforce. *Business Insurance* (Electronic version]. Retrieved June 9, 2006, from http://www.compbenefits.com/BIdental.pdf

Zoller, H. M. (2004). Dialogue as global issue management: Legitimizing corporate influence in the TranSatlantic Business Dialogue. *Management Communication Quarterly, 18*(2), 204–240.

New Millennium Thought

Perspectives and Trends

> *Praxis and Consciousness Raising*
> A Feminist Organization: Casa de Esperanza (House of Hope)
>
> TRENDS INFLUENCING ORGANIZATIONS TODAY
> Globalization of the Marketplace and Global Competitive Pressures
> Gender and Diversity
> Quality and Customer Satisfaction
> Political and Legal Pressures on Organizations
> Stress at Work
> Inadequately Educated Workforce
> Critical Questioning of Corporate Values
> Stakeholder Perspectives

In this first decade of the new millennium, organizational stakeholders and researchers are raising a number of important questions. Among these questions are (a) What will be the impact of decreased access to crude oil and continued population growth? (b) What forms of organizing make the best use of human resources? (c) What constitutes a humane working environment? (d) How can organizations operate effectively in a globally competitive environment? (e) What are the benefits and challenges of sustaining a diverse workforce? (f) How do organizational operations need to change in order to protect the environment? and (g) How can workers be empowered in ways that allow them to accomplish individual and organizational goals? In this chapter, we will address these questions by focusing on recent theoretical developments in organizational studies. First, we will discuss traditional, interpretive, and critical perspectives on the new millennium. Second, our discussion of the critical perspective will lead to a consideration of possibilities for worker emancipation in the 21st century and an overview of empowering workplace structures such as self-managed work teams, democratic workplace systems, and feminist organizations. Finally, we will discuss trends influencing organizations today.

PERSPECTIVES ON THE NEW MILLENNIUM

As the first decade of the new millennium continues to unfold and we look toward the future, there are very different trajectories that organizations may follow. One critical factor appears to be the continued availability of cheap energy. Large-scale production requires significant amounts of cheap energy and many scientists believe that the era of cheap energy, in the form of oil, may soon be ending. Another important factor is that the basis of the world economic system is predicated on continued growth of population and consumption. Many environmental scientists, however, argue that our finite planet has only so many resources. Some argue that we have already passed the point of maximum population, whereas others argue that point looms on the horizon.

What implications do these observations have for the new millennium? The end of cheap energy and population growth will significantly affect the type of world in which we live. As you will see in the sections to follow, the most significant changes will be smaller and more local forms of organizing. Large corporations will no longer exist in this environment. People will be organized in smaller communities that may need to be self-sufficient in energy and agricultural production. Consumer products will be produced in cottage businesses.

Are these changes inevitable? If so, when will they occur? These questions are difficult to answer, and complete answers are beyond the scope of the present text. Some of the sources cited below provide our readers with a starting place to find out what the scientific community is saying about these issues.

In the sections that follow, we also consider the possibility that technological solutions to our energy problems will allow us to proceed with business as usual, at least for the coming decade or two. Given this possibility, we also offer a more conventional vision of the future.

TRADITIONAL PERSPECTIVES AND THE NEW MILLENNIUM

In the final stages of preparing this book for publication in the fall of 2007, the traditional perspective of organizing is still being played out in the global marketplace. Large corporations continue to compete with one another for market share by producing products in mass quantities at ever-higher levels of efficiency. Sadly, as we observed earlier in Chapter 11, efficiency often requires cheap labor where workers are not paid a living wage, whether at Wal-Mart in the United States or in a manufacturing company in China.

The continuation of the traditional model, however, requires the availability of huge amounts of cheap energy to fuel large-scale production processes. And the era of cheap energy appears to be coming to a rapid end. Crude oil prices are at $76.70 per barrel (New York Mercantile Exchange, 2007), and most experts believe that prices will only continue to increase. Why is crude oil so expensive? The answer is complex. Part of the problem is the instability in the Middle East, the major oil-producing region in the world. So, security costs now have to be factored into oil production and delivery. The two Gulf Wars have also damaged many oilfields in Iraq (a major producer) to the point that extraction costs now exceed the oil yield from those fields. These damages may have eliminated access to billions of barrels of oil, a significant loss to the world market (Orlov, 2006).

Most troublesome is the belief held by many scientists that we have reached or soon will reach the state of peak oil production. Peak oil is that point at which the production of oil will start a continual decline. Another way of looking at it is that when we reach peak oil, only half of the amount of oil that exists on the planet remains. On the one hand, that's a lot of oil. On the other hand, worldwide consumption of oil continues to increase every year. Furthermore, the oil we have accessed up to now was the easiest and least inexpensive to extract because it was closer to the surface. The oil that remains is more expensive to extract and will only become more so. At a certain point, drilling is no longer viable because it will cost more energy to remove the oil than that oil produces. So, we will never be able to gain the use of all the oil that remains because of the increasing costs of extraction.

Why all this focus on oil? Well, oil is the cheapest and most efficient energy source for large organizations to use to produce and transport products. Oil is also the cheapest form of energy to heat homes, produce electricity, and fuel vehicles. If oil continues to become more expensive, we will need to rely increasingly on other forms of energy (solar, wind, hydrogen, nuclear, battery, hydroelectric, etc.). The problem with these alternatives is none is as efficient as oil as a producer of energy; they cannot, at present, come close to meeting world energy needs; and some of them are unreliable. So, without the availability of cheap, efficient, and reliable energy, the traditional model of large-scale production will end.

Some argue that we will discover new technologies that will meet our increasing energy needs, but most scientists are not so optimistic (Heinberg, 2003; Hickerson, 2004; Pfeiffer, 2006). The implication of the eventual end to cheap energy is a collapse of large-scale production and a return to simpler models of preindustrial production. Sophisticated technologies requiring huge amounts of energy will no longer be available. Simple production by small groups of individuals using hand tools may become the norm, at least during a transition period as we redefine how we organize ourselves. The way we live, how we travel, the education we will need, and the jobs we choose will all be affected by this profound shift.

One very interesting source that describes the impact of peak oil is James Howard Kunstler's (2005) *The Long Emergency.* He believes that developed countries such as the United States will need to make new arrangements in a postindustrial age for the manufacture, distribution, and sale of ordinary goods. Specifically, goods will probably be made on a "cottage industry" basis rather than on the factory model because the scale of available energy will be much lower. The selling of products will also need to occur on the local level so merchandise needs to be moved only short distances. Although there is no way to predict when these changes may occur, in the next five to 10 years it will become increasingly clear what road we will be traveling down.

INTERPRETIVE PERSPECTIVES AND THE NEW MILLENNIUM

How society socially constructs reality during the end of the cheap oil era will have a significant bearing on the world we live in. Ignoring the problem will not make it go away. Furthermore, the cheap oil era has had significant environmental impacts, including global warming. Rising temperatures and ocean levels and more catastrophic storms will affect where people may live and work.

One way to socially construct reality in this era is taking a Darwinian "survival of the fittest" perspective. Nations will compete for access to cheap oil, and oil wars are not out of the question according to the Research and Development Center of the U.S. Army Corps of Engineers (Westervelt & Fournier, 2005). Of course, this competition will ultimately fail because of the massive amounts of energy required to fight the battles to gain access to oil. Also, by competing, we lose the advantages of cooperation. Specifically, to face the complex problems associated with the end of the fossil fuel era, we need to work collaboratively with one another, thereby tapping the best creative minds of the world. This is a very different construction of reality than the competitive model that exists at present. The U.S.

is showing no signs of reducing its thirst for oil, and neither is India or China. The United States and China, in particular, have also shown a commitment to competition in seeking access to the cheapest oil available.

Another dominant interpretive frame that may emerge in the next several years is aggressive pursuit of technological solutions to the energy problem. This pursuit may also be either competitive or cooperative. What makes this frame unique is that it is driven by the belief that science will produce an answer to our energy needs that will allow us to sustain not only our present energy usage but also increasing needs in the future. Those who hold onto this interpretive frame are advocates of continuing the traditional model of large-scale organizing and production.

If society embraces the possibility of finding a technological solution to the energy problem to allow continued growth, we will eventually need to challenge the problems associated with growth. When economists use the term growth, they are referring to more people buying more products and services. Obviously, this means continued increases in population. If population continues to expand, we will need to harvest more of the world's resources, including metals, wood, and agricultural land.

The final interpretive frame challenges the economic and population growth model in exchange for a conservation model. Dr. M. King Hubbert, the first scientist to discuss peak oil, observed

> For most of human history the population doubled every 32,000 years. Now it's down to 35 years. That is dangerous. No biologic population can double more than a few times without getting seriously out of bounds. The world is seriously overpopulated right now. There can be no possible solutions to the world's problems that do not involve stabilization of the world's population. (quoted in Hickerson, 2004, p. 1)

It is critical to stabilize the world's population because humans continue to need more natural resources and energy in order to survive. Most of the world's scientists agree that current population and energy trends are unacceptable and not sustainable. According to the U.S. Army Corps of Engineers, "the impact of excessive, unsustainable energy consumption may undermine the very culture and the activities it supports" (Westervelt & Fournier, 2005, p. 2). Given these problems, what options may frame our vision of the future?

In place of the growth model is a steady-state model in which world population is stabilized (perhaps at reduced levels) and the economy neither grows nor shrinks. Of course, this framework raises numerous moral, ethical, and social issues for many people. There are also economists who challenge the viability of a steady-state economy. Support for this framework does exist, however (Czech & Daly, 2004; Hickerson, 2004). Two leading advocates of the steady-state model of population and economics are Brian Czech, a wildlife biologist, and Herman Daly, a former economist at the World Bank and author of *Beyond Growth: The Economics of Sustainable Development* (1997). These two researchers argue that a steady-state model is inevitable given the fundamental conflict between economic growth and the conservation of life (all species) on the planet. Humans have gone too far in abusing the environment and harvesting the earth's resources. Survival in the future will depend on positioning our population and economic activity within a steady state where the earth may replenish its resources for continued use over time.

The health of a steady-state model is also dependent on shifting away from the focus on competition that dominates capitalistic industrial society. In place of the competitive model is one of cooperation and community. Even in developed countries people may find themselves living in smaller towns organized into neighborhood associations, neighborhood watch programs, community gardens, and existing friend and family networks. Agriculture will be localized with community gardens providing certain food needs. The remaining food needs of townspeople will require forming cooperative networks with communities of farmers (Wolf, 2006). In the cooperative communities envisioned by Wolf, editor of *Uncommon Thought Journal,* building knowledge and skills among community members will be critical. Community members will need knowledge so they can become self-sufficient in basic survival skills related to food production, constructing and maintaining shelter, maintaining transportation systems (e.g., bicycle and small engine repair), and protecting the environment. Skills such as working with hand tools, using herbal medicine, making septic systems, paper making, candle making, glass blowing, and blacksmithing may all become highly desirable skills in small self-sufficient cooperative communities. In order to build this knowledge base and the requisite skills needed to promote community health, community colleges may become critically important. Although the changes that are implied in the shift from a competitive capitalistic model to a cooperative community model are significant, they are possible. Preparation, planning, and community building will be necessary. As Wolf (2006) concludes, "the more we can do now, and the more we can build and move into an alternative organization and economy, the more likely we are to successfully meet the future that will come."

CRITICAL PERSPECTIVES AND THE NEW MILLENNIUM

The way we manage the present energy crisis and the environmental problems fossil fuel use and overpopulation have created will have a tremendous impact on the world we live in. Some critical theorists anticipate a struggle between the most powerful for a continuation of business as usual (in terms of economic growth and energy use) that further disadvantages the masses and further separates the rich from the poor. From this perspective, those with money or power win, and the rest lose. Increasingly, power will be concentrated in the hands of fewer people, and the numbers of poor will swell.

Critical theorists are not exclusively pessimistic, however. As we have explained in previous chapters, critical theory also focuses on empowerment and emancipation. Given the preceding observations we have made concerning the challenges the world faces in the next decade or so, we would like to propose two scenarios. First, let's consider that the energy crisis requires a significant shift in the way we live, returning us to a preindustrial age. Empowerment and emancipation may be experienced in a return to a simpler life of people living in communities where there are close relationships among neighbors. People derive satisfaction and a sense of connection by growing their own food, being more closely connected to family and friends, and leading a more local existence. Work will be hard and physical, but we will also be able to rely on other community members for some specialized tasks that only a few perform. Perhaps we even barter for services from one another.

This is a very different life than we live now, but it is not a life without value, purpose, and joy. As an example, consider the co-housing arrangement described by Christine Johnson (2006):

> With 48 other families, we own homes and a common house situated on five acres in an urban area. The development is legally structured as a condominium with each family or individual holding title to the interior of their home; together we hold a title in common to the "common house," a workshop, gardens, and the acreage upon which the community is sited. We intend to put in an organic garden, to keep chickens for eggs and meat, and we will participate in community-supported agriculture. We will harvest both rainwater and graywater for irrigation. We'll enjoy shared meals several times a week in the common house, which is built with a commercial kitchen, a large dining/meeting room, laundry room, library, exercise room, craft room, play room, and kid's play area just outside in a courtyard visible from the dining area. The most important aspect of this community is our shared desire for cooperative living and consensus democracy. (Johnson, 2006)

The amount of work the community members must do themselves depends on the amount of energy they will be able to purchase from utilities versus the amount they must generate themselves. The more energy co-housing communities must generate themselves, the more preindustrial the living standards will be. But, this is a life free of the tensions of a technology-saturated world where workers can never escape their jobs.

Although the life described in these smaller cooperative communities is vastly different from the experiences of people today living in large urban centers, such communities are a central part of the human experience. As Johnson (2006) notes, "people have always joined together to support each other, to trade with each other, and to make a good life together" (p. 2). People who are able to anticipate the changes that may confront us will be able to find others who support their views and create a warm and sustainable community of friends. As Kunstler (2005) explains, there may be many benefits in close communal relations in which people work closely and physically with their neighbors. In such communities, we will join enterprises that really matter to us and we will become engaged in "meaningful social enactments instead of being merely entertained to avoid boredom" (Kunstler, 2005, p. 238).

The second alternative path to emancipation will occur if we find some combination of technological solutions to our energy problems that allow us to sustain large organizations with many members and levels of hierarchy. If this occurs, we may consider possibilities for emancipation in the following ways.

The Concept of Emancipation in Organizational Studies

When organizational researchers refer to the term "emancipation," they are describing the process "through which individuals and groups become free from repressive social and ideological conditions, in particular those that place socially unnecessary restrictions on the development and articulation of human consciousness" (Alvesson & Willmott, 1992, p. 432). The purpose of critical organizational theory is to facilitate this process through raising the consciousness of oppressed members so they can gain a clear understanding of the nature of the oppression they face. Once worker consciousness is raised, they can consider alternative means of organizing and communicating that offer opportunities for empowerment and emancipation. In fact, communication is essential to the emergence of meaningful empowerment and emancipation. As Albrecht (1988) concluded, empowerment "is essentially an interactional process, where a sense of personal control results from believing it is one's communication behavior that can produce a desired impact on others" (p. 380).

Some researchers, as well as practicing managers and corporate owners, scoff at the idea of employee emancipation because it minimizes the interests of those organizational stakeholders who want to control the actions of employees for their own ends (e.g., organizational survival, profitability, and so on). However, this does not mean that worker emancipation always threatens organizational survival and effectiveness. Human relations approaches, quality of life programs, and calls for workplace democracy can promote the realization of higher order human needs (e.g., self-actualization) while simultaneously improving job satisfaction and increasing productivity (Alvesson & Willmott, 1992). The key is to discover ways in which employee desires for emancipation dovetail with improved organizational performance.

Self-Reflection and Self-Transformation

Fostering an environment in which worker emancipation is possible is not simple and it is not without drawbacks. Employees must engage in a painful process of resistance so they can overcome socially unnecessary restrictions such as the fear of failure and sexual and racial discrimination. As Alvesson and Willmott (1992) observed:

> [A]ny substantial and lasting form of emancipatory change must involve a process of critical self-reflection and associated self-transformation. From this perspective, emancipation is not to be equated with, or reduced to, piecemeal social engineering directed by a somewhat benevolent management. Rather, its conception of the emancipatory project encompasses a much broader set of issues that includes the transformation of gender relations, environmental husbandry, the development of workplace democracy, and so forth. (p. 434)

Central to critical theory is the belief that human reason possesses emancipatory potential. Through critical reflection people can come to understand how the reality of the social world and the construction of the self are socially produced. In other words, the social and structural arrangements that exist in organizations are produced by members who interact with one another. Furthermore, a person's self-perceptions emerge through interacting with other people (e.g., in talking with others we receive feedback concerning our actions in different social situations). Importantly, actions that are socially produced are open to transformation. This point is made most clearly by Giddens (1979), who observed that every social actor within a system has the capacity to exercise power and control through resist-ing and challenging dominant meaning systems.

Microemancipation

One argument that critical theorists face when addressing the issue of worker emancipa-tion is that their claims are too grandiose. For example, if workers free themselves from the controls of management, will they be able to produce products or provide services at a level that sustains organizational competitiveness and ensures survival? This has led some the-orists to call for "microemancipation." Alvesson and Willmott (1992) explain that **microe-mancipation** focuses attention on "concrete activities, forms, and techniques that offer themselves not only as means of control, but also as objects and facilitators of resistance and, thus, as vehicles for liberation" (p. 446).

A microemancipatory practice could involve redefining a verbal symbol advanced by management for a particular purpose. For example, managers sometimes try to promote a family metaphor to encourage employees to work together in the pursuit of organizational (family) goals. Just as families pull together in tough times, workers would be expected to pitch in by working overtime or increasing the pace of their activities so the organization can continue to survive. However, employees could recognize how they are being manipu-lated by this metaphor and redefine it in ways that are empowering for them. Families, for instance, encourage self-development for their children. This means that children can be expected to resist rules put forth by parents as a sign of their independence. Family members also engage in heated conflicts when any member attempts to enforce a rule that limits the options available to other members. These conflicts can result in certain members not talking or listening to one another for prolonged periods of time. So, workers who feel oppressed by the family metaphor can redefine it in ways that are empowering. Indeed, workers can say to their managers that families argue, challenge unfair rules, and encour-age individuality and separateness as well as closeness. If this redefinition is accompanied by resistant action to the more confining family metaphor advocated by management, a form of microemancipation surfaces for employees.

Questioning, Utopian, and Incremental Emancipation

In addition to their description of microemancipation, Alvesson and Willmott (1992) propose three other types of emancipatory projects. The first type, **questioning**, involves workers who challenge and critique dominant forms of thinking within the organization. The aim here is to resist authority by contesting what is taken for granted. For example, workers could resist a management directive to perform a certain task because it is both inefficient and potentially dangerous. However, the challenge to managerial authority occurs without proposing an alternative action.

The second type of emancipation is called **utopian**. This form of emancipation surfaces when employees present management "with a new form of ideal which aims at opening up consciousness for engagement with a broader repertoire of alternatives" (Alvesson &

Willmott, 1992, p. 450). Utopian emancipation represents an invitation to consider alternative ways of thinking rather than a suggestion for a ready-made course of action. The feminist call for holistic or integrative thinking instead of cause-effect linear thinking as a guide for decision making is representative of utopian emancipation.

Between these two types of emancipation is a third type called **incremental**. This type of emancipation is concerned with liberation from certain specific forms of oppression. A demand for a higher level of employee participation in organizational decision making is an example of this type of emancipation.

If we refer back to our descriptions of workplace democracy and the various perspectives posed by feminist theorists, other paths to emancipation can also be identified. A democratic workplace empowers and emancipates employees as their voices become a central part of organizational decision making. An organization that is structured and influenced by feminist principles empowers women and other groups who are marginalized by the dominant themes that pervade most modern organizations (e.g., competitive individualism, cause-effect linear thinking, separation and autonomy, and so on). So, although worker emancipation cannot occur without attention to such organizational realities as the need to sustain productivity, various types and levels of emancipation are clearly possible. Perhaps the most interesting potential outcome linked to worker emancipation is the possibility that it may increase the productive capacity of workers by giving them more control over their actions and decisions.

Now that we have considered some of the possibilities for worker emancipation in the 21st century, let's take a look at the types of workplace structures and theories that may become more common in the future. We'll start by focusing on self-managed work teams and the emergence of concertive control systems.

Self-Managed Work Teams and Concertive Control

One of the most interesting and popular alternatives to bureaucratic structure is to shift from multilayered organizational hierarchies to a flat collection of **self-managed work teams**. For example, over the last several years Xerox, General Motors, and Coors Brewing have initiated this sort of change (Barker, 1993). One reason for the shift to self-managed teams is that bureaucratic constraints stifle worker creativity and innovation. Also, when worker-run teams are responsible for completing work assignments, the organization can eliminate unneeded supervisors and other bureaucratic staff (Barker, 1993).

As more organizations shift to various forms of self-management, there will be significant changes in the daily experiences of employees. As Barker (1993) explains

> Instead of being told what to do by a supervisor, self-managing workers must gather and synthesize information, act on it, and take collective responsibility for those actions. Self-managing workers generally are organized into teams of 10 to 15 people who take on the responsibilities of their former supervisors. Top management often provides a value-based corporate vision that team members use to infer parameters and premises (norms and rules) that guide their day-to-day actions. Guided by the company's vision, the self-managing team members direct their own work and coordinate with other areas of the company. (p. 413)

Organizations that utilize self-managed teams require team members to complete specific, clearly defined tasks. Often, team members are cross-trained so that any member can perform all of the tasks needed to complete a given job. Also, team members are given "the authority and responsibility to make the essential decisions necessary to complete the function" (Barker, 1993, p. 413). In addition to performing specific tasks assigned to the team, self-managed workers establish their own work schedules, order needed materials, and coordinate their actions with other workgroups. Importantly, researchers have found that systems of self-management increase employee motivation, productivity, and commitment (Mumby & Stohl, 1991; Osbourne, Moran, Musselwhite, & Zenger, 1990; Wellins, Byham, & Wilson, 1991).

On the surface it would seem that self-managed teams give workers the sort of flexibility and empowerment that is not possible within bureaucracies. Workers establish their own work rules and norms, emphasis is placed on working collaboratively with others to reach co-determined goals, and worker creativity and innovation are encouraged. However, recent examinations of work teams in different organizations show that there is a negative side to the control mechanisms workers establish for themselves. In order to clarify how and why this occurs, we need to describe the different forms of organizational control.

Edwards (1981) originally identified three strategies of control in organizations: **simple, technological,** and **bureaucratic.** Simple control is the direct, personal control of work by supervisors who oversee the performance of subordinates. Technological control emerges from the physical technology used in an organization. Computer systems that monitor worker performance exemplify this form of control. Bureaucratic control emanates from hierarchically based social relations within an organization. This form of control is based on rational-legal rules that reward compliance and punish noncompliance.

Self-managed teams often enact a form of control referred to as **concertive control** (Tompkins & Cheney, 1985). Concertive control is built on the three traditional control strategies we described above. Specifically, concertive control systems require a shift in control from management to workers who collaborate with one another to create rules and norms that govern their behavior. So, in these systems, control emanates from the concertive, value-based actions of an organization's members. Top management stimulates this collaborative process by providing a value-based corporate vision "that team members use to infer parameters and premises (norms and rules) that guide their day-to-day actions" (Barker, 1993, p. 413). Using the corporate vision statement as their guide, workers collaborate with one another to create social rules that "constitute meaning and sanction modes of social conduct" (p. 412).

Identification

For concertive control systems to be effective in regulating worker behavior, the workers must **identify** with a set of value and factual premises that guide their decision making and work activities (Barker & Tompkins, 1994). These decision premises are accepted in exchange for incentives offered by the organization such as wages, salary, and continued employment. As we explained above, concertive control systems emerge when top management produces a value-based corporate vision that is intended to serve as a guide for member behavior and decision making. Workers then exhibit their **identification** with this vision when, in making a decision, they perceive the organization's values or interests as relevant in evaluating the alternatives of choice (Tompkins & Cheney, 1983). Through identification the decision maker's range of "vision" is narrowed "by selecting particular values, particular items of empirical knowledge, and particular behavior alternatives for consideration, to the exclusion of other values, other knowledge, other possibilities" (Simon, 1976, p. 210). Indeed, the organization member "sees" that with which he or she identifies. When considering decision options, a member is limited to alternatives linked to his or her identifications; "other options will simply not come into view, and therefore will not be considered" (Tompkins & Cheney, 1985, p. 194).

Disciplinary Techniques

The concept of identification is clearly linked to concertive control systems. Also important to consider within these systems are disciplinary techniques. More specifically, worker designed systems of control include microtechniques of discipline to regulate and normalize individual and collective action in organizations. When members internalize these disciplinary techniques (because of their identification with the organizational value system), they become part of "standard operating procedure." Of course, organizations cannot operate without some form of discipline. As Barnard (1938/1968) argued more than a half-century ago, the master paradox of organizational life is that "to accomplish our individual goals, we must frequently relinquish some autonomy to the organizational system" (p. 17). Barker and Cheney (1994) extend this line of reasoning by observing that disciplines are "enabling because they allow us to create reality in concert with others, and simultaneously constraining because the disciplines shape our behavior in directions that are functional for the organization" (p. 30).

Discursive Formations

Foucault (1968/1972, 1975/1977) provides a particularly rich description of microtechniques of discipline. According to Foucault (1968/1972), disciplines are **discursive formations**. Discipline functions as a social force in the organization, "demarcating good behavior from bad, providing a context for organizational interaction, and, in general, shaping day-to-day organizational activity" (Barker & Cheney, 1994, p. 26). Thus, Foucault presents us with an encompassing notion of disciplinary discourse. Such discourse emerges in those social relations that serve to control, govern, and normalize individual and collective behavior. Disciplinary discourse leads to the construction of "apparatuses of knowledge and a multiplicity of new domains of understanding" (Foucault, 1980, p. 106). Eventually, social production of the apparatuses of knowledge and domains of understanding lead organizational actors to the conclusion, "that's the way we do things around here."

Let's take a moment to clarify Foucault's notion of discipline as a discursive process. Foucault believes that disciplinary systems emerge through conversations among organization members. In these conversations, workers develop rules and norms to govern their behavior as they attempt to reach individual, group, and organizational goals. Importantly, as we explained earlier, employees are motivated to develop rules and norms that are consistent with the values communicated by management in its vision statement (e.g., we at ACE Manufacturing are committed to producing high-quality merchandise at a reasonable price), because they identify strongly with this statement and the organization. The techniques of discipline the workers then produce allow them to accomplish work-related goals.

Microtechniques of discipline both punish and reward. Foucault (1975/1977) refers to "micropenalties" as the practice of "making the slightest departures from correct behavior subject to punishment, and of giving punitive function to the apparently indifferent elements of the disciplinary apparatus" (p. 178). Within this disciplinary apparatus, "everything might serve to punish the slightest thing; each subject finds himself caught in a punishable, punishing universality" (Foucault, 1975/1977, p. 178). Conversely, disciplinary systems also reward by means of awards. Subjects are judged against a norm or average in a way that continually creates ranks. Those judged to be significantly better than the norm are rewarded by the fact of the judgment itself.

When workers within a concertive control system identify strongly with an organization, disciplinary systems are created that allow members to reach work-related goals. Although these control systems can empower workers in ways that elude them in traditional bureaucracies, these systems can also limit behavioral options open to employees. As Barker (1993) explained, the irony of this shift from management-designed control systems to worker-designed systems is that workers may create forms of control that are more powerful, less apparent, and more difficult to resist than that of the former bureaucracy. In order to clarify how and why this occurs, let's consider a couple of examples.

Barker and Cheney (1994) conducted an investigation of disciplinary techniques in a manufacturing organization (called "Tech USA" to protect confidentiality) that relied on a system of concertive control. During the course of conducting the study, one of the work teams faced a problem. On a Thursday afternoon, the workers began to recognize that they were in jeopardy of missing a deadline to ship a customer's order out by Friday. The only way they could meet the deadline was to work overtime. One of the team leaders (Teri) called everyone together and addressed the team. The scenario unfolded in the following manner:

> You know we all said that we were going to have these boards ready to go
> by tomorrow. It ain't gonna happen unless we stay late. Who's gonna help out
> here?" [Teri]
>
> After some exchanging of conspicuous looks at each other, Johnny, another one
> of the team's leaders stood up and exclaimed: "We all agreed and committed
> ourselves to get this out on time. We have a responsibility here. I'm gonna stay
> here, who else will?"
>
> The other team members began to raise their hands, except for Vicki, whom
> the team viewed as someone who tended to 'shirk' her fair share of overtime. All
> eyes turned toward her as she said: "Look, I've got to pick up my kids at 3 PM.
> [long pause] Let me do that and I'll come in at 5:30 tomorrow [one and a half
> hours early] and start packing [for shipment] when you get finished tonight."
>
> The team members expressed satisfaction with this "deal." Vicki complied with
> her commitment and the team did complete this order on time. (Barker & Cheney,
> 1994, pp. 33–34)

The preceding vignette shows how powerful concertive control systems can be. These workers were not being paid to work overtime, but they were motivated to do so because they had collectively made a commitment to fulfill a customer order by the next day. So, there was pressure to acquiesce to Teri's request, and she reminded the team members of their commitment. A manager is not needed to demand the overtime because these workers operate under peer pressure to abide by their agreement to meet the customer's deadline. This peer pressure is the form of discipline workers enact to gain compliance from resistant members. Although Vicki had planned to pick up her children at 3:00 (after her shift had ended), she felt compelled to offer the team something to make up for leaving before the order was finished. Of course, arriving at work by 5:30 a.m. the next day may also have caused inconveniences for her and her children. Also, note that Vicki was perceived as an employee who shirked her fair share of overtime. What this means is that workers are establishing (with some regularity) deadlines that are difficult to meet in a normal 40-hour workweek. This raises issues of fairness, particularly because workers are pressured to sacrifice their personal lives and time with their families to meet team goals. Barker (1993) commented on this peer pressure when he observed, "If [workers] want to resist their team's control, they must be willing to risk their human dignity, being made to feel unworthy as a 'teammate'" (p. 436).

Papa, Auwal, and Singhal (1997) also conducted a study that focused on concertive control systems. The organization selected for their study was the Grameen Bank in Bangladesh. This financial institution is dedicated to helping the poorest of the poor by offering them social services, economic programs, and loans for small business development. The bank has been incredibly successful over the past 20 years. More than two million borrowers have received loans, and the bank sustains a remarkable 99% loan recovery rate. One of the main reasons for the success of this institution is the exceptional dedication of the bank field workers who administer the loan programs. Working under a system of concertive control in which they establish their own norms and rules, the workers exhibit an almost fanatical devotion to upholding the humanitarian mission of the bank. For example, Atiquar Rahman is a bank field worker who regularly works 12-hour days and often works for months at a time without a single day off. When asked why he works so diligently, he responded, "How can I let down the other field workers and the poor people we serve? We work together as a team, and in working together we help the poor to improve their lives" (Papa et al, 1997, p. 223). Furthermore, if a field worker experiences problems with loan recovery in a given branch office, he or she will be criticized by fellow field workers and pressured to do whatever is necessary to recover the loan (including working extra hours to help a loan recipient with his or her small business). As Papa and colleagues conclude

> The field workers so strongly identify with the Grameen's goal of uplifting the poor that they socially construct standards that place extraordinary pressure on everyone to succeed. Not surprisingly, the depth of their organizational commitment clouds their ability to assess objectively the micro-techniques of discipline that are part of the bank's concertive control system. (p. 234)

Are there systems of concertive control within organizations that do not result in an oppressive environment for workers? Certainly, it seems possible that workers can design humane concertive control systems. The key to designing more humane control systems may be linked to the emergence of competing value systems to guide member behavior. If workers are concerned only with responding to management's vision statement, then they may design a control system that pressures them to place organizational goals over individual needs. As an alternative framework, workers may need to consider how they may "do well and do good" (Whetten, 1996a, 1996b). When workers do well, they act in ways that ensure the effectiveness and success of the organization. All organizations and the workers within them also need a "moral logic," however. As Barker (1999) explains, "they have to act, individually and collectively, in moral and 'good' ways, both toward themselves and toward their external environment and stakeholders" (p. 179). Importantly, in acting in good and moral ways toward one another workers may find ways of navigating the concertive control system in ways that promote humane treatment. Designing a more humane workplace may also require managers and workers to consider more democratic forms of decision making and governance. So, let's now turn to a discussion of workplace democracy.

Workplace Democracy

Although democracy as a form of political governance has a long and rich history, the application of democratic principles to the workplace, or **workplace democracy**, is a relatively recent phenomenon. Indeed, Cheney (1995) observed, "Surely one of the great ironies of the modern world is that democracy, imperfect as it is in the political realm, seldom extends to the workplace" (p. 167). Why has this been the case? Well corporate owners and top management personnel have long viewed it as their job to direct, manage, and coordinate the efforts of those people who work for them to ensure the continued attainment of organizational goals. McGregor's Theory X provides us with a clear example of this perspective in that threat and coercion are considered the primary ways to assure employee compliance with managerial directives.

Because so many organizations have experienced success with nondemocratic forms of management, why is the issue of workplace democracy important for us to consider now? Well, over the last 30 years a number of organizations have benefited from involving employees more directly in various forms of decision making. Remember the examples we cited of AS & W Steel and Saturn in previous chapters. Furthermore, on a theoretical level, McGregor's Theory Y and Likert's system 4 both emphasize the value of employee participation in workplace decisions. However, just because employees participate in decision making does not mean that a democratic form of workplace governance exists. So, let's turn to a definition of workplace democracy that was advanced by Cheney (1995):

> [W]orkplace democracy is broadly defined as a system of governance which truly values individual goals and feelings (e.g., equitable remuneration, the pursuit of enriching work and the right to express oneself) as well as typically organizational problems (e.g., effectiveness and efficiency, reflectively conceived), which actively fosters the connection between those two sets of concerns by encouraging individual contributions to important organizational choices, and which allows for the ongoing modification of the organization's activities and policies by the group. (pp. 4–5)

What are the key components of the preceding definition? Clearly, the goals and feelings of individual employees are valued in democratic workplace systems. However, individual goals and feelings cannot be considered independent of organizational problems. Cheney is arguing that organizational survival depends on a certain level of effectiveness and efficiency in attaining important organizational goals (e.g., sales, profits, providing services, and so on). So, in a democratic workplace the employees play an active role in determining how individual and organizational goals can be accomplished simultaneously. Importantly, in their conversations with one another workers play a role in deciding what the organization's goals should be and how they should be reached. Finally, employees are also expected to evaluate and, if necessary, modify the organization's activities and policies to accomplish new goals.

Worker Cooperatives

Although workplace democracy is not widely practiced, various forms of democracy do exist in different types of organizations. Most examples of workplace democracy are found in varying forms of **worker cooperatives** and in certain types of employee-owned organizations (Clarke, 1984; Gherardi & Masiero, 1987; Harrison, 1994; Mellor, Hannah, & Stirling, 1988). These organizations tend to be employee owned in a collective sense, meaning that members typically "equalize share ownership (or membership) and voting rights between individuals, usually through a one person-one vote formula" (Harrison, 1994, p. 261). Such worker-owned cooperatives can be found in the United States and in other countries around the world. One very interesting description of a worker-owned cooperative is provided by Cheney (1995), who spent time researching the Mondragon worker cooperatives in the Basque region of Spain. The first of these cooperatives opened for business in 1956, making it one of the oldest worker-owned cooperatives in the world. As of 2006, there were more than 260 of these cooperatives employing over 83,000 people in a wide array of businesses (e.g., a supermarket chain, a bank, machine tool manufacturers, an electronics firm, and so on).

Employee Stock Ownership Plans

Certain larger organizations with **employee stock ownership plans** (ESOPs) also practice forms of workplace democracy. In democratically run ESOPs, ownership is linked to owning shares of the firm. These shares can be distributed on the basis on seniority, pay scale, or some other formula. The basis for participation is linked to one's status as a shareholder, and organizations differ in terms of how they allocate voting power. For example, in some organizations owners may possess votes equal to the number of shares they own. Other organizations follow a one person, one vote rule. Finally, some organizations vary the formula for participation depending on the issue (Blasi, 1987).

Participatory Versus Representative Democracy

Workplace democracy is often enacted differently depending on the size of the organization (an issue we will return to later). The most basic difference is practicing a participatory versus a representative form of democracy. **Participatory** forms are more common in smaller organizations where a one person, one vote formula is used. In larger organizations, for the purposes of efficiency in decision making, representative forms of democracy are more common. In a **representative** form of democracy, workers elect representatives to present their interests to the main decision-making body of the organization. In order to clarify the differences between these two forms of democratic participation, let's consider a couple of examples.

In small organizations where democracy is practiced, group meetings are the only routinized form of interaction. Other interaction among members occurs when and as it is needed (Harrison, 1994). Relying on a one person, one vote decision-making formula, these organizations "are committed to achieving consensus and strive to make decisions that are satisfactory to all" (Harrison, 1994, p. 264). Of course the interaction that occurs in these meetings can be long and fraught with conflict as members assert their individuals needs and interests. For example, Hafen (1993) conducted a study of a small worker-owned restaurant in Athens, Ohio. There are 33 worker-owners in this restaurant who all participate in decisions concerning organizational operations (e.g., shift assignments, menu development, ordering food, marketing, and so on). Interestingly, the workers have different perceptions of this participative system. One worker-owner stated, "We're just too big to make decisions by 100% consensus. We're going to have to make more decisions among small groups of people. . . . Our lives are indebted to consensus ruling, and it's time consuming and inefficient and expensive" (p. 19). Another worker-owner also recognized the challenges associated with consensus decision making, but ultimately felt it was worth it:

> If there's one person who says, "I think what you're doing is a big mistake,
> I cannot in any conscience let you go through with that decision," that one person
> can block that decision. And that's happened in the past, and its been very
> cumbersome and very difficult—but we have always reached a better decision
> because of it. (Hafen, 1993, pp. 19–20)

In larger organizations, it is simply not practical to include every member in every decision that needs to be made. So, in larger organizations, "opportunities for participatory and representative decision-making are woven together in an effort to maximize individual autonomy within a large group" (Harrison, 1994, p. 264). One example of a larger organization that practices democratic decision making is Hoedads, a reforestation cooperative that comprises approximately 300 members. The members of this organization plant trees, thin forests, construct forest trails, and fight fires. This work is performed by teams or crews that work for weeks at a time in locations that are distant from the central office (see Gunn, 1984). Harrison (1994) offered the following description of Hoedads's decision-making system:

> Decisions are distributed into three tiers of responsibility: individual crews act as
> autonomous work groups in the conduct of day-to-day activities; a council,
> composed of members elected from each of the crews, considers issues that affect
> the cooperative as a whole; and, task forces, whose membership may be open to
> the crews or elected, are created to research problems that require specific
> information or particular expertise. General meetings, which can last for several
> days, take place a couple of times a year to consider task force issues as well as any
> other issues that are known by the council as likely to be controversial. (p. 264)

Principles and Practices of Workplace Democracy

Now that we have covered some of the decision-making strategies in democratic organizations, let's consider some of the broader principles and practices that are linked to workplace democracy. Cheney (1995) provides an overview of five major principles and practices of workplace democracy: (a) interaction with external systems; (b) size, structure, and patterns of interaction; (c) maintaining integrity; (d) self-reflection and self-generation; and (e) consistency between goals and process. These five principles and practices provide the basis for our subsequent discussion.

Interaction With External Systems. Because most organizations are not structured by democratic principles, Cheney contends that democratic organizations must be buffered from outside pressures to alter their core values and practices. This can be accomplished in one of two ways. First, the democratic organization can embed itself in a network of relationships with organizations that also practice forms of democracy. This, of course, is contingent on finding a sufficient number of organizations in reasonable proximity that practice democracy. If relationships can be formed with suppliers and other allied partners, the democratic organization buffers itself from outside pressures to operate in a more bureaucratic manner. Alternatively, the democratic organization can "try to sustain a special identity while also doing business with other types of organizations" (Cheney, 1995, p. 7). For example, Cheney recommends that democratic organizations establish and maintain certain "sacred" values, principles, practices, and rituals "that help to remind members of where their organization 'stands' with respect to the rest of the organizational world" (p. 7).

Size, Structure, and Patterns of Interaction. Regarding size, structure, and pattern of interaction, Cheney focuses on the challenges of sustaining democracy in large organizations. Indeed, he makes the observation that the "intense face-to-face interaction required by real democratic participation cannot be maintained in something larger than what we call a small group" (Cheney, 1995, p. 8). As an alternative, large organizations (as we noted earlier) need to enact a representational form of democracy. However, Cheney raises another important issue, namely, what can be done when the majority enacts decisions that become a source of oppression for the minority of employees who adopt dissenting views? Here Cheney recommends an *adversarial* model of democracy in which competing interests are institutionalized and have proportional representation and influence. Of course, such an adversarial form of democracy is likely to engender more frequent conflict, but a larger percentage of workers are likely to feel supported within this system.

Maintaining Integrity. Maintaining integrity, the third of Cheney's democratic principles and practices, refers to sustaining workplace democracy despite the pressures to become more bureaucratic. This position can be linked to Weber's (1922/1978) inevitable "march of rationalization." According to Weber, most organizations exhibit a tendency to move toward bureaucratic order. What can be done to resist this? Cheney recommends that democratic organizations can occasionally restructure themselves in order to preserve spontaneous aspects. For example, new types of groups can be formed within the larger organization to prevent any established group from becoming too dominant and creating a hierarchical system of control.

Self-Reflection and Self-Regeneration. Self-reflection and self-regeneration constitute the most challenging aspects of sustaining democracy in organizations. The starting point for self-reflection is to define the deep value consensus that unifies organization members. For example, an organization may be held together by values such as democratic participation and equality. However, for democratic organizations to sustain themselves over time, members must be willing to discuss critically the benefits of sustaining their particular value consensus. Indeed, a given democratic form of governance should not be accepted blindly as the only form of democracy that is possible. Democratic structures and processes should be viewed as evolutionary. This means that the particular form of democracy that an organization adopts needs to change as the beliefs and values of the members change. As Cheney (1995) observes, "the values of the organization and their pursuit must be available to both members and outside observers for review and critique. In particular, sacred notions of democracy and participation must themselves be open to criticism" (p. 12).

Cheney observed the processes of self-reflection and self-regeneration in his association with the Rocky Mountain Peace Center of Boulder, Colorado. One of the most interesting facets of this organization is that members periodically reexamine what peace, nonviolence, and sustainable development mean for different people at different times. This ongoing process of reflection and discussion makes individual members aware of the different viewpoints that exist within the organization. "As a result, both the structure and some of the practices of the organization are distinctly different now from what they were ten years ago: Today, for instance, the organization has a radial design with work groups that involve numerous citizens that elect representatives to a core group" (pp. 12–13).

Obviously, there are challenges associated with sustaining an environment in which employees challenge one another's ideas, values, and actions. However, sustaining such an environment is at the core of what democracy really is. So, if a diversity of opinions exist within the organization, how can these diverse views be recognized and valued? One way is to advocate what Cheney referred to earlier as an adversarial form of democracy. Another way is to promote dialogue among members who hold differing viewpoints. Eisenberg (1994) suggests three guidelines to promote dialogue in organizations. First, every person has the right to be heard, and they are given the opportunity to present their views. Second, members must exhibit empathy for different perspectives, ideas, and opinions. Third, members must be encouraged to speak from personal experience. By following these guidelines, members who hold diverse views may find a superordinate goal that links them together, or they may discover that their interests dovetail on certain critical issues. Perhaps the strongest rationale for sustaining dialogue in the workplace is provided by Evered and Tannenbaum (1992):

> [Dialogue] is one of the richest activities that human beings can engage in. It is the thing that gives meaning to life, it's the sharing of humanity, it's creating something. And there is this magical thing in an organization, or in a team, or in a group, where you get unrestricted interaction, unrestricted dialogue, and this synergy happening that results in more productivity, and satisfaction, and seemingly magical levels of output from a team. (p. 8)

Consistency Between Goals and Process. The final principle of workplace democracy advocated by Cheney is to ensure consistency between goals and process. What this means is that the goal of a democratic workplace can exist only if democratic, participative processes are sustained within the system. Monge and Miller (1988) contend that three factors should be considered in evaluating an organization's commitment to employee participation. First, employee input must cover a wide range of issues. Second, employees must be able to exhibit influence over matters that are important to them (e.g., wages, policies, and so on). Third, participation must be exhibited at all levels of the organization and employees must be empowered to deal with higher level issues.

Organizational survival in the 21st century will be linked to the creativity and innovation exhibited by employees. One way of harnessing worker creativity is to create a democratic workplace where employees are encouraged to challenge one another's ideas, actions, and values. Now let's consider another recent theoretical development in organizational studies that also promotes equality and participation. Specifically, feminist theorists have offered provocative and insightful insights into the nature of communicating and organizing within the workplace.

Feminist Theories and Organizational Communication

Before describing some of the major feminist perspectives, let's consider a comment by Kathy Ferguson in her 1984 book *The Feminist Case Against Bureaucracy*:

> Real social change comes about when people think and live differently. Feminist discourse and feminist practice offer the linguistic and structural space in which it is possible to think, live, work, and love differently, in opposition to the discursive and institutional practices of bureaucratic capitalism. At least it is a start. (p. 212)

The reason we selected the preceding passage is that is gets to the heart of what feminist perspectives offer to all of us. Too many management systems disqualify or minimize the contributions of certain groups or participants, especially women and minorities (Bullis, 1993; Deetz, 1992). As a result, the organizational benefits of including their diverse perspectives are not realized (Maruyama, 1994). In an era of global competition, worker creativity and innovation are central to organizational survival and success. One way to promote creativity and innovation is to bring people together who have different ways of viewing the world. The perspectives of women and minority group members are often unique because of different socialization experiences that shape their worldviews. So, to increase the pool of creative and innovative ideas within organizations, managers must empower members whose views have typically been silenced and include their diverse perspectives in all important forms of decision making. Now that we have presented our rationale for focusing on feminist perspectives, let's take a moment to consider what is meant by the term "feminist ideology."

At a general level, feminist ideology views women as a "sex-class" and acknowledges that women are oppressed and disadvantaged as a group (Martin, 1990). This oppression is rooted in social arrangements (e.g., in the home, at work, in government, etc.) in which the values and interests of men are privileged over those of women. So, in order for women to be empowered, social, political, and economic changes are needed in society (Eisenstein,

1981). At the core of all of these changes is recognition that women's experiences and meanings need to be honored and valued (Natalle, Papa, & Graham, 1993).

It is important to note that there is no single feminist perspective. Rather, there are many diverse perspectives that are unified by the themes of cooperation, caring for others, integrative thinking, connectedness, and openness to the environment (Marshall, 1989). Buzzanell (1994) identified eight major feminist approaches: liberal, Marxist, radical, psychoanalytic, contemporary socialist, existentialist, postmodern, and revisionist. Each of these approaches takes a somewhat different stance toward the sort of individual and societal changes that are necessary for women to be empowered. Let's briefly consider the sorts of changes advocated by each feminist perspective.

Liberal feminists believe that legal remedies can balance the power between men and women by ensuring that women are not systematically disadvantaged in their competition with men for scarce resources. For the liberal feminist, empowerment means that women obtain their fair share of control of institutions formerly dominated by men.

Marxist feminists draw attention to a societal class structure that devalues women's contributions and excludes them from owning the means of production. This group of feminists argues for equality in the satisfaction of material (e.g., economic) needs and for an educational system that emphasizes the pursuit of common rather than individual goals. From the Marxist perspective, women's empowerment must also include ownership of the means of production in an economy.

Radical feminists argue that patriarchal (male-controlled) institutions must be torn down so that new ones can be built on the basis of feminist principles.

Psychoanalytic feminists posit that the experience of sexuality must be socially constructed rather than defined solely from the male perspective.

Contemporary socialist feminists point to systemic power relations that oppress women. For example, domestic labor is devalued in comparison to earning wages. Changes advocated by this group include valuing and mainstreaming women's perspectives. Also, contemporary socialists contend that women's values and activities must be considered an essential part of the survival and success of any system (e.g., family, organizational, political, and so on).

Existential feminists claim that women have historically been marginalized and treated as "the other" in society. So, the key to women's empowerment is a form of self-development in which women recognize and internalize a belief in their value to society and its various institutions.

Postmodern feminists believe in the value of societal and institutional diversity (as reflected in women's views and the views of other marginalized groups such as racial and ethnic minorities). They also argue that dominant (male-oriented) value systems and activities must be deconstructed so that women's perspectives can be integrated into all of society's institutions.

Finally, **revisionist** feminists observe that women are oppressed by a dominant male value system and by stereotypes that minimize their contributions to society. This oppression can be eliminated only by a re-valuing of women's values and activities (see Buzzanell, 1994, for a more complete description of these eight feminist perspectives; also see Adamson, Briskin, & McPhail, 1988; Donovan, 1985; Jaggar, 1983; Langston, 1988; Nye, 1988; Tong, 1989).

Traditional Versus Feminist Views of Organizations

From the perspective of organizational communication theorizing, how do the various feminist perspectives alter traditional (male-oriented) views of organizational operations? Buzzanell (1994) offered some valuable theoretical insights into this very question. First, she explains that feminist organizational communication theorizing "discusses the moral commitment to investigate the subordinated, to focus on gendered interactions in ordinary lives, and to explore the standpoints of women who have been rendered invisible by their absence in theory and research" (p. 340). More specifically, she observed that traditional views of organizations are associated with three primary themes: competitive individualism, cause-effect linear thinking, and separation or autonomy. Conversely, feminist perspectives emphasize the cooperative enactment of organization, integrative thinking, and connectedness. In order to understand the differences that underlie these contrasting themes, let's examine each one in detail.

Competitive Individualism Versus Cooperative Enactment. The ethic of **competitive individualism** separates people and organizations into winners and losers. An employee is viewed as a winner if his or her performance exceeds all other coworkers (who consequently become losers). Of course, organizations also battle one another (frequently over market share). Organizations that survive are the winners, whereas those that must close their doors are the losers. Importantly, an emphasis on winning within organizations brings with it some serious negative consequences such as "distrust, lower self-esteem, neglected family and friendships, and health problems" (Buzzanell, 1994, p. 345).

Feminist organizational communication theory can provide us with insight into the ways women emphasize a **cooperative** ethic in their talk and behavior. For example, when a group of workers is encouraged to work cooperatively on a project, their success is linked to how much they help one another. Consider for a moment a group of sales representatives who are required to work cooperatively with one another to increase the number of cars that are sold in a given geographic area. Would this emphasis on cooperation result in lower sales than a system that encourages the sales representatives to compete against one another? Of course, both models (competitive and cooperative) can yield positive results. But how do workers perceive each system? The competitive system produces winners and losers, whereas the cooperative system allows all workers to excel. Cooperation does not mean accepting substandard or inferior performance. Rather workers can labor together in pursuit of common goals (Lugones & Spelman, 1987).

A cooperative environment exists when decisions are made by consensus and the voices of all members are heard. When success is equated more with value fulfillment (e.g., producing environmentally safe products) than personal advancement within a hierarchy, workers realize that cooperation produces its own rewards. Of course, for a cooperative workplace environment to flourish workers need to understand how they are interconnected and interdependent. In addition, they need to engage in dialogue so they can figure out how to coordinate their efforts in the pursuit of common goals. Only through such cooperation can the unique talents of each worker be tapped for the attainment of personal and organizational goals (Wachtel, 1983).

Tapping the unique talents of workers, particularly those whose views have traditionally been excluded from mainstream decision making, can provide enormous benefits to organizations. As Mary Parker Follett (1924/1951) stated, "society flourishes through the interweaving of human [not individual] desire" (p. 49). Furthermore, as Maruyama (1994) observed, a diverse workforce is a valuable organizational asset waiting to be discovered. Indeed, genuine creativity is made possible by the interaction of ideas among many people. So, through fostering cooperation among diverse workers and empowering those workers, organizations can fully realize the benefits of diversity.

Cause-Effect Linear Thinking Versus Integrative Thinking. The second traditional (male-oriented) theme identified by Buzzanell (1994) is **cause-effective linear thinking**. This form of thinking is preferred in most organizations because it is viewed as rational, direct, and solution oriented. Linear thinking assumes that there is one best way to accomplish organizational activities, so the goal of employee interaction is to discover this best approach and then to enact it.

Cause-effect linear thinking also privileges traditional social science research over interpretive or critical approaches. Working from the traditional social science model, "issues can be dissected and examined linearly; situations can be analyzed to uncover true and solitary symptoms and solutions; and deviations can be controlled" (Buzzanell, 1994, p. 360). Results stemming from social science research can then be applied to the bottom-line interests of organizational owners and management (e.g., effectiveness, efficiency, profitability, and so on).

In contrast to cause-effect linear thinking, feminist theorists emphasize holistic or **integrative thinking**. For example, feminists argue that women tend to engage in more contextual thinking. This means considering how any given action or decision will influence workers' lives, contribute to power imbalances, or affect the environment. So instead of considering only how a decision will improve productivity, women are more likely to be concerned with the broader implications of implementing that decision. As Buzzanell (1994) notes, employees often lapse into forgetting that there are alternatives to addressing any issue or situation.

In taking a holistic perspective on decision making, many feminists focus on how organizational decisions affect environmental issues. In order to protect the environment, feminists advocate alternative approaches to solving organizational problems. Maruyama (1994) provides an excellent example that shows the organizational benefits of sustaining a concern for the environment by promoting alternative thinking:

> When the environmentalist movement was mounted in the U.S., most firms opposed stricter regulations, but one firm made use of the movement: a fish-farming firm devised a system to remove toxic elements from water beyond the current requirement, and pressed the government to establish a new requirement that the firm could meet but its competitors could not. (p. 12)

Although women engage in interaction that contributes to the bottom-line interests of management, they also interact to enhance the socioemotional climate, to nurture others, and to share power. Integrative thinkers recognize that there is more going on in organizations than pursuing goals, sustaining profits, and engaging in strategic decision making.

Workers form relationships with one another, they express their emotions; they pursue dreams and endure failure. Furthermore, leading a full life requires balancing family, leisure, work, and community activities (Buzzanell, 1994). These are issues that feminists believe should be central to workplace conversations.

Let's refer back to Barker's (1993) example of the self-managed team that needed to work overtime to fulfill a customer's order. What issues were considered when the workers accepted the customer's deadline? Was the only concern making money from that particular contract? Feminists would be more likely to raise questions such as (a) What is a fair workload? or (b) How often should we be required to work overtime? Balancing family and leisure time with work means that work cannot always dominate one's life. By drawing attention to such questions, feminists can make important contributions to creating a more humane workplace.

Feminists encourage researchers to focus more directly on the lived experiences of workers within organizations. Organizational communication research should not be confined to the examination of issues or problems that are linked to bottom-line results such as efficiency or productivity. Researchers can also point us toward the examination of communication processes that "encourage community, value diversity and integration, promote alternatives, and demonstrate caring and cooperative ethics" (Buzzanell, 1994, p. 365). Such research can be executed from a traditional social science perspective or from an interpretive or a critical perspective.

Separation and Autonomy Versus Connectedness. The third traditional (male-oriented) theme identified by Buzzanell (1994) is **separation** and **autonomy**. She explains that socialization practices "urge men to distinguish themselves as individuals through action, work, and status; men learn to separate truth and fairness from emotionality" (pp. 365–366). From this perspective, qualities such as nurturance and cooperation are considered weak. So, within organizations, women must often denounce their values of cooperation, relationships, interdependence, continuity, and collective success (Buzzanell, 1994).

Women contrast the values of separateness and autonomy with a concern for connectedness. **Connectedness** refers to attempts to integrate the mind, body, and emotions in making sense of the world around us. Humans are holistic beings not limited to displays of rationality; rather, there is an emotional side to all of us. As Buzzanell (1994) observes, "Until we embrace and integrate human emotion into standard organizational communication theory and research, we cannot truly value difference, accept the hidden fears in all humans, and change the motif of organizational life to promote diversity and connectedness" (p. 369).

Consistent with the standpoint of many feminists, organizational researchers are increasingly giving attention to the central role of emotions in the workplace. For example, Fineman (2003) argues that emotions infuse most practices in organizational life: leading, decision making, organizational change, gender relations, stress, and downsizing. It is also important to recognize that emotions have both positive and negative effects on workers. On the constructive side, positive emotions can increase creativity (Madjar, Oldham, & Pratt, 2002), motivate helping behavior and cooperation (Isen & Baron, 1991), and reduce aggression against both the organization and coworkers (Fox, Spector, & Miles, 2001). In addition, pride has been associated with increases in citizenship behavior (Hodson, 1998), and intrinsic motivation is "characterized by the fact that employees *love* their work" (Hess, 2003,

p. 8). On the negative side, anger has been linked to theft, vandalism, and aggression toward coworkers (Fox et al., 2001). Sadness leads to employees wanting to quit their jobs (Grandey, Tam, & Brauburder, 2002), and envy and jealousy have been associated with stress and a desire to quit (Vecchio, 2000).

If we turn to the issue of sexual harassment in the workplace, we can contrast the perspectives of separateness and autonomy with connectedness. One way of addressing sexual harassment is to listen to the accusations of the person making the complaint, focus on the behaviors committed by the violator, evaluate those behaviors in terms of corporate policy, and engage in corrective action if it is deemed necessary. Of course, if a man who sexually harasses women is fired from his job, a more humane workplace is created for the remaining men and women. However, who is attending to the emotional experiences of the women who were harassed? Do those emotional feelings end upon the termination of the violator's job contract? The harassed women are living, feeling human beings, and their emotions cannot be forgotten because one harasser is no longer around to humiliate them. For an excellent treatment of this very subject, you may wish to turn to a special issue of the *Journal of Applied Communication Research* (Eadie, 1992). In this issue, academic men and women describe their emotional experiences with sexual harassment in powerful detail.

Women's connectedness may also be promoted by specific organizing activities. For example, Papa, Singhal, Ghanekar, and Papa (2000) examined the organizing activities of women dairy farmers in India who joined together in local dairy cooperative societies (DCS). Many of the women they interviewed in their study recognized the importance of women's unity and organizing as necessary for meaningful empowerment to occur. Specifically, empowerment was linked to contact with other women in public places and the opportunity to share personal stories. For example, Nisha, from the village of Tisangi, explained, "All women in our village came together and started the women's club. I now have the courage to speak in public situations. Therefore I can express my feelings" (Papa et al., 2000, p. 105). Sarju Devi, from the village of Mamtori-Kalan, remarked, "Earlier we were not able to meet other women. We now meet other ladies at the milk collection center and discuss various issues" (p. 105). Finally, Banarasi Devi, from the village of Sitarampura, observed, "The DCS is the contact place for village women. When we meet at the DCS we develop a sense of togetherness" (p. 105). For these women, the local dairy cooperative societies and women's clubs provide places of contact where they share their stories and initiate organizing processes for their subsequent empowerment. Importantly, interpersonal contact and connectedness provide the spark for this empowerment.

Praxis and Consciousness Raising

In terms of organizational communication theorizing, the feminist concern for connectedness is clearly relevant. For example, Marxist feminists are committed to the concept of **praxis**. Praxis refers to the linkage between theory and action. More specifically, praxis links theory and action so the members of an oppressed group come to understand fully the nature of their oppression. This is referred to as **consciousness raising**. Once workers recognize how and why they are oppressed, they can search for ways to change their circumstances through empowerment and emancipation.

Consciousness-raising sessions among women may help spark a shift away from traditional (male-dominated) practices toward feminist practices. However, this shift is likely to be neither simple nor swift. For example, Gibson and Schullery (2000) examined the shifting meanings that occurred in a traditional manufacturing company when management decided to initiate a philanthropic program that embodied feminist principles such as cooperative enactment, integrative thinking, and connectedness. Although Gibson and Schullery were able to locate feminine values within the organization, they also discovered tensions that were "associated with the melding of traditional and feminist organizing principles, specifically, in the decision-making, resource seeking, coping, reframing, negotiating, socializing, group problem-solving and consciousness-raising processes that emerged as thematic stages in the program" (p. 225).

In other words, this manufacturing organization did not become a feminist organization because it initiated a philanthropic program. Rather, a traditionally structured organization adopted a program that reflected feminist principles. This may be a necessary first step, however, to becoming a feminist organization. This leads us to our next section, a description of a feminist organization.

A Feminist Organization: Casa de Esperanza (House of Hope)

When Casa de Esperanza was founded in 1982, its purpose was to provide shelter to Latinas who were victims of domestic violence. On the basis of the experiences of the founders in "consciousness-raising groups," they decided to creative a new type of organization called a *collective.* This was a purposeful choice because they wanted the collective to operate differently than the "competitive and male-dominated organizations and bureaucracies that prevailed in the social service arena" (Sandfort, 2005a, p. 372). In contrast, Casa de Esperanza was egalitarian, supportive of differences, and nurturing. More specifically, the organization's founding members created a participatory, nonhierarchical structure that included staff and ex-shelter residents on the board of directors. Because the origin of the organization was precipitated through consciousness-raising groups, they viewed the cause of domestic violence as patriarchal power or male dominance over women (Sandfort, 2005a).

The core services offered by Casa de Esperanza resemble those of most domestic violence shelters. First, this organization offers a safe house where women and children can flee when violence erupts in their home. Second, they offer support through a variety of activities and programs that help the women and children exit the violent relationship. As Sandfort (2005a) explains:

> In the Women's program, they offered support groups, advocacy in existing human and health services, supportive listening, and goal setting. Staff and a cadre of volunteers operated a 24-hour crisis hotline that responded to calls from the community for support and shelter. Staff also developed a Children's Program that provided sessions for children to explore their feelings about violence in their homes. Children's advocates helped meet kids' concrete needs, securing clothing and medical services while they were at the shelter. They also offered structured daily activities, such as therapeutic dance and Spanish classes. Finally, staff

realized that during their stays at the shelter women would need to develop new skills to allow them to leave their abuser and live new lives. As a result, they developed a Women's Empowerment program which provided resources to foster independent living, including securing and maintaining housing, employment, education, and social support. (p. 378)

Casa de Esperanza continued to expand during the 1980s and 1990s by expanding their services beyond the shelter and beginning a community education and outreach program to reach more Latinas. One group of women initiated a "culture circle" where oral histories were shared and materials for education were created that focused on community values of family and religion. These same women, in conjunction with other volunteers and Casa staff, organized *Rompiendo el Silencio* (Breaking the Silence). This program offered a day of workshops, entertainment, and a march attended by more than 100 participants.

Recognizing the significance of the domestic violence problem, Casa began to network with other Hispanic organizations and other domestic violence programs. They formed coalitions and engaged in public advocacy to confront domestic violence. As these connections were forged and they expanded their outreach, they began to recognize the diversity of women seeking shelter. This led to a lesbian outreach program that included the production of the movie, *My Girlfriend Did It*. Now they offer advocacy services to women battered by other women and provide training concerning homophobia to other social service agencies (Sandfort, 2005a, p. 379).

Since Casa's founding in 1982, it has experienced tremendous expansion. The present executive director is Lupe Serrano (Casa de Esperanza, 2006). In a typical year, Casa provides shelter to 145 women and an additional 175 children. Volunteers at the Information and Resource Center assisted more than 5,700 visitors in 2005, and 89% of these people said they found solutions to daily problems at the Center. In addition, more than 4,000 calls were made to the crisis hotline in 2005, and 549 Latinas and their children were supported by the organization's Family Advocates program. Finally, senior staff at Casa provided training or consultation to more than 1,400 people representing 179 social service organizations at local and national levels (Casa de Esperanza, 2006).

Casa de Esperanza continues its ambitious mission to confront the problem of domestic violence both locally and nationally. In order to sustain these ambitions, it must be aggressive in fund-raising. In 2005, it raised more than $1.8 million in grants and contributions and had expenditures of more than $1.3 million (Casa de Esperanza, 2006). Given the continued financial support it has received from thousands of people and organizations, it holds to the goal of being a leading feminist organization devoted to the problem of domestic violence. As Sandfort (2005b) explains

Casa de Esperanza is trying to change the field of domestic violence. We believe that the strongest chance to achieve this is to place the primary responsibility for change in the hands of everyday people. We are trying to change attitudes and behaviors. We are trying to change mainstream systems by holding them accountable for serving all battered women, including those whose primary language is not English. We are trying to change the way that many Latinas,

Latinos, and mainstream individuals accept domestic violence as "part of our culture." We are trying to create a better community for our children and our families. (p. 107)

TRENDS INFLUENCING ORGANIZATIONS TODAY

In the first decade of the new millennium, a number of trends have surfaced that are influencing the way organizations do business and the way organization members communicate with one another. Among the most discussed trends are (a) globalization of the marketplace and global competitive pressures, (b) gender and diversity, (c) quality and customer satisfaction, (d) political and legal pressures on organizations, (e) stress at work, (f) an inadequately educated workforce, (g) critical questioning of corporate values, and (h) stakeholder perspectives. Let us consider each of these trends.

Globalization of the Marketplace and Global Competitive Pressures

The **globalization of the marketplace** refers to improvements in transportation and marketing capability that permit businesses to access sources of supplies and to sell goods and services to more distant customers. In this global marketplace, business owners may seek out markets anywhere in the world. Of course, any organization in any country has the same option, so competition is becoming increasingly fierce. To survive and remain competitive, organizations must be efficient in the production of goods and services, respond rapidly to the tastes and needs of consumers, and use effective marketing strategies. New information and telecommunications technologies allow business owners to meet these requirements; however, greater worldwide competition means that corporate owners must conduct careful research before pursuing any particular business option (Economic Trends Affecting Businesses, 2006).

Global competitive pressures raise critically important issues and concerns that need to be considered for organizational survival and fair treatment of employees. Increasingly, as a result of instantaneous worldwide communication via computer networks, more businesses need to operate globally in order to survive by selling products in markets all over the world. One implication of this reality is that prices of goods produced by an organization need to keep pace with prices charged elsewhere. It is irrelevant if labor costs are higher in the United States than in China. A U.S. business must be priced competitive by improving productivity, restructuring, and downsizing, if necessary. Sadly, layoffs in many industries will be inevitable, as fewer people will be needed to do more work for businesses to survive (Seltzer, 2006).

During the Industrial Revolution in the United States, businesses faced similar competitive pressures at the national level. Many workers labored for 16-hour days and were barely paid enough money to feed and house their families. Government leaders needed to intervene to ensure that workers were treated fairly and humanely and were given living wages. We are at a point in history now where the same spirit of cooperation is needed internationally. Many labor agreements will be needed to level the business playing field worldwide to ensure that workers are able to sustain an acceptable standard of living in terms of pay, working conditions, and number of hours worked (Seltzer, 2006).

Gender and Diversity

In the United States, the days of European American men controlling all organizations are long gone. This does not mean that all organizations have realized the full benefits of gender and racial and ethnic diversity. **Gender and diversity** must be considered carefully by all organizations worldwide. From the standpoint of good business practice, when groups of diverse people are brought together, an organization increases its creative potential by employing workers who approach problem solving in ways uniquely attributable to their experiences and ways of viewing the world. Simply stated, what is creativity but a bringing together of differences in a way that produces something unique and new? In addition, diversity contributes to an organization's bottom line by "making it easier to retain good employees, lowering costs by developing skills in-house, and developing a reputation that helps attract new employees" (Ethnic Majority, 2006). Importantly, gender and racial and ethnic diversity should not be limited to entry-level positions. For the benefits of diversity to be fully realized, it must exist in a company's workforce as a whole, among the highest salaried workers, and at the officer, board of director, and senior management positions (Ethnic Majority, 2006).

Quality and Customer Satisfaction

Because we live in an increasingly competitive world, consumers are in the position to demand higher levels of quality and service. **Quality and customer satisfaction** have become buzzwords that attract the attention of organizational leaders worldwide. To be successful in this arena, companies need to do more than respond to consumer demands. Instead, companies need to be "proactive in the way they manage quality and continuously seek to improve levels of customer satisfaction" (EuroMaTech, 2006). One approach to focusing on quality and customer satisfaction is total quality management (TQM). An effective TQM program takes a "developmental" approach to transforming the organization to focus on quality and customer satisfaction in all aspects of work, production, service, and management. This means proactively seeking out information from consumers about what their needs are now and how those needs may change in the future. When products are produced and services are provided, the needs of the customer are kept in mind to improve levels of customer satisfaction (Choi & Behling, 1997). This is accomplished by not only meeting the basic requirements of customers but by enhancing and differentiating products and services for competitive advantage (Stark, 1998). In this way, consumers are more likely to continue buying from your organization.

Political and Legal Pressures on Organizations

Political and legal pressures on organizations have changed as different problems have emerged. Recently, political and legal pressure has been brought to bear on organizations concerning worker rights. In developing countries, the issue of worker rights is of particular concern. For example, in China millions of workers are paid wages that trap them in poverty. There are also problems such as "forced labor, child labor, discrimination against women and rural workers, and virtually no freedom of association" (Meyers, 2005, p. 56).

When independent trade union organizers attempt to confront these problems, they are often arrested and jailed for their activities. Political and legal pressure will be necessary to promote worker rights in China. Hopefully, new international rules linking trade and labor practices and greater awareness and activism among consumers using their purchasing power to press for worker rights will help (Meyers, 2005).

Political and legal pressures are also being applied to U.S. corporations for unethical and illegal activities. In the year 2000, Enron was the seventh largest company in the United States with a value in excess of $70 billion. However, the company used every accounting trick and unethical public relations tactic to pump up its share price well in excess of its true value. When Enron finally admitted it was insolvent in December 2001, 20,000 employees lost their jobs, their health insurance, and their pensions. Shareholders were told that their investments were worthless (Enron: The Fraud That Changed Everything, 2006).

As a result of the Enron collapse, U.S. politicians were forced to act. Corporate financial statements may no longer be taken on trust. Now, corporate directors must sign off personally on their accuracy. There are also now tough new rules on how accounts are to be checked. Although this adds millions of dollars to the costs of running a public company in the United States, many believe the price is worth it to protect investors and employees (Enron: The Fraud That Changed Everything, 2006).

Wal-Mart, the second largest corporation in the United States, has been beset with lawsuits in recent years. In December 2005, a California jury awarded $172.3 million to workers who claimed they were denied meal breaks. This may just be the beginning of their legal troubles, however. Robert Bonsignore is an attorney representing more than 1.5 million current and former Wal-Mart employees in states from Hawaii to Maine. The company is facing more than 50 lawsuits from Bonsignore and others alleging that Wal-Mart failed to pay employees for all the time they worked. These class-action suits may have a significant material impact on Wal-Mart if the allegations prove to be true (Chediak, 2006).

Stress at Work

The National Institute for Occupational Safety and Health (NIOSH) is a federal agency that is responsible for conducting research and making recommendations for the prevention of work-related illness and injury (Sauter, 2006). Because the nature of work is changing so rapidly and global competitive pressures often require fewer workers to do the work of many, **stress at work** poses a threat to workers more than ever before. In the United States, for example, one-fourth of employees view their jobs as the number one stressor in their lives, and three-fourths of employees believe the worker has more on-the-job stress today than a generation ago (Sauter, 2006). In addition, problems at work are more strongly associated with health complaints than are any other life stressor (Princeton Survey Research Associates, 1997).

Sauter (2006) defines job stress as the "harmful physical and emotional responses that occur when the requirements of the job do not match the capabilities, resources, or needs of the worker" (p. 4). Given increasing expectations for high output and productivity, the design of tasks for many workers is a key contributor to stress. Specifically, many of today's workers are given heavy workloads, infrequent breaks, and long hours. Hectic and routine tasks that have little inherent meaning, do not utilize workers' skills, and provide little sense of control also contribute to stress. Finally, the availability and use of portable communications technologies and computers does not allow many workers to escape work at home or even while on vacation.

When workers endure stress at work for long periods of time, research tells us that it may lead to cardiovascular disease, musculoskeletal disorders, psychological disorders, workplace injuries, suicide, cancer, ulcers, and impaired immune function (Sauter, 2006). Although some employers view workplace stress as a necessary evil in a hypercompetitive economic climate, research challenges this view. "Studies show that stressful workplace conditions are associated with increased absenteeism, tardiness, and intentions by workers to quit their jobs—all of which have a negative effect on the bottom line" (Sauter, 2006, p. 11). Thus, corporate leaders and human resource professionals need to figure out ways of designing work tasks in ways that maximize productivity while keeping job stress under control. Simply focusing on productivity to the exclusion of job stressors will inevitably backfire and cost the company more than it gains.

Inadequately Educated Workforce

Technological advances at work require employees to master the use of sophisticated equipment including computers and communications devices. The skillful and productive use of such equipment demands that workers be educated. However, an **inadequately educated workforce** is one of the most significant problems that corporations face worldwide. *The Global Competitiveness Report 2005–2006* was based on an international survey of business and political leaders in 104 countries asking them to identify the most problematic factors in doing business in their own country. The problem ranked sixth was an inadequately educated workforce (Porter, Schwab, & Lopez-Claros, 2006). This problem even exists in the United States, which at one time had the world's most educated workers. In fact, because of substandard school systems and high levels of poverty in many urban and rural areas, the United States now ranks 14th in high school graduation rates behind countries such as France, Germany, and Japan (Porter et al., 2006).

The problem of an inadequately educated workforce is not easy to solve in any country. Providing a quality education is expensive. Developing countries face a particularly daunting problem because there are few resources available to publicly fund education. When there are many poor people in a developing country, families cannot afford to pay tuition to send their children to school for more than a few years. In developed countries, problems exist as well. Publicly funded education becomes more expensive as new building facilities, teacher salaries, and administrative costs continue to increase. The costs of education are just one side of the problem, however. The costs of *not* providing a high-quality education to the largest possible number of children will produce greater costs. If workers are not adequately educated, they will not be able to perform productively in the types of jobs likely to be in demand in the future. Political, business, and community leaders must work together to confront this problem so living wages may be earned by workers in the future.

Critical Questioning of Corporate Values

In recent years, companies around the world have adopted formal statements of **corporate values**. In fact, Van Lee, Fabish, and McGaw (2005) report that senior executives "now routinely identify ethical behavior, honesty, integrity, and social concerns as top issues on their companies' objectives" (p. 54). This recent renewed interest in values needs to be evaluated carefully, however. Are values being espoused because companies are truly committed to them, or are values being marketed to different publics to manipulate how companies are perceived? This requires us to engage in a **critical questioning of corporate values**.

The importance of critically questioning corporate values is linked to the fact that the recent resurgence in value statements has occurred against the backdrop of economic problems worldwide and spectacular corporate scandals. The bursting of the dot-com bubble and the bear market that ensued caused many of the economic problems we experienced in the first few years of the 21st century. Financial scandals the last several years have led to the collapse of Enron and WorldCom, accounting fraud charges against Tyco and Time Warner, and Medicare fraud by Health South and United Health Care. Problems such as these have led many companies to "question the quality of their management systems and their ability to inculcate and reinforce values that benefit the firm, its various constituencies, and the wider world" (Van Lee et al., 2005, p. 55).

There appears to be a growing body of evidence to suggest that companies are going beyond simply devising value statements. Rather, many companies are performing values-driven management improvement efforts including "training staff in values, evaluating executives and staff on their adherence to values, and hiring organizational experts to help address how values affect corporate performance" (Van Lee et al., 2005, p. 56). One example of how companies are beginning to exhibit little patience for executives who commit unethical behavior occurred at Boeing. When Boeing's board of directors discovered that their CEO Harry Stonecipher was having a sexual affair with an employee, they fired him. Only 15 months earlier, Stonecipher had been hired to help Boeing after a series of ethical breaches had threatened the company's standing with its largest customer, the Pentagon. Although the board did not specify what ethical rule the CEO had violated, they decided that any ethical lapse could create financial problems for the business (Lucier, Schuyt, & Tse, 2005). *What do you think of the actions taken by the Boeing board in this case? Were they justified in ousting the CEO over his affair with an employee?*

What exactly are the most frequently stated corporate values? A study by the Booz Allen Hamilton/Aspen Institute in 2004 surveyed 365 senior executives from corporations around the world. They discovered the following 14 values were most frequently identified by the executives (in descending order): ethical behavior/integrity, commitment to customers, commitment to employees, teamwork and trust, commitment to shareholders, honesty/openness, accountability, social responsibility/corporate citizenship, innovativeness/entrepreneurship, drive to succeed, environmental responsibility, initiative, commitment to diversity, and adaptability (Van Lee et al., 2005).

In the same study, senior executives were asked why they committed themselves to specific values. Most of the executives believe that values influence two important strategic areas: *reputation* and *relationship* with suppliers, customers, and employees. Although few thought that values were related directly to earnings and revenue growth, most thought a focus on reputation and relationships was a vital aspect of the company's risk management program (Van Lee, 2005).

For CEOs to be successful in promoting values in a way that employees internalize and that strengthens the company's commitment to them, they must back up their endorsement of values through their words and behavior. In addition, they must provide support for "ongoing corporate activities that consistently articulate what the company's values are" (Van Lee, 2005, p. 36).

When efforts to support corporate values fail, it is often because of a lack of commitment by the CEO and the management team to show how their actions are consistent with the written value statements that appear on plaques and in company documents. Van Lee (2005) explains, "If the company's managers espouse one thing but do another, employees may view values as another management scheme that requires them to do most of the heavy lifting while their supervisors are free to ignore the high-minded principles" (p. 38). In companies where managers behave in ways that contradict value statements, there will be little if any commitment on the part of employees to those values.

One interesting case in point of a contradiction between corporate value statements and corporate action is Enron. Goldsmith (2005) reported that he had an opportunity to review Enron's value statements before the company's collapse in 2001.

> I was shown a wonderful video on Enron's ethics and integrity. I was greatly impressed by the company's espoused high-minded beliefs and the care that was put into the video. Examples of Enron's good deeds in the community and the professed character of Enron's executives were particularly noteworthy. It was one of the most smoothly professional presentations on ethics and values that I had ever seen. Clearly, Enron spent a fortune "packaging" these wonderful messages. It didn't really matter. Despite the lofty words, many of Enron's top executives either have been indicted or are in jail. (p. 58)

For a company to live up to its values, it must focus on how employees, managers, and corporate leaders act. Actions will say much more to employees and the public about values than words ever can. As Goldsmith (2005) explains, "If our actions are wise, no one will ever care if the words on the wall are not perfect. If our actions are foolish, the wonderful words on the wall will only make us look more ridiculous" (p. 59). Consumers, investors, employees, and local communities should critically question corporate values if the company fails to deliver results that show those values in action. Although a "belief in corporate values may be in vogue, the cynics will remain skeptical until corporations can prove that they are committed to using values to create value" (Van Lee, 2005, p. 37).

Stakeholder Perspectives

In identifying a firm's stakeholders, one focuses on the "individuals, groups, or other organizations that are affected by and also affect the firm's decisions and actions" (Helms, 2005, p. 813). Depending on the organization, there may be many different stakeholders. Employees, shareholders, suppliers, distributors, and the community in which the organization is located are one important collection of stakeholders. The media may play an important stakeholder role, as well as government agencies (Securities and Exchange Commission, Internal Revenue Service, Environmental Protection Agency, etc.), social activist groups (National Organization for Women, Greenpeace, etc.), and self-regulatory agencies (Better Business Bureau, National Advertising Review Board, etc.). Although there are different ways of characterizing different stakeholder perspectives, Helms (2005) provides a helpful categorization in the *Encyclopedia of Management*. In her article on stakeholders she describes three broad categories: the **separation perspective**, the **ethical perspective**, and the **integrated perspective**.

According to the separation perspective on stakeholders, managers are the agents of the organization's owners. As agents, managers should always strive to act in the best interests of the owners. The only reason managers would act in a way to benefit nonowner stakeholders is if that action ultimately rewarded the owners in some way. Even if a managerial action would serve the greater good of society, the action would be taken only if the owners received a tangible benefit. So, let's say that a new technology lowers the level of pollution that an organization produces, providing benefits to the surrounding community. However, this technology is expensive, and the organization already meets the minimum requirements of the Environmental Protection Agency. From the standpoint of the separation perspective, because the owners' profits would suffer by adopting the new technology, the managers dismiss any consideration of the benefits to the community.

The ethical perspective on stakeholders takes the position that businesses have an obligation to treat each stakeholder group fairly. "This view does not disregard the preferences and claims of shareholders, but takes shareholder interests in consideration only to the extent that their interests coincide with the greater good" (Helms, 2005, p. 814). The ethical perspective has its roots in the philosophy of Immanuel Kant. According to Kant's normative view of ethics, "an ethically correct action should supercede actions based solely on self-interest, thus making managerial decisions and actions that impact stakeholders based on universal standards of right and wrong that managers should follow" (Helms, 2005, p. 815). However, in the reality of the 21st century there may be different standards of right and wrong that need to be taken into account. Given the nature of capitalistic competition, doing the "right thing" may bankrupt a business, thus denying opportunities for employment and returns on investment by shareholders. So overemphasizing the greater good of the community may result in ignoring the reality of self-interest, particularly regarding the ethical obligation to maximize shareholder wealth (Helms, 2005).

The integrated perspective suggests that organizations operate in a complicated stakeholder environment where the interests of various stakeholder groups are interconnected. So, separating shareholders from nonowner stakeholders is not always possible. If managers focus on one group to the exclusion of others, they may risk organizational survival or miss opportunities for innovative action that serves the interests of multiple groups. By integrating the components of the separation and the ethical perspective, organizational leaders may serve the self-interests of owners and display corporate responsibility to nonowner stakeholders so economic growth may coexist with social responsibility. Consider the following example:

> Maytag [recently] found that by balancing a plant closure with adequate notice, the reputation of the firm was held intact—a benefit to owners—at the same time that competing stakeholder interests were considered. In this situation, Maytag's Galesburg, Illinois refrigeration assembly plant announced it would be moving operations to a location with less expensive labor and other operational costs, but

took the unusual move of giving the firm's 1,000 employees, its local suppliers, and the small Galesburg community two years to prepare. Maytag allowed local employment agencies to set up job training within the Maytag plant to prepare its employees for employment after the plant closure. This illustrates how integration of multiple stakeholder interests can move beyond only self-interest or only ethics by integrating both of these. (Helms, 2005, p. 817)

Before closing this section on trends influencing organizations today, let's link the last two trends on corporate values and the stakeholder perspective. In developing corporate values it may be overly simplistic to take the view that managers should always do the "right thing." As our consideration of the different stakeholder perspectives shows, the right thing to do is not always clear. Organizations cannot abandon their ethical obligations to owners to provide a reasonable return on their investments. Alternatively, the owners' concern with self-interest does not justify an abandonment of corporate or social responsibility. So, integrating multiple perspectives gives managers the opportunity to balance the interests of different stakeholder groups in a way that harmonizes the interests of these groups.

SUMMARY

In considering traditional, interpretive, and critical perspectives on the new millennium, we positioned our observations against the current energy crisis and resource depletion brought about by constant economic and population growth. There are a variety of opinions and projections on this issue with wildly different scenarios for the future. Some economists predict that we will find technological solutions to our energy problems that will allow us to live the sorts of lives we lead today. Even if that is true, few biologists believe that we can sustain life as we know it without capping or reducing the human population. Alternatively, there are many scientists who believe we are on the precipice of a new age brought on by the end of the fossil fuel era. The end of this era will require significant reductions in energy use worldwide and a return to a preindustrial age. Perhaps when the next edition of this book is written it will be clearer which road we are traveling down.

If we are able to sustain large-scale organizations, the concept of emancipation in organizational studies will be critically important to consider. Although worker emancipation cannot occur without attention to organizational concerns (e.g., profits, survival, etc.), workers can be freed from many of the restrictions placed on them in bureaucracies. By giving workers a greater say in how to accomplish individual and organizational goals, they can simultaneously realize higher order human needs such as self-actualization while also increasing productivity. Through carefully examining those organizations that encourage employee emancipation, we will learn more about alternative forms of communicating and organizing in the workplace.

We also looked at some of the most recent theoretical developments in organizational communication. First, we described the shift from bureaucratic forms of control to self-managed work teams. Although self-managed work teams offer opportunities for worker participation and self-governance, workers are not always pleased with their experiences in these workgroups. Of particular concern has been the emergence of concertive control systems in which workers display more intense levels of control and discipline than exist in many bureaucracies. This chapter also examined democratic workplace systems as a form of governance that can offer clear opportunities for worker participation and empowerment. Particularly interesting are those organizations that empower employees to reconsider the very nature of organizational goals in order to sustain a vibrant, evolutionary form of democracy. Feminist theorists have highlighted paths to employee empowerment, especially by focusing on such themes as cooperation, integrative thinking, and connectedness. The enactment of these themes in the workplace maximizes the contributions of diverse members (e.g., women and racial and ethnic minorities) who are typically silenced in more traditional management systems.

DISCUSSION QUESTIONS/ACTIVITIES

1. How can the members of self-managed work teams sustain a balance between the attainment of individual and organizational goals? What do these employees need to do to prevent the sorts of problems reflected in the Barker and Cheney (1994) study?

2. What are the key advantages and disadvantages of enacting various forms of workplace democracy? How would worker experiences differ under participatory versus representative forms of democracy?

3. What are the key challenges to implementing feminist themes (e.g., cooperation, integrative thinking, connectedness) into the workplace? What are the major individual and organizational benefits of valuing these themes?

4. Is the concept of employee emancipation a utopian dream? What actions do workers need to take to experience some form of emancipation from repressive workplace rules?

5. How will the processes of communicating and organizing be different if we return to a preindustrial age in which the average person uses significantly less energy than he or she uses today?

REFERENCES

Adamson, N., Briskin, L., & McPhail, M. (1988). Entering the world of the women's movement. In N. Adamson, L. Briskin, & M. McPhail (Eds.), *Feminist organizing for change: The contemporary women's movement in Canada* (pp. 3–26). Toronto: Oxford University Press.

Albrecht, T. L. (1988). Communication and control in empowering organizations. In J. A. Anderson (Ed.), *Communication yearbook 11* (p. 380–390). Newbury Park, CA: Sage.

Alvesson, M., & Willmott, H. (1992). On the idea of emancipation in management and organization studies. *Academy of Management Review, 17,* 432–464.

Barker, J. R. (1993). Tightening the iron cage: Concertive control in self-managing teams. *Administrative Science Quarterly, 38,* 408–437.

Barker, J. R. (1999). *The discipline of teamwork: Participation and concertive control.* Thousand Oaks, CA: Sage.

Barker, J. R., & Cheney, G. (1994). The concept and practices of discipline in contemporary organizational life. *Communication Monographs, 61,* 19–43.

Barker, J. R., & Tompkins, P. K. (1994). Identification in the self-managing organization: Characteristics of target and tenure. *Human Communication Research, 21,* 223–240.

Barnard, C. (1968). *The functions of the executive.* Cambridge, MA: Harvard University Press. (Original work published in 1938)

Blasi, J. R. (1987). *Employee ownership through ESOPs: Implications for the public corporation.* New York: Pergamon.

Bullis, C. (1993). At least it is a start. In S. A. Deetz (Ed.), *Communication Yearbook 16* (pp. 144–154). Newbury Park, CA: Sage.

Buzzanell, P. (1994). Gaining a voice: Feminist organizational communication theorizing. *Management Communication Quarterly, 7,* 339–383.

Casa de Esperanza. (2006). *Making a difference in people's lives: Casa de Esperanza annual report: 2005.* St. Paul, MN: Casa de Esperanza.

Chediak, M. (2006, January 27). Worker lawsuits stack up at Wal-Mart. *Orlando Sentinel.* Retrieved April 9, 2006, from http://wakeupwalmart.com/news/20060127-os.html

Cheney, G. (1995). Democracy in the workplace: Theory and practice from the perspective of communication. *Journal of Applied Communication Research, 23,* 167–200.

Choi, T. Y., & Behling, O. C. (1997). Top managers and TQM success: One more look after all these years. *Academy of Management Executive, 11*(1), 37–47.

Clarke, T. (1984). Alternative modes of co-operative production. *Economic and Industrial Democracy, 5,* 97–129.

Czech, B., & Daly, H. E. (2004). In my opinion: The steady state economy—what it is, entails and connotes. *Wildlife Society Bulletin, 32*(2), 598–605.

Daly, H. E. (1997). *Beyond growth: The economics of sustainable development.* Boston, MA: Beacon.

Deetz, S. A. (1992). *Democracy in an age of corporate colonization: Developments in communication and the politics of everyday life.* Albany: State University of New York Press.

Donovan, J. (1985). *Feminist theory: The intellectual traditions of American feminism.* New York: Frederick Unger.

Eadie, W. F. (Ed.). (1992). Sexual harassment issue. *Journal of Applied Communication Research, 20*(4).

Economic Trends Affecting Businesses. (2006). Retrieved April 9, 2006, from http://www.ces.ncsu.edu/resources/economics/cd45

Edwards, R. C. (1981). The social relations of production at the point of production. In M. Zey-Ferrell & M. Aiken (Eds.), *Complex organizations: Critical perspectives* (pp. 156–182). Glenview, IL: Scott, Foresman.

Eisenberg, E. M. (1994). Dialogue as democratic discourse: Affirming Harrison. In S. A. Deetz (Ed.), *Communication yearbook 17* (pp. 275–284). Thousand Oaks, CA: Sage.

Eisenstein, Z. (1981). *The radical future of liberal feminism.* New York: Longman.

Enron: The fraud that changed everything. (2006, April 9). *The Independent.* Retrieved April 9, 2006, from http://news.independent.co.uk/business/analysis_and_features/article356600.ece

Ethnic Majority. (2006). Corporate culture and diversity. Retrieved April 9, 2006, from http://www.ethnicmajority.com/corporate_diversity.htm

EuroMaTech. (2006). Managing service quality and customer satisfaction. Retrieved April 9, 2006, from http://www.euromatech.com/seminar06/pr4610.htm

Evered, R., & Tannenbaum, R. (1992). A dialogue on dialogue. *Journal of Management Inquiry, 1,* 43–55.

Ferguson, K. (1984). *The feminist case against bureaucracy.* Philadelphia: Temple University Press.

Fineman, S. (2003). *Understanding emotion at work.* London: Sage.

Follett, M. P. (1951). *Creative experience.* New York: Peter Smith. (Original work published 1924)

Foucault, M. (1972). *The archaeology of knowledge* (A. Sheridan, Trans.). New York: Vintage. (Original work published 1968)

Foucault, M. (1977). *Discipline and punish* (A. Sheridan, Trans.). New York: Vintage. (Original work published 1975)

Foucault, M. (1980). *Power/knowledge* (G. Gordon, L. Marshal, J. Mepham, & K. Soper, Trans.; L. Gordon, Ed.). New York: Pantheon.

Fox, S., Spector, P. E., & Miles, D. (2001). Counterproductive work behavior (CWB) in response to job stressors and organizational justice: Some mediator and moderator tests for autonomy and emotions. *Journal of Vocational Behavior, 59,* 113–140.

Gherardi, S., & Masiero, A. (1987). The impact of organizational culture in life-cycle and decision-making processes in newborn cooperatives. *Economic and Industrial Democracy, 8,* 323–347.

Gibson, M. K., & Schullery, N. M. (2000). Shifting meanings in a blue-collar worker philanthropy program: Emergent tensions in traditional and feminist organizing. *Management Communication Quarterly, 14,* 189–236.

Giddens, A. (1979). *Central problems in social theory.* Berkeley: University of California Press.

Goldsmith, M. (2005, Summer). Leaders make values visible. *Strategy + Business, 10*(4), 58–59.

Grandey, A. A., Tam, A. P., & Brauburger, A. L. (2002). Affective states and traits in the workplace: Diary and survey data from young workers. *Motivation and Emotion, 26,* 54–79.

Gunn, C. (1984). Hoedads co-op: Democracy and cooperation at work. In R. Jackall & H. Levin (Eds.), *Worker cooperatives in America* (pp. 141–170). Berkeley: University of California Press.

Hafen, S. (1993, October). *Worker-owners and the experience of myness: A phenomenological study at Restaurant Casa Nueva.* Paper presented at the second annual Kentucky conference on narrative, Lexington, KY.

Harrison, T. M. (1994). Communication and interdependence in democratic organizations. In S. A. Deetz (Ed.), *Communication yearbook 17* (pp. 247–274). Thousand Oaks, CA: Sage.

Heinberg, R. (2003). *The party's over: Oil, war, and the fate of industrial societies.* Denver, CO: New Society Publishers.

Helms, M. M. (Ed.). (2005). *Encyclopedia of management.* Farmington Hills, MI: Thomson Gale.

Hess, U. (2003). *Emotion at work.* Montreal, Canada: Cirano.

Hickerson, R. L. (2004). Hubbert's prescription for survival, a steady state economy. Retrieved April 21, 2006, from http://survivingpeakoil.com

Hodson, R. (1998). Pride in task completion and organizational citizenship behaviour: Evidence from ethnographic studies. *Work and Stress, 4,* 199–222.

Isen, A. M.., & Baron, R. A. (1991). Positive affect as a factor in organizational-behavior. In B. M. Staw & L. L. Cummings (Eds.), *Research in organizational behavior* (pp. 208–236). Greenwich, CT: JAI.

Jaggar, A. (1983). Political philosophies of women's liberation. In L. Richardson & V. Taylor (Eds.), *Feminist frontiers: Rethinking sex, gender, and society* (pp. 332–329). New York: Random House.

Johnson, C. (2006). Co-housing. Retrieved April 21, 2006, from http://www.survivingpeakoil.com

Kunstler, D. (2005). *The long emergency.* New York: Basic.

Langston, D. (1988). Feminist theories and the politics of difference. In J. W. Cochran, D. Langston, & C. Woodard (Eds.), *Changing our power* (pp. 10–21). Dubuque, IA: Kendall/Hunt.

Lucier, C., Schuyt, R., & Tse, E. (2005). *CEO succession 2004: The world's most prominent temp workers.* McLean, VA: Booz Allen Hamilton, Inc.

Lugones, M. C., & Spelman, E. V. (1987). Competition, compassion, and community: Models for a female ethos. In V. Miner & H. E. Longino (Eds.), *Competition: A feminist taboo?* (pp. 234–247). New York: Feminist Press, The City University of New York.

Madjar, N., Oldham, G. R., Pratt, M. G. (2002). There's no place like home: The contributions of work and nonwork creativity support to employees' creative performance. *Academy of Management Journal, 45,* 412–437.

Marshall, J. (1989). Re-visioning career concepts: A feminist invitation. In M. B. Arthur, D. T. Hall, & B. S. Lawrence (Eds.), *Handbook of career theory* (pp. 275–291). Cambridge: Cambridge University Press.

Martin, P. Y. (1990). Rethinking feminist organizations. *Gender & Society, 4,* 182–206.

Maruyama, A. (1994). *Mindscapes in management: Use of individual differences in diversity management.* Hanover, NH: Dartmouth.

Mellor, M., Hannah, J., & Stirling, J. (1988). *Worker cooperatives in theory and practice.* Milton, Keynes, England: Open University Press.

Meyers, L. (2005, March 24). Report on China finds workers' rights violations, but also signs of hope. *Cornell Chronicle, 36*(27), 56–57.

Monge, P. R., & Miller, K. I. (1988). Participative processes in organizations. In G. M. Goldhaber & G. A. Barnett (Eds.), *Handbook of organizational communication* (pp. 213–229). Norwood, NJ: Ablex.

Mumby, D. K., & Stohl, C. (1991). Power and discourse in organizational studies: Absence and the dialectic of control. *Discourse & Society, 2,* 313–332.

Natalle, E. J., Papa, M .J., & Graham, E. E. (1993). Feminist philosophy and the transformation of organizational communication. In B. Kovacic (Ed.), *New approaches to organizational communication* (pp. 245–270). Albany: State University of New York Press.

New York Mercantile Exchange. (2007, June 26). Light sweet crude oil. Retrieved June 26, 2007, from http://www.nymex.com/lsco_fut_cso.aspx

Nye, A. (1988). *Feminist theories and the philosophies of man.* London: Croon Helm.

Orlov, D. (2006). Post-Soviet lessons for a post-American century. Retrieved April 26, 2006, from http://www.survivingpeakoil.com

Osbourne, J. D., Moran, L., Musselwhite, E., & Zenger, J. H. (1990). *Self-directed work teams: The new American challenge.* Homewood, IL: Irwin.

Papa, M. J., Auwal, M. A., & Singhal, A. (1997). Organizing for social change within concertive control systems: Member identification, discursive empowerment, and the masking of discipline. *Communication Monographs, 64,* 219–249.

Papa, M. J., Singhal, A., Ghanekar, D. V., & Papa, W. H. (2000). Organizing for social change through cooperative action: The [dis]empowering dimensions of women's communication. *Communication Theory, 10,* 90–123.

Pfeiffer, D. A. (2006). A call for action. Retrieved April 21, 2006, from http://www.survivingpeakoil.com

Porter, M. E., Schwab, K., & Lopez-Claros, A. (Eds.). (2006). *The global competitiveness report 2005–2006: Policies underpinning rising prosperity.* New York: Palgrave Macmillan.

Princeton Survey Research Associates. (1997). *Labor Day survey: State of workers.* Princeton, NJ: Author.

Sandfort, J. (2005a). Casa de Esperanza. *Nonprofit Management & Leadership, 15*(3), 371–382.

Sandfort, J. (2005b). Casa de Esperanza [Part C]. *Nonprofit Management & Leadership, 16*(1), 101–108.

Sauter, R. (2006). Stress at work. Retrieved April 9, 2006, from http://www.cdc.gov/niosh/stresswk.html

Seltzer, R. (2006). Global competition and the long road to general prosperity. Retrieved April 9, 2006, from http://www.samizdat.com/global.html

Simon, H. (1976). *Administrative behavior.* New York: Free Press.

Stark, J. (1998). A few words about TQM. Retrieved April 9, 2006, from http://www.johnstark.com/fwtqm.html

Tompkins, P. K., & Cheney, G. (1983). Account analysis of organizations: Decision-making and identification. In L. L. Putnam & M. E. Pacanowsky (Eds.), *Communication and organizations: An interpretive approach* (pp. 123–146). Beverly Hills, CA: Sage.

Tompkins, P. K., & Cheney, G. (1985). Communication and unobtrusive control in contemporary organizations. In R. D. McPhee & P. K. Tompkins (Eds.), *Organizational communication: Traditional themes and new directions* (pp. 179–210). Beverly Hills, CA: Sage.

Tong, R. (1989). *Feminist thought: A comprehensive introduction.* Boulder, CO: Westview.

Van Lee, R. (2005, August 25). Corporate value statements—do they mean it? *Advertising Age, 66,* 35–38.

Van Lee, R., Fabish, L., & McGaw, N. (2005, Summer). The value of corporate values. *Strategy + Business, 10*(4), 55–58, 60–61.

Vecchio, R. P. (2000). Negative emotion in the workplace: Employee jealousy and envy. *International Journal of Stress Management, 7,* 236–259.

Wachtel, P. L. (1983). *The poverty of affluence: A psychological portrait of the American way of life.* New York: Free Press.

Weber, M. (1978). *Economy and society,* 2 vols. (G. Roth & C. Wittich, Trans.). Berkeley: University of California Press. (Original work published 1922)

Wellins, R. S., Byham, W. C., & Wilson, J. M. (1991). *Empowered teams: Creating self-directed work groups that improve quality, productivity, and participation.* San Francisco: Jossey-Bass.

Westervelt, E. T., & Fournier, D. F. (2005). Energy trends and implications for U.S. Army installations. Retrieved April 26, 2006, from http://www.erdc.usace.army.mil

Whetten, D. A. (1996a). *If beauty is only skin deep, what about virtue? Applying the concept of identity congruence to socially responsible businesses.* Unpublished manuscript, Brigham Young University, Center for the Study of Values in Organizations, Provo, UT.

Whetten, D. A. (1996b). *The costs and benefits of business' commitment to "doing good and doing well."* Unpublished manuscript, Brigham Young University, Center for the Study of Values in Organizations, Provo, UT.

Wolf, S. R. (2006). Community is necessary to survival. Retrieved April 26, 2006, from http://www.surviving peakoil.com

Author Index

Bouchard, T. J., Jr., 119
Bowditch, J. L., 104
Bradbury, T. N., 324
Bradford, L. J., 208
Bradley, P. H., 214
Bradshaw, S., 241
Brauburder, A. L., 405
Brenton, A. L., 280, 284
Briggs, R. O., 171, 173, 178
Brillouin, L., 33
Briskin, L., 401
Brown, M. H., 147
Browning, L. D., 215
Bruce, P., 35
Bruner, M. S., 368
Bruning, F., 202
Brynjolfsson, E., 164
Buch, K., 58
Buchholz, R., 360
Buller, D., 118
Bullis, C., 400
Burawoy, M., 302
Bureau of Labor Statistics, 219, 220
Burke, R. J., 320, 321
Burns, J. M., 265
Burns, J. P., 368
Burrell, N. A., 321, 334
Buss, D. M., 121
Buzzanell, P. M., 15, 215–217, 321, 334, 401–404
Byham, W. C., 391

Cabezas, H., 110
Cafferty, T. P., 338
Cahill, D. J., 41–42
Cameron, G., 364
Campbell, D. T., 113
Canary, D. J., 322–324, 342
Capps, C. J., 110
Carey, A., 91
Catalyst, 213
Cazale, L., 262
Census Bureau, U.S., 220
Center, A. H., 359
Cesaria, R., 5
Chacko, H. E., 277
Chaffee, E. E., 350–352, 363
Chakravorty, J., 211
Chamber of Commerce, U.S., 356
Chandler, T. A., 151, 152, 268, 269
Chase, W. H., 360–362
Chediak, M., 410

Chen, W., 169
Cheney, G., 133, 151, 152, 156, 195, 304, 391–393, 395–396, 398, 399
Cheng, H., 364
Chester, N. L., 216
Chilberg, J. C., 177, 251
Chiles, A. M., 137, 138
Choi, T. Y., 409
Cil, I., 177
Clarke, T., 396
Clegg, S., 298, 302
Clifford, J., 129
Clinebell, S. K., 199
Coates, J., 360
Coates, V., 360
Cohen, G., 144
Cole, T., 119, 122
Coleman, J., 35
Conrad, C., 2, 23, 199, 280, 321, 350
Contractor, N. S., 71, 72
Cooper, R., 311
Corman, S. R., 50, 51, 65, 67, 140–142
Cose, E., 222
Cosmides, L., 119, 120–121
Costantino, C. A., 326
Cotton, J. L., 58
Cox, T., Jr., 199
Crawford, J. S., 12
Cronen, V., 3, 116
Crum, M. R., 270
Culbert, S. A., 61
Cummins, R. C., 245
Cunningham, M. A., 25
Cupach, W. R., 235, 322, 323
Curran, K. E., 34
Curry, J., 271
Curtis, E., 241
Cutlip, S. M., 359
Cyert, R. M., 67
Czarniawska-Joerges, B., 197
Czech, B., 385

Daft, R. L., 176
Dahl, R., 292, 294
Daly, H. E., 385
Daly, J. A., 34
Damhorst, M. L., 34
Dance, F. E. X., 30–32, 42
Daneke, G. A., 110
Daniels, T. D., 34, 53, 96, 271, 272, 421
D'Aprix, R., 108–109

Subject Index

About the Authors

Michael J. Papa is a professor in the Department of Communication and Dramatic Arts at Central Michigan University, where he served as chair from 2003 to 2006. He has also held faculty positions at Michigan State University, Ohio University, Bangkok University, and the University of North Carolina at Greensboro. Michael has pursued a diverse research agenda over the past 20 years and has authored numerous research articles, book chapters, and conference papers, as well as three books including one on social change in developing countries. He has been involved in the design, evaluation, and documentation of various organizing for social change initiatives in Bangladesh, India, Thailand, and the United States. Projects include evaluation studies of the Grameen Bank in Bangladesh (recipient of the 2006 Nobel Peace Prize), the Cooperative Development programs of India's National Dairy Development Board, HIV/AIDS prevention programs in Thailand, entertainment-education initiatives in rural Uttar Pradesh and Bihar, India, and a program of feeding the poor in Appalachia. Most recently, Michael has served as a consultant to the Conflict Resolution Program at The Carter Center in Atlanta, Georgia. His work has involved documenting President Carter's approach to negotiating peace with a focus on the settlement reached between Uganda and Sudan. Michael has received 10 research awards for top papers from the National Communication Association and the International Communication Association. He and his wife Wendy live in Mount Pleasant, Michigan with their two children, Andrew and Samantha. In his spare time, Michael enjoys riding his bicycle, sailing, and downhill skiing.

Tom D. Daniels is a professor of communication studies in the Scripps College of Communication at Ohio University. He has worked at Ohio University since 1984, serving at various times as an associate dean, associate provost, and in interim administrative posts in addition to his faculty appointment. Before 1984, he was an assistant professor at the University of New Mexico and at the University of Wisconsin, Green Bay. A teacher and writer on subjects in organizational communication for many years, Tom also teaches quantitative research methods. He and his wife, Gretchen, a performing arts administrator, share a home with several dogs and cats in the woods of southern Ohio where they are visited occasionally by children and grandchildren. If they are not at work and not at home, they are probably on the water in their kayaks.

Barry K. Spiker brings more than 20 years' experience leading organizational change and directing human capital development and management. A teacher, management consultant, business strategist, and theoretician, Spiker draws from his background in the private sector as both corporate executive and start-up entrepreneur and from his knowledge as an educator and researcher. An expert on related subject matters, he has published nine books and more than 15 refereed articles in applied research, communication, organizational development, and systems theory.